CAMPAIGNS

A Century of Presidential Races

From the Photo Archives of The New York Times

NEW YORK CITY
BOARD OF ELECTIONS

The New York Times

CAMPAIGNS

A Century of Presidential Races

From the Photo Archives of The New York Times

Introduction by Alan Brinkley

Text by Ted Widmer

DK

London, New York, Sydney, Delhi,
Paris, Munich, and Johannesburg

DK Publishing
Project & Photo Editor/Photo Captions: Barbara M. Berger
Book Designer: Russell Hassell
Senior Art Editor: Mandy Earey
Art Directors: Tina Vaughan and Dirk Kaufman
Publisher: Sean Moore
Production Director: David Proffit

The New York Times
Original Concept Development/Photo Research: Mark Bussell
Project Editor: Mitchel Levitas, Editorial Director, Book Development
Consulting Editor: Nancy Lee, Director, Business Development
Photo Research: Margaret O'Connor, Picture Editor; Jeff Roth, Picture Archivist; Lonnie Schlein, National Picture Editor
Photo Scanning: Paul Hacker

First American Edition, 2001
00 01 02 03 04 05 10 9 8 7 6 5 4 3 2 1
Published in the United States by
DK Publishing, Inc.
95 Madison Avenue
New York, New York 10016

Library of Congress Cataloging-in-Publication Data
Brinkley, Alan.
Campaigns : a century of presidential races from the photo archives of the New York Times / text by Alan Brinkley and Ted Widmer.
p. cm.
Includes index.
ISBN 0-7894-7135-3 (alk. paper)
1. Presidents—United States—Election—History—20th century—Pictorial works. 2. Presidential candidates—United States—History—20th century—Pictorial works. 3. Political campaigns—United States—History—20th century—Pictorial works. 4. United States—Politics and government—20th century—Pictorial works. I. Widmer, Edward L. II. New York times. III. Title.
E176.1 .B86 2001
324.973'09—dc21 00-065814

Reproduced by Colourscan, Singapore
Printed in the United States
See our complete catalog at
www.dk.com

Contents

INTRODUCTION

Every Four Years

by Alan Brinkley

The nomination and election of the President of the United States is the greatest civic ritual of American politics. It displays the majesty and, at times, the tawdriness of our messy, fractious, and on the whole remarkably successful democratic system. And like almost every other aspect of American public life, it changes constantly. Laments about the corruption and degradation of our political world are as old as the nation itself; but while the complaints are constant, the realities they describe are not. In the twentieth century alone, the process of selecting a president has changed dramatically, both for better and for worse.

Choosing a president has always been the subject of broad popular interest. The astute British observer of American life, Lord Bryce, wrote in 1888 that "America suffers from a sort of intermittent fever. . . . Every fourth year there come terrible shakings, passing into the hot fit of the presidential election." But when Bryce wrote those words, presidential campaigns bore almost no relation to those we know today. The parties were supreme, and the candidates themselves virtually invisible—refraining from active campaigning because, most Americans believed, such efforts were beneath the dignity of the office to which they aspired. Today, parties are little more than shells, and candidates have no inhibitions about displaying their lust for office. They are omnipresent—marketed, packaged, poll-tested, and scripted, constantly visible in the press, on radio and television, and now on the Internet—and unapologetic about their relentless self-promotion.

The remarkable photographs collected in this book—and the vivid text that accompanies them—give us a powerful view of a vanished political world, and a revealing view of our present one. On the one hand, we see the frenzied parades and the packed town squares and meeting halls in which campaigns were fought through the first half of the century and beyond. We see Theodore Roosevelt, Woodrow Wilson, Franklin Roosevelt, Wendell Willkie, Harry Truman, John Kennedy, and Lyndon Johnson electrifying great crowds and seeking to make direct contact with as many voters as possible. And we see the bumper stickers and campaign buttons and sidewalk party booths that were part of the everyday life of communities into the 1960s. On the other hand, we see the governing reality of more recent campaigns—best symbolized, perhaps, by the famous scene from the 1984 Republican convention in which Nancy Reagan waves fondly at the televised image of her husband on a giant screen behind the podium. Instead of photographs of great crowds, we mostly see now the carefully crafted images candidates create for television: sitting in classrooms surrounded by

Bill Clinton plays football at Midway Airport in Chicago, during one of many campaign stops, October 1992.

students; visiting churches to demonstrate sympathy for minorities and ethnic groups; posing in casual situations (George Bush on his speedboat in Maine, Bill Clinton catching a football). If one looks at the first pictures in this book—pictures of highly public campaigns conducted in the presence of vast throngs of people—and compares them with the pictures toward the end—images of candidates in intimate, even private settings broadcast to millions—one can see the passage of American presidential campaigning from its highly public character at the dawn of the twentieth century to its more insulated, even private character at the dawn of the twenty-first.

The Age of Parties

As late as 1900, when William McKinley ran for reelection as president, it was possible for a candidate to remain almost entirely out of view during the national campaign and allow other party leaders to do virtually all the work of mobilizing voters. Successful presidential candidates in the nineteenth century accepted election almost as if it were a gift from the people—a gift that they pretended never to have sought and that they had made no active efforts to accept (although of course they had almost always worked incessantly if quietly to obtain it). The few departures from this tradition almost always harmed the politician who attempted it. When President Andrew Johnson left the White House in 1866 to campaign openly—not for himself but for his supporters in congressional contests—he was the subject of ferocious criticism. His opponents made his notorious "swing around the circle" a count in the impeachment effort waged against him in Congress two years later. He had, the impeachment article claimed, brought "the high office of the President of the United States into contempt, ridicule, and disgrace" by stumping so openly and intemperately. Almost no subsequent president or presidential candidate dared break the traditional ban on campaigning for almost thirty years.

The public aloofness of most presidential candidates gave an aura of nonpartisan dignity to the election process and kept alive the vision of the nation's founders of a political world free of parties and factions. George Washington had warned of "the baneful effects of the spirit of party" in his Farewell Address and, for more than a century after that, presidential campaigning—and American politics as a whole—strove to maintain the myth of a factionless nation.

But myth is all it was. Even in the early years of the Republic, when almost no one believed that organized parties should be a part of the nation's political life, there were bitter partisan divisions—indeed so bitter that they make modern campaigns seem remarkably tame and positive by contrast. By the 1820s, most Americans were

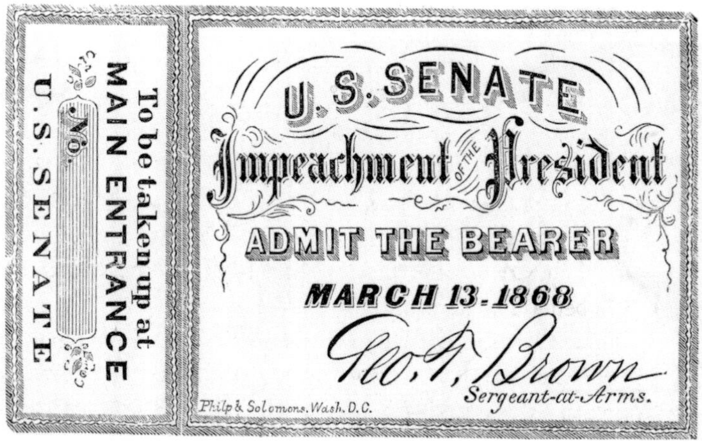

After Andrew Johnson narrowly avoided impeachment in 1868 (one of the charges was that he "disgraced" Congress by "blatantly" campaigning for his supporters), no presidential candidates openly campaigned for almost thirty years. This ticket admitted a bearer to the trial, a huge event in Washington.

ready to discard the myth of a partyless nation and to embrace the idea that permanent, organized parties could actually contribute to the workings of democracy. Even then, however, they continued to embrace the notion of a president who stood above the passions of party competition.

The irony of presidential campaigning before the twentieth century was that the non-partisan sobriety and dignity of presidential candidates contrasted so sharply with the wild passions that so many Americans came to invest in the political parties themselves. Indeed, the strength of political parties is probably the most striking difference between mid- to late-nineteenth-century politics and the politics of our time. Nineteenth-century parties were immensely powerful, in ways almost inconceivable to us today. They were the center of public life. The vast majority of white male Americans (virtually the only people who could vote), and many non-voting women and others as well, had strong, almost unshakable loyalties to one or another of the major parties, loyalties often as powerful as those to community, region, or church. The idea of independent voters was almost unheard of. When movements arose occasionally that rejected party loyalty—as, for example, when reformers broke with the Republican party in the 1870s and 1880s and dubbed themselves the Independent Republicans—most Americans viewed them as freakish aberrations, even as dangerous and subversive.

The power of the parties was not just emotional. It was based in their real control of the instruments of public influence. Most important newspapers in the United States were party sheets—often boasting of their connections in their titles. Papers called themselves the *Democrat* or the *Republican* or the *Whig*. Many of them were actually owned by party organizations, and they presented the news in predictably partisan fashion. Parties controlled the ballot directly and openly. Until the last decades of the nineteenth century, there was no secret ballot as we know it today. Most voters came to the polls carrying ballots (or "tickets"), printed and distributed by local party organizations, and dropped them in the ballot box in full view of the party observers in the room. Ticket splitting was almost impossible (and almost unheard of). For the large number of new citizens for whom English was not their native language, the "ticket" offered party machines an easy way to mobilize and manipulate voters.

Parties were, by almost any measure, the most important political institutions in the United States, indeed one of the very few truly national organizations—more visible in the lives of most Americans than the small, remote, and to most people largely irrelevant federal government. Party bosses were often more powerful than elected officials, and party machines functioned almost as unelected governments. It was little wonder that presidential candidates kept a low profile and let the parties do the work. Their own power was utterly dependent on the workings of their parties.

Nowhere, in fact, was the power of party more visible than in presidential elections. It was visible, first, in the extraordinarily high voter turnout the parties were able to produce through much of the nineteenth century. The heyday of party power was in the four decades after the Civil War. Between 1860 and 1900, years in which presidential candidates did virtually no campaigning and in which the parties themselves had few fundamental differences on major issues, turnout averaged 78.5 percent of all eligible voters (no election since then has attracted much more than 60 percent). Even in off-year elections, between 60 and 80 percent of the voters went to the polls. There were, of course, enormous groups of people who were not eligible to vote: women in all but a few states; most blacks and some poor whites in the South; Native Americans; most Mexican-Americans; and many others. Still, for white males in most of the country, there were virtually no franchise restrictions; and so this remarkable turnout represents a genuinely mass-based presidential politics, with parties able to retain and mobilize the loyalties of the vast majority of the eligible voters.

The loyalty to party in the late nineteenth century was largely unaffected by issues or events, for the major parties seldom dealt with important issues or produced significant public initiatives. As Bryce wrote of political leaders, "Neither party has any principles, any distinctive tenets. . . . All has been lost, except office or the hope of it." But for most voters, party loyalty was an almost unquestioned part of their sense of self. In some places, that loyalty was rooted in part in material self-interest. Party machines often provided important services to their voters: jobs, emergency assistance, help with the law. Another reason was that party identification usually had its roots not in issues, but in community identity. Most people were Democrats or Republicans because their parents had been, or because their town or county or region was identified with one or the other, or because the members of their faith were committed to one or another party.

The passions the parties attracted were in some ways comparable to, although much more enduring than, the passions some Americans invest today in a sports team. As the French observer of American life Alexis de Tocqueville wrote of popular politics in his classic 1835 work, *Democracy in America*:

> To take a hand in the regulation of society and to discuss it . . . is [the American's] biggest concern and, so to speak, the only pleasure an American knows. . . . Even the women frequently attend public meetings and listen to political harangues as a recreation from their household labors. Debating clubs are, to a certain extent, a substitute for theatrical entertainments.

In the heat of the campaign, he added:

> . . . the whole nation glows with feverish excitement; the election is the daily theme of the press, the subject of every private conversation, the end of every thought and action, the sole interest of the president.

Presidential campaigns were waged mostly at the local level, and they were often the most important public event in a community. Party organizations staged picnics and barbecues. They organized great torchlight parades in which hundreds, sometimes thousands of excited supporters marched on behalf of their candidates. They built clubhouses and meeting halls and taverns where the party faithful gathered for both public events and informal conversation. Bryce was astonished at the intensity of these displays, at "the demonstrations, the parades, the receptions, the badges and brass bands and triumphal arches" and at "the disproportion that strikes a European between the merits of the presidential candidate and the blazing enthusiasm which he evokes." But he misread the real meaning of the activities he observed. The excitement was not about the candidates, but about the parties themselves. For partisanship was an intense, even emotional force, widely admired, akin to (and often identified with) patriotism.

One example of that was David B. Hill, an otherwise obscure Democratic governor of New York in the late 1880s. He once attended a meeting where dissidents were threatening to desert the party. Hill stood up and made a speech in which he said he would never bolt the party, no matter what it did or whom it nominated, because, he said, "I am a Democrat." That single sentence became one of the great rallying cries of the era, repeated constantly all over the country as a statement of profound emotional force and moral significance. It made David Hill a national hero to his party and, for a time, a highly touted presidential candidate. And it was a statement that, by our standards, is almost meaningless—because to Hill, as to most other Americans at the time, party loyalty was not connected to any clear ideological stance. But Hill's statement meant a great deal to his contemporaries. To them, partisanship was something to be valued for its own sake—and the vast majority of those who voted for president did so simply as an expression of their intense loyalty to their parties. That was what made possible the genteel tradition of the "front porch" campaign, in which the presidential nominee stayed at home except occasionally to appear on his front porch to greet visiting delegations of supporters.

The Birth of the Modern Campaign: From Roosevelt to Roosevelt

William McKinley's successful reelection effort in 1900 was, however, one of the last of the true "front porch" campaigns (even though McKinley spent most of the electoral season not on his front porch in Ohio, as he had four years earlier, but in the White House). In 1904, when Theodore Roosevelt ran for reelection (having succeeded to the presidency in 1901 when McKinley was assassinated), he bridled at the ban on campaigning and made some first, tentative steps out of the White House and onto the stump. He had campaigned widely and enthusiastically as a candidate for vice president in 1900, and chafed at the

Theodore Roosevelt—one of America's most demonstrative presidents—forever changed the way candidates campaigned. Here he makes a campaign speech in 1912 while running for president on the Progressive Party ticket.

restrictions incumbency placed on him. In 1908, both presidential candidates—William Howard Taft and William Jennings Bryan—campaigned strenuously and openly. Almost all presidential candidates, challengers and incumbents alike, have done so ever since.

That change was a result in part of personalities. Roosevelt was perhaps the most extroverted president the country had ever seen. He was as incapable of sitting on the sidelines in the thick of political battle as he had been incapable of sitting on the sidelines during the Spanish-American War, when he resigned his position as assistant secretary of the Navy to lead the Rough Riders in Cuba. William Jennings Bryan, the Democratic candidate in 1896, 1900, and 1908, was similarly restive with the tradition of self-restraint and had stumped openly and actively, if unsuccessfully, in 1896—despite the complaints of more traditional political observers who charged that he "is begging for the presidency as a tramp might beg for a pie." And Woodrow Wilson, after he became president in 1912, moved even further in the direction of making the president himself an active and independent political figure. He lobbied members of Congress personally, circumventing party leaders; he became the first president since Jefferson to appear before Congress to deliver a State of the Union address in person. And in 1916, he became the first incumbent president to abandon all restraints against campaigning for his own reelection.

But the shift away from a party-dominated to a candidate-dominated presidential campaign was also a result of a series of larger changes in American politics—changes that made parties less central both to elections and to the lives of citizens, and changes that made individual candidates far more visible and far more important to the voters considering them.

The Rise of Interest Groups

Through much of the nineteenth century, no other national organizations—not even the small and, to most Americans, largely invisible federal government—could compete with the political parties in influence, prestige, and size. But by the beginning of the twentieth century, that dominance was eroding. As the industrial economy became more integrated and more national, new organizations began to emerge expressing national interests and exercising national power. Parties, in other words, began to face competition for the loyalties of citizens not just from each other but also from other organizations and groups.

The rise of national organizations was among the most striking characteristics of turn-of-the-twentieth-century America. That era saw the birth of the first great national corporations—symbolized, perhaps, by the creation of United States Steel in 1901, a billion-dollar giant with plants, and influence, in most areas of the country. Alongside the corporations emerged a host of other non-party institutions. Professions were becoming more truly national in these years, and by the end of the nineteenth century many of them had created national professional organizations capable of exercising substantial political power on matters that affected them. Among them were such still-familiar groups as the American Medical Association, the American Bar Association, the National Association of Manufacturers, the United States Chamber of Commerce, the National Education Association, the National Farm Bureau Federation, and many others. There was a great network of women's organizations, which merged in the 1890s to create the General Federation of Women's Clubs and which by 1900 had over a million members. The General Federation became a powerful force in promoting issues of concern to its mostly middle-class members. Workers, too, struggled to create national organizations through the late nineteenth century, beginning in the 1860s with the short-lived National Labor Union, continuing in the 1870s with the rise of the Knights of Labor, and culminating near the end of the century in the American Federation of Labor, which has survived into our own time.

These new national organizations were not equal to one another in power. Labor unions could rarely match the power of corporations, for example. Farm organizations could not compete effectively with the railroads and the champions of industry. But together, these new organizations formed the basis of a genuinely new kind of politics: a politics less of parties than of interest groups; a politics in which more and more voters saw the parties not as things to which they formed an unbreakable bond, but as objects they would try to influence on behalf of their own particular interests. Having once attracted the primary loyalty of voters, parties increasingly came to be secondary or tertiary forces in the lives of citizens. Eventually, of course, they came to play no important role at all in the lives of most Americans.

Members of the Executive Council of the American Federation of Labor pose for a portrait at the Atlantic City Labor Convention, June 10, 1919. Clockwise from top left: William Grier; Joseph Valentine; Frank Morrison, secretary; Samuel Gompers, president; and James Duncan, vice president.

The decline of parties was visible in many ways as the nineteenth century came to an end. It was evident, first, in the rise of powerful third party alternatives to the Republicans and Democrats: the People's Party (or the Populists) in the 1890s, which attracted nearly 9 percent of the vote in the 1892 presidential election; the Socialist Party, which consistently received 3 percent of the national vote and once as much as 6 percent for its presidential candidates in the early twentieth century; and the Progressive Party of 1912—the basis of Theodore Roosevelt's "Bull Moose" campaign for the presidency—which received over 27 percent of the vote and outpolled the Republicans. The erosion of party power was also visible in the decline of voter turnout in the early twentieth century. In 1896, over 79 percent of the eligible electorate voted in the presidential election. By 1912, turnout had declined to just under 59 percent, and would never again go much above that. Many factors contributed to this decline, but one of the most important was the inability of the major parties any longer to retain the fervent loyalty of their followers and thus their increasing inability to mobilize their voters to go to the polls. And in this new political world, in which each political party was just one of many national organizations, in which voters had many groups and movements competing for their loyalties, presidential candidates had to emerge from the shadows of the "front porch" and begin to mobilize voters on their own.

The Birth of the Primaries

The problem facing the political parties in the early twentieth century was not just the emergence of powerful new competitors in the form of national interest groups. It was also the rise of a powerful anti-party sentiment, led by influential reformers bent on changing the political system to eliminate the "boss" and the "machine" and to elevate the "people." This assault on the parties had implications for every level of American politics. Eventually, it helped transform the nature of presidential campaigns.

The beginnings of anti-party sentiment could be seen in the late nineteenth century in third-party and independent movements committed to reform. The Greenbackers of the 1870s, the Independent Republicans (known derisively, as "mugwumps") in the 1880s, and the populists in the 1890s all made attacks on party dominance central to their appeal. Their popularity, however short-lived, put pressure on major party politicians to respond to their demands, often by distancing themselves from the party organizations from which they had emerged. Equally powerful was a growing popular outcry against the corruption of politics by bosses and special interests. By 1900, reformers had already succeeded in introducing the secret ballot in almost every state, eroding the ability of local party organizations to control the way their constituents voted. They had begun to create new newspapers in many major cities unconnected with either party. (In addition to papers named *Republican* and *Democrat*, there began to appear papers named *Independent*.)

Horace White, an editor of the *Chicago Tribune* and, later, the *New York Post*, expressed this new view of an independent, professional journalism: "I think the greatest service a public journal can render to its readers is to encourage them to form independent opinions. This can only be done by holding out to them an example of independence." And the late nineteenth century saw as well the beginnings of a new view of political debate among many middle-class Americans—what some then called a new "educational politics," in which issues more than party loyalty would be the focus of attention. Whitelaw Reid, vice president under Benjamin Harrison and a long-time editor of the *New York Tribune,* argued in the early 1890s that what the nation needed was a turn away from empty spectacle and toward the "dry diet of public education." By the end of the nineteenth century, both parties—largely in response to the successful presidential campaign of Grover Cleveland in 1884, whic had distanced itself from party bosses and stressed issues—were struggling to make their campaigns more substantive. As one New York Republican leader stated after Cleveland's victory:

> All men who were active in that campaign will remember the surprise that came when the brass band, the red light, and the mass meeting seemed suddenly to have lost their power. That was the beginning of a change of political discussion from the open field, as in Lincoln's day, to the private home where each family began to examine and discuss for itself the policy of the parties to find which party promised the most for the elevation and comfort of that special home. It was an evolutionary result, arising from the demand of changing conditions from sentimental to economic issues,—the evolution into education as the superior force in American politics.

He was excessively optimistic. Educational politics did not become the norm, then or later. But it did mark a gradual move away from the politics of partisan spectacle, mass mobilization, and broad participation; from politics as a major cultural activity and commitment toward politics as a calculation of interests. Torchlight parades, ribald political rallies, party bands, campaign barbecues: in the twentieth century those things would become increasingly rare and increasingly irrelevant to the political experience of most Americans. And one result, already faintly visible as early as the 1880s, was a growing voter apathy. There were recurring phrases in reports from party organizers during the 1892 campaign about the response of voters to the new, more issue-oriented campaign style: "astonishing lethargy," "political lassitude," "no enthusiasm, no activity, rather a feeling of indifference," "so much *apathy*." There were complaints that this new style was, in fact, driving people away from political activity altogether. And the people making those complaints were right. Voter participation in presidential elections began declining as early as 1892, when the turnout was 75 percent. That was still very high by modern standards, but it was the lowest since before the Civil War.

Reformers, however, were not content with this grudging shift by parties toward so-called educational politics. They wanted to rescue elections form the parties altogether. At the state level, they campaigned for the initiative (by which citizens could use the state ballot to force the state legislature to consider legislation that the legislators themselves did not support); the referendum (by which voters could themselves pass laws, circumventing the legislatures altogether); and the recall (by which the public could remove elected officials from office before the end of their terms). Reformers transformed municipal elections into non-partisan contests to limit the power of bosses to choose candidates. They reconstructed city governments to limit the power of elected officials entirely, by creating commission governments and professional city managers. And they struggled, ultimately successfully, for a constitutional amendment to end the system by which United States Senators were elected by the members of the state legislatures. The Seventeenth Amendment, finally ratified in 1913, established the direct election of Senators by the people of each state.

Inevitably, this anti-party movement began to challenge the way presidents were selected as well. In 1905, Governor Robert M. La Follette of Wisconsin, one of the great figures in the history of American reform, persuaded the Wisconsin legislature to establish a direct popular election—controlled by state officials, not party organizations—to select delegates to the national presidential nominating conventions. "No longer," he promised, "will there stand between the voter and the official a political machine with a complicated system of caucuses and conventions, by the manipulation of which it thwarts the will of the voter." Several years later, Oregon established aprimary in which

Governor Robert M. La Follette, one of the great figures in the history of American reform, persuaded the Wisconsin legislature to establish a direct popular election to select delegates.

voters expressed a preference for aparticular presidential candidate, whom delegates would be obligated to support through the first ballot at the convention. Most other primary states eventually adopted this system.

By 1912, twelve states had established mandatory presidential primaries. Former President Theodore Roosevelt, challenging President William Howard Taft for his party's nomination, called that year for a national presidential primary to eliminate the role of party "middlemen" altogether. President Woodrow Wilson called for the same thing a year later. In the meantime, eight more states established their own presidential primaries; by 1916, there were twenty such elections.

The primaries did not soon end party control of the nominating process. Between 1917 and 1945, in fact, only one additional state added a primary election (Alabama, largely as a tool to block black voting) and eight states that had introduced primaries abolished them. Even in the heyday of early twentieth-century primaries, urban machines and party leaders continued to play the dominant role in selecting candidates, as Theodore Roosevelt discovered in 1912 when, after having won every primary, he was nevertheless denied the Republican nomination for president. But primaries did establish an alternative route to political prominence for candidates out of favor with party establishments. Franklin Roosevelt in 1932 helped overcome the skepticism of many party leaders by winning almost every primary. Primaries, in short, introduced a popular voice into what had been a largely closed, boss- controlled nominating process. And they created a precedent for a system that eventually would make all other aspects of the nominating process virtually irrelevant.

The Conventions

Even as the power to choose presidents moved slowly out of the hands of the political parties, the national nominating conventions remained a cardinal moment in the electoral process. The conventions were the largest, most riotous, and most ebullient of all the partisan displays in the presidential election year, and they remain so even today, though they have lost virtually all their other functions. But until well into the second half of the century, they also remained important decision-making bodies. Indeed their importance seemed in many ways to expand as the power of the parties declined. In the twentieth century, delegates to conventions represented not just the innumerable party organizations scattered throughout the country. Many of them were representatives chosen by popular vote in primaries. Others were delegates, directly or indirectly, of powerful interest groups. The movement of political power out of the hands of a few party bosses and into a much wider group of actors made conventions both harder to control and, as a result, sometimes more powerful.

The modern convention has often been criticized as an undemocratic institution—one reason being that its nominating function has now been entirely usurped by the primary system. But the first conventions were designed precisely to make the process of nominating presidents more democratic. In the early years of the Republic, presidential candidates were selected by the congressional caucus, in which members of Congress gathered in closed party meetings in Washington to choose their presidential nominees. To much of thevoting public, however, the caucus system soon began to seem corrupt and undemocratic. And so in the 1830s, party leaders replaced it with the national convention, which would, they believed, be more democratic, more representative of popular sentiment than Congress or state legislatures. It would be a great conclave of thepeople in which ordinary citizens, not officeholders or professional politicians, could shape the party's decisions.

Indeed, the creation of the convention was part of a much larger process of extending democracy in America: a process that was intended to expand the electorate (at least among white males), attack privilege, and make the political system more responsive to the people and less responsive to the elite. The first major-party convention, held by the Democrats in 1832, was in many ways a celebration of the idea of increased democracy with which Andrew Jackson had identified the party.

By the late nineteenth century, conventions had lost most of their early democratic aura and had become gatherings of party bosses and other luminaries. But that did not keep them from being the sites of dramatic and often tumultuous political struggle. This was particularly true of the Democratic party's conventions, largely because the Democrats remained saddled with a rule, adopted at their first convention in 1832, that presidential candidates needed the support of two-thirds of the delegates to win nomination. In the nineteenth century, the two-thirds rule had, in effect, given the slave South a veto over the party's candidates—one reason that antislavery Democrats eventually left the party. In the twentiethcentury, the rule continued to give disproportionate power to the South and to frustrate the efforts of the party's new urban leaders to establish their dominance.

Nowhere was that more visible than in the infamous Democratic convention of 1924 in Madison Square Garden in New York. It was the first convention whose proceedings were available to national audiences over the radio, and the first of many in which broadcasting did not serve the party's interests. An epic battle—between rural, Protestant Democrats united behind Senator William Gibbs McAdoo of California, and urban, ethnic, mostly Catholic Democrats united behind Governor Al Smith of New York—paralyzed the convention for 102 ballots until a pallid compromise candidate, the Wall Street lawyer John W. Davis, managed to win the necessary two thirds of the delegates. Davis went on to lose decisively to Calvin Coolidge.

The 1924 convention was unusual, however, only for the degree of its fractiousness. Both parties' gatherings were marked at times by bitter battles and unexpected passions: the 1912 Republican convention, for example, in which Theodore Roosevelt stormed out with his delegates after being denied the nomination by party leaders of the Old Guard; the 1916 Democratic convention, in which the wholly predictable renomination of Woodrow Wilson became the occasion of the unexpected and apparently spontaneous decision of the delegates to identify the party with non-intervention in World War I. The delegates attached the slogan "He kept us out of War" to a president who was by now unsure that he would be able to continue

Delegates gather in Chicago for the July 1896 Democratic National Convention.

to do so. In 1924, the Democrats battled not only over their presidential candidates, but also over the Ku Klux Klan, which the party narrowly failed to denounce after a bitter platform battle; and over prohibition, which remained a powerful divisive force within the party until the Volstead Act's repeal in 1933.

But in 1932, the role of the convention was suddenly transformed by a dramatic symbolic event. A century earlier, when the Democrats had held their first convention, their great leader Andrew Jackson was nowhere to be seen. And for the next hundred years, at virtually every convention of every party, the presidential candidate remained conspicuously absent. Tradition required him to remain at home and wait to be called upon, often several weeks later, to be formally notified of his nomination by a party delegation. But Governor Franklin D. Roosevelt of New York, after winning the presidential nomination on the fourth ballot, shattered that tradition. Traveling by airplane from Albany to Chicago (the first presidential candidate ever to fly), he appeared in person before the convention to accept the nomination with a dramatic speech, broadcast nationally by radio, in which he promised "a new deal for the American people." At virtually every Democratic and Republican convention since, the presidential candidate has appeared in person to accept the nomination. One exception, ironically, was Roosevelt himself. Weary, sick, and preoccupied with the war, he did not attend the 1944 Democratic convention and accepted its nomination by radio.

The combination of radio broadcasting and the introduction of the candidate himself into the convention ritual changed the dynamic of the meeting profoundly. After 1932, conventions became less important as meetings of the party faithful and more important as showcases for the candidates. The great oratorical battles over platform planks; the dramatic nominating speeches by party grandees; the contrived and often ribald demonstrations on the convention floor that at times continued for hours; the strident ideological debates; the displays of vanity as "favorite son" candidates had themselves nominated for office: these and other traditional features of national conventions began fading away, victims both of the increasing influence of the candidates over the proceedings and, even more, the awareness of the delegates that what excited the audience in the convention hall could often sound silly and trivial to radio listeners at home. Also gone were the prolonged battles over the presidential nominees, especially after the Democrats finally repealed the two-thirds rule in 1936.

Demonstrators tout their candidate, Governor Alf Landon of Kansas, at the Republican National Convention in Cleveland, June 1936.

The transformation of the convention from a gathering of party leaders to an image-making event for presidential candidates symbolizes the larger transformation of elections in the first half of the century. By the end of World War II, the race for the presidency had moved almost entirely out of the shadows of party governance and had become squarely centered on the candidates themselves. The lavish apparatus of the modern, media-centered campaign was already becoming visible. All presidential campaigns were heavily invested in the use of radio by 1945. All made significant use of public opinion polls to guide their efforts. All were receiving advice from advertisers, public relations experts, and other professionals who were already coming to be known as "handlers." And yet even after all these changes, the outward form of the presidential campaign still looked very much the same as it had more than a generation earlier. But not for long. The second half of the twentieth century would transform the process of choosing a president even more profoundly than had the first.

Campaigning for President in the Age of Television and Citizens' Rights

Historians looking back from some future date on the political history of the last fifty years might well conclude that we live in unusually contradictory, even paradoxical times. On the one hand, postwar American life—and postwar American politics—saw an almost unprecedented expansion of citizens' rights. Previously disenfranchised voters won access to the polls. Obstacles to voter registration were dramatically reduced. The ability of citizens to control the process by which candidates for the presidency and other offices were chosen dramatically increased, as primaries swept the nation and replaced selection by party bosses and organizations almost everywhere. Not since at least the mid-nineteenth century had the United States seen such a dramatic increase in political democratization.

One might expect—and most reformers did expect—that this increased democratization of the political process would produce greater citizen involvement in politics. But in reality, quite the contrary was the case in these turbulent years. For at the same time that the process of voting became at last open to almost everyone, much of the electorate developed a virtually unprecedented antipathy for the political system and its leaders. The decline in voter turnout that had begun early in the twentieth century and then leveled off suddenly accelerated in the 1970s. Allegiance to political parties declined rapidly and perhaps permanently; for the first time, more voters called themselves independents than claimed allegiance to any major party. Disillusionment with politics, with politicians, with government, and with public policy was widespread, rising in tandem with the system's increasing democratization. And Americans everywhere—ordinary citizens, influential figures in the media, scholars, business leaders, even politiciansthemselves—seemed to compete with one another in expressing their contempt for the nation's public life.

Many things produced this profound change in the role of politics in American life. Great political and policy disasters—the Vietnam War, Watergate, failed social and economic programs, and others—played a role. So did the emergence of the new global economy, which limited government's influence over the economy, and the sharply rising levels of instability and inequality that came in its wake. A culture of scandal (fueled, of course, by a number of actual scandals) has come to permeate both the workings of government and the behavior of a more aggressive press. And there was a broad and related shift in American culture, stretching now over more than forty years, that emphasized individual freedom, consumption, and personal fulfillment over older notions of discipline, restraint, repression, and duty to the community. Partly as a result, traditional patterns of authority have frayed. Fewer Americans any longer have an instinctive respect for public institutions; many more have come to believe that in the world of our time, every individual is largely on his or her own. There is much to be said for this new culture and for the liberation from artificial and repressive restraints it has helped to produce. But it has also created an environment in which politics, government, and many other institutions have much more difficulty winning popular respect.

And yet if one were to ask almost any knowledgeable observer of American politics what single thing has been most responsible for the dramatic change in the nation's public life in the last fifty years, one would very likely receive a simple and emphatic answer: television. And whether one concludes that television caused, or simply reflected, the vast changes in the way Americans approach politics, there can be little doubt that it played a tremendous role in reshaping today's public world.

America in the postwar era became a participatory democracy to a degree it had never been before. It also became an electronic democracy. And it is hard to decide which of those great changes was the more important.

Participatory Democracy

The rise of a more participatory democracy in the postwar era moved along many fronts: the civil rights movement, which enfranchised a black population in the South that had lost the vote to Jim Crow many decades before; a New Left that persuaded many young people in the 1960s that existing political structures were undemocratic and must be transformed; and a series of other "liberation" movements (for women, for Native Americans, for Latinos and Asian-Americans, for gays and lesbians, and others), which introduced a host of new voices to public discourse. Out of these many new forces pushing politics into a more democratic direction emerged a dramatic change in the nature of presidential politics, of which perhaps the most important was the triumph of the primaries.

The first wave of creating state primaries to determine delegates to presidential nominating conventions had run out of steam around the end of World War I, and for the next half-century the primary system had actually contracted. Even many of the primaries that survived gradually came to exercise only a modest effect on the nominating process. Some were simply devices for pledging delegates to a "favorite son," who had no hope of nomination but could use his delegate strength to exercise power at the convention; others, in parts of the South, were devices for disenfranchising black voters and some poor whites as well. By the early 1930s, primaries were in wide disrepute. In North Dakota, for example, a commission examining the state's 1932 primary (which no major presidential candidate had chosen to enter) concluded that "so far as expressing the preference of the . . . voters of the state was concerned, the election was a farce which cost the taxpayers $135,635." By 1940, the presidential primary system had reached its lowest ebb since 1912, with little-noticed elections in only thirteen states.

For the primary system genuinely to revive and expand, candidates and voters would have to believe not only that primaries were democratic, but that they were effective. In the thirty years after World War II, a series of important primary campaigns gradually proved that the system could make a difference. In 1948, for example, Harold Stassen, the young ambitious governor of Minnesota, launched a credible, and nearly successful, challenge to the Republican front-runner by defeating

Policemen in riot gear stand with their rifles ready at the scene of the turbulent 1968 Democratic National Convention in Chicago.

Governor Thomas E. Dewey of New York in a series of early primaries. Four years later, Dwight D. Eisenhower, a political neophyte, proved his vote-getting potential by running well in the Republican contests against the established party figure Robert Taft. And in 1960, John Kennedy overcame the doubts of party leaders by winning a series of crucial victories in that year's Democratic primaries, most notably in a celebrated contest in West Virginia against Senator Hubert Humphrey of Minnesota. There were still only sixteen states with primary elections, and nearly two-thirds of the delegates to both party conventions were still chosen by other means. But it was becoming difficult for party leaders in states without primaries to ignore these demonstrations of popular sentiment.

Perhaps most crucial of all was the 1968 Democratic convention, in which Vice President Hubert Humphrey received the party's nomination without having run in a single primary and without having aroused the enthusiasm of any significant group within the party. That convention produced scenes of unprecedented turbulence. Some of it—the most visible to the rest of the nation—came from demonstrators on the streets of Chicago protesting furiously (and in full view of television cameras) against what they claimed was the undemocratic character of the party's proceedings. Pictures of their violent clashes with police became part of the iconography of the age. But some of the turbulence came inside the conventional hall itself, as Democratic delegates pledged to Robert Kennedy (who had been assassinated several months earlier) and Eugene McCarthy (the quixotic anti-war candidate who had won the loyalty of millions of young people) repudiated the convention's rules, tried at times to disrupt the meeting, and expressed contempt for the process by which Humphrey had, they claimed, been imposed upon them from above.

In the aftermath of this political disaster, the Democratic party began working to reform its own rules to satisfy at least some of the demands of the insurgents. The result was the McGovern Commission—chaired by Senator George McGovern of South Dakota, who in 1972 became the first beneficiary of his committee's work. It reformed the Democratic delegation-selection process in ways that did not formally require primary elections but left few alternatives to them. In the future, delegates would need to be much more fully representative of the character of the party's, and the nation's population, and could not consist simply of party activists. In the aftermath of these reforms, the role of primaries quickly and dramatically increased. By 1980 the number of presidential primaries had risen from 15 to 35; by the 1990s there were primaries in 38 states, choosing more than 80 percent of the delegates. Indeed, so decisive has the primary system become that the party convention now plays virtually no role in selecting a candidate. In the last seven presidential elections, with only two exceptions (the Ford–Reagan contest in 1976 and the Carter–Ted Kennedy battle in 1980), candidates have locked up the nomination well before the end of the primary season. Not since 1952 has any convention needed more than one ballot to choose its nominee.

The rise of the primary has coincided with the first major reform of ballot access since early in the twentieth century—a reform of voter registration signed by President Bill Clinton in 1993 that required states to provide several sites at which citizens can register to vote, as alternatives to the often inaccessible offices of voter registrars. The most common new site was motor vehicle departments, which up to 80 percent of Americans visit periodically to acquire or renew drivers' licenses (hence the frequent, if somewhat derisive, term "motor voter law" to describe the new rules). The result was a substantial expansion of the voter rolls—nine million in under two years.

Reformers had argued for years that changing the rules of political behavior—limiting the power of bosses and machines in the selection of candidates and making voter registration easier and more accessible—would expand public engagement with the process and increase voter turnout. That has not happened. Indeed, at the very time that these reforms were taking effect, participation by voters in elections declined precipitously. One reason for that was the profound changes in the forms (as opposed to the rules) of political behavior that accompanied the rise of television.

Electronic Democracy

High above the floor of the 1948 Democratic National Convention in Philadelphia, tucked in the rafters almost out of sight, was an entirely new feature of the presidential election process: a television camera. Only a few thousand Americans owned television sets by then, and the medium was still a novelty in the minds of most politicians. So the single camera was installed under the roof, where the cameramen and newscasters had to speak over the flapping and cooing of pigeons—a far cry from the imperial glass booths, the legions of floor reporters, and the extensive prime-time coverage that would soon transform conventions into a spectacle designed almost entirely for and by television.

By 1952, however, over 19 million Americans had televisions in their homes. And while televised coverage of the conventions that year—still crude and modest—did little to establish the medium as a major political force, a sensational event in the fall campaign did. Richard Nixon, the Republican candidate for vice president and a young senator from California, came under attack in September for a controversial fund established on his behalf by wealthy business leaders in his home state. Dwight D. Eisenhower, the presidential nominee, had made corruption one of the principal targets of his campaign. "Let's Clean House with Ike" was one of his slogans. So he was particularly alarmed by the accusations of corruption against his own running mate. Eisenhower gave Nixon the chance to explain himself on national television, with the implied warning that if he did not succeed he would be removed from the ticket. Nixon's speech, in which he laid out his private (and very modest) finances and humiliated his wife (who sat grimly behind him on the flimsy television set) by showing how little they had, ended with a mawkish description of how, although he had almost always resisted gifts from supporters, he had accepted one: a small dog, Checkers, which he took for his daughters. The "Checkers Speech" became the first great television event in American political history. It attracted the largest audience the new medium had ever produced—over 30 million people and a vast radiolistenership as well. Not until another political innovation—the Kennedy–Nixon debates in 1960—would any television event, political or otherwise, attract a larger audience. Nixon's speech also produced a vast outpouring of support for the beleaguered candidate, saving his place on the ticket and his political career. It established television as the most powerful vehicle in American politics, and almost nothing in the world of elections would ever be the same again.

Richard Nixon's "Checkers Speech"—a nationally televised plea for sympathy and exoneration of any wrongdoing in regard to his personal finances—established television as the most influential medium in American politics, September 23, 1952.

In 1948, Harry Truman had won the presidency in the most famous upset in American political history by campaigning relentlessly all over the country from the back of a train. He made some radio speeches, and his campaign made effective use of advertising. But the enduring image of the 1948 contest was the scrappy Truman standing on the rear platform speaking aggressively and apparently spontaneously about the "do-nothing, good-for-nothing" Republican Congress. Compared to the slick, smooth campaign of Thomas E. Dewey, Truman's heavily favored opponent, the Democrats's whistle-stop, "give 'em hell" tactics seemed honest, authentic, and uncalculating (even though they were the result of careful and elaborate planning).

In every subsequent presidential campaign, the most enduring images would be televised ones: images of candidates giving their acceptance speeches at their now fully televised party conventions; images of television advertisements, which quickly became among the most important vehicles of campaigning; images of televised presidential debates, which started in 1960 and became regular features of presidential contests starting in 1976; and, of course, images of candidates battling personal or political crises on television—the "Checkers Speech" in 1952, Lyndon Johnson withdrawing from the race in 1968, Edmund Muskie crying during the New Hampshire primary campaign and George McGovern dumping Thomas Eagleton from his ticket in 1972, Bill Clinton defending his personal life on *60 Minutes* in 1992.

In many respects, television greatly improved the quality of political discourse and the seriousness of campaigns. Televised debates were the most important innovations in presidential campaigning since candidates began taking to the stump for the first time in the early twentieth century, and the debates gave voters an unparalleled opportunity to make informed, comparative judgments about the candidates they were considering. Many more Americans received news about candidates and information about the issues they were promoting through television than had ever received such news through the print media, radio, or newsreels; and as television news proliferated in the late twentieth century on cable and satellite channels, it could fairly be said that more information about political questions was available to the American public, and was more easily accessible, than ever before in the nation's history. Television stripped presidential candidates of many of the barriers and defenses they had enjoyed in the past and forced them to face the public directly, rather than through the screen of their parties. When people vote for president in the television age, they are more likely than they were in the past to vote for an individual candidate whom they have come to know at least reasonably well. No longer do they choose among mythologized images hidden from public view.

But the costs of television to the quality of presidential politics has been at least as high as its benefits. As the

Harry S. Truman's 1948 spirited whistle-stop campaign—in which he visited approximately 230 cities and towns from September 6 to November 1—was the last presidential campaign undefined by television imagery.

candidate's personality became a far more critical element of his appeal than it had been in the past, the qualities that voters came to value in their candidates began to shift as well. Personal qualities (what became known as the "character" issue) became more important, and it often became easy for issues to lose their power to persuade. In 1952 and 1956, the single most potent idea of the presidential campaigns was the one captured in the Republican slogan, "I Like Ike." The beaming, photogenic candidate with the dazzling smile and the comfortingly inarticulate public demeanor perfectly captured the mood of a prosperous nation eager for security and stability. In 1960, the handsome, youthful, charming John F. Kennedy—who, like Eisenhower, was not closely identified with any particular issues—squeaked out a victory over his much better-known opponent Richard Nixon largely by virtue of his television skills, and his performance in the first presidential debates in particular. Richard Nixon reinvented himself in 1968 on the basis of the most elaborately crafted television and advertising strategy any campaign had ever devised and won election without ever explaining clearly what he would do as president. Jimmy Carter emerged from the obscurity of his single term as governor of Georgia by virtue of a telegenic smile and an intimate speaking style that worked better on television than it did before an audience. And Ronald Reagan, the most successful media president of the last half-century, owed his political rise to a powerful television speech he gave in 1964 in the last days of the failing Goldwater campaign; and he sustained his visibility, and his popularity, over the next 25 years through his unfailing skill—unsurprising for an accomplished actor—before the cameras. Most voters

Ronald Reagan, known as the "Great Communicator," demonstrates his charismatic persona as he accepts the presidential nomination at the July 1980 Republican National Convention.

knew of Reagan's roots in the most conservative wing of the Republican party; but Reagan won election less because of his right-wing past than because his comforting television demeanor persuaded many voters that he was less ideological than in fact he was.

By the same inevitable logic, public figures who might in another age have become successful presidential candidates have found themselves left behind because they did not fit comfortably into the new media age. The annals of modern politics are filled with talented, experienced, distinguished men whose presidential hopes were dashed at least in part because of poor television skills or disastrous televised mistakes: Robert Taft, Barry Goldwater, George Romney, Edmund Muskie, Walter Mondale, Michael Dukakis, Bob Dole.

Television rewarded candidates who were telegenic enough to make effective use of the electronic media and well-funded enough to be able to afford it. But it also changed the relationship between voters and the men and women they were asked to support. Grass-roots mobilization, party organization, doorbell ringing, bumper stickers, campaign buttons, and all the other activities and accoutrements that have come to be called "retail politics" became much less important—and hence received much less attention from campaigns—once it became possible to reach millions of people at once over television. Candidates continued to travel the country and to speak at rallies and even, at times, to make whistle-stop railroad tours—but now mostly as backdrops for local or national television coverage, not primarily as ways to reach individual voters or communities. Party organizations became largely adjuncts of the presidential campaigns—their leaders chosen by the presidential candidates themselves, the committees shriveling back into near invisibility in the years between elections.

The primacy of television created a vast gulf between the experience of individual voters and the reality of presidential campaigns. Citizens might see more of their candidates and learn more about them than they had previously been able to discover. But the sense of personal connection and direct involvement with the political process itself, which had been so important a part of American political life in the nineteenth century and even (if in somewhat diminished form) in the first half of the twentieth century, gradually vanished altogether.

In the past, many Americans had taken an interest in politics because it was something in which they could participate—as members of local organizations; as participants in rallies, parades, and barbecues; as workers in community-based campaign offices. These may have been trivial activities, but they gave many people the feeling of being a part of the public world and that created lifelong habits of political participation. By the late twentieth century, however, presidential campaigns—to an increasing degree, the only campaigns to which most voters paid any serious attention—had become, and remain still, something very different. Politics had moved out of local party offices, out of the streets and auditoriums, indeed out of any significant place in the lives of communities and families and individuals, and into consulting firms, advertising offices, and television studios. Politics had become both more constantly visible and at the same time more remote, impersonal, and unapproachable.

The sense of distance between ordinary voters and the presidential campaigns they are asked to support has been greatly increased by the new and corrosive role of money in a politics driven by the need to buy expensive television time. Beginning in earnest in the 1960s, but accelerating rapidly through the decades that followed, one of the principal activities of major political candidates has become the effort to raise money; and increasingly, the only way to raise large sums of money is through courting wealthy people and powerful groups and interests. It is hard to fault the candidates themselves too much for this. Campaigns are expensive, and if any candidates refrain from raising the money they need, their opponents surely will not. But the centrality of money to modern campaigns, and the increasingly unattractive ways in which candidates seek to raise it, has disillusioned millions of ordinary Americans, who have come to feel that they are now secondary figures in contests dominated by large contributors. The rise of campaign finance reform as an issue in presidential campaigns in the 1990s, and the intermittent popularity of such advocates of reform as Ross Perot, John McCain, and Bill Bradley, is only one of many signs of how money has eroded public trust in a process that used to be an intimate part of the lives of many citizens.

And so most Americans have simply ceased to participate very often, or even think very often, about public life. Instead, politics has become for them an almost entirely passive activity, which most voters encounter rarely and glancingly. They read capsule descriptions of campaigns in newspapers and magazines. They listen to the radio. Above all, they watch television. And occasionally, in ever dwindling numbers, they go to the polls and vote. In 1996, for only the second time since 1824, fewer than half the eligible voters participated in a presidential election. In 2000, in the most closely contested race in recent history, only 51 percent of thevoters participated.

The Future of Presidential Politics

Despite all the signs of decline—the popular apathy, the cynicism, the disenchantment, the declining voter turnout—presidential politics continue to attract substantial interest at times. Those who do vote usually do so on the basis of real conviction; and even many of those who do not form strong opinions about the candidates vying for their support. There are, moreover, signs of a continuing if usually unfulfilled yearning for political engagement, of the appeal of an older style of grass-roots politics. Those signs were visible in the enthusiasm with which thousands of people, black and white, participated in the civil-rights and antiwar movements in the 1960s; in the enormous success of environmentalism in mobilizing people of all ages and classes behind its goals; in the commitment with which gays and lesbians have fought for equal rights through political action and with which AIDS activists have struggled to win attention to a terrible disease; and in the passions with which women and men have embraced the pro-life and pro-choice movements and have worked actively to promote them. It is also visible occasionally within the formal political system.

One example was the first stage of the presidential campaign of Ross Perot in 1992, which illustrated the appeal of an older political style. Perot, a wealthy Texas businessman with a penchant for publicity, announced his candidacy by denouncing the moral corruption of both parties and calling for common sense and business principles to solve the nation's problems. Eventually, Perot's campaign became an almost entirely personal vehicle driven by the obsessions, the ego, and the money of the erratic candidate himself. But in the beginning, whether by design or not, it was very different. It produced something that had long been missing from presidential politics, and it enjoyed astonishing (if short-lived) success as a result. For it gave millions of voters the chance to feel that they were part of a genuine popular movement. The enthusiasm of those citizens was not just for, perhaps not even mainly for, Perot himself, about whom most of his supporters actually knew relatively little; it was an enthusiasm for the idea of political participation: for collecting signatures, organizing local campaign committees, passing out buttons and bumper stickers. Perot gave his supporters the chance to feel that they were controlling the process and not being controlled by it. Perot's campaign demonstrated, if nothing else, that a yearning for political empowerment remains strong in America. For many voters, apparently, Perot's position on issues (or his unwillingness to take positions on them) was beside the point. For a brief moment, it gave them something they considered more important: a chance to feel democracy at work.

Billionaire Ross Perot jolted the 1992 election and the status quo with his grass-roots Reform Party campaign.

As the twenty-first century begins its unpredictable history, an increasing number of Americans are expressing their unhappiness with the style and structure of modern political life and are looking to another electronic medium to rescue it: the Internet. The Internet, they claim, makes possible a re-creation, in virtual form, of the personal engagement with politics that was once the norm of public life. It offers a chance to engage citizens in discussion and debate, even to give them control over policy decisions in a direct and immediate way. It gives every voter a chance to make his or her views available to the public through a website or participation in an Internet forum. It is, at least for now, perhaps the most intensely democratic and participatory mass medium ever created. Whether the Internet will become the site of a genuinely new kind of popular politics, and whether it would be a good thing if it did, remains to be seen.

The tumultuous and controversial conclusion to the 2000 presidential election—in which the candidate who received the most popular votes lost the presidency for the first time since 1888, and in which a bitter contest over disputed ballots in Florida convinced supporters of both candidates that the election was in danger of being "stolen"—raised new questions about, and new possibilities for, the character of presidential politics:

In this unprecedently close election, the candidacy of Ralph Nader, representing the new Green Party, almost certainly affected the outcome. Nader received fewer than 1 percent of the vote nationally, but won enough support in several states—including the crucial state of Florida—to deny the Democratic candidate (from whom Nader drew most of his support) a victory. Will this new influence strengthen the appeal of third party candidacies or discredit them?

While the Supreme Court was in chambers considering the Bush campaign's request for a stay of the Florida Supreme Court's ruling, demonstrator's marched outside, December 9, 2000.

That Al Gore received over 300,000 more votes than George Bush in the national election and still lost, demonstrated to many Americans the tremendous significance of the electoral college, the device created by the Constitution for determining the results of presidential elections. Will the apparent unfairness of the 2000 result lead to efforts to eliminate the electoral college? Or will the great difficulties in counting the votes in Florida persuade reformers that a close national popular vote might be the source of even greater difficulties and controversies?

And will the extraordinary closeness of the 2000 contest, in which a few hundred votes eventually helped determined the outcome, convince voters that their votes really do count? Will it persuade many more voters to come to the polls in subsequent elections? Or will the tawdry process by which the election was finally decided—including the shocking actions of the United States Supreme Court in terminating the contest and, in effect, choosing a winner—simply reinforce the already widespread belief that elections do not reflect the popular will but, rather, the machinations of privileged elites?

In short, how will Americans in the twenty-first century resolve the tension, which stretches back over well over a century, between the disenchantment of voters with the political process and the continued yearning for some personal connection to the great, majestic, and increasingly remote pageant through which our nation chooses leaders?

The American Century began with a referendum on America's rapidly changing relationship to the rest of the world. Flush with prosperity and recent victory in the Spanish-American War, the Republicans renominated President William McKinley. The Democrats renominated William Jennings Bryan, still remarkably young at 40.

Although the candidates were the same as in 1896, the nation had come far in four years. What Secretary of State John Hay called a "splendid little war" had a huge effect on American foreign policy, bringing the United States forcefully into the world arena.

The chief drama of the conventions was the selection of the vice presidents. In Kansas City, the Democrats chose Adlai Stevenson (the grandfather of Adlai Stevenson II, Governor of Illinois and Democratic candidate for president in 1952 and 1956), Grover Cleveland's second VP. The Republicans deflected Bryan's youth and energy by picking New York Governor Theodore Roosevelt, whose courageous (and artfully publicized) charge up San Juan Hill in Cuba had brought his name before millions of newspaper readers. Yet Roosevelt's nomination was no foregone conclusion. He was proposed by Thomas Platt, New York's boss of bosses, who was tired of dealing with an obstreperous governor back home. Mark Hanna, the party kingmaker, loathed the idea, andused all his clout to thwart Roosevelt at the convention, but to no avail.

Left to right:
William McKinley (1843–1901)
William Jennings Bryan (1860–1925)

William Jennings Bryan, the "Boy Orator of the Prairie," was still only 40 in 1900, the second time he ran for president.

Amidst the tumult, he warned, "Don't any of you realize that there's only one life between that madman and the presidency?" Ominously, he instructed President McKinley, "Your duty to the country is to live for four years."

To Hanna's surprise, Roosevelt proved himself a brilliant campaigner. McKinley was expected to stay presidential by staying put, but Roosevelt was out on the hustings every day (he logged 673 speeches). "Teddy" intuitively grasped the power of personality to shape publicity, and the papers were flooded with colorful stories about the Rough Riders and other legends that nourished the cult of TR. He was especially popular in the West, "where they regard me as a fellow barbarian, and like me much."

Bryan was no wallflower, either. The Great Commoner matched Roosevelt's energy and then some. He often gave a dozen speeches a day, hammering away at the superiority of "republic" to "empire," and of democracy to plutocracy. Americans hungered for glory, and new territory fed that hunger. An improving economy dulled the luster of Bryan's earlier crusade against the gold standard. The Democrats were also vulnerable to charges of ignoring lynchings in the South while defending human rights in the Philippines.

The result was a foregone conclusion. It was 1896 all over again, only more so. Bryan won the solid South and much of the West. Everything else went to McKinley, creating an impressive mandate for a strong President and a nation yearning to be taken seriously on the world stage.

A few bit players worked the sidelines. The Socialists nominated Eugene V. Debs for the first of five times and included the radical pledge of female suffrage on their platform. The United Christian Party acknowledged Christ as the sovereign ruler of all nations. If that claim hearkened back to America's evangelical past, then the sense that other countries mattered foreshadowed the busy century to come. Despite warnings from naysayers like Mark Twain and Andrew Carnegie, the voters were enthusiastic for an expansive America.

Having led the United States to victory in its first foreign war in over five decades, McKinley was unbeatable.

Although President William McKinley did not personally campaign in 1900, he received the largest popular majority ever given a presidential candidate up to that time, and led in electoral votes, 292 to 155. Here he poses for a formal portrait, c. 1901.

William Jennings Bryan called for income tax, direct elections, an end to "federal interference," and liberalization of the Supreme Court, among other reforms. By the time of this photograph, he had already lost for a second time to William McKinley, c. 1901.

Four of the most powerful men of the era *(above)* pose for a group portrait at the White House: from left, steel magnate Andrew Carnegie; William Jennings Bryan; J. J. Hill, president of the Great Northern Railway Company; and John Mitchell, president of the United Mine Workers of America, c. 1900.

Before embarking on the 1900 campaign, Bryan was a key figure at the Trans Mississippi International Exposition and Indian Congress of 1898 in Omaha, Nebraska *(right)*, which brought together 500 Native Americans from 35 tribes. Over 2,600,000 people visited the exposition between June 1 and November 1, 1898.

Vice Presidential candidate Theodore Roosevelt addresses a suffragette rally from the his home porch in Oyster Bay, Long Island, 1900.

The men of the 1st U.S. Volunteer Cavalry, known as the "Rough Riders," flank their leader, Lt. Col. Roosevelt (center), on San Juan Hill, Cuba, 1898.

President McKinley gives his inaugural address *(left)*, Washington, D.C., March 4, 1900.

A horse-drawn carriage ferries McKinley (in hat) to the inauguration at the Capitol *(right)*. To his right is Senator Mark Hanna of Ohio, chairman of the Republican National Committee, Washington, D.C., March 4, 1900.

SUNDAY, THREE CENTS. DAILY, ONE CENT.

"All the News That's Fit to Print."

The New York Times.

THE WEATHER.
Partly cloudy; fresh southerly winds.

VOL. L...NO. 15,860. NEW YORK, WEDNESDAY, NOVEMBER 7, 1900.–SIXTEEN PAGES. ONE CENT In Greater New York, Elsewhere, and Jersey City. TWO CENTS.

M'KINLEY RE-ELECTED

McKinley 284
Bryan 155

REPUBLICANS CARRY

NEW YORK,
INDIANA,
WEST VIRGINIA,
DELAWARE,
MARYLAND,
KANSAS,
NORTH DAKOTA,
SOUTH DAKOTA,
CALIFORNIA,
WYOMING.

DEMOCRATS CARRY

NEVADA,
KENTUCKY.

DOUBTFUL

NEBRASKA.

Total Electoral Vote	447
Necessary to a choice	224
William McKinley	284
William J. Bryan	155
McKinley over Bryan	121

The expected has happened. The Republican Presidential ticket has swept the country.

William McKinley of Ohio, the Republican candidate for President of the United States, has been re-elected to that office, and Theodore Roosevelt of New York has been chosen Vice President.

The Republicans carried twenty-seven States and the Democrats eighteen.

In 1896 the Republicans carried twenty-three States, including California and Kentucky, in each of which the Democrats secured one Electoral vote. The Democrats carried twenty-two States.

The Republicans have regained the States of Kansas, South Dakota, Washington, Utah, and Wyoming.

The Democrats have recovered the State of Kentucky.

Kentucky has given her entire Electoral vote to Bryan.

While victorious in Kentucky in securing the Electors for Bryan, the Democrats have suffered a great defeat in the election of John W. Yerkes, Republican, as Governor, over Beckham, the successor to Gov. Goebel.

Colorado's Electoral vote will be cast for Bryan.

A fusion Legislature has been elected in Colorado. It will elect an opposition Senator to succeed Edward O. Wolcott, Republican, whose term will expire March 3, 1901.

Delaware has chosen Electors favorable to McKinley and Roosevelt.

The election in Delaware of a Democratic Legislature assures the election of two Democratic Senators, one to fill a vacancy and another to succeed Senator Richard R. Kenney, Democrat, whose term will expire March 3, 1901.

Idaho's Electoral vote will go to Bryan and Stevenson.

The victory in Idaho for the fusion legislative ticket assures the election of an opposition Senator to succeed George L. Shoup, Republican, whose term will expire next March.

Kansas has decided to cast her Electoral vote for McKinley.

The election in Kansas of a Republican Legislature will give to that State a Republican Senator to succeed Lucien Baker, Republican, whose term will expire March 3, 1901.

Montana persists in its allegiance to free silver and to Bryan and will give him its Electoral vote.

Although Montana has chosen a Democratic Legislature, it is not yet certain that the partisans of William A. Clark can command votes enough to elect him. The Daly Democrats and Republicans may combine to choose Senator Thomas H. Carter, Republican, to succeed himself, and a Democrat of the Daly faction for the short term.

South Dakota has returned to the Republican column and will cast her Electoral vote for McKinley and Roosevelt.

Senator Richard F. Pettigrew, who calls himself a silver man, the most active and bitter opponent of the Administration in the United States Senate, will be succeeded by a Republican, South Dakota having chosen a Republican Legislature.

Utah has reversed the position occupied by that State four years ago, and will give its three Electoral votes to McKinley.

Having elected a Republican Legislature, Utah will choose a Republican Senator to fill the vacancy created in that State by failure to elect.

West Virginia adheres to the Republican Party, and will give its Electoral vote to McKinley.

The election in West Virginia of a Republican Legislature will be followed by the return to the United States Senate of Stephen B. Elkins, whose term will expire March 3, 1901.

McKinley's plurality of the popular vote is about 550,000.

This is smaller than his plurality of 603,514 in 1896, which was exceeded only by Grant's plurality over Greeley, in 1872, of 762,991.

REPUBLICAN.	
California	9
Connecticut	6
Delaware	3
Illinois	24
Indiana	15
Iowa	13
Kansas	10
Maine	6
Maryland	8
Massachusetts	15
Michigan	14
Minnesota	9
New Hampshire	4
New Jersey	10
New York	36
North Dakota	3
Ohio	23
Oregon	4
Pennsylvania	32
Rhode Island	4
South Dakota	4
Utah	3
Vermont	4
Washington	4
West Virginia	6
Wisconsin	12
Wyoming	3
Total	284

DEMOCRATIC.	
Alabama	11
Arkansas	8
Colorado	4
Florida	4
Georgia	13
Idaho	3
Kentucky	13
Louisiana	8
Mississippi	9
Missouri	17
Montana	3
Nevada	3
North Carolina	11
South Carolina	9
Tennessee	12
Texas	15
Virginia	12
Total	155

DOUBTFUL.	
Nebraska	8

McKinley's majority 121

FIERCE RIOT ON BROADWAY.

Police Commissioner Hess Buffeted by the Crowd.

The sidewalk in front of the Rossmore Hotel was the scene of a fierce riot shortly before 2:30 o'clock this morning. It was precipitated by a number of Columbia students.

Before peace was restored by the reserves from the Tenderloin Station Police Commissioner Hess had been buffeted by the crowd and Samuel B. Harry, a hunchback, of 506 East Sixth Street, had been trampled underfoot on the pavement and so badly injured that he had to be removed in a carriage by some friends who witnessed the affray.

About 300 of the college boys, all of whom were shouting for Bryan, started the trouble by lining up on the sidewalk and striking at every passer-by who came between their lines.

On some they used their canes and on others fists and gloves, and nobody attempted to interfere with them until a band of hilarious young Republicans, each man of whom bore an American flag, came between the lines.

One of the students cried: "Why should they have a monopoly of the flag?" and seized it. Several others supported him, and in an instant there were a dozen free fights in progress along the street.

Commissioner Hess ran out of the hotel and shouted:

"Stop this disorder."

The rioters then turned on him, and, after beating him, threw him back into the hotel and held the doors so that he could not again come out.

He sent an alarm to Police Headquarters over the hotel telephone, and a few moments later two Sergeants with forty of the reserves were being hurried up Broadway in the patrol wagon.

The police did not try to make arrests, but used their clubs freely, and before long the fighters had broken and run, and a guard of policemen was stationed about the hotel to prevent the young men from again assembling there.

Only one prisoner was taken, Frank Butler, a newspaper man, who was pointed out by Rufus Silberman of 306 West Forty-seventh Street, as being the instigator of the riot.

Butler had many friends who protested that he had nothing to do with it, but Silberman, who was one of the McKinley paraders, insisted that he be locked up.

Harry, the cripple, when picked up from where he had fallen, was bleeding profusely. The police wanted him to go to a hospital, but he declined to do so.

Before the fighting was over many who were not students had been drawn into it.

CONGRESS BOTH HOUSES REPUBLICAN

About 24 Majority in Senate.

About 47 Majority in House.

REPUBLICAN GAINS IN MANY STATES.

Clean Sweep in Maryland—General Overturn in Nebraska—Increased Republican Majority in Both Houses.

The Fifty-seventh Congress will be Republican in both branches.

In the Senate the Republicans will have a majority of sixteen on a straight party vote.

There will be a Republican majority in the House of Representatives of 47.

In the Fifty-sixth Congress the Republicans have majorities in both houses. The Senate, with 86 members, consists of 51 Republicans and 35 in the opposition, giving a majority of 16. There are four vacancies.

The House of Representatives, consisting of 357 members when full, consists of 185 Republicans and 167 Democrats and others, showing a Republican majority of 18. There are five vacancies to be filled at this election.

The Republican majority in the House, 18 in the present House, will be 47 in the next.

Maryland elects a solid Republican delegation.

The Republicans succeeded in breaking into the North Carolina delegation. James M. Moody, Republican, is elected in the Ninth District.

In all probability Spencer Blackburn (Rep.) is also elected in the Eighth District by 500 plurality.

One of the most surprising results was the defeat of William McAleer in the rock-ribbed Democratic Third District of Pennsylvania. His successor is Henry Burke, a Republican.

The Democrats reclaimed the district in Texas now represented by Hawley and made the delegation solid.

Bryan's own State overturned her Congressional delegation. In the present House she is represented by two Republicans and four Fusionists and Democrats. In the next she will be represented by five Republicans and one Fusionist.

One of the biggest changes is in New York. In the Fifty-sixth Congress she is represented by 15 Republicans and 18 Democrats. In the Fifty-seventh Congress New York will have 20 Republicans and 14 Democrats.

"Billy" Lorimer, the Republican boss in Chicago, is defeated by John J. Feeley.

Two districts are in doubt. One is Congressman Lentz's district in Ohio. The Republicans made strenuous efforts to defeat Lentz because of his violent attacks on the Administration in the last session. Tompkins, his opponent, is probably elected, but not by more than 100 majority.

The Third Massachusetts is claimed by Washburn, (Rep.,) by 300 majority, and by Thayer, (Dem.,) by 200. Thayer is probably elected.

UNITED STATES SENATE.

Next Senate—Republicans	57
Opposition	33
Republican majority	24
Present Senate—Republicans	51
Opposition	35
Republican majority	16

HOUSE OF REPRESENTATIVES.

Fifty-seventh Congress—	
Republicans	202
Opposition	155
Republican majority	47
Fifty-sixth Congress—	
Republican	185
Opposition	167
Republican majority	18

CLOSE IN KANSAS.

One-third of a Number of Precincts Show a Gain for Bryan.

Special to The New York Times.

TOPEKA, Kan., Nov. 6.—Seventeen Kansas precincts, one-third counted, show a gain for Bryan over 1896 of 15 per cent. The result in the State is close and cannot be known before to-morrow.

Election day dawned clear and pleasant throughout the State. The polls in this city opened at 8 o'clock. The vote was extraordinarily heavy during the morning, due to splendid weather.

The heaviest vote in years has been polled in Southern Kansas. Democratic hopes lie in the country districts. The fair weather caused nearly all the farmers to go to the polls.

Wichita will probably go Republican.

Fusion Headquarters claim the State for Bryan and the Fusion ticket. W. E. Stanley, Republican candidate for Governor, predicts his own election.

DEMOCRATS CONCEDE NEBRASKA.

CHICAGO, Nov. 6.—Henry C. Payne has received the following message from the Assistant Secretary of War, Meiklejohn, at his home in Fullerton, Neb.: "The Democrats concede Nebraska to McKinley by 7,000."

CLOSE IN NEBRASKA.

Special to The New York Times.

OMAHA, Neb., Nov. 6.—The returns from the State are coming in very slowly, but the Republicans are showing gains on an average of ten to a precinct. There are 1,250 precincts in the State. At this rate the State will give a Republican majority for the electoral ticket of at least 10,000.

At 10 o'clock this evening Vice Chairman Edmisten of the Populists' National Committee and also Chairman of the Populist State Committee, said:

"The returns received by us indicate that Bryan has carried Nebraska by 15,000 votes. I do not care to comment on National returns. They show for themselves."

The State Journal claims Nebraska by a small majority for the Republicans, if the present ratio of gain holds out.

The Republican State Committee claims the State by 10,000.

The State ticket will be close, but the indications now are that the Republicans will elect the full State ticket and the Legislature.

A dispatch from Lincoln says the Congressional ticket is very favorable to the Republicans. G. J. Burkett is elected in the First District, David H. Mercer in the Second, and John R. Hays in the Third, all Republicans.

McKinley in Lincoln has a majority of 1,602, a gain of 555 over 1896.

In the Fourth the returns indicate the election of John D. Pope, (Rep.,) and the Fifth and Sixth are in doubt, but will probably be carried by the Fusionists A. C. Shallenberger and William Neville.

Nine precincts outside of Omaha and Douglass give McKinley 1,392; Bryan, 849. The same precincts in 1896 gave McKinley, 1,097; Bryan, 815.

Fourteen precincts out of twenty in Lincoln give McKinley a gain of 562 over 1896.

The Fusion managers are very much disconcerted, and the State news, together with information of overwhelming majorities for McKinley received from the East, has caused considerable depression among the Fusionists.

As the news is received here on the street the scenes beggar description, the excitement being intense. Many thousands of dollars were wagered on the last moment on Nebraska by Republicans, and it is estimated that $100,000 changed hands in Omaha on the result at odds in favor of Bryan of from 1 to 3.

The weather throughout Nebraska today could not be improved on, being far above the average of November temperature, with the skies clear throughout the State. In Omaha the polls were open at 8 o'clock. The early voting was unusually heavy. The leaders were out early, getting their men in line, and conditions were favorable for the full vote being polled.

The number of votes registered at noon broke the record.

At Kearney, where there was no registration this year, several challenges were made and some arrests threatened for illegal voting.

GOV. ROOSEVELT'S COMMENT.

He Hears the News at Oyster Bay and Sends Message to the President.

OYSTER BAY, L. I., Nov. 6.—Gov. Roosevelt, surrounded by his family, to-night received the returns at his home on Sagamore Hill. The Governor at no time during the evening seemed anxious about the result. He did not make any special arrangements to receive the news, and depended on messages to be brought from the telegraph office in the railroad station, nearly three miles away.

The first definite information of the Republican victory was conveyed to the Governor at about 10 o'clock. He was in the reception room with his wife and daughter. When he appeared at the door to meet a newspaper correspondent he was in evening dress. He invited his visitor into the parlor and closely scrutinized the returns and briefly commented on the result. After reading the message, he said:

"Isn't that fine. It shows what the American people are. It shows that they want the good times to continue, and are in favor of honest money and are for the flag."

The Governor at once dictated the following dispatch to President McKinley:

To President William McKinley, Canton, Ohio:
I congratulate you and far more the Nation. You have my heartfelt gratitude over the result.
THEODORE ROOSEVELT.

Gov. Roosevelt also sent messages of congratulations to Senator Hanna and Mr. Odell.

MR. ODELL JUBILANT.

Says the General Result of the Election Far Exceeds His Expectations.

Governor-elect Odell, talking to THE NEW YORK TIMES over the telephone from his home in Newburg at 11 o'clock last night, said:

"The general result of the election far exceeds my expectations. President McKinley appears to have carried every doubtful State. The story is one of increased majorities everywhere. The people have not only given a grand indorsement of President McKinley's Administration, but they have administered a rebuke to Mr. Bryan and his party leaders which will retire them from the councils of the Democratic Party, and which will put an end to the theories which they have been advocating.

"To the Republican Party has been given a full measure of power in the National Government, and the country is safe.

"So far as this State is concerned, it seems now that the Republican ticket has won by 150,000 majority. My estimate of 100,000 for the party was given out as conservative, and the vote justifies the prediction. I scarcely looked for so sweeping a victory.

"Mr. Croker has carried New York County for Mr. Bryan as he said he would, and Greater New York appears to have given Mr. Bryan a majority, but while Mr. Croker has done this he has heard from the 'men from cornfields' for whom he has expressed such contempt. The result in the State demonstrates his unfitness for State leadership.

"Of course I regard my own election with great satisfaction. It proves that the people are not afraid to elect a Governor simply because he has been able to serve his party as a practical politician. As Governor I shall try to bring into use the same practical, businesslike methods as I have tried to apply as a party leader."

CROKER'S MESSAGE TO BRYAN.

Richard Croker said just before leaving Tammany Hall at 11:15 last evening that he would give out only one statement about the election returns received by him. Here is the statement:

"I can't say what caused the defeat of Mr. Bryan, if he has been defeated, and I don't admit that he has been. I cannot attribute it to anybody, but I can say that we in New York have done everything in our power to elect Mr. Bryan, and we have made a splendid showing."

"This ends Mr. Bryan's political career so far as the Presidency is concerned," said a reporter.

"Not by any means," replied Mr. Croker. "Mr. Bryan is a natural leader of the people, and he will be heard from again."

Before leaving Tammany Hall Richard Croker caused the following telegram to be sent to William J. Bryan at Lincoln, Neb.:

As you no doubt already know, this State has gone heavily against us, but whereas this county in 1896 gave McKinley 23,000, it gives you today 32,000, a gain of 55,000.
We are defeated but not discouraged.
RICHARD CROKER.

Mr. Croker announced again that he would make no further statement under any circumstances about the election, and he left Tammany Hall to go to the Democratic Club. He was accompanied by John F. Carroll.

ODELL ELECTED GOVERNOR

110,559 PLURALITY

LEGISLATURE REPUBLICAN

16 Maj. in Senate.
58 Maj. in House.

McKINLEY RUNS ABOUT 3,000 AHEAD OF ODELL.

The State of New York has given a plurality of over 140,000 to William McKinley, Republican candidate for President, and a plurality of 110,559 to Benjamin B. Odell, Jr., Republican candidate for Governor.

Both Bryan and Stanchfield have carried the counties of New York, Queens, Richmond, and Schoharie. Mr. Stanchfield also has carried the County of Chemung by 584, although the county gave McKinley a plurality of about 403. In 1896 McKinley carried every county in the State except Schoharie, and Black, the Republican candidate for Governor, did the same.

Mr. Odell had a narrow escape from losing Greene County, where his plurality is only 6 votes. Mr. McKinley's plurality in Greene County is 107, which is 19 above his plurality in 1896.

Elmira, Mr. Stanchfield's home, supported him handsomely. While Mr. Bryan's plurality in that city was 172, Mr. Stanchfield's was over 800.

STATE VOTE FOR PRESIDENT.

County.	Pluralities. McKinley. Rep.	Bryan Dem.
Albany	4,080	
Allegany	3,475	
Broome	3,800	
Cattaraugus	3,750	
Cayuga	3,950	
Chautauqua	8,618	
Chemung	403	
Chenango	1,894	
Clinton	2,067	
Columbia	1,489	
Cortland	2,078	
Delaware	3,200	
Dutchess	4,308	
Erie	5,500	
Essex	3,155	
Franklin	3,700	
Fulton & Ham	3,522	
Genesee	2,146	
Greene	107	
Herkimer	2,900	
Jefferson	4,850	
Kings	3,492	
Lewis	1,500	
Livingston	1,725	
Madison	3,290	
Monroe	7,000	
Montgomery	2,135	
New York		27,800
Nassau	2,000	
Niagara	1,974	
Oneida	6,388	
Onondaga	9,842	
Ontario	2,055	
Orange	4,820	
Orleans	1,810	
Oswego	4,683	
Otsego	1,700	
Putnam	851	
Queens		1,094
Rensselaer	3,000	
Richmond		695
Rockland	165	
St. Lawrence	8,700	
Saratoga	2,900	
Schenectady	1,800	
Schoharie		875
Schuyler	600	
Seneca	557	
Steuben	1,800	
Suffolk	4,152	
Sullivan	900	
Tioga	1,704	
Tompkins	1,559	
Ulster	2,000	
Warren	2,302	
Washington	4,880	
Wayne	3,479	
Westchester	2,989	
Wyoming	2,131	
Yates	1,200	
Total		
plurality, 1896		
plurality, 1898		

STATE VOTE FOR GOVERNOR.

County.	Pluralities. Odell Rep.	Stanchfield Dem.
Albany	1,284	
Allegany	3,325	
Broome	3,730	
Cattaraugus	3,249	
Cayuga	3,600	
Chautauqua	8,126	
Chemung		584
Chenango	1,730	
Clinton	1,748	
Columbia	1,374	
Cortland	1,982	
Delaware	3,000	
Dutchess	2,970	
Erie	3,049	
Essex	3,137	
Franklin	3,650	
Fulton and Hamilton	3,850	
Genesee	2,121	
Greene	6	
Herkimer	2,600	
Jefferson	4,500	
Kings	1,332	
Lewis	1,430	
Livingston	1,475	
Madison	3,182	
Monroe	5,000	
Montgomery	1,722	
New York		34,883
Nassau	2,000	
Niagara	1,000	
Oneida	5,151	
Onondaga	8,300	
Ontario	2,000	
Orange	4,200	
Orleans	1,734	
Oswego	4,599	
Otsego	1,700	
Putnam	803	
Queens		1,989
Rensselaer	2,800	
Richmond		993
Rockland	42	
St. Lawrence	8,500	
Saratoga	3,000	
Schenectady	1,300	
Schoharie		380
Schuyler	450	
Seneca	100	
Steuben	3,300	
Suffolk	3,885	
Sullivan	800	
Tioga	1,470	
Tompkins	1,376	
Ulster	1,500	
Warren	2,300	
Washington	4,789	
Wayne	3,351	
Westchester	1,989	
Wyoming	1,975	
Yates	1,180	
Total	149,468	38,909
Odell's plurality		110,559

THE NEXT LEGISLATURE.

The Senate.	
Republicans	33
Democrats	17
Republican majority	16
The Assembly.	
Republicans	104
Democrats	46
Republican majority	58

Yesterday's election gives the Republicans a safe working majority of 16 in the Senate and 58 in the Assembly. The present Senate is made up of 27 Republicans and 23 Democrats, and the Assembly of 93 Republicans, 56 Democrats, and 1 Independent Democrat. This gives the Republicans a gain of 12 in the Senate and 21 in the Assembly and a majority of 74 on joint ballot.

Republicans marked R; Democrats, D; re-elected, *.

SPEECH BY MR. M'KINLEY

Addresses a Few Words to Canton Crowd, in Response to a Tremendous Ovation—How He Received the News.

CANTON, Ohio, Nov. 7.—At midnight Canton was in a frenzy of enthusiasm which knew no bounds. The crowds which had been burning red fire down town marched en masse to the McKinley residence with bands playing, rockets sending lurid streaks across the sky, and tumultuous cheers mingling with the din of horns and steam whistles.

The crowd was stilled for a time with some of the cheering news received. This included dispatches from the Kansas Chairman, claiming that State by 40,000; from Secretary Heath of the Republican National Committee, saying Indiana gave McKinley 29,000 plurality; from the Iowa Chairman, saying Iowa's Republican plurality was 100,000, and from the Union League Club, Chicago, giving the President glowing congratulations on the triumphant indorsement given him by the American people. But the crowd soon clamored for the President, and he appeared, waving his acknowledgment of the deafening cheers. Mr. McKinley said:

"Fellow Citizens: I thank you for the very great compliment of this call on this inclement night, and at this late hour. Of the many gratifying reports from every part of the country, none have given me more genuine and sincere gratitude than those from my own city and my own county of Stark. And I appear now only to do as I have done on so many former occasions, to thank you once more for the warm and hearty indorsement which you have to-day given my public acts."

President McKinley received the election returns to-night at his home, surrounded by a large number of his old friends and neighbors, including many women who came as the guests of Mrs. McKinley.

Direct wires connected the house with the Republican National Headquarters at New York and Chicago, with Senator Hanna at the Union Club in Cleveland, and with the home of Gov. Roosevelt, at Oyster Bay, so that the President was in constant telegraphic touch with his associate on the ticket and with the campaign leaders.

The President made his headquarters in his library, where most of the men guests congregated, while Mrs. McKinley entertained the women in another room.

Secretary Cortelyou read most of the dispatches, some of the more cheering announcements being heartily applauded by the guests. Most of the early advices were fragmentary, and inconclusive, but the strong indications that New York and probably Illinois had gone for McKinley were received with great satisfaction.

The President's first congratulations from headquarters came from J. H. Manley, at New York, as follows:

"Praise God, from whom all blessings flow. Your triumphant re-election is conceded by Democratic managers. I tender my earnest congratulations. We are very happy at headquarters."

Even at 11 o'clock the President had given no intimation to those nearest to him as to his own opinion of the results, although it was the general view of those at the house that his re-election was assured beyond a doubt. The advices from headquarters had been uniformly favorable. The announcement that Croker conceded New York and Illinois to McKinley was greeted with applause. There was another outburst when strong assurances were received that Missouri and Indiana would be in the McKinley column. The Kentucky headquarters sent word that the contest was very close.

SECRETARY GAGE'S VIEWS.

He Says the Result of the Election Will Be New Confidence and Courage Everywhere.

WASHINGTON, Nov. 6.—The jubilation here over President McKinley's re-election broke all bounds. Never, except at inauguration times, did such crowds surge up and down Pennsylvania Avenue, cheering, singing, and blowing horns.

In the absence of the President there was no gathering at the White House, and such advices as were received there were conveyed by telephone to the members of the Cabinet now in Washington. Only three are here—Secretaries Hay, Gage, and Root—the last-named reaching the city this evening after casting his ballot in New York. Secretary Hay was feeling indisposed, and remained at his home during the evening, but Secretary Gage was at the Treasury Department and with a number of friends heard the results there. Mr. Gage said:

"The result will bring a sense of gratification and triumph to the rank and file, as well as to the leaders of the Republican Party.

"If this were all which the result involved one could look on it with a sense of comparative indifference. To my mind, however, this is but the most minor consideration. It is to the broad industrial and commercial interests that the result must bring a feeling of profound thankfulness. It is not necessary to descant upon the propositions of the opposition.

"These propositions have been rejected, and we have the assurance that no serious interruption to the on-going of business affairs is to occur. The country, that portion of it at least which carries the burdens and risks of enterprise and industry, will give a sigh of relief that we have been delivered from dangers which could not be measured. Thus relieved, new confidence and courage will everywhere be felt, and the good conditions in finance, trade, and industrial activity, now so observable on every hand, ought to and undoubtedly will be strengthened and advanced.

"It is to be hoped that the victorious party will realize that its triumph only serves to increase its responsibility; not to its adherents merely, but to all the people. The protests and criticisms of the minority, when made in good faith, may justly demand honest and patient consideration from the party invested with legislative and administrative power.

"Protests and criticism have filled the air with clamorous tongue. Intensified by partisan heat though they have been, the elements of truth they may carry are educational, and may bring light to National councils.

"My own deep conviction—freed as far as possible from political bias—is that every right-minded man and woman in our land is to be congratulated upon the result. I know, if I know anything, that in the President-elect the country may impose its trust with full sense of security. He is superior to mere party advantages. He loves his country better than his party, and his highest aim is to secure it, as a whole, conditions of domestic peace and economic well-being. This opinion is, I believe, fully shared by those of the opposing party, whether from the North or South, who, representing their constituents in the halls of the National Legislature, have come into contact with his spirit and motives during the four years of Administration now drawing to a close."

NEW YORK CITY

Bryan Carries It By About 28,000.

BELMONT ELECTED

RUPPERT WINS

McClellan and Cummings Re-elected.

DOUGLAS DEFEATS HILL

Manhattan Gives Bryan Over 28,000 Plurality.

Kings County for McKinley By Small Margin.

JACOB WORTH DEFEATED IN BROOKLYN.

VAN COTT-CREAMER CONTEST

Mr. Bryan carried the City of New York by a plurality of about 31,000 over Mr. McKinley. The total vote cast for the Presidential candidates in the five boroughs of New York was about 690,000. The total registration was 642,654.

The latest returns from the entire city, with forty-one election districts missing out of a total of 1,522, show that Mr. McKinley received 273,179 votes and Mr. Bryan 301,309, a plurality of 28,130.

The Boroughs of Manhattan and the Bronx, with 33 districts missing out of 822, give Mr. Bryan a plurality of 28,620.

Richard Croker sent a telegram to Mr. Bryan saying that New York County had gone for him by 32,000, an increase of 55,000 over the vote of '96, and he wrote, "We are defeated, but not discouraged."

The vote in Brooklyn was very close, but the plurality for Mr. McKinley is about 2,000. With fifty-two districts the vote for Mr. McKinley was 97,931 and for Mr. Bryan 94,433.

In the Borough of Queens, with twelve missing election districts, Mr. Bryan carries the county by 1,994. The vote was as follows: McKinley, 10,069; Bryan, 12,063.

The complete returns from the Borough of Richmond show that this district was closely contested. Mr. McKinley received 6,038 and Mr. Bryan received 6,733, a plurality on the latest returns of 696 for the Democratic ticket.

The registration was: Brooklyn, 230,439; Queens, 29,318, and Richmond, 13,982.

Tammany has probably elected eight Congressmen. There was some doubt expressed as to whether Richard Van Cott had defeated Assistant Corporation Counsel Thomas Creamer in the Eighth District.

The latest news received by Richard Croker from the Assembly District leaders last evening at Tammany Hall showed that if Creamer was elected it would be by a small majority.

The young candidate, J. Sprunt Hill, whom Mr. Richard Croker put up in the Fourteenth District, was defeated by the Republican candidate, William H. Douglass.

George B. McClellan defeated Herbert Parsons in the Twelfth District by about 4,500, according to Congressman McClellan's report to Mr. Croker at Tammany Hall.

O. H. P. Belmont was elected over William R. Willcox in the Thirteenth District.

Jacob Ruppert, Jr., succeeded in defeating Elias Goodman, Republican, in the Fifteenth District.

In the other Congressional districts the contests resulted as follows:

Nicholas Muller, Democrat, defeated Gen. J. R. O'Beirne in the Seventh District.

Henry M. Goldfogle, Democrat, defeated Theodore Cox in the Ninth District.

Amos J. Cummings, Democrat, defeated John Glass, Jr., in the Tenth.

William Sulzer, Democrat, defeated Charles Schwick in the Eleventh.

There were some surprises in the contests in New York and Brooklyn.

In the Eighth Assembly District Charles Adler has always succeeded in being elected to the Assembly when nominated on the Republican ticket, although the district is strongly Democratic.

In Brooklyn the Republican and Democratic politicians alike were surprised at the defeat of Jacob Worth for Congress.

Mr. Worth has also been one of the Republicans who always able to win in a Democratic district. The Democratic leaders in Kings County conceded the election of Jacob Worth by about 1,000 votes a few days before election.

There are two election contests in New York in which the vote is so evenly divided that the result may not be accurately known until the official canvass is made.

In the Eighth Congressional District the returns wavered from Thomas Creamer, Democrat, to Richard Van Cott, Republican, several times before 1 o'clock A. M. The news Mr. Croker received at Tammany Hall was that Mr. Van Cott had been defeated.

The police returns given out at 1 A. M. showed that Mr. Van Cott was elected by a very small plurality. Later the vote on

New York, Wednesday, November 7, 1900.

M'Kinley Re-Elected

McKinley 284
Bryan 155

Republicans Carry
New York, Indiana, West Virginia,
Delaware, Maryland, Kansas, North Dakota,
South Dakota, California, Wyoming.

Democrats Carry
Nevada, Kentucky.

Doubtful
Nebraska.

Total Electoral Vote 447
Necessary to a choice 224
William McKinley 284
William J. Bryan 155
McKinley over Bryan 121

The expected has happened. The Republican Presidential ticket has swept the country.

William McKinley of Ohio, the Republican candidate for President of the United States, has been re-elected to that office, and Theodore Roosevelt of New York has been chosen Vice President.

The Republicans carried twenty-seven States and the Democrats eighteen.

In 1896 the Republicans carried twenty-three States, including California and Kentucky, in each of which the Democrats secured one Electoral vote. The Democrats carried twenty-two States.

The Republicans have regained the States of Kansas, South Dakota, Washington, Utah, and Wyoming.

The Democrats have recovered the State of Kentucky.

Kentucky has given her entire Electoral vote to Bryan.

While victorious in Kentucky in securing the Electors for Bryan, the Democrats have suffered a great defeat in the election of John W. Yerkes, Republican, as Governor, over Beckham, the successor to Gov. Goebel.

Colorado's Electoral vote will be cast for Bryan.

A fusion Legislature has been elected in Colorado. It will elect an opposition Senator to succeed Edward O. Wolcott, Republican, whose term will expire March 3, 1901.

Delaware has chosen Electors favorable to McKinley and Roosevelt.

The election in Delaware of a Democratic Legislature assures the election of two Democratic Senators, one to fill a vacancy and another to succeed Senator Richard R. Kenney, Democrat, whose term will expire March 3, 1901.

Idaho's Electoral vote will go to Bryan and Stevenson.

The victory in Idaho for the fusion legislative ticket assures the election of an opposition Senator to succeed George L. Shoup, Republican, whose term will expire next March.

Kansas has decided to cast her Electoral vote for McKinley.

The election in Kansas of a Republican Legislature will give to that State a Republican Senator to succeed Lucien Baker, Republican, whose term will expire March 3, 1901.

Montana persists in its allegiance to free silver and to Bryan and will give him its Electoral vote.

Although Montana has chosen a Democratic Legislature, it is not yet certain that the partisans of William A. Clark can command votes enough to elect him. The Daly Democrats and Republicans may combine to choose Senator Thomas H. Carter, Republican, to succeed himself, and a Democrat of the Daly faction for the short term.

South Dakota has returned to the Republican column and will cast her Electoral vote for McKinley and Roosevelt.

Senator Richard F. Pettigrew, who calls himself a silver man, the most active and bitter opponent of the Administration in the United States Senate, will be succeeded by a Republican, South Dakota having chosen a Republican Legislature.

Utah has reversed the position occupied by that State four years ago, and will give its three Electoral votes to McKinley.

Having elected a Republican Legislature, Utah will choose a Republican Senator to fill the vacancy created in that State by failure to elect.

West Virginia adheres to the Republican Party, and will give its Electoral vote to McKinley.

The election in West Virginia of a Republican Legislature will be followed by the return to the United States Senate of Stephen B. Elkins, whose term will expire March 3, 1901.

McKinley's plurality of the popular vote is about 550,000.

This is smaller than his plurality of 603,514 in 1896, which was exceeded only by Grant's plurality over Greeley, in 1872, of 762,991.

Teddy Roosevelt so completely dominated the political scene that his initials were enough to attract voters—and the Rough Rider hat on this campaign pin added to his appeal.

At 42, Theodore Roosevelt became the youngest president ever when he succeeded William McKinley, assassinated in Buffalo in September 1901. Though deliberative at first, Roosevelt soon captured the fancy of the American people with a series of bold initiatives and an irrepressible style that stood out brilliantly against the monochrome of late nineteenth-century presidential history.

In foreign policy, he strengthened the Monroe Doctrine, and added the Roosevelt Corollary asserting Washington's right to intervene anywhere within the hemisphere. In economic matters, he stole a page from Bryan by dismantling one of J.P. Morgan's trusts (Northern Securities). He won further approval by the simple fact that he spoke his mind frequently, threw open the doors of the White House to photographers, and initiated a modern presidency that was interactive and interventionist—a "bully pulpit," he called it. Best of all, he enjoyed it so much.

For all Roosevelt's confidence, he felt vulnerable as the election loomed. Detractors called him "His Accidency" to remind voters how he had inherited the presidency. No former vice president had been elected since Martin Van Buren in 1836. Roosevelt also had rivals within

Left to right:
Theodore Roosevelt (1858–1919)
Alton B. Parker (1852–1926)

In 1901, Roosevelt boldly invited the African-American leader Booker T. Washington to dine with him at the White House—to the horror of segregationists.

the party, including his old nemesis, Senator Mark Hanna of Ohio, who entertained ideas of a run of his own. But Teddy outmaneuvered all challengers, thanks in part to his travels around America, and an unassailable hold on the affection of voters.

The Democrats went in a very different direction from either Roosevelt or William Jennings Bryan, who had lost two elections in a row. The party's eastern wing reclaimed control, and after flirting with the idea of a third run for Grover Cleveland, nominated the dull but virtuous Alton B. Parker, a New York judge. They gave the second spot to an octogenarian, Henry Davis of West Virginia. This was not exactly an electrifying team. Despite Parker's habit of skinny-dipping in the Hudson every day, he was a far cry from TR, and so taciturn that he was called "The Sphinx." He disliked stumping, and would have preferred a "front porch" campaign of the kind McKinley had won only eight years earlier. But the times now demanded excitement.

Teddy delivered it, but at a price. Amazingly, Roosevelt had an attack of nerves near the end of the campaign, and sought large loans from Henry Frick and Edward Harriman to keep his campaign lubricated. It was a doubly bad decision, because it gave Parker one of the few issues he could exploit, and it forced TR into a relationship with plutocrats he had no intention of honoring in the way they expected. Frick put it bluntly: "We bought the son of a bitch and then he did not stay bought."

In the end, these problems proved irrelevant, as Roosevelt won in a landslide. "I am no longer a political accident," he exulted. But flush with victory, Teddy committed a blunder that would haunt him for the rest of his life. Announcing formally that he would not run in 1908, he impetuously removed himself from the future, and laid the foundation for the presidencies of Taft and Wilson. (TR later said he would cut off his hand to be able to retract the pledge.) For all of Roosevelt's popularity then and now, 1904 proved to be the only presidential campaign he ever won.

Alton B. Parker and Henry G. Davis—resembling men of the 19th century more than the 20th—offered no serious competition to the vigorous Roosevelt.

Judge Alton B. Parker accepts the Democratic nomination *(left)* at Rosemont, his home in Esopus, New York, 1904

President Theodore Roosevelt stumps on the campaign trail *(right)*, 1904.

The Parker family poses for a campaign publicity photograph in Cortland, New York. From left: Alton Parker Hall, Mrs. Alton Parker, Mrs. Charles Mercer Hall, Mrs. Parker Sr., Judge Parker, and Mary Parker Hall. The unusual color picture was taken and printed by the Quadri-Color Company of New York City, in October 1904.

The Roosevelts pose for a portrait *(above)* in front of their home at Sagamore Hill, Long Island—the "summer White House." From left: Quentin, Roosevelt, Ted, Archie, Alice, Kermit, Edith Roosevelt, and Ethel, 1903.

Teddy Roosevelt delivers a campaign address *(right)* to a rapt crowd—some of whom watch from rooftops and powerlines, New York City, 1904.

"All the News That's Fit to Print."

The New York Times.

THE WEATHER.
Partly cloudy; possibly local showers; light winds.

VOL. LIV...NO. 17,114. NEW YORK, WEDNESDAY, NOVEMBER 9, 1904.--SIXTEEN PAGES. ONE CENT In Greater New York, Jersey City and Newark. | Elsewhere, TWO CENTS.

ROOSEVELT

Sweeps North and West and Is Elected President.

SAYS HE WILL NOT RUN AGAIN

Will Have 325 Electoral Votes—Republican Gains in Congress—Folk, La Follette and Douglas Win Governorship Fights.

Theodore Roosevelt was yesterday elected President of the United States for four years more, overwhelming majorities having been given to the Republican Electoral tickets in all of the States which had been classed as doubtful. The returns received up to midnight indicate that Roosevelt will have **325** votes in the Electoral College to **151** for his opponent, Alton B. Parker. The total number of votes in the Electoral College is **476**, of which **239** are necessary to a choice. Mr. Roosevelt, therefore, will have a majority in the Electoral College of **174**. The only State about whose Electoral vote there was any doubt at a late hour was Maryland. The returns indicated that it had gone Republican by several thousand, but the Democratic State Committee had not abandoned hope.

As soon as it became certain that he had carried the country Mr. Roosevelt issued the following statement at the White House, in Washington:

"Washington, Nov. 8, 1904.

"I am deeply sensible of the honor done me by the American people in thus expressing their confidence in what I have done and have tried to do. I appreciate to the full the solemn responsibility this confidence imposes upon me, and I shall do all that in my power lies not to forfeit it. On the Fourth of March next I shall have served three and one-half years, and this three and one-half years constitutes my first term. The wise custom which limits the President to two terms regards the substance and not the form. Under no circumstances will I be a candidate for or accept another nomination."

The polls closed in New York at 5 o'clock, and the people were not kept long in suspense as to the result in New York State and the Nation. As early as 7:30 o'clock August Belmont, who was at the Democratic National headquarters receiving returns, conceded the election of President Roosevelt by "an overwhelming majority." By 8 o'clock those in charge of returns at Democratic headquarters were willing to concede that Mr. Roosevelt had carried every doubtful State in the country.

The figures which came in from New York, New Jersey, Connecticut, Indiana, and West Virginia were stunning to the Democratic managers. In none of the bulletins was there a single ray of hope for the Democrats, and as early as 8:30 o'clock a telegram was sent to Judge Parker informing him of his defeat.

Returns from New York State up to midnight indicated that Roosevelt would have a plurality of **186,000** in the State. His indicated plurality above the Bronx line was **223,000**, while Parker's indicated plurality in New York City was **37,000**. Higgins's plurality for Governor will be about **85,000**.

The Republicans of the State of New York retained their hold on the Legislature, electing on the face of the returns as this edition of THE TIMES went to press, **36** members of the Senate, to **14** Democrats, and **104** members of Assembly to **46** Democrats. This is a clean Republican gain of **7** in the Senate and **7** in the Assembly. Districts that went Republican only when McKinley ran in 1896 were this year again turned into the Republican column.

The returns for Congress show that the Republicans have elected **229** members of the House, and the Democrats **157**, thus giving the Republicans **72** majority.

In New Jersey the indicated plurality for Roosevelt is **60,000**, and the Republican candidate for Governor, Edward C. Stokes, will have about **35,000**.

Connecticut gave a plurality of **25,000** for Roosevelt. A. Heaton Robertson, the Democratic candidate for Governor, ran ahead of his ticket, but Henry Roberts, the present Lieutenant Governor, was elected by a plurality of about **20,000**.

Indiana went **50,000** for Roosevelt.

The latest returns indicated **50,000** plurality for the Republican Electoral ticket in Wisconsin. La Follette, the regular Republican candidate for Governor in Wisconsin, ran behind the Electoral ticket, but the returns indicate his election.

West Virginia, the home State of Henry Gassaway Davis, the Democratic candidate for Vice President, gave **23,000** plurality for Roosevelt and Fairbanks.

The latest returns from Colorado indicate that the State went for Roosevelt by a small plurality and that Peabody, the Republican candidate for Governor, won by a narrow margin.

Maryland was claimed by both sides at midnight, but the latest returns indicated that the State would be Republican by a small plurality.

Massachusetts furnished a surprise by electing William L. Douglas, Democrat, Governor of the State, although the plurality for Roosevelt and Fairbanks was in the neighborhood of **80,000**.

Joseph W. Folk is elected Governor of Missouri by a plurality estimated at **40,000**, but the returns indicated that Parker was running behind. He probably will carry the State by **35,000**.

While complete returns were lacking at 1:30 o'clock it seemed probable that the Democrats had elected Governors in Nebraska and possibly West Virginia. In the latter State the vote is very close, but the indications are that Cornwell, the Democratic candidate, has outrun the National ticket and will pull through.

Montana also reverses her Electoral vote on State issues and elects a Democratic Governor.

PARKER TO ROOSEVELT.

Sends His Congratulations at 8:30 P. M. —The President Replies.

ESOPUS, Nov. 8.—Judge Parker to-night sent this telegram to the President:

"Rosemount,

"Esopus, N. Y., 8:30 P. M., Nov. 8.

"The President, Washington, D. C.:

"The people by their votes have emphatically approved your Administration and I congratulate you.

"ALTON B. PARKER."

WASHINGTON, Nov. 8.—President Roosevelt's reply to Judge Parker's telegram was as follows:

"Alton B. Parker, Rosemount, N. Y.:

"I thank you for your congratulations.

"THEODORE ROOSEVELT."

THE ELECTORAL VOTE.

ROOSEVELT.

California	10
Colorado	5
Connecticut	7
Delaware	3
Idaho	3
Illinois	27
Indiana	15
Iowa	13
Kansas	10
Maine	6
Maryland	8
Massachusetts	16
Michigan	14
Minnesota	11
Montana	3
Nebraska	8
New Hampshire	4
New Jersey	12
New York	39
North Dakota	4
Nevada	3
Ohio	23
Oregon	4
Pennsylvania	34
Rhode Island	4
South Dakota	4
Utah	3
Vermont	4
Washington	5
West Virginia	7
Wisconsin	13
Wyoming	3
Total	325

PARKER.

Alabama	11
Arkansas	9
Florida	5
Georgia	13
Kentucky	13
Louisiana	9
Mississippi	10
Missouri	18
North Carolina	12
South Carolina	9
Tennessee	12
Texas	18
Virginia	12
Total	151

Total number of votes in Electoral College, 476. Necessary to a choice, 239.

HIGGINS THANKS THE TIMES.

In Message on Election Result He Recalls the Furnaceville Case.

Special to The New York Times.

Olean, N. Y., Nov. 8.

To the Editor of The New York Times:

The magnificent majority received by President Roosevelt in his home State, in my opinion, is due to his unquestioned integrity, high character, great ability, and devotion to the welfare of the masses of the people.

In my recent campaign tour through the State the Republicans were all united and earnest for his election, and at every place we visited Democrats openly and frankly expressed their intention of supporting him.

I feel that the Republicans of the State, as well as myself, personally are indebted to THE NEW YORK TIMES for the broad integrity with which they handled the Furnaceville case.

FRANK W. HIGGINS.

CITYVOTE

Parker's Plurality Over 37,000.

HERRICK BY 76,000.

Roosevelt Carries Brooklyn by Narrow Margin — Republicans Win 19 Assembly Districts in the City.

Alton B. Parker's plurality in the City of New York will be more than **37,000** when the final count is made. With fifty-five election districts still to be heard from, he ran about **36,000** ahead of Roosevelt in the five boroughs, but the Republican candidate carried Brooklyn by about **2,000** votes.

D Cady Herrick, Democratic candidate for Governor, carried every borough, and his plurality in the city will be about **76,000**.

Parker made a little better showing than Bryan in 1900. The Democratic plurality in the city that year was **29,181**, while Brooklyn Borough went for McKinley by **2,745**.

Manhattan and the Bronx gave Parker a plurality of more than **34,000**. In Queens he won by about **4,000** and in Richmond by nearly **600** votes.

The Republican Presidential candidate carried nineteen Assembly districts in the greater city.

In Manhattan the districts that went for Roosevelt were the Fifth, Eighth, Tenth, Sixteenth, Nineteenth, Twenty-first, Twenty-fifth, Twenty-seventh, Twenty-ninth, and Thirty-first, and probably the Twelfth and Twenty-third, where the voting was very close. In this number are three that were not carried by McKinley in 1900—the Eighth, Tenth, and Sixteenth.

The Brooklyn districts that went for Roosevelt were the First, Fourth, Fifth, Sixth, Tenth, Twelfth, Sixteenth, Seventeenth, Eighteenth, Twentieth, and Twenty-first, while the result in the Thirteenth was very close, Parker winning by less than **100** votes. The Eleventh, which was carried by McKinley four years ago, returned to the Democratic column.

Of the twelve State Senators chosen in New York County, nine will be Democrats. Three out of seven in Brooklyn, too, belong to the victorious party. The one Queens Senator is a Democrat.

Democratic Assemblymen were successful in twenty-six districts and Republicans in nine in New York City. In Brooklyn there are twelve Democratic and nine Republican Assemblymen. The two from Queens and the one from Richmond are Democrats.

Victor J. Dowling (Dem.) was elected Justice of the Supreme Court in New York County, and Joseph I. Green (Dem.) Judge of the City Court.

The votes for the Presidential candidates of the other parties—Thomas E. Watson, Populist; Dr. Silas E. Swallow, Prohibitionist, and Eugene V. Debs, Social Democrat—are not estimated at more than **35,000** or **40,000** altogether.

STATE PLURALITIES.

REPUBLICAN.

California	40,000
Colorado	5,000
Connecticut	25,000
Delaware	2,500
Idaho	5,000
Illinois	100,000
Indiana	70,000
Iowa	150,000
Kansas	80,000
Maine	37,000
Maryland	2,000
Massachusetts	82,000
Michigan	125,000
Minnesota	100,000
Montana	2,000
Nebraska	30,000
New Hampshire	18,000
New Jersey	50,000
New York	186,000
Nevada	4,000
North Dakota	25,000
Ohio	125,000
Oregon	30,000
Pennsylvania	370,000
Rhode Island	5,000
South Dakota	15,000
Utah	8,000
Vermont	31,000
Washington	20,000
West Virginia	20,000
Wisconsin	75,000
Wyoming	7,000

DEMOCRATIC.

Alabama	25,000
Arkansas	40,000
Florida	15,000
Georgia	45,000
Kentucky	12,000
Louisiana	35,000
Mississippi	47,000
Missouri	35,000
North Carolina	22,000
South Carolina	40,000
Tennessee	15,000
Texas	250,000
Virginia	30,000

NEBRASKA.

(Voted for Presidential Electors, Congressmen, Governor and State officers, and a Legislature, to elect a United States Senator. Vote in 1900: Rep., 121,833; Dem., 114,013.)

LINCOLN, Neb., Nov. 8.—Roosevelt will probably carry Nebraska by 30,000. This is the estimate of the State Central Committee. Roosevelt's election is conceded by the Fusion Committee. Berge, Fusionist for Governor, seems to be elected. The Legislature will probably be Republican. The Watson vote seems to be a trifle smaller in Nebraska than Parker's vote. Five precincts in this (Lancaster) county outside of Lincoln show a net loss to Mickey (Rep.) for Governor of 52. A loss of three votes to the precinct for the State would defeat Mickey.

Precincts in Omaha reporting thus far indicate a Republican gain on the National ticket and a corresponding loss on the State ticket.

Outside returns are similar, and with the present ratio of Republican loss on the State ticket, Berge will be elected. The Republican State Committee claims the State for Roosevelt by 30,000.

Ten out of twenty-six voting precincts in the city of Lincoln give Roosevelt a plurality of 928. The same precincts gave McKinley a plurality of 840. The city of Lincoln will give Roosevelt close to 1,900 plurality against 1,777 for McKinley. Eleven Lincoln precincts show a net loss for Mickey (Rep.) for Governor, of 161.

HIGGINS, TOO

Behind His Ticket, But Elected Governor by 85,000.

UP-STATE PLURALITY 162,000

Legislature Will Be Republican by a Majority of 80 on Joint Ballot—Depew's Successor To Be a Republican

WISCONSIN REPUBLICAN.

Roosevelt Carries the State—La Follette Wins.

(Voted for Presidential Electors, Congressmen, Governor and State officers and a Legislature, to elect a United States Senator. Vote in 1900: Rep., 265,866; Dem., 159,285.)

Special to The New York Times.

MILWAUKEE, Nov. 8.—The latest returns received from the election in Wisconsin indicate that Roosevelt has carried the State by a large plurality, probably 75,000, and La Follette, (Rep.), has been elected Governor over Peck, Dem., by 25,000 plurality.

There are no figures at this time upon which to make an estimate on the next Legislature.

So far seven Republicans and one Democrat have been elected to Congress, and three districts are to be heard from.

MINNESOTA, 100,000.

Democratic Governor Elected by 10,000 Majority—One Congress District in Doubt.

(Voted for Presidential Electors, Congressmen, Governor and State officers and a Legislature, to elect a United States Senator. Vote in 1900: Rep., 190,461; Dem., 112,901.)

Special to The New York Times.

ST. PAUL, Nov. 8.—Chairman Martin of the Minnesota State Central Committee claims a plurality for Roosevelt of 100,000.

The great contest here was on Governor. The Republicans cut their nominee to such an extent that Johnson (Dem.) was elected by from 10,000 to 30,000 majority.

The Fifth Congressional District is in doubt. Figures at a late hour give the Democratic candidate a good lead, but only half the returns are completed. All other Congressmen are Republicans.

WASHINGTON.

Conceded to Roosevelt—State Ticket Is Still in Doubt.

(Voted for Presidential Electors, Congressmen, Governor and State officers and a Legislature, to elect a United States Senator. Vote in 1900: Rep., 57,456; Dem., 44,833.)

Special to The New York Times.

TACOMA, Nov. 8.—The Democrats concede Washington on National issues, but claim the State ticket, which is still in doubt.

The candidates for Governor are Albert E. Mead (Rep.) and George Turner, (Dem.) There are also Prohibition, Socialist, and Socialist-Labor tickets.

Frank W. Higgins was swept into the Governorship yesterday by the tidal wave which gave Roosevelt a record-breaking plurality in New York State, but the "Odell tag" caused his plurality to fall to about **85,000**. His plurality north of the Bronx was probably about **162,000**, but Herrick's great vote in the city reduced this figure.

The Republicans made important gains in the Legislature. The indications are now that they have gained **7** Senators and **7** Assemblymen, thus making the Senate stand **36** Republicans to **14** Democrats, and the Assembly **104** Republicans to **46** Democrats. On joint ballot the Republicans have a majority of **80** votes. This insures the election of a Republican to succeed Chauncey M. Depew in the Senate of the United States.

STATE VOTE FOR GOVERNOR.

County.	Pluralities— Higgins, Rep.	Herrick, Dem.
Albany	4,000	.....
Allegany	3,300	.....
Broome	2,550	.....
Cattaraugus	5,716	.....
Cayuga	3,380	.....
Chautauqua	9,316	.....
Chemung	1,108	.....
Chenango	2,187	.....
Clinton	1,975	.....
Columbia	1,600	.....
Cortland	2,100	.....
Delaware	3,500	.....
Dutchess	2,603	.....
Erie	3,200	.....
Essex	2,907	.....
Franklin	3,319	.....
Fulton	1,020	.....
Genesee	2,676	.....
Greene	584	.....
Hamilton	100	.....
Herkimer	1,885	.....
Jefferson	4,939	.....
Kings	.....	13,096
Lewis	1,200	.....
Livingston	2,079	.....
Madison	3,801	.....
Monroe	8,000	.....
Montgomery	1,375	.....
New York	.....	51,497
Nassau	2,300	.....
Niagara	2,300	.....
Oneida	500	.....
Onondaga	6,164	.....
Ontario	2,002	.....
Orange	4,500	.....
Orleans	175	.....
Oswego	4,150	.....
Otsego	1,600	.....
Putnam	730	.....
Queens	.....	5,608
Rensselaer	3,200	.....
Richmond	.....	604
Rockland	.....	100
St. Lawrence	9,103	.....
Saratoga	2,100	.....
Schenectady	2,740	.....
Schoharie	.....	485
Schuyler	1,250	.....
Seneca	300	.....
Steuben	4,317	.....
Suffolk	2,434	.....
Sullivan	400	.....
Tioga	1,304	.....
Tompkins	1,346	.....
Ulster	2,300	.....
Warren	1,980	.....
Washington	5,200	.....
Wayne	3,418	.....
Westchester	6,000	.....
Wyoming	2,058	.....
Yates	1,000	.....
Total	168,478	90,697

*Estimated.

200,000 IN ILLINOIS.

Gain of Three Republican Congressmen —W. P. Harrison Defeated.

(Voted for Presidential Electors, Congressmen, Governor and State officers, and a Legislature. Vote in 1900: Rep., 597,985; Dem., 503,061.)

CHICAGO, Nov. 8.—The latest indications are that the Republican National ticket had carried Illinois by about 150,000. The Chairman of the Republican State Central Committee asserted that Roosevelt would certainly have a plurality of 200,000. The Democrats declared that the figures were greatly exaggerated, but admitted that Roosevelt would have a plurality not far from 100,000.

The returns on Congressmen are slow, but it looks as if the Republicans had gained at least three Congressmen, two of them in Chicago. William P. Harrison, the brother of Mayor Harrison of Chicago, is defeated for Congress.

Roosevelt has apparently carried Chicago by about 80,000 and Cook County by 90,000 to 100,000.

Charles S. Deneen, the Republican candidate for Governor, will have about the same plurality.

The Republicans have probably carried the First and Eighth Congressional Districts, hitherto Democratic.

MAP SHOWING HOW THE DIFFERENT STATES VOTED.

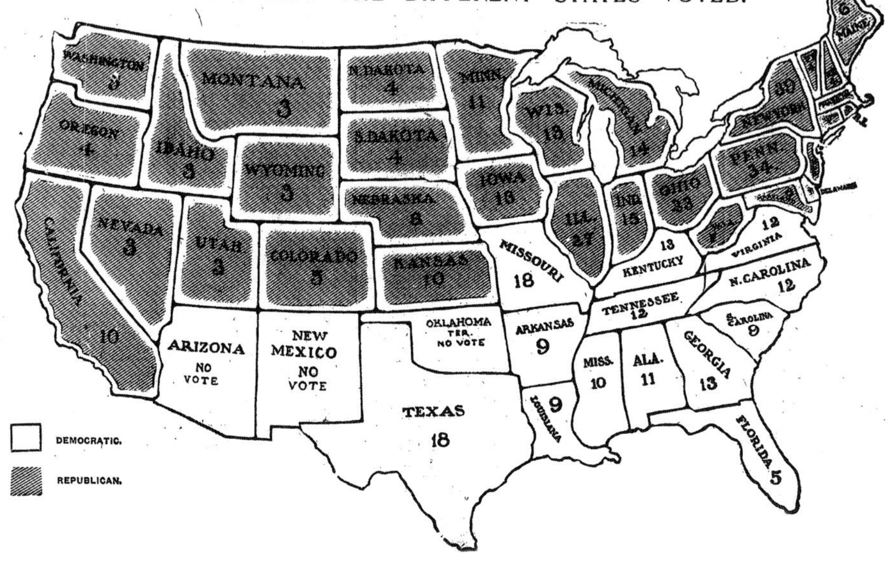

Wednesday, November 9, 1904

Roosevelt

Sweeps North and West and Is Elected President.

Says He Will Not Run Again

Will Have 325 Electoral Votes—Republican Gains in Congress—Folk, La Follette and Douglas Win Governorship Fights.

Theodore Roosevelt was yesterday elected President of the United States for four years more, overwhelming majorities having been given to the Republican Electoral tickets in all of the States which had been classed as doubtful. The returns received up to midnight indicate that Roosevelt will have 325 votes in the Electoral College to 151 for his opponent, Alton B. Parker. The total number of votes in the Electoral College is 476, of which 239 are necessary to a choice. Mr. Roosevelt, therefore, will have a majority in the Electoral College of 174. The only State about whose Electoral vote there was any doubt at a late hour was Maryland. The returns indicated that it had gone Republican by several thousand, but the Democratic State Committee had not abandoned hope.

As soon as it became certain that he had carried the country Mr. Roosevelt issued the following statement at the White House, in Washington:

"Washington. Nov. 8, 1904.

"I am deeply sensible of the honor done me by the American people in thus expressing their confidence in what I have done and have tried to do. I appreciate to the full the solemn responsibility this confidence imposes upon me, and I shall do all that in my power lies not to forfeit it. On the Fourth of March next I shall have served three and one-half years, and this three and one-half years constitutes my first term. The wise custom which limits the Presidency to two terms regards the substance and not the form. Under no circumstances will I be a candidate for or accept another nomination."

The polls closed in New York at 5 o'clock, and the people were not kept long in suspense as to the result in New York State and the Nation. As early as 7:30 o'clock August Belmont, who was at the Democratic National headquarters receiving returns, conceded the election of President Roosevelt by "an overwhelming majority." By 8 o'clock those in charge of returns at Democratic headquarters were willing to concede that Mr. Roosevelt had carried every doubtful State in the country.

The figures which came in from New York, New Jersey, Connecticut, Indiana, and West Virginia were stunning to the Democratic managers. In none of the bulletins was there a single ray of hope for the Democrats, and as early as 8:30 o'clock a telegram was sent to Judge Parker informing him of his defeat.

Returns from New York State up to midnight indicated that Roosevelt would have a plurality of 186,000 in the State. His indicated plurality above the Bronx line was 223,000, while Parker's indicated plurality in New York City was 37,000. Higgins's plurality for Governor will be about 85,000.

The Republicans of the State of New York retained their hold on the Legislature, electing on the face of the returns as this edition of The Times went to press, 36 members of the Senate to 14 Democrats, and 104 members of Assembly to 46 Democrats. This is a clean Republican gain of 7 in the Senate and 7 in the Assembly. Districts that went Republican only when McKinley ran in 1896 were this year again turned into the Republican column.

The returns for Congress show that the Republicans have elected 229 members of the House, and the Democrats 157, thus giving the Republicans 72 majority.

In New Jersey the indicated plurality for Roosevelt is 60,000, and the Republican candidate for Governor, Edward C. Stokes, will have about 35,000.

Connecticut gave a plurality of 25,000 for Roosevelt. A. Heaton Robertson, the Democratic candidate for Governor, ran ahead of the ticket, but Henry Roberts, the present Lieutenant Governor, was elected by a plurality of about 20,000.

Indiana went 50,000 for Roosevelt. The latest returns indicated 50,000 plurality for the Republican Electoral ticket in Wisconsin. La Follette, the regular Republican candidate for Governor in Wisconsin, ran behind the Electoral ticket, but the returns indicate his election.

West Virginia, the home State of Henry Gassaway Davis, the Democratic candidate for Vice President, gave 23,000 plurality for Roosevelt and Fairbanks.

The latest returns from Colorado indicate that the State went for Roosevelt by a small plurality and that Peabody, the Republican candidate for Governor, won by a narrow margin.

Maryland was claimed by both sides at midnight, but the latest returns indicated that the State would be Republican by a small plurality.

Massachusetts furnished a surprise by electing William L. Douglas, Democrat, Governor of the State, although the plurality for Roosevelt and Fairbanks was in the neighborhood of 80,000.

Joseph W. Folk is elected Governor of Missouri by a plurality estimated at 40,000, but the returns indicated that Parker was running behind. He probably will carry the State by 35,000.

While complete returns were lacking at 1:30 o'clock it seemed probable that the Democrats had elected Governors in Nebraska and possibly West Virginia. In the latter State the vote is very close, but the indications are that Cornwell, the Democratic candidate, has outrun the National ticket and will pull through.

Montana also reverses her Electoral vote on State issues and elects a Democratic Governor.

Theodore Roosevelt designed the 1908 campaign as a going-away party for himself. It didn't quite turn out that way, because he had trouble leaving the festivities, as Americans would learn four years later. But 1908 did signal the last hurrah for William Jennings Bryan, waiting since 1900 for what he considered his last, best hope for the presidency. It didn't turn out his way, either. Instead, William Howard Taft, a man with none of their charisma, was elected to the White House by a comfortable margin, and Americans settled in for four more years of prosperity and watered-down progressivism.

Constrained by his 1904 promise not to run again, Roosevelt needed a loyalist to build upon his legacy. Eventually, the nod went to Taft, his Secretary of War, whom Roosevelt admired for his loyalty and amiability. Taft deserved his trust—he was an able administrator, with deep experience in government. He had served competently as a judge in Cincinnati, Solicitor General, civil governor of the Philippines, and increasingly, as a roving trouble shooter for Roosevelt, who felt safe leaving the government with Taft "sitting on the lid" (all 297 pounds of him).

But Taft had a fatal flaw—he was a maladroit campaigner, uncomfortable with the give and take of a bruising election. Nearly all of his political jobs had been appointive. He

Left to right:
William Howard Taft (1857–1930)
William Jennings Bryan (1860–1925)

Despite facing his weakest opponent, Bryan's third and final campaign ended with the same results as his two previous.

admitted, "Politics, when I am in it, makes me sick." To make matters worse, his wife Helen followed the campaign closely, always monitoring his performance. Jealous of Roosevelt, she timed their ovations at the convention.

The Democrats sensed Taft's vulnerability. Bryan had positioned himself to reclaim the nomination from the party's eastern wing (he had embarked on a year-long world tour to create a presidential aura), and secured the nomination at Denver. Under his influence, the Democratic platform pitched leftward again, criticizing monopolies, special interests, and corporate influence on the campaign. "The Great Commoner" gave up to 30 speeches a day. A commentator called him "a talking machine" who can "set his mouth in action, and go away and leave it, sure that it will not stop until he returns."

Like Bryan, Eugene V. Debs also ran for the third time, on the Socialist ticket. He chartered a three-car train dubbed the "Red Special," visiting 300 communities in 33 states.

Despite good intentions, TR was constitutionally incapable of staying out of the action. He called Bryan "the cheapest faker we have ever proposed for President," and cajoled Taft to be more aggressive ("Hit them hard, old man!"). Taft responded, traveling an impressive 180,000 miles. Some joked that Taft stood for "Take Advice From Theodore"—but his performances grew better.

For all the zeal of his adversaries, Taft won easily, capturing every major state outside the South. Bryan agonized over "the mystery of 1908." The reason was simple: the fresh young face of 1896 had become old hat.

But even after winning, Taft wrote nervously, "I feel just a bit like a fish out of water." He was right. In New Jersey, a rising star of the Democratic party was waiting in the wings, ready to profit from the exhaustion of the Bryan campaigns, and the Republican turmoil that erupted soon enough.

Illustrations of Taft and his running mate, Congressman James Sherman of New York, decorate a plate honoring GOP standard bearers going back to Fremont and Lincoln.

William Howard Taft (center, standing on podium) campaigns in New Brunswick, New Jersey, 1908.

William Jennings Bryan at work in his home office in Omaha, Nebraska *(right)*, where—from 1901 to 1923—he published his political newspaper, the *Commoner*, 1908.

Bryan delivers one of his rousing campaign speeches *(left)*, as the women in the front row transcribe, 1908

Bryan campaigns to a group of loggers *(below)*, 1908.

Taft visits Hot Springs, Arkansas, going Oyster Bay one better and reaching out for the farmer's vote, August 1908.

Bryan receives notification of the Democratic nomination at the State House in Lincoln, Nebraska, August 1908.

Taft and his wife, Helen "Nellie" Herron Taft *(above),* on the drive to his inauguration, Washington, D.C., April 3, 1909.

President Taft sits on the porch of his summer home in Beverly, Massachusetts *(left),* 1909.

"All the News That's Fit to Print."

FOURTH EDITION

The New York Times.

THE WEATHER.
Fair to-day; fair, colder to-morrow; westerly gales.

4 A. M.

VOL. LVIII...NO. 18,547. * * * * NEW YORK, WEDNESDAY, NOVEMBER 4, 1908.—SIXTEEN PAGES ONE CENT In Greater New York, Jersey City, and Newark | Elsewhere, TWO CENTS.

TAFT WINS

Falls Only 22 Short of Roosevelt's Electoral Vote.

GETS 187,902 IN THIS STATE

Has 314 Electoral Votes — The House Republican by Increased Majority -- But Some Western States Vote for Bryan.

William H. Taft will be the twenty-seventh President of the United States, having swept the country by a vote which will give him **314** ballots in the Electoral College against Mr. Bryan's **169**, or only **22** less than Mr. Roosevelt had in 1904. His majority will be **145**. William J. Bryan yesterday suffered his third and most crushing defeat in his twelve-year run for President of the United States.

To enforce his policies President Taft will have an overwhelmingly Republican Congress, the Senate being as strongly Republican as before, and the House increasing its Republican majority from **57** to **65**.

About every so-called doubtful State went Republican, though Indiana is still in doubt. It was noticeable that the majorities in the East were greater than those in the West. In New York, for instance, Taft beat the great Roosevelt majority of 1904, getting **187,902** majority, as against Roosevelt's **175,000**.

The greatest surprise of the election was the Republican victory in New York City, where Taft's majority was **9,378**. Never before this has this city gone Republican in a Presidential election except in 1900, when it voted for McKinley as against Bryan. Chanler's plurality in the city was **56,000**.

Taft's plurality on the popular vote is estimated at **1,098,000**, as against Roosevelt's plurality of **2,545,515** over Parker.

Bryan, however, has improved on Parker's run by carrying Missouri, Nevada, and apparently his own State of Nebraska, though later returns may change the last-named State's position in the Electoral College.

In his great sweep of this State Taft carried with him Gov. Hughes, though the Governor's majority fell far below his, being only **71,189**.

Speaker Cannon will be able to make the race to succeed himself, having downed his opponent in the Danville district by about **10,500** majority in spite of Samuel Gompers's efforts.

Morris Hillquit, the Socialist candidate for Congress in the Ninth New York District, was defeated by Republican votes which were cast for his opponent Judge Goldfogle.

A noticeable feature of the election was the increase of the Republican vote in the Southern States. In Florida, for example, it increased so much that early in the evening there was a report that the State had gone Republican. Everywhere in the Southern States along the Atlantic Coast there was this unusual Republican vote.

In Illinois, which Bryan's managers had claimed, there was a smashing vote against him. Cook County, where Roger Sullivan is supreme, went against him by **50,000**. The majority in the State is estimated at **170,000**.

Indiana is still in doubt, and it seems likely that Thomas R. Marshall, the Democratic candidate for Governor, has been elected, though the State may have cast its vote for Taft.

Maryland, which was claimed by the Democrats and almost conceded by the Republicans—actually conceded, in fact, by President Roosevelt—has gone Republican by a majority of about **5,000**. Kentucky is for Bryan by about **15,000**.

The biggest surprise was in Senator La Follette's State of Wisconsin, where knifing of the ticket was freely predicted even by Republican observers, and where nobody looked to see Taft do more than squeeze through. He has bettered Roosevelt's 1904 majority there, and the La Follette men have apparently played fair.

Michigan may have elected a Democratic Governor. That State is still in doubt on its Gubernatorial ticket, though it has voted for Taft.

Connecticut's majority is as usual, and Representative Lilley has been elected Governor by **15,000**.

Taft carried his own State, Ohio, by **49,000**, but Harmon (Dem.) is elected Governor.

New Jersey went Republican by over **65,000**.

The city election was full of surprises, not the least being the victory here of Taft and Chanler. In Kings County McCarren made good by carrying it for Chanler by **5,241**, though it went for Taft by **22,500**. These extraordinary results led to the report that wholesale trading had been going on in the greater city.

Texas is actually in doubt on the Governorship. Cecil Lyon's prediction, at which everybody laughed at Chicago last June, that a Republican might be elected Governor this year, may come true. Col. Simpson, an old Confederate cavalryman, is Boss Lyon's candidate.

STATE VOTE FOR PRESIDENT.

County.	Pluralities. Taft. Rep.	Bryan. Dem.
Albany	5,500	—
Allegany	4,000	—
Broome	4,100	—
Cattaraugus	3,187	—
Cayuga	4,000	—
Chautauqua	3,230	—
Chemung	1,500	—
Chenango	2,231	—
Clinton	1,593	—
Columbia	500	—
Cortland	2,000	—
Delaware	2,622	—
Dutchess	452	—
Erie	6,870	—
Essex	2,940	—
Franklin	3,100	—
Fulton	2,000	—
Genesee	2,533	—
Greene	430	—
Hamilton	400	—
Herkimer	2,400	—
Jefferson	5,072	—
Kings	21,364	—
Lewis	1,400	—
Livingston	2,100	—
Madison	3,400	—
Monroe	10,353	—
Montgomery	2,344	—
New York	—	9,835
Nassau	4,622	—
Niagara	2,500	—
Oneida	5,000	—
Onondaga	10,370	—
Ontario	2,300	—
Orange	4,000	—
Orleans	2,274	—
Oswego	4,500	—
Otsego	1,800	—
Putnam	812	—
Queens	—	1,456
Rensselaer	4,026	—
Richmond	—	695
Rockland	700	—
St. Lawrence	8,600	—
Saratoga	1,500	—
Schenectady	2,947	—
Schoharie	—	500
Schuyler	600	—
Seneca	1,000	—
Steuben	4,084	—
Suffolk	4,300	—
Sullivan	3,048	—
Tioga	1,573	—
Tompkins	1,286	—
Ulster	1,650	—
Warren	1,800	—
Washington	4,400	—
Wayne	3,582	—
Westchester	9,000	—
Wyoming	3,200	—
Yates	1,400	—
Total	200,888	12,486
Taft's plurality		187,002

THE ELECTORAL VOTE.

TAFT.

California	10
Colorado	5
Connecticut	7
Delaware	3
Idaho	3
Illinois	27
Indiana	15
Iowa	13
Kansas	10
Maine	6
Maryland	8
Massachusetts	16
Michigan	14
Minnesota	11
Montana	3
New Hampshire	4
New Jersey	12
New York	39
North Dakota	4
Ohio	23
Oregon	4
Pennsylvania	34
Rhode Island	4
South Dakota	4
Utah	3
Vermont	4
Washington	5
West Virginia	7
Wisconsin	13
Wyoming	3
Total	314

BRYAN.

Alabama	11
Arkansas	9
Florida	5
Georgia	13
Kentucky	13
Louisiana	9
Missouri	18
Mississippi	10
North Carolina	12
Nevada	3
Nebraska	8
Oklahoma	7
South Carolina	9
Tennessee	12
Texas	18
Virginia	12
Total	169

Total number of votes in Electoral College, 483; necessary to a choice, 242.

PARIS HEARS NEWS.

Taft's Election Known to Throng of Americans in Cafes at 2 A. M.

PARIS, Nov. 4.—The cafés and restaurants, where the election returns from the United States were received, were thronged until early morning by Americans.

Definite news of Mr. Taft's election reached here about 2 o'clock and was made the occasion of great merrymaking, as the supporters of the Republican nominee were largely in the majority.

LAMB CONCEDES NOTHING.

CHICAGO, Nov. 3.—At midnight John E. Lamb, Vice Chairman of the Democratic National Committee, in charge of Western headquarters, refusing to admit defeat, issued the following statement:

"I do not care to estimate the probable final result, although we do not concede anything. It looks as though we had won Montana, Nebraska, and Colorado. We have not enough from Ohio, West Virginia, or Maryland to give any indications."

CITY VOTE

Taft Carries New York by 9,378.

CHANLER BY 56,000

Hughes Loses Kings by 5,241 and Queens by 4,635—Trading at Bryan's Expense Shown in Brooklyn.

This city contributed one of the great surprises of the election, William H. Taft carrying it by a probable plurality of 9,378. The heaviest Taft vote was in Kings County, where the Republican plurality of about **22,500** was amply sufficient to overcome the Bryan plurality of **9,835** in Manhattan and the Bronx. This is with some ninety districts missing.

Chanler's vote in the city ran far below the expectations of every one, including the Republican leaders. He developed great strength in Kings County, and this, taken in connection with the heavy Taft vote there, was regarded as evidence of trading, the assumption being that Senator McCarren traded Bryan votes for Chanler votes very successfully.

In Manhattan and the Bronx, while Bryan ran behind Chanler, there was not so much evidence of trading. Chanler's plurality in the whole city will not be above **50,000**, about half what was expected.

Gov. Hughes developed great strength in New York County especially, and Queens did not do as well by Chanler as the Democrats had hoped. Chanler's plurality in that borough will be apparently about 5,146.

There will be no change in the city's representation in Congress as a result of the election. Morris Hillquit, the Socialist, running in the Ninth District was again beaten by Goldfogle. Bennet and Olcott both hold their districts, though hard fights were made on them. In Brooklyn, Foelker, who as Senator, saved the anti-race track gambling bills, was elected to Congress from the Third District.

As far as the Assembly is concerned, the representation from this city will be about the same. The Republicans make a gain in the First and Fifteenth Districts of Kings, but two districts in New York County which were won last time by Republicans with Independence League indorsements have gone Democratic again. The State Senate remains practically as it was as far as this city's representation is concerned.

The Independence League ticket did not poll as heavy a vote as was expected. Hisgen and Shearn ran about evenly, getting approximately 28,000 votes in the whole city.

The Tammany county ticket has seemingly been elected by a reduced plurality. The general belief is that the new registration law is responsible for the reduced Tammany pluralities.

Surrogate Beckett, whose nomination was indorsed by practically the whole of the New York Bar, was defeated by John P. Cohalan, 640 districts out of 891 in Manhattan and the Bronx, giving Cohalan a lead of something like 28,000.

Mr. Beckett early this morning, however, was still hopeful that complete returns might show his election.

"I have the greatest confidence," he said, "and if this is justified my success will be due to the strenuous support given to my cause by the whole bar."

Tammany's two City Court Judges, La Fetra and Lynch, were elected by pluralities of approximately 34,000. Wasservogel and Matthewson going down to defeat.

STATE PLURALITIES.

REPUBLICAN.

California	45,000
Colorado	20,000
Connecticut	40,000
Delaware	2,500
Idaho	20,000
Illinois	175,000
Indiana	5,000
Iowa	45,000
Kansas	26,000
Maine	31,500
Maryland	5,000
Massachusetts	70,000
Michigan	100,000
Minnesota	80,000
Montana	7,000
New Hampshire	20,000
New Jersey	65,000
New York	190,000
North Dakota	10,000
Ohio	49,000
Oregon	25,000
Pennsylvania	350,000
Rhode Island	16,000
South Dakota	32,000
Utah	20,000
Vermont	28,000
Washington	40,000
West Virginia	10,000
Wisconsin	100,000
Wyoming	1,000
Total	1,629,000

DEMOCRATIC.

Alabama	45,000
Arkansas	20,000
Florida	21,000
Georgia	40,000
Kentucky	15,000
Louisiana	40,000
Mississippi	50,000
Missouri	30,000
Nevada	5,000
Nebraska	10,000
North Carolina	40,000
Oklahoma	25,000
South Carolina	40,000
Tennessee	20,000
Texas	100,000
Virginia	30,000
Total	531,000

Taft's Plurality over Bryan, 1,098,000.

TIMES'S BULLETINS IN BERLIN

American Colony Cheers Taft Victory at Hotel Adlon.

Special Cable to THE NEW YORK TIMES.

BERLIN, Nov. 4.—At 4 A. M. Wednesday Berlin's American colony, headed by Ambassador Hill, is bivouacked in the lobby of the Hotel Adlon. All through the night they have been awaiting the bulletins from THE NEW YORK TIMES.

Early indications of Taft's victory were greeted vociferously, men and women breaking out into cheers, while the orchestra struck up "Yankee Doodle."

Among those who held the long vigil were American Minister to Persia Jackson, Consul General Thackara of Berlin, Consul General Gaffney of Dresden, Secretaries Hitt, Grew, and Orr of the American Embassy; Vice Consul General Cauldwell of Berlin and President Hessenberg of the American Chamber of Commerce.

HUGHES, TOO

Runs Behind Taft, but Wins by 71,189 Plurality.

BIG CUT IN UP-STATE CITIES

Rural Districts Return Large Vote for Republican Candidate, Offsetting Democratic Gains Elsewhere.

Charles Evans Hughes was re-elected Governor of New York State yesterday by a plurality of **71,189**. His plurality two years ago when he ran against William Randolph Hearst was **57,897**. In nearly all the counties of the State Gov. Hughes ran behind the Republican candidate for President, whereas in 1906 the votes cast for Hughes exceeded by from about **60,000** to **70,000** the votes cast for his running mates on the Republican State ticket.

The early returns which came from the cities up the State showed that the Governor had been cut to the extent, in some of the larger cities, of many thousand votes. The returns from the rural districts of the up-State counties, however, saved the day for the Republican candidate for Governor, bringing him down to the Bronx with a plurality of about 127,500 over Lewis Stuyvesant Chanler, his Democratic opponent. Chanler's plurality in New York City was **56,000**, reducing Gov. Hughes's net plurality to **71,189**.

In Erie and Saratoga Counties, where the Personal Liberty League was very active, the fight against Gov. Hughes was reflected in heavy losses from the Republican vote two years ago in Buffalo and Saratoga Springs. In Buffalo, where Taft received yesterday a plurality over Bryan of over **4,000** votes, Chanler piled up a plurality against Hughes of over **5,000** votes. The Saratoga Springs vote for Chanler was offset by the returns from other districts in that county, and Saratoga County remained in the Republican column with a plurality of about **1,000** for Hughes and about **1,500** for Taft. The total vote in Erie County gave Taft a plurality of **7,000** and Chanler a plurality of about **3,000**. Two years ago Hughes had a plurality of **1,282** in Erie County.

In Onondaga County Gov. Hughes proved stronger than the rest of his ticket, running several hundred votes ahead of Horace White, candidate for Lieutenant Governor on the Republican ticket.

FORAKER EXPECTED IT, TOO.

Ohio Senator Says So—Will Not Comment Further on Result.

CINCINNATI, Nov. 3.—Senator Joseph B. Foraker, when asked for an expression on the election said:

"It is just as I expected."

He would not discuss the matter further.

STATE VOTE FOR GOVERNOR.

County	Pluralities. Hughes Rep.	Ch'nl'r Dem.
Albany	5,900	—
Allegany	3,900	—
Broome	3,800	—
Cattaraugus	3,150	—
Cayuga	2,786	—
Chautauqua	3,100	—
Chemung	1,000	—
Chenango	2,200	—
Clinton	1,184	—
Columbia	300	—
Cortland	2,425	—
Delaware	2,200	—
Dutchess	200	—
Erie	—	3,000
Essex	2,080	—
Franklin	2,761	—
Fulton	1,900	—
Genesee	2,221	—
Greene	400	—
Hamilton	100	—
Herkimer	1,930	—
Jefferson	3,765	—
Kings	—	2,182
Lewis	1,200	—
Livingston	1,900	—
Madison	2,897	—
Monroe	7,209	—
Montgomery	1,700	—
New York	—	43,033
Nassau	2,700	—
Niagara	1,000	—
Oneida	4,000	—
Onondaga	8,167	—
Ontario	2,500	—
Orange	2,700	—
Orleans	2,005	—
Oswego	3,600	—
Otsego	1,700	—
Putnam	—	—
Queens	—	5,146
Rensselaer	2,470	—
Richmond	—	1,310
Rockland	—	—
St. Lawrence	6,800	—
Saratoga	141	—
Schenectady	1,612	—
Schoharie	—	520
Schuyler	500	—
Seneca	480	—
Steuben	3,015	—
Suffolk	3,500	—
Sullivan	650	—
Tioga	1,561	—
Tompkins	1,175	—
Ulster	1,473	—
Warren	1,400	—
Washington	3,200	—
Wayne	3,426	—
Westchester	7,000	—
Wyoming	2,400	—
Yates	1,425	—
Total	131,552	60,363

Hughes's plurality, 71,189.

NEBRASKA FOR BRYAN.

His Plurality 10,000—Republican Precincts Change.

NEBRASKA—Voted for Presidential electors, Congressmen, Governor, and State officers, and a Legislature. Vote in 1904: Republican, 138,558; Democrat, 51,876.

Special to The New York Times.

LINCOLN, Neb., Nov. 4, 1 A. M.—Nebraska has gone Democratic. The State may give more than 10,000 majority for Bryan if returns now on hand hold good throughout. T. S. Allen, Chairman of the Democratic State Central Committee, claims the State by 15,000 and the Republican State Committee has no statement to make. Many Republican precincts in the State have given a strong Democratic majority.

Shallenberger, (Dem.) for Governor is also elected.

OMAHA, Neb., Nov. 3.—At midnight only 284 out of the 1,800 precincts outside of Omaha and Douglas Counties had reported. In those precincts Bryan's plurality is 1,550. At this ratio Bryan's majority in the State will not reach the figures named. Shallenberger, the Democratic candidate for Governor, is losing his heavy lead over Gov. Sheldon. However, he will carry the State by about 3,000. The entire Democratic State ticket was elected.

The Omaha Bee claims that Taft has carried Nebraska by 12,000.

Omaha complete gives Bryan, 10,732; Taft, 10,600; Shallenberger, (Dem.) for Governor, 10,918; Sheldon, (Rep.,) 9,875. The first precinct to come in gave Taft, 305; Bryan, 405, a gain of 100 for Bryan.

Indications are that Bryan has nearly overturned a normal Republican plurality of 1,600 in the City of Lincoln. Three precincts complete give Bryan 542; Taft 498. Estimates on the remainder show that Taft will not carry the city by more than 200 plurality.

Bryan carried his precinct 106 to 62 for Taft.

Scattering returns from Nebraska indicate a heavy loss to Bryan in the country precincts, with a gain in Omaha and Lincoln. The State is claimed for Taft by Republican managers by between 7,000 and 10,000 majority.

The first country precinct reporting, Ravenna, Buffalo County, showed a gain for Taft of 54 over that for McKinley eight years ago, and a gain for Bryan of 15 over his own vote eight years ago.

Blue Springs, Gage County, showed a net gain of one vote for Taft.

Bryan is making slight gains over eight years ago at Grand Island, and Taft shows a loss compared with the vote for McKinley.

Forty-one precincts outside of Lincoln and Omaha give: Taft, 5,332; Bryan, 5,602. The same precincts in 1900 gave: McKinley, 4,778; Bryan, 4,812. Bryan probably has carried the State by from 8,000 to 14,000.

Nine precincts out of a total of twenty-one in Lincoln gave Bryan a plurality of 288 votes. The Republicans are already conceding the city and county to Bryan. Returns from thirty precincts throughout the State give Bryan a plurality of 41. With this gain it is estimated that Bryan will carry the State by about 1,000. Mr. Bryan carried his home district by 57 votes.

Map Showing How the Country Voted.

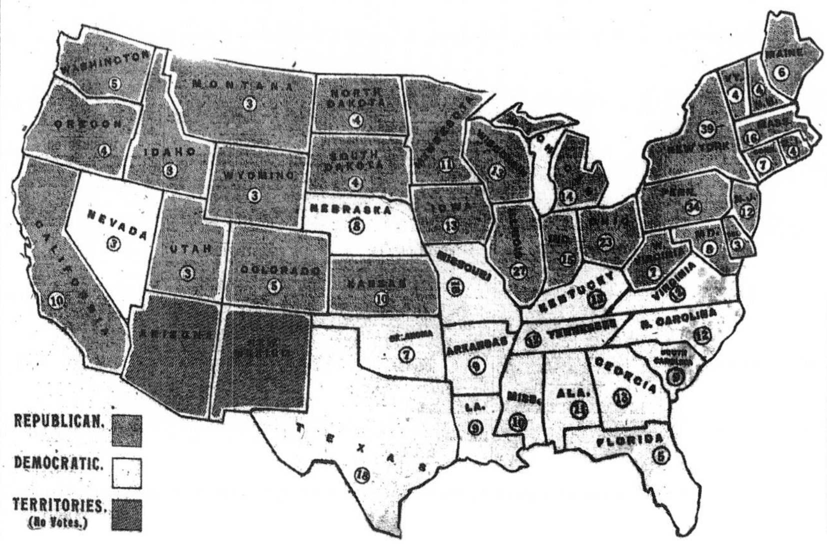

Wednesday, November 4, 1908.

Taft Wins

Falls Only 22 Short of Roosevelt's Electoral Vote.

Gets 187,902 In This State

Has 314 Electoral Votes—The House Republican by Increased Majority—But Some Western States Vote for Bryan.

William H. Taft will be the twenty-seventh President of the United States, having swept the country by a vote which will give him 314 ballots in the Electoral College against Mr. Bryan's 169, or only 22 less than Mr. Roosevelt had in 1904. His majority will be 145. William J. Bryan yesterday suffered his third and most crushing defeat in his twelve-year run for President of the United States.

To enforce his policies President Taft will have an overwhelmingly Republican Congress, the Senate being as strongly Republican as before, and the House increasing its Republican majority from 57 to 65.

About every so-called doubtful State went Republican, though Indiana is still in doubt. It was noticeable that the majorities in the East were greater than those in the West. In New York, for instance, Taft beat the great Roosevelt majority of 1904, getting 187,902 majority, as against Roosevelt's 175,000.

The greatest surprise of the election was the Republican victory in New York City, where Taft's majority was 9,378. Never before this has this city gone Republican in a Presidential election except in 1900, when it voted for McKinley as against Bryan. Chanler's plurality in the city was 56,000.

Taft's plurality on the popular vote is estimated at 1,098,000, as against Roosevelt's plurality of 2,545,515 over Parker.

Bryan, however, has improved on Parker's run by carrying Missouri, Nevada, and apparently his own State of Nebraska, though later returns may change the last-named State's position in the Electoral College.

In his great sweep of this State Taft carried with him Gov. Hughes, though the Governor's majority fell far below his, being only 71,180.

Speaker Cannes will be sure to make the race to succeed himself, having downed his opponent in the Danville district by about 10,500 majority in spite of Samuel Gompers's efforts.

Morris Hillquit, the Socialist candidate for Congress in the Ninth New York District, was defeated by Republican votes which were cast for his opponent Judge Goldfogle.

A noticeable feature of the election was the increase of the Republican vote in the Southern States. In Florida, for example, it increased so much that early in the evening there was a report that the State had gone Republican. Everywhere in the Southern States along the Atlantic Coast there was this unusual Republican vote.

In Illinois, which Bryan's managers had claimed, there was a smashing vote against him. Cook County, where Roger Sullivan is supreme, went against him by 50,000. The majority in the State is estimated at 170,000.

Indiana is still in doubt, and it seems likely that Thomas R. Marshall, the Democratic candidate for Governor, has been elected, though the State may have cast its vote for Taft.

Maryland, which was claimed by the Democrats and almost conceded by the Republicans—actually conceded, in fact, by President Roosevelt—has gone Republican by a majority of about 5,000. Kentucky is for Bryan by about 15,000.

The biggest surprise was in Senator La Follette's State of Wisconsin, where knifing of the ticket was freely predicted even by Republican observers, and where nobody looked to see Taft do more than squeeze through. He has bettered Roosevelt's 1904 majority there, and the La Follette men have apparently played fair.

Michigan may have elected a Democratic Governor. That State is still in doubt on its Gubernatorial ticket, though it has voted for Taft.

Connecticut's majority is as usual, and Representative Lilley has been elected Governor by 15,000.

Taft carried his own State, Ohio, by 49,000, but Harmon (Dem.) is elected Governor.

New Jersey went Republican by over 45,900.

The city election was full of surprises, not the least being the victory here of Taft and Chanler. In Kings County McCarren made good by carrying it for Chanler by 5,241, though it went for Taft by 22,500. These extraordinary results led to the report that wholesale trading had been going on in the greater city.

Texas is actually in doubt on the Governorship. Cecil Lyon's prediction, at which everybody laughed at Chicago last June, that a Republican might be elected Governor this year, may come true. Col. Simpson, an old Confederate cavalryman, is Boss Lyon's candidate.

Eugene V. Debs won over 900,000 votes and even defeated President Taft in a few states.

The presidential campaign came of age in 1912, when the polite approach to electioneering was abruptly abandoned. Living up to the Bull Moose mantle, Teddy Roosevelt lumbered through the china shop of American politics, leaving a trail of shards. Some voters thought it ominous; most found it entertaining. Either way, personality was forever a part of the changed democratic landscape, increasingly chronicled by newsreel footage and newspaper photography. For oratory, drama, and pure spectacle, it ranks with any election before or since.

Prior to 1912, campaigns were largely conducted behind the scenes. Candidates refrained from invective, or for that matter, from campaigning. Former presidents were expected to retire gracefully to their country retreats. Roosevelt changed all that by launching an aggressive drive for reelection, and calling his protégé, President Taft, a "fathead" with the "brains of a guinea pig." For half a century, elections had been somber, two-party affairs. Suddenly, a new party existed, powered by the charisma of a star performer who delighted reporters and audiences alike.

In February 1912, Roosevelt shocked the nation by announcing that he was seeking the Republican nomination over the President he had installed. Roosevelt was outraged by Taft's growing conservatism. A pugilistic tone was set when Roosevelt proclaimed, "The fight is on

Left to right:
Woodrow Wilson (1856–1924)
Theodore Roosevelt (1858–1919)
William Howard Taft (1857–1930)
Eugene V. Debs (1855–1926)

For the first time in U.S. history, delegates to the GOP convention in Chicago were selected through state primaries.

and I am stripped to the buff!" Taft, he said, was a creature of "the bosses." The normally good-natured Taft responded in kind, calling Roosevelt's followers "radicals" and "neurotics." For the first time, a President actively campaigned for reelection, driven by a desire "to keep that madman out of the White House."

At a chaotic convention in Chicago, Taft's regulars thwarted the unruly Roosevelt supporters, who rubbed sandpaper whenever they disliked a speech. A disgusted Roosevelt then bolted and held a tumultuous convention of his own, also in Chicago, which launched the Progressive or "Bull Moose" Party, pursuing the reformist instincts then percolating across America. TR brought down the house with an apocalyptic appeal: "We stand at Armageddon and we battle for the Lord." Political and religious purists were aghast.

Roosevelt's blasphemy was music to Democrats, who had a fighting chance for the first time in two decades. Their convention nearly chose Champ Clark, the Speaker from Missouri. But delegates sensed that new winds were blowing, and nominated a compromise candidate on the 46th ballot: Woodrow Wilson, the former president of Princeton University, and now governor of New Jersey. Despite his academic pedigree, Wilson emerged as a robust candidate, articulating a reform platform called "the New Freedom" (in subtle contrast to Roosevelt's "New Nationalism").

A nasty campaign nearly turned lethal when Roosevelt was shot in the chest before an appearance in Milwaukee. With great courage, and an astonishing flair for the dramatic, he gave the speech anyway, holding up its blood-soaked pages for all to see, then speaking for an hour and a half.

Even that was not enough. Wilson trounced the divided Republicans, carrying 40 states, with 435 electoral votes. Roosevelt ran well for an independent, capturing six states. Taft got just two—Utah and Vermont (even the Socialist Eugene Debs beat Taft in a few states). From 1912 on, presidential elections were something new: a contest dominated by flashbulbs, toothy grins, catchy slogans, and the roar of the crowd.

Southern by birth, northern by education and experience, the former Princeton president had a surprisingly wide appeal and a deft political touch.

The "Bull Moose," a reminder of Teddy Roosevelt's hunting prowess, became the symbol of the Progessive Party. But the Bull Moosers faded after TR's acrimonious defeat.

Rivals Roosevelt (on left) and Taft stand for a portrait at the White House *(above)*, 1912.

President Taft speaks outside the Manassas Courthouse in Virginia *(left)*, 1911.

TH
A NEW

Eugene V. Debs addresses a Socialist Party meeting *(left)* in New York City, 1912.

Teddy Roosevelt runs on the Progressive Party ticket *(above)*, 1912.

Woodrow Wilson casts his vote in New Jersey *(right)*, November 5, 1912.

Roosevelt submits his ballot in Oyster Bay, Long Island, November 5, 1912.

President Wilson meets with his newly appointed cabinet at the White House *(above)*; William Jennings Bryan, named Secretary of State, sits to the President's right, 1913.

Wilson gives his inauguration speech at the Capitol *(right)*, Washington, D.C. March 4, 1913.

"All the News That's Fit to Print."

The New York Times.

THE WEATHER.
Increasing cloudiness to-day and probably followed by rain to-night or to-morrow.
For full weather report see Page 23.

VOL. LXII...NO. 20,010. NEW YORK, WEDNESDAY, NOVEMBER 6, 1912—TWENTY-FOUR PAGES. ONE CENT In Greater New York, Jersey City, and Newark. | Elsewhere, TWO CENTS.

WILSON WINS

He Gets 409 Electoral Votes; Roosevelt, 107, and Taft, 15.

206,000 OVER TAFT IN NEW YORK

Illinois and Pennsylvania for Roosevelt, but Close—House Democratic By 157—May be Senate, Too—Cannon Beaten

Woodrow Wilson was elected President yesterday and Thomas R. Marshall Vice President by an Electoral majority which challenged comparison with the year in which Horace Greeley was defeated by Grant. Until now that year has always been the standard of comparison for disastrous defeats, but the downfall of the Republican Party this year runs it a close second.

The apparent results at 4 o'clock this morning gave Wilson **409** Electoral votes, Roosevelt **107**, and Taft **15**.

Wilson carried 38 States, Roosevelt 6, and Taft 4.

The Republican Party is wiped off the map. Nearly everywhere Taft ran third, with Roosevelt capturing a large majority of the old Republican vote, and in many States Taft's vote was almost negligible.

New York gave Wilson a plurality over Taft of about 206,000. Wilson's vote in the State was 698,000, Taft's 498,000, and Roosevelt's 419,000.

The Democratic plurality in the House of Representatives will not be less than **157**, and the United States Senate will probably be Democratic also.

The Democrats swept New York, electing Sulzer Governor, with Hedges running second and Straus a poor third.

Throughout the night the most interesting features were the fluctuations in Illinois and Pennsylvania, the returns from which every minute or two put first one candidate and then another in possession of the two States. This morning it is apparently certain that Roosevelt has carried them both.

New Jersey produced a majority of about **50,000** for Wilson over Roosevelt, and the Democrats have apparently gained three Congressmen. The Legislature is overwhelmingly Democratic, insuring the election of a Democrat to succeed Senator Briggs and a Democratic Governor to succeed Wilson.

In Idaho, where Senator William E. Borah is running for re-election as a Republican, though a Progressive at heart, the Legislature is badly split.

There is a close race for the Senate in Oregon, with Senator Bourne, who ran independently, utterly out of it.

Maine went for Wilson by probably 7,500, with Roosevelt second. The indications are that Wilson has 47,500, Roosevelt 40,000, and Taft 27,000.

The returns from California, which Roosevelt has been expected to carry, are naturally meagre, owing to the three hours' difference in time to New York, but Wilson has carried San Francisco by 20,000 and the State seems to have gone for Wilson. The reason, of course, is that the Taft Republicans, having no opportunity to vote for candidates of their own under the California law, have voted in a body for Wilson.

Ohio has gone overwhelmingly for Wilson, electing Cox (Dem.) for Governor. President Taft's defeat in his own State was as complete as Col. Roosevelt's in his State.

Massachusetts not only went for Wilson by a great majority, but for the first time in her history she elected a Democratic State ticket and a Democratic Legislature. This means a Democratic Senator from the Bay State in the place of Winthrop Murray Crane.

One of the features of the election was the heavy vote Roosevelt polled in the South, particularly Alabama and Georgia. At one time it seemed as if Congressman Underwood, the Democratic leader in the House, might be defeated because of the heavy vote for the Bull Moose in his district. The first three counties to be heard from in Georgia reported that Roosevelt had carried them.

Iowa has apparently gone for Roosevelt by between 4,000 and 5,000, despite Gov. Cummins's failure to take any active part in the campaign after Mr. Roosevelt's failure to take his advice about not running a State ticket.

Nebraska, which had been expected to cast an overwhelming majority for the Democrats since Mr. Bryan took an active part in the campaign, did not do so well as had been expected. Wilson has apparently carried the State, but the fight over both the Senatorship and the Governorship is close, and it is possible that Senator Brown, (Rep.,) who was looked upon as a sure loser, may win.

"Uncle Joe" Cannon went down to defeat in the Danville district, and will be missing from the Capitol for the first time since his defeat in 1890, the only other defeat he has ever met with since he began representing that district in the 70's of the last century.

Roosevelt and Taft each carried their home towns handsomely. Oyster Bay went for Roosevelt by a majority of 292, giving him 510, Wilson 218, and Taft, 67. Gov. Wilson's birthplace, Staunton, Va., gave him 632, Taft, 287, and Roosevelt, 65.

In Vermont Taft won by 924 votes, but Roosevelt is close behind him.

New Hampshire is Democratic. Wilson carried Connecticut by nearly 7,000, and Baldwin was re-elected Governor.

Victor L. Berger, the Socialist Congressman from Milwaukee, is defeated by William H. Stafford, the Republican candidate. His majority was over **2,000**.

In New York City Wilson defeated Roosevelt by 123,000, but Roosevelt had 59,000 more than Taft.

Wilson lost 6,000 votes in Erie because of the double ballot. They have voting machines there, and that many voters pushed the knob for Sulzer, but did not push the knob for Wilson, forgetting that both knobs had to be pushed.

The Electoral Vote

Wilson

Alabama	12
Arizona	3
Arkansas	9
California	13
Colorado	6
Connecticut	7
Delaware	3
Florida	6
Georgia	14
Indiana	15
Kansas	10
Kentucky	13
Louisiana	10
Maine	6
Maryland	8
Massachusetts	18
Minnesota	12
Mississippi	10
Missouri	18
Montana	4
Nebraska	8
Nevada	3
New Hampshire	4
New Jersey	14
New Mexico	3
New York	45
North Carolina	12
North Dakota	5
Ohio	24
Oklahoma	10
Oregon	5
Rhode Island	5
South Carolina	9
Tennessee	12
Texas	20
Virginia	12
West Virginia	8
Wisconsin	13
Total	409

Roosevelt

Illinois	29
Iowa	13
Michigan	15
Pennsylvania	38
South Dakota	5
Washington	7
Total	107

Taft

Idaho	4
Utah	4
Vermont	4
Wyoming	3
Total	15

Total number of votes in Electoral College, 531; necessary to a choice, 266.

NEBRASKA.

NEBRASKA.—Voted for Presidential Electors, Congressmen, Governor, and State officers and a Legislature to choose a successor to United States Senator Brown, (Rep.,) and a Constitutional amendment. Vote in 1908: Democratic, 131,099; Republican, 126,997.

OMAHA, Nov. 5.—Returns from Omaha and Lincoln and scattered precincts over the State show a clear plurality for Gov. Wilson. Should the remainder of the State show the same results the New Jersey Governor will have the electoral vote by a safe plurality.

William J. Bryan to-night sent the following telegram to Gov. Wilson:

"I most heartily congratulate you and the country upon your election. Your splendid campaign has borne fruit in a great victory. I am sure your administration will prove a blessing to the Nation and a source of strength to our party."

Normal precinct, where William J. Bryan voted, gave Wilson 77; Roosevelt, 47; Taft, 26. This precinct, which is just outside Lincoln, in 1908 gave Bryan 111; Taft, 52.

CITY VOTE

Wilson Takes New York by 122,777 Plurality.

SULZER BY 110,529

All Minor Democratic Candidates In on the Party Tide—Roosevelt and Straus Second.

Woodrow Wilson carried New York City by a plurality of **122,777** over Theodore Roosevelt, and beat President Taft by **182,262** votes.

With complete returns in from all but eighteen election districts the totals of the city vote for President were: Wilson, **309,202**; Roosevelt, **186,425**, and Taft, **126,940**. Manhattan and the Bronx gave Wilson **164,211** votes, against **96,929** for Roosevelt and **61,577** for the President.

The city voted for William Sulzer for Governor by a plurality of **110,529** over Oscar S. Straus, who ran second. The vote, with 97 election districts missing, was: Sulzer, **287,980**, Straus **105,775**, Hedges **177,451**.

The county ticket, the judiciary ticket, the Congressional and Legislative tickets followed the Presidential and Gubernatorial; all the Democratic candidates, according to the early returns, being victors by substantial margins.

New York County will send a solid Democratic delegation to support President Wilson in the next Congress. In Kings County Calder is apparently the only Republican Congressman who will save his seat. Ex-Controller Herman Metz is one of the new Democratic Congressmen.

In the First Congressional, Col. Roosevelt's own district, which is partly in Queens and partly in Nassau, Lathrop Brown, Democrat, has a strong lead over W. Bourke Cockran, the Bull Moose nominee, and is likely to be elected.

In the judiciary contests the Democratic nominees for Supreme Court in Manhattan, Donnelly and Whittaker, each polled more votes than were cast for the Republican and Bull Moose candidates together.

Returns from the Senate and Assembly contests were extremely scant at midnight, but the indications are that the Democratic hold upon both houses of the Legislature has been greatly strengthened.

In fact from end to end of the city it was a clean Democratic sweep.

Apparently the Bronx voted "Yes" on the constitutional amendment to create a new county for the borough. With nineteen election districts out of 205 missing the vote on the amendment was: Ayes, **33,532**; noes, **23,607**; majority for the amendment was **9,925**.

Wilson to the People.

A great cause has triumphed. Every Democrat, every true progressive of whatever alliance, must now lend his full force and enthusiasm to the fulfillment of the people's hopes, the establishment of the people's rights, so that justice and progress may go hand in hand.

—First statement of President-elect Wilson in a telegram to Chairman McCombs.

MICHIGAN.

MICHIGAN.—Voted for Presidential Electors, Congressmen, Governor, and State officers, and a Legislature to choose a successor to United States Senator Smith, (Rep.) Vote in 1908: Democratic, 175,771; Republican, 333,580.

DETROIT, Mich., Nov. 5.—Col. Roosevelt appears to have carried the State by 30,000. Gov. Wilson ran second and President Taft third.

The State was divided between the three Presidential candidates. The upper peninsula was apparently Taft's, but Roosevelt was strong in the lower peninsula.

In 350 out 2,048 precincts outside of Detroit the vote was: Roosevelt, 47,136; Wilson, 40,502, and Taft, 30,273.

The vote for Governor in 221 precincts was Ferris, (Dem.,) 18,085; Musselman, (Rep.,) 15,711, and Watkins, (Prog.,) 15,380.

Roosevelt's best vote was in Grand Rapids, where the early returns gave him a clear majority. In Detroit, with 8,000 ballots counted, Taft had a lead of 750. The total vote will exceed 600,000.

Woodbridge N. Ferris, Democratic candidate for Governor, is running ahead of Wilson everywhere, and the Democratic State Committee claims his election.

The vote on woman suffrage apparently is close. In Detroit it is a few votes behind. In Grand Rapids it was turned down by a two to one vote, but in other up-State towns it has a majority. The suffragists have claimed that if they made even a fair showing in Detroit the farmers would pull them through.

Congressman Doremus, Democrat, in the First (or Detroit) District, in all probability has been re-elected, being within 200 votes of Beechler, the Republican candidate, in precincts which two years ago gave Debs a plurality of 2,000.

The Legislature probably will be Republican, and will re-elect United States Senator William Alden Smith.

NORTH DAKOTA.

NORTH DAKOTA.—Voted for Presidential Electors, Congressmen, Governor, and State officers. Vote in 1908: Democratic, 32,885; Republican, 57,680.

GRAND FORKS, N. D., Nov. 5.—With the returns at hand at 11:45 o'clock to-night the indications were that Gov. Wilson had carried North Dakota, but by what majority it was at that time impossible to estimate. Taft and Roosevelt ran close together, but far behind Wilson.

Indications were that the Republican State ticket, headed by Congressman L. B. Hanna for Governor, had won.

SOUTH DAKOTA.

SOUTH DAKOTA.—Voted for Presidential Electors, Congressmen, Governor, and State officers, and a Legislature to elect a successor to United States Senator Gamble, (Rep.) Vote in 1908: Democratic, 40,266; Republican, 67,536.

YANKTON, S. D., Nov. 5.—With fully half the precincts missing and many counties yet to hear from, the returns from South Dakota at 1 o'clock this morning indicate that Roosevelt has carried the State by not less than 5,000.

MINNESOTA.

MINNESOTA.—Voted for Presidential Electors, Congressmen, Governor, and State officers, and a Legislature to choose a successor to United States Senator Nelson, (Rep.) Vote in 1908: Democratic, 109,401; Republican, 195,843.

Special to The New York Times.

ST. PAUL, Minn., Nov. 5.—It looked at 11:30 P. M. as if Wilson had won in Minnesota. Returns from 105 precincts out of 3,063 in Minnesota gave Taft, 6,330; Wilson, 9,178; Roosevelt, 8,188.

Gov. Eberhardt, Republican, up for re-election, was leading the State ticket.

SULZER, TOO

Elected Governor of New York by 215,000 Over Hedges.

STRAUS SECOND IN THE CITY

Sulzer's Lead in Greater New York About 110,000—Hedges Beaten Only 21,000 Up the State.

William Sulzer, Democrat, was elected Governor of New York by an estimated plurality of **215,000** over Job E. Hedges, Republican.

Hedges ran a close second up the State, where he was beaten by only about **21,000**.

In Greater New York Oscar S. Straus, Progressive, ran second to Sulzer, who defeated him by **110,000**.

The total vote in the entire State was:

Sulzer, **664,488**.
Hedges, **448,918**.
Straus, **380,899**.

In the city the vote was:

Sulzer, **287,980**.
Hedges, **105,775**.
Straus, **117,451**.

Above the Bronx the vote was:

Sulzer, **358,000**.
Hedges, **337,000**.
Straus, **201,000**.

Buffalo gave Sulzer **29,326**, Hedges **16,979**, Straus **20,801**.

Rochester gave Sulzer **14,887**, Hedges **14,626**, Straus **12,092**.

Both branches of the Legislature will be Democratic by splendid majorities. Only half a dozen Progressives were elected to the law-making body. Schenectady replaced its present Socialist member in the lower house with a Democrat.

In the City of Schenectady the Socialists polled a heavy vote, their candidate, Russell, receiving **1,500** votes more than Straus, and nearly as many as Hedges. The vote was: Sulzer **4,760**, Hedges **3,944**, Straus **2,199**, Russell **3,641**.

In Auburn Sulzer beat Hedges out by **2,552** to **2,497**, Straus receiving **1,050**.

Troy gave Sulzer **8,561**, Hedges **6,061**, and Straus **2,328**.

Of the up State counties Sulzer carried Columbia, Erie, Greene, Rensselaer, Seneca, Suffolk, Sullivan, Tompkins, Ulster, Westchester.

CALIFORNIA.

CALIFORNIA.—Voted for Presidential Electors and Congressmen and on three proposed Constitutional amendments. Vote in 1908: Democratic, 127,492; Republican, 214,398.

Special to The New York Times.

SAN FRANCISCO, Nov. 5.—"Wilson by 20,000," says Chairman Davis. Scattering returns from forty precincts in this city give Wilson 2,507, Roosevelt, 1,829. This means a plurality of 15,000 in the city. Roosevelt will come from the South with a lead of 25,000, but a heavy Wilson vote in the interior valleys will probably be enough to break it down.

STATE VOTE FOR PRESIDENT.

County.	WILSON Dem.	TAFT Rep.	ROOSEVELT Prog.
Albany	19,000	15,400	10,000
Allegany	3,200	4,000	3,000
Broome	6,681	8,313	2,550
Cattaraugus	6,500	6,000	4,400
Cayuga	6,800	6,700	2,900
Chautauqua	4,000	10,000	11,000
Chemung	7,200	4,000	3,125
Chenango	4,100	4,800	1,750
Clinton	3,267	3,827	1,187
Columbia	5,398	4,530	1,850
Cortland	2,300	3,300	1,300
Delaware	5,746	5,702	2,444
Dutchess	9,600	10,000	2,000
Erie	40,000	23,000	31,000
Essex	1,740	3,020	1,700
Franklin	3,700	4,700	1,600
Fulton	2,530	3,782	2,187
Genesee	2,484	3,288	2,019
Greene	3,104	2,342	700
Hamilton	600	400	300
Herkimer	6,400	5,300	3,600
Jefferson	7,100	5,400	4,420
Kings	106,190	50,380	70,747
Lewis	2,500	2,100	1,800
Livingston	2,600	4,300	2,100
Madison	3,600	4,600	2,800
Monroe	18,211	16,902	14,880
Montgomery	5,300	6,100	1,500
Nassau	5,300	4,500	6,900
New York	161,220	60,627	95,868
Niagara	8,800	7,000	4,900
Oneida	14,680	13,100	8,769
Onondaga	19,060	18,000	12,500
Ontario	5,500	5,625	3,000
Orange	9,000	11,500	3,600
Orleans	3,100	2,500	1,500
Oswego	5,500	7,600	4,500
Otsego	6,600	6,300	2,100
Putnam	1,238	1,425	647
Queens	27,421	9,232	14,519
Rensselaer	14,500	11,500	4,600
Richmond	8,443	3,033	3,741
Rockland	4,223	2,066	2,319
St. Lawrence	5,900	9,000	5,300
Saratoga	6,500	5,000	3,700
Schenectady	5,572	6,430	2,712
Schoharie	3,800	2,300	1,286
Schuyler	1,710	[illegible]	[illegible]
Seneca	2,482	[illegible]	1,323
Steuben	8,880	7,994	4,344
Suffolk	7,609	5,100	4,800
Sullivan	4,600	4,300	900
Tioga	2,600	3,300	1,400
Tompkins	3,204	2,112	1,328
Ulster	9,940	8,075	3,385
Warren	3,000	2,800	2,000
Washington	3,900	5,400	2,800
Wayne	4,142	4,938	2,840
Wyoming	2,900	3,100	2,300
Westchester	22,600	15,750	14,700
Yates	1,518	2,028	783
Total	681,290	474,716	390,149

Plurality for Wilson, 206,333.

STATE VOTE FOR GOVERNOR.

County.	SULZER Dem.	HEDGES Rep.	STRAUS Prog.
Albany	1,900	23,500	3,300
Allegany	2,173	2,895	1,916
Broome	5,741	7,281	1,880
Cattaraugus	6,500	6,000	4,400
Cayuga	4,873	6,249	2,478
Chautauqua	4,823	8,098	6,102
Chemung	7,300	4,150	3,200
Chenango	3,193	4,280	1,383
Clinton	3,276	3,827	1,187
Columbia	5,690	5,010	1,428
Cortland	2,200	3,130	2,381
Delaware	5,746	5,702	2,444
Dutchess	9,350	10,650	1,820
Erie	37,041	22,472	25,300
Essex	1,830	3,100	1,640
Franklin	2,789	4,025	1,410
Fulton	2,550	3,782	2,187
Genesee	2,484	3,288	2,019
Greene	3,623	2,830	800
Hamilton	600	400	200
Herkimer	8,400	7,172	4,940
Jefferson	5,412	3,688	2,760
Kings	201,720	48,004	62,951
Lewis	2,278	[illegible]	1,208
Livingston	3,600	4,800	2,100
Madison	3,221	3,851	1,858
Monroe	18,716	18,801	15,229
Montgomery	6,200	6,100	1,836
Nassau	6,404	4,172	5,114
New York	149,726	46,137	99,617
Niagara	8,600	7,000	4,300
Oneida	14,600	13,100	8,700
Onondaga	19,000	18,000	12,300
Ontario	3,500	5,000	3,600
Orange	10,380	11,400	2,988
Orleans	2,412	2,898	1,388
Oswego	2,627	2,898	1,778
Otsego	6,600	6,300	2,190
Putnam	1,330	1,400	900
Queens	22,671	6,927	8,822
Rensselaer	11,676	9,290	3,642
Richmond	7,016	2,580	3,373
Rockland	4,283	2,096	2,319
St. Lawrence	5,900	9,600	5,296
Saratoga	6,500	5,000	3,700
Schenectady	5,572	5,430	2,713
Schoharie	3,800	2,200	3,700
Schuyler	1,710	1,200	300
Seneca	2,489	2,310	943
Steuben	8,880	2,900	1,800
Suffolk	7,588	5,278	6,332
Sullivan	4,650	4,450	750
Tioga	1,331	1,761	694
Tompkins	2,300	2,150	2,100
Ulster	11,278	9,197	3,840
Warren	3,800	4,200	1,200
Washington	3,211	4,230	2,206
Wayne	4,142	4,939	[illegible]
Wyoming	1,616	2,390	1,047
Westchester	23,950	16,800	17,800
Yates	1,518	2,028	793
Total	664,488	448,570	380,899

Plurality for Sulzer, 215,918.

KANSAS.

KANSAS.—Voted for Presidential Electors, Congressmen, Governor, and State officers, and a Legislature to choose a United States Senator. Preference vote for United States Senator. Vote in 1908: Democratic, 161,209; Republican, 197,216.

TOPEKA, Kan., Nov. 5.—Thirty-three scattered precincts in Kansas of 2,300 give Wilson a lead over Roosevelt of 500. On the basis of these returns Wilson will carry the State by from 25,000 to 40,000 over Roosevelt.

Indications are that Taft will have a total of 70,000 votes in the State. Judge Thompson (Dem.) has certainly defeated Gov. Stubb (Bull Moose) for Senator.

The estimated Thompson majority will be 40,000.

The Democrats claim the election of Congressmen in the Second, Fourth, Fifth, Sixth, and Seventh Districts.

Wilson's lead indicates the election of the Democratic State ticket by from 15,000 to 30,000.

Returns received indicate that woman suffrage has carried by a small majority.

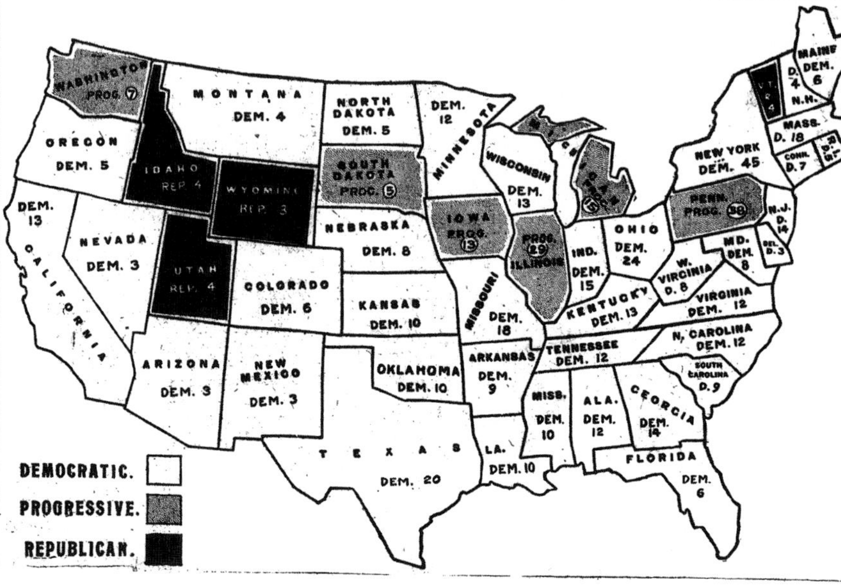

Wednesday, November 6, 1912

Wilson Wins

He Gets 409 Electoral Votes; Roosevelt, 107, and Taft, 15.

206,000 Over Taft in New York

Illinois and Pennsylvania for Roosevelt, but Close—House Democratic By 157—Maybe Senate, Too—Cannon Beaten

Woodrow Wilson was elected President yesterday and Thomas R. Marshall Vice President by an Electoral majority which challenged comparison with the year in which Horace Greeley was defeated by Grant. Until now, that year has always been the standard of comparison for disastrous defeats, but the downfall of the Republican Party this year runs it a close second.

The apparent results at 4 o'clock this morning gave Wilson 409 Electoral votes, Roosevelt, 107, and Taft, 15.

Wilson carried 38 States, Roosevelt 6, and Taft 4.

The Republican Party is wiped off the map. Nearly everywhere Taft ran third, with Roosevelt capturing a large majority of the old Republican vote, and in many States Taft's vote was almost negligible.

New York gave Wilson a plurality over Taft of about 206,000. Wilson's vote in the State was 698,000, Taft's 493,000, and Roosevelt's 419,000.

The Democratic plurality in the House of Representatives will not be less than 157, and the United States Senate will probably be Democratic also.

The Democrats swept New York, electing Sulzer Governor, with Hedges running second and Straus a poor third.

Throughout the night the most interesting features were the fluctuations in Illinois and Pennsylvania, the returns from which every minute or two put first one candidate and then another in possession of the two States. The morning, it is apparently certain that Roosevelt has carried them both.

New Jersey produced a majority of about 50,000 for Wilson over Roosevelt, and the Democrats have apparently gained three Congressmen. The Legislature is overwhelmingly Democratic, insuring the election of a Democrat to succeed Senator Briggs and a Democratic Governor to succeed Wilson.

In Idaho, where Senator William E. Borah is running for re-election as a Republican, though a Progressive at heart, the Legislature is badly split.

There is a close race for the Senate in Oregon, with Senator Bourne, who ran independently, utterly out of it.

Maine went for Wilson by probably 7,500, with Roosevelt second. The indications are that Wilson has 47,500, Roosevelt 40,000 and Taft 27,000.

The returns from California, which Roosevelt has been expected to carry, are naturally meagre, owing to the three hours' difference in time to New York, but Wilson has carried San Francisco by 20,000 and the State seems to have gone for Wilson. The reason, of course, is that the Taft Republicans,having no opportunity to vote for candidates of their own under the California law, have voted in a body for Wilson.

Ohio has gone overwhelmingly for Wilson, electing Cox (Dem.) for Governor. President Taft's defeat in his own State was as complete as Col. Roosevelt's in his State.

Massachusetts's not only went for Wilson by a great majority, but for the first time in her history she elected a Democratic State ticket and a Democratic Legislature. This means a Democratic Senator from the Bay State, in the place of Winthrop Murray Crane.

One of the features of the election was the heavy vote Roosevelt polled in the South, particularly Alabama and Georgia. At one time, it seemed as if Congressman Underwood, the Democratic leader in the House, might be defeated because of the heavy vote for the Bull Moose in his district. The first three counties to be heard from in Georgia reported that Roosevelt had carried them.

Iowa has apparently gone for Roosevelt by between 4,000 and 5,000, despite Gov. Cummins's failure to take any active part in the campaign after Mr. Roosevelt's failure to take his advice about not running a State ticket.

Nebraska, which had been expected to cast an overwhelming majority for the Democrats since Mr. Bryan took an active part in the campaign, did not do so well as had been expected. Wilson has apparently carried the State, but the fight over both the Senatorship and the Governorship is close, and it is possible that Senator Brown (Rep.), who was looked upon as a sure loser, may win.

"Uncle Joe" Cannon went down to defeat in the Danville district, and will be missing from the Capitol for the first time since his defeat in 1890, the only other defeat he has ever met with since he began representing that district in the 70's of the last century.

Roosevelt and Taft each carried their home towns handsomely. Oyster Bay went for Roosevelt by a majority of 292, giving him 510, Wilson, 218, and Taft, 67. Gov. Wilson's birthplace, Staunton, Va., gave him 632, Taft, 287, and Roosevelt, 65.

In Vermont, Taft won by 924 votes, but Roosevelt is close behind him.

New Hampshire is Democratic. Wilson carried Connecticut by nearly 7,000, and Baldwin was re-elected Governor.

Victor L. Berger, the Socialist Congressman from Milwaukee, is defeated by William H. Stafford, the Republican candidate. His majority was over 2,000.

In New York City Wilson defeated Roosevelt by 123,000, but Roosevelt had 59,000 more than Taft.

Wilson lost 6,000 votes in Erie because of the double ballot. They have voting machines there, and that many voters pushed the knob for Sulzer, but did not push the knob for Wilson, forgetting that both knobs had to be pushed.

The 1916 campaign was closely fought between two parties more evenly matched than they had been in decades. Culturally, it was also a watershed moment for a nation torn between global aspirations and an intense desire to avoid the war roiling Europe.

Democrats were proud of President Wilson's record. Though he had won by default in the three-way election of 1912, he could point to real achievement in his first term, including tariff and banking reform and trust regulation. But the incumbent was vulnerable for personal and politican reasons. His first wife had died in 1914, leaving him depressed, and while his early remarriage to Edith Galt in 1915 revived him, it also scandalized others.

As the election approached, Wilson was beset by new problems, chiefly in the nternational sphere. When the revolutionary Pancho Villa crossed the border in March 1916 with 600 men and attacked Columbus, New Mexico—killing 17 American citizens—Wilson ordered a punitive expedition into Mexico, sorely testing relations. In the summer of 1916, Marines were sent into Haiti to establish order (they stayed until 1934). And across the Atlantic, it seemed like civilization itself was ending. Wilson strove for neutrality in the World War, despite outrages committed by both sides, including the sinking of the passenger liner *Lusitania* by a German U-boat in 1915. But slowly America was drawn into the conflict.

Left to right:
Woodrow Wilson (1856–1924)
Charles E. Hughes (1862–1948)

An oddly bellicose button for a candidate whose chief appeal was that "he kept us out of war."

Sensing the importance of capturing the Progressive vote, the Democrats shifted course at their St. Louis convention, and advocated greater government intervention. A slogan emerged when crowds responded fervently to a speech repeating the mantra: "He kept us out of war." Wilson's slogan would not remain true for long, but it was a powerful argument in a time of growing unease.

Republicans, too, were nervous. Were Theodore Roosevelt to maintain his Progressive insurgency, the schism would cripple their chances. With him back in the fold, they were confident of recapturing the White House they had occupied almost without exception since the Civil War. The chief drama of the Republican convention in Chicago lay in Roosevelt's failure to sway the delegates he had alienated four years earlier.

TR accepted his defeat, and went along as the party anointed Charles Evans Hughes, a Supreme Court justice and former New York Governor. Hughes did not want the nomination, but he accepted it, resigned from the Court, and launched his campaign with a stunningly dull oration that promised greater "efficiency." Roosevelt called him "the bearded iceberg." Hughes had legitimate progressive credentials, having once led a crusade against New York City utilities, but he failed to connect with swing voters, especially out West.

Wilson ran a smart campaign, with a smaller war chest than the Republicans. He gave a few speeches at his summer house in New Jersey, but his policy was "never to murder a man who is committing suicide." Accordingly, he ignored Hughes and acted presidentially, responding to the international crisis, and solving a labor impasse that threatened to shut down the railroads.

The election was so close that it took days to tally the result. *The New York Times* called it for Hughes. In the end, with the slow trickling of Western returns, Wilson was reelected. It was a tremendous affirmation of his leadership—though it also proved to be the last Democratic victory for 16 years.

Hughes's slogan, like his campaign, failed to electrify the American people.

Wilson makes a campaign speech *(above)*, 1916.

President Wilson accepts the Democratic nomination at his summer residence in Long Branch, New Jersey *(left)*, June 1916.

Charles Hughes sits for a formal campaign portrait, 1916.

Hughes empasizes a point during a campaign rally, 1916.

Hughes speaks at a crowded Republican rally, 1916.

Woodrow Wilson sits in the box seats with his second wife, Edith, at the opening baseball game of the season, the Senators and the Yankees, at the Polo Grounds, New York City. The Senators won 3–2, April 12, 1916.

President Wilson calls for quiet as he addresses a crowd, 1917.

"All the News That's Fit to Print."

The New York Times.

THE WEATHER
Partly cloudy, colder; tomorrow overcast; strong west winds.
For full weather report see Page 21.

VOL. LXVI...NO. 21,475. NEW YORK, FRIDAY, NOVEMBER 10, 1916.—TWENTY-TWO PAGES. ONE CENT In Greater New York, Jersey City and Newark. | Elsewhere TWO CENTS

WITH 272 ELECTORAL VOTES, WILSON WINS; GETS CALIFORNIA, NORTH DAKOTA, NEW MEXICO

GERMANY FAVORS LEAGUE OF PEACE WITH CONDITIONS

But Bethmann Hollweg Says the Entente Allies Must Renounce Their Annexation Schemes.

DENOUNCES "BRUTE FORCE"

Abolition of "Aggressive Coalitions" Put as First Step Toward International Harmony.

ANSWERS VISCOUNT GREY

Asserts That England Plunged Europe Into War by Encouraging France and Russia.

Special Cable to THE NEW YORK TIMES.

BERLIN, Nov. 9.—Answering Viscount Grey, Chancellor von Bethmann Hollweg, in the course of his speech before the Main Committee of the Reichstag today said:

"Germany is at all times ready to join a league of nations—yes, even to place herself at the head of such a league—to keep in check the disturbers of peace."

BERLIN, Nov. 9, (by Wireless to Sayville.)—Chancellor von Bethmann Hollweg announced today before the Main Committee of the Reichstag that after the end of the war Germany would co-operate in an endeavor to find a practical means for procuring a lasting peace by means of an international league. The Chancellor also presented a new version of events in the last days before the outbreak of the war, particularly in connection with Russia's mobilization and efforts to avert hostilities.

The Chancellor, according to the Overseas News Agency, connected the two subjects in his speech, and in doing so replied to the speech made by Lord Grey, the British Foreign Secretary, to foreign newspapermen, in which he said that the origin of the present war must influence peace conditions, and that Germany would be entitled to ask for guarantees against future attacks if the present war really were forced upon Germany. Of course, Lord Grey at once added that Germany's interpretation of the origin of the war was incorrect, and that the war was not forced upon Germany, but was forced by Germany upon Europe.

Little Faith in Arbitration Courts.

Referring to the question of an international league for the preservation of peace, the Chancellor said:

"We never concealed our doubts whether peace could be guaranteed permanently by international organizations, such as arbitration courts. I shall not discuss the theoretical aspects of the problem in this place. But from the standpoint of matters of fact we now and in peace must define our position with regard to this question.

"If at and after the end of the war the world will only become fully conscious of the horrifying destruction of life and property, then through the whole of humanity there will ring out a cry for peaceful arrangements and understandings which, as far as is within human power, will avoid the return of such a monstrous catastrophe. This cry will be so powerful and so justified that it must lead to some result.

"Germany will honestly co-operate in examination of every endeavor to find a practical solution, and will collaborate for its possible realization. This all the more if the war, as we expect and trust, shall create political conditions that do full justice to the free development of all nations, of small as well as great nations. Then the principle of justice and free development, not only on the Continent, but also on the seas, must be made valid. This, to be sure, Lord Grey did not mention."

Denounces British "Brute Force."

The Chancellor pointed out that Lord Grey's ideas in regard to international guarantees of peace seemed to possess a peculiar character, in that they took into consideration only British wants. Neutrals, who during the war had to accept in silence British domination of the seas, were to form a union after the war when, England hoped, she would have conquered Germany, in order to guarantee that the British plans should prevail under the new conditions. The Chancellor said it was known on reliable authority that in 1915 Great Britain and France promised to Russia dictatorial domination of Constantinople, the Bosporus and the west shore of the Dardanelles, with the hinterland, and that Asia Minor should be divided among the Entente powers. These plans, he continued, probably were of interest for neutrals, who were expected to guarantee this order of things. The British Government, he asserted, has kept silent in regard to these plans, in spite of questions asked in Parliament.

"Such a policy of brute force," the Chancellor added, "cannot be the basis of an efficient international league for peace.

"These are the plans of our enemies

Continued on Page 6.

Suffrage Amendment Defeated in Two States

Woman suffrage amendments were evidently beaten in the two States that voted on the question last Tuesday. In South Dakota, with 200 precincts still to be heard from, the vote stood 22,934 for and 25,248 against the amendment.

West Virginia, the other State to vote on the proposition, rejected it overwhelmingly. The returns from 843 out of the 1,713 precincts in the State showed 33,887 for and 73,463 against it.

ASQUITH EXPOUNDS ESSENTIALS OF PEACE

Must Insure Security of Weak, Liberties of Europe, and Free Future of World.

TRADE OF NEUTRALS SAFE

German Talk of Wall Against It Called Childish Fiction—Ready for Next Channel Raid.

LONDON, Nov. 9.—The banquet of the new Lord Mayor of London, Sir William Henry Dunn, was given at the Guildhall tonight, and was attended by Cabinet Ministers, members of the Diplomatic Corps, including Walter Hines Page, the American Ambassador, and men prominent in the military and naval world, among them Lord Fisher, Chairman of the Invention Board; Arthur J. Balfour, First Lord of the Admiralty, and Sir William R. Robertson, Chief of the Imperial Staff at Army Headquarters.

The leading speech of the evening was delivered by Premier Asquith, who, in alluding to peace, declared that nobody had greater reason than Great Britain to desire peace, but that it was desired on only one condition—that the sacrifices of the war should not have been made in vain. A feature of the speeches was the warm tribute of admiration on the stand made by Rumania and the expression of the opinion that although the attack on Rumania had not yet been defeated, it had been successfully stayed.

Turkey a "Subservient Agent."

Mr. Asquith began his speech with a reference to Turkey, which country he described as a subservient agent of German interests and ambition, as was instanced, he said, by the fact that by lifting a finger Germany might have arrested the Armenian horrors, but instead looked on unmoved, acquiescent and possibly even complacent.

"That," said the Premier, "is a significant sample of what a continuance of the rule of Germanic Turkey in Europe will mean."

Mr. Asquith said he would refrain from any detailed review of the naval and military situation. He dwelt, however, on the continued Entente allied successes and said the British Navy was ready, and more than ready, whenever opportunity was offered to it.

With regard to the Greek situation Mr. Asquith said he wished he could speak with as much confidence as hope. The Entente Allies went to Saloniki as friends of both Greece and Serbia, he said. Their sole desire was to prevent Greece from becoming enmeshed in the Germanic net and to save her from internal strife. Whatever apparently drastic measures had been taken were dictated solely by the necessity of preventing Athens from becoming the centre of German propaganda and intrigue.

Declaring that the Entente Allies were in hearty sympathy with Eleutherios Venizelos, former Premier, Mr. Asquith, asked how Greece could possibly stand aloof from a war for the emancipation of smaller States.

"Greece," Mr. Asquith continued, "first lit the torch of liberty in Europe and withstood the inrush of eastern barbarism and tyranny. May Greece rekindle her lamp and show herself worthy of her immortal past."

Dealing with the general situation, Mr. Asquith said:

"Let there be no illusion about our enemies. They are great organizers and fine fighters in the field. They are also, if not skillful, yet indefatigable workers in the sphere of propaganda, where they have a double motive—to divide the Allies and capture neutral opinion."

No Designs Against Neutrals.

In this connection Mr. Asquith characterized the German suggestion of a sinister design on the part of the Entente Allies to combine against neutral countries and build up an impenetrable stone wall against their trade as childish fiction, which could only mean that the Allies were bent upon economic suicide. He said it ought to be unnecessary to affirm that when the time came for peace nothing would be more essential for the Entente Allies from the standpoint of simple self-interest than to establish and maintain the best industrial and financial relations with neutrals.

Alluding to the different methods of propaganda which he said were employed at different places with a view to dividing the Allies and influencing

Continued on Page 8.

WON'T CONCEDE WILSON VICTORY WITHOUT RECOUNT

Both Sides Should Be Anxious to Remove All Doubt, Willcox Says.

FOUR STATES IN QUESTION

New Hampshire, New Mexico, North Dakota, and California Returns Scrutinized.

THE OLD GUARD CONFERS

Willcox Not Invited to Meeting of Crane, Barnes, and Others Ignored in the Campaign.

The Republican campaign managers will not concede the State of California to President Wilson until after the result of the official count of the vote which is scheduled to begin on Monday has been announced. And even then it is more than likely that if the result of the official canvass should give the State to the President they will go into the courts and ask that the ballot boxes be reopened and the ballots recounted.

After a conference with Charles E. Hughes, in which former United States Attorney General George W. Wickersham participated, Chairman William R. Willcox of the Republican National Committee announced last night that California was only one of four States in which recount proceedings were probable. The other States are New Hampshire, New Mexico and North Dakota. In New Hampshire and New Mexico Mr. Hughes was leading on the late returns yesterday, but it was assumed by the Republican leaders that in the event of their winding up in the Hughes column, the Democrats would ask for a new count under the auspices of the courts.

"I think there ought to be a recount in those four States," said Mr. Willcox. "I assume the other side is just as anxious as we are to have any cloud on the title removed by a recanvass in States where the vote is close. Just think of it! There are States where in 400,000 votes or more the margin of the winning candidate promises to be 400 votes or less. Where the election of a President of the United States hinges on such a slender plurality I think the natural thing would be to have a recount."

Seek New Hampshire Recount.

In New Hampshire, where the vote fluctuated all day yesterday slightly in favor of the two candidates in turn, the Republicans took the preliminary steps looking to a recount while the odds seemed to favor Mr. Wilson. Republican National Committeeman Frank W. Estabrook, who has been attached to National Headquarters here, hurried home and took charge of the situation when it seemed to indicate that the State might be lost to the Republican nominee. He sent word last night that he had retained lawyers who were procuring from the Town and County Clerks certified copies of the vote returned from the various voting precincts.

The Old Guard Republican leaders held an important conference at the Hotel Manhattan last night which Chairman Willcox was not invited to attend. The leading spirits at this gathering were men who while they are shrewd and experienced in political campaigning have not been consulted much in connection with the campaign for the election of Mr. Hughes. Among those present were W. Murray Crane, the Republican leader in Massachusetts; United States Senator John W. Weeks from that State, who has been in charge of the Republican campaign throughout the country for the recapture of the United States Senate; William Barnes, and former Chairman Charles D. Hilles of the Republican National Committee, Charles B. Warren, the Republican National Committeeman from Michigan, was the only man at the conference who has been attached to the staff of Chairman Willcox at Republican National Headquarters.

Gloom pervaded the meeting of the Old Guard. They had been in close touch with Republican leaders in States which were catalogued as "doubtful" and had learned that in California, where the electoral votes were essential to a Hughes victory, there was little hope that the Republican nominee would come out ahead. From North Dakota, where a Hughes majority was regarded as safe, but where it had changed into a majority for President Wilson, word had come from United States Senator McCumber that the best to be expected was about an even break between President Wilson and the Republican candidate.

"There should be no man in the White House with a clouded title," said one leader. "It seems to me that the recount is the only means to clear the title by definitely establishing the fact that the ballots have been counted right."

It is understood that this view has the

Continued on Page 2.

News of Wilson's Election Sent to Him by Wireless

Special to The New York Times.

ASBURY PARK, N. J., Nov. 9.—To President Wilson aboard the yacht Mayflower, en route to Williamstown, Mass., this message was wirelessed shortly before midnight tonight by Secretary Tumulty:

"I am here surrounded by the loyal Democrats of old Monmouth, and beg leave to send you our greeting and congratulations. The cause you have so nobly represented has at last triumphed, and we greet you. Our hearts, our thoughts and our affections go to you."

M'CORMICK JOYFUL AT NEWS OF VICTORY

Crowd in Democratic National Headquarters Cheers as California Goes to Wilson.

HIS OPTIMISM UNFLAGGING

Chairman All Day Had Claimed 288 Votes, and Announced: "We've Got It Sewed Up!"

Scenes of growing jubilation at Democratic National headquarters here, which were in evidence throughout the day yesterday, reached a culmination last night when word was received that THE TIMES had bulletined that California had gone for President Wilson, and that the President was re-elected. Face to face with the success which they had hoped for confidently for many anxious hours, several hundred Democratic workers, including many women, cheered, leaped into the air, clapped their hands, and slapped each others' backs in an excess of the delight of victory.

When the result in California became definitely known, the Democratic National Committee issued this statement:

"The President has carried the country by a popular plurality of from 200,000 to 300,000. With an electoral vote of 272 absolutely sure, and with Minnesota, West Virginia, and New Hampshire still to be decided, to say there will be any contest is an insult to the intelligence of the American people.

"There is nothing to add to our statements previously made. We have claimed the re-election of President Wilson since early Tuesday morning. We knew we had it. We have been fighting especially for the Western States."

Vance McCormick, Chairman of the Democratic National Committee, left headquarters at 11:30 o'clock saying that he was satisfied that the President had been re-elected.

The large crowd at Democratic Headquarters that had been watching the returns all evening broke loose into a riot of applause when the California result was posted. Hundreds in the street immediately fell in behind several bands and a parade was started down Forty-second Street to Fifth Avenue. After a march of only a few blocks, however, the paraders returned to headquarters and soon dispersed.

Close on the California information came the news from Republican Headquarters that Republican Chairman Willcox "had nothing to say." The pent up enthusiasm broke its bounds again and again. For many of those in headquarters it meant rest for the first time in seventy-two hours. Many others had not slept for two days.

The crowd at headquarters had one short period of anxiety when the news came from Republican headquarters at 5:30 o'clock that Mr. Hughes was ahead in California by 298 votes. A correction of this report was soon received, however, and the crowd cheered again. Chairman McCormick had said at noon:

"It's all over, boys. We are going to clean them up, and I still stick to my figures that the President will have 288 electoral votes. The New Hampshire vote has been counted, and it is in our favor. The count is still going on in the other States, but in California we are running well ahead and we will get it. There is no question about that. We have got it sewed up! President Wilson is re-elected beyond any shadow of a doubt."

President Was Confident.

During the day many well-known Democrats called upon the Chairman and congratulated him. Among them were Alton B. Parker and Morgan J. O'Brien. The Chairman denied that they had called in connection with possible recount proceedings. He said he had called up President Wilson at Shadow Lawn frequently and told him how things were proceeding. He said the President informed him that he was thoroughly satisfied that he had been re-elected.

A telegram was received at headquarters from Dudley Field Malone, Collector of the Port, who is in California, saying that the State was safe for the President, no matter what anybody might say to the contrary. Word also came from the National Committee's Western Headquarters in Chicago that a message had been received that The San Francisco Chronicle and The Los Angeles Times, both Republican newspapers, had conceded Wilson's success in the State. Secretary of the Treasury McAdoo added his quota of comfort by showing a telegram he had received from J. B. Coulson of California, a personal friend, which read: "Fully convinced that it is impossible to overcome President's lead of over 4,000 in California."

Regarding Minnesota, Chairman McCormick said he was content to accept the estimate of Frederick B. Lynch, Democratic National Committeeman for that State, who had advised him over the telephone that the President's plurality there would be 300 at least. This, he said, would include the soldier vote, which had been checked up as far as possible by local leaders who were familiar with conditions. The count in Minnesota was proceeding slowly, Mr McCormick said, because the system there permitted the mailing of votes, and many of these had not been received.

"The final count will show Minne-

Continued on Page 2.

WILSON AHEAD IN CALIFORNIA BY OVER 3,100

Republican Chairman Concedes State on Face of the Returns.

36 PRECINCTS ARE MISSING

These Cannot Change Result, Reached After Day of Great Political Tension.

FULL RECOUNT IS CERTAIN

Both Sides Carefully Watching the Canvass—Much Talk of a Split Vote.

SAN FRANCISCO, Cal., Nov. 9.—California has given her electoral vote to Woodrow Wilson.

The Republican Chairman, C. H. Rowell, admitted at 8:25 o'clock tonight that, barring some exceptional errors in the count, the President had carried the State.

Mr. Rowell conceded the State after reviewing returns showing a plurality of 2,970 for Wilson, with only forty-eight scattered precincts of the 5,870 in the State not complete. These figures were: Wilson, 465,194; Hughes, 462,224.

These returns showed forty-two of fifty-eight counties in the State completed. In all but ten counties in the State returns had been back-checked and corrected. The possibility of error was thus reduced to a minimum.

Returns were received later from further precincts, reducing the number missing to thirty-six. The totals in the 5,834 precincts available at a late hour were: Wilson, 465,669; Hughes, 462,538. This would make Wilson's plurality 3,131.

After conceding California to Wilson, Chairman Rowell talked by wire with George W. Perkins in the office of the National Republican Committee in New York, and later gave out this statement:

"While the face of the returns as compiled by The Associated Press shows Wilson ahead in California, so many startling changes have happened in the count during the last twelve hours that it will not do to reach final conclusions on anything less than final information. The official count begins Monday, and we shall watch the counting of every vote in every county seat in the State.

"I estimate that there will be a difference of 4,000 or 5,000 between the high and low man on the electoral tickets, and this is greater than any possible majority in California. This means a split electoral vote."

O. K. Cushing, Chairman of the Democratic Central Committee:

"From the information we have received from all counties in the State we confidently expect that President Wilson's majority in California will not be less than 3,200."

The result in the State was made certain after a day of great tension, with hopes rising and falling in the rival political camps as the added returns changed the small but continuing plurality for Wilson over Hughes.

Starting the day with a lead of more than 3,000, Wilson lost ground as additional Los Angeles County precincts were heard from, and a rectification of figures was made in Alameda County. These, benefiting Hughes by 1,830 votes, cut the Wilson lead to 600 votes soon after noon.

In the late day, however, remote districts came in with consistent Wilson pluralities, until at night a decisive Democratic lead was re-established.

Mountain fastnesses and desert wastes hid most of these missing precincts. To many of these there was no telephonic communication. Humboldt County, in the extreme northwestern part of the State, awaited anxiously returns from eight precincts, reached only by stage. For more than 500 miles the snow peaks of the Sierras blocked communication in a half score of counties, passes and trails being drifted over.

The large cities and the fertile valleys which reach for hundreds of miles north and south from San Francisco were well accounted for, as were the seacoast counties in the main.

Up to a late hour today few of Sierra County's sixteen precincts had been heard from, and twenty-six of another mountain district, Tuolumne County, were likewise missing. Lack of telephone communication was largely responsible for the delay. These same districts elected James D. Phelan, Democrat, to the United States Senate two years ago, after ex-Congressman Joseph R. Noland had been in the lead more than twenty-four hours on urban returns.

Efforts are being continued tonight to bring in the few remaining isolated precincts. There are two or three to the county in most instances.

One precinct on the border of Lake Tahoe might be missing for days, it was said. The telephone was broken, and all efforts to communicate from Placerville, forty miles away, were fruitless.

The concession of the State to Wilson on the face of the returns altered in no way the determination of both parties to keep a sharp watch on the semi-official count by County Clerks and the final official count by the Secretary of State.

With a plurality of not less than 3,000

Continued on Page 2.

THE ELECTORAL VOTE.

Total, 531; necessary to a choice, 266.

State.	WILSON Vote.	State.	HUGHES Vote.
Alabama	12	Connecticut	7
Arizona	3	Delaware	3
Arkansas	9	Illinois	29
California (By 3,131 votes, 36 precincts missing.)*	13	Indiana	15
Colorado	6	Iowa	13
Florida	6	Maine	6
Georgia	14	Massachusetts	18
Idaho	4	Michigan	15
Kansas	10	Minnesota (By 1,084 votes, 85 precincts missing.)	12
Kentucky	13	New Hampshire (By 131 votes, 23 precincts missing.)	4
Louisiana	10	New Jersey	14
Maryland	8	New York	45
Mississippi	10	Oregon	5
Missouri	18	Pennsylvania	38
Montana	4	Rhode Island	5
Nebraska	8	South Dakota	5
Nevada	3	Vermont	4
New Mexico (By 1,750 votes, 105 precincts missing.)	3	*West Virginia	8
North Carolina	12	Wisconsin	13
North Dakota (By 1,618 votes, 28 precincts missing.)	5		
Ohio	24		
Oklahoma	10		
South Carolina	9		
Tennessee	12		
Texas	20		
Utah	4		
Virginia	12		
*Washington	7		
Wyoming	3		
Total	272	Total	259

*Vote for deceased Democratic Elector may give one Elector to Hughes.

*Substituted elector's name omitted from some ballots; may give one elector to Wilson.

No States are classified as doubtful in the above table. Under the close States the latest returns are given.

Hughes's Lead Is Up in Minnesota; Wilson Holds N. Dakota, New Mexico

New Hampshire, on Latest Returns, Shows a Hughes Lead of 131, With Twenty-five Districts Missing—Democrats Claim the State.

MINNESOTA.

ST. PAUL, Minn., Nov. 9.—Three nights of unofficial canvassing have failed to take Minnesota from the doubtful column of the Presidential race.

Charles E. Hughes maintained a slight lead over President Wilson throughout today; the standing continued so close that politicians of both parties declared tonight that only the official count would settle the contest.

Errors in the transmission of returns from several precincts in Minnesota were discovered late tonight, changing the standing somewhat in the Presidential contest. In 2,939 precincts out of 3,024 in the State the corrected figures gave Hughes 176,545 and Wilson 175,511, a lead of 1,034 for Hughes.

Most of the remaining precincts to be heard from are in counties where Wilson has a plurality. Wilson's rate of gain, however, is not likely to cut his opponent's plurality down to below 500.

Except for President, Minnesota delivered its customary big Republican majority, as shown in the pluralities of Governor Burnquist and Frank B. Kellogg, candidate for the United States Senate. Republicans also were uniformly successful on the rest of the State ticket.

Hughes's lead in the State was threatened several times today by returns from the northern part of the State, but always some other section added the necessary votes to the Republican candidate's column to keep him ahead.

The closeness of the vote attracted intense interest throughout the State, which normally has questioned only the size of the plurality of the Republican candidates. Bulletin boards in all the larger cities held throngs all day.

Several prominent politicians expressed the belief that the vote cast by the Minnesota guardsmen at the Mexican border would be the deciding factor in the Presidential contest.

The State Canvassing Board is to meet next Tuesday to check the tabulation sheets sent in by local officials to county auditors, and by the county auditors to the Secretary of State, who takes charge of them. At that time the result of the guardsmen's vote will be known.

So far as can be learned no extraordinary precautions have been taken to guard ballot boxes in any precinct. State officials well acquainted with gathering of returns in Minnesota advance various reasons for the delay in hearing from some of the district. In some of the counties the distances are great. One precinct in Cook County is forty miles from the county seat, with poor means of transportation.

Returns from a village on The Lake of the Woods must be brought across Canadian territory to the county seat of Beltram County. Some of the election officials in small towns mailed their tabulation sheets without notifying the County Auditors of the result. Some, more interested in local fights and figuring that Minnesota would give its usual Republican majority for the national ticket, delayed counting the Presidential returns.

Some of the country election judges apparently locked up their ballot boxes without counting the votes. Several counties reported that returns "from certain precincts were unavailable, as the boxes had been sealed and sent to the depot for shipment to St. Paul."

Fred P. Lynch, Democratic National Committeeman from Minnesota, telegraphed President Wilson this afternoon that Minnesota would give him a plurality of 1,000. Later he said what he had said before, that Wilson would carry Minnesota "by from 500 to 1,000," but that the vote of the State's National Guardsmen on the Mexican border would be necessary to decide the contest. Of these 3,600 guardsmen 2,136 voted, and the Commissioners taking the vote are reported as saying two-thirds of them voted for Hughes. These ballots will not be counted until next Tuesday.

Federal authorities today began an investigation of alleged election frauds in Minnesota. Accompanied by a large staff of special agents, Hinton G. Clabaugh of Chicago, Chief of the Western Division of the Bureau of Investigation of the Department of Justice, arrived in St. Paul early in the day. After a conference with officials at the United States District Attorney's office he went to Minneapolis to "nose around a little," it was said.

The Federal authorities are said to have received numerous complaints of fraudulent voting, stuffing of ballot boxes, and irregularities in counting the votes. One small lumber camp near Duluth is said to have turned in over 3,000 votes.

"The charges must be pretty serious, or the investigators would not come here at this time," said Alfred Jaques, District Attorney, who conferred with Mr. Clabaugh this morning. "I understand Mr. Clabaugh will distribute his agents throughout St. Paul, Minneapolis, and Duluth in order to keep a close tab on the situation."

On instructions from Democratic Headquarters in New York, Fred B. Lynch, Democratic National Committeeman, has instructed all the Democratic County Chairmen in Minnesota to employ legal aid in the election fight.

"The grave importance of Minnesota's vote," said Mr. Lynch, "and the fact that the fate of the nation for the next four years may depend on what Minnesota does, brought about this action. We don't want any suspicion to attach to the counting of the votes. The election will be conducted legally and honestly if we can have it so."

Republicans discredit the charges of fraud and are following a policy of watchfulness.

Claims Minnesota for Wilson.

By Telegraph to the Editor of THE NEW YORK TIMES.

ST. PAUL, Minn., Nov. 9.—Hughes leads Wilson in Minnesota 700 votes at this time, with 120 precincts to be heard from. These are mainly in the northern part of the State, in the woods, and are remote from railroads. Ordinarily these precincts are Republican, but this year, so far as reported, these people have been voting for the President. They are mostly foreigners and but few Germans are among them. When these precincts are in Hughes will have about 300 plurality in this State, subject to minor errors in the returns, which should about balance.

To offset this our report claims that the Minnesota troops on the border will give the President 600 majority, and the so-called absentee vote of this State will give the President about 300 more. Under one of our laws a voter temporarily absent from his precinct may send his vote in by mail and have it counted where he lives. Here this applies principally to railroad employes absent on their runs and traveling men. Twelve hundred of these votes are registered, and we think 900 of them will be voted. From returns already in they vote two to one for the president.

"I think I am safe in claiming this State for Wilson by 500.

F. B. LYNCH,
Democratic National Committeeman from Minnesota.

NORTH DAKOTA.

FARGO, N. D., Nov. 9.—North Dakota's five votes in the Electoral College were conceded to President Wilson late tonight by William Lemke, Chairman of the Republican State Central Committee, when returns from all but thirty-three precincts in the State gave the President a plurality of 1,560 over Hughes.

Later returns received up to the time when the tabulators ceased labor for the night, reduced the missing precincts to twenty-eight. The totals in the 1,831 precincts available at that time were: Wilson, 54,449; Hughes, 52,831. The President's lead thus being 1,618.

Forty per cent. of the unreported precincts are in counties that have been giving Wilson majorities, about 30 per cent. are in counties in which Hughes has been leading, and the remaining precincts are districts that have favored neither candidate decisively.

While Mr. Lemke estimated Wilson's plurality in the State at less than 900, Fred McLean, Chairman of the Democratic State Central Committee, asserted that the President's vote would exceed that of Hughes by 1,400.

Returns from several precincts will not be available for the official canvass, as the ballot boxes in these districts have been sealed up by the election officials and will not be opened until the official canvassing boards meet next week.

When Wilson's plurality in the State mounted to 1,500 this afternoon, several leading Republican newspapers conceded that he had carried the State. Returns from 1,745 precincts out of 1,859 in the State gave Wilson 53,125 and Hughes 51,598.

Charges that attempts were being made to tamper with the ballot boxes in a number of precincts in the western part of the State were laid before United States District Attorney Hildreth this afternoon by United States Mar-

Continued on Page 4.

CALIFORNIA DECIDES

Result Was in Doubt Till Republicans Gave It Up at 11:25 P. M.

MINNESOTA STILL CLOSE

Hughes's Lead Going Up There; Wilson Gains in Other Close States.

CONTESTS ARE PROMISED

Charges of Fraud Are Already Under Investigation in Some Districts.

ONE CITY PLAYS BIG PART

Women and Progressives of San Francisco Deciding Factor in National Result.

HOUSE CONTROL IN DOUBT

Minor Parties May Have Balance of Power—Senate Is Safely Democratic.

Woodrow Wilson and Thomas R. Marshall have been again elected President and Vice President. Soon after 11 o'clock last night all the doubtful States, except New Hampshire and Minnesota, had given Wilson such a steady lead that his election was no longer in doubt. When, at 11:25, the news came that Chester H. Rowell, the Republican State Chairman in California, had conceded the State to the Democrats, the disputed election of 1916 was no longer in dispute.

Wilson's indicated vote in the Electoral College is 272, that of Hughes being 259. With 272 votes in sight, President Wilson has six to spare for a possible split of Electors in California, or a sudden reversal in New Mexico.

Yesterday morning the States in doubt were California and North Dakota, in which Wilson was leading by small pluralities; Minnesota and New Mexico, in which Hughes was leading by still smaller ones. Later in the day New Hampshire, which had been given to Hughes, became doubtful, and New Mexico swung over to the Wilson column.

After that the only hope of the Republicans was in California, which Hughes must carry, in addition to Minnesota. But the California returns, as they kept on coming in, only served to strengthen Wilson's assurance of the State. He did not gain much, but he did not lose, and with every new return the hope of hearing from some Hughes stronghold which would overturn the Wilson plurality became fainter. When the southern part of the State was nearly all on record, and had failed to cut Wilson down any further, while the northern part confirmed his plurality, it became certain that California had given the Democrats the victory in the nation.

All the news of the day was Wilson news. The back settlements of New Mexico, which were so long coming in, reversed Hughes's apparent lead when they did come, and turned the State over to Wilson by what, for that sparsely settled State, is a large majority. Hughes lost nothing in Minnesota, but the hope of a change in North Dakota was not realized, and the dwindling of his plurality in New Hampshire until the Democrats were claiming the State was the finishing blow.

San Francisco Did It.

California, however, was the pivot on which the election of 1916 swung. The big vote for Wilson in San Francisco was what gave Wilson his first lead. But that was not decisive, and Republican hopes turned to Los Angeles, which responded with a Hughes majority that was slightly in excess of San Francisco's Democratic majority. It all depended then on the northern and southern parts of the State, and there the Progressive vote failed Hughes and gave the State to Wilson. But without the City of San Francisco Woodrow Wilson would have had to quit the White House on March 4 next.

It is San Francisco which has elected Wilson. His lead in California up to

Friday, November 10, 1916.

With 272 Electoral Votes, Wilson Wins; Gets California, North Dakota, New Mexico

California Decides

Result Was In Doubt Till Republicans Gave It Up At 11:25 P.M.

Minnesota Still Close

Hughes's Lead Going Up There; Wilson Gains In Other Close States.

Contests Are Promised

Charges Of Fraud Are Already Under Investigation in Some Districts.

One City Plays Big Part

Women and Progressives Of San Francisco Deciding Factor in National Result.

House Control in Doubt

Minor Parties May Have Balance of Power—Senate Is Safely Democratic.

Woodrow Wilson and Thomas R. Marshall have been again elected President and Vice President. Soon after 11 o'clock last night all the doubtful States, except New Hampshire and Minnesota, had given Wilson such a steady lead that his election was no longer in doubt. When, at 11:25, the news came that Chester H. Rowell, the Republican State Chairman in California, had conceded the State to the Democrats, the disputed election of 1916 was no longer in dispute.

Wilson's indicated vote in the Electoral College is 272, that of Hughes being 250. With 272 votes in sight, President Wilson has six to spare for a possible split of Electors in California, or a sudden reversal in New Mexico.

Yesterday morning the States in doubt were California and North Dakota, in which Wilson was leading by small pluralities; Minnesota and New Mexico, in which Hughes was leading by still smaller ones. Later in the day New Hampshire, which had been given to Hughes, became doubtful, and New Mexico swung over to the Wilson column.

After that the only hope of the Republicans was in California, which Hughes must carry, in addition to Minnesota. But the California returns, as they kept on coming in, only served to strengthen Wilson's assurance of the State. He did not gain much, but he did not lose, and with every new return the hope of hearing from some Hughes stronghold which would overturn the Wilson plurality became fainter. When the southern part of the State was nearly all on record, and had failed to cut Wilson down any further, while the northern part confirmed his plurality, it became certain that California had given the Democrats the victory in the nation.

All the news of the day was Wilson news. The back settlements of New Mexico, which were so long coming in, reversed Hughes's apparent lead when they did come, and turned the State over to Wilson by what, for that sparsely settled State, is a large majority. Hughes lost nothing in Minnesota, but the hope of a change in North Dakota was not realized, and the dwindling of his plurality in New Hampshire until the Democrats were claiming the Sate was the finishing blow.

San Francisco Did It.

California, however, was the pivot on which the election of 1916 swung. The big vote for Wilson in San Francisco was what gave Wilson his first lead. But that was not decisive, and Republican hopes turned to Los Angeles, which responded with a Hughes majority that was slightly in excess of San Francisco's Democratic majority. It all depended then on the northern and southern parts of the State, and there the Progressive vote failed Hughes and gave the State to Wilson. But without the City of San Francisco Woodrow Wilson would have had to quit the White House on March 4 next.

It is San Francisco which has elected Wilson. . . .The Republicans finally rested their hopes on Southern California. They carried Los Angeles County, but the returns were incomplete from the other parts of the immense territory comprised in the southern part of the State. Finally word came that the count in Los Angeles had been stopped for the night and the ballot boxes locked up.

But meanwhile that part of Los Angeles County which lies outside of the city reported a Hughes majority of 16,158, and right on the heels of this came the news that six of the southern counties had given him a majority of 4,808.

Since if Wilson carried either Minnesota or California, he would need only the three votes of New Mexico to win, the course of that State was followed with intense anxiety.

North Dakota, which had apparently gone for Wilson, became doubtful during the day and with California, Minnesota and New Mexico, made a total of thirty-three doubtful votes. West Virginia remained shaky throughout the evening, but at midnight the chances favored Hughes by a safe though small plurality, which, unless disturbed by later returns, might remain at 3,000. In North Dakota the slight swing away from Wilson was maintained.

Indiana was claimed by the Democrats as doubtful, but there seems to be no sufficient reason. At 1:30 A.M. 2,801 precincts out of 3,143 in Indiana had given Wilson 305,186 and Hughes 311,697, with Hughes leading by 6,561.

> Congress is to have its first woman member—Miss Jeanette M. Hankin, a Republican . . . from Montana.

It may be that the vote of the soldiers on the Mexican border will determine the election. That will not be the case if California is the pivotal State, probably, for the majority in that State is not likely to fall so low that her 400 soldier votes will affect it. But Minnesota, which see-sawed from Wilson to Hughes last night, and was for Wilson by 386 at midnight and for Hughes by 224 an hour later, has 4,047 men on the border, and West Virginia, where Hughes has apparently not more than 3,000 majority, has 1,058. New Hampshire also may be swung to Wilson if there should be a strong vote for him among the 1,375 men she has in Texas.

A dispatch from McArlen, Texas, to The Times says that the total vote of the Minnesota brigade is indicated [at] 1,906, apportioned as follows: Minnesota Artillery, 360; First Infantry [456], Second Infantry, 413; Third Infantry, 657. An unofficial ballot in the First Regiment went three to one for Wilson, but the officers say that in the other units the Republican vote was predominant.

Death as a Factor.

With the election so close, importance attaches even to individual electors. There appears to be a possibility that, although Wilson carried Washington, Hughes may get one of that State's seven votes. The death of A. Stream, a Democratic candidate for elector, shortly before election, and the substitution of E. M. Connor in his place on the ticket, came so late that in many counties the name of Stream, not Connor, appeared on the ballot. All votes cast for Stream will be invalid.

A similar question may arise in Missouri, in which State an elector committed suicide before election. In West Virginia an elector withdrew.

Though most of the great States of the Union went for Hughes by large majorities, the small majorities cast one way or the other by the smaller States were a curious feature of the result. Delaware went for Hughes by only 856 and was long in doubt. The Democrats actually claimed New Hampshire, so small was the Hughes majority there.

It was also noticeable that Hughes was weaker than his party in the smaller States of the East. Vermont gave him only 17,000, Maine only [5,000], Rhode Island 4,800. Vermont emphasized her vote by giving Graham, the Republican candidate for Governor, 25,000, and by re-electing Senator Page by an even larger plurality.

The most mixed result of all, however, was not in the East but in the West. Washington went for Wilson, but re-elected Senator Poindexter, Republican, and also re-elected Governor Lister, Democrat, and chose a solid Republican Congress delegation.

Kansas made it plainly manifest that the Progressive vote had not been coaxed back, so far as Hughes was concerned. That State went for Wilson, but at the same time re-elected the Republican Governor, Capper.

Two of the figures most constantly in the public eye were defeated for re-election. They both came from Illinois. One was Frank Buchanan, the labor leader, who was indicted for his pro-German activities, which were alleged to have transgressed the bounds of law, and who retaliated by getting Congress to investigate United States District Attorney Marshall of this city with a view to his impeachment. The other was Clyde H. Tavenner, noted for his opposition to an army and navy of any size and his semi-socialistic oratory. Both were Democrats.

Congress is to have its first woman member. She will be Miss Jeannette M. Hankin, a tall and red-haired Republican, who was elected Representative-at-Large from Montana. Montana went Democratic, and it was presumably the woman vote which saved this one Republican candidate from the defeat.

Friday, November 10, 1916.

WON'T CONCEDE WILSON VICTORY WITHOUT RECOUNT

Both Sides Should Be Anxious
to Remove All Doubt, Willcox Says.

Four States in Question

New Hampshire, New Mexico,
North Dakota, and California
Returns Scrutinized.

The Old Guard Confers

Willcox Not Invited to Meeting
of Crane, Barnes, and Others Ignored
in the Campaign.

The Republican campaign managers will not concede the State of California to President Wilson until after the result of the official count of the vote which is scheduled to begin on Monday has been announced. And even then it is more than likely that if the result of the official canvass should give the State to the President they will go into the courts and ask that the ballot boxes be reopened and the ballots recounted.

After a conference with Charles E. Hughes, in which former United States Attorney General George W. Wickersham participated, Chairman William R. Willcox of the Republican National Committee announced last night that California was only one of four States in which recount proceedings were probable. The other States are New Hampshire, New Mexico and North Dakota. In New Hampshire and New Mexico Mr. Hughes was leading on the late returns yesterday, but it was assumed by the Republican leaders that in the event of their winding up in the Hughes column, the Democrats would ask for a new count under the auspices of the courts.

"I think there ought to be a recount in those four States," said Mr. Willcox. "I assume the other side is just as anxious as we are to have any cloud on the title removed by a recanvass in States where the vote is close. Just think of it: There are States where in 400,000 votes or more the margin of the winning candidate promises to be 400 votes or less. Where the election of a President of the United States hinges on such a slender plurality I think the natural thing would be to have a recount."

Seeks New Hampshire Recount

In New Hampshire, where the vote fluctuated all day yesterday slightly in favor of the two candidates in turn, the Republicans took the preliminary steps looking to a recount while the odds seemed to favor Mr. Wilson . . . The Old Guard Republican leaders held an important conference at the Hotel Manhattan last night which Chairman Willcox was not invited to attend.

Gloom pervaded the meeting of the Old Guard. They had been in close touch with Republican leaders in States which were catalogued as "doubtful" and had learned that in California, where the electoral votes were essential to a Hughes victory, there was little hope that the Republican nominee would come out ahead. From North Dakota, where a Hughes majority was regarded as safe, but where it had changed into a majority for President Wilson, word had come from United States Senator McCumber that the best to be expected was about an even break between President Wilson and the Republican candidate.

"There should be no man in the White House with a clouded title," said one leader. "It seems to me that the recount is the only means to clear the title by definitely establishing the fact that the ballots have been counted right."

It is understood that this view has the full approval of Chairman Willcox. He said yesterday that practically the only means of putting the quietus on the Democratic cries of fraud was by a recount in the so-called doubtful States.

Former United States Attorney General George W. Wickersham, who, it is expected, will take an active part in mapping out the recount program in doubtful States, said last night that there was little likelihood that the contest would come before the House of Representatives for final arbitrament in this instance, as it did in the Hayes-Tilden contest in 1876. The present House, which would be the arbiter, has a Democratic majority.

Mr. Wickersham asserted that the legislation enacted by Congress in 1887, very largely as a result of developments in that historic contest, made the States sovereign in pronouncing judgment in a recount on the Presidential vote and that only in the case of a tie that might result from the death or retirement or the refusal to vote on the part of the Electors, or in case a State should return two sets of Electors, as might be possible as a result of factional fights, would the House be called on to give a decision.

Although jailed for sedition throughout the campaign, the perennial Socialist candidate Eugene V. Debs received an impressive 919,799 votes—his high-water mark.

The 1920 election was summed up by the word "normalcy." Accidentally coined by Warren G. Harding (he meant normality), it captured the widespread desire to move beyond the unsettling changes that followed the Great War, from female suffrage to prohibition, race riots, and red-baiting. Of the four candidates on the Democratic and Republican tickets, three would ultimately occupy the Oval Office.

For all its early promise, Woodrow Wilson's presidency ended in disarray. He was hailed as a conquering hero in Europe, but back home he could not persuade Americans to join the League of Nations. His long, futile campaign for the League raised partisan tensions, and brought on the stroke that crippled him in 1919. For most of his last year in office, the President's access to others and their access to him was strictly controlled by his wife and physician.

But Wilson did not fade into the sunset willingly, and refused to foreclose on a third run until it became obvious that he could not win. A large crowd of pretenders gathered at the San Francisco convention, and Ohio Governor James M. Cox won the nomination. His running mate was a relatively obscure former Assistant Secretary of the Navy named Franklin D. Roosevelt, only 38 years old.

A swarm of Republicans campaigned fiercely for their party's nomination, sure that it and the presidency were the same. Warren Harding was an undistinguished first-term Senator

Left to right:
Warren G. Harding (1865–1923)
James M. Cox (1870–1957)
Eugene V. Debs (1855–1926)

A beanie supporting James M. Cox, the only major party candidate for president or vice president in 1920 who failed to one day become president.

who had published a paper in his hometown of Marion, Ohio. His chief strength was that he had few enemies; his nomination was assured in a legendary "smoke-filled room" at the Chicago convention. Interestingly, the apostle of normalcy had quite a few mysteries in his past, including persistent rumors that he was partly African-American and had a daughter out of wedlock. His quirky slogan was "Let's Be Done With Wiggle and Wobble." Calvin Coolidge, the governor of Massachusetts, was picked as his running mate, largely for quelling a Boston police strike in 1919.

Cox and Roosevelt hit the ground running, traveling thousands of miles across the country. FDR especially came into his own as a formidable campaigner. The Democrats promoted the League of Nations, but found a more effective issue in campaign funding. Cox lambasted the Republicans for accepting huge corporate donations, but near the end of the campaign, he went overboard, calling them traitors, for which he was widely censured.

For most of the campaign, Harding remained in Marion, welcoming reporters to relax and chat on his front porch. The former publisher knew how to charm the press, and most newspapers openly supported him. His message of small-town neighborliness and morality was a powerful tonic in 1920.

The election result was a larger repudiation of Wilson and the Democrats than anyone thought possible. On November 2, 1920, Harding's fifty-fifth birthday, he was overwhelmingly elected (404 electoral votes to 127 for Cox). In his fifth campaign, the Socialist Eugene V. Debs won 919,799 votes, despite running from a jail cell in Atlanta, where he had been sent after giving anti-war speeches in 1918.

Americans settled in happily for a new decade. Most were optimistic, with the notable exception of Mrs. Harding, who said, "I can see but one word over his head if they make him President, and that word is Tragedy."

This sheet music cover pays tribute to the first president of the Jazz Age—Warren G. Harding.

As a publicity stunt, Warren Harding becomes a printer again for a day, assembling the front page of his Ohio newspaper, the *Marion Star*, Marion, Ohio, August 14, 1920.

James Cox and Franklin D. Roosevelt motorcade past Union Station during a campaign stop in Washington, D.C., July 1920.

A crowd of 3,000 gathers in Marion, Ohio, to hear Harding accept the Republican nomination *(above)*, June 1920.

Debs, in Atlanta Federal Prison, is formally notified of his nomination for presidency *(right)* by a New York delegation of the Socialist Party, May 29, 1920.

Debs took his first railroad job at 15, and in later years became a leader in organizing and building the early railroad unions. He continued to crusade on behalf of workers *(above)* after his release from prison, 1921.

Eugene Debs smiles after walking out of prison on Christmas Day *(right)*, Atlanta, 1921. After Harding was elected he commuted Debs's sentence but did not restore his citizenship (it was eventually reinstated in 1976).

James Cox does a bit of harness racing while campaigning at the Minnesota State Fair, Saint Paul, 1920.

Cox places a wreath on the grave of suffragist Susan B. Anthony while visiting Rochester, New York, October 1920.

Harding gives a speech while on the campaign trail in the Pacific Northwest *(above)*, 1920.

In an early form of mass communication, Harding records a speech about "Americanism" on a phonograph *(right)* for use in his campaign.

"All the News That's Fit to Print."

The New York Times.

THE WEATHER
Fair and colder today; Thursday fair; strong southwest to west winds.
For full weather report see Page 15.

VOL. LXX....No. 22,929. NEW YORK, WEDNESDAY, NOVEMBER 3, 1920. TWO CENTS In Greater New York | THREE CENTS Within 200 Miles | FOUR CENTS Elsewhere

HARDING WINS; MILLION LEAD HERE; BIG REPUBLICAN GAINS IN CONGRESS; MILLER LEADS SMITH FOR GOVERNOR

MILLER BY 57,000

But Democrats Refuse to Concede Governor's Defeat.

SMITH'S SURPRISING RUN

In Some Up-State Strongholds He Surpassed His Former Vote.

WINS EVERY CITY BOROUGH

Strongest in Manhattan, but Could Not Overcome Miller's Up-State Lead.

75,000 VICTORY, GLYNN SAYS

Republicans Here Accuse Tammany of Holding Back City Returns.

WADSWORTH IS ELECTED

Plurality Betters Miller's, but is Far Behind That on Presidential Ticket.

NEW YORK—Voted for Presidential Electors, United States Senator, Congressmen, Governor and other State officials and on an amendment to the Constitution. Vote in 1916: Democratic, 750,426; Republican, 869,115.
Polls closed at 6 P. M.

After a neck-and-neck race all evening ex-Judge Nathan L. Miller defeated Alfred E. Smith, his Democratic opponent, for the Governorship on the latest returns by about 57,000 plurality. Despite the big Harding landslide, it seemed probable for some time that Governor Smith would be able to pull through, but late returns from rural Republican districts overcame a record vote for him in New York City.

The Democratic managers refused, however, to give up hope, and early this morning still claimed the election of Mr. Smith. The Governor did not put forth any claim himself, asserting that he preferred to wait until remote up-State districts had been heard from. The Democratic leaders based their hopes for final success upon the fact that late returns showed that the Governor had increased his average majority in each election district in the city from 115 to 118 votes. They did not take into account, however, that Mr. Miller had also increased his average in up-State districts from 75 to 83.

If the present ratios are maintained, ex-Judge Miller will have an up-State lead of 379,725, while Governor Smith's plurality in New York City will be 322,494, giving the Republican candidate a plurality in the entire State of 57,231. Republican leaders claimed the election of Mr. Miller by approximately 75,000. Democratic leaders said Smith's plurality would be around 40,000.

Smith Led at First.

Early reports all evening showed the Tammany Governor in the lead, but when reports from rural Republican strongholds came in Mr. Miller's vote picked up considerably and shoved him well into the lead. At the same time Smith's vote in outlying districts in New York City did not keep pace with the huge vote he received in other parts of the city, and the indications were that ex-Judge Miller would be elected by a small plurality.

Some of the members of the Republican County Committee shortly before midnight made the charge that election returns were being held up in some Tammany districts until Mr. Miller's full strength had been reported. The First, Third and Fourth Assembly Districts, in lower Manhattan, where Tammany's strength is greatest, were among those mentioned at Republican county headquarters.

Deputy Attorney General Berger, accompanied by several members of the committee, set out for the polling places in the districts to learn the true state of affairs.

Wadsworth Elected.

United States Senator James W. Wadsworth, Jr., although running behind Senator Harding did not have any difficulty in defeating his Democratic

Continued on Page Four.

State Pluralities.
FOR PRESIDENT.

REPUBLICAN	
California	500,000
Connecticut	100,000
Colorado	40,000
Delaware	5,000
Idaho	25,000
Illinois	800,000
Indiana	200,000
Iowa	200,000
Kansas	200,000
Maine	75,000
Maryland	20,000
Massachusetts	300,000
Michigan	400,000
Minnesota	100,000
Missouri	40,000
Montana	50,000
Nebraska	100,000
New Hampshire	30,000
Nevada	4,000
New Jersey	200,000
New York	1,000,000
Ohio	400,000
Oregon	5,000
Pennsylvania	750,000
Rhode Island	50,000
South Dakota	80,000
Utah	30,000
Vermont	45,000
Washington	150,000
West Virginia	50,000
Wisconsin	300,000
Wyoming	8,000
DEMOCRATIC.	
Alabama	70,000
Arkansas	100,000
Florida	
Georgia	
Kentucky	20,000
Louisiana	
Mississippi	
New Mexico	
North Carolina	60,000
Oklahoma	7,500
South Carolina	
Tennessee	40,000
Texas	50,000
Virginia	75,000
DOUBTFUL.	
Arizona	
North Dakota	

CITY'S VOTE GOES TO HARDING AND SMITH

For Republican President by 443,000 and Democratic Governor by 325,000.

SEPARATE BALLOTS HELPED

But Some Charges Heard That Tammany Traded Votes—Socialists Make Gains.

New York City, in yesterday's election, gave its vote overwhelmingly to Senator Warren G. Harding, Republican candidate for President; to Calvin Coolidge, Republican candidate for Vice President, and to Alfred E. Smith, Democratic candidate for Governor.

Senator Harding carried every Assembly District in the Greater City with one exception—the First Assembly District, which is Governor Smith's home district. This gave Cox a plurality of about 400 votes.

In the minor contests the Republicans made some gains, although these were nothing like what might have been expected from the overwhelming sweep made by the Presidential ticket.

This result was greatly facilitated by the three ballots instituted by the Board of Elections, one for the Presidency, one for the State ticket (which also included the Congressional candidates), and one for the constitutional amendment and bonus proposal. The separation made ticket splitting easy, and the voters took full advantage of it.

Harding's victory in the city was overwhelming. At 3 A. M. today, on the returns then available, the plurality of the Republican candidate for the Presidency in the city was indicated as about 443,000.

Manhattan gave a Republican Presidential plurality of about 136,000; the Bronx, 62,000; Brooklyn, 177,000; Queens, 61,000, and Richmond, 7,000.

Striking Support of Smith.

But on the State ticket it was quite a different story. The same hour that found Harding victorious by 443,000 in the normally Democratic city of New York, showed Alfred E. Smith, Democrat, leading Judge Nathan Miller, his

Continued on Page Three.

OHIO FOR HARDING; 400,000 PLURALITY IS NOW ESTIMATED

Republicans Ahead in Nearly All the Large Cities of the State.

BIG LEAD IN CINCINNATI

Harding's Margin in Hamilton County Believed to be 20,000.

VICTORY IN CLEVELAND

Cuyahoga County About Two to One—Sweep in Toledo Also.

OHIO—Voted for Presidential Electors, United States Senator, Congressmen, Governor and other State officials. Vote in 1916: Democratic, 604,161; Republican, 516,733.
Polls closed at 5:30 P. M. (6:30 P. M. New York time).

COLUMBUS, Ohio, Nov. 2.—Returns from 2,987 precincts out of a total of 7,146 in the State give Harding 469,355, Cox 336,352.

If this ratio is maintained, the indications are that Senator Harding carried Ohio by more than 400,000 plurality.

Under instructions from State officials county election boards counted Presidential returns first. This made returns on the State ticket and the United States Senatorship unusually slow. Many scratched ballots were voted on the State ticket.

Returns from 128 precincts on the Governorship race show Davis (R), 15,690; Donahey (D), 10,833.

Returns from 66 precincts for United States Senator give Willis (R), 6,341; Julian (D), 4,794.

Senator Harding has probably carried every large city in the State from which normally the Democrats get their majorities. In some instances his pluralities have been tremendous. He is running even in Columbus, and may have carried it.

Many of the country districts are holding up to normal for Governor Cox. In some instances he is making slight gains there.

Chairman Clark claims the election of the Republican State ticket, including Harry L. Davis for Governor, by 100,000, while Chairman Durbin claims the election of A. V. Donahey (Dem.) for Governor by at least 50,000.

The vote in Cuyahoga County, including Cleveland, is running about two to one for Harding, indicating the sentiment in Northern Ohio. Four years ago Wilson carried the county two to one. Seventy-eight precincts out of 571 in the city of Cleveland gave Harding 13,840, Cox 7,937. In Cuyahoga County, outside of Cleveland, nine precincts out of 133 give Harding 2,826, Cox 830.

Hamilton County, in which Cincinnati is situated, will give 20,000 plurality for Harding.

The first twenty-two precincts to re-

Continued on Page Three.

United States Senators Elected.

REPUBLICANS, 20.	DEMOCRATS, 14.
S. Shortridge, Calif.	O. W. Underwood, Ala.
S. D. Nicholson, Col.	J. T. Heflin, Ala.
F. B. Brandegee, Conn.	M. A. Smith, Ariz.
F. R. Gooding, Idaho.	T. H. Caraway, Ark.
W. B. McKinley, Ill.	D. U. Fletcher, Fla.
J. E. Watson, Ind.	T. E. Watson, Ga.
A. B. Cummins, Iowa.	J. C. W. Beckham, Ky.
C. Curtis, Kan.	E. S. Broussard, La.
O. E. Weller, Md.	C. B. Henderson, Nev.
S. B. Spencer, Mo.	L. S. Overman, N. C.
G. H. Moses, N. H.	S. Ferris, Okla.
J. W. Wadsworth, Jr., N. Y.	G. E. Chamberlain, Ore.
E. F. Ladd, N. Dakota.	E. D. Smith, S. C
F. B. Willis, Ohio.	C. Glass, Va.
B. Penrose, Pa.	
P. Norbeck, S. Dakota.	
R. Smoot, Utah.	
W. P. Dillingham, Vt.	
W. L. Jones, Wash.	
I. L. Lenroot, Wis.	

INDIANA IS SWEPT BY REPUBLICANS

Early Returns Indicate That Harding Will Carry State by Upward of 200,000.

WATSON LEADING TAGGART

He Trails Ticket, but on Basis of Returns His Election Is Expected by 135,000 Plurality.

INDIANA—Voted for Presidential Electors, United States Senator, Congressmen, Governor and other State officials. Vote in 1916: Democratic, 334,063; Republican, 341,005.
Polls closed at 6 P. M. (7 P. M. New York time).

Special to The New York Times.

INDIANAPOLIS, Ind., Nov. 2.—Late returns coming in from the rural districts have piled up the Harding plurality in the State with every indication pointing that the Republican landslide will be the largest in the history of Indiana. It was estimated late tonight that Cox will be defeated by at least 200,000 votes. The former Republican plurality record for Indiana in a Presidential race was held by Roosevelt with 93,000.

Of 1,002 precincts out of the 3,384 in the State, Harding has received 330,767 votes and Cox, 239,621.

Warren T. McCray of Kentland, Republican Gubernatorial nominee, has been swept into office by an overwhelming plurality over Dr. Carlton B. McCulloch of Indianapolis, his Democratic opponent. Although James E. Watson ran behind the ticket in several districts in his race for re-election to the Senate against Thomas Taggart, it is estimated that he will trail Harding less than 15,000 votes. Watson ran especially strong in the rural districts, while Taggart made his best showing in the laboring centres.

On the face of incomplete returns it appears that eleven of the thirteen Congressional Districts have piled up a suf-

Continued on Page Three.

ILLINOIS TREBLES REPUBLICAN VOTE

Returns Indicate Harding Has More Than 800,000 Plurality in the State.

McKINLEY CHOSEN SENATOR

Governor, State Officers and Entire Delegation to Congress Probably Republican.

ILLINOIS—Voted for Presidential Electors, United States Senator, Congressmen, Governor and other State officials and on an amendment to the Constitution. Vote in 1916: Democratic, 950,229; Republican, 1,152,549.
Polls closed at 5 P. M. (6 P. M. New York time).

CHICAGO, Nov. 2.—Upon the basis of returns received up to a late hour tonight Harding and Coolidge have carried Illinois by a plurality of more than 800,000. At this hour Harding has an indicated plurality of 331,000 in Chicago. His plurality down State is estimated to be not less than 316,000.

Harding's plurality in Chicago is apparently larger than any ever given a candidate by the city. It exceeds the famous 147,477 which Mayor Thompson got in 1915.

In 966 of 5,750 Illinois precincts, including 475 in Chicago, Harding had 218,913 votes, against 78,906 for Cox.

McKinley, for Senator, had a plurality of 57,621 over Waller, and Small was leading Lewis nearly two to one for Governor.

The Republican sweep apparently is even stronger than in 1904, when Roosevelt carried Cook County by 126,000, the women not voting then. Four years ago Hughes carried the county by 56,000 over Wilson, but Harding's lead over Cox is more than five times greater.

By 1 o'clock it was estimated that 60 per cent. of the 884,000 registered voters had visited the polls. During the afternoon they kept swarming in, and closing time saw many still waiting in line.

Early returns indicate about 825,000 votes were cast in Chicago. The plurality

Continued on Page Three.

CONGRESS HEAVILY REPUBLICAN, GAINS IN BOTH HOUSES

Party Will Have a Majority of 12 in the Senate and 113 in the House.

54 REPUBLICAN SENATORS

House Stands: Republicans 274, Democrats 158, Independents 2, Drys 1.

IRRECONCILABLES ELECTED

Brandegee in Connecticut and Moses in New Hampshire Returned.

President Harding will have a Republican Congress to support his policies in the first two years at least of his Administration. Returns received up until the time this edition of THE TIMES goes to press show that the party which was triumphant at the polls yesterday will have increased majorities in both Houses, with that in the House approaching 300.

Returns in the elections for Senators and Representatives are meager from some important States, but the trend of voting in those States in the Presidential and Gubernatorial contests indicates the probable result as far as the Senate is concerned. The returns received indicate that the two houses in the next Congress will stand as follows:

Senate—Republicans, 54 Democrats, 42.

House—Republicans, 274; Democrats, 158; Independents, 2; Prohibitionist, 1.

This gives the Republicans a majority of 12 in the Senate and a majority of 113 in the House. The present Republican majority in the Senate is 2 and in the House 39.

Senator Moses of New Hampshire and Senator Brandegee of Connecticut, both Republicans of the irreconcilable treaty group in the Senate, were strongly opposed on account of their opposition to the League of Nations, but have carried their States by substantial majorities. Senator Brandegee also had the opposition of many women on account of his effort to prevent the ratification of the Nineteenth Amendment.

Phelan Loses California.

Samuel Shortridge, Republican, who supported Senator Hiram Johnson's irreconcilable opposition to the League of Nations, appears to have been elected to the Senate, defeating Senator James D. Phelan, Democrat, a firm friend of the Wilson Administration. Senator James E. Watson, Republican, has been re-elected from Indiana, defeating ex-Senator Thomas Taggart, Democrat. Returns from Iowa are not nearly complete, but they indicate that in spite of the opposition of organizations of farmers and laborers and a great many Re-

Continued on Page Three.

Electoral Vote.

HARDING.	
California	13
Colorado	6
Connecticut	7
Delaware	3
Illinois	29
Indiana	15
Idaho	4
Iowa	13
Kansas	10
Maine	6
Maryland	8
Massachusetts	18
Michigan	15
Minnesota	12
Missouri	18
Montana	4
Nebraska	8
Nevada	3
New Hampshire	4
New Jersey	14
New York	45
Ohio	24
Oregon	5
Pennsylvania	38
Rhode Island	5
South Dakota	5
Utah	4
Vermont	4
Washington	7
West Virginia	8
Wisconsin	13
Wyoming	3
Total	371
COX.	
Alabama	12
Arkansas	9
Florida	6
Georgia	14
Kentucky	13
Louisiana	10
Mississippi	10
New Mexico	3
North Carolina	12
Oklahoma	10
South Carolina	9
Tennessee	12
Texas	20
Virginia	12
Total	152
Doubtful or Insufficiently Reported	
Arizona	3
North Dakota	5
Total	8

Total number of votes in Electoral College, 531; necessary to a choice, 266.

PRESIDENT HEARD FIRST VOTES ONLY

He Retired at 9 o'Clock, His Physician Leaving the White House Earlier.

NO COMMENT ON RETURNS

Wilson at Afternoon Cabinet Meeting Expressed Confidence in Success of League.

Special to The New York Times.

WASHINGTON, Nov. 2.—Although messages to the White House tonight brought the news that Harding was leading in very nearly all the doubtful localities the attitude seemed to be sit tight and concede nothing until the actual result was ascertained. The experience of the Hughes débâcle four years ago appeared to hold out a lesson in the wisdom of this course for the White House circle.

No public expressions of any kind were made. The atmosphere lacked the gloom usually associated with the news of a reversal. Visitors to the White House found the Secretaries and other members of the staff in perfect good humor.

President Wilson heard bulletins until about 9 o'clock, and this being his usual bed hour, he retired, so it was said. Admiral Cary T. Grayson, his personal physician, left the White House for his home about 8:30 o'clock. This fact seemed to set aside theories that the President would be in a nervous condition if he realized that Senator Harding was far ahead in the Presidential race.

Joseph P. Tumulty, Private Secretary

Continued on Page Four.

GIGANTIC MAJORITIES

Pennsylvania, 750,000; Illinois, 800,000; Ohio, 400,000.

MAY BE 6,000,000 IN ALL

More Than 370 Electoral Votes Won by Harding and Coolidge.

BIG GAINS IN THE WEST

Indiana, Wisconsin, Michigan, Iowa, Kansas, Nebraska and California Won.

NEW JERSEY BY 200,000

Maine, with 75,000, Beats the Plurality She Gave in September.

SOLID SOUTH UNBROKEN

Unless Late Figures Change Tennessee—Cox May Lose All Western States.

By majorities unprecedented in American politics, Warren G. Harding was elected President and Calvin Coolidge Vice President yesterday on Senator Harding's fifty-fifth birthday. Though the addition of women to the electorate might have been expected to make the margins of successful candidates somewhat larger than in past years, it could hardly account for any such unheard of majorities as were rolled up yesterday. From coast to coast records were broken.

Harding's total pluralities in the States he carried may reach 6,500,000 and his net plurality over Cox may be 6,000,000. This surpasses by 3,500,000 the previous record, which was that of Theodore Roosevelt's victory over Alton B. Parker.

The highest State plurality ever previously recorded, Roosevelt's margin of 500,000 over Parker in Pennsylvania in 1904, was surpassed by at least four States yesterday. New York State went for Harding by nearly 1,100,000; Pennsylvania gave him a plurality of 750,000; Illinois gave him 800,000; California, which went for Wilson four years ago by a majority of 2,700, gave Harding a plurality of perhaps 500,000 over James M. Cox. Ohio, the home State of both candidates, went for Harding by 400,000.

At 4 o'clock this morning it seemed that Harding's majority on electoral votes would equal or surpass the record-breaking landslide by which Roosevelt beat Alton B. Parker.

Cox held the solid South, and Kentucky and perhaps Oklahoma among the border States; but West Virginia and Missouri had apparently gone for Harding, as they went for Roosevelt in 1904. Late reports indicate that Cox might possibly lose Tennessee.

The latest reports give Harding 371 electoral votes and Cox 152, with eight votes—those of Arizona and North Dakota—still uncertain. This, however, seems to be due to inadequate reports; the probability is that they are all for Harding.

All over the country the Harding pluralities broke records. Boston, which has been consistently Democratic in recent years, except in 1896, when McKinley carried it over Bryan, showed the effect of the drift of the Irish vote by giving Harding a plurality of more than 20,000.

New York City, however, was even more surprising. The city went for Taft in 1908 by less than 16,000; it seems to have given Harding a plurality of more than 443,000. Buffalo gave Harding a plurality of 46,247.

The effect of the Harding sweep showed everywhere. Though the Southern States stood fast, Harding had carried two wards in Atlanta and two Louisiana parishes. In the Middle West, Indiana and Kansas each gave him more than 200,000 plurality, Iowa about the same; Michigan nearly 400,000; Wisconsin nearly 300,000.

Maine, which surprised observers last September by a Republican plurality of 70,000 in the Gubernatorial election, surpassed this figure by several thousand

MAP SHOWING HOW THE STATES VOTED

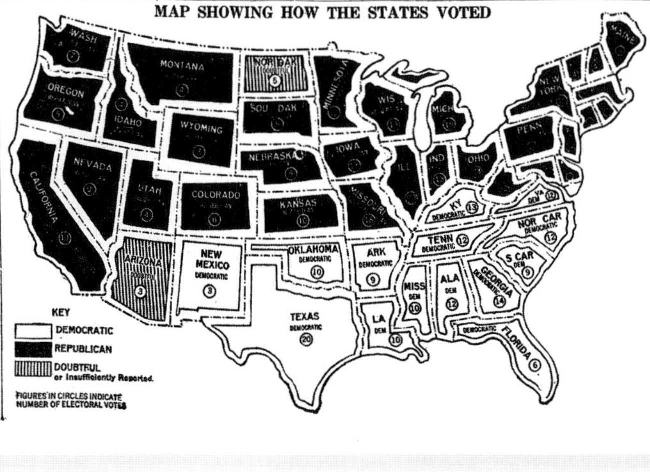

Wednesday, November 3, 1920.

Harding Wins; Million Lead Here; Big Republican Gains in Congress; Miller Leads Smith for Governor

Gigantic Majorities

Pennsylvania, 750,000;
Illinois, 800,000;
Ohio, 400,000.

May Be 6,000,000 in All

More than 370 Electoral Votes
Won by Harding and Coolidge.

Big Gains in the West

Indiana, Wisconsin, Michigan, Iowa,
Kansas, Nebraska and California Won.

New Jersey by 200,000

Maine, with 75,000, Beats the
Plurality She Gave in September.

Solid South Unbroken

Unless Late Figures Change Tennessee—
Cox May Lose All Western States.

By majorities unprecedented in American politics, Warren G. Harding was elected President and Calvin Coolidge Vice President yesterday on Senator Harding's fifty-fifth birthday. Though the addition of women to the electorate might have been expected to make the margins of successful candidates somewhat larger than in past years, it could hardly account for any such unheard of majorities as were rolled up yesterday. From coast to coast records were broken.

Harding's total pluralities in the States he carried may reach 6,500,000 and the net plurality over Cox may be 6,000,000. This surpasses by 3,500,000 the previous record, which was that of Theodore Roosevelt's victory over Alton B. Parker.

The highest State plurality ever previously recorded, Roosevelt's margin of 500,000 over Parker in Pennsylvania in 1904, was surpassed by at least four States yesterday. New York State went for Harding by nearly 1,100,000; Pennsylvania gave him a plurality of 750,000; Illinois gave him 800,000; California, which went for Wilson four years ago by a majority of 2,700, gave Harding a plurality of perhaps 500,000 over James M. Cox. Ohio, the home State of both candidates, went for Harding by 400,000.

At 4 o'clock this morning it seemed that Harding's majority on electoral votes would equal or surpass the record-breaking landslide by which Roosevelt beat Alton B. Parker.

Cox held the solid South, and Kentucky and perhaps Oklahoma among the border States; but West Virginia and Missouri had apparently gone for Harding, as they went for Roosevelt in 1904. Late reports indicate that Cox might possibly lose Tennessee.

All over the country the Harding pluralities broke records.

The latest reports give Harding 371 electoral votes and Cox 152, with eight votes—those of Arizona and North Dakota—still uncertain. This, however, seems to be due to inadequate reports; the probability is that they are all for Harding.

All over the country the Harding pluralities broke records. Boston, which has been consistently Democratic in recent years, except in 1896, when McKinley carried it over Bryan, showed the effect of the drift of the Irish vote by giving Harding a plurality of more than 20,000.

New York City, however, was even more surprising. The city went for Taft in 1908 by less than 16,000; it seems to have given Harding a plurality of more than 443,000. Buffalo gave Harding a plurality of 46,247.

The effect of the Harding sweep showed everywhere. Though the Southern States stood fast, Harding had carried two wards in Atlanta and two Louisiana parishes. In the Middle West, Indiana and Kansas each gave him more than 200,000 plurality, Iowa about the same; Michigan nearly 400,000; Wisconsin nearly 300,000.

Maine, which surprised observers last September by a Republican plurality of 70,000 in the Gubernatorial election, surpassed this figure by several thousand yesterday. New Jersey gave Harding more than 200,000.

Reports from the Far West, due to the wide extent of territory and the difference in time, were slow in coming in, but there was every indication that the Western States which had re-elected Wilson in 1916 when almost all the East went for Hughes had turned over solidly to the Republican nominee this year.

> The effect of the Harding sweep showed everywhere.

Harding carried his home precinct, 373 to 76. It was Democratic four years ago, though there has been a reapportionment since. Governor Cox's home precinct was carried by Harding by 12 votes. In Northampton, Mass., Coolidge's home town, the Republicans won by two to one. Four years ago Hughes carried it by a very narrow margin. Harding carried Hyde Park, N. Y., the home town of Franklin D. Roosevelt, Democratic nominee for Vice President, by 279 votes to 194, and he carried President Wilson's home district at Princeton, N. J., by a majority estimated at about five to one.

At 11 o'clock last night Governor Cox's newspaper, The Dayton News, conceded the election of Harding, and George White, Chairman of the Democratic National Committee, followed his candidate's example a few minutes later.

Governor Alfred E. Smith seems to have been defeated, although he ran nearly 300,000 ahead of the Democratic national ticket up-State and more than three quarters of a million ahead of the national ticket in the city. His plurality in this city at 4 o'clock this morning, was estimated at 315,000, but Judge Nathan L. Miller, the Republican candidate, had a margin of apparently 370,000 in the up-State vote. Democratic leaders, however, refused at 4 o'clock this morning to concede Governor Smith's defeat.

> From coast to coast veteran and popular Democrats fell in the general collapse.

The Republican sweep carried with it considerably increased majorities in both houses of Congress. Indications at 2 o'clock this morning were that the Republicans would have fifty-four Senators to the Democrats forty-two, but Will H. Hays, Chairman of the Republican National Committee, was claiming a majority of fourteen. The present Senate has forty-nine Republicans and forty-seven Democrats.

In the House the Republicans will apparently have 273 and the Democrats 159. Two independents and one Prohibitionist have been elected. The present House has a Republican majority of 38 over all; it will be increased in the next to 111. It appears that the Democrats will have only 13 of the 43 seats from New York.

Ogden L. Mills (Rep.) defeated Representative Pell in the Seventeenth District here.

In each house of the New York Legislature the Democrats have lost six seats. The next Senate will have 37 Republicans and 14 Democrats; the next Assembly 116 Republicans, 29 Democrats and 5 Socialists. Four of the five Socialists expelled from the Assembly last Winter were re-elected, and the Socialists gained another seat in the Bronx.

Senator James W. Wadsworth, Jr., was elected easily, despite the opposition of the woman suffragists, who were embittered by his consistent antagonism to their cause in recent years. His plurality over Harry C. Walker, the Democratic nominee, seems to be about 365,000, although Republican headquarters are claiming 500,000.

In Connecticut Senator Frank B. Brandegee, also opposed by the woman suffragists and by some League Republicans because of his outspoken hostility to the League, will probably have a margin of 35,000 or more over Congressman Augustine Lonergan, his Democratic opponent.

From coast to coast veteran and popular Democrats fell in the general collapse. The disaster which seems to have beaten Alfred E. Smith out of the Governorship of New York has also defeated Senator James D. Phelan for re-election in California, despite his great popularity throughout the State. In Indiana, Thomas Taggart, candidate for the Senate against James E. Watson, the present holder of the seat, was thought likely a few weeks ago to win his fight; but though Watson has apparently run behind the Presidential ticket by many thousands, he seems sure of election.

Factional fights in Illinois and Wisconsin did not disturb the Republicans. The battle in the primaries between the Thompson and Lowden factions in Illinois had caused bitter animosities, and several Republican papers, including The Chicago Tribune, supported James Hamilton Lewis, the Democratic nominee for Governor, against Len Small, the Thompson Republican candidate. But Lewis was overwhelmingly defeated, and William B. McKinley, the Lowden Republican candidate for the Senate, was elected by a huge majority over Waller, his Democratic opponent.

In Wisconsin Senator Irvine Luther Lenroot, a mild reservationist on the League question, was opposed by James Thompson, a La Follette man and representative of the bitter-end anti-League faction. But Lenroot won handily, and Paul S. Reinsch, former Minister to China, who was the Democratic candidate, did no more than beat the Socialist for third honors. In New Hampshire Senator George H. Moses, one of the bitter opponents of the League, had been disturbed in his campaign by echoes from the primary fight against a pro-League Republican, but he too won with ease.

Socialist managers claimed a vote of more than 2,000,000, as against less than 600,000 four years ago, but the early returns did not provide a basis for judging the reliability of their estimates. They seem to have a heavy vote in Illinois.

Wednesday, November 3, 1920.

PRESIDENT HEARD FIRST VOTES ONLY

He Retired at 9 o'Clock, His Physician Leaving the White House Earlier.

No Comment on Returns

Wilson at Afternoon Cabinet Meeting Expressed Confidence in Success of League.

Special to The New York Times.

WASHINGTON, Nov. 2—Although messages to the White House tonight brought the news that Harding was leading in very nearly all the doubtful localities the attitude seemed to be sit tight and concede nothing until the actual result was ascertained. The experience of the Hughes débacle four years ago appeared to hold out a lesson in the wisdom of this course for the White House circle.

No public expressions of any kind were made. The atmosphere lacked the gloom usually associated with the news of a reversal. Visitors to the White House found the Secretaries and other members of the staff in perfect good humor.

President Wilson heard bulletins until about 9 o'clock, and this being his usual bed hour, he retired, so it was said. Admiral Cary T. Grayson, his personal physician, left the White House for his home about 8:30 o'clock. This fact seemed to set aside theories that the President would be in a nervous condition if he realized that Senator Harding was far ahead in the Presidential race.

. . . President Wilson appeared this afternoon at a Cabinet meeting, where he expressed confidence that Governor Cox would be elected. The President took the ground, as he has all along, that the country was in favor of the League of Nations and would show its preference at the polls.

. . . Practically every Senator and member of the House of Representatives is now away from Washington, as are other politicians of note. Republican and Democratic headquarters were dreary spots, compared to the hives of activity in New York and Chicago. Still the election means much to Washington, as this city's heart is purely Governmental and great crowds sought bulletin boards, newspaper offices and all other sources of information.

. . . The representatives here of the various foreign Governments have been keeping in close touch with the developments of the campaign. While they have been refraining carefully from saying anything of a partisan character, or participating in any way in any phase of the campaign, they have been eager seekers after information from whatever sources available as to the trend of events.

By a logic that seems fuzzy in retrospect, Americans chose Calvin Coolidge to lead them through the uproar of the Jazz Age. Though "Silent Cal" lacked charisma, the taciturn New Englander was was a perfect foil against the corruption charges stemming from the Harding Administration's Teapot Dome scandal, in which public oil reserves in Wyoming were secretly leased to an oil company with ties to the Secretary of the Interior. Ordinary Americans found Coolidge's quirky ways endearing, even when they laughed at him. One commentator guessed he had been "weaned on a pickle."

Vice President Coolidge had accidentally assumed the presidency when Warren G. Harding died in 1923, but he consolidated real power by 1924. The Republican convention in Cleveland aroused so little controversy that Will Rogers complained the city should open its churches to enliven the proceedings. Chagrined by the allegations of corruption, the GOP understood that the best strategy was to "keep cool with Coolidge." The main suspense lay in the selection of his running mate. Americans had a newfound respect for the vice presidency, thanks to Coolidge's example and the near accession of Thomas Marshall when Wilson's health failed. The GOP found a robust second in Charles G. Dawes, a brigadier general and banker. Despite his dislike for

Left to right:
Calvin Coolidge (1872–1933)
John W. Davis (1873–1955)
Robert M. La Follette (1855–1925)

"Fighting Bob" La Follette led the strongest third party challenge since the Bull Moose excitement of 1912.

This poster is a surprisingly effervescent advertisement for the reserved Coolidge.

"pinhead politicians," Dawes was an enthusiastic campaigner, and did much of the heavy lifting during the campaign.

The Democrats had a harder time, their energy drained by a marathon 16-day convention in New York City. Through the grueling days and nights, the party schisms lying close to the surface erupted in the old Madison Square Garden: South vs. North, country vs. city, dry vs. wet, nativist vs. immigrant. Even more damaging to the party, the arguments were broadcast live on the infant medium of radio.

The divisions centered around a bruising battle for the nomination. William Gibbs McAdoo of California, Woodrow Wilson's son-in-law and Treasury Secretary, appealed to southern and western Democrats. Northerners had an appealing candidate of their own in New York Governor Al Smith, dubbed "the Happy Warrior" by FDR in a nominating speech that revived his own career after a polio attack three years earlier. After an agonizing 102 ballots, the decision went to a compromise candidate on the 103rd: the unremarkable John W. Davis of West Virginia.

The Democratic cause was further weakened by a new Progressive party led by Wisconsin's feisty Senator, Robert "Fighting Bob" La Follette. With his attacks on monopoly and his call for government supervision of transportation, La Follette appealed to workers and farmers.

As usual, the Democrats tried to buck the odds by outcampaigning the Republicans. Coolidge barely spoke in public, and when he did, he said things like, "I am for economy. After that I am for more economy." It worked—the Republicans won another landslide. Coolidge won almost twice as many votes as Davis (almost 16 million to 8 million; 4 million for La Follette), and nearly every state outside of the South.

Times were changing rapidly—which may have been the key to Coolidge's reassuring, laconic appeal. In a noisy age, the last candidate left standing was the least outspoken one of all.

John W. Davis, the compromise nominee, had been a negotiator at Versailles and Ambassador to the Court of St. James.

President Coolidge (seated, wearing boater) attends a picnic rally *(left)* in Ardmore, South Dakota, July 24, 1924.

Coolidge after being nominated *(right)* at the Republican National Convention in Cleveland, June 1924.

John W. Davis sits at the throttle of the Saratoga Express *(below)*, en route to a meeting with FDR in Poughkeepsie, New York, August 1924.

Wisconsin Senator and Progressive Party candidate Robert M. La Follette at home *(above)* with his family, 1924.

Robert "Fighting Bob" La Follette *(right)* in a characteristic pose, makes the first radio speech of his campaign, 1924.

Wyoming cowboys greet Democratic candidate for vice president *(opposite)* Governor Charles W. Bryan, August 1924.

The president signs his absentee ballot as a resident of Massachsetts, from the White House lawn *(left)*, November 1924.

The entire voting population *(below)* of Somerset, Vermont, October 1924.

The only living ex-president gets the returns: Chief Justice Taft at a radio set in the home of Miss Mabel Boardman in Washington, D.C., November 1924.

"All the News That's Fit to Print."

The New York Times.

EXTRA 5 A. M.

THE WEATHER—Fair today.

VOL. LXXIV....No. 24,392. NEW YORK, WEDNESDAY, NOVEMBER 5, 1924. TWO CENTS In Greater New York | THREE CENTS Within 200 Miles | FOUR CENTS Elsewhere

COOLIDGE WINS, 357 TO DAVIS'S 136; LA FOLLETTE CARRIES WISCONSIN; SMITH BEATS ROOSEVELT BY 140,000

CITY ELECTS SMITH

Big Manhattan and Bronx Vote Wins for Governor.

UP-STATE STRONGLY G. O. P.

Roosevelt Carries Buffalo and Several Large Industrial Centres.

BROOKLYN GOES TO SMITH

Kings County Gives Him 152,000 Plurality, Although Coolidge Carries It by 80,000.

LEGISLATURE REPUBLICAN

Democrats Lose Control of Senate and Their Numbers in Assembly Are Reduced.

SOME OFFICES IN DOUBT

Whole Smith Ticket May Not Be Elected—Vote for the Socialist Nominee, Thomas, Is Small.

Overcoming a Republican Presidential sweep that reached nearly a million plurality, Alfred E. Smith was re-elected Governor of New York in yesterday's election, defeating his Republican opponent, Colonel Theodore Roosevelt, by an estimated plurality of 140,000.

As a vote-getter the Governor surpassed his performance of four years ago when, in the Harding landslide, he went down to defeat, although running more than a million votes ahead of his ticket.

By an enormous city vote the Governor overcame a heavy handicap, for Colonel Roosevelt captured the rock-ribbed Republican counties up-State. The Colonel, reversing the record of Nathan L. Miller, also carried Democratic city strongholds above the Bronx which Governor Smith easily carried two and four years ago.

At 1:30 o'clock this morning Colonel Roosevelt at Oyster Bay issued a statement conceding the election of Governor Smith. He said he congratulated the Governor and also expressed satisfaction over the election of President Coolidge.

While the Governor was taking the measure of his Gubernatorial opponent, President Calvin Coolidge carried the State by 920,000 plurality. His vote up-State not only reached 800,000, but he carried every borough in the City of New York with a plurality over John W. Davis, his Democratic opponent, of 130,000.

La Follette Polls 400,000.

Senator Robert M. La Follette, running for President on a Third Party ticket, polled 400,000 votes in the State but ran third.

While Governor Smith was elected by a safe margin there was considerable uncertainty as to the fate of the rest of the State Democratic ticket. Lieutenant Governor George R. Lunn appeared to be safe although he ran fully 100,000 votes behind the Governor in the city. The rest of the ticket was lost in the count of votes for the Governorship.

The Governor's triumph was marred somewhat by the Republican gains in the Legislature. It was admitted by the Democrats that the Republicans elected enough State Senators to take control of that body from the Democrats and had materially increased their majority in the Assembly.

George K. Morris, Republican State Chairman, made the following statement at 1:30 o'clock this morning:

"Indications are that Governor Smith has been re-elected by between 50,000 and 85,000. But we have made substantial gains in the Assembly and have regained control of the State Senate, which will now be 28 to 23 in favor of the Republicans, instead of 26 to 25 in favor of the Democrats. We gained two Senators in Erie County, one in Rensselaer County and one in New York County, with probably an additional gain of one or more in other Senatorial districts. We have undoubtedly elected the entire State ticket with the exception of Colonel Roosevelt."

Continued on Page Two.

GOVERNORS ELECTED.

REPUBLICAN.

Connecticut	Hiram Bingham
Delaware	Robert P. Robinson
Illinois	Len Small*
Idaho	Charles C. Moore*
Indiana	Ed Jackson
Iowa	John Hammill
Kansas	Ben S. Paulen
Massachusetts	Alvan T. Fuller
Michigan	Alex J. Groesbeck
Nebraska	Adam McMullen
New Hampshire	John G. Winant
Rhode Island	Aram J. Pothier
South Dakota	Carl Gunderson
Vermont	Franklin K. Billings
Washington	Roland H. Hartley
West Virginia	Howard M. Gore
Wisconsin	John J. Blaine*

DEMOCRATIC.

Florida	John W. Martin
Georgia	Clifford Walker*
New York	Alfred E. Smith*
North Carolina	A. W. McLean
South Carolina	T. G. McLeod
Tennessee	Austin Peay*
Texas	Mrs. Miriam A. Ferguson

*Re-elected.

COOLIDGE AND SMITH CARRY THIS CITY

The President's Plurality About 130,000 and the Governor's About 500,000.

LA FOLLETTE VOTE 250,000

Coolidge Wins in Every Borough—Democrats Elect All Local Officers.

New York City gave its vote at yesterday's election to Calvin Coolidge, Republican nominee for President, and Charles G. Dawes, Republican nominee for Vice President, and at the same time rolled up a record plurality for Governor Alfred E. Smith, electing him Chief Executive of New York State for the third time.

As in the Presidential election of 1920, Governor Smith's personal popularity, apparent satisfaction with his administration and possibly some weakness of his opponent, Colonel Theodore Roosevelt, combined to give the Governor a lead never before obtained by any candidate for any office in this city.

President Coolidge obtained a total of approximately 130,000 plurality in New York City and carried every borough, according to fairly complete returns.

The indications were that he would have a plurality of about 9,000 in Manhattan, 4,300 in the Bronx, 75,000 in Brooklyn, 39,000 in Queens and 2,200 in Richmond.

500,000 Plurality for Smith.

Governor Smith, however, carried the city by about 500,000, the "spread between his vote and that for Davis, the Democratic Presidential candidate, being about 630,000, or nearly equal to the difference between his vote and that for Cox four years ago. Governor Smith carried every borough heavily.

The indications on incomplete returns were that he had carried Manhattan by more than 195,000, Brooklyn by approximately 136,000, the Bronx by 166,000, Queens by 43,000 and Richmond by 9,800.

Governor Smith apparently carried every Assembly district in the city but one, the Twenty-first District, in Brooklyn. La Follette showed his greatest proportionate strength in the Bronx, where he led in the Third, Fourth and Fifth Assembly Districts and was running close in the Seventh.

The vote in the Nineteenth, Manhattan, Assembly District, which includes a large part of Harlem's "black belt," showed that the negroes here remained true to the Republican Party's national candidates, but voted for Governor Smith on the Ku Klux Klan issue. With seven districts missing out of forty-four, the

Continued on Page Five.

MRS. FERGUSON WINS 2 TO 1 IN TEXAS RACE FOR GOVERNORSHIP

Incomplete Returns Indicate That She Will Have a Majority of 225,000 Over Republican.

RUNS BEHIND IN CITIES

But the Big Majorities in the Rural Districts Carry Her to Victory.

LARGE KLAN VOTE IS CAST

Party Lines Are Ignored as Ku Klux Vote for Republican, While Negroes Vote for Democrat.

Special to The New York Times.

AUSTIN, Texas, Nov. 4.—Returns from the rural districts of Texas coming in late this evening show that Mrs. Miriam A. Ferguson will probably receive a majority of about 225,000 votes over Dr. George C. Butte, Republican, for Governor.

Of a total of about 700,000 votes cast about 218,000 have been counted, giving Mrs. Ferguson a lead of 62,000 votes. According to unofficial returns, the lead which Dr. Butte started with by returns from the larger cities was quickly overcome by the rural returns.

At 10 o'clock the vote for Governor, including returns from 310 towns and cities, stood:

Mrs. Ferguson, 117,343.

Dr. Butte, 68,145.

Interest in the election was intensified by the prominence of the Ku Klux Klan issue in the campaign and it caused an outpouring of people at the polls. It is estimated that nearly 800,000 votes were cast. This is only a few thousand less than the total number polled in the run-off primary. Perfect weather prevailed all over the State, and this was a factor in favor of Mrs. Ferguson, as it meant passable roads for the farmer to travel to the precinct voting boxes.

The early returns show that Mrs. Ferguson's principal strength was in the rural districts. The count in the larger cities is progressing slowly. It shows that Dr. George C. Butte, the Republican candidate for Governor, is running well ahead of Mrs. Ferguson in Dallas, Austin, Houston, Beaumont and other of the larger cities.

Butte is also running ahead of Mrs. Ferguson in a number of the populous counties of North Texas and is making a strong showing in parts of Central Texas. The rural districts, however, are piling up in the early count an almost solid vote for Mrs. Ferguson.

According to these returns, she swept East Texas and the territory south of San Antonio and more than broke even with Butte in other rural districts. It is practically conceded by the Republican leaders that if the estimate that 800,000 votes were polled is correct Mrs. Ferguson's election by the usual big Democratic majority is assured. These leaders contend, however, that the total vote was not more than 600,000 and that this means that Butte has a chance of winning.

The Ku Klux Klan strongholds gave a surprisingly large vote for Butte. It is apparent that he received the bulk of the Klan vote. Party lines were largely lost sight of and thousands of veteran Democrats today cast their first vote for a Republican candidate for office. The election marked the greatest political revolution that ever took place in Texas. Irrespective of the indication that Butte was not elected. Practically all of the German vote, more than 30,000 in number, which is nominally Republican, went to Mrs. Ferguson because of the Klan issue. The same is true of the negro vote which went solid for the woman candidate.

TEMPLE, Texas, Nov. 4.—Mrs. Miriam A. Ferguson of Temple, who on the face of returns in today's general election

Continued on Page Five.

La Follette Wins Koenig's Home District; Coolidge Captures Davis's and Olvany's

Senator La Follette carried the home election district of Samuel S. Koenig, Manhattan Republican leader, with a vote of 285 to 138 for Coolidge and 169 for Davis. La Follette received 175 of these votes as the Progressive candidate and 111 as the Socialist candidate. Four years ago the same district gave Cox 40 and Harding 285.

The Rev. Norman Thomas, the Socialist Gubernatorial candidate, ran a poor third in his own home district, polling only 19 votes as compared with 282 for Smith and 152 for Roosevelt.

Governor Smith's district on the lower east side was carried by Davis with a vote of 165. La Follette ran second with 110 and Coolidge third with 54. Four years ago this district gave Cox 289 and Harding 278.

Governor Smith carried his home district by a vote of 494 to 40 for Roosevelt and 2 for Thomas. Two years ago the same district gave Smith 484 and Miller 29.

President Coolidge carried the home district of Tammany Leader George W. Olvany with a vote of 462. Davis had 191 and La Follette 91. The President also defeated John W. Davis in the latter's home district at Locust Valley, L. I. The vote was: Coolidge 471 and Davis 176.

Colonel Roosevelt at Oyster Bay received in his own voting district, the Tenth, a smaller vote than President Coolidge, getting 185 to Coolidge's 193. In the same district Governor Smith received 120 votes, while John W. Davis polled 99.

The home city of Lieut. Governor Lunn was carried by Colonel Roosevelt by a plurality of 5,000.

United States Senators Elected

REPUBLICANS—18.

Colorado	*L. C. Phipps
Colorado	†Rice W. Means
Delaware	T. C. du Pont
Idaho	*William E. Borah
Illinois	C. S. Deneen
Kansas	*Arthur Capper
Kentucky	F. M. Sackett
Massachusetts	F. H. Gillett
Michigan	‡James Couzens
Nebraska	*G. W. Norris
New Hampshire	*H. W. Keyes
New Jersey	*W. E. Edge
Oklahoma	W. B. Pine
Oregon	*C. L. McNary
Rhode Island	‡J. H. Metcalf
South Dakota	W. H. McMaster
West Virginia	Guy D. Goff
Wyoming	*F. E. Warren

DEMOCRATS—10.

Alabama	*J. T. Heflin
Arkansas	*J. T. Robinson
Georgia	*W. J. Harris
Louisiana	*J. E. Ransdell
Mississippi	*Pat Harrison
North Carolina	*F. M. Simmons
South Carolina	C. L. Blease
Tennessee	L. D. Tyson
Texas	*M. Sheppard
Virginia	*Carter Glass

Result in Iowa, Minnesota, Montana and New Mexico is in doubt.

*Re-elected.

†Elected for short term to fill vacancy in present Senate.

‡Elected for both short and long terms.

LEGISLATURE AGAIN SOLIDLY REPUBLICAN

Party Recovers Control of the Senate, With a Probable Majority of Four.

STRONGER IN THE ASSEMBLY

J. A. McGinnies of Chautauqua Is Slated for Speaker—One Woman Elected.

Returns from the legislative elections throughout New York State yesterday showed that the Republicans had recaptured control of the State Senate, which during the last two years has been Democratic by the slender majority of one vote. The returns indicated also that the Republicans had increased their lead in the Assembly, which remained Republican during the two years of Governor Smith's present Administration.

Figures, which in some instances have been estimated, give the Republicans a working majority of four in the upper house of the Legislature, with the possibility that this may be increased through changes based on more complete returns.

In the normally Republican Fifteenth Senate District on the upper west side in Manhattan, Senator Nathan Straus won a signal victory, which will return him to the Senate for a third term. He defeated Assemblyman Victor R. Kaufman, whom the Republicans had nominated.

The latest figures received indicate that the Republicans, who have twenty-five members in the present Senate, will have at least twenty-nine in the body elected yesterday.

They gained one Senator in the Seventeenth District, located on the upper west side in Manhattan, where, on partial returns, the election of Courtland Nicoll, the Republican candidate, appeared assured. His Democratic opponent was the present incumbent, Senator Meyer Levy.

In the Eighth Senatorial District in Brooklyn, where early returns indicated re-election of the present incumbent, Dr. W. L. Love, more nearly complete figures pointed to his defeat by R. C. Ellis, his Republican opponent.

Gains by Republicans.

Other gains by the Republicans included the Thirty-first Senate District, which takes in Rensselaer County, where Senator John F. Williams, the Democratic incumbent, was defeated by John R. Williams, a Republican newcomer in the Legislature. In the Forty-ninth, which takes in part of Erie County, Robert C. Lacey, the present Democratic Senator, who enjoyed wide popularity in labor circles and has served two years in the Senate, will be replaced by L. R. Lipowicz, his Republican opponent.

Returns from the Assembly elections showed an increased Republican majority in the lower house of next year's Legislature, where the Republicans this year have a working majority of twelve. In the table a number of the districts within the city were estimated on partial returns from a small number of election districts and the result was subject to change on more complete returns.

Despite the huge pluralities run up by the Republicans for Coolidge and Dawes in New York City, the Democrats retained their hold, with few exceptions, on Senate and Assembly districts in the city which are represented by Democrats in the present Legislature.

The Republican Assembly gains were made up-State for the most part. There they won in Sullivan County, in the First District of Rensselaer, in the First and Third Albany Districts, in the Second Onondaga District and the First District in Schenectady County, all of which sent Democrats to the present Legislature in the election a year ago.

Republican Gain in Kings.

About the only gain made by the Republicans in this city was in the Seventeenth Assembly District in Kings, normally Republican, but for the last two or three years represented by a Demo-

Continued on Page Two.

COOLIDGE AND EDGE WINNERS IN JERSEY

Record Vote Gives President Plurality Which Is Estimated at 350,000.

MRS. NORTON IS ELECTED

First Woman in Congress From the East—Tunnel Bond Issue Adopted.

New Jersey, breaking all previous records in the size of its vote, gave large pluralities to Coolidge and Senator Edge, and increased the Republican majorities in both branches of the State Legislature. The proposed $8,000,000 bond issue for finishing the Hudson vehicular tunnels and the Camden Bridge was receiving large majorities.

The polls were closed at 7 o'clock and the size of the vote was so unprecedented that the first returns were made long after the customary time for reporting them. At 3 o'clock this morning Coolidge had a lead of 167,686 in 1,181 of the 2,559 election districts in New Jersey. On the basis of these figures his estimated plurality reached 350,000 for all the districts.

In the Senatorial contest Edge was leading Donnelly by 27,537 in 324 of the 2,559 districts. Senator Edge declared last night that the Coolidge-Dawes plurality as well as his own would reach 200,000.

The Republicans elected ten members of Congress and the Democrats only two, including Mrs. Mary T. Norton of Jersey City, who won a sweeping victory in the Twelfth District in Hudson County, a Democratic stronghold. Mrs. Norton ran against Douglas D. T. Storey, Republican, and she will be the first woman to go to Congress to represent an Eastern State.

She Thanks the Voters.

When her election was assured Mrs. Norton, in an interview, expressed her gratitude to Mayor Frank Hague of Jersey City for having placed her in nomination in the Twelfth District, which is a Democratic stronghold.

"I congratulate Mayor Hague," she said, "on his foresight and justice in placing New Jersey among the first States of the Union to send a woman to Congress. I thank the organization and I thank the voters. I shall do everything in my power for the people of New Jersey and for the nation."

The success of the Democratic candidate in the Twelfth District of New Jersey was a foregone conclusion. Mrs. Norton was nominated by Mayor Hague with the full approval of other Democratic leaders. Her nomination was hailed at the time as a tribute to her years of work in the interests of the party.

Mrs. Norton cast her ballot in the Twenty-first Election District, in the Eleventh Ward, Jersey City. She was accompanied by her husband when she went to the polling place in a small candy store. Her husband is Robert E. Norton, who is in the cooperage business in Jersey City.

Five election districts in Camden County gave Coolidge 705 votes, Davis 360 and La Follette 80. One election district in Morris County gave Coolidge 118, Davis 25 and La Follette 4. Twenty of the 2,559 election districts in

Continued on Page Seven.

THIRD PARTY POLLS 4,000,000 VOTES IN WHOLE COUNTRY

Showing in Electoral College Far Behind Strength in Popular Support.

CARRIED ONLY WISCONSIN

Mid-West Deserted the Senator but Industrial Districts in Cities Helped Him.

COLLAPSE IN CALIFORNIA

But the Senator Ran Second in That State, the Dakotas, Minnesota, Montana and Nevada.

Returns from the Eastern and Southern States, and a few States in the West, showed that the Progressive Party movement, headed by Senator Robert M. La Follette of Wisconsin, fell far short of the expectations of its leaders. Senator La Follette, apparently, has run a poor third in all States east of the Mississippi River, except his own State of Wisconsin, which he carried and Minnesota, where he is running second. He is running second in Montana, Nevada, California, Iowa and the two Dakotas. Apparently his total vote in the country is about 4,000,000.

La Follette's greatest collapse was in California, where, so far from his carrying the State, as he expected, the Republicans have it by a great majority.

The following table shows the estimated La Follette vote in the various States.

California	350,000
Illinois	350,000
Iowa	275,000
Indiana	80,000
Kansas	90,000
Michigan	125,000
Minnesota	450,000
New York	410,000
Montana	50,000
Nebraska	90,000
North Dakota	100,000
New Jersey	60,000
Ohio	200,000
Pennsylvania	250,000
South Dakota	90,000
Washington	120,000
Wisconsin	375,000

His vote in other States varied from 1,000 or less in Arizona to about 45,000 in Maryland.

The forecasts by the Progressive Party leaders that La Follette and Wheeler would carry Illinois, Ohio and probably a few Eastern States were not made good. In both Illinois and Ohio Senator La Follette was many thousand votes behind John W. Davis, Democratic nominee, and the Wisconsin Senator received only a fraction of the total vote given to President Coolidge.

In New York State, where the backers of La Follette had predicted that the Progressive ticket would carry New York City, La Follette was a bad third. La Follette received fewer than half the votes recorded for Mr. Davis, and President Coolidge beat the Third Party candidate in New York five or six to one. Most of the La Follette strength in New York, as in other Eastern States, was concenerated in a few industrial centres.

In Massachusetts, where President Coolidge beat Mr. Davis six or seven to one, Mr. Davis beat La Follette more than two to one. Even in Boston, a city which La Follette leaders had professed confidence of carrying, Senator La Follette received but a negligible vote.

In Connecticut, another State where the Progressive Party leaders claimed great strength, early returns showed that President Coolidge was getting more than six votes for each given La Follette and that Mr. Davis was leading La Follette about two to one.

Poor Showing in South and West.

The Progressive Party had expected to run first or second in New Hampshire, according to the predictions made, but the returns indicated that President Coolidge would beat Senator La Follette by fifteen to one or better, and that Davis was running ahead of La Follette at the rate of eight votes to one.

Another example of the collapse of the La Follette movement was supplied

Continued on Page Five.

State Pluralities Rolled Up by Coolidge.

The following table shows President Coolidge's estimated pluralities on the returns so far received from the States carried by him:

California	*300,000	New Jersey	350,000
Colorado	70,000	New York	900,000
Delaware	15,000	North Dakota	*120,000
Illinois	750,000	Ohio	500,000
Indiana	400,000	Pennsylvania	1,100,000
Iowa	*225,000	Rhode Island	35,000
Kansas	250,000	South Dakota	*45,000
Maine	50,000	Utah	4,000
Maryland	10,000	Washington	100,000
Massachusetts	250,000	West Virginia	35,000
Michigan	400,000		
Nebraska	50,000		

*Over La Follette.

Electoral Vote

COOLIDGE.

California	13
Colorado	6
Connecticut	7
Delaware	3
Idaho	4
Illinois	29
Indiana	15
Iowa	13
Kansas	10
Kentucky	13
Maine	6
Maryland	8
Massachusetts	18
Michigan	15
Missouri	18
Nebraska	8
New Hampshire	4
New Jersey	14
New York	45
North Dakota	5
Ohio	24
Oregon	5
Pennsylvania	38
Rhode Island	5
South Dakota	5
Vermont	4
Utah	4
Washington	7
West Virginia	8
Wyoming	3
Total	357

DAVIS.

Alabama	12
Arkansas	9
Florida	6
Georgia	14
Louisiana	10
Mississippi	10
North Carolina	12
Oklahoma	10
South Carolina	9
Tennessee	12
Texas	20
Virginia	12
Total:	136

LA FOLLETTE.

Wisconsin	13
Total	13

DOUBTFUL.

Arizona	3
Minnesota	12
Montana	4
Nevada	3
New Mexico	3
Total	25

Total number of votes in Electoral College, 531; necessary to a choice, 266.

Some of the States in the above list are placed as doubtful only because, due to the difference in time, the returns are inadequate.

REPUBLICANS MAKE GAINS IN CONGRESS

Retain Control of Senate and May Increase House Majority to 50.

BROOKHART LIKELY TO LOSE

Stanley of Kentucky and Walsh of Massachusetts, Democratic Senators, Apparently Beaten.

While the returns on the elections of United States Senators and members of the House of Representatives are incomplete, the indications early this morning were that the Republican Party would retain majorities in both houses of Congress for the two-year period beginning March 4, 1925, the first half of President Coolidge's new administration.

There have been Republican gains in the House sufficiently large to make it apparent that the present majority in that body, which was fifteen when the Congress adjourned in June and has been reduced to ten by resignations and deaths of Republican members, will be considerably exceeded. As for the Senate, Republican candidates have very generally held their own in States from which complete or fairly complete returns have been received.

Figures compiled from the latest returns give the following showing for the next Senate as a result of the elections yesterday:

Republicans, 52; Democrats, 38; Farmer-Labor, 1; four in doubt, with one vacancy not filled yesterday.

The majority the Republicans will have in the House is uncertain but that it will be much larger than the mere nominal majority obtained by the Republicans in the Congressional elections of two years ago is indicated by the following political alignment, based on returns up to an early hour this morning: Republicans, 232; Democrats, 181; Socialists, 1; Farmer-Labor, 2; in doubt, 19. This indicates a sure Republican

Continued on Page Four.

NEW YORK BY 900,000

Coolidge's Plurality in This State Little Below Harding's

DAVIS GETS THE SOUTH ONLY

La Follette Apparently Only His Own State, but Large Industrial Vote.

CALIFORNIA FOR COOLIDGE

Doubtful States of the Far West Lean to the President as Returns Increase.

DAVIS LOSES WEST VIRGINIA

Refused at Late Hour to Concede Defeat and Hoped for Upset From the West.

BRYAN'S STATE TO COOLIDGE

Plurality of 50,000 in Nebraska for the President Indicated in Latest Dispatches.

Calvin Coolidge has been elected President of the United States in a victory of impressive proportions.

At 5 o'clock this morning the returns indicated that President Coolidge had secured 357 electoral votes, Davis 136 and La Follette 13, and that 25 votes in five Western States were still in doubt. The principal overtures in the late returns were in Kentucky and Missouri. In Kentucky, in 3,431 out of 3,971 precincts, seven-eighths of the State, Coolidge had 337,838, against 331,244 for Davis. It was the opinion of the most competent observers in the State that later returns would not take the State away from the President.

In Missouri Coolidge has 251,602, against Davis's 238,896 in 1,934 out of 4,069 precincts. Correspondents in the State believed that the Republican rural precincts were sure to give the State to the President. The St. Louis Globe-Democrat estimates that Coolidge will carry the State by 50,000.

The five States remaining in doubt are Minnesota, Montana, Nevada, Arizona and New Mexico.

In Montana Coolidge has a slight lead, but the returns are too scant to justify giving the State to him at present. Arizona and New Mexico are close, with indications of going for Davis. In Nevada Coolidge has a lead of 600 votes over La Follette, who is running second, in a little less than one-half the State.

It is not probable that Davis's vote in the Electoral College will exceed 142, which it will be if he carries Arizona and New Mexico. Apparently he has no chance in Minnesota, Montana and Nevada, where he is running third, La Follette being second. On the other hand, it is possible that Coolidge may carry Minnesota, Montana and Nevada, giving him a total of 376, or, with Arizona and New Mexico added, 382 as his utmost limit.

An extreme possibility, but not a very strong one, for La Follette, is the addition of Minnesota, Montana and Nevada, to the one State that he has surely carried, Wisconsin, which would give him a total of 32.

Senator Robert M. La Follette is leading in his home State, Wisconsin, and will undoubtedly win there and get its 13 electoral votes.

Mr. Coolidge is the sixth Vice President to become President through the death of the incumbent and the second to be elected President immediately afterward. The other was Theodore Roosevelt.

Coolidge Victory Overwhelming.

The victory which returns President Coolidge to office and elects Brig. Gen. Charles G. Dawes of Illinois Vice President is overwhelming in the East and Middle West, and early indications are that the Republicans have registered heavily even in the Far West. Such States as North and South Dakota, which the La Follettites claimed for the Third Party, have gone to President Coolidge. So also has Oregon, which some expected to see in the Third Party column.

Nebraska also has apparently gone for Coolidge by about 50,000, according to the latest returns.

Mr. Davis, however, went to bed at midnight refusing to accept the fact

Wednesday, November 5, 1924.

Coolidge Wins, 357 to Davis's 136; La Follette Carries Wisconsin; Smith Beats Roosevelt by 140,000

New York By 900,000

Coolidge's Plurality in This State Little Below Harding's

Davis Gets the South Only

La Follette Apparently Only His Own State, but Large Industrial Vote.

California for Coolidge

Doubtful States of the Far West Lean to the President as Returns Increase.

Davis Loses West Virginia

Refused at Late Hour to Concede Defeat and Hoped for Upset From the West

Bryan's State to Coolidge

Plurality of 50,000 in Nebraska for the President Indicated in Latest Dispatches

Calvin Coolidge has been elected President of the United States in a victory of impressive proportions.

At 5 o'clock this morning the returns indicated that President Coolidge had secured 357 electoral votes, Davis 136 and La Follette 13, and that 25 votes in five Western States were still in doubt. The principal overtures in the late returns were in Kentucky and Missouri. In Kentucky, in 3,431 out of 3,971 precincts, seven-eighths of the State, Coolidge had 337,838 against 331,244 for Davis. It was the opinion of the most competent observers in the State that later returns would not take the State away from the President.

In Missouri Coolidge has 251,802, against Davis's 238,896 in 1,934 out of 4,069 precincts. Correspondents in the State believed that the Republican rural precincts were sure to give the State to the President. The *St. Louis Globe-Democrat* estimates that Coolidge will carry the State by 50,000.

The five States remaining in doubt are Minnesota, Montana, Nevada, Arizona and New Mexico.

In Montana Coolidge has a slight lead, but the returns are too scant to justify giving the State to him at present. Arizona and New Mexico are close, with indications of going for Davis. In Nevada Coolidge has a lead of 600 votes over La Follette, who is running second, in a little less than one-half the State.

It is not probable that Davis's vote in the Electoral College will exceed 142, which it will be if he carries Arizona and New Mexico. Apparently he has no chance in Minnesota, Montana and Nevada, where he is running third, La Follette being second. On the other hand, it is possible that Coolidge may carry Minnesota, Montana and Nevada, giving him a total of 376, or, with Arizona and New Mexico added, 382 as his utmost limit.

An extreme possibility, but not a very strong one, for La Follette, is the addition of Minnesota, Montana and Nevada, to the one State that he has surely carried, Wisconsin, which would give him a total of 32.

Senator Robert M. La Follette is leading in his home State, Wisconsin, and will undoubtedly win there and get its 13 electoral votes.

Mr. Coolidge is the sixth Vice President to become President through the death of the incumbent and the second to be elected President immediately afterward. The other was Theodore Roosevelt.

Coolidge Victory Overwhelming.

The victory which returns President Coolidge to office and elects Brig. Gen. Charles G. Dawes of Illinois Vice President is overwhelming in the East and Middle West, and early indications are that the Republicans have registered heavily even in the Far West. Such States as North and South

Dakota, which the La Follettites claimed for the Third Party, have gone to President Coolidge. So also has Oregon which some expected to see in the Third Party column.

Nebraska also has apparently gone for Coolidge by about 80,000, according to the latest returns.

Mr. Davis, however, went to bed at midnight refusing to accept the face of the returns and concede defeat for himself and his running mate, Governor Charles W. Bryan of Nebraska. Mr. Davis then believed the returns from Western States, some of which might not come in until 6 o'clock in the morning, would throw the election into the House. Mr. Davis was alone in his prediction of such a result.

Mr. Davis has carried the solid South, except Kentucky, winning Tennessee by apparently 30,000.

The Democratic national ticket appears to have made no serious inroads in the border States. West Virginia apparently is President Coolidge's by 25,000. Mr. Davis's inability to carry his own State is accompanied by failure to win Maryland, where the President seems to have triumphed by a plurality of some 12,000 votes.

La Follette's Vote Industrial.

If the heavy vote rolled up by President Coolidge be taken as an outcome fully expected and generally forecast, the surprise of the election is the heavy vote that La Follette managed to pile up in the industrial districts in the East. His estimated totals include 410,000 in New York State, nearly two-thirds of which was polled in New York City.

Senator La Follette's estimated popular vote of 4,000,000 is interesting because of the assertions of himself and his party leaders that the present campaign was waged chiefly in the interest of founding a third party and that the movement would not be abandoned after the present election. The approximate La Follette vote compares strikingly with the popular total of the last third party candidate—Theodore Roosevelt—whose Bull Moose movement away from the Republicans in 1912 resulted in a nation-wide vote for him of 4,126,024.

While Senator La Follette appears to have registered nearly as many votes as did the late Colonel Roosevelt, his Electoral College showing is much poorer than that of the 1912 thirty party. La Follette has carried only one State, his own Wisconsin, with its thirteen electoral votes, whereas Roosevelt carried six States—Pennsylvania, Michigan, Minnesota, South Dakota, California and Washington, with an Electoral college vote of 90.

The vote polled by President Coolidge and his Republican running mate, while naturally falling behind the landslide figures of the 1920 Harding victory, if only because the vote this year was split three ways, is one of huge totals in the East and the Middle West, topped by 920,000 in New York, 350,000 in New Jersey and 1,100,000 in Pennsylvania.

The Republican national figures in other States include Ohio 500,000; Indiana, 225,000; Illinois, 750,000; Kansas, 250,000; Michigan, 400,000; West Virginia, 35,000; Maryland, 10,000; and Delaware, 15,000. The last returns from California indicated a plurality there for Coolidge of 300,000.

Mr. Coolidge is the sixth Vice President to become President through the death of the incumbent and the second to be elected President immediately afterward. The other was Theodore Roosevelt.

In Minnesota, Magnus Johnson, one of the two Farmer-Labor Senators now in Congress, was trailing far behind his Republican opponent, Representative T. D. Schall, in the early morning returns.

Charles D. Hilles, Vice Chairman of the Republican National Committee, at 4 o'clock this morning estimated the popular vote as follows—Coolidge, 18,000,000; Davis, 8,000,000; La Follette, 4,000,000.

City Vote Elected Smith.

Alfred E. Smith has been re-elected Governor of New York, according to all indications, with three-quarters of the vote tabulated. The defeat of Colonel Theodore Roosevelt, the Republican candidate, is due to the huge majority piled up by the Democratic Governor in his race in New York City. Indications are that Governor Smith has the State by about 140,000, although Colonel Roosevelt came down to the Bronx with an up-State majority around 385,000. Governor Smith's majority in the Greater City will be about 500,000.

Of outstanding interest in the up-State result is the shift of many cities to the Republican column, although Governor

Smith carried them against Nathan L. Miller two years ago, when he was elected for his second term. Of the first eight cities to report, Colonel Roosevelt carried Rome, Poughkeepsie, Buffalo, Newburgh, Binghamton, Gloversville and Syracuse. Of these eight, Governor Smith managed to keep tucked away only Troy, and his majority there dropped about two-thirds.

President Coolidge has carried New York City by probably 130,000, winning every borough, including, apparently, Manhattan, in which, however, the returns were shifting and close.

Governor Smith's majority of about 800,000 in New York apparently carries with it the whole Democratic slate.

The effect of the big Republican vote in the State, so far as the early returns showed, has been to make the State Senate safely Republican, changing its complexion from that at the last legislative session. The Republicans also will have an increased lead in the Assembly.

Congress Changes.

In the country at large the Republican sweep brings the party very close to control of both houses of Congress. The apparent complexion of the Senate is Republicans, 50; Democrats, 38; Farmer-Laborites, 1; vacancy to be filled, 1; in doubt, 6. Necessary to a majority, 49, with the Republican showing up to an early hour this morning exceeding that figure.

In the House the Republicans seem to have obtained a fairly good majority. The present tally stands: Republicans, 232; Democrats, 180; Socialists, 2; Farmer-Laborites, 2; in doubt, 19. Necessary to a majority, 218.

This gives the Republicans a present indicated majority of 48 over the Democrats, Socialists and Farmer-Laborites, whose election seem assured or 30 over the combined opposition, granting it success in all the 19 doubtful districts.

Among the outstanding results indicated in the United States Senate are the election of General T. Coleman du Pont, Republican, in Delaware; the election in Oklahoma of W. B. Pine, Republican, who contested for the seat with ex-Governor Jack Walton.

The returns from Iowa foreshadow the defeat of Senator Brookhart, La Follette Republican, by Daniel F. Steck.

Klan Defeat and Victories.

The Ku Klux Klan, which figured heavily in the political battles of several States, appears to have won most of its fights and also to have suffered one notable defeat. That defeat brings into office the first woman Governor ever to hold the executive chair of a State—"Ma" Ferguson of Texas. Mrs. Ferguson has won the office lost to her husband by impeachment, overcoming strenuous Klan-Republican opposition.

The outcome in the other Gubernatorial contest in which a woman figured still is in doubt. Mrs. Nellie T. Ross, the Democratic candidate, is running a neck-and-neck race in Wyoming with Eugene J. Sullivan, the Republican nominee. Mrs. Ross was nominated by the Democrats when her husband, then Governor, died recently in office.

The Klan, which fought altogether on the Republican side, has won a victory in Oklahoma, where W. B. Pine has been elected to the United States Senate over the Democratic opposition of ex-Governor Walton, who made a straight-out anti-Klan fight. Another Klan victory has been scored in Kansas, where the Republican candidate, Ben S. Paulen, has been elected Governor, defeating Jonathan M. Davis, the Democratic incumbent, and William Allen White, who took the field in the hope of downing the masked and hooded element.

Again in Indiana the Klan has triumphed, putting its Gubernatorial candidate, Ed Jackson, the Republican contestant, in the Governor's chair.

Opponents of a proposed amendment to the State Constitution of Michigan, which would abolish parochial schools, were far in the lead on the face of early returns.

The ranks of women in official public life probably have been swelled by the election to the national House of Representatives of Mary T. Norton of Jersey City, candidate in the overwhelmingly Democratic Hudson County. The first figures received also show that Nellie Cline, Democrat, of Kansas is endangering the seat in the House now held by Representative Tincher.

Radio Tells the News Early.

A new feature in the national elections this year was the broadcasting throughout the country of the returns as fast as they were gathered. Many millions kept in touch in that way with the hour-to-hour tallying of the votes and went to bed knowing the outcome both of the Presidential race and even of the local contests in which they were interested. One result of the broadcasting was to keep down the election crowds on the streets, hordes of people gathering around loud speakers in homes, clubs and other meeting places.

Almost everywhere the balloting was carried on under favorable skies, although there were some slight showers on the Pacific Coast and in some of the Northwestern States. Early tabulations, taken in connection with the country-wide increase in registration, indicated that a record vote had been cast throughout the country. That result was attributed in part to the weather, in part to the interest aroused by the lively fight among the three principal parties and in part to campaigns by candidates, civic organizations and the press to persuade the recalcitrant or indifferent citizen to do his duty at the polls.

The 1928 campaign really began on August 2, 1927, when Calvin Coolidge, vacationing in South Dakota, gave a note to reporters that read, "I do not choose to run for President in nineteen twenty eight." Many wondered if Coolidge actually hoped to be drafted, but his words were ultimately taken at face value, and support shifted to his Secretary of Commerce, Herbert Hoover.

Fate has not been kind to Hoover. His passivity when confronted by the Great Depression has preserved the image of a helpless executive, paralyzed by a problem too big to solve. Yet of all Americans, none had a better reputation for crisis management and old-fashioned American know-how. Hoover won fame during World War I, when "The Great Engineer" supervised American efforts to bring relief to starving children in Belgium. He was touted as presidential timber in 1920, though only 46 years old. Eight years later, he appeared to be at the height of his powers, refreshingly dynamic in comparison to Coolidge.

The GOP convention in Kansas City nominated Hoover on the first ballot. The platform sounded familiar themes of prosperity, international goodwill, and preservation of the status quo.

Left to right:
Herbert C. Hoover (1874–1964)
Alfred E. Smith (1873–1944)

The brown derby worn by Al Smith became a political symbol in its own right—though far more meaningful to urban Democrats than to rural Southerners and Westerners.

The Democrats, meeting in Houston, were still a house divided, with deep disagreements separating the northern wing from the rural South and West. But they were determined not to repeat the disastrous 1924 convention, and they succeeded, thanks to William Gibbs McAdoo, who withdrew his name from consideration in the interest of party unity. That left a clear field for New York Governor Al Smith, his rival in 1924, and once again nominated with a stirring speech by Franklin D. Roosevelt. Smith won on the second ballot.

Nevertheless, Smith's softness on Prohibition remained an issue for many voters. So did his Irish origins, his New York accent, and more than anything, his Catholicism. Hoover defended his opponent against religious attacks. But the anti-Rome specter of the 1928 campaign would hang over politics for many years. Not until 1960 was another Catholic nominated, and John F. Kennedy's election finally put the religious issue to rest.

The Democrats went after the prize with enormous gusto. Smith campaigned everywhere with his cigar and brown derby hat, comfortable in the open air, telling jokes and speaking to any crowd who would listen. In contrast, following Republican tradition, Hoover did not campaign much. He avoided mentioning Smith by name, and refused to debate him.

Once again, the American people voted overwhelmingly for the GOP, proving that stamina and charm are not enough to win elections. Republicans even made inroads into the South—winning Virginia, North Carolina, Tennessee, Texas and Florida. Al Smith won Massachusetts, Rhode Island and the rest of the South.

The Republicans had lost just twice in the previous 32 years. But the party with prosperity at the heart of its plank was about to learn a hard lesson in accountability. Hoover's acceptance speech proclaimed that poverty was on the run and "the poohouse is vanishing from among us." Before long, thousands of new poorhouses appeared—in places called Hoovervilles.

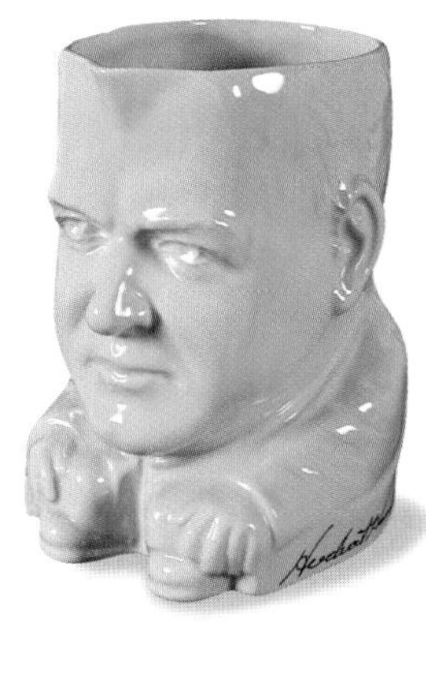

Hoover cruised to an easy victory over the "Happy Warrior," Governor Al Smith of New York.

Herbert Hoover campaigns from the Baltimore Special.

Hoover meets with former New York representative William H. Hill, his campaign manager in New York State for the Republican presidential nomination, Washington, D.C., 1928.

Hoover waves to crowds on a campaign trip through New Jersey. Accompanying Hoover, from left, are his wife, Lou Henry Hoover, and New Jersey politicans Morgan Larson (gubernatorial candidate) and Hamilton Kean (senatorial candidate), September 18, 1928.

Al Smith takes the stage at Tammany Hall to commemorate Tammany's 139th anniversary, a day before the organization's building on East 14th Street was demolished, July 4, 1928.

The day's catch is proudly displayed *(above)* by Arkansas senator Joseph T. Robinson—Al Smith's running mate (on right)—and a friend, August 1928.

Kansas senator Charles Curtis poses at home with his sister after receiving news of his nomination as Republican vice presidential candidate *(opposite)*, Topeka, June 1928.

An Al Smith banner is unfurled at the Democratic National Convention *(above)*, Houston, June 26, 1928.

Smith goes on air after his defeat to address his supporters *(right)*, urging them to maintain an aggressive policy over the next four years, New York City, February 2, 1929.

NBC
NBC

The first electoral votes in the 1928 election are received at the office of Vice President Charles Dawes by his secretary E. Ross Bartley, Washington, D.C., January 19, 1929.

Hoover delivers an address to a packed audience at Madison Square Garden, New York City.

"All the News That's Fit to Print."

The New York Times.

LATE EDITION
5:30 A. M.
WEATHER—Fair today; cloudy tomorrow.

VOL. LXXVIII....No. 25,855. NEW YORK, WEDNESDAY, NOVEMBER 7, 1928. TWO CENTS In Greater New York | THREE CENTS Within 200 Miles | FOUR CENTS Elsewhere in the U. S.

HOOVER WINS 407 TO 69; DOUBTFUL 55; SMITH LOSES STATE; SOUTH BROKEN; ROOSEVELT IS ELECTED GOVERNOR

HOOVER CARRIES ILLINOIS, SWEEPING IN THE STATE TICKET

Smith Wins in Chicago, but His Republican Rival Gets Big Down-State Vote.

IOWA STRONG FOR HOOVER

Nebraska Puts Republican in Lead and His Victory Seems Certain.

MICHIGAN ALSO REPUBLICAN

Hoover Sweeps Ohio by a Big Majority—Entire State Ticket Elected.

Special to The New York Times.

CHICAGO, Nov. 6.—Illinois went Republican today. Herbert Hoover and the State ticket, headed by Louis L. Emmerson, candidate for Governor, and Otis F. Glenn, nominee for United States Senator, won by such large figures in down-State territory that close battles over some of the places in Cook County were eliminated.

Although he apparently lost Chicago to Governor Smith, incomplete returns indicated that Hoover had carried Cook County, which was counted upon by the Democrats as certain for their entire ticket.

The figures received as this is written forecast a Smith victory in Chicago by about 40,000 and informal reports from the suburbs of the county promised a Republican lead of 75,000.

The vote of 3,208 precincts out of 6,942, including 1,816 from Cook County, gave Hoover 741,167; Smith 604,811. The Republican nominee for President apparently won the State by about 400,000.

Emmerson and his fellow contestants for State executive office apparently fell considerably behind Hoover both in Cook County and down-State, but all apparently were safe on the face of the incomplete figures.

Close Race for Senatorship.

The closest race of all was that for United States Senator which the first reports indicated might be a neck and neck race because of the way that Anton J. Cermak, the "wet" Democrat ran ahead of Governor Smith in Chicago. The first big batch of city precincts to be heard from promised him a Chicago lead of from 250,000 to 275,000.

It was thought that Glenn might not be able to overcome this in the down-State territory because the figures on the Governorship which had been received more fully did not indicate that Emmerson would carry down-State by quite that big a margin. But when the outside counties began to report the returns forecast a margin for Glenn outside Chicago in excess of 350,000.

Cermak was the only Democrat who leaped ahead of his national ticket in Chicago. Floyd E. Thompson, Democratic gubernatorial entry, was allowed by his party to trail Governor Smith and also Thomas J. Courtney, nominee for Attorney General against Oscar E. Carlstrom, the Republican who now holds that office.

The returns on these offices were far ahead of those for the rest of the offices on the State ticket, but Hoover's lead and the leads of Glenn, Emmerson and Carlstrom were taken as proof that all the Republican entries had carried the State.

On incomplete returns Judge William J. Lindsay, Democrat, was leading Judge John A. Swanson, Republican, for State's Attorney, the centre of the battle over Cook County offices.

In the battle over lucrative berths on the Board of Review, Thomas D. Nash, Democrat, is leading Edward R. Litsinger, Republican.

Much Splitting of Votes.

Scattering precinct figures from all the wards, indicate a day of prodigious vote splitting.

The Crowe-Thompsonites whetted their axes for the Dineen Republican candidates, and vice versa. Indications are that if Judge Lindsay maintains his early lead, the entire Democratic ticket may win. Figures on other candidates are slow in arriving but they indicate that the Crowe-Thompson machine was caught in another avalanche, similar to the one that struck it in the popular uprising at the April primaries.

In the fight for drainage trusteeships, where the Crowe-Thompson

Continued on Page Four.

U. S. Senators Elected

REPUBLICAN—18

California	*H. W. Johnson
Connecticut	‡F. C. Walcott
Delaware	John G. Townsend Jr.
Idaho	§John Thomas
Illinois	§Otis F. Glenn
Indiana	*A. R. Robinson
Maine	‖Frederick Hale
Maryland	‡P. L. Goldsborough
Michigan	†A. H. Vanderberg
Nebraska	*Robert B. Howell
New Jersey	‡Hamilton F. Kean
North Dakota	*Lynn J. Frazier
Ohio	*Simeon D. Fess
Ohio	§T. E. Burton
Pennsylvania	*David A. Reed
Rhode Island	‡Felix Hebert
Vermont	*Frank L. Greene
Wisconsin	*R. M. La Follette Jr.

DEMOCRATS—9

Arizona	*Henry F. Ashurst
Florida	*Park Trammell
Massachusetts	*David I. Walsh
Mississippi	*H. D. Stephens
New York	*R. S. Copeland
Tennessee	*Kenneth McKellar
Texas	‡Tom Connally
Utah	*William H. King
Virginia	*C. A. Swanson

FARMER-LABORITE—1

Minnesota . . *Henrik Shipstead

IN DOUBT—7

Missouri, New Mexico, Montana, Washington, Nevada, West Virginia, Wyoming

*Re-elected for full term ending March 3, 1935.
†Elected for both long and short terms.
‡Elected for full term ending March 3, 1935.
‖Re-elected Sept. 10, 1928, for full term ending March 3, 1935.
§Elected for short term ending March 3, 1933.

BAY STATE IS CLOSE, WITH SMITH AHEAD

Walsh, Democrat, Re-elected to Senate and Cole Is in Front for Governor.

SMITH WINS RHODE ISLAND

But State Ticket Goes Republican—Other New England States for Hoover.

Special to The New York Times.

BOSTON, Mass., Nov. 7.—At 4:30 o'clock this morning, after one of the liveliest election nights ever known in Massachusetts, and when it appeared that the Democrats had swept the State, there was a possibility that Herbert Hoover, though trailing Governor Smith, might receive the eighteen electoral votes of this State.

At the same time there was a a probability that the fianl returns would show Frank G. Allen winner of the Gubernatorial contest over his Democratic opponent, General Charles H. Cole, despite the latter's lead.

Senator David D. Walsh, Democrat, running 10,000 votes ahead of Governor Smith, was clearly re-elected over Benjamin Loring Young, Republican.

Smith Carries Textile Cities.

From early in the evening, when Hoover had built up a substantial lead, the returns from Boston and some textile centres pulled him down and pushed Smith out in front.

Then followed a see-sawing back and forth, with Smith slowly forging ahead in the early morning hours, largely as a result of 10,000-vote margins which were given to him in Fall River and Lowell, 4,000 in New Bedford, 5,000 in Salem, 7,000 in Holyoke, and lesser votes in other cities.

For President, 952 precincts out of the 1,605 in the State gave Hoover 405,125, Smith 426,509.

For Governor, 848 precincts, including 300 of the 339 in Boston, gave Allen (R.) 346,495, Cole (D.) 351,091.

For Senator, 848 precincts gave Young (R.) 312,866, Walsh (D.) 321,002.

Unofficial Boston figures for 310 precincts out of 339 gave Hoover

Continued on Page Two.

NEW JERSEY GIVES REPUBLICAN SLATE A HEAVY MAJORITY

Incomplete Figures for State Show Hoover Leads Smith by 116,944.

LARSON AHEAD OF DILL

Victory for Republican by 166,340 Is Indicated in Gubernatorial Race.

KEAN BEATING EDWARDS

Strong Republican Showing Is a Damaging Blow to Prestige of Hague as Leader.

Herbert Hoover's indicated plurality in New Jersey was 309,420 early this morning when the tabulation of returns from 1,102 of the 2,920 districts gave Hoover 303,792 and Smith 186,848. In the metropolitan district of New Jersey the Republican and Democratic candidates ran a close race.

In Essex County, which includes Newark, tabulation of the vote in 150 of the 481 districts showed that it stood, Hoover, 39,122; Smith, 31,810.

Hamilton F. Kean was leading Senator Edward I. Edwards, Democrat, by 91,021 in 1,102 districts and his indicated plurality was 239,440.

Larson in the Lead.

In the Gubernatorial contest the returns from 1,102 districts gave Larson 269,391 and Dill 205,692, giving Larson, Republican, a lead of 63,699 and an indicated plurality of 166,340.

In 75 of 506 districts in Hudson County, the stronghold of Mayor Frank Hague, the vote was: Hoover 9,106, Smith 18,302, Kean 10,204, Edwards 18,896, Larson 10,302, Dill 18,107.

Increasing Republican pluralities reported from the counties of Southern New Jersey were not offset by expected Democratic gains in the metropolitan area.

Republican candidates for Congress were leading their opponents in all counties except Hudson, and Republican candidates for the Assembly were reported generally in the lead in all but counties which are now represented in the Assembly by Democrats.

While the Republicans of Camden County were celebrating the success of their State and national tickets there, State Senator Joseph H. Forsyth was reported to be dying from influenza at his home at Haddonfield. He was stricken several days ago. He was elected in 1926 for three years.

Reports from Trenton were to the effect that a plurality of from 150,000 to 200,000 for Hoover was indicated by the early returns. According to The Associated Press fifty-six districts out of 2,920 in strongly Republican territory gave Hoover a lead of 5,456 over Smith. The vote was Hoover 9,078 and Smith 3,622.

The first 12,000 ballots tabulated in Jersey City gave Smith 7,761 votes, Hoover 4,024, Edwards 7,405, Kean 4,037, Dill 7,276, Larson 4,320.

Forty-five districts reported in the United States Senatorial and Gubernatorial races. These gave Kean, Republican, 7,080; Senator Edwards, Democrat, 3,217. The Governorship figures were William L. Dill, Democrat, 3,580; Morgan F. Larson, Republican, 6,989.

The indicated heavy pluralities of the Republican candidates for United States Senator and Governor were a damaging blow to the prestige of Mayor Hague, Vice Chairman of the Democratic National Committee, whose Democratic stronghold in Hudson has been sufficiently powerful in three Gubernatorial elections to stem the Republican tide in other sections of New Jersey and send Democratic candidates to the Governor's Mansion and to the Senate.

Fight in Hudson County.

The fight of Mayor Frank Hague of Jersey City, Democratic leader in Hudson County, was responsible for the action of election officials in striking the names of apporximately 29,000 voters from the enrollment lists. It was reported that several thousand voters had been disfranchised in Hudson County because of inability of the Commissioner of Registration to deal with the situation resulting from the County Board of Election's ruling at the eleventh hour. Election officials re-

Continued on Page Eighteen.

Gov. Smith's Message to Mr. Hoover

Governor Smith sent the following telegram just after midnight to his successful rival:

Hon. Herbert Hoover,
Palo Alto, Cal.:

I congratulate you heartily on your victory, and extend to you my sincere good wishes for your health and happiness and for the success of your Administration.

ALFRED E. SMITH.

Electoral Vote

HOOVER.

Arizona	3	Nevada	3
California	13	New Hampshire	4
Colorado	6	New Jersey	14
Connecticut	7	New Mexico	3
Delaware	3	New York	45
Florida	6	Ohio	24
Idaho	4	Oklahoma	10
Illinois	29	Oregon	5
Indiana	15	Pennsylvania	38
Iowa	13	South Dakota	5
Kansas	10	Tennessee	12
Kentucky	13	Utah	4
Maine	6	Vermont	4
Maryland	8	Virginia	12
Michigan	15	Washington	7
Minnesota	12	West Virginia	8
Missouri	18	Wisconsin	13
Montana	4	Wyoming	3
Nebraska	8	Total	407

SMITH.

Alabama	12	Mississippi	10
Arkansas	9	Rhode Island	5
Georgia	14	South Carolina	9
Louisiana	10	Total	69

DOUBTFUL.

Massachusetts	18	Texas	20
North Carolina	12	Total	55
North Dakota	5		

Total number of votes in Electoral College, 531; necessary to a choice, 266.

HOOVER BREAKS THE SOLID SOUTH

He Carries Virginia and Probably Florida and North Carolina—Leads in Texas Also.

Special to The New York Times.

RICHMOND, Va., Nov. 6.—Herbert Hoover has carried the Old Dominion and broken the Solid South.

State Democratic headquarters authorized the statement before midnight:

"he unofficial returns indicate that Virginia has gone for Hoover."

At a late hour he had obtained a 21,000 lead over Governor Smith, with two-thirds of the State polled. His plurality had been steadily mounting from the start.

The totals in 1,429 precincts out of 1,665 were: Hoover, 145,641; Smith, 124,520.

Fifteen of forty precincts in Richmond gave Hoover 2,253 and Smith 2,391.

Danville has gone for Hoover. It is a Ku Klux Klan stronghold, but Democrats were as thoroughly organized there as anywhere in the State. Hoover, as expected, polled heavy votes in the first and second districts while Smith showed great strength in the fourth.

Only in the ninth district did the returns look normal. There were fewer Democratic defections than in other parts of the State, and Hoover and Smith were running neck and neck.

Hoover Leads in Texas.

DALLAS, Texas, Nov. 6 (AP).—The possibility that a Republican Presidential candidate might carry Texas for the first time in history loomed late tonight as Herbert Hoover, for the third time during the tabulation of the vote, went into the lead.

The 11 o'clock tabulation of the Texas Election Bureau showed the Republican ahead by 2,855 votes, with more than half of the ballots counted. It was the largest lead either candidate had gained in the nip and tuck race. Hoover's total, as computed by the bureau, was 208,415, Smith's 205,560. Later a count of 214 counties out of 253, four

Continued on Page Two.

CITY GIVES SMITH 430,000 MAJORITY

Incomplete Count Also Indicates Like Lead for Roosevelt for Governor.

Governor Smith carried New York City by about 430,000 plurality over Mr. Hoover, or about 88,000 less than the plurality he received over Theodore Roosevelt in 1924, which was the largest plurality the city gave him in any of his Gubernatorial campaigns.

With only 28 out of the 3,493 election districts of the city missing, Smith had 1,106,524 against 680,074 for Hoover, a plurality of 426,450. Norman Thomas, Socialist candidate, received less than 50,000 in the city.

Franklin D. Roosevelt, Democratic candidate for Governor, ran behind Smith in the city. With 90 districts missing, Roosevelt had 1,087,418 against 699,441 for his Republican opponent, Attorney General Albert Ottinger, a plurality of 387,977.

Herbert H. Lehman, Democratic candidate for Lieutenant Governor, and United States Senator Royal S. Copeland, Democratic candidate for re-election to the Senate, ran ahead of their ticket in the city.

Lehman Has Big Lead.

With 193 districts missing, Lehman received 1,106,088 votes, against 614,241 for Mr. Lockwood, his Republican opponent, a plurality of 491,847.

With 668 districts missing, Copeland had 958,401 to 498,699 for Alanson B. Houghton, former Ambassador to Germany and Great Britain, the Republican candidate, a plurality of 459,702 for Copeland.

Albert Conway, Democratic candidate for Attorney General, and Maurice S. Tremaine, Democratic candidate for re-election as State Controller, also ran ahead of Smith in the city. With 382 districts missing, Conway had 1,020,620 votes against 564,486 for Hamilton Ward, Republican, a plurality of 456,134. With 258 districts missing, Tremaine had 1,058,027, against 588,780 for

Continued on Page Seven.

ROOSEVELT IS VICTOR BY SLIM PLURALITY; COPELAND ALSO WINS

Democratic Nominee Captures Governorship by Margin Indicated to Be 40,000.

SENATOR IN BY 56,000

Re-elected Over Houghton After Running Up Lead of 523,000 in the City.

LEAVES SMITH FAR BEHIND

Polls 90,000 More Votes Than the Governor—Lehman, Conway and Tremaine Leading.

Franklin D. Roosevelt, Democrat, defeated Attorney General Albert Ottinger, Republican, for the Governorship of New York State, on the basis of returns from 7,718 election districts out of the 8,267 in the State. A plurality of about 40,000 for Mr. Roosevelt was indicated on these figures, and it is possible that this plurality might be cut somewhat by the returns from the missing districts but not enough to give Mr. Ottinger the State.

Senator Royal S. Copeland, candidate for re-election on the Democratic ticket, apparently had won from former Ambassador Alanson B. Houghton by an indicated plurality of about 56,000. Senator Copeland ran surprisingly well in New York City, where his plurality seems likely to reach 523,000, or about 90,000 more than the plurality received by Governor Smith, heretofore regarded as the strongest candidate in the city, personally.

The victories for Mr. Roosevelt and Senator Copeland went some distance toward assuaging the local Democrats for Governor Smith's defeat. Governor Smith's indicated plurality in New York City was about 430,000, and his defeat in the State by about 125,000 was indicated.

Roosevelt Lead 68,568.

Mr. Roosevelt had an actual lead of 68,568, with 549 out of the 8,267 election districts in the State missing, the vote being Roosevelt 2,073,372 and Ottinger 1,954,754.

Outside New York City 4,298 election districts out of 4,774 gave Roosevelt 929,953 and Ottinger 1,257,002, an actual plurality of 327,049 and an indicated up-State plurality for Ottinger of 367,598.

In New York City 3,400 out of 3,393 election districts gave Roosevelt 1,093,369 and Ottinger 697,752, an actual plurality of 395,617 and an indicated plurality of 405,188.

Mr. Roosevelt ran ahead of Governor Smith in virtually every county up-State, while Mr. Ottinger cut into the Democratic vote somewhat in New York City, but not as much as expected.

Senator Copeland's run in New York City was surprising. In 3,144 out of the 3,493 election districts in the city he received 1,033,048 and Houghton 561,539, an actual plurality of 471,509 and an indicated plurality of 523,950.

To offset this tremendous plurality, seemingly the largest ever received in the city by any candidate, Mr. Houghton in 3,645 out of 4,774 Up-state election districts received 1,069,464 to 713,173 for Senator Copeland. This is an actual plurality of 356,291 and an indicated plurality of 467,852 for Mr. Houghton Upstate.

The delay in the returns from about a thousand up-State districts led Mr. Roosevelt to charge early this morning that there were indications which led him to suspect fraud up-State. He announced that Edward S. Dore, Chairman of the Law Committee of the Democratic State Committee, would leave for up-State this morning with a hundred lawyers ready to resist or prevent any fraud which might be attempted.

"Owing to the extreme delay with which about 1,000 districts up-State are sending in election returns, the Democratic State Committee has become convinced that fraud is being committed in an attempt to elect Ottinger as Governor of the State of New York," Mr. Roosevelt said.

"Accordingly, Mr. Dore, John Godfrey Saxe and Maurice Bloch, minority leader of the Assembly, are leaving New York City on the Empire State Express this (Wednesday) morning for up-State cities, together with a staff of 100 lawyers to uncover such frauds as have been com-

Continued on Page Two.

HOOVER CARRIES NEW YORK BY 125,000

Republican Nominee Captures New Jersey, Takes Wisconsin; Breaks Solid South, Winning Virginia, Florida

GAINING IN NORTH CAROLINA AND BAY STATE

Most of Farm Belt in Republican Column in Record-Breaking Vote—Kentucky, Missouri and Tennessee Lost to Democrats.

Voting in unprecedented numbers, a myriad of American citizens yesterday chose Herbert Hoover of California for President of the United States and Charles Curtis of Kansas for Vice President.

How pronounced is the victory of these candidates of the Republican Party over their Democratic competitors, Governor Alfred E. Smith of New York, nominee for President, and Joseph T. Robinson of Arkansas, the Vice Presidential nominee, cannot be determined until the stupendous task of counting 40,000,000 or more votes is completed, but a Republican landslide took place at the polls, and it will be reflected in a heavy Hoover-Curtis majority of the 531 ballots in the Electoral College.

400 Electoral Votes for Hoover

Mr. Hoover is assured of more than 400 electoral votes. It is probable that his majority will increase as further returns are received. He has broken the traditionally Democratic Solid South. He has carried Virginia and returns from Florida indicate that he has won in that State. His tally in the Electoral College may go as high as 444 votes if North Carolina, North Dakota and Texas, which are very close, are added to his strength, or even to the stupendous total of 462, if the count now proceeding in Massachusetts turns in his favor.

Such an outcome would give Mr. Hoover a majority of 397 electoral votes over Governor Smith. It is already apparent that no Presidential candidate of any major party has been beaten as badly as Governor Smith, with the exception of William H. Taft, who got only 8 votes in the Electoral College in his contest for re-election against Woodrow Wilson and Theodore Roosevelt.

According to the latest returns received from Massachusetts, North Carolina, North Dakota and Texas, these States are still in the doubtful column either by reason of inadequate returns or on account of the closeness of contests as the count proceeds, and while Governor Smith may be shown to have carried some of them, his tally of electoral votes may not exceed seventy.

New York Spells Smith's Doom.

Governor Smith's hope of victory began to fade within a few hours after the polls closed in New York State when it was indicated that he had carried New York City, his great stronghold, by less than 450,000, which was much short of the estimate of his managers. As returns began to roll in from up-State it became apparent that the Hoover plurality in that strong Republican area would materially overcome the showing for Governor Smith in New York City, with the prospect that the Republican nominee would carry the State by a lead in the neighborhood of 125,000.

With New York's forty-five electoral votes placed in the Hoover column it became merely a matter of waiting until the full returns determined what the Republican candidates' majority will be in the Electoral College. The tremendous onsweep of the Hoover following was emphasized when State after State in which the Democrats had placed hope of victory went over into the Republican camp.

New Jersey was carried by the Republican national ticket by a heavy majority. Maryland followed suit. Late returns show that Hoover also took Missouri. Of other border States, he captured Kentucky and Oklahoma. Minnesota, which the Smith management was also hopeful of carrying on account of the defection among Republican voters because of Mr. Hoover's attitude on the McNary-Haugen bill, gave him a heavy plurality.

Smith States Only in South.

As for Governor Smith, there is no assurance that he has carried any State outside of the South. With the results in Florida and Texas still in doubt he seems to be certain of having carried only Alabama, Georgia, Louisiana, Mississippi and South Carolina. In the early morning hours late returns had Hoover forging ahead even in North Carolina. Tennessee was conceded to the Republican candidate.

His victories in Alabama and North Carolina are a set back for Senator J. Thomas Heflin and Senator Furnifold M. Simmons, who deserted their party allegiances to oppose him, Simmons on the ground of Governor Smith's anti-prohibition policy and Senator Heflin for the openly stated reason that Governor Smith was a Catholic.

In the early morning hours returns from Wisconsin indicated that the portion of the State outside of Milwaukee had voted so heavily for Hoover that Smith's lead in the metropolis made famous by beer had been overcome and that the State's thirteen electoral votes would be added to the steadily mounting Hoover column.

It was after 4 o'clock this morning before virtually complete returns from Rhode Island showed that Smith had carried Rhode Island, the only State outside the Solid South that can with certainty be placed to his credit. He seems to have carried it by a small majority, probably not exceeding 2,000.

Maine, New Hampshire, Vermont and Connecticut joined the Republican procession. At an early hour this morning the prospect was that where the eighteen electoral votes of Massachusetts would go could not be made certain until late today.

Republican Congress Assured.

The victory for the Republican national ticket is accompanied by the assurance that, as President, Mr. Hoover will have the support of a Congress controlled by those of his own party. While returns are incomplete, the indications are that the Republican majority in the House of Represen-

Wednesday, November 7, 1928

Hoover Wins 407 to 69; Doubtful 55; Smith Loses State; South Broken; Roosevelt Is Elected Governor

Hoover Carries New York by 125,000

Republican Nominee Captures New Jersey, Takes Wisconsin; Breaks Solid South, Winning Virginia, Florida

Gaining in North Carolina and Bay State

Most of Farm Belt in Republican Column in Record-Breaking Vote—Kentucky, Missouri and Tennessee Lost to Democrats

Voting in unprecedented numbers, a myriad of American citizens yesterday chose Herbert Hoover of California for President of the United States and Charles Curtis of Kansas for Vice President.

How pronounced is the victory of these candidates of the Republican Party over their Democratic competitors, Governor Alfred E. Smith of New York, nominee for President, and Joseph T. Robinson of Arkansas, the Vice Presidential nominee, cannot be determined until the stupendous task of counting 40,000,000 or more votes is completed, but a Republican landslide took place at the polls, and it will be reflected in a heavy Hoover-Curtis majority of the 531 ballots in the Electoral College.

400 Electoral Votes for Hoover

Mr. Hoover is assured of more than 400 electoral votes. It is probable that his majority will increase as further returns are received. He has broken the traditionally Democratic Solid South. He has carried Virginia and returns from Florida indicate that he has won in that State. His tally in the Electoral College may go as high as 444 votes if North Carolina, North Dakota and Texas, which are very close, are added to his strength, or even to the stupendous total of 462, if the count now proceeding in Massachusetts turns in his favor.

Such an outcome would give Mr. Hoover a majority of 397 electoral votes over Governor Smith. It is already apparent that no Presidential candidate of any major party has been beaten as badly as Governor Smith, with the exception of William H. Taft, who got only 8 votes in the Electoral College in his contest for re-election against Woodrow Wilson and Theodore Roosevelt.

According to the latest returns received from Massachusetts, North Carolina, North Dakota and Texas, these States are still in the doubtful column either by reason of inadequate returns or on account of the closeness of contests as the count proceeds, and while Governor Smith may be shown to have carried some of them, his tally of electoral votes may not exceed seventy.

New York Spells Smith's Doom.

As for Governor Smith, there is no assurance that he has carried any State outside of the South. With the results in Florida and Texas still in doubt he seems to be certain of having carried only Alabama, Georgia, Louisiana, Mississippi and South Carolina. In the early morning hours late returns had Hoover forging ahead even in North Carolina. Tennessee was conceded to the Republican candidate.

His victories in Alabama and North Carolina are a set back for Senator J. Thomas Heflin and Senator Furnifold M. Simmons, who deserted their party allegiances to oppose him, Simmons on the ground of Governor Smith's anti-prohibition policy and Senator Heflin for the openly stated reason that Governor Smith was a Catholic.

In the early morning hours returns from Wisconsin indicated that the portion of the State outside of Milwaukee had voted so heavily for Hoover that Smith's lead in the metropolis made famous by beer had been overcome and that the State's thirteen electoral votes would be added to the steadily mounting Hoover column.

It was after 4 o'clock this morning before virtually complete returns from Rhode Island showed that Smith had carried Rhode Island, the only State outside the Solid South that can with certainty be placed to his credit. He seems to have carried it by a small majority, probably not exceeding 2,000.

Maine, New Hampshire, Vermont and Connecticut joined the Republican procession. At an early hour this morning the prospect was that where the eighteen electoral votes of Massachusetts would go could not be made certain until late today.

Republican Congress Assured.

The victory for the Republican national ticket is accompanied by the assurance that, as President, Mr. Hoover will have the support of a Congress controlled by those of his own party. While returns are incomplete, the indications are that the Republican majority in the House of Representatives, now thirty-six over the combined opposition, will be increased, and the mere constructive majority of the Republicans in the Senate, where Insurgent members of that party hold the balance of power, will be augmented so materially as to permit Mr. Hoover's political associates to dominate that body.

Early this morning as returns began to come in from Far West they bore out predictions that Hoover would sweep those sections of the country. He captured California, his home State, while the returns from Oregon showed him leading Smith by three to one. Idaho seems to have given him double the vote obtained by Smith.

A Republican landslide took place at the polls, and it will be reflected in a heavy Hoover-Curtis majority of the 531 ballots in the Electoral College.

A two to one lead was also indicated by the first returns from Colorado, a State which the Democrats hoped to carry. So it was also with New Mexico, which the Republicans were fearful of losing. Arizona showed that the race was close, with Hoover less than 100 votes in the lead on limited reports. Smith forged ahead in Nevada in the early tally, but later Hoover passed him. Montana, which was another State that the Democrats had hopes of capturing, gave the lead to Hoover in late returns.

In the Western farming states where dissatisfaction over agricultural conditions has been very marked, Hoover has done better than Smith. Nothing has appeared in the returns from these States, where Robert M. La Follette's Presidential candidacy was extremely marked four years go, to show that Smith got the benefit of the La Follette following as Chairman Raskob of the Democratic National Committee had predicted.

From many parts of the country where the result as between Hoover and Smith was in doubt, returns came in very slowly. This was especially true of doubtful Western States, with the exception of Texas. The lack of information was accounted for chiefly by the difference in time and the late closing of the polls in some of these States.

In the three Pacific Coast States, California, Oregon and Washington, the polls did not close until 8 o'clock, Pacific Coast Time, which was 11 o'clock, Eastern Standard Time.

In Kansas, some polling places closed at 7 and others at 9 o'clock, which, translated into Eastern Standard Time, meant 8 and 10 o'clock, while in North Dakota the polls closed at 8 and 9 o'clock, or one hour later in the East.

What Early Returns Indicated.

Early returns from the Texas cities indicated that Hoover was running slightly ahead of Smith in the cities, but as the returns came in Smith took a very slight lead. Texas has heretofore been rock-ribbed Democratic territory and one of the solidest States of the Solid South.

Florida, too, showed a tendency toward Hoover in the early returns. The first information from these two Southern States appeared to give the color of accuracy to predictions made by their Republican leaders and anti-Smith Democrats that they would be found in the Republican column.

A tendency toward Hoover was shown also in early returns from Oklahoma. While this State is normally Democratic, although it had cast its electoral vote for Warren G. Harding in the Republican landslide of 1920, the opinion of most neutral political observers was that it was inclined to give a majority to Hoover. In Oklahoma Governor Smith's religion appeared to be the chief issue, taking precedence in importance there to the prohibition question. Four of the principal Democratic newspapers in the State bolted their party and declared for Hoover, and there were marked incidences of Democration defection, especially in the southern part of Oklahoma, which is chiefly settled by Texas Democrats and their descendants.

The religious issue was also foremost in Texas and Florida, as it was in every State of the Solid South and in the border States. It was on account of the opposition to Governor Smith within the ranks of his own party on his stand for the modification of the Volstead act and because of his Roman Catholic religion that the possibility of a break in the South's Democratic solidarity was seen, although the more widespread opinion of those versed in politics was that the South would cling to its traditional loyalty to the Democratic Party.

Hoover Spurts in Illinois.

Early returns from Chicago indicated a tremendous Smith trend but later reports from the Illinois metropolis reduced the lead of the Democratic Presidential candidate considerably, so considerably as to lead to predictions that he would lose Illinois by a big majority. When the country districts of the State began to be heard from and Governor Smith's plurality in Chicago was estimated as not exceeding 100,000, the political forecasters made confident claims that Hoover would get the twenty-nine electoral votes of Illinois by a large plurality.

The religious issue was also foremost in Texas and Florida, as it was in every State of the Solid South and in the border States.

Illinois is similar to New York State in political elections, in that the heavy Democratic vote in Chicago and the heavy Democratic vote in New York City frequently enter into a battle royal with what is known as Downstate Illinois and Upstate New York, where rural communities furnish a solid foundation of Republican strength.

The great interest revealed in the political reactions of normally Republican States in the Central West and Northwest, where the Democrats placed high hopes of making gains, was manifested particularly in the outcome of the Presidential contest in Nebraska, Minnesota, North Dakota and South Dakota. All these States were regarded as doubtful by the more conservative political prognosticators, although it was regarded as likely that all of them, with the exception of North Dakota, would be found in the column of Republican electoral votes.

But the doubt increased considerably when Senator George W. Norris of Nebraska, leader of the Republican Insurgent flock in the Senate, announced in a speech at Omaha that he favored Governor Smith's election as President.

Hoover Leads at Start.

It was predicted by Democrats and anti-Hoover farm leaders that this would swing Nebraska to Governor Smith and probably carry Minnesota and perhaps South Dakota along with Senator Norris's State. But even Nebraska went for Hoover along with Minnesota and South Dakota.

Opinion among politicians in these States was that, because of this antagonism to Mr. Hoover, the disposition among the generality of Republican farmers was to vote against him, but considerable doubt was expressed that large numbers of them would cast their ballots for the Smith-Robinson ticket in view of Governor Smith's religion, his wet slant and his Tammany Hall affiliations.

The predicted trend to Governor Smith in Wisconsin was borne out in early returns from that State.

Senator John J. Blaine, one of the Republican Progressive leaders of the Badger State, announced himself for Governor Smith and called upon his following to vote for the Democratic national ticket. His colleague, Senator Robert M. La Follette, Jr., did not go quite so far as Senator Blaine in making a comparison of the candidacies of Smith and Hoover but indicated very plainly that he preferred the former to the latter. Newspaper polls were construed as showing that Smith would carry the normally Republican city of Milwaukee by a fair majority but would lose heavily to Hoover in the rural sections of the State.

For the American people and their shifting political traditions, 1932 was arguably the pivotal year of the century. The election of Franklin D. Roosevelt brought a dynamic leader to the White House and ended seven decades of near-total Republican dominion. But it signaled far more than a partisan shift. FDR brought a vastly more active philosophy of government to grapple with the profound social conflicts exposed by the Great Depression. With confidence and charisma, he also overhauled the rules of campaigning.

The Hoover Administration was barely under way when the stock market crashed in October 1929. Hoover was more interventionist than any previous president, but his proposals did little to ameliorate the misery and few believed that prosperity was "just around the corner." He won renomination, but his popularity plummeted with the ugly repression of the "Bonus Army"—thousands of veterans who marched on Washington in the summer of 1932 to demand benefits, only to be chased with tanks and tear gas by Army troops led by Douglas MacArthur.

On the Democratic side, Roosevelt was the front-runner, having won election as New York governor in 1928 and again, overwhelmingly, in 1930. But FDR's detractors thought he was a

Left to right:
Franklin Delano Roosevelt (1882–1945)
Herbert C. Hoover (1874–1964)
Norman Thomas (1884–1968)

Franklin D. Roosevelt rewrote the rules of campaigning in 1932, presaging the revolution he would bring to the presidency.

Hooverites warned never to "swap horses" mid-stream; but for Americans living in Hoovervilles, that warning was a little too late.

lightweight. His predecessor and former ally, Al Smith, who fought desperately for a third chance to run, argued that even "the one-eyed O'Leary could win" in 1932. Walter Lippman dismissed Roosevelt as an "amiable Boy Scout." Others, playing on his initials, called him "Feather Duster."

Like the Republicans, the Democrats convened in Chicago. Al Smith led a drive against Roosevelt, who won only after some hard-nosed bargaining. To win the delegates of Texas and California, he promised the vice presidency to Speaker John Nance Garner, and reached an agreement with the press lord William Randolph Hearst. Dramatically, FDR flew to Chicago in person to accept the nomination, boldly dispensing with the polite tradition of waiting weeks for ersatz notification.

It was a brilliant stroke, demonstrating his physical endurance as well as his political skills. In a celebrated speech, he pledged "a new deal" for the American people. The phrase was picked up by a cartoonist and immediately defined the campaign and the public's hunger for change. The Democratic platform was uncharacteristically bold, demanding the repeal of Prohibition, unemployment relief, and better protection for labor.

Throughout the summer and fall, FDR was ebullient, speaking often and well. Unlike Hoover, who still wrote his own plodding speeches, Roosevelt had a skilled team of professional wordsmiths. Though many of the early promises of the New Deal were vague, it was easy to believe, watching his smile, that happy days were indeed here again.

Hoover made a last-ditch effort to catch up, but for all his talents, he failed to sense that a political revolution was at hand (even Norman Thomas, the six-time Socialist candidate, ran well). FDR won by an overwhelming margin: 22.8 million votes to 15.7 million for Hoover—and an even wider discrepancy in the electoral tally, 472 to 59. Roosevelt had a sweeping mandate for change, and few presidents before or since have interpreted a mandate more broadly.

Norman Thomas, a former clergyman and journalist, garnered nearly 900,000 votes for the Socialist ticket.

Hoover accepts the Republican nomination for reelection at the Constitution Hall, Washington, D.C., August 11, 1932.

Governor Roosevelt and his family wave good-bye to Albany as he leaves for a speaking tour through fourteen states aboard the Roosevelt Special, September 1932.

Hoover campaigns in Huntington, West Virginia *(left)*, October 1932.

Norman Thomas addresses a peace rally *(below)*, New York City, February 1932.

The Tammany delegation *(right)* sits in the front row of the Democratic convention in Chicago. New York City Mayor Jimmy Walker is third from left, June 27, 1932.

Texas delegate W. L. Rea *(below)* calls for order in the hall during a demonstration at the Democratic convention, June 27, 1932.

Roosevelt's running mate, John "Cactus Jack" Nance Garner *(left)*, of Texas, 1932.

Former mayor of New York John F. Hylan whispering to James Farly *(below)*, campaign manager for Roosevelt, July 1932.

Bishop James Cannon Jr., one of the foremost drys of the country, examines a bottle of bay rum offered to him by Virgin Islands' delegate Lucius J. Malmin, *(opposite, top)*, at the Republican convention, June 1932.

Will Rogers winks and former Alabama governor William Brandon waves *(opposite, bottom)* at the Democratic convention, June, 1932.

A demonstration in Des Moines on a "Farmer's Holiday" draws sympathizers from all over Iowa, previous to President Hoover's arrival, October 4, 1932.

Roosevelt campaigns in Seattle, September 1932.

"All the News That's Fit to Print."

The New York Times.

5 A. M. EDITION
WEATHER—Rain today; tomorrow fair and colder.
Temperatures Yesterday—Max., 56; Min., 50.

VOL. LXXXII....No. 27,318. Entered as Second-Class Matter, Postoffice, New York, N. Y. NEW YORK, WEDNESDAY, NOVEMBER 9, 1932. * * * * * TWO CENTS In New York City | THREE CENTS Within 200 Miles | FOUR CENTS Elsewhere Except in 7th and 8th Postal Zones

ROOSEVELT WINNER IN LANDSLIDE! DEMOCRATS CONTROL WET CONGRESS; LEHMAN GOVERNOR, O'BRIEN MAYOR

BIG VOTE FOR M'KEE

O'Brien Is 245,464 Behind Ticket as Protests Rise

BUT FINAL LEAD IS 616,736

Pounds Concedes Defeat Early, Saying 'Day of Miracles Is Past.'

McKEE TOTAL IS 137,538

Thousands of "Write-In" Votes Are Wasted as Backers Fail to Record Choice Properly.

HILLQUIT POLLS 248,425

Gets Greatest Vote in History of City for a Socialist—Runs Far Ahead of Party.

Surrogate John P. O'Brien, Tammany's candidate, was elected Mayor of New York yesterday, but overshadowing his victory, which was a foregone conclusion, was the tremendous "write-in" vote cast for Acting Mayor Joseph V. McKee.

Final returns from the city showed Judge O'Brien to have received a plurality of 616,736 over his nearest opponent, Lewis H. Pounds, Republican. Judge O'Brien's vote was 1,055,768, Mr. Pounds polled 439,032, and Morris Hillquit, Socialist, polled the highest vote ever given a candidate of his party in the city by receiving 248,425 votes.

Vote Listed by Boroughs.

By boroughs, the totals were as follows:

	O'Brien.	Pounds.	Hillquit.
Manhattan	309,256	113,273	39,398
Bronx	181,345	45,284	67,949
Brooklyn	358,005	155,478	112,740
Queens	176,237	105,461	25,821
Richmond	30,221	16,511	2,517
City total	1,055,768	439,032	248,425

The vote for Mr. McKee, put early this morning at 137,538, actually was far more than that, if ballots in which the voters had abbreviated his name, or used initials, or spelled it wrongly, were counted.

The vote was unprecedented, particularly as the use of voting machines made it much more difficult for a name to be writen in than on the old paper ballots.

Judge O'Brien had a clear majority of 215,000 votes over the combined vote of Pounds, Hillquit and McKee, but the McKee ballots cast aside as void would have reduced this, it was pointed out last night.

The vote for Mr. McKee by boroughs was as follows:

Manhattan, 26,326, with ten election districts missing.
Bronx, 24,453, complete.
Brooklyn, 43,325, complete.
Queens, 36,303, complete.
Richmond, 6,790, complete.
City total, 137,538.

The vote for Mr. McKee, made without any campaign on his part, and in the face of his own disavowal of the movement kept him in the political picture as a candidate to be reckoned with for the full four-year term, to be voted on in 1933.

The term for which Judge O'Brien was elected starts on Jan. 1, 1933, and ends on Jan. 1, 1934.

The vote for Mr. O'Brien indicated he ran 381,263 votes behind Governor Roosevelt in the city, in actual votes cast, though his plurality was only 245,464 smaller than that given to the Presidential candidate.

Mr. Pounds conceded Mr. O'Brien's victory as early as 9:30 in the evening, and he sent the latter a telegram of congratulation.

He said later he could have been elected only by a miracle, and that the days of miracles were past. Mr. McKee, receiving election returns at the Park Lane, also sent a short

Continued on Page Seven.

THE GOVERNOR-ELECT.

© New York Times Studio.
Colonel Herbert H. Lehman.

JUDGES IN 'DEAL' WIN; PROTEST VOTE HEAVY

Steuer and Hofstadter Elected With Lydon and Leary to Supreme Court Bench.

290,000 FOR INDEPENDENTS

Bar Leaders Elated by Big Count for Deutsch and Alger—Call It 'Warning to Bosses.'

City Court Justice Aron Steuer and State Senator Samuel H. Hofstadter were elected yesterday over their independent opponents, Bernard S. Deutsch and George W. Alger, by a vote of about 2 to 1.

The protest vote against the so-called deal by which Senator Hofstadter and Justice Steuer received bipatrisan nominations for two of four vacancies on the Supreme Court bench in the first judicial district exceeded all expectations, but it was not enough to upset the combined strength of the Republican and Democratic organizations.

Justice Richard P. Lydon, who was nominated by both major parties for re-election, and Municipal Court Justice Timothy A. Leary, who had the Democratic nomination for the fourth vacancy on the bench, were elected with comfortable margins. Municipal Court Justice George L. Genung, who had the Republican nomination, trailed far behind the independent candidates.

Since Justice Lydon's re-election was virtually uncontested, his totals were not computed in the early returns. Of the other, Justice Steuer and Judge Leary were running slightly ahead of Senator Hofstadter, whose lead was large enough, however, to preclude the possibility of his being overtaken by Mr. Deutsch, his nearest rival.

The Complete Returns.

The complete returns for the entire first judicial district, comprising the boroughs of Manhattan and the Bronx, follow:

Steuer	565,405
Leary	547,112
Hofstadter	544,032
Deutsch	293,125
Alger	287,167
Genung	205,222

The totals recorded for the judiciary candidates in Manhattan follow:

Steuer	367,295
Hofstadter	357,430
Leary	331,442
Deutsch	147,886
Alger	145,346
Genung	138,304

Final returns from the Bronx, where the independent candidates ran strongest, showed the following totals:

Leary	215,670
Steuer	198,110
Hofstadter	186,602
Deutsch	145,239
Alger	141,821
Genung	66,918

The independent candidates did not

Continued on Page Twelve.

STATE VICTORY SOLID

Lehman Gets Record Party Plurality of 887,000.

WAGNER CLOSE TO HIM

National Ticket Has Margin of 615,000—Full Slate Is Elected.

RELIEF BONDS ARE VOTED

Republicans Have Narrow Edge Up-State—Hill Admits 'Protest' Defeated Them.

By JAMES A. HAGERTY.

Lieut. Gov. Herbert H. Lehman, Democratic nominee for Governor, defeated Colonel William J. Donovan, Republican, yesterday, in the Democratic whirlwind that swept New York State, by a plurality of about 887,000, a record for a Democratic candidate in this State.

Governor Franklin D. Roosevelt and Speaker John N. Garner, the Democratic candidates for President and Vice President, carried the State by a plurality of about 615,000, as against Governor Roosevelt's heretofore record Democratic plurality of 725,000, which he received as candidate for re-election to the Governorship two years ago.

With Governor Roosevelt and Colonel Lehman were swept into office the other Democratic candidates on the State-wide ticket, United States Senator Robert F. Wagner, candidate for re-election; M. William Bray, for Lieutenant Governor; State Controller Morris S. Tremaine, Attorney General John J. Bennett Jr. and the two candidates for Representatives-at-Large, Elmer E. Studley and John Fitzgibbons.

Colonel Lehman led Governor Roosevelt by 88,279 in actual votes cast in New York City and also led the Governor in many cities and counties up-State. His indicated plurality exceeded that of Governor Roosevelt by more than 250,000, but exceeded the indicated plurality for Senator Wagner by only about 35,000.

Returns on the proposition and proposed constitutional amendment were slow in coming in, but a large majority for the proposal to issue $30,000,000 in bonds for unemployment relief was indicated, and scattering returns indicated that the constitutional amendment to throw open the forest reserve to the development of recreational facilities had been beaten.

The vote for President and State-wide candidates follows:

FOR PRESIDENT.

New York City, complete—Roosevelt, Democrat, 1,437,231; Hoover, Republican, 575,031; Thomas, Socialist, 120,486; actual plurality for Roosevelt, 862,200.

Up-State, 431 election districts missing—Roosevelt, 1,022,121; Hoover, 1,254,032; actual plurality for Hoover, 231,911; indicated plurality for Hoover, 247,107; indicated plurality for Roosevelt in the entire State, 615,093.

FOR GOVERNOR.

New York City, complete—Lehman, Democrat, 1,525,510; Donovan, Republican, 542,492; plurality for Lehman, 983,018.

Up-State, 561 election districts missing—Lehman, 1,056,088; Donovan, 1,141,735; actual plurality for Donovan, 85,647; indicated plurality for Donovan, 95,817.

Indicated plurality for Lehman in the entire State, 887,201.

FOR UNITED STATES SENATOR.

New York City, complete—Wagner, Dem., 1,438,343; Medalie, Rep., 517,733; plurality for Wagner, 920,610.

Up-State, 1,301 districts missing—Wagner, 915,699; Medalie, 964,418;

Continued on Page Sixteen.

The President's Message To the President-Elect

From a Staff Correspondent.

PALO ALTO, Cal., Nov. 8.—President Hoover conceded his defeat for re-election at 9:17 o'clock tonight, Pacific Time, and dispatched this telegram of congratulations to Governor Roosevelt:

Palo Alto, Cal., Nov. 8, 1932.

The Hon. Franklin D. Roosevelt,
Biltmore Hotel,
New York, N. Y.

I congratulate you on the opportunity that has come to you to be of service to the country and I wish for you a most successful administration. In the common purpose of all of us I shall dedicate myself to every possible helpful effort.

HERBERT HOOVER.

Governor Roosevelt had not received President Hoover's message when he left for his home shortly before 2 o'clock this morning. Pending its receipt he said he preferred not to make reply or comment on the message.

DEMOCRATS CONTROL STATE SENATE, 26-25

Republican Margin in Assembly of 6 Votes Is Reduced to 2—Lose by 4 Up-State.

ALSO TWO SENATE SEATS

Moffatt Is Re-elected, While Hastings and Dr. Love Are Defeated in City Race.

The slender working majority of two votes by which the Republicans control the present State Senate was swept away in yesterday's Democratic landslide. The next Senate will be made up of 25 Republicans and 26 Democrats, giving the Democrats a majority of one. The present Senate has 27 Republican and 25 Democratic members. Twenty-six votes are required to pass a bill in that branch of the Legislature.

In the Assembly, where 76 votes are required to control legislation, the Republican majority of six is cut down to two in the 1933 Legislature. The Republicans won 77 seats and the Democrats 73 at yesterday's elections for the Assembly.

The Democrats won four Assembly districts north of the Bronx away from the Republicans; one district in Monroe County, one district in Oneida and two in Sullivan and Schoharie counties. The Republicans, however, reduced the up-State Democratic gains by recapturing from them Schuyler county in the southern tier, where last year they succeeded in electing their candidate for the Lower House.

Post Is Defeated.

The Republicans also managed to strengthen their New York City representation by electing Herbert Brownell Jr. in the Tenth (Manhattan) District. This was the district where Langdon W. Post, Democratic incumbent was turned down by Tammany for supporting legislation to broaden the powers and continue the Hofstadter Committee and ran as an independent, polling 5,053 votes. Mr. Brownell defeated his Tammany opponent by a scant plurality of 307 votes. He received 8,907 votes, Sylva La Chappelle, the Democrat, 8,600.

The Democrats gained two Senate districts up-State, the Thirty-first, made up of Rensselaer County, and the Thirty-sixth, made up of Oneida. In the Thirty-fourth, composed of St. Lawrence and Franklin Counties, Warren T. Thayer, the present Republican incumbent, managed to win again after a hard fight.

The New York City Republicans will have three representatives in the Legislature, Senator-elect George Blumberg, who won by a plurality of approximately 500 over Senator John A. Hastings, Democratic incumbent in the Seventh Senatorial

Continued on Page Five.

OVERTURN IN SENATE

Bingham, Watson, Moses and Smoot Are Defeated.

DEMOCRATIC MAJORITY 12

Party Adds to Control in House—May Rule Both Branches This Winter.

LA GUARDIA LOSES SEAT

Mrs. Pratt Defeated, Wadsworth Wins—Texas Sends Garner Back to the House.

The Democratic wave of victory yesterday gave that party complete control of Congress and in its onrush carried down to defeat the four Republican leaders of the Senate.

Senator Smoot of Utah, Republican dean of the Senate and chairman of the powerful Finance Committee; Senator Watson of Indiana, floor leader; Senator Moses, president pro tempore and Senator Jones of Washington, chairman of the Appropriations Committee, all were relegated to the ranks of "lame ducks." No such upset has occurred in recent history.

While returns early this morning showed the new Senate will be Democratic by a majority of twelve and the House overwhelmingly Democratic, there was a possibility that in the session of the old Congress convening on Dec. 5, the Democrats will achieve a slender control of the whole body.

Changes in Coming Session.

They now have a majority of one in the House, in the old Congress that still is to hold a "lame-duck" session; in the Senate the numbers were evened with the defeat of Senator Barbour of New Jersey for the short term beginning next month, and there was, early this morning, an even chance that Colorado would elect Walter Walker, a Democrat, also for the short term. In that event the Senate in December would be: Democrats 49, Republicans 46, Farmer-Labor 1.

On the basis of incomplete returns, the new Senate stood at Democrats 54, Republicans 34, Farmer-Labor 1, and seven States still in doubt.

The next Congress not only will be Democratic; it will be wet.

New York Republicans fared especially ill in the election, which saw Representative La Guardia, fiery "liberal" Republican who led a bloc that controlled the House temporarily in the last session, defeated by J. J. Lanzetta, Democrat. Representative Ruth Pratt also failed of re-election.

Moses Loses in Close Race.

Of the most prominent Republicans who were unseated Senator Watson went down first, conceding his defeat by Frederick Van Nuys, Democrat.

Senator Moses ran nip and tuck with Fred H. Brown, Democrat, until after midnight in the poll of ballots, when returns from Manchester, N. H., spelled his certain defeat.

Senator Smoot was defeated by Professor E. D. Thomas and Mr. Jones by Homer T. Bone. Both of the victors were Democrats. Senator Jones, who is better known as the author of the "five-and-ten" law than for his important committee chairmanship, was defeated coincident with adoption of a State referendum in Washington repealing that State's prohibition law.

An important Republican defeat in the House was that of Representative Haugen of Iowa, co-author of the McNary-Haugen bill, who went down before F. Bierman, Democrat.

McAdoo Wins Seat.

William Gibbs McAdoo, former Democratic Secretary of the Treasury, who was credited with switching the Democratic National Convention to Franklin D. Roosevelt through

Continued on Page Six.

THE PRESIDENT-ELECT.

© New York Times Studio.
Franklin D. Roosevelt.

The Electoral Vote

ROOSEVELT 448.

Alabama	11	Nebraska	7
Arizona	3	Nevada	3
Arkansas	9	New Jersey	16
California	22	New Mexico	3
Colorado	6	New York	47
Florida	7	North Carolina	13
Georgia	12	North Dakota	4
Idaho	4	Ohio	26
Illinois	29	Oklahoma	11
Indiana	14	Rhode Island	4
Iowa	11	South Carolina	8
Kansas	9	South Dakota	4
Kentucky	11	Tennessee	11
Louisiana	10	Texas	23
Maryland	8	Utah	4
Massachusetts	17	Virginia	11
Minnesota	11	Washington	8
Mississippi	9	West Virginia	8
Missouri	15	Wisconsin	12
Montana	4	Wyoming	3

HOOVER 59.

Connecticut	8	New Hampshire	4
Delaware	3	Pennsylvania	36
Maine	5	Vermont	3

DOUBTFUL 24.

Michigan	19	Oregon	5

Votes in Electoral College, 531; needed to elect, 266.

Wets in Control in Both Houses, But Short of Two-Thirds in Senate

Modification of Volstead Act Appears Certain, and House Has Easy Majority for Repeal, but Upper Chamber Support Is Uncertain on Basis of Returns.

Complete control of the next Congress by forces opposed to Federal prohibition was one of the results which came with the political upheaval that took place with yesterday's election.

With full returns from the major portion of the country and definite trends established in the remainder, it appeared certain that those demanding a change in the dry laws would hold between fifty and fifty-five seats in the Senate and 300 or more in the House of Representatives.

Up until an early hour this morning, only nineteen outspoken drys had been returned definitely to the House, while twenty-four Senators, most of whom did not come up for re-election this year, remained among the prohibitionists. Around 100 House seats still were in doubt, and several Senators and re-elected Representatives were yet undecided how to align themselves on the question.

The aggregation chosen yesterday represented a veritable checker-board of views on prohibition reform, but the extent of the majorities indicated a good chance for immediate modification of the Volstead act to allow light wines and beer. The gains in both Houses were chiefly among Democrats, whose party has been pledged to that course.

Modification in the next Congress appeared much more probable on the basis of yesterday's election than outright repeal of the Eighteenth Amendment. Sixty-four Senate seats and 290 in the House will be required for the latter, whereas only a bare majority of 49 in the Senate and 218 in the House would be needed to change the national prohibition (Volstead) law.

The House was sure of the necessary two-thirds for repeal, as early this morning the anti-prohibitionists had already captured 292 seats; the

Continued on Page Eight.

SWEEP IS NATIONAL

Democrats Carry 40 States, Electoral Votes 448.

SIX STATES FOR HOOVER

He Loses New York, New Jersey, Bay State, Indiana and Ohio.

DEMOCRATS WIN SENATE

Necessary Majority for Repeal of the Volstead Act in Prospect.

RECORD NATIONAL VOTE

Hoover Felicitates Rival and Promises 'Every Helpful Effort for Common Purpose.'

Roosevelt Statement.

President-elect Roosevelt gave the following statement to THE NEW YORK TIMES early this morning:

"While I am grateful with all my heart for this expression of the confidence of my fellow-Americans, I realize keenly the responsibility I shall assume and I mean to serve with my utmost capacity the interest of the nation.

"The people could not have arrived at this result if they had not been informed properly of my views by an independent press, and I value particularly the high service of THE NEW YORK TIMES in its reporting of my speeches and in its enlightened comment."

By ARTHUR KROCK.

A political cataclysm, unprecedented in the nation's history and produced by three years of depression, thrust President Herbert Hoover and the Republican power from control of the government yesterday, elected Governor Franklin Delano Roosevelt President of the United States, provided the Democrats with a large majority in Congress and gave them administration of the affairs of many States of the Union.

Fifteen minutes after midnight, Eastern Standard Time, The Associated Press flashed from Palo Alto this line: "Hoover concedes defeat."

It was then fifteen minutes after nine in California, and the President had been in his residence on the Leland Stanford campus only a few hours, arriving with expressed confidence of victory.

A few minutes after the flash from Palo Alto the text of Mr. Hoover's message of congratulation to his successful opponent was received by THE NEW YORK TIMES, though it was delayed in direct transmission to the President-elect. After offering his felicitations to Governor Roosevelt on his "opportunity to be of service to the country," and extending wishes for success, the President "dedicated" himself to "every possible helpful effort * * * in the common purpose of us all."

This language strengthened the belief of those who expect that the relations between the victor and the vanquished, in view of the exigent condition of the country, will be more than perfunctory, and that they may soon confer in an effort to arrive at a mutual program of stabilization during the period between now

New York, Wednesday, November 9, 1932.

Roosevelt Winner in Landslide! Democrats Control Wet Congress; Lehman Governor, O'Brien Mayor

Sweep Is National

Democrats Carry 40 States, Electoral Votes 448.

Six States for Hoover

He Loses New York, New Jersey, Bay State, Indiana and Ohio.

Democrats Win Senate

Necessary Majority for Repeal of the Volstead Act in Prospect.

Record National Vote

Hoover Felicitates and Promises 'Every Helpful Effort for Common Purpose.'

Roosevelt Statement.

President-elect Roosevelt gave the following statement to *The New York Times* early this morning:

"While I am grateful with all my heart for this expression of the confidence of my fellow-Americans, I realize keenly the responsibility I shall assume and I mean to serve with my utmost capacity the interest of the nation.

"The people could not have arrived at this result if they had not been informed properly of my views by an independent press, and I value particularly the high service of *The New York Times* in its reporting of my speeches and in its enlightened comment."

By Arthur Krock.

A political cataclysm, unprecedented in the nation's history and produced by three years of depression, thrust President Herbert Hoover and the Republican power from control of the government yesterday, elected Governor Franklin Delano Roosevelt President of the United States, provided the Democrats with a large majority in Congress and gave them administration of the affairs of many States of the Union.

Fifteen minutes after midnight, Eastern Standard Time, The Associated Press flashed from Palo Alto this line: "Hoover concedes defeat."

It was then fifteen minutes after nine in California, and the President had been in his residence on the Leland Stanford campus only a few hours, arriving with expressed confidence of victory.

A few minutes after the flash from Palo Alto the text of Mr. Hoover's message of congratulation to his successful opponent was received by *The New York Times*, though it was delayed in direct transmission to the President-elect. After offering his felicitations to Governor Roosevelt on his "opportunity to be of service to the country," and extending wishes for success, the President "dedicated" himself to "every possible helpful effort . . . in the common purpose of us all."

This language strengthened the belief of those who expect that the relations between the victor and the vanquished, in view of the exigent condition of the country, will be more than perfunctory, and that they may soon confer in an effort to arrive at a mutual program of stabilization during the period between now and March 4, when Mr. Roosevelt will take office.

The President-elect left his headquarters shortly before 2 A.M. without having received Mr. Hoover's message.

As returns from the Mountain States and the Pacific Coast supplemented the early reports from the Middle West and the eastern seaboard, the President was shown to have surely carried only five States with a total of 51 electoral votes. It is probable that Mr. Roosevelt has captured forty-two States and 472 electoral votes. With two States in doubt he has taken forty States and 448 votes. Only 266 are required for the election of a President. It also appeared certain that the Congress elected by the people yesterday will be wet enough not only to modify the Volstead Act, as pledged in the Democratic platform, but to submit flat repeal of national prohibition.

Republican Strongholds Fall.

The States carried by the President, after weeks of strenuous appeal for re-election on his record, seemed early this morning to have been Delaware, Maine, New Hampshire, Pennsylvania and Vermont. It is possible that complete returns may deprive him of one or more of these, but Connecticut seems to have returned to the Republican standard.

In 1928 Mr. Hoover defeated Alfred E. Smith by a popular plurality of more than 6,300,000 and with a tally of 444 electoral votes to 87. Not only will this equation be more than reversed, according to all indications, but in the final accounting it may be shown that Mr. Smith, who aided powerfully in Governor Roosevelt's cause with especial effects in Massachusetts, Rhode Island, New York and New Jersey was a much less badly defeated candidate than his successful rival of four years ago.

Late returns indicate that such Republican fortresses as Michigan, Ohio, Indiana, Illinois, Kansas, New Jersey, Oregon, Utah, Wisconsin and Wyoming—and even the President's birth State of Iowa and resident commonwealth of California—will join New York and the eleven Southern States which led the van of Governor Roosevelt's overwhelming victory.

A message to *The New York Times* from Ohio, which seemed for a time to be in doubt, is that it will choose the Democratic nominee by more than 200,000, and 100,000 for Mr. Roosevelt is claimed in a telegram from Michigan, where the requirement for Democratic success was to change 100 votes per precinct. In Minnesota and Washington, reporting late, Mr. Roosevelt is leading.

Votes National Grouch.

The country was voting a "national grouch" against three years of business stagnation, against farm foreclosures, bank failures, unemployment and the Republican argument that "things could have been worse." The President's single-handed fight against Democratic changes in the Hawley-Smoot tariff and efforts to impress the country with fear of a change of administration were as futile in the final analysis as straw votes and the reports of newspaper observers indicated that it would be.

Mr. Hoover joins in history Benjamin Harrison and William Howard Taft as the only Republican Presidents who sought and were denied re-election. In the sum, his defeat was greater even than Mr. Taft's in 1912, for while his electoral and popular vote will be greater, he had a united party organization behind him and Mr. Taft was opposed by Theodore Roosevelt and the Bull Moose party.

Political Monuments Fall.

Illinois turned down Senator Otis F. Glenn in favor of Representative William Dietrich. New Jersey refused to re-elect Senator W.W. Barbour, giving his Senate place to Representative Percy H. Stewart. The latest word from Utah was that Senator Reed Smoot, apostle of the Republican high tariff and watchdog of the Treasury, was defeated for re-election.

California appears to have chosen for its Senator W. G. McAdoo, the Democrat who delivered to Governor Roosevelt at Chicago the votes he required to be nominated, over Reverend "Bob" Shuler.

F. Ryan Duffy, opposed as Democratic Senate nominee in Wisconsin by Mr. Hoover's protégé, John B. Chapple, apparently was successful. On every front Republicans were falling and Democrats triumphing in one of those great reversals of party preference by which the American people occasionally signify their acceptance of the dictum that they are "sovereign voters."

The party contest was so close in some States that they veered from Hoover to Roosevelt several times throughout the night.

The party contest was so close in some States that they veered from Hoover to Roosevelt several times throughout the night. Connecticut, which showed a substantial Democratic lead for hours, went into the Republican column at 2 A.M. The same thing was true of candidates for State offices. Thus Senator George H. Moses of New Hampshire, whom Al Smith called "Hawkshaw the detective," was in front for a long time, but about an hour after midnight *The Manchester Union* conceded his defeat by former Governor Brown, Democrat.

In Wisconsin former Governor Walter Kohler and the Democratic candidate for Governor, Mayor A. C. Schmederman of Madison, see-sawed in the tally, with the Mayor on top as dawn approached. There was at no time, however, any doubt that Missouri had elected in the Senate the son of the late Speaker, Colonel Bennett Champ Clark, or that when Kentucky counts tomorrow Senator A. W. Barkley will have been re-elected. Pennsylvania re-elected Senator James J. Davis.

This closeness in some States and local contests may bring the popular vote of the two major candidates nearer than the distance between their electoral vote totals would suggest. Perhaps more than 40,000,000 votes were cast, but Mr. Roosevelt, the overwhelming victor, conceivably might have a plurality of not more than 6,000,000. Norman Thomas, the socialist candidate, seems to have polled more than 1,000,000, but less than the 2,000,000 toward which goal he had set his face.

The defeat of Senator Barbour, and the possible election of a Democrat in Colorado, both victors to take office in December, would mean that the Democrats control the Senate which meets in December and would be able to organize it at once. What will be done about chairmanships for the Progressive Republicans who have helped governor Roosevelt, and what Senator Huey P. Long of Louisiana will do with his "personal bloc," will be earlier issues than March 4 will present. It depends on Colorado.

Defeat Privately Conceded.

Before 9 o'clock, following the discouraging news from New York, Connecticut, Illinois, Massachusetts and Indiana, Republican leaders privately conceded their defeat, although they withheld official acknowledgments. President-elect Roosevelt came early to his headquarters at the Biltmore Hotel, in New York City, where, surrounded by a happy and confident group, he heard the returns and smiled when his campaign and pre-nomination manager, National Chairman James A. Farley, reiterated his often-asserted but now disproved claim that Mr. Hoover would not carry one State.

The President was at his home in Palo Alto for the news. He had reached there this afternoon, weary after thousands of miles and active days and nights of campaigning, but expressing confidence that the people would give him a vote of confidence.

Business as represented by Wall Street has already discounted the result of the election and has expressed its confidence in the future by a general rise in stocks on Monday of this week. When the rise came, the betting was as high as 7 to 1 on Governor Roosevelt and few important members of the financial community doubted that the odds were accurate.

Democrats Elect Governors.

So tremendous a party victory as this one, accomplished by the secession of Republicans and independents from the standard to which they usually rally, insures the victory of many candidates who ordinarily would have no chance.

For this reason there is a possibility that Iowa has elected Louis R. Murphy, a Democrat, to the Senate, and that there will be a Democratic Governor in Michigan, William S. Comstock.

Massachusetts re-elected Governor Joseph B. Ely, a Democrat, and in Illinois the governor will be Judge Henry Horner, the nominee of the party which swept the State and the nation.

In Texas Mrs. Miriam A. Ferguson successfully resisted the fusion movement in the interest of Orville Bullington, Republican nominee for Governor, and she and "Jim" will go back as a governing team to the State Capitol at Austin.

Late returns from Tennessee, where an independent Democrat was contesting with Hill McAlister, the regular Democratic candidate for Governor, are that Mr. McAlister will have a plurality of 25,000.

Returns from Washington, on the Pacific slope, are meager, but the indications favor Homer T. Bone to succeed Senator Wesley I. Jones, author of the prohibition "five-and-ten" act. In Kansas the reports are that John R. Brinkley, the independent "goat gland" candidate for Governor, has been defeated by Governor Harry Woodring, a Democrat.

Indiana sent to its State House Paul V. McNutt, former national commander of the American Legion. Ruth Pratt, New York City's woman Representative, and Representative Fiorello H. LaGuardia went down in the shambles, but a distinguished survivor of the party rout was former Senator James W. Wadsworth of Genesee, N.Y., who was elected to the House of Representatives.

Other curiosities of the returns were that Speaker John N. Garner, the Democratic nominee for Vice President, who was also running for re-election to the House, was successful in both quests, while Governor Roosevelt carried his home district in Dutchess County, New York, but lost his "home town" of Hyde Park.

In Ohio Senator Robert J. Bulkley, a pioneer repealist, was re-elected, as was Senator Robert F. Wagner in New York. Both are Democrats. It also seemed certain that a former Democratic national chairman, Governor George White of Ohio, had successfully resisted the challenge offered by David S. Ingalls, former Assistant Secretary of the Navy for Aviation.

This pin, evoking the Sunflower State, helped Alf Landon to carry his native Kansas—but not much else.

Despite the way it finally turned out, the 1936 campaign made Roosevelt's New Deal strategists anxious. Discordant voices roiled the Democratic party. Al Smith complained of "socialism" and threatened to bolt. Charles Coughlin, a popular and influential anti-Semitic radio preacher, and Huey Long, the populist Governor of Louisiana, seemed poised to form incendiary new movements (Long was assassinated in September 1935). And the Republicans, shocked by new forms of government regulation and an alphabet soup of new agencies, were set to reclaim their historic hold on the executive branch.

But like a long succession of Republicans before him, FDR enjoyed great advantages before the contest even began. As president, he was able to communicate freely and directly with the American people whenever he chose to, which was often. In his first term, he revived the press conference, meeting reporters 337 times, and invented the "fireside chat" to convey his thoughts informally to a receptive audience. These chats continued well into election season, provoking a justifiable outcry from Republicans who knew too well how political they really were.

Left to right:
Franklin Delano Roosevelt (1882–1945)
Alfred Landon (1887–1987)

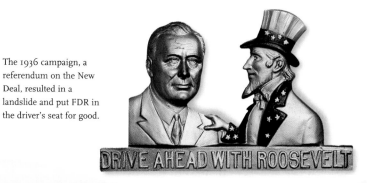

The 1936 campaign, a referendum on the New Deal, resulted in a landslide and put FDR in the driver's seat for good.

If the Republicans were going to occupy the White House again, they needed a candidate who could be equally persuasive. Governor Alf Landon of Kansas, while appealing in many ways, was simply not that man. Landon was a moderate who admired certain aspects of the New Deal. But his campaign was lackluster, and his voice did not exactly electrify radio listeners. He also could not shake off the Roosevelt-haters on the Republican fringe, and toward the end of his campaign, he too drifted into unwise attacks on the administration's "socialism."

For the most part, Roosevelt ignored Landon. The Democratic convention at Philadelphia cheered another memorable FDR speech, invoking a generation's "rendezvous with destiny." FDR attacked his opponents as "economic royalists" and "malefactors of great wealth," which gave more than a tinge of class conflict to the contest.

The campaign was also memorable for its unprecedented reliance on mass communication and a new emphasis on the science of polling. Although a prominent poll taken by the *Literary Digest* before the election predicted a Landon landslide—proving then, as now, that polls are imperfect—both sides realized the importance of taking the pulse of the nation, and deployed agile communication to convert shifting moods into votes.

Another salient feature of the campaign was Democratic success in attracting African-American voters, historically loyal to the party of Lincoln. The Democratic platform, for all its talk of democracy, was silent on race issues but the convention was notable for its symbolic inclusion of black delegates, journalists and speakers. African-Americans noticed, and responded.

By the time election day rolled around, it was clear that Roosevelt would be reelected, but the result exceeded all expectations. He won 523 electoral votes from 46 states, while only Maine and Vermont, with their 8 votes, went Republican. Receiving the news of his triumph in his family home at Hyde Park, New York, FDR blew a smoke ring and said, "Wow."

FDR loved this felt hat, which softened his aristocratic pedigree before an adoring public.

Delegates at the Republican Convention (left) in Chicago raise their glasses in defiance of Wet Laws, 1932.

Just before Alf Landon enjoys Sunday noon roast beef, mashed potatoes, and ice cream at Mrs. A. Young's home *(below)*, "Aunt" Molly Baird has a chance to see what kind of a man the baby she nursed back in the 1880s had grown into—with sixty photographers and reporters and part of the population of West Middlesex, Pennsylvania, still following along, August 1936.

Elephants take part in a Landon parade *(right)* in Indianapolis, October 1936.

E
L
C
O
M
E

FDR makes his acceptance speech at the Democratic convention in Philadelphia, *(above)*, June 1936.

Miss Marion Fore, the Democratic Convention Queen, amid the Texas delegation *(right)*, June, 1936.

YOUNG
DEMOCRATIC
CLUBS
MAINE
WILL
WIN
WITH
SEVELT

Landon is greeted with waving flags *(above)* as he steps out on the platform of the Cleveland Municipal Auditorium, scene of the June Republican convention, October 18, 1936.

FDR confers with his son, John, on the eve of the election *(left)*, November 1936.

"All the News That's Fit to Print."

The New York Times.

FINAL EXTRA
Rain and much colder today. Tomorrow fair, with little change in temperature.
Temperatures Yesterday—Max., 72; Min., 65

VOL. LXXXVI....No. 28,774. Entered as Second-Class Matter, Postoffice, New York, N. Y. NEW YORK, WEDNESDAY, NOVEMBER 4, 1936. TWO CENTS In New York City. | THREE CENTS Within 200 Miles. | FOUR CENTS Elsewhere Except in 7th and 8th Postal Zones.

ROOSEVELT SWEEPS THE NATION; HIS ELECTORAL VOTE EXCEEDS 500; LEHMAN WINS; CHARTER ADOPTED

FEW HOUSE SHIFTS

Democrats May Add to Vast Majorities in Both Chambers

THREE SENATORS TRAIL

Barbour, Hastings and Metcalf Appear to Have Lost Seats.

90 HOUSE RACES IN DOUBT

Democrats Elect 254, While Republicans Obtain 84, and Progressives 6.

By TURNER CATLEDGE

Republican hopes of making heavy inroads upon the huge Democratic majorities in Congress were apparently smothered under the pro-Roosevelt landslide in yesterday's election.

As the size of the New Deal avalanche continued to grow into the early morning hours the Democrats gave promise of actually increasing their lop-sided majority in the Senate and were offsetting Republican gains of new House seats by capturing places now held by anti-New Dealers. If the trend of the count persists in the tardy tabulations today the Democrats may hold their own or actually add to their majorities in both branches of Congress.

In the wreckage left by the Democratic sweep also appeared the Senatorial careers of three outstanding Republican Senators—Barbour of New Jersey, Hastings of Delaware and Metcalf of Rhode Island. As the count from their respective States stood early today, these three incumbents appeared defeated.

Moreover, the Democrats threatened to pick up still another Republican Senate seat, that formerly occupied by the late Senator Couzens, and they were pressing hard upon Senator Lester J. Dickinson of Iowa, whose opposition to the administration's farm relief program won for him the enmity of many farmers in his State.

Lodge Leading Curley

The only present Democratic Senate seat which appeared definitely lost to the Democrats was that held by Senator Marcus Coolidge of Massachusetts. Henry Cabot Lodge 2d, Republican, was well ahead of Governor James M. Curley for this post, despite the State's substantial majority for the remainder of the Democratic national and State ticket.

Still another Democratic berth was threatened. Senator W. J. Bulow, Democrat, was trailing Chandler Gurney, Republican, by a slight margin in South Dakota.

The veteran Senator Norris, who left the Republican fold to stand for re-election as an Independent in Nebraska, was increasing his lead over former Representative Robert G. Simmons, Republican, and Terry Carpenter, "regular" Democrat.

Representative Ernest Lundeen, Farmer-Labor candidate, was piling up a commanding lead over former Governor Theodore Christianson, Republican, in Minnesota.

Senator Borah, Republican dean of the Senate, was doing the same to his opponent, Governor C. Ben Ross, Democrat.

As the Senate count stood early today, the Democrats appeared to have elected twenty of the thirty-six Senators who were up for election this year and the Republicans six, while ten were still in doubt. On this showing the Democrats would have a membership of at least sixty-seven Democrats in the new Congress, the Republicans seventeen, Farmer-Laborites one, and Progressives one. The Democrats stood a good chance to pick up still others out of the ten in

Continued on Page Three

Landon Congratulates President, Who Replies

Special to THE NEW YORK TIMES.

TOPEKA, Wednesday, Nov. 4.—Governor Landon conceded his defeat in a message of congratulation to President Roosevelt at 1:30 o'clock this morning, Eastern standard time.

His message read as follows:

"The nation has spoken. Every American will accept the verdict and work for the common cause of the good of our country. That is the spirit of democracy. You have my sincere congratulations."

"ALF M. LANDON."

Governor Landon decided to send the message after he had retired for the night at the Executive Mansion, with the word that no statement would be issued during the night.

Special to THE NEW YORK TIMES.

HYDE PARK, N. Y., Wednesday, Nov. 4.—Half an hour after receiving Governor Landon's message President Roosevelt sent the following reply:

"I am grateful to you for your generous telegram and I am confident that all of us Americans will now pull together for the common good. I send you every good wish."

UNION PARTY VOTE FAR BELOW BOASTS

Coughlin Group Appears to Have Exercised Little Influence on the Electorate.

SUPPORT OF LEMKE WEAK

Even in Ohio and South Dakota His Showing in the Early Returns Is Poor.

By F. RAYMOND DANIELL

Representative William Lemke, the Presidential candidate of the so-called "lunatic fringe," made scarcely a dent in the great totals the nation piled up for President Roosevelt and Alfred M. Landon in yesterday's voting.

Showing his greatest strength in Illinois, Pennsylvania and Massachusetts, the North Dakota Representative, who had the backing of the Rev. Charles E. Coughlin, Dr. Francis E. Townsend and the Rev. Gerald L. K. Smith, still remained a negligible factor in the outcome of the election.

Despite confident predictions by the Union party's backers last August that Mr. Lemke would take enough votes from Mr. Roosevelt to deprive him of a majority in the Electoral College, thus throwing the election into the House of Representatives, nowhere did he poll a substantial enough vote to hurt either major party candidate.

In his home State of North Dakota the co-author of the Frazier-Lemke bill was trailing far behind the President and his Republican opponent. The first seventy-eight precincts reporting gave Mr. Lemke only 1,280 to Mr. Roosevelt's 11,644 and Mr. Landon's 5,333.

Here in New York, Father Coughlin's candidate for the House of Representatives in the Sixteenth Assembly District was snowed under. He was former State Senator John A. Hastings, an intimate friend of former Mayor James J. Walker. His opponent was Representative John J. O'Connor, who incurred Father Coughlin's wrath by threatening to kick the priest of Royal Oak from the Capitol to the White House. Mr. O'Connor seemed an easy winner in the Sixteenth.

Two reasons were advanced to explain the failure of Mr. Lemke to make a better showing. The first was that Father Coughlin, the Rev. Mr. Smith and Dr. Townsend all were inflationists when it came to estimating the size of their following, which each placed in the neighborhood of 6,000,000 voters. The second was that the men and women who cheered so loudly at the Cleveland conventions of the National Union for Social Justice and Old Age Revolving Pensions Ltd., became Republicans and Democrats again after returning home.

The early vote for Representative William Lemke, even in States where Father Coughlin's National Union for Social Justice boasts a

Continued on Page Five

BIG CHARTER VOTE

8-Hour System for Firemen Also Wins Easily

VOTING CHANGE APPROVED

Brunner Is Victor Over Morris by Large Plurality.

ROOSEVELT SWEEP HERE

President's Vote and Margin, Which Reached 1,356,458, Set Highest City Record.

By RUSSELL B. PORTER

President Roosevelt piled up the largest vote and plurality ever accorded to a candidate for any office in the history of New York City at yesterday's election.

With all the city's 3,799 election districts in, the President had the extraordinary plurality of 1,356,458, which was considerably larger even that his campaign managers had estimated.

This was about 50 per cent larger than his 1932 plurality and about three times former Governor Alfred E. Smith's city plurality when he ran against Herbert Hoover for the Presidency in 1928.

The total Presidential vote was 2,747,240, or over 500,000 more than the total vote cast in the 1932 Presidential election and the 1933 Mayoralty election, the previous records.

Governor Lehman ran behind the President, but had a plurality of 921,938 with no election districts missing. He ran about 2 to 1 ahead of William F. Bleakley, his Republican opponent, while President Roosevelt's ratio was 3 to 1 over Governor Landon. Governor Lehman's plurality was not as large as in 1932, when it was 989,844, but was larger than two years ago, when it was 803,956.

Brunner an Easy Winner

In the day's only election for city office, William F. Brunner, Democrat, had a final plurality of 891,880 over Newbold Morris, Republican, in the contest for president of the Board of Aldermen, with no election districts missing.

The voters approved all three local questions on which referenda were taken. They accepted the new city charter by 927,396 to 583,044, an affirmative majority of 344,354, with 689 election districts missing.

With 78 election districts missing, they voted 898,389 for and 551,914

Continued on Page Four

Smith Plans Comment On the Election Today

Alfred E. Smith, former Democratic candidate for President who espoused the cause of Alfred M. Landon in this campaign said last night that he probably would issue a statement today setting forth his views on President Roosevelt's sweeping victory.

Earlier in the evening he had called THE NEW YORK TIMES to ask how the election was going. He was informed that President Roosevelt was leading in all but a handful of States. He made no comment but when he was asked if he were going to a party of Jeffersonian Democrats in the apartment of Raoul Desvernine, Liberty League lawyer, to which he had been invited, he replied:

"No, I'm going to bed."

P. S.—The former Governor did not retire at once. He called up an hour later to get the latest returns.

DEMOCRATS RETAIN STATE SENATE LEAD

They Are Assured of 30 Seats of the 51, One More Than Their Previous Number.

FAIL TO WIN ASSEMBLY

Republicans Are Beaten for Five Places, but Still Hold a Bare Working Majority.

By W. A. WARN

The Democrats will control the State Senate by a subsantial majority and the Republicans will have a bare working majority in the Assembly, according to complete returns from the legislative elections.

The latest returns give the Democrats thirty seats out of fifty-one in the Senate, a net gain of one over their present quota. The Republicans suffered a loss of five seats in the Assembly, but still retain seventy-six seats, which gives them the constitutional majority necessary to pass bills and prevail on important parliamentary motions.

The result in not a few of the districts, however, on the face of the latest returns was so close that in some instances a demand may be made by the losers for recount proceedings.

This city will lose its only Republican Senator through the defeat of Senator Joseph C. Baldwin 3d in the Seventeenth Senatorial District, situated in Manhattan. Leon A. Fischel, Democrat, carried the district by a plurality somewhat below 5,000.

The Democratic solidarity of Albany County in its legislative representatives surprisingly was broken. A Republican candidate for Assembly, John McBain, nominated in

Continued on Page Five

Roosevelt, Speaking to Victory Procession At Hyde Park, Predicted Record Sweep

By CHARLES W. HURD
Special to THE NEW YORK TIMES.

HYDE PARK, Nov. 3.—With wire returns indicating a landslide for President Roosevelt far in excess of the majority necessary to re-elect him, President Roosevelt said tonight that he thought the "sweep" might carry every section of the United States.

Speaking to several hundred loyal followers who staged a victory procession through rain from Hyde Park to Mr. Roosevelt's home, Hyde Park House, at 10:30 P. M., he said:

"The returns are not all in yet, so I can't say anything official or final, but it looks as though we are going to have one of the largest sweeps ever heard of in the United States."

"As a matter of fact, from the returns now, it looks as though this sweep has carried every single section of the country," he exclaimed.

The President, laughing and happy, spoke while standing on the open porch of his house, looking out over a crowd whose faces were illuminated by red-fire torches and the calcium flares used for light for motion pictures.

He waved aside sound microphones, saying: "This is just a home party."

The crowd cheered the President, Mrs. Roosevelt, and his mother, Mrs. Sara Delano Roosevelt.

The assemblage cheered loudly when Mr. Roosevelt said one of his happiest moments came with the word that he had carried the village of Hyde Park, although he lost the township.

The crowd remained for half an hour, with some enthusiastic persons shouting "How about 1940?"

Mr. Roosevelt leaned on the arm of his son, Franklin Jr. Beside him were his wife and mother. Grouped behind him was a small party including his daughter, Mrs. Anna Boettiger, and Mr. Boettiger, Mrs. James Roosevelt, his daughter-in-law, and other relatives.

Others in the party included Secretary and Mrs. Morgenthau, Judge and Mrs. Sam Rosenman, Frederick A. Delano and members of the White House staff and newspaper correspondents.

LEHMAN VOTE CUT

Bleakley Gets a Surprising Total in the City

SWEEP HELPS GOVERNOR

Roosevelt Strong in Industrial Cities—Gets Big Up-State Poll.

OTHER DEMOCRATS SAFE

Bray, Tremaine, Bennett and Others of State Ticket Regarded Certain of Victory.

By JAMES A. HAGERTY

Governor Herbert H. Lehman was re-elected Governor of New York yesterday for a third term. The indicated plurality for the Governor over former Supreme Court Justice William F. Bleakley, his Republican opponent, was about 600,000.

Governor Lehman, who was urged to become a candidate for re-election to help President Roosevelt, ran far behind the President in New York City. With all the election districts reported, his plurality in New York City was 921,938 as compared with the city plurality of 1,356,458, or more than the million and a quarter predicted by Postmaster General Farley, for President Roosevelt. President Roosevelt's plurality in the State was indicated at about 1,150,000.

The tremendous vote for President Roosevelt in New York City and the failure of Governor Landon to carry up-State by much more than 200,000 indicated that the defection of former Governor Alfred E. Smith and other Jeffersonian Democrats had little effect on the Presidential vote, although there apparently were influences within the Democratic party working against Governor Lehman in New York City.

With New York City complete and 480 election districts missing out of 5,151 up-State, the vote for President was:

	Roosevelt.	Landon.
Up-State	1,187,201	1,370,516
New York City	2,016,204	659,746
Totals	3,213,405	2,030,262

Actual plurality for Roosevelt, 1,183,143.

With New York City complete and 892 election districts missing up-State, the vote for Governor was:

	Lehman.	Bleakley.
Up-State	1,060,564	1,338,892
New York City	1,795,124	873,186
Totals	2,855,688	2,212,078

Actual plurality for Lehman, 643,610.

The tremendous vote for President Roosevelt swept to victory the other State-wide Democratic candidates for re-election, Lieut. Gov. M. William Bray, Controller Morris S. Tremaine, Attorney General John J. Bennett Jr., and Mrs. Caroline O'Day and Matthew J. Merritt, Representatives at Large.

Incomplete returns also indicated the election of Harlan W. Rippey, Democratic candidate for Associate Judge of the Court of Appeals over Supreme Court Justice James P. Hill, Republican candidate.

City Margin Is Unprecedented

President Roosevelt carried New York City by the unprecedented plurality of 1,356,458, the total vote being 2,016,204 for the President and 659,746 for Governor Landon. This was more than 50,000 in excess of the results forecast in the surveys made by the five Democratic county leaders, which they believed should be scaled down 10 per cent to give the probable results.

Governor Lehman's New York City plurality increased with the late returns, and he did not run as far behind the President as the early returns had indicated he would do.

With all election districts reported, the vote for Governor in New

Continued on Page Five

©New York Times Studio Photo.

FRANKLIN D. ROOSEVELT

DEMOCRATS SWEEP ALL PENNSYLVANIA

President Wins by More Than 550,000 in First National Party Victory in 70 Years.

PHILADELPHIA IS CARRIED

Whole State Government and the Legislature Go to Democratic Control.

Special to THE NEW YORK TIMES.

PHILADELPHIA, Wednesday, Nov. 4.—Pennsylvania, the Keystone State of Republicanism, was swept yesterday by the Democrats for the first time in a Presidential election since the Civil War era.

With unprecedented Democratic pluralities in Philadelphia and Allegheny Counties, with greatly diminished Republican pluralities in the commuting counties about Philadelphia, and with even the rural districts only half heartedly Republican, President Roosevelt carried the State by a margin which exceeded 550,000 votes.

Returns from 6,733 of the State's 8,010 divisions gave:

Roosevelt, 2,010,343.
Landon, 1,469,679.
Lemke, 44,253.

Complete returns from the 1,291 divisions in this city gave:

Roosevelt 521,941.
Landon, 322,229.

This city plurality of 199,712 exceeds that for Herbert Hoover in 1932 for the whole State by 40,000.

The Democratic victory, the size of which amazed even the leaders of that party, not only gave to President Roosevelt this State's thirty-six electoral votes, but put the State government wholly in the hands of the Democrats.

Democrats Get Legislature

George H. Earle in 1934 seized the Governorship for the Democrats for the first time in forty-four years. Since assuming office he has been at odds constantly with a Republican-controlled State Senate, which has succeeded in balking many of his plans for putting a "little New Deal" in effect in Pennsylvania.

As a result of yesterday's election

Continued on Page Three

JERSEY'S 16 VOTES SAFE FOR NEW DEAL

Upsets in Republican Areas Add to Huge Pluralities in Democratic Counties.

SMATHERS SEEMS WINNER

Senate Aspirant Runs Behind Roosevelt but Has Lead Over Barbour, Incumbent.

New Jersey's sixteen electoral votes seemed at 5 o'clock this morning in possession of President Roosevelt. Reports from 1,719 of the State's 3,581 election districts gave him 493,071 votes to 295,794 for Governor Landon.

Hudson County, the great Democratic stronghold run by the State leader, Mayor Frank Hague of Jersey City, was responsible for this tremendous lead in what had been a doubtful State until the count began. It seemed quite likely that, although Mr. Landon made gains in other areas, he never could overcome the Hudson County handicap, particularly since several normally powerful Republican communities deserted Landon for Roosevelt.

Keeping pace with President Roosevelt in the Democratic territories, but dropping behind him in many Republican sections which the President dominated, State Senator William H. Smathers, Democrat, had in 1,656 districts a total of 404,546 for United States Senator.

His Republican opponent, W. Warren Barbour, the incumbent, was gathering many hundreds here and there, outside Hudson County, having a total in the same districts of 297,000. Though this seemed a difficult lead to overcome, Mr. Barbour was quite confident that the great number of unreported districts would offset the Smathers advantage and pull him through for another stay in Washington.

Even Mayor Hague's prediction of 125,000 plurality in Hudson County for Roosevelt was so far surpassed as to give him a happy surprise. In 545 districts out of 634 in that county, the President received 204,-

Continued on Page Eleven

POLL SETS RECORD

Roosevelt Electoral Vote of 519 Seen as a Minimum

NO SWING TO THE BOLTERS

'Jeffersonian Democrats' Fail to Cause Rift as Expected.

NEIGHBORS HAIL PRESIDENT.

Landon Concedes Defeat and Sends His Congratulations to Victorious Rival.

By ARTHUR KROCK

Accepting the President as the issue, nearly eight million more voters than ever before had gone to the polls in the United States—about 45,000,000 persons—yesterday gave to Franklin Delano Roosevelt the most overwhelming testimonial of approval ever received by a national candidate in the history of the nation.

Except for the small corner of New England occupied by Maine, Vermont and New Hampshire—which was oscillating between Republican and Democratic in the early morning hours of Wednesday—the President was the choice of a vast preponderance of the voters in all parts of the country, and with him were re-elected as Vice President John N. Garner of Texas and an almost untouched Democratic majority in the House of Representatives. The Democratic national ticket will have a minimum of 519 electoral votes and a possible popular majority of ten millions.

The Republican candidates for President and Vice President, Governor Alfred M. Landon of Kansas and Colonel Frank Knox of Illinois, are the worst-beaten aspirants for these offices in the political annals of the United States, with the exception of William H. Taft in 1912, when Colonel Theodore Roosevelt led a formidable revolt in the Republican party and Mr. Taft carried only Vermont and Utah. Yesterday Utah was also in the President's campaign bag. He had carried forty-five States as contrasted with the forty-two he won from Herbert Hoover in 1932. And to assure his reputation as the greatest vote-getter in the annals of the United States he—a Democrat—had overwhelmingly swept Pennsylvania, unfailingly Republican for generations in national elections.

The following table contains a list of the States carried by the President, with a total of 519 electoral votes, to which the four of New Hampshire may yet be added:

Alabama	11	Nebraska	7
Arizona	3	Nevada	3
Arkansas	9	New Jersey	16
California	22	New Mexico	3
Colorado	6	New York	47
Connecticut	8	North Carolina	13
Delaware	3	North Dakota	4
Florida	7	Ohio	26
Georgia	12	Oklahoma	11
Idaho	4	Oregon	5
Illinois	29	Pennsylvania	36
Indiana	14	Rhode Island	4
Iowa	11	South Carolina	8
Kansas	9	South Dakota	4
Kentucky	11	Tennessee	11
Louisiana	10	Texas	23
Maryland	8	Utah	4
Massachusetts	17	Virginia	11
Michigan	19	Washington	8
Minnesota	11	West Virginia	8
Mississippi	9	Wisconsin	12
Missouri	15	Wyoming	3
Montana	4		

Landon Sends Congratulations

After hours of hopeful waiting on rural districts in the Northeast States, Mr. Landon and the Republican national chairman, John D. M. Hamilton, announced their intentions of letting the night pass before agreeing to the fact of the stupendous party defeat. But about 1 A. M. in Topeka, Mr. Landon sent the customary message of congratulation to the President at Hyde Park, and at 1:45 A. M., at headquarters in Chicago, Mr. Hamilton followed suit. All the important newspapers supporting the Republican ticket (about 90 per cent of the metropolitan and country

Continued on Page Three

New York, Wednesday, November 4, 1936.

Roosevelt Sweeps the Nation; His Electoral Vote Exceeds 500; Lehman Wins; Charter Adopted

Poll Sets Record

Roosevelt Electoral Vote of 519 Seen as a Minimum

No Swing to the Bolters

'Jeffersonian Democrats' Fail to Cause Rift as Expected.

Neighbors Hail President.

Landon Concedes Defeat and Sends His Congratulations to Victorious Rival.

By Arthur Krock

Accepting the President as the issue, nearly eight million more voters than ever before had gone to the polls in the United States—about 45,000,000 persons—yesterday gave to Franklin Delano Roosevelt the most overwhelming testimonial of approval ever received by a national candidate in the history of the nation.

Except for the small corner of New England occupied by Maine, Vermont and New Hampshire—which was oscillating between Republican and Democratic in the early morning hours of Wednesday—the President was the choice of a vast preponderance of the voters in all parts of the country, and with him were re-elected as Vice President John N. Garner of Texas and an almost untouched Democratic majority in the House of Representatives. The Democratic national ticket will have a minimum of 519 electoral votes and a possible popular majority of ten millions.

The Republican candidates for President and Vice President, Governor Alfred M. Landon of Kansas and Colonel Frank Knox of Illinois, are the worst-beaten aspirants for these offices in the political annals of the United States, with the exception of William H. Taft in 1912, when Colonel Theodore Roosevelt led a formidable revolt in the Republican party and Mr. Taft carried only Vermont and Utah. Yesterday Utah was also in the President's campaign bag. He had carried forty-five States as contrasted with the forty-two he won from Herbert Hoover in 1932. And to assure his reputation as the greatest vote-getter in the annals of the United States he—a Democrat—had overwhelmingly swept Pennsylvania, unfailingly Republican for generations in national elections.

The following table contains a list of the States carried by the President, with a total of 519 electoral votes, to which the four of New Hampshire may yet be added:

Alabama 11	Nebraska 7
Arizona 3	Nevada 3
Arkansas 9	New Jersey 16
California 22	New Mexico 3
Colorado 6	New York 47
Connecticut 8	North Carolina 13
Delaware 3	North Dakota 4
Florida 7	Ohio 26
Georgia 12	Oklahoma 11
Idaho 4	Oregon 5
Illinois 29	Pennsylvania 26
Indiana 14	Rhode Island 4
Iowa 11	South Carolina 8
Kansas 9	South Dakota 4
Kentucky 11	Tennessee 11
Louisiana 10	Texas 22
Maryland 8	Utah 4
Massachusetts 17	Virginia 11
Michigan 19	Washington 8
Minnesota 11	West Virginia 8
Mississippi 9	Wisconsin 12
Missouri 15	Wyoming 3
Montana 4	

Landon Sends Congratulations

After hours of hopeful waiting on rural districts, Mr. Landon and the Republican national chairman, John D. M. Hamilton, announced their intentions of letting the night pass before agreeing to the fact of the stupendous party defeat. But about 1 A.M. in Topeka, Mr. Landon sent the customary message of congratulation to the President at Hyde Park, and at 1:45 A.M., at headquarters in Chicago, Mr. Hamilton followed suit. All the important newspapers supporting the Republican ticket (about 90 per cent of the metropolitan and country press) had given up many hours before.

Among the casualties in the voting, along with Governor Landon, Colonel Knox, Chairman Hamilton and a number of Republican Senators and Representatives, were Father Charles E. Coughlin and his Union for Social Justice ticket, headed by Representative William Lemke, who polled a negligible vote, even in his own State of North Dakota, and other minor Socialists. William E. Borah of Idaho and George W. Norris of Nebraska, venerable Senate leaders, were victorious; the youthful Henry Cabot Lodge 3d, Republican, was running far ahead of Governor Curley for the Senatorship in Massachusetts, and two Republican Senators who voted against the Social Security Act, on which the party managers made a last-minute attack—Hastings of Delaware and Metcalf of Rhode Island—were also rejected by the voters in their States. Another Republican casualty was Senator W. Warren Barbour of New Jersey.

South Piles Up a Huge Vote

The "Jeffersonian Democrats," led by such well-known and supposedly influential Democrats as Alfred E. Smith, John W. Davis and James A. Reed, and on whose rejection of the new Deal the Republicans had greatly depended to cut into Southern votes and swing the Northeast away from the President, proved as ineffectual foes as did the Republican campaign candidates and management. The South rolled up tremendous Roosevelt pluralities, and the President carried Philadelphia, Chicago, New York City and Boston by large margins.

Labor, the unemployed and the colored voters, on whose support the Democrats had counted, were visible in the stunning returns from Illinois, Pennsylvania, New York, Ohio and Michigan.

Several thousand neighbors, bearing torches and accompanied by a band playing "Happy Days Are Here Again," visited the President at Hyde Park after it appeared that his victory was established. He stood facing them in a light drizzle and said that, "While I can't say anything official, it appears that the sweep is covering every section." The President, on the arm of his son Franklin, urged press photographers to get through with him because "I've got to get back and get the returns from California."

Soon after 11 P.M. Mr. Farley issued a formal statement in which he congratulated the nation on the results of the election and praised the President for his administrative efforts. He said the final results would show that the President had received "probably the greatest vote of confidence" ever accorded in the United States. The victory was in large measure a personal triumph for Mr. Farley himself, who takes rank as the most successful political manager in the history of the Democratic party. Since he was a steady personal target throughout the Republican campaign, his share in the outcome is particularly gratifying to his associates.

Contest Is Close in Kansas

From a standpoint of sentiment there was a great interest in the close contest between the President and Governor Landon in the Republican nominee's home State of Kansas. The margin was as thin as a razor's edge between them, and shifted several times as the night wore on.

Dissension in the Republican party over chairman Hamilton's conduct of the campaign was foreshadowed early last night when Representative Hamilton Fish of New York criticized the attack on the Social Security Act, for which a large Republican majority in Congress, including the Senate and House leaders, had voted.

The first of the President's non-political leaders to issue a formal statement was John L. Lewis, president of the United Mine Workers of America, to whom is given great credit for the Democratic victory in Pennsylvania—the first in modern political history.

"The people could not be deceived," he said in part. "Labor's Non-Partisan League has justified the expectations and claims of its founders. . . . Labor's strength is being demonstrated in each of the industrial states. Without this unanimity of support the result would have been otherwise."

The outstanding events in the early returns were the colossal majority given to the President in Chicago and his foreshadowed capture of Pennsylvania. Soon after these astonishing facts were being digested, Ohio showed a pro-Roosevelt trend which could give him a majority of 200,000 in a State estimated to be "close," and where 50,000 was the private figure on both sides.

So well was the President running in New England that *The Providence Journal*, a Landon supporter, early conceded that State to Mr. Roosevelt by 30,000 votes.

Every sign, as the returns piled up, was that Republican campaign strategy had come to a disastrous finish. A year ago the prevailing idea among Republican leaders was to make a front assault on the New Deal with an outstanding Eastern candidate, such as Senator Vandenberg of Michigan. Subtler counsels, however, were adopted, and it was decided to swallow half of the New Deal in the platform and nominate a nationally unknown candidate who would provide a powerful personal contrast to the forceful personality of the President. This was done in the selection of Governor Landon.

Outlay Possibly Fifty Millions

Although a year ago the Republicans had little or no hope of electing a President in 1936, the spirit of the Cleveland convention fired them to hope, and this was highly stimulated by the public desertions of their party by such prominent Democrats as Alfred E. Smith, John W. Davis, Lewis W. Douglas and T. Jefferson Coolidge, and by the refusal of Democratic newspapers like *The Baltimore Sun, The St. Louis Post-Dispatch* and *The Omaha World-Herald* (once edited by William Jennings Bryan) to support the President.

The result of this new-found enthusiasm was persuasion of Republican leaders that they could defeat the President, and from this viewpoint came a much more active and expensive campaign than any one would have predicted a year ago. Activity on the Republican side produced a corresponding acceleration of pace, with consequent expense, in Chairman Farley's staff.

The two national committees have and will have confessed to the expenditure of nearly $10,000,000. But, considering the sums spent personally by Republican enthusiasts of great wealth in their own communities and in the nation at large, it is perhaps no wild estimate to conclude that $50,000,000 were expended in the name of politics in the United States between the Cleveland convention in June and yesterday.

Pay Envelope Campaign Starts

The campaign was not particularly interesting in so far as speeches and situations were concerned. But because of the strategy employed and the emotional mood in which partisans on both sides soon found themselves, it will probably stand out in American political history. The issues offered at first by the Republicans—the Presidential candidate, the Vice Presidential candidate and the national committee—were "dictatorship" and general accusations of administration designs against individual liberty; waste, extravagance, political manipulation of relief and spoilsmanship generally; and contempt for the Constitution.

But by mid-October reports from midland States which Mr. Landon had to carry to win were so unsatisfactory that the national committee discharged a petard in reserve. That was an attack in the industrial centers on the Social Security Act in an effort to win back unorganized labor. The payroll contribution of employees was stressed without mention of the employers' levy, and it was contended that, since collections were placed in a Treasury general fund, contributors were always in danger of having any Congress take their money for an extraneous purpose. This propaganda was circulated in payroll envelopes.

When word came to Chairman Farley that the attack on the Social Security Act was affecting labor—one of the President's greatest group reliances—a counter-attack was launched, led by the President himself. This dispute marked the last week of the campaign, and managing politicians were accordingly on tiptoe all last night for returns from such labor centers as Chicago, Detroit, Gary, Indiana, and Pittsburgh.

"Master" Speech Seized Upon

The President himself furnished the Republicans with another eleventh-hour hope in certain passages of his speech at Madison Square Garden in New York City last Saturday night. He said that he "welcomed" the "hatred" of "organized money," and added the hope that, having found his first administration its "match," "organized money" would find his second administration its "master." These remarks, taken from their context, were reported to have alienated many Northeastern voters who were preparing to vote for the President. The campaign ended with a great deal of money being spent by the Republicans to hammer these words home with as much sinister implication as both fact and fancy could furnish.

Throughout the four months between the Cleveland convention and the election, Republican strategy was a matter of revision and change, suggesting that the President's description of the New Deal in his famous "quarterback" simile could be applied to the attack of his political foes. Governor Landon made more speeches than he had planned at first, and the "front porch" Kansas campaign plan went glimmering. In his speech of acceptance he pleaded for quiet and tolerance, but by October he was charging the President with a wish to be dictator, and in the middle of that month he made a sudden trip to California to garner votes of those expectant of the benefits of Dr. Townsend's plan to pay old people $200 a month each.

Roosevelt Extended Schedule

The President's managers, alarmed by the rise in Republican hopes and activities and by news that such States as Massachusetts, New York and Illinois were too close for comfort, prevailed on Mr. Roosevelt greatly to extend his speaking schedule, with the result that he almost duplicated his effort of 1932.

Several factors in addition to control of the executive branch of the government and Congress were in the balance as the voters went to the polls yesterday. The next President will in all likelihood have several appointments to make for justices of the Supreme Court. The party leadership will almost inevitably shift back to this side of the Mississippi River and Chairman John D. M. Hamilton will have to make way for another. Also, Mr. Landon will not be renominated, and the star of Senator Arthur H. Vandenberg of Michigan will rise for 1940.

The waging of the 1940 campaign was almost a secondary concern for Roosevelt as he struggled to prepare America for its inevitable engagement with the Axis powers.

Nineteen forty was that rare campaign shaped by conditions far from America's shores. For Roosevelt, neither renomination nor reelection was a foregone conclusion. His second term had been marred by a series of frustrations, and the taboo against third terms, dating back to George Washington himself, was not easily dismissed. Perhaps as a ploy, Roosevelt professed to seek retirement—he would tell any reporter who asked him about a third term to put on a dunce cap and sit in the corner.

But extraordinary times called for extraordinary measures, and as the grim reality of World War II unfolded, more Americans accepted the inevitable. The Democratic convention in Chicago took place a month after the fall of France, lending a genuine air of emergency to the proceedings. A little chicanery was also involved, and at one point, the convention was drowned out by deafening shouts for Roosevelt, later traced by a *New York Times* reporter to a basement room, where Chicago's Superintendent of Sewers was screaming into a secret loudspeaker. FDR's choice of Henry Wallace to succeed John Nance Garner (who resigned) as Vice President did not go down well among party conservatives, but Wallace proved an able adjutant in speaking to farmers and Midwesterners.

Left to right:
Franklin Delano Roosevelt (1882–1945)
Wendell L. Willkie (1892–1944)

A Willkie button states the most powerful argument of the Republican campaign but voters stuck with FDR despite reluctance to break precedent.

Stung by their last two defeats, the Republicans found an unlikely but formidable campaigner in Wendell Willkie. Willkie was barely a Republican—he was still listed in *Who's Who* as a Democrat, and had never held political office. But the affable, tousle-haired lawyer knew how to sway people. In a sense, he was the first celebrity candidate. In the spring of 1940, Willkie rose like a bamboo shoot in the public eye, propelled by friendly profiles in *Time* and *Life*. Soon, half a million people had joined 4,000 Willkie Clubs. The *Times* called him "the biggest smash since Mickey Mouse." And when Republicans were deadlocked between the early frontrunners, Governor Thomas Dewey of New York, and Senator Robert Taft of Ohio, the delegates flocked to Willkie.

Following his nomination, Willkie gave an acceptance speech in his hometown, Elwood, Indiana. Refreshingly, it showed a man who thought for himself. Willkie endorsed many aspects of the New Deal, and initially refused to attack FDR's foreign policy of active engagement. He then launched an energetic campaign around the nation, traveling 18,759 miles by train, 8,884 by plane, and 2,000 by car. Willkie spoke often, but as the campaign wore on, his attacks on FDR grew harsh, including accusations of "totalitarian" tendencies, and a vitriolic response to the Lend-Lease program, which allowed FDR to send the Allies arms in exchange for deferred payments.

For months, FDR stayed above it all, rejecting Willkie's call for a debate. It was good politics, but he also had much to worry about in the fall of 1940. London was in flames, Hitler seemed invincible and the Allies were turning to America in desperation. Finally, Roosevelt was roused to respond in October, stung by Willkie's attacks and his rising poll figures. In a series of five speeches, he demolished the opposition.

On Election Day, FDR won another landslide, with 449 electoral votes to Willkie's 82. After the election, Willkie and the President resumed cordial relations, and Roosevelt sent Willkie around the world as his personal emissary. There was even short-lived talk of a joint ticket in 1944.

This slogan inadvertantly hints at the great global conflict already under way, which would soon engulf all Americans.

After eight years of New Deal legislation, Republicans were seeking relief from the administration's relief effort.

A Willkie motorcade is ready to ride all the way to Elwood, Indiana, from New York City, August 16, 1940.

Willkiettes stand in formation outside the National Republican Club, New York City, August 1940.

FDR and New York Governor Henry H. Lehman (center) take a hansom ride through New York City on their way to a Democratic rally, October 28, 1940.

FDR gestures during a speech at Madison Square Garden in New York; listening, from left, are former Democratic committee chairman James A. Farley, Tammany leader Christopher Sullivan, and Democratic committee chairman Edward J. Flynn, October 28, 1940.

Former Democratic vice president John Nance Garner makes a call before leaving his office for the last time *(left)*, January 1941.

Willkie tunes in the Democrats *(opposite)*, July 1940.

In an Indiana grove with the temperature 102 degrees in the shade, Wendell L. Willkie faces a coatless throng to deliver his speech accepting the Republican presidential nomination *(below)*, August 1940.

FDR responds to the crowd during a Democratic rally in Madison Square Garden, New York, October 28, 1940.

"All the News That's Fit to Print."

The New York Times.

LATE CITY EDITION
Cloudy, much colder today. To-morrow partly cloudy and rather cold
Temperatures Yesterday—Max., 68; Min., 52

VOL. XC. No. 30,237. Entered as Second-Class Matter, Postoffice, New York, N. Y. NEW YORK, WEDNESDAY, NOVEMBER 6, 1940. THREE CENTS NEW YORK CITY and Vicinity | FOUR CENTS Elsewhere Except in 7th and 8th Postal Zones.

ROOSEVELT ELECTED PRESIDENT; CERTAIN OF 429 ELECTORAL VOTES; DEMOCRATS KEEP HOUSE CONTROL

RETAIN HOUSE GRIP

Democrats, Holding 225 Seats, Gain at Least Ten From Rivals

65 ARE NOW IN DOUBT

Latest Figures Indicate Republican Gain of 1 to 3 Senators

By TURNER CATLEDGE

Unless further complete returns today show more Republican winners in yesterday's election, the Democrats not only will have met successfully the challenge of their opponents to control the house but may actually repair some of the damage to their huge majority in cthe 1938 Congressional election.

The Republicans, on the other hand, may have added from one to three to their roster in the Senate, but this remains to be determined by complete reports.

Returns received up to 4 o'clock this morning indicated that the President's party had dropped only four seats to the opposition, while they had picked up at least ten now held by Republicans. This made the count 225 Democrats, 143 Republicans, one Independent Democrat and one American Labor ,with sixty-five seats still in doubt.

The present House is composed of 259 Democrats, 167 Republicans, one Farmer-Laborite, two Progressives and one American Labor member, with five vacancies due to deaths and resignations.

The status of the Senatorial tabulation at that hour, with thirty-six States in contest—thirty-three for full and three for unexpired terms—showed Democrats, 18; Republicans, 7, and 11 still in doubt. This made sure that the new Senate would have at least 62 Democrats, 22 Republicans, 1 Independent, leaving the 11 in doubt. The present ratio of the Senate is 69 Democrats, 24 Republicans, 1 Progressive, 1 Independent and 1 Farmer-Laborite (Senator Shipstead of Minnesota, who ran this year as a Republican).

The Senate's lone Progressive, Senator Robert M. La Follette, trailed Fred H. Clausen, his Republican opponent, in the earlier returns from Wisconsin, but along in the morning hours he forged ahead and word from the Badger State indicated that he might pull through in the toughest fight of his career.

The four seats dropped by Democrats to Republicans were in the Eighth Oklahoma, Sixteenth New York, Fourth California and the Sixth Misouri districts. More than offsetting these were the ten picked up by the Democrats, including the First, Second and Fourth Connecticut districts and the Congressman at Large of that State; the First and Second Rhode Island districts, the Fift and Twenty-second Pennsylvania districts and the Forty-first New York and the Sixteenth Ohio districts. The Democrats made a clean sweep of the delegations in Connecticut and Rhode Island, annexing six seats held in these two States. Perhaps the greatest upsets in the House were the defeats of Representative Phil Ferguson, Democrat, of Oklahoma by Ross Rizley, Republican, and of the Democratic Representative James Fay of the Sixteenth New York by William E. Pheiffer, Republican.

Incumbent Democrats Sticking

Incumbent Democrats were holding tenaciously to leads in most of the other contests in which they were involved and New Deal nominees were threatening sitting Republican Congressman in a number of districts, particularly in States where the Roosevelt victory was assuming landslide proportions in the popular vote.

The Republicans had entertained no hope from the start of capturing the leadership of the Senate, but they claimed chances of picking up from five to ten new seats to add to the twenty-four they now have.

Continued on Page Two

THE VOTE FOR PRESIDENT

State.	Districts Total.	Districts Reported.	Roosevelt, Democrat.	Willkie, Republican.	Thomas, Socialist.	Electoral Vote Roosevelt.	Electoral Vote Willkie.
Alabama	2,300	1,107	140,984	21,224	....	11	..
Arizona	430	270	40,287	21,603	....	3	..
Arkansas	2,169	642	37,258	8,586	....	3	..
California	13,692	9,594	1,043,200	743,522	....	22	..
Colorado	1,610	387	43,150	54,301	....	..	..
Connecticut	169	166	412,648	358,159	....	8	..
Delaware	249	200	50,890	40,312	....	3	..
Florida	1,451	896	246,183	82,531	....	7	..
Georgia	1,720	896	196,657	29,046	....	12	..
Idaho	792	300	36,113	30,155	....	..	..
Illinois	8,378	6,017	1,514,763	1,375,092	....	29	..
Indiana	3,898	2,185	576,754	576,872	....	..	..
Iowa	2,453	1,505	356,657	376,859	....	..	..
Kansas	2,734	1,377	147,821	216,802	....	..	9
Kentucky	4,341	2,240	297,223	193,622	....	11	..
Louisiana	1,712	481	137,518	22,987	....	10	..
Maine	629	623	154,732	163,782	....	..	5
Maryland	1,331	1,194	351,234	241,447	....	8	..
Massachusetts	1,810	1,151	636,856	575,950	....	17	..
Michigan	3,630	1,349	287,245	387,758	....	..	19
Minnesota	3,696	910	258,715	216,433	....	11	..
Mississippi	1,668	635	87,190	4,179	....	9	..
Missouri	4,479	2,914	526,667	480,110	....	..	..
Montana	1,196	262	43,057	26,829	....	4	..
Nebraska	2,043	1,227	124,825	169,083	....	..	7
Nevada	260	177	15,545	11,213	....	3	..
New Hampshire	294	287	115,932	103,671	....	4	..
New Jersey	3,630	2,038	529,922	564,294*	....	..	16
New Mexico	914	413	60,999	39,300	....	3	..
New York	9,319	9,297	3,231,032	3,021,536	....	47	..
North Carolina	1,926	,686	560,558	175,507	....	18	..
North Dakota	2,262	631	73,669	73,330	....	..	..
Ohio	8,675	7,722	1,485,514	1,385,759	....	26	..
Oklahoma	3,613	2,805	355,766	249,117	....	11	..
Oregon	1,693	923	89,971	89,639	....	..	..
Pennsylvania	8,113	7,132	1,912,401	1,670,032	....	36	..
Rhode Island	259	259	181,881	138,432	....	4	..
South Carolina	1,277	963	81,867	4,144	....	8	..
South Dakota	1,936	1,034	61,211	83,369	....	..	4
Tennessee	2,300	1,891	257,724	119,836	....	11	..
Texas	254	244	504,433	118,198	....	23	..
Utah	831	345	63,298	39,941	....	4	..
Vermont	246	246	64,244	78,355	....	..	3
Virginia	1,714	1,622	223,388	103,030	....	11	..
Washington	3,018	1,083	184,500	102,032	....	8	..
West Virginia	2,300	1,016	217,064	155,680	....	8	..
Wisconsin	3,038	1,782	408,666	377,717	....	12	..
Wyoming	696	490	32,889	31,765	....	..	..
						429	51

*Hudson County returns incomplete.

ROOSEVELT WINNER IN MASSACHUSETTS

Indicated Margin Is Below That of 1936—Saltonstall Ahead in a Close Race

Special to THE NEW YORK TIMES.

BOSTON, Nov. 5—President Roosevelt carried Massachusetts over Wendell Willkie in today's election. Indications tonight were that his margin would be smaller than the 174,000 by which he captured the State's 17 electoral votes four years ago.

The Democratic surge was great enough to re-elect Senator Walsh over Henry Parkman Jr. by a substantial margin and to endanger Governor Leverett Saltonstall's re-election in his contest with Attorney General Paul A. Dever.

Lieut. Gov. Cahill, State Secretary Cook, State Treasurer Hurley and State Auditor Cook apparently were re-elected, while Robert T. Bushnell seemed to have won his contest for Attorney General on the basis of returns which had been counted late tonight.

President Roosevelt was Strongest in the industrial cities outside Boston. He carried Lynn by almost 6,000 votes and New Bedford by a ratio of nearly 2 to 1. It was estimated that Roosevelt's margin in Boston would approach 100,000. He carried Somerville by 4,100 votes.

Governor Saltonstall fared much

Continued on Page Four

The War

Leading developments yesterday in the war, accounts of which appear on Page 25—the first page of the second section, —were as follows:

1. A German pocket battleship appeared in mid-Atlantic and shelled a British convoy.

2. Prime Minister Churchill emphasized before the Commons the growing U-boat threat and said bases in Ireland were needed by Britain.

3. In the Greek-Italian hostilities Rome reported an advance in the Yanina sector, the Greeks were said to be closing in on Koritza and a Yugoslav town was bombed by Italian-type planes.

The summary headed "International Situation" also appears on Page 25.

NEW JERSEY VOTE GOES TO PRESIDENT

Willkie Margin Cut in Normal Republican Areas—Edison and Barbour Win

By RUSSELL B. PORTER

On the basis of incomplete returns at 4 o'clock this morning, President Roosevelt appeared to have carried New Jersey with its sixteen electoral votes by a safe plurality—over Wendell Willkie—drastically reduced from 364,000 margin in 1936, and closer to his 31,000 edge in 1932.

The same returns indicated the election of Charles Edison, former Secretary of the Navy and son of the late Thomas A. Edison, the inventor, over his Republican opponent, State Senator Robert C. Hendrickson. Mr. Edison appeared to have polled more votes than the President.

United States Senator W. Warren Barbour, Republican candidate for re-election, ran far ahead of his ticket, and decisively defeated James H. R. Cromwell, former Minister to Canada and husband of Doris Duke, the tobacco heiress.

Eight hours after the polls closed at 8 P. M. there was still uncertainty over State-wide totals. Only one-half of the State's 3,631 election districts had reported their results by that time, and only a few comparatively of these were from the strong Democratic counties—Hudson, where Mayor Frank Hague of Jersey City, vice chairman of the Democratic National Committee, piled up a big Roosevelt vote, and Camden and Middlesex, where big industries with strong Roosevelt labor strength are located.

Big Vote Adds to Delay

The delay in recording the vote from these counties was caused partly by the record-breaking vote, brought out by perfect weather and unprecedentedly heavy registration, partly by the fact that voting machines are not used in these counties, and partly by the traditional withholding of the Hudson County vote until after the Republican counties have reported.

Surrogate John H. Gavin of Hudson County, spokesman for Mayor Hague, estimated early this morning, with the vote still incomplete, that Hudson would give the President and Mr. Edison a plurality of 110,000, including 60,000 in Jersey City. Mr. Cromwell was running far behind.

Four years ago Mr. Roosevelt re-

Continued on Page Twelve

CITY MARGIN WIDE

Lead Totals 727,254—Queens, Richmond Won by Willkie

P. R. SYSTEM UPHELD

Abolition Move Defeated by About 206,550—Simpson Is Elected

By LEO EGAN

Franklin D. Roosevelt piled up a plurality of 727,254 in New York City yesterday as voters in record-breaking numbers went to the polls under clear skies to record their choice for President. This was far short of the 1,375,396 plurality given to him in 1936, when he was a candidate for a second term.

The President carried the three most populous counties in the city but lost Queens and Richmond. Queens gave Wendell Willkie a plurality of 36,875.

Senator James M. Mead, seeking re-election on the Democratic ticket, ran slightly ahead of the President. He carried the city by 845,063, carrying all five counties.

The President's pluralities of 350,610 in Kings, 219,066 in the Bronx and 195,017 in Manhattan were much less than his supporters had counted on except in Manhattan, but they were enough to please them. The Manhattan plurality was larger than expected.

Results in Other Contests

Other features of yesterday's voting in the city were the defeat by an indicated plurality of 206,550 of the proposal to repeal the proportional representation method of selecting members of the City Council, the apparent defeat of Representative James H. Fay in the Sixteenth District, the election of Kenneth F. Simpson, New York County Republican leader, for the Congressional seat now held by Representative Bruce Barton; the election of John Cashmore and Samuel S. Leibowitz, the Democratic candidates for Borough President and County Judge, respectively, in Brooklyn, and the re-election of Representative Vito Marcantonio, outstanding Congressional foe of conscription and the Roosevelt defense program, in the Twentieth Congressional District on Manhattan's upper East Side.

The President carried all but two Assembly districts in Manhattan, losing the Fifteenth and Tenth, and all but three in King's losing the Ninth, Tenth and Twentieth. He swept all eight districts in the Bronx and lost three out of six in Queens.

In all but one borough the friends of proportional representation were able to beat down the proposal to repeal it. If the proposal had been carried the voters would have elected Councilmen next year on the basis of State Senate districts with

Continued on Page Four

WINNERS OF PRESIDENCY AND VICE PRESIDENCY
Franklin Delano Roosevelt — Henry Agard Wallace

DEMOCRATS CARRY STATE BY 230,000

Mead, O'Day, Merritt and Desmond Join President in New York Victory Column

By JAMES A. HAGERTY

For the third time President Franklin D. Roosevelt carried his home State of New York with its forty-seven electoral votes in yesterday's election, this time by a plurality of about 230,000, over Wendell L. Willkie, his Republican opponent.

The vote in New York City with 40 election districts missing out of 4,051 gave Willkie 1,241,501 and Roosevelt 1,937,017, an actual plurality for Roosevelt of 695,516 and an indicated plurality of 700,823.

Outside New York City in 5,004 out of 5,268 election districts, the vote was Willkie 1,685,043, Roosevelt 1,219,817, an actual plurality of 465,276 for Willkie and an indicated plurality of 489,924. This gave the President an actual plurality of 230,240 on these returnst and an indicated plurality of 215,000, which may be slightly higher because of the small number of votes in the unreported districts.

Bruce Barton, Republican candi-

Continued on Page Ten

Bonfires of All Buttons Urged to Heal Bitterness

Public bonfires of all the Democratic and Republican campaign literature and buttons was suggested yesterday by William Allen White, national chairman of the Committee to Defend America by Aiding the Allies, as a means of "healing partisan bitterness and for launching a nation-wide campaign to safeguard American democracy."

Mr. White, in a statement issued last night, urged "unity mass meetings" as soon as possible after election, in a message to the representatives of the group's 717 local chapters in the forty-eight States.

The meetings should be held, he said, "not in the spirit of exaltation on the part of the victorious party but with the idea that we destroy the symbols of partisan bitterness and unite now on a national program of safeguarding American democracy."

PRESIDENT TAKES KEYSTONE STATE

Republican Chairman Concedes Pennsylvania—Guffey Ahead in Senate Race

Special to THE NEW YORK TIMES.

PHILADELPHIA, Wednesday, Nov. 6—Aided by impressive strength in the industrial areas, President Roosevelt apparently duplicated his feat of 1936 and won the thirty-six electoral votes of traditionally Republican Pennsylvania in yesterday's election.

The trend in the senatorial contest between Senator Joseph F. Guffey, Democrat, and Jay Cooke, chairman of the Philadelphia Republican Committee, was in the direction of the re-election of Mr. Guffey, who campaigned on his record of "100 per cent Roosevelt support."

The Democrats, it seemed likely, would gain an undetermined number of seats in the State's Congressional delegation, which had been Republican by nineteen to fifteen, and they appeared to have an even chance of wresting control of the State House of Representatives from the Republicans, who took it over with the election of Governor James two years ago. The Republicans were hopeful of salvaging their majority in the State Senate.

James F. Torrance, Republican State Chairman, conceded Pennsyl-

Continued on Page Four

Willkie Retires Refusing to Give Up; He Declines Any Statement Before Today

Grimly clinging to his avowed determination not to give up the fight, Wendell L. Willkie said at 1:30 this morning that he intended to go to bed in his suite at the Hotel Commodore, and that he would have no statement to make concerning the election until some time after he wakes up this morning.

This information, relayed from his fourteenth-floor suite to the waiting crowd of reporters in the press headquarters downstairs, was the only word that came from Mr. Willkie after he had briefly appeared before a crowd of cheering campaign workers at 12:20 A. M., to say that he was neither afraid nor disheartened, and repudiate indignantly suggestions that he should concede his defeat.

When he appeared at that time before about 1,500 faithful supporters in the Grand Ball Room of the Commodore Hotel, Mr. Willkie pleaded with them not to quit and expressed his confidence that the fight they had jointly waged would eventually be won.

His appearance before his campaign workers came after hours of seclusion in his private suite, where he repeatedly characterized the election as "a horse race" and predicted that the result would not be known definitely until some time today. Mr. Willkie appeared before the crowd of campaign workers at 12:19 A. M.

Holding up both hands to ask for silence while they gave him an earsplitting ovation, Mr. Willkie said:

"Fellow workers: I first want to say to you that I never felt better in my life. I congratulate you in being a part of the greatest crusade of this century. And that the principles for which we have fought will prevail is as sure as that the truth will always prevail.

"And I hope that none of you are either afraid or disheartened because I am not in the slightest.

"I just wanted to come down and thank you so much for being my fellow fighters in this struggle—to

Continued on Page Five

ROOSEVELT LOOKS TO 'DIFFICULT DAYS'

But Tells Celebrators That He Will Carry On for the Country 'Just the Same'

By CHARLES HURD

Special to THE NEW YORK TIMES.

HYDE PARK, Wednesday, Nov. 6—Standing on the portico of his mother's home here, Franklin D. Roosevelt early today acknowledged his re-election with a promise to continue to be "the same Franklin Roosevelt you have known."

He made this statement to several hundred residents of Hyde Park and vicinity who formed a torchlight procession that carried out a tradition marking Democratic political victories with rallies at the old house, a parade formed by Democrats as soon as returns indicated the victory.

"We are facing difficult days in this country," Mr. Roosevelt told the throng, "but I think you will find me in the future just the same Franklin Roosevelt you have known a great many years."

The President beamed on the crowd as he leaned on the arm of his third son, Franklin Jr., in the bright light of flares set in place by motion-picture camera men.

He smiled and waved while hundreds of persons trooped through the grounds from cars parked first in the driveways and afterward on the Albany Post Road, some of them a quarter of a mile away.

President Faces His Neighbors

Behind the President were grouped about forty guests who had been entertained by Mrs. Roosevelt at supper at her cottage at Val-Kill. But the President faced a crowd in which there were no prominent politicians, no industrial leaders.

These were exclusively his neighbors, who bear to him the same relationship as the villagers bore to his father when he was a minor Democratic leader and a friend of President Cleveland.

President Roosevelt walked on to the front porch of Hyde Park house just before midnight, when he finally broke a vigil over tables on which he marked election returns behind locked doors in the dining room of his home.

The first glare of red flares was seen far off down the driveway. Ten minutes later, exactly at midnight, a town band marched into the car park in front of the house.

The President, with Franklin Jr., stood at the right side of the porch.

Continued on Page Two

BIG ELECTORAL VOTE

Large Pivotal States Swing to Democrats in East and West

POPULAR VOTE CUT

First Time in History That Third Term Is Granted President

By ARTHUR KROCK

Over an apparently huge popular minority, which under the electoral college system was not able to register its proportion of the total vote in terms of electors, President Roosevelt was chosen yesterday for a third term, the first American in history to break the tradition which began with the Republic. He carried to victory with him Henry A. Wallace to be Vice President, and continued control of the House of Representatives by the Democrats was also indicated in the returns.

But in many of the larger States so many precincts were still missing early this morning, and the contest in these States was so close, that Wendell L. Willkie, the Republican opponent, whose name Mr. Roosevelt never mentioned throughout the campaign, refused to concede defeat. He said it was a "horse race," and that the result would not be known until today. He went to bed in that frame of mind.

As the returns mounted there seemed little, however, to sustain Mr. Willkie's hope. New York, Massachusetts, Connecticut, Rhode Island, Pennsylvania, Ohio and Illinois, of the greater States, all appeared to have been carried safely by the President. The Solid South had resisted all appeals to revolt against Mr. Roosevelt's quest for a third term. The Pacific and Mountain States were following the national trend.

States for Mr. Roosevelt

States sure or probable for the President are:

Alabama, Arizona, Arkansas, California, Connecticut, Delaware, Florida, Georgia, Illinois, Kentucky, Louisiana, Maryland, Massachusetts, Missouri, Minnesota, Mississippi, Montana, Nevada, New Hampshire, New Jersey, New Mexico, New York, North Carolina, Ohio, Oklahoma, Pennsylvania, Rhode Island, South Carolina, Tennessee, Texas, Utah, Virginia, West Virginia and Wisconsin—electoral votes, 429.

States sure or probable for Mr. Willkie:

Kansas, Maine, Michigan, Nebraska, North Dakota, South Dakota, Vermont—electoral votes 51.

States doubtful or insufficiently reported:

Colorado, Idaho, Indiana, Iowa, Oregon, Washington and Wyoming—electoral votes, 51.

The Electoral Vote

Listing as doubtful nine States, including several like California, Ohio and Indiana, which seem certain to join the Democratic column, there were at 3 A. M. only 51 electoral votes in possible dispute. The President had an apparently certain total of 429, while with more or less security in Mr. Willkie's column were only 51 votes.

No shift or series of shifts could affect the electoral result and the indications were that the President's total would reach from 420 to 470.

Either figure would be much less than the nearly clean sweeps he had in 1932, when he carried forty-two States, and in 1936, when only Maine and Vermont went Republican. And unless the Far West and the Mountain States shall be shown to have given incredible majorities and late returns from the Eastern States pile up the President's votes higher than indications seem to make possible, Mr. Roosevelt's popular majority will be far less than he had against Herbert Hoover and Alf M. Landon.

It appeared early this morning that a maximum of 5,000,000 and a minimum of 2,000,000 would represent the final difference between the popular votes cast for the two major Presidential candidates. The Associated Press tabulation at 1:50 A. M. was 14,879,930 for Mr. Roose-

Continued on Page Two

New York, Wednesday, November 6, 1940.

Roosevelt Elected President; Certain of 429 Electoral Votes; Democrats Keep House Control

Big Electoral Vote

Large Pivotal States Swing to Democrats in East and West

Popular Vote Cut

First Time in History That Third Term Is Granted President

By Arthur Krock

Over an apparently huge popular minority, which under the electoral college system was not able to register its proportion of the total vote in terms of electors, President Roosevelt was chosen yesterday for a third term, the first American in history to break the tradition which began with the Republic. He carried to victory with him Henry A. Wallace to be Vice President, and continued control of the House of Representatives by the Democrats was also indicated in the returns.

But in many of the larger States so many precincts were still missing early this morning, and the contest in these States was so close, that Wendell L. Willkie, the Republican opponent, whose name Mr. Roosevelt never mentioned throughout the campaign, refused to concede defeat. He said it was a "horse race," and that the result would not be known until today. He went to bed in that frame of mind.

As the returns mounted there seemed little, however, to sustain Mr. Willkie's hope. New York, Massachusetts, Connecticut, Rhode Island, Pennsylvania, Ohio and Illinois, of the greater States, all appeared to have been carried safely by the President. The Solid South had resisted all appeals to revolt against Mr. Roosevelt's quest for a third term. The Pacific and Mountain States were following the national trend.

States for Mr. Roosevelt

States sure or probable for the President are:

Alabama, Arizona, Arkansas, California, Connecticut, Delaware, Florida, Georgia, Illinois, Kentucky, Louisiana, Maryland, Massachusetts, Missouri, Minnesota, Mississippi, Montana, Nevada, New Hampshire, New Jersey, New Mexico, New York, North Carolina, Ohio, Oklahoma, Pennsylvania, Rhode Island, South Carolina, Tennessee, Texas, Utah, Virginia, West Virginia and Wisconsin—electoral votes, 429.

States sure or probable for Mr. Willkie:

Kansas, Maine, Michigan, Nebraska, North Dakota, South Dakota, Vermont—electoral votes 51.

States doubtful or insufficiently reported:

Colorado, Idaho, Indiana, Iowa, Oregon, Washington and Wyoming—electoral votes, 51.

Over an apparently huge popular minority . . . President Roosevelt was chosen yesterday for a third term, the first American in history to break the tradition which began with the Republic.

The Electoral Vote

Listing as doubtful nine States, including several like California, Ohio and Indiana, which seem certain to join the Democratic column, there were at 3 A.M. only 51 electoral votes in possible dispute. The President had an apparently certain total of 429, while with more or less security in Mr. Willkie's column were only 51 votes.

No shift or series of shifts could affect the electoral result and the indications were that the President's total would reach from 420 to 470.

Either figure would be much less than the nearly clean sweeps he had in 1932, when he carried forty-two States, and in 1936, when only Maine and Vermont went Republican.

And unless the Far West and the Mountain States shall be shown to have given incredible majorities and late returns from the Eastern States pile up the President's votes higher than indications seem to make possible, Mr. Roosevelt's popular majority will be far less than he had against Herbert Hoover and Alf M. Landon.

It appeared early this morning that a maximum of 5,000,000 and a minimum of 2,000,000 would represent the final difference between the popular votes cast for the two major Presidential candidates. The Associated Pess tabulation at 1:50 A.M. was 14,879,930 for Mr. Roosevelt and 11,980,499 for Mr. Willkie. The United Press figures about the same time were Roosevelt 13,130,419, Willkie 10,726,517.

Mr. Willkie told a cheering group of his supporters assembled . . . "I hear some people shouting 'don't give up!'" he said, "I guess those people don't know me."

President Greets Neighbors

The President, early today, greeted a torchlight procession of his Hyde Park neighbors and, standing on the portico of his mother's house, gave a promise to continue to be "the same Franklin Roosevelt you have known."

Mr. Willkie would not accept the increasing statistics of his opponent's victory, and at 12:30 o'clock this morning he told a cheering group of his supporters assembled at the Hotel Commodore to keep stout hearts and the fight will ultimately be won. About 1,500 persons were present.

"I hear some people shouting 'don't give up!'" he said, "I guess those people don't know me."

Remembering the eye-lash finish of 1916, when the States west of the Mississippi River joined Ohio to re-elect Woodrow Wilson, this was a natural attitude for Mr. Willkie to take. But Ohio had already been conceded by the Cleveland Plain Dealer, one of his chief press supporters. In Indiana, his home State, he was trailing.

In Pennsylvania the story was the same. Connecticut, center of the defense industry, had already entered the Democratic column.

In these circumstances no set of other States can give Mr. Willkie the 266 electoral votes required for a majority.

The campaign which now has drawn to a successful conclusion for the President has been remarkable in many ways. First there was the unexpected nomination of Mr. Willkie by the Republicans. Then there was the so-called "draft" of the President at Chicago, followed by his long inaction as a candidate.

There followed the sledge-hammer campaign of Mr. Willkie which so alarmed the Democratic strategists that they prevailed on Mr. Roosevelt to abandon his plan and to make a vigorous campaign. This he did, with the indicated result of having turned a close and possibly adverse political situation into an electoral landslide.

First Third Term in History

Mr. Willkie based his attack on "politics and incompetence" in the defense program, the spending and deficits of the New Deal, the "drift toward war" which, he said, the President was abetting and the general New Deal philosophy, and defended the two-term tradition.

The Democratic defense was that domestic issues were unimportant, that it was perilous to interrupt the foreign policy of the President and Secretary Hull, and that the Axis powers were anxious for Mr. Roosevelt's defeat.

The President not only did not mention his opponent by name at any time in the campaign; he never discussed the third-term issue or made any defense of his domestic policies or record. Everything was pitched on foreign policy and the mass benefits conferred by the New Deal, and this, plus the personality of Mr. Roosevelt, was successful in making the President the first Chief Executive in history to whom the two-term limitation was not applied. Also he is the first President in history to have been nominated for a third term.

His triumph, though great, was marked by a considerable recession of political strength from his high tide of 1936; by the defection of his own Vice President, John N. Garner, and by the long though passive insurgency of James A. Farley, twice the President's campaign manager.

Of all the voters recorded Vice President Garner was not among them, having apparently refrained from voting for the only time in his long career as a test against the third term and the "draft."

All over the country the vote was heavy and was registered early in the day. Rain, sleet, snow and cold weather here and there did not appear to have cut down the volume.

The President . . . never discussed the third-term issue or made any defense of his domestic policies or record. Everything was pitched on foreign policy and the . . . New Deal, and this, plus the personality of Mr. Roosevelt, was successful in making the President the first Chief Executive in history to whom the two-term limitation was not applied.

Considering the bitterness of the campaign, the personal attacks made on the Presidential candidates and one another by speakers, and also Mr. Willkie's assaults on the Democratic bosses in New York, Chicago and Jersey City, the continuous report of an orderly election throughout the country was not the least of its unusual features.

The control of the House of Representatives was also at stake in the election, but not of the Senate, since it is almost mathematically impossible—and certainly impossible politically—for the Republicans to overcome the Democratic majority there. That will endure until 1942.

Wednesday, November 6, 1940

PRESIDENT'S TALK TO FRIENDS

Special to The New York Times

HYDE PARK, Wednesday, Nov. 6—President Roosevelt's informal talk to a gathering of neighbors early today was as follows:

You know, this is a perfectly tremendous surprise. I learned about it—I learned about this party first from the news ticker an hour and a half ago. And the news ticker said something else. It said that neighbors and boosters from the Roosevelt Home Club planned a torchlight parade to the Hyde Park House shortly before midnight. And you could have knocked me down with a feather.

And then the report went on to say of course, it was probably written by a kid—that this has been a regular custom on election night since the Chief Executive entered the field of national politics.

A Memory of Childhood

It seems to me that I and most of us go further back than that. We go back, first, to the campaigns of 1928 and 1930. And then a few old graybeards like me—we go back to 1912 and 1910.

But I think that, except for a very few people in Hyde Park, I go back even further than that. I claim to remember it, but the family say that I do not, and that was the first election of Grover Cleveland in 1884.

I was one and a half years old at that time, and I remember the torchlight parade that came down here that night. As they say, "believe it or not."

. . . We haven't got the full returns yet . . . However, it looks all right.

Pride in Battle for Counties

And one of the things that makes me very happy about this thing is the fact that we have won a very great victory in these three counties of Dutchess, Putnam and Orange, because even though our present Congressman may have been re-elected by a very small majority, the victory of Mr. Steeholm is just as big, nevertheless.

. . . I don't need to tell you that we face difficult days in this country, but I think you will find me in the future just exactly the same Franklin Roosevelt that you have known for a great many years.

My heart has always been here. It always will be. And, by Jove, you know some day, when Elmer (Van Wagner) gets tired of running for Supervisor—oh, I don't know when—ten or twenty years—I might take a shot at that job myself.

It has been fine to see you. Thanks ever so much and I am going to be back here, as you know, just as much as the government of the United States will let me.

Thanks very much!

Having lost three elections in a row to Franklin D. Roosevelt, the Republicans played the youth card in 1944. Thomas Dewey was 42 years old, and the first national candidate born in the twentieth century. He had matinee idol looks, though it was also true, as Alice Roosevelt Longworth jibed, that he resembled the groom on a wedding cake. And he possessed a credible record as both governor of New York, Roosevelt's former launching pad, and a gang-busting district attorney in Manhattan.

In truth, Roosevelt looked haggard in 1944. The pressures of three terms, along with the burden of leading the war effort, had left their mark. The Republicans sounded out several candidates, including General Douglas MacArthur (who withdrew), but in the absence of a clear favorite settled on Dewey, a strong candidate in 1940 before the Willkie boom. He won the nomination on the first ballot, along with a conservative running mate, John W. Bricker, Governor of Ohio. Their platform proclaimed that government interfered too much with business, but in most other respects it remained true to the spirit of the New Deal, a fact FDR made sport of, since the Republicans had spent so much time opposing those very policies.

Left to right:
Franklin Delano Roosevelt (1882–1945)
Thomas E. Dewey (1902–71)

Despite a feeble effort in his final campaign, FDR had come to personify the arsenal of democracy.

There was far less uncertainty about FDR's intentions in 1944 than in 1940. He was renominated in Chicago without a fuss. The key question quickly became the vice presidency. In 1940, the President's choice of Henry Wallace had not gone down well with conservative Democrats. Now, the slot was more critical than ever, considering FDR's declining health. Though Wallace gave a rousing speech seconding Roosevelt's nomination and was cheered by delegates, party bosses had no intention of handing him the job. Amidst a great deal of intrigue, various candidates were rejected as either too liberal (Wallace) or too conservative (James Byrnes). Soon, a "Missouri Compromise" emerged in the form of Harry Truman—a well-liked Senator and staunch New Dealer who had won respect by leading a committee to eliminate wasteful military spending. The wisdom of the selection—probably the most important vice presidential nomination in American history—would take decades to fully appreciate.

As usual, Roosevelt did little campaigning. Dewey relentlessly disparaged the "tired old men" of the New Deal, and later in the campaign, he fastened upon a new accusation, the Administration's alleged links to Communists. An angry FDR called it "the meanest campaign of my life" and counterattacked with a memorable speech before the Teamsters union that excoriated the Republicans for misrepresenting him, and ridiculed the claim that FDR had sent a destroyer to Alaska to rescue his Scotch terrier, Fala.

Dewey responded with fury, but to little effect. Though he worked hard, he remained a stiff campaigner ("the Boy Orator of the Platitude"). Again, pollsters predicted a close election. Again, they were wrong. Roosevelt won his fourth and final election with 432 electoral votes to Dewey's 99. It was a gratifying victory. When Dewey finally conceded at 3 A.M., Roosevelt muttered, "I still think he is a son of a bitch."

Governor Thomas E. Dewey of New York was the young face of the future—or so he thought in 1944.

President Roosevelt stumps on behalf of Senator Robert Wagner of New York at Ebbets Field in Brooklyn *(above)*, October 21, 1944. Mayor Fiorello LaGuardia stands to FDR's far left.

Governor Dewey looks at a cake *(left)* made in the form of the United States Capitol during a visit to his headquaters at the Hotel Roosevelt, in New York City, July 1944.

New Yorkers go to the polls early on Election Day to cast their ballots; this line formed by noon on East Forty-eighth Street, Tuesday, November 7, 1944.

The Dewey entourage gets a Wild West welcome in Valentine, Nebraska, replete with flag-waving cavalrymen, September 1944.

President and Mrs. Roosevelt tour the Hudson Valley, an Election Eve custom, Poughkeepsie, New York, November 6, 1944.

FDR chats with Elmer Van Wagner, town supervisor, after voting at Hyde Park, November 7, 1944.

"All the News That's Fit to Print"

The New York Times.

LATE CITY EDITION
POSTSCRIPT
Considerable cloudiness and milder today; moderate winds.
Temperatures Yesterday—Max.,51; Min.,37
Sunrise, 7:15 A. M.; Sunset, 5:45 P. M.

VOL. XCIV No. 31,700. Entered as Second-Class Matter, Postoffice, New York, N. Y. NEW YORK, WEDNESDAY, NOVEMBER 8, 1944. THREE CENTS NEW YORK CITY

ROOSEVELT WINS FOURTH TERM; RECORD POPULAR VOTE IS CLOSE; DEMOCRATS GAIN IN THE HOUSE

2-DAY LUZON BLOWS SMASH 440 PLANES, 30 JAPANESE SHIPS

Halsey's Fliers Destroy 249 Aircraft, Sink Four Vessels in Sunday Sweep

MANILA FIELDS RAVAGED

Ports and Installations Hit Hard—Enemy Lines to Leyte Defenders Are Strained

BY GEORGE HORNE
By Telephone to The New York Times.

PEARL HARBOR, Nov. 7—Admiral William F. Halsey's Third Fleet carriers spread death and damage over southern Luzon Island in the Philippines for the second successive day on Sunday, sinking another five ships and destroying 249 additional enemy aircraft.

It was a major air strike, apparently an all-out effort to annihilate the Japanese air forces supporting enemy counter-attacks on Leyte, where American military leaders have reported the campaign nearing its final stages.

Over the two days, according to Admiral Chester W. Nimitz's communiqué today, the enemy has lost 440 aircraft, 327 of which were caught and destroyed on the ground and 113 shot down in the air. The principal plane concentrations were found on seven fields in the Manila network. They were Nichols, Clark, Nielson, Lipa, Tarlac, Bambam and Mabalacat.

[The two-day toll of enemy ships sunk or damaged was about thirty.]

Unable to Rise in Strength

As the widespread attacks continue, the enemy air opposition is becoming steadily weaker, as is evidenced by the fact that on the second day all but a few of the lost enemy aircraft were caught on the ground, unable to get into the air.

Terrific damage is being inflicted on port facilities and ground installations in and around Manila harbor. In addition to ships sunk and planes destroyed, many air and surface craft were listed as damaged. Reports on the action were still of a preliminary nature and there was no count of our own losses.

Admiral Nimitz said three oil storage areas were left blazing at the northern section of Clark Field and at the northeast of the field a tremendous explosion was observed, followed by fire. North of Malvar a railroad engine and five tank cars were blown up.

Five Ships Sunk at Manila

In the harbor of Manila the fighters, torpedo planes and dive-bombers sank three cargo ships and an oil tanker, probably sank a destroyer and damaged two destroyers, two destroyer escorts, a trawler and several cargo ships. Fourteen cargo ships were damaged during the two-day attack, in which wave after wave of American planes swept in from the sea to wipe out available enemy strength that might be used to bolster the hard-pressed Japanese forces on Leyte.

Meanwhile the steady attacks on the Bonins and Kuriles are continuing. On Sunday a Liberator of the Eleventh Army Air Force, flying hundreds of miles from our Aleutian bases, hit three small transports off Onnekotan Island in the Kuriles and other Liberators flying with it concentrated on land targets of the island base.

Seven enemy fighters fought the big bombers in a running battle, and guns from three Liberators brought down one and probably destroyed another. Two Liberators were damaged.

Otomari and Tori Island, also in the Kuriles, were attacked.

Seventh Air Force Liberators

Continued on Page 19, Column 2

War News Summarized

WEDNESDAY, NOVEMBER 8, 1944

Japanese Lose 440 Planes

Japanese air power in the Philippines received a staggering blow on Saturday and Sunday when Third Fleet carrier planes destroyed 440 enemy aircraft in the Manila and southern Luzon areas. Nearly thirty ships, including a number of warcraft, were also destroyed or damaged. Our fliers reaped their greatest harvest at seven airfields where they wiped out 327 planes on the ground. Port and ground installations suffered terrific damage. Reports were still incomplete and our own losses were not known. [1:1.]

Nov. 8, 1944
Luzon fields pounded from air

Battle Joined on Leyte

American troops on Leyte were battling elements of four Japanese divisions in the hills north of Ormoc and repulsed three heavy attacks, inflicting great loss on the enemy. The area of Valencia, north of Ormoc, was under American artillery fire. [19:1, with map.]

Tokyo Sees B-29's

The jittery Japanese reported more Superfortresses on reconnaissance flights over Tokyo and surrounding territory. They also said that the Bonins and Volcanos had been bombed. [19:2.] In China the enemy scored by driving to within twenty miles of Liuchow, but in Burma the British captured Kennedy Peak and threatened Fort White and Paletwa. [21:1.]

Grim Fight Below Aachen

The United States First Army fought its way back into the streets of Vossenack in some of the bitterest fighting of the war.

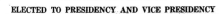

Three German counter-attacks from Schmidt were repulsed. The Sixth Army Group made important advances in the Vosges Mountains and in the Netherlands Allied troops were mopping up the liberated areas. [19:8, with map.]

Soviet Drive Forecast

Behind the lull on Russia's fighting fronts the Red Army was reported to be preparing for a great new offensive. [19:4.] The Athens radio announced that the Greek Government had ordered dissolution of the guerrilla bands Edes and Elas. [19:5.]

Robot Blows at U. S. 'Possible'

A joint Army-Navy statement said that it was "entirely possible" for flying bombs to reach the United States from Europe, but gave no indication such an attack was expected. [19:6-7.]

FISH IS DEFEATED; CLARE LUCE WINS

Congress Veteran Concedes Bennet's Victory—Close Finish in Connecticut

Special to The New York Times.

NEWBURGH, N. Y., Wednesday, Nov. 8—Representative Hamilton Fish, for twelve terms a Republican member of the House and a leading isolationist and critic of President Roosevelt's foreign policy, conceded his defeat by Augustus W. Bennet just before 1 o'clock this morning.

"From reports I have received to date, it looks like I have lost the district by a 5,000 vote majority," he said.

"It looks as if the Republicans have lost the House, and if that is so, as much as I regret it, I have no great desire to continue to serve as a minority member, which I have for the last fourteen years in an uphill fight."

Mr. Bennet, in a victory statement, paid tribute to those who had supported him from all parties, "including the much-abused Political Action Committee." He hailed his election as the result of the citizens' determination "to eliminate Ham Fish from Congress."

Factors in the Result

Heavy Republican defections to Mr. Bennet in Orange County and strong support for Mr. Fish's opponent in the parts of the district in Rockland, Sullivan and Delaware counties sent the Republican nominee down to defeat in the bitterest Congressional election in this part of the State in years.

Complete returns from Orange County gave Fish 35,126 votes to 27,371 for Bennet, a majority for Fish of 7,755. This indicated that Mr. Bennet's majority for the whole Twenty-ninth Congressional District would be about 5,600.

Complete returns from Rockland County gave Bennet 19,706 votes to 12,323 for Fish, a majority of 7,383.

In Sullivan County, with twenty-four election districts missing, including those where Mr. Bennet was expected to run strongest, the vote was Fish 3,877, Bennet 3,776,

Continued on Page 2, Column 7

ROOSEVELT VICTORY CLAIMED IN JERSEY

Hague Spokesmen Also Say Wene Will Win—Constitution Revision Is Rejected

Despite greatly reduced pluralities in Hudson County, Democratic stronghold of New Jersey, lieutenants of Mayor Frank Hague of Jersey City, Democratic boss of the State, predicted shortly before 4 A. M. today that the State's sixteen electoral votes would be delivered to President Roosevelt, largely by virtue of an estimated plurality of 75,000 votes in Hudson. In 1940 Mr. Roosevelt carried the county by a plurality of 100,877.

Mayor Hague's spokesman also predicted victory for the party nominee for the United States Senate, Representative Elmer H. Wene, although by a close vote, and rejection of the proposed revised State Constitution by a substantial margin.

Mr. Hague himself left headquarters in Jersey City early today without making any statement.

The Jersey City predictions were made depsite the fact that eight of the twelve wards in the city had not reported returns up to that hour, but the estimates on the fate of charter revision appeared to be borne out by State-wide returns. At 4 A. M., with 1,311 of the State's 3,657 election districts missing, the vote for rejection was 480,503 to 381,686 for approval.

At the same hour Mr. Dewey was leading Roosevelt by a vote of 481,677 to 456,275, with 1,819 districts missing, and H. Alexander Smith, Mr. Wene's Republican opponent, was leading the Democratic nominee by a vote of 562,261 to 503,763, on the basis of returns from 2,226 districts.

Five Hudson Communities Bolt

The apparent failure of the Hague machine earlier to deliver the expected large Democratic plurality in the county had caused some political observers to place the State in the doubtful class.

Continued on Page 9, Column 4

GET 11 TO 20 SEATS

Victories Blast Hopes of Rivals to Control the House

SENATE UNCHANGED

Democrats Have 180 in House, Republicans 155, 98 in Doubt

By TURNER CATLEDGE

Democratic gains of from eleven to twenty seats in the House and a possible new place or two in the already one-sided Senate, appeared on returns received up to 5 A. M. today to have followed in the wake of yesterday's fourth-term landslide for President Roosevelt.

Republican hopes of controlling the House appeared to have been blasted beyond any possibility of realization and what in the earlier count seemed to portend a G. O. P. gain in the Senate began to fade with the later returns.

These same reports showed the defeat of Representative Hamilton Fish, Republican, of New York, one of the most controversial figures in the lower house; the possible defeat of Senator John A. Danaher, Republican, of Connecticut; a victory for Mrs. Clare Luce, Republican, in a close race in the Fourth Connecticut Congresional District; a trend in the early count against Senator Gerald P. Nye, Republican "isolationist" of North Dakota, and a neck-and-neck contest in which Senator James J. Davis, Republican, of Pennsylvania, was trailing his Democratic opponent, Representative Francis J. Myers, by a slight margin.

Leading Senators Re-elected

These returns also revealed the re-election of Senator Alben W. Barkley, Democratic Majority Leader, in Kentucky; of Senator Scott Lucas, Democrat, in Illinois; of Senator Robert A. Taft, Republican, in Ohio; of Senator Millard Tydings, Democrat, in Maryland, and numerous other sitting Senators, both Democratic and Republican.

With 98 House seats still in doubt, the Democrats had clinched 180 seats in the House of Representatives of the Seventy-ninth Congress; the Republicans were certain of at least 155; the American Labor party of 1 an dthe Progressives of 1.

Seventeen Senate places were still awaiting the decision of the final count, but the Democrats were certain of 49, or an actual majority. The Republicans appeared certain of thirty-one and the Progressives of one.

With the latest returns received the Democrats had garnered a net

Continued on Page 2, Column 5

ELECTED TO PRESIDENCY AND VICE PRESIDENCY

Franklin D. Roosevelt © Perskie

Harry S. Truman Chase-Statler

ROOSEVELT STRONG IN WAR VOTE TALLY

Partial Count of Ballots of Armed Forces Increases President's Majority

By CHARLES GRUTZNER Jr.

The majority given to President Roosevelt by civilian voters who went to the polls throughout the nation yesterday was increased by the count of war ballots marked, some of them as long as two months ago, by members of the armed forces in camps here and in far-flung theatres of operations.

The decisiveness of the President's victory over Governor Dewey removed the possibility that the outcome of the election might hinge on the soldier vote in some of the eleven States that delayed counting their war ballots, but partial returns from States that counted their war ballots yesterday made it clear that the support of the men and women in the armed forces would be a strong factor in building up the final majority of their Commander in Chief.

A breakdown of the vote into civilian and war ballots was slow in coming in from nearly all of the thirty-seven States that counted their soldier vote yesterday, because election officials were concerned chiefly with transmitting

Continued on Page 4, Column 2

Roosevelt Leads as Davis Trails, In Mounting Pennsylvania Count

Special to The New York Times.

PHILADELPHIA, Wednesday, Nov. 8—On the basis of partial returns from all but three of the sixty-seven counties in Pennsylvania, it appeared early that President Roosevelt for the third successive time had captured the State's electoral votes.

Swept on the Roosevelt wave, it appeared, was Representative Francis J. Myers in his race to unseat James J. Davis, 71-year-old Republican Senator who was elected first in 1932 and re-elected six years ago.

Whether the Roosevelt impetus would be sufficient to sweep into office the Democratic candidates for the five State offices remained in doubt. Reports in these instances, lagging far behind the count on the two top contests, were inconclusive.

With 6,012 of 8,202 precincts reporting, President Roosevelt was leading Governor Dewey, 1,282,392, to 1,238,986. Among the returns were all the 1,338 precincts in this city where the President gained a lead of 117,000.

The returns showed that once again the soft coal miners in western Pennsylvania and the anthracite miners in the East repudiated John L. Lewis, president of the United Mine Workers of America, by turning in thumping pluralities for Mr. Roosevelt.

On the other hand, with less than half the precincts reporting and Governor Dewey reducing the President's lead, Republican leaders were hoping that late returns and a fair share of the soldier vote, to be counted on Nov. 22, would mean victory for the party in the State.

Although the President seemed

Continued on Page 8, Column 4

New York for Roosevelt; Wagner Re-elected Senator

By JAMES A. HAGERTY

For the sixth consecutive time, four times as a candidate for President and twice as a candidate for Governor, President Roosevelt carried his home State of New York in yesterday's election and won its forty-seven electoral votes. With 3,609 of the 3,700 election districts in New York City and with 4,978 of the 5,421 election districts outside New York City reporting, President Roosevelt had an actual lead over Governor Dewey, his Republican opponent, of 300,831 and a plurality of about 283,000 for the President in the State was indicated.

Returns from 3,609 election districts out of 3,700 in New York City gave Dewey 1,240,216, Roosevelt 1,966,539. This is an actual plurality of 726,273 and an indicated plurality of 743,700 for for Roosevelt.

Returns from 4,978 election districts out of 5,421 outside New York City gave Dewey 1,585,771, Roosevelt 1,160,329. This is an actual plurality of 425,442 and an indicated plurality of 460,785 for Dewey.

Re-elected in the sweep for the President was United States Senator Robert F. Wagner, who defeated Secretary of State Thomas J. Curran by a plurality probably greater than that for Mr. Roosevelt. Also elected was Associate Judge of the Court of Appeals, Marvin R. Dye, who defeated John Van Voorhis, Republican. The President, Senator Harry S. Truman, candidate for Vice President, Senator Wagner and Mr. Dye, all Democrats, also were nominees of the American Labor and Liberal parties.

Returns from 3,566 election districts of the 3,700 in New York City gave Curran 1,183,020, Wagner 1,957,026. This is an actual plurality of 774,006, and an indicated plurality of 802,900 for Wagner.

Returns from 4,797 of 5,421 election districts outside of New York City gave Curran 1,468,985, Wagner 1,086,736. This is an actual plurality of 382,249, and an indicated plurality of 433,680 for Curran.

Both Houses of the State Legislature remain Republican. Among the greatest upsets in the State was the defeat of former Mayor Rolland B. Marvin of Syracuse, Republican candidate for State Senator in the Forty-third Senatorial District, by Richard P. Byrne, Democratic and American Labor party nominee. On incomplete returns, Senator John J. Dunnigan, Democratic leader of the

Continued on Page 6, Column 4

DEWEY STATEMENT ADMITS HIS DEFEAT

Candidate Concedes Loss of Election at 3:12 A. M. and Congratulates Victor

Gov. Thomas E. Dewey, Republican candidate for President, conceded defeat at 3:12 o'clock this morning.

His statement was made at Republican National Headquarters in the Hotel Roosevelt, where both he and Herbert Brownell Jr., chairman of the National Committee, earlier had refused comment on the growing indication of a lop-sided elcetrical college vote for his Democratic opponent, President Franklin D. Roosevelt.

Mr. Dewey said:

It is clear that Mr. Roosevelt has been re-elected for a fourth term, and every good American will whole-heartedly accept the will of the people.

I extend to President Roosevelt my hearty congratulations and my earnest hope that his next term will see speedy victory in the war, the establishment of lasting peace and the restoration of tranquuillity among our peoples.

I am deeply grateful for the confidence expressed by so many million Americans for their labors in the campaign.

The Republican party emerges from the election revitalized and a great force for the good of the country and for the preservation of free government in America.

I am confident that all Americans will join me in a devout hope that in the years ahead Divine Providence will guide and protect the President of the United States.

President Roosevelt, from his Hyde Park home, acknowledged, at 3:28 o'clock this morning Gov-

Continued on Page 3, Column 2

DEWEY CONCEDES

His Action Comes as Roosevelt Leads in 33 States

BIG ELECTORAL VOTE

Late Returns in Seesaw Battles May Push Total Beyond 400

By ARTHUR KROCK

Franklin Delano Roosevelt, who broke more than a century-old tradition in 1940 when he was elected to a third term as President, made another political record yesterday when he was chosen for a fourth term by a heavy electoral but much narrower popular majority over Thomas E. Dewey, Governor of New York.

At 3:15 A. M. Governor Dewey conceded Mr. Roosevelt's re-election, sending his best wishes by radio, to which the President quickly responded with an appreciative telegram.

Early this morning Mr. Roosevelt was leading in mounting returns in thirty-three States with a total of 391 electoral votes and in half a dozen more a trend was developing that could increase this figure to more than 400. Governor Dewey was ahead in fifteen States with 140 electoral votes, but some were see-sawing away from him and back again. Typical of these were Wisconsin, where he overtook the President's lead about 2 A. M.; Nevada' where Mr. Roosevelt passed him at about the same time, and Missouri.

In the contests for seats in Congress, the Democrats had shown gains of 11 to 20 in the House of Representatives, assuring that party's continued control of this branch. In the Senate the net of losses and gains appeared to be an addition of one Republican to the Senate, which would give that party twenty-eight members—far short of the forty-nine necessary to a majority. A surprise was the indicated defeat of the veteran Pennsylvania Republican, Senator James J. Davis.

Mrs. Luce's Opponent Concedes

The Congressional races were featured by a mass Democratic attempt, in which the President and Vice President Henry A. Wallace personally participated, to unseat Representative Clare Boothe Luce of Connecticut. But shortly after 3 A. M., following a night in which the lead had swung back and forth, her election was conceded by her opponent, Miss Margaret Connors. Some hours before, to his neighbors at Hyde Park, the President had expressed rejoicing over Mrs. Luce's "defeat." Her success is the vitriol in the Democratic honey.

Despite the great general victories by the Democrats, the popular vote will evidently show a huge minority protest against a fourth term for the President. Tabulations by the press associations indicated that the disparity between the ballots cast for the two candidates will be so small that a change of several hundred thousand votes in the key States, distributed in a certain way, would have reversed the electoral majority. At 4:40 A. M. The Associated Press reported 16,387,999 for Mr. Roosevelt and 14,235,051 for Mr. Dewey from more than one-third of the country's election districts. This ratio, if carried through, would leave only about 3,000,000 votes between the candidates.

One of the most interesting struggles for the Presidency was that in Wisconsin, where Mr. Dewey took an early lead, lost it and regained it again. Wisconsin is the State where the late Wendell L. Willkie made his stand for renomination, posing the issue of

Continued on Page 2, Column 3

New York, Wednesday, November 8, 1944.

Roosevelt Wins Fourth Term; Record Popular Vote Is Close; Democrats Gain in the House

Dewey Concedes

His Action Comes as Roosevelt Leads in 33 States

Big Electoral Vote

Late Returns in Seesaw Battles May Push Total Beyond 400

By Arthur Krock

Franklin Delano Roosevelt, who broke more than a century-old tradition in 1940 when he was elected to a third term as President, made another political record yesterday when he was chosen for a fourth term by a heavy electoral but much narrower popular majority over Thomas E. Dewey, Governor of New York.

At 3:15 A.M. Governor Dewey conceded Mr. Roosevelt's re-election, sending his best wishes by radio, to which the President quickly responded with an appreciative telegram.

Early this morning Mr. Roosevelt was leading in mounting returns in thirty-three States with a total of 391 electoral votes and in half a dozen more a trend was developing that could increase this figure to more than 400. Governor Dewey was ahead in fifteen States with 140 electoral votes, but some were see-sawing away from him and back again. Typical of these were Wisconsin, where he overtook the President's lead about 2 A.M.; Nevada, where Mr. Roosevelt passed him at about the same time, and Missouri.

In the contests for seats in Congress, the Democrats had shown gains of 11 to 20 in the House of Representatives, assuring that party's continued control of this branch. In the Senate the net of losses and gains appeared to be an addition of one Republican to the Senate, which would give that party twenty-eight members—far short of the forty-nine necessary to a majority. A surprise was the indicated defeat of the veteran Pennsylvania Republican, Senator James J. Davis.

Mrs. Luce's Opponent Concedes

The Congressional races were featured by a mass Democratic attempt, in which the President and Vice President Henry A. Wallace personally participated, to unseat Representative Clare Booth Luce of Connecticut. But shortly after 3 A.M., following a night in which the lead had swung back and forth, her election was conceded by her opponent, Miss Margaret Connors. Some hours before, to his neighbors at Hyde Park, the President had expressed rejoicing over Mrs. Luce's "defeat." Her success is the vitriol in the Democratic honey.

Despite the great general victories by the Democrats, the popular vote will evidently show a huge minority protest against a fourth term for the President. Tabulations by the press associations indicated that the disparity between the ballots cast for the two candidates will be so small that a change of several hundred thousand votes in the key States, distributed in a certain way, would have reversed the electoral majority. At 4:40 A.M. The Associated Press reported 16,387,999 for Mr. Roosevelt and 14,235,051 for Mr. Dewey from more than one-third of the country's election districts. This ratio, if carried through, would leave only about 3,000,000 votes between the candidates.

One of the most interesting struggles for the Presidency was that in Wisconsin, where Mr. Dewey took an early lead, lost it and regained it again. Wisconsin is the State where the late Wendell L. Willkie made his stand for renomination, posing the issue of "isolationism" versus "internationalism." He ran last in the Presidential primary and expressed the belief, in then withdrawing from the race, that isolationism controlled the thinking of Wisconsin Republicans.

The close race between the President and Mr. Dewey, however, supported the view of others that Mr. Willkie was defeated by a combination between the followers of Mr. Dewey and Harold E. Stassen and that his contrary interpretation was not sound.

Stiff Fight in Pennsylvania

Pennsylvania was another scene of an intense struggle. Mr. Roosevelt got a much reduced majority in Philadelphia, but Allegheny County (Pittsburgh) exceeded expectations, and at 4 A.M. the State's thirty-five electors seemed moving toward Mr. Roosevelt's list.

In Ohio Mr. Dewey's early lead was being cut sharply by the President early this morning. New York's forty-seven electoral votes are certain for Mr. Roosevelt, and, with Illinois, Minnesota, Massachusetts, Connecticut and the 127 electors of the old Confederacy plus Tennessee in his column, the President was far beyond the 266 electors who constitute a majority.

The States in which Mr. Roosevelt was leading at 4 A.M. were:

Alabama, 11; Arizona, 4; Arkansas, 9; California, 25; Connecticut, 8; Delaware, 3; Florida, 8; Georgia, 12, Idaho, 4; Illinois, 28; Kentucky, 11; Louisiana, 10; Mississippi, 9; Maryland, 6; Missouri, 15; Montana, 4; Massachusetts, 16; Minnesota, 11; New Hampshire, 4; New Mexico, 4; New York, 47; Nevada, 3; North Carolina, 14; Oklahoma, 10, Pennsylvania, 35; Rhode Island, 4; South Carolina, 8; Tennessee, 12; Texas, 23; Virginia, 11; West Virginia, 8; Washington, 8, and Utah, 4—Total of 391.

Dewey Leads in New Jersey

The States with margins for Mr. Dewey were:

Colorado, 6; Indiana, 13; Iowa, 10; Kansas, 8; Maine, 5; Michigan, 19; Nebraska, 6; New Jersey, 16; North Dakota, 4; Ohio, 25; Oregon, 6; South Dakota, 4; Vermont, 3; Wisconsin 12, Wyoming, 3—a total of 140.

To win Mr. Dewey was obliged to effect a combination of Massachusetts (or Connecticut), New York (or Pennsylvania), the Border States, the Midwestern States and Oregon on the Pacific Coast. This is because the President, despite the midsummer "revolts" in Texas, South Carolina, Mississippi and Louisiana, was sure to start with 127 certain electors—the old South, plus Tennessee. Mr. Dewey failed to come within spyglass distance of this feat.

Wallace Proves Right

The popular vote ran so close until after 11 o'clock that even the most optimistic supporters of the President were cautious in their claims. But Mr. Wallace was not so timorous. He established a national record as a forecasting statistician by announcing at 9:30 P.M. that the President had been re-elected by a large electoral majority, that he had been given a Democratic House with a "mandate" to carry out his war and post-war program and that "bi-partisan isolationism has been destroyed."

When Mr. Wallace issued this statement few were ready to accept his conclusion. But an hour later he had become a major prophet.

Hillman's Group Effective

Early in the day, throughout the United States, it became evident that the heavy registration was the true portent of a larger vote than was anticipated when the campaign began. Soon after the national conventions were held the predictions in both political camps were for a vote well below that of 1940, under 45,000,000 and perhaps little more than 40,000,000.

Faced with this prospect, Democratic spokesmen openly conceded that so light a vote meant the re-election odds would be against the President and that only with a tally of 45,000,000 or more could his true strength be registered—in which event they were confident of success.

But within a few weeks after the nominations, the Political Action Committee of the Congress of Industrial Organizations, under the chairmanship of Sidney Hillman, began its effort to bring out the vote. Pamphlets urging citizens to go to the polls, and making arguments for Mr. Roosevelt's re-election, were distributed in great numbers in all parts of the country, but particularly in the large cities and even more intensively in those areas where war industry had sprung up and the normal population was much enlarged.

The popular vote ran so close until after 11 o'clock that even the most optimistic supporters of the President were cautious in their claims.

When the registration periods arrived it was demonstrated that these activities of Mr. Hillman's group were very effective. By the end of this period a vote that may exceed 500,000,000 (including ballots from the armed services) was indicated, and Democratic hopes rose accordingly. Reports from the sections where CIO-PAC had been busiest accentuated the view that, in bringing out votes which otherwise might not have been registered, Mr. Hillman's committee had been more vigilant and more successful than the regular Democratic organizations.

One interesting phase of this new note in national political campaigns was that the Hillman group did not neglect the Solid South, where Democratic nomination is equivalent to election and the November vote accordingly is light. To make sure that the President's popular vote would represent his real November strength, and to avert any possibility of an electoral victory without a popular majority—or a popular vote far below the electoral vote of the Democratic national ticket in percentage—the CIO-PAC besought Southern Democrats, especially the war industrial workers, to go to the polls and swell Mr. Roosevelt's general totals.

Not until the returns are all in will it be possible to make an estimate of the degree to which this innovation materialized. But there was no doubt in the minds of the professional politicians, after registration, that in the areas of normally close party division the CIO-PAC has done notable work in preventing a light poll this year.

The proof of this in every large industrial city was received with mixed feelings by the regular Democratic organizations, which hitherto have had all the credit for the votes registered and cast for their ticket. They were obliged to accept a competitor which, they were certain, would not be hesitant in pointing to its contribution in the event of the President's election to a fourth term which, on analysis, would prove to have been achieved by the voters in the large industrial areas where the CIO-PAC is strong and has been very active. This would presage a rivalry for influence and reward in the next administration to which dispute Mr. Hillman and his group could bring impressive support of their claims.

For a space in the campaign, when the Republican orators and organizers concentrated their fire on Mr. Hillman, and he was put down as a liability, the Democratic National Committee subordinated the role of his group as best it could and declined to certify its members as official spokesmen of the President's re-election.

But as the voters turned out yesterday in unusual and unexpected numbers, the dispute was suspended in the mutual wish to win, to be resumed in the event of Mr. Roosevelt's re-election by citizens in PAC territory and demonstrably responsive to its influence. Before the campaign ended Robert E. Hannegan, chairman of the Democratic National Committee, was vigorously defending Mr. Hillman from the Republican attacks and making the PAC cause his own in so far as he could.

Wednesday, November 8, 1944

DEWEY STATEMENT ADMITS HIS DEFEAT

Candidate Concedes Loss of Election at 3:12 A.M. and Congratulates Victor

Gov. Thomas E. Dewey, Republican candidate for President, conceded at 3:12 o'clock this morning.

His statement was made at Republican National Headquarters in the Hotel Roosevelt, where both he and Herbert Brownell Jr., chairman of the National Committee, earlier had refused comment on the growing indication of a lopsided electoral college vote for his Democratic opponent, President Franklin D. Roosevelt.

Mr. Dewey said:

It is clear that Mr. Roosevelt has been re-elected for a fourth term, and every good American will whole-heartedly accept the will of the people.

I extend to President Roosevelt my hearty congratulations and my earnest hope that this next term will see speedy victory in the war, the establishment of lasting peace and the restoration of tranquility among our peoples.

I am deeply grateful for the confidence expressed by so many million Americans for their labors in the campaign.

The Republican party emerges from the election revitalized and a great force for the good of the country and for the preservation of free government in America.

I am confident that all Americans will join me in a devout hope that in the years ahead Divine Providence will guide and protect the President of the United States.

President Roosevelt, from his Hyde Park home, acknowledged at 3:28 o'clock this morning Governor Dewey's concession of defeat in the Presidential election, saying: "I thank you for your statement which I have heard over the air a few minutes ago."

Stephen T. Early, the President's press secretary, in telling correspondents of the President's message to Governor Dewey, denied the radio report that the President had retired and was sleeping.

"The President remained at work at the table throughout the evening and is still there," Mr. Early said.

Earlier in the day Mr. Dewey had limited his comment to a statement that he believed, regardless of the outcome of the balloting, that the Republicans had made a mighty effort toward unity, the war effort and a successful peace.

Former vice president Henry Wallace tried to run in the shadow of FDR, but his leftist politics frustrated many New Dealers, including Eleanor Roosevelt.

The election of 1948 will be forever defined by the photograph of Harry Truman beaming next to the *Chicago Daily Tribune*'s premature headline, "Dewey Defeats Truman." More than half a century later, it still ranks as one of the great upsets in election history.

Truman, who inherited the presidency upon Roosevelt's death in April 1945, had more than his share of adversaries in 1948. The Cold War was growing dangerous, and the Middle East was in chaos. In 1946, Republicans captured Congress for the first time since 1930. Millions of returning GIs urgently needed jobs and housing. Truman's job was not made easier by the lingering fears among both parties that he was less than presidential, especially in comparison to the sainted Roosevelt.

The Republicans mulled over a plethora of candidates, including Harold Stassen, Robert Taft and Douglas MacArthur, but again chose Thomas Dewey as their standard bearer. From Philadelphia, their convention proceedings were beamed into American homes through the new technology of television. The Democrats also met at Philadelphia, where a bitter struggle broke out over the phrasing of a plank on civil rights, a volatile issue for Southern Democrats and the rising number of African-American voters needed by Truman.

Proponents of a strong statement won, but at a heavy cost. Before long, two new parties splintered from the Democrats: the segregationist Dixiecrats, who nominated Governor Strom

Left to right:
Harry S. Truman (1884–1972)
Thomas E. Dewey (1902–71)
James Strom Thurmond (b. 1902)
Henry A. Wallace (1888–1965)

Despite energetic marketing, Dewey never quite escaped Alice Roosevelt Longworth's barb that he resembled the groom on a wedding cake.

Thurmond of South Carolina, and the leftist Progressives, who nominated Henry Wallace, and called for a softer line toward Moscow. The Dixiecrats thought Truman was going too far, too fast on civil rights (he integrated the armed forces that summer by executive order), and the Progressives thought he should go faster.

The highlight of the Philadelphia convention was Truman's delivery of a rip-roaring speech attacking the Republicans, then calling Congress into a summer session. The basic themes of the campaign were set early: Truman hammered away relentlessly at the "Do Nothing" Congress and presented himself as the champion of the New Deal and Fair Deal.

The pace quickened on Labor Day, when Truman began a series of "whistlestop" railroad tours that continued right up to the election. In small towns across America, Truman was blunt, funny and persuasive, especially when ridiculing Congress.

Dewey also crossed America by train, but his speeches were bland in comparison—intentionally so, since he thought he had the election wrapped up. Two-thirds of the nation's dailies had endorsed him (in contrast to 15 percent for Truman), and throughout the campaign, his poll numbers were well above Truman's. But the science of polling was inexact, and failed to capture a large shift for Truman in the final weeks. Despite more than a million votes for each of the splinter parties, Truman captured 303 electoral votes to Dewey's 189—to the amazement and amusement of the electorate.

1948 has been remembered as the triumph of a man who never stopped believing in himself. It was also a reminder that issues matter as much as candidates do. For all his detractors, Truman succeeded in articulating a real program that addressed the future as much as the past. If in some ways this campaign celebrated a disappearing America of small towns and straight talk, it also presaged a contentious debate over a host of divisive issues that would not go away soon.

Truman's whistlestop campaign was the most populistic since FDR's attack on "economic royalists" in 1936, and echoed the campaigns of the Great Commoner, William Jennings Bryan.

Southern Democrats, angered by encroaching ideas about civil rights nominated Governor Strom Thurmond of South Carolina and Governor Fielding Wright of Mississippi as the "Dixiecrat ticket.

LOUISIANA

JOE
'MAHONEY

ALTERNATE
Coca-Cola

Truman

President Truman receives the FDR Memorial Brotherhood Medal from Dr. C. Asapansa Johnson, president of the Interdenominational Ministers, while visiting Harlem *(above)*, October 29, 1948.

Delegates at the Democratic Convention in Philadelphia *(previous pages)*, July 1948.

Thomas E. Dewey holds a press conference in the Governor's mansion in Albany, October 10, 1948.

Delegates rally at the Dixiecrat Convention in Birmingham, Alabama *(left)*, July 17, 1948.

Governor Strom Thurmond of South Carolina accepts the Dixiecrat nomination at the Birmingham convention *(below)*. Convention chairman Walter Stillers, on the left, raps for order, July 17, 1948.

Candidates Henry Wallace and Senator Glen Taylor of Idaho (holding his two-year old son) acknowledge delegates' applause *(right)* at the Progressive Party convention, July 24, 1948.

Campaign supporters wave legal tender at a Henry Wallace rally in Peoria, Illinois *(below)*, May 1948.

Governor Dewey campaigns in Spencer Park, Rock Island, Illinois, September 20, 1948.

Republican headquarters after defeat, November, 3, 1948.

Long before all the votes were counted on election night, the Chicago Daily Tribune published an early edition with the premature banner headline "DEWEY DEFEATS TRUMAN." Truman triumphantly displays the paper on the morning of November 3, 1948, in St. Louis, Missouri.

President Truman and Vice President Alben W. Barkley toast each other with coffee at their inaugural, January 20, 1949.

"All the News That's Fit to Print"

The New York Times.

LATE CITY EDITION
Rain ending tonight. Partly cloudy and mild tomorrow.
Temperature Range Today—Max., 64; Min., 56
Temperature Yesterday—Max., 61; Min., 46
Full U. S. Weather Bureau Report, Page 59

Copyright, 1948, by The New York Times Company.

VOL. XCVIII..No. 33,157. Entered as Second-Class Matter, Postoffice, New York, N. Y. NEW YORK, THURSDAY, NOVEMBER 4, 1948. Times Square, New York 18, N. Y. Telephone LAckawanna 4-1000 THREE CENTS IN NEW YORK CITY

TRUMAN WINS WITH 304 ELECTORAL VOTES; DEMOCRATS CONTROL SENATE AND HOUSE; EUROPE SEES FOREIGN POLICY CONTINUING

NATIONS ARE UNITED IN ASSEMBLY VOTE FOR PEACE PACTS

Marshall and Vishinsky Back Mexican Resolution in U. N. to Bring About Treaties

ATOMIC DEBATE FOLLOWS

Austin Expresses Hope Russia Will Accept the Majority View to Effect Control

By A. M. ROSENTHAL
Special to The New York Times.

PARIS, Nov. 3—The United Nations General Assembly unanimously asked the Big Five today to start a new era of cooperation and a few hours later heard the United States invite Russia to "high level" atomic control negotiations.

Without debate the plenary session of the Assembly gave quick approval to the Mexican resolution calling on the major powers to try again to settle their quarrels and come to agreement on the terms of peace treaties with Germany and Japan.

Mexico's resolution was introduced to leaven the atmosphere of tension and animosity caused by the thrashing out of all major Soviet-West disputes in the full Assembly and in committee rooms. From the beginning it had the support of every member of the Big Five and all small and middle sized powers.

Marshall, Vishinsky Vote Yes

When Dr. Herbert Evatt of Australia, Assembly President, asked for a vote the delegates saw something they had not seen at a plenary session of this Assembly on any important issue. Secretary of State Marshall and Andrei Y. Vishinsky of Russia both raised their hands to vote yes.

But that about ended agreement for the day. The next major item on the agenda was the atomic control controversy, and the Assembly settled down to hear a rehashing of the arguments from the majority and the minority.

The two main documents are before the committee—the Canadian resolution adopted by the Political and Security Committee, and the rejected Soviet motion.

Canada's proposal approves the majority control plan, continues the life of the Atomic Energy Commission and suggests that the sponsors of the United Nations' atomic control idea—Canada and the Big Five—get together to try to break the deadlock.

On the other hand, the Russian resolution would ignore the majority control reports, but would instruct the Atomic Commission to continue. The Russian motion also contains a controversial proposal for simultaneous signing of conventions outlawing the atomic bomb and establishing atomic control.

Austin Accents Talks

The first and only speaker today was Warren R. Austin of the United States. He gave full support to the Canadian resolution, but put the accent on the paragraph dealing with private Big Five Canada talks.

"It is the desire of the United States that these consultations should be at a high level and principally concerned with the cause of the Soviet Union's finding itself at present unwilling or unable to take a cooperative part with other nations in the necessary measures for the maintenance of peace," he said.

Mr. Austin made it clear that he did not expect differences to disappear at the first consultation. But the United States, he said, believes the time is ripe for "quiet and mature discussion in an atmosphere of intelligent deliberation."

"We believe that the terrible problem of atomic energy would provide the framework which would keep constantly before the consulting powers the urgent necessity for agreements on measures which would resolve the present difficulties and which would lift from the hearts of nations the overshadowing fear of atomic warfare," said the United States delegate.

The tenor of the former Vermont Senator's speech was probably the most moderate of any made on the high-powered atomic dispute. He told the delegates that the United States felt that some day Russia would come to believe that it was in her interests to accept foolproof atomic control.

Mr. Austin acknowledged that the United States had gone into the session "just about" convinced that a continuation of the Atomic Commission would be futile. But many other delegates announced

Continued on Page 25, Column 7

10 U. S. Fliers Crash In B-29 in Britain

Special to The New York Times.

LONDON, Nov. 3—A United States B-29 Superfortress, on a routine flight between Scampton airfield in Lincolnshire and the Burtonwood air depot in Lancashire, crashed today with its crew of three officers and seven enlisted men.

Seven bodies had been recovered by nightfall. It was presumed that all aboard had been killed. The crash occurred in one of the lonliest regions of the British Midlands — atop Kinder Scout, a 2,000-foot mountain near Glossop in Derbyshire.

United States Air Force headquarters said tonight that no identification of crew members could be made until the next of kin had been notified. The plane, however, was revealed to be part of the 301st Bomb Group in the United Kingdom.

JAPAN HELD GUILTY OF AGGRESSIVE WAR

Court Cites Attack on China and Designs on Allies in Prelude to Tojo Verdict

By The Associated Press.

TOKYO, Thursday, Nov. 4—The International Military Tribunal held today that Japan was guilty of waging wars of aggression against China and planning similar hostilities against the United States, Britain, Russia and other allied powers.

The ruling came in the first day's reading of the voluminous judgment in the war crimes trial of former Premier Hideki Tojo and twenty-four co-defendants. It covered the period from 1928 to 1938.

The eleven-nation court narrowed the issues down to the simplest terms:

Was Japan guilty of waging aggressive war in violation of international treaties?

Were the twenty-five defendants responsible for making and carrying out those policies?

Were the defendants responsible for crimes against humanity and violations of the laws of war?

Thus far in its reading, the tribunal has declared that "militarists and their supporters" seized control of Japan's Government. This in effect means that any who joined in the seventeen Cabinets since 1928 adopted the militarists' policy as their own.

The court ruled that the Manchurian conquest of 1931 and the full-scale war against China, which opened July 7, 1937, were instigated by militarists and deliberately provoked on the part of Japan.

Earlier, the tribunal cleared the twenty-five defendants of thirty-eight of the fifty-five counts in their war crimes indictment.

It held that in the early 1930's the Japanese Government began preparations for war not only against China but against Russia, Britain, the United States and other Western powers.

The court has not reached the individual verdicts against the prisoners, however.

The tribunal blamed the Japanese Army for fomenting the Sept. 18, 1931, Mukden incident which gave Japan the excuse to seize Manchuria. And the war with China in 1937, it said, was a direct result of the foreign policy adopted

Continued on Page 32, Column 3

WEST IS HOPEFUL

Sees Marshall Plan Aid and Truman Doctrine Being Carried Out

END OF SNARLS FORECAST

Observers on Continent Say Berlin and Other Issues Will Be Discussed Soon

By C. L. SULZBERGER
Special to The New York Times.

MADRID, Nov. 3—As an immediate result of President Truman's astonishing electoral victory, many major foreign political developments that had been halted until after the voting in the United States almost certainly will be activated now more swiftly than had been expected.

Not only has Mr. Truman's reelection established his position in a fashion relatively more impressive to foreign eyes than it was in the past, but the shift in the Congressional picture is bound to convince other nations of the solidity of the United States administration and the permanence of the programs and attitudes adopted by the White House during the last two years.

[Astonishment and relief were expressed in London. Paris sources saw the continuance of the Truman Doctrine and the Marshall Plan. At the United Nations session John Foster Dulles said he believed President Truman would continue the "bipartisan foreign policies that have proved their worth." Dr. Herbert V. Evatt of Australia said the world owed Mr. Truman a tribute for his battles for mankind.]

It is obvious from the views foreign sources expressed before the vote that both the extreme Left and the extreme Right in Europe are disappointed. Likewise the center and non-Communist Left—the so-called "Third Force"—is bound to be delighted because it has derived considerable support from United States diplomacy.

It was generally considered that Moscow would have preferred a Republican victory. One Communist tactic used whenever possible was to attempt to disrupt the center forces and group the anti-Communist opposition as much as possible into coalitions that Kremlin propaganda could label the Right Wing.

One may assume that such would have been the Communist strategy in attacking a Dewey Administration as Rightist, even though it represented a scant change.

The Soviet Union obviously also must have been severely disappointed at the wretched showing of Henry A. Wallace.

Mr. Truman's moral position with "Third Force" elements must certainly now be high, because there was considerable interest abroad in his attitude on civil rights, even though this question

Continued on Page 24, Column 4

SWEEP IN CONGRESS

Democrats Obtain 54-42 Margin in Senate by Winning 9 GOP Seats

CERTAIN OF 258 IN HOUSE

Republicans Have 167, With 9 Still in Doubt—Shifts in Chairmanships Slated

By WILLIAM S. WHITE

The Democrats swept all of Congress yesterday, recapturing the supposedly impregnable Republican House by a landslide and seizing firm control of the Senate in one of the great political revolutions of American history.

As the story of Tuesday's elections yet unfolded in the late counts from the voting places, the first Republican Congress since 1932 looked out upon a scene of catastrophe as it prepared to relinquish its brief two-year tenure of leadership.

Broken were the great bastions of Republican Congressional strength; vanished was the almost universal presumption that no matter what happened to the Senate, the House would stay in Republican hands.

The labor vote, implacably angry over the Taft-Hartley Act and resentful over Republican tax reductions, had moved with strength and determination against the Republican incumbents.

Farm Vote Disappoints GOP

The farm vote had bitterly disappointed the Republicans. Where it did not turn upon them outright, the Democrats made sharp inroads in the grain belts.

President Truman's long campaign against the Eightieth Republican Congress, which he had called either "the worst" or "the second worst" of all time, apparently had a strong appeal at the ballot boxes.

Thus, last night, with all the votes not yet counted, the Democrats had taken in overflowing measure their revenge for their own Congressional rout of 1946.

The clear prospect was that in the Eighty-first Congress of next January the House would be overwhelmingly Democratic with as

Continued on Page 6, Column 3

A VICTORY SMILE AND SALUTE GIVEN BY THE PRESIDENT

Mr. Truman acknowledging plaudits of a crowd outside his hotel in Kansas City. He had just received Governor Dewey's message of congratulations.
Associated Press Wirephoto

DEWEY 'SURPRISED'; WILL NOT TRY AGAIN

Congratulates Truman, Asks Support for Him to Aid National Unity, Peace

By RUSSELL PORTER

After conceding defeat and sending congratulations to President Truman yesterday, Governor Dewey announced he did not intend to seek a third Presidential nomination. He said he had "no plans" about a third term as Governor and denied a reported intention of resigning. His term has two years to run.

In his telegram and in a press conference the Governor urged public support of the President for the sake of national unity and world peace. At the press conference he emphasized "most earnest-

Continued on Page 5, Column 1

Truman Humble in Pledging Service to American People

By ANTHONY LEVIERO
Special to The New York Times.

INDEPENDENCE, Mo., Nov. 3—President Truman accepted this day of supreme triumph in a spirit of humility and with a simple pledge to serve the American people for prosperity and peace. The fire-breathing campaigner, who "passed a miracle" unsurpassed in American political history, today was more like the man who appeared so overawed when he assumed the succession to the late Franklin D. Roosevelt.

Correspondents who have been recording his words in many weeks of hard campaigning gave him an opportunity to have an "I-told-you-so" fling at Thomas E. Dewey and the poll-takers. He had said that today they would be the reddest-faced people in the United States. Mr. Truman did not take the opportunity.

To the American people he rededicated himself to four years of the Presidency with these words:

"I feel very deeply the responsibility which has fallen to my lot as the result of the election. I shall continue to serve the American people to the best of my ability. All my efforts will be devoted to the cause of peace in the world and the prosperity and happiness of our people here at home."

In fewer words, but as feelingly expressed, was his message to Mr. Dewey, who until yesterday was the almost universally acknowledged winner.

"I thank you sincerely for your congratulations and good wishes. Your fine sportsmanship is deeply appreciated. We jointly own con-

Continued on Page 7, Column 3

CHIEF RACE DELAYS REFERENDA COUNT

But Some States Decide Such Issues as War Bonus, Old-Age Aid, Labor Controls

By The Associated Press.

WASHINGTON, Nov. 3—In the general election voters of several states were called upon to decide upon bonuses for veterans of World War II, increased old-age pensions, labor issues and various tax and bond proposals.

The closeness of the Presidential race was delaying today reports on most of the results.

Twelve states posed veterans' benefit questions to their electorates. Reports from six show that Indiana, South Dakota and Louisiana approved bonuses; Nebraska and Wisconsin did not. The Indiana action is not binding on the 1949 Legislature. North Dakota defeated a proposal for a levy for a veterans' rehabilitation fund.

Eight states, in addition to Kansas, had the perennial wet vs. dry issue on the ballot in one form

Continued on Page 18, Column 4

OHIO POLL DECIDES

It Clinches for President in Race Called Miracle of Electioneering

NO RECORD BALLOT IS SEEN

Dedicating Himself to Peace, Prosperity, Truman Says He Wants to Deserve Honor

By ARTHUR KROCK

The State of Ohio, "mother of Republican Presidents," furnished the electoral bloc early yesterday forenoon which assured to President Harry S. Truman a four-year term in his own right as Chief Executive of the United States. Until this late accounting of votes cast in Tuesday's general election put Ohio firmly in Mr. Truman's column, after it had fluctuated throughout the night, he was certain of but 254 electoral votes, which were twelve less than the 266 required.

The historic role played by Ohio was only one of the dramatic and extraordinary phases of the election of 1948. The President, opposed by the extreme right and left wings of the Democratic party, won a minimum of 304 electoral votes as against 189 acquired by his Republican opponent, Gov. Thomas E. Dewey of New York; carried a Democratic majority in Congress along with him after the Republicans had held this for two years; and gained victory through a multi-sectional combination of states that did not include New York, New Jersey, Pennsylvania and four of the Southern states in normal Democratic territory.

Miracle of Electioneering Seen

In the political history of the United States this achievement by Mr. Truman will be set down as a miracle of electioneering for which there are few if any parallels. His victory made him the undisputed national leader of the Democratic party, which, though bitterly divided for the past few years, has acknowledged none since the death of Franklin D. Roosevelt, whom Mr. Truman succeeded from the office of Vice President.

When it was assured that he would have Ohio's electors and hence the majority he needed, and Governor Dewey had wired his congratulations and publicly conceded defeat, the President dedicated his official future to world peace and domestic prosperity and said to his brother, J. Vivian Truman, simply: "I just want to deserve the honor."

No Record Vote Indicated

In the result, unexpected by nearly everyone who qualified as a judge of elections except the President himself, there were these other attendant circumstances:

1. The popular vote, expected to reach 51,000,000 or 52,000,000 and thus break the record poll of about 49,548,000 in the Presidential contest of 1940, will probably be far short of the 1940 total.

2. It is possible that Mr. Truman's plurality over Mr. Dewey will not exceed 2,000,000 and may be less than that, which is smaller than the electoral division of 304 to 189 would ordinarily indicate. But this can be partly attributed to the fact that two splinter Democratic tickets were in the field—the States' Rights Democrats headed by Gov. J. Strom Thurmond of South Carolina, and the Progressives headed by Henry A. Wallace, which will poll almost 2,000,000 votes more than probably would have gone in large measure to the national Democratic ticket in normal circumstances.

3. To the vote cast for Mr. Wallace can be traced definitely the failure of the President to carry only one state, New York, with forty-seven electors.

4. California, after see-sawing all Tuesday night and yesterday morning as in 1916, ended in the Truman column as it did in Woodrow Wilson's contest with Charles E. Hughes thirty-two years ago. But then California made the drama of victory for Wilson; this year Ohio

Continued on Page 3, Column 1

World News Summarized

THURSDAY, NOVEMBER 4, 1948

President Truman's victory in Tuesday's election was assured yesterday when Ohio's final figures gave him that state. He was then certain of at least 304 electoral votes, with 189 for Governor Dewey and 38 for Governor Thurmond on the States' Rights ticket. [1:8.]

The President accepted his victory with humility. Thanking Governor Dewey for his congratulations, Mr. Truman said they both were indebted to the American people, who had shown the world once again "the vitality of our free institutions." [1:6-7.] Mr. Dewey, conceding defeat, urged national unity behind the President "to keep our nation strong and free and establish peace in the world." [1:5.]

Henry A. Wallace did not congratulate the President, but called on him to fulfill his campaign promises. [20:1.]

The Democrats' sweep of Congress in all sections gives them control of the House, with a majority that may reach 100. [1:4], and of the Senate, where the majority reached twelve. [2:2.]

Few immediate changes were seen in the Cabinet. Secretary Marshall wishes to retire to his farm and Secretary Forrestal may resign upon unifying the armed forces. [15:3.]

Labor support and general dissatisfaction with high prices were held responsible for cutting Governor Dewey's plurality in New York to 42,777. [18:3.] The Democrats gained nineteen seats in the Assembly and ten in the Senate. [12:4.]

In the eyes of foreign diplomats, the Truman victory assured a steadier and more vigorous American foreign policy than was possible with a Democratic President and a Republican Congress. [1:3.] A form of lend-lease arms assistance for Western Europe, it was said in Washington, will be started even before the new Congress takes office. [33:2-3.]

Britain saw the Marshall Plan undisturbed as a result of Mr. Truman's election [22:2] and the British people admired his fight. [22:4.] The French felt that their Third Force had been strengthened. [23:2-3.] Germans were encouraged [20:3], as were the Italians. [19:4.] South America felt there would be no important change in the diplomatic corps. [23:4.] The Chinese, however, were disappointed, having looked for more liberal help from Governor Dewey. [1:2-3.] Arab states saw Israel strengthened. [23:6.]

John Foster Dulles and Warren R. Austin, both Republicans, declared in Paris that the bipartisan policy would not be disturbed. [21:1.]

The United Nations General Assembly unanimously approved a Mexican resolution urging the big powers to settle their differences and to speed peace treaties. [1:1.]

The uncoordinated state of internal security controls is a grave threat to the nation's security, Secretary Forrestal told the President and the National Security Council. [33:1.]

The International Military Tribunal for the Far East, reconvening to pass judgment on Tojo, found Japan guilty of waging aggressive war. [1:2.]

Truman Vote Disappoints Nanking; Hope of Full Aid From Dewey Gone

By HENRY R. LIEBERMAN
Special to The New York Times.

NANKING, Thursday, Nov. 4—Manifestly hoping for a Republican victory in the United States elections, high Chinese officials were unable to conceal their disappointment today as the balloting returns, broadcast by American shortwave radio, showed President Truman's re-election.

The surprising vote figures were being carefully tallied in the Government Information Office yesterday afternoon, while Generalissimo Chiang Kai-shek conferred with Premier Wong Wen-hao and tried to persuade the latter not to resign in the midst of the present military, economic and psychological crisis in China.

Other Nanking officials telephoned American correspondents for the last word on the returns that the correspondents themselves were getting by shortwave radio.

Dr. Wong has submitted his resignation three times, but it has not been accepted by the Generalissimo. Before he conferred with Generalissimo Chiang, the harassed Premier asserted his determination to resign at a full meeting of the Cabinet yesterday morning. He was authorized by the Cabinet, as a matter of formal constitutional procedure, to report its resignation to the Generalissimo orally. However, each member was reportedly left free to carry on at his own discretion.

Encouraged by the Republican party platform and Gov. Thomas E. Dewey's campaign statements asserting Democratic neglect of China, the Government had been anticipating fuller American aid under a new administration after it took office in January. But with the time factor made critical by a series of morale-shattering, civil war defeats the Government seemed to be counting even more on the immediate magic

Continued on Page 25, Column 5

Kansas Votes Prohibition Repeal After 68 Years of Dry Experience

By The Associated Press.

TOPEKA, Kan., Nov. 3—Kansas voted repeal of its sixty-eight-year-old constitutional prohibition amendment. Wet forces piled up an apparent 46,000-vote majority in yesterday's voting.

Repeal of the amendment, however, was just the beginning of the fight for legalized liquor in Kansas. The issue now goes to the Legislature where some seats were upset as a result of the repeal vote. Many observers said the vote, which trailed the balloting for national and state offices in this Republican stronghold, was merely a division of wets and drys.

Kansas still has a "bone dry" law on the books which bans transportation and possession of liquor. The Constitution prohibited only manufacture and sale. Repeal means that the Legislature can decide what needs to be done but offers no solution for eliminating the "bone dry" law.

Prohibition leaders, apparently expecting repeal, were working on state legislators before the election. The city voting put repeal across but western dry counties control the State House.

The vote on repeal pulled with it another state matter of major interest to the legislators. They now will get a pay increase.

The end of prohibition as a political issue was predicted yesterday by leaders of the liquor industry when the repeal victory in Kansas was made known. Defeat of prohibition measures in California, Washington and Colorado acted to strengthen this belief.

Vice Admiral F. E. M. Whiting, president of the Licensed Beverage Industries, an association representing all major liquor producers made this comment:

"Kansas can now be added to the list of seventeen countries and provinces which have tried prohibi-

Continued on Page 13, Column 2

Thursday, November 4, 1948.

Truman Wins with 304 Electoral Votes; Democrats Control Senate and House; Europe Sees Foreign Policy Continuing

Ohio Poll Decides

It Clinches for President in Race Called Miracle of Electioneering

No Record Ballot Is Seen

Dedicating Himself to Peace, Prosperity, Truman Says He Wants to Deserve Honor

By Arthur Krock

The State of Ohio, "mother of Republican Presidents," furnished the electoral bloc early yesterday forenoon which assured to President Harry S. Truman a four-year term in his own right as Chief Executive of the United States. Until this late accounting of votes cast in Tuesday's general election put Ohio firmly in Mr. Truman's column, after it had fluctuated throughout the night, he was certain of but 254 electoral votes, which were twelve less than the 266 required.

The historic role played by Ohio was only one of the dramatic and extraordinary phases of the election of 1948. The President, opposed by the extreme right and left wings of the Democratic party, won a minimum of 304 electoral votes as against 189 acquired by his Republican opponent, Gov. Thomas E. Dewey of New York; carried a Democratic majority in Congress along with him after the Republicans had held this for two years; and gained victory through a multi-sectional combination of states that did not include New York, New Jersey, Pennsylvania, and four of the Southern states in normal Democratic territory.

Miracle of Electioneering Seen

In the political history of the United States this achievement by Mr. Truman will be set down as a miracle of electioneering for which there are few if any parallels. His victory made him the undisputed national leader of the Democratic party, which, though bitterly divided for the past few years, has acknowledged none since the death of Franklin D. Roosevelt, whom Mr. Truman succeeded from the office of Vice President.

When it was assured that he would have Ohio's electors and hence the majority he needed, and Governor Dewey had wired his congratulations and publicly conceded defeat, the President dedicated his official future to world peace and domestic prosperity and said to his brother, J. Vivian Truman, simply: "I just want to deserve the honor."

No Record Vote Indicated

In the result, unexpected by nearly everyone who qualified as a judge of elections except the President himself, there were these other attendant circumstances:

1. The popular vote, expected to reach 51,000,000 or 52,000,000 and thus break the record poll of about 49,548,000 in the Presidential contest of 1940, will probably be far short of the 1940 total.

2. It is possible that Mr. Truman's plurality will not exceed 2,000,000 and may be less than that, which is smaller than the electoral division of 304 to 189 would ordinarily indicate. But this can be partly attributed to the fact that two splinter Democratic tickets were in the field—the States' Rights Democrats headed by Gov. J. Strom Thurmond of South Carolina, and the Progressives headed by Henry A. Wallace, which will poll almost 2,000,000 votes more than probably would have gone in large measure to the national Democratic ticket in normal circumstances.

3. To the vote cast for Mr. Wallace can be traced definitely the failure of the President to carry only one state, New York, with forty-seven electors.

4. California, after see-sawing all Tuesday night and yesterday morning as in 1916, and as Ohio did this year, ended in the Truman column as it did in Woodrow Wilson's contest with Charles E. Hughes thirty-two years ago. But then California made the drama of victory for Wilson; this year Ohio had taken the laurels by an hour or two.

5. The winning combination of states for Mr. Truman bore some resemblance to Wilson's in 1916, but there were notable exceptions, such as Iowa and Illinois which the President carried Tuesday in his group of twenty-eight states. His popular and electoral majority differed from Wilson's also in that it was supplied by an unusual combination of

large popular blocks with grievances against the Republican Eightieth Congress which the President had accentuated—such as union labor—contented farmers in normal Republican territory who like the current price levels and did not want to take a chance on a new regime in which they might decline, and urban consumers who, though disturbed over prices, were more disturbed over emotional issues like "civil rights" and Palestine.

6. In the wake of the President's attacks on the record of the Eightieth Congress, centering on tax reduction and the Taft-Hartley Act, a minimum of 258 Democrats were returned to the House of Representatives (the last one had 185) and a minimum of fifty-four to the Senate which, when it recessed, contained only forty-five. The Republicans in the House exchanged 254 for 167, with more losses in sight, and, in the Senate, forty-two members for fifty-one. The fly in this ointment, however, is that under the Democratic label in Congress are two bitterly divided wings of the party which has been unable to cooperate very often for years.

Missouri Maintains Record

7. Missouri, Mr. Truman's home state, maintained the record it has had since 1904 of being on the winning side of every Presidential contest. But Maryland, which had a much longer lien on that record, lost it Tuesday by giving its electors to Governor Dewey.

8. For the first time since the death of President Roosevelt, the United States will have a Vice President and the Senate a President in the person of Albert W. Barkley, now a member of the Senate from Kentucky, the present minority and former majority leader. And Representative Sam Rayburn of Texas will be restored to the Speaker's dais in the Eighty-first Congress.

9. More than fifty members of Congress who helped to make the Taft-Hartley Act into law over Mr. Truman's veto were defeated for re-election. This will likely be reflected in the President's labor legislative policy which he will doubtless present to the Eighty-first Congress.

10. In contests for Governor, Democrats defeated Republican incumbents in eight States, were ejected in one and may be in another—Washington—a net gain of six or seven. The major parties each had twenty-four Governors on election day.

Truman Carries 28 States

The President's victory was so complete and so surprising to almost everyone except himself that analyses of the reasons will recur for years and began yesterday as soon as Ohio's decision was known. But, assuming that California will stay in his column, it was enough for his opponents temporarily to realize that Mr. Truman carried twenty-eight states, in addition to the other victories to which he led his party, and Mr. Dewey sixteen, as follows:

Truman—Arizona, Arkansas, California, Colorado, Florida, Georgia, Idaho, Illinois, Iowa, Kentucky, Massachusetts, Minnesota, Missouri, Montana, Nevada, New Mexico, North Carolina, Ohio, Oklahoma, Rhode Island, Tennessee, Texas, Utah, Virginia, Washington, West Virginia, Wisconsin, Wyoming.

Dewey—Connecticut, Delaware, Indiana, Kansas, Maine, Maryland, Michigan, Nebraska, New Hampshire, New Jersey, New York, North Dakota, Oregon, Pennsylvania, South Dakota, Vermont.

Mr. Wallace carried no state. Governor Thurmond got the 38 electors of Alabama, Louisiana, Mississippi and South Carolina, while 2 of Tennessee's 12 electoral votes are pledged to him, but are in dispute.

It was plain from the above division that the inter-sectional combination of voting groups effected by President Roosevelt after 1932 and held by him in sufficient number to maintain victory through the election of 1944 has been renewed as a national majority by Mr. Truman, for the time being at any rate. This pattern was not many minutes old when Governor Dewey, summoning a press conference, said that he would never again seek the Presidency. It was his third try—twice as the Republican nominee (1944 and 1948) and once (1940) as an unsuccessful candidate for the nomination.

During the long hours of Tuesday night and yesterday morning, when it seemed possible that the Presidential contest might be carried into the next House of Representatives, many persons were deeply disturbed over the possible effects of this on the international situation and the pressing problems of the domestic economy that underlie it. But, with the decision of Ohio and California, and the establishment of the new complexion of Congress, these fears subsided in a feeling that the continuity of the American Government was one of the most definite results of the general election of 1948.

Thursday, November 4, 1948

THE COMMON MAN DAZED BY ELECTION

He Reads News, Hears Radio, Talks to Strangers—Calls Papers to Confirm Miracle

By Meyer Berger

The common man walked, or rode, to work yesterday a little stunned by the miracle he passed when he r'ared up on Tuesday and re-elected President Truman.

He reacted to his achievement as any little man might act when he shouts in a wilderness and hears the echo, tremendously amplified.

Walking in a daze to the subway, or sitting dreamy-eyed in the commuters' train, he scanned newspapers to confirm his miracle. He paused by blaring shop radios to hear it reconfirmed.

On Broadway, in Brooklyn, in The Bronx, Queens and Staten Island he relished it again and again, but it tasted oddly in his own mouth when he discussed it with neighbors and with utter strangers on New York's sidewalks.

"Can't Quite Believe It"

One man in Times Square said: "It's something like the night President Roosevelt died. You can't quite believe it. You have to talk it over with someone—anyone—to make sure you've got it right."

Just after 11 o'clock, when the radio carried the news that Governor Dewey had officially conceded the election, public reception was varied but still followed the trance pattern.

From windows high in Times Square, shreds of paper were thrown to the wet wind. They twisted in the air, blew northward, and lay against heaps of Election Night debris.

In the garment center, too, windows flew open briefly and brilliantly colored cloth remnants—red and yellow and blue and green—were given to the damp wind. The remnants clung to ledges and to window sills, to taxicab roofs and bus tops.

Yet there was little cheering. The voters had not come out of their daze. They snatched newspapers from newsstands an hour later to stare raptly at the black-type legend "TRUMAN WINS," but their eyes betrayed something that spelled less than complete comprehension.

The police anticipated a spontaneous celebration. They sent extra mounted men clattering into the garment district and into the Square. But there was no celebration. That was still not the public mood. The people who had performed the miracle had not yet accepted it.

Seeking still further confirmation of this wonder they had created, thousands of persons turned from raucous radios and from bold-face headlines to call newspaper offices. The New York Times had more than 25,000 such calls between 9 A.M. to 6 P.M.

The Times pressed thirty-four of its workers and a number of job applicants into service immediately to handle these calls and to repeat: "Yes, it's true. President Truman is re-elected. Governor Dewey has conceded it." The calls set a Times record.

Still the crowds moved through the city streets in their common daze. In The Bronx, in Flatbush, in downtown Brooklyn, in Queens and on Staten Island, men and women talked freely with strangers and a note of awe was in their voices.

The talk in one-arm restaurants, in barber shops and in the subways took on a familiar pattern. It was generally to the effect that—as one Brooklyn waitress put it—"Dewey didn't look like the man to be President. He was for the rich and Truman was for us poor people."

And others spoke of the President, oddly, as an underdog. "You got to remember, he was the underdog. It was like in American sports. You always root for the little guy who's getting a pushing around from the big one."

There was other talk, mostly about the President's courage. It seemed a little singular that the President's campaign wind-up visit last week had bred a kind of affection. Cab drivers and policemen kept referring to him as "Harry." Just plain "Harry."

Although the story of Governor Dewey's concession screamed from newsstand headlines and from the radio to penetrate every corner of the city, The Times was deluged with requests to bring its running electric bulletin board into day-light play for election details.

Electric Bulletin Sign Goes On

Service was resumed before 1 P.M., and throngs paused in their daily routine in mist and in drizzle all afternoon to read the figures and reports the sign carried.

A reporter coming late to Times Square to study crowd reaction saw a huddle of vehement men at the north end of Times Tower violently selling one another the thought that they had figured, in some mysterious way, long ago, that the President would win.

The disillusioned policeman in the information booth was asked if this group—from 200 to 250, all told—was what was left of the crowds that had formed after Governor Dewey's message of congratulation had gone to the White House.

"Young feller," he said, "those men you see there, they broke the Hindenberg Line—the day, or the hour after they read it on the bulletin board. They broke the Maginot Line, the same way. They figured the landing in North Africa, and D-Day the same way. And they're re-electing President Truman the same way—after they've seen it on the bulletin board."

New faces and new technology marked the election of 1952. Not since 1924 had there been a campaign without a New York governor. Four years after Truman's whistlestops, the candidates zoomed around the country in airplanes, speaking to Americans on television, the device that would forever alter the way candidates and voters perceived each other.

Democrats were deeply vulnerable after two decades in the White House. Truman's embattled presidency had given the Republicans ammunition—from war in Korea to charges of corruption and Communism at home. When Truman opted out of the race in March, few lamented his departure.

The Republicans were split between their conservative wing, which admired Douglas MacArthur and Senator Robert Taft, and the moderates who had twice championed Dewey. Dewey himself proposed Dwight Eisenhower in 1950. With dazzling credentials (war hero, former president of Columbia University, NATO commander), Ike was wooed by both parties. In early 1952, friends entered him in the New Hampshire primary and confirmed that he was a Republican. Though Eisenhower was still in Europe with NATO, he won the primary and the stampede began.

The consummate insider, Taft was strong going into the convention at Chicago. But the Eisenhower forces shrewdly played for delegates and won the nomination. The surprise choice for vice president was Richard M. Nixon, a 39-year old Senator from California who had built his reputation on anti-communism and the Alger Hiss perjury case.

Left to right:
Dwight David Eisenhower (1890–1969)
Adlai Stevenson (1900–65)

After a widely reproduced photograph revealed a hole in the bottom of Stevenson's shoe, both sides took advantage. Democrats cited their candidate's bond with the common voter (as illustrated in this button), while Republicans were satirical.

Among the Democrats, Senator Estes Kefauver of Tennessee had won a following as a result of televised hearings that exposed the influence of organized crime. His primary victory in New Hampshire had helped Truman decide to retire. But momentum soon shifted to the eventual nominee, Governor Adlai Stevenson of Illinois, respected widely for his eloquence and his aspiration to "talk sense to the American people."

Eisenhower's "Great Crusade" was shaken in September when the press reported a slush fund created for Nixon by friendly businessmen. Fighting for his political life, Nixon addressed the largest TV audience yet assembled, defended his innocence, and proclaimed his affection for his cocker spaniel, Checkers. The speech was hugely successful with the public, confirming TV's power as a political tool. Nixon roared back, sneering at Stevenson as "Adlai the Appeaser" and worse. Senator Joseph McCarthy jumped on the bandwagon and helped turn the election into a referendum on Americanism by suggesting that Democrats were soft on Communists.

At times, Ike expressed disgust with the rightward drift of his crusade and its tight management by advertising executives, but by and large, he went along with it. The slogan "I Like Ike" perfectly captured the moment, and his promise to go to Korea to end the war, while vague, seemed better than military stalemate. Mamie Eisenhower also filled a useful role, calling subtle attention to Stevenson's divorce.

Both candidates used television effectively, but Stevenson was more comfortable with language, both in substantive speeches and frequent jests (he called the GOP "Grouchy Old Pessimists"). For all his efforts, he was branded an "egghead"—a disparaging epithet that stuck.

Until the last minute, pollsters predicted a dead heat, but they were wrong again. Ike won 442 electoral votes to Stevenson's 89. After two decades of depression and war, Americans wanted nothing more than stability and a chance to get ahead. Even with his rhetorical vagueness, and perhaps because of it, Eisenhower was a stronger voice for these inchoate aspirations.

This Republican poster alludes to the allegations of corruption and mismanagement that bedeviled the Truman Administration.

It is hard to imagine General Eisenhower actually wearing these "I Like Ike" sunglasses, but thousands of his supporters did.

A preconvention huddle at Topeka's Jayhawk Hotel, April 13, 1952.

Dwight Eisenhower hosts a rally at his Gettysburg farm, Pennsylvania, June 13, 1952.

Adlai Stevenson campaigns in Florida, 1952.

Stevenson addresses a rally in the Garment Center *(above)*, New York City October 29, 1952.

Stevenson meets with reporters after a conference at the White House *(right);* on the left is Stevenson's running mate, Senator John Sparkman of Alabama, August 13, 1952.

Nixon's famous "Checkers Speech" was seen and heard by approximately 30 million television viewers and a vast radio audience, September 23, 1952.

Eisenhower greets an enthusiastic crowd at the Chicago Republican convention, July 6, 1952.

"All the News That's Fit to Print"

The New York Times.

ELECTION EXTRA
Fair, warmer today. Some cloudiness and turning cooler tomorrow.
Temperature Range Today-Max., 62; Min., 38
Temperatures Yesterday—Max., 52; Min., 39
Full U. S. Weather Bureau Report, Page 35

VOL. CII No. 34,619. Entered as Second-Class Matter. Post Office, New York, N. Y. NEW YORK, WEDNESDAY, NOVEMBER 5, 1952. Times Square, New York 36, N. Y. Telephone LAckawanna 4-1000 FIVE CENTS

EISENHOWER WINS IN A LANDSLIDE; TAKES NEW YORK; IVES ELECTED; REPUBLICANS GAIN IN CONGRESS

G.O.P. HOUSE LIKELY

But the Senate Margin Hangs in the Balance of Two Close Races

LODGE TRAILING RIVAL

President Eisenhower May Lack a Working Majority in Congress

By JAMES RESTON

It appeared at 4:30 this morning that control of the United States Senate could be determined by the outcome of the Senatorial races in Michigan and Massachusetts.

At that time the Republicans appeared to have picked up five new seats and lost three others, thus enabling them to wipe out the two-seat advantage held by the Democrats at the end of the Eighty-second Congress.

To assure the power to organize the Senate and place their Republicans at the head of its important committees, however, Senator Henry Cabot Lodge Jr., Republican of Massachusetts, would have to overcome an advantage of more than 75,000 held by Representative John F. Kennedy, his opponent.

And Representative Charles E. Potter, Republican of Michigan had to retain the 47,000 lead he held over the Democratic incumbent, Senator Blair Moody of Michigan.

Morse May Be Vital

So close was the Senate race that there was a possibility that control of the upper chamber could be determined by the decision of Senator Wayne Morse of Oregon, who was elected as a Republican, but who broke with his party during the campaign, and announced that hereafter he was an "independent."

Though it appeared that the Republicans had won control of the House, one thing was certain: that President Dwight D. Eisenhower would not have a comfortable working majority in either house and would require all his gifts of persuasion to win consent for his policies on Capitol Hill.

Several factors in the Senate race were noteworthy:

¶Of the ten so-called isolationist or extremist Republicans who went before the voters yesterday, seven seemed fairly sure of victory. These were Senators Joseph R. McCarthy of Wisconsin; John W. Bricker of Ohio; William E. Jenner of Indiana; Edward Martin of Pennsylvania; Arthur V. Watkins of Utah, George W. Malone of Nevada and Hugh Butler of Nebraska.

Three other Republicans in this same category, however, were in serious trouble if they had not actually been defeated. They were:

Continued on Page 15, Column 1

M'Carthy Is Winner, But Is Last on Ticket

By RICHARD J. H. JOHNSTON
Special to The New York Times.

MILWAUKEE, Wednesday, Nov. 5—Wisconsin went to the Republicans today for the third time in a national election since 1920.

The predicted Republican sweep of the state and capture of its twelve electoral votes became a certainty a few minutes after midnight.

Gen. Dwight D. Eisenhower, the Republican Presidential nominee ran second on the G. O. P. ticket with Gov. Walter J. Kohler Jr. leading the slate in his bid for re-election.

As the returns neared the final count, Gen. Dwight D. Eisenhower's vote indicated he would emerge as leader of the G. O. P. slate in Wisconsin. With 2,036 of the state's 3,224 vtoing precincts reported, his vote was 554,369 to Gov. Adlai E. Stevenson's 356,218.

Gov. Walter J. Kohler, seeking

Continued on Page 22, Column 6

Electoral Vote by States

	Eisenhower	Stevenson		Eisenhower	Stevenson
Ala.	—	11	Neb.	6	—
Ariz.	4	—	Nev.	3	—
Ark.	—	8	N. H.	4	—
Calif.	32	—	N. J.	16	—
Colo.	6	—	N. M.	4	—
Conn.	8	—	N. Y.	45	—
Del.	3	—	N. C.	—	14
Fla.	10	—	N. D.	4	—
Ga.	—	12	Ohio	25	—
Idaho	4	—	Okla.	8	—
Ill.	27	—	Ore.	6	—
Ind.	13	—	Pa.	32	—
Iowa	10	—	R. Isl.	4	—
Kan.	8	—	S. C.	—	8
*Ky.	—	10	S. D.	4	—
*La.	—	10	*Tenn.	11	—
Me.	5	—	Texas	24	—
Md.	9	—	Utah	4	—
Mass.	16	—	Vt.	3	—
Mich.	20	—	Va.	12	—
Minn.	11	—	Wash.	9	—
Miss.	—	8	W. Va.	—	8
Mo.	13	—	Wisc.	12	—
Mont.	4	—	Wyo.	3	—
			Total	442	89

*Trend.

EISENHOWER TAKES JERSEY BY 300,000

Senator Smith Is Re-elected—Bond Issues Supported in Record Balloting

By RUSSELL PORTER

With more than three-quarters of New Jersey's vote counted early this morning, Gen. Dwight D. Eisenhower appeared headed toward a plurality of close to 300,000 in the state over Gov. Adlai E. Stevenson. This far exceeded Governor Dewey's 1948 plurality of 85,669 over President Truman.

United States Senator H. Alexander Smith, Republican candidate for re-election, won a sweeping victory over his Democratic opponent, Archibald S. Alexander, though Mr. Smith ran behind the head of his ticket. His indicated plurality was about 200,000.

The returns were:

PRESIDENT
3,461 precincts out of 3,840:

Eisenhower	1,203,120
Stevenson	921,375

UNITED STATES SENATOR
3,399 precincts out of 3,840:

Smith	1,089,883
Alexander	903,533

The Republicans appeared to have retained their majority of nine to five in New Jersey's delegation in the House of Representatives.

Both bond issues on the ballot

Continued on Page 23, Column 2

STATE LEAD 850,000

General's Upstate Edge Tops Million—He Loses City by Only 362,674

PROTEST VOTE SEEN

Albany County, Other Areas in Democratic Column Switch

State Presidential Vote

CITY SUMMARY

	Eisenhower (Rep.)	Stevenson (Dem.-Lib.)
Manhattan	300,234	447,877
Bronx	241,545	393,052
Brooklyn	447,148	656,278
Queens	449,505	331,633
Richmond	55,981	28,247
Total	1,494.413	1,857,087
Upstate	2,413,299	1,147,510
Grand total	3,907,712	3,104,597

4,394 election districts out of 4,394 in the city reporting and 5,222 out of 5,954 upstate.

By JAMES A. HAGERTY

Gen. Dwight D. Eisenhower, Republican nominee for President, carried New York State with its forty-five electoral votes with a plurality of landslide proportions that will reach nearly 850,000.

With 33 election districts missing, all outside this city, General Eisenhower led Gov. Adlai E. Stevenson, his Democratic opponent, by an actual plurality of 846,020 and an indicated plurality of 840,034.

To carry his adopted state by this astounding plurality, General Eisenhower held Governor Stevenson down to an actual plurality of 362,674 in this city, far less than the supporters of the Democratic candidate expected.

With the 33 election districts missing, General Eisenhower carried the state outside the city by an actual plurality of 1,265,789 and, assuming that his vote held up in the missing districts, by an indicated plurality of about 1,270,000.

Governor Stevenson carried Manhattan by 147,633, the Bronx by 151,597 and Brooklyn by 209,130, all far below Democratic expectations. General Eisenhower carried Queens by 117,872 and Richmond by 27,834, well above

Continued on Page 24, Column 3

Hill Battle Spurts in Korea; Allies Press 'Triangle' Fight

By LINDESAY PARROTT
Special to The New York Times.

TOKYO, Wednesday, Nov. 5—The hard-fighting South Korean infantry, driving for the third time in three days up the slopes of the central Korean ridges, drove a penetration today into the Communist lines on the western flank of "Triangle Hill," a strategic position north of Kumhwa.

Early this afternoon, the Republic of Korea (R. O. K.) troops had captured one of the twin peaks that project from "Triangle"—named "Jane Russell Hill." The sharp, indecisive combat continued.

The attack on the twin peaks was tied in with a new drive against the central pyramid of "Triangle Hill." The South Koreans again thrust within yards of the crest.

The Chinese Reds struck again just to the east in a new attempt to capture the summit of "Sniper Ridge," flanking "Triangle" on the United Nations' right.

The crest of "Triangle" had been lost to the Chinese Communists after the United Nations limited objective offensive took it last month. The South Koreans pushed up southern slopes today to within fifty yards of the Reds' lines.

Some reports said the fighting again today was as furious as during the attacks Sunday and Monday, when the South Koreans desperately struggled to regain the positions.

Allied warplanes were out against the enemy guns. About fifty sorties had been flown by Fifth Air Force fighter-bombers before noon against Red artillery on high Papasan Mountain, the Communists' strongpoint just to the north of the central front.

At every opportunity, Allied guns pounded the Reds on the crest of "Triangle."

The Reds' guns dropped 5,000 rounds on the United Nations positions near "Heartbreak Ridge" and the "Punchbowl" in the mountainous eastern watershed, where the heaviest fighting of yesterday occurred. A North Korean battalion hit Allied defense positions on "Heartbreak" on the heels of the barrage, but the enemy failed to make a penetration.

On "Triangle Hill" and the twin peaks to the west of it, contact was light yesterday. At least temporarily, the South Koreans broke off attempts to storm two positions they had lost to the Chinese Reds' counter-attacks, after the United Nations limited objec-

Continued on Page 2, Column 3

New President and Vice President

DWIGHT D. EISENHOWER

RICHARD M. NIXON

The New York Times

IVES IS RE-ELECTED BY RECORD MARGIN

Defeats Cashmore by Biggest Plurality of Any Republican —Harding Mark Topped

Vote for Senator

CITY SUMMARY

	Ives (Rep.)	Cashmore (Dem.)	Counts (Lib.)
Manh'n	303,040	322,157	88,797
Bronx	233,548	277,506	101,014
B'klyn	398,498	522,751	147,370
Queens	429,225	265,812	62,558
Rich'd	51,939	28,742	2,044
Total	1,416,250	1,416,968	401,783
Up-state	2,399,770	1,099,842	52,259
Gr Totl	3,816,020	2,516,810	454,042

4,394 election districts out of 4,394 in the city reporting and 5,854 out of 5,954 up-state.

By LEO EGAN

Senator Irving M. Ives won re-election in a three-cornered race yesterday by the largest plurality ever obtained by a Republican candidate in New York State, topping President Warren G. Harding's record-setting margin of 1,089,929 in 1920 by more than 200,000 votes.

The former majority leader of the State Assembly and co-sponsor of New York's law against racial discrimination in employment thus became the first Republican Senator to win re-election in New York since the late James W. Wadsworth performed that feat in the Harding landslide of 1920.

Not only did Senator Ives carry the normally Republican upstate area by a plurality that may reach 1,297,972, but he came within 718 votes of capturing normally Democratic New York City as well.

The complete Senate vote in the city gave Senator Ives 1,416,250 to 1,416,968 for Borough President John Cashmore of Brooklyn, the Democratic candidate. Thus Mr. Cashmore's plurality within the city was held to 718 votes.

With 5,854 of the 5,954 districts outside the city totaled, Senator Ives had an actual plurality of 1,299,928. On this basis, his final up-state margin should reach 1,300,000.

Dr. George S. Counts, the Liberal party candidate, polled 454,042 votes in the same districts tabulated for Senator Ives and Mr. Cashmore. On this basis his final vote could reach 460,000. Corliss Lamont, the American Labor can-

Continued on Page 21, Column 2

NEW YORK TIMES news bulletins are broadcast over WQXR every hour.

Eisenhower Cracks South, Heads for Victory in Texas

By WILLIAM S. WHITE

Gen. Dwight D. Eisenhower, the Republican Presidential candidate, has smashed the traditionally Democratic Solid South in his national victory over Gov. Adlai E. Stevenson. He has carried outright Florida and Virginia, with their twenty-two electoral votes. This morning unofficial observers gave him the greatest Southern prize of all—Texas and its twenty-four electoral votes, the sixth biggest bloc in the United States.

Confirmation of this indicated loss would involve a Democratic disaster.

Apart from all this and from receiving the greatest popular ballot ever given a Republican in the South, General Eisenhower was first narrowly leading and then narrowly trailing this morning in Tennessee, which has eleven electoral votes. In Tennessee, the position was so close that the result probably will not be known until late this afternoon.

In Louisiana and South Carolina Governor Stevenson had slight leads after trailing often in the early returns.

Only the hardest of the hard core of the Old South has remained wholly faithful to the old Democratic tradition.

Mississippi, Arkansas, North

Continued on Page 22, Column 3

CONNECTICUT G. O. P. SEATS 2 IN SENATE

Benton and Ribicoff Concede to Purtell and Bush While Eisenhower Sweeps State

Special to The New York Times.

HARTFORD, Conn., Wednesday, Nov. 5—Gen. Dwight D. Eisenhower swept to an amazing landslide victory in Connecticut yesterday, winning by a margin of nearly 130,000 votes over Gov. Adlai E. Stevenson in final returns from the 169 cities and towns in the state.

The victory astounded Republicans as well as Democrats. Prior to the election, Republican leaders had made cautious claims of victory by about 25,000 or 30,000 votes, while Democrats privately thought they had a chance to win the state.

The tremendous Eisenhower sweep carried two Republican United States Senators into office with him. Senator William A. Purtell of West Hartford defeated William Benton, Democrat, for the full six-year term by a margin of 90,286, and Prescott S. Bush, Greenwich banker, defeated Representative Abraham A. Ribicoff of Hartford, Democrat, by 30,373 votes. Mr. Ribicoff made a spectacular uphill run but was edged out by Mr. Bush's lead in the small towns that are traditionally Republican.

Final returns were:

PRESIDENT
169 precincts out of 169:

Eisenhower	610,989
Stevenson	481,482

UNITED STATES SENATOR
(For six-year Term)
169 precincts out of 169:

Purtell (R.)	575,445
Benton (D.)	485,159

(For Four-year Term)

Bush (R.)	559,586
Ribicoff (D)	529,213

The Eisenhower sweep enabled the Republicans to win five of the six seats from Connecticut in the House of Representatives, a gain

Continued on Page 28, Column 3

GENERAL APPEALS FOR UNITED PEOPLE

He Vows Not to Give 'Short Weight' as President — Thanks Rival for Pledge

By WILLIAM R. CONKLIN

A jubilant Gen. Dwight D. Eisenhower accepted his election as President early this morning with a pledge to the American people that he would not give "short weight" in the execution of his new responsibilities in Washington.

With his wife by his side, the Republican President-elect told 2,000 campaign supporters in the grand ballroom of the Commodore Hotel at 2:05 A. M. that it would take the support of a united people to carry his Administration to success in its efforts to build a "better future for America."

His remarks were carried by radio and television to all parts of the country.

He read a message he had sent a few minutes before to his defeated rival, Gov. Adlai E. Stevenson of Illinois, thanking him for his promise of assistance. General Eisenhower expressed hope that Americans of both parties would speedily forget campaign bitter-

Continued on Page 20, Column 2

Stevenson Concedes the Victory As Weeping Backers Cry 'No, No'

By WILLIAM M. BLAIR
Special to The New York Times.

SPRINGFIELD, Ill., Wednesday, Nov. 5—Gov. Adlai E. Stevenson conceded defeat early today to his Republican opponent, Gen. Dwight D. Eisenhower, and pledged the support "he will need to carry out the great tasks that lie before him."

The Governor came from the Executive Mansion to the Democratic Headquarters in the Leland Hotel to make his announcement before a jammed ballroom of supporters, many of whom broke into tears and cried, "No, no."

Governor Stevenson said:

"General Eisenhower has been a great leader in war. He has been a vigorous and valiant opponent in the campaign. These qualities will now be dedicated to leading us all through the next four years.

"It is traditionally American to fight hard before an election.

"It is equally traditional to close ranks as soon as the people have spoken. From the depths of my heart I thank all of my party, and all of those independents and Republicans who supported Senator Sparkman and me."

The Governor said he had dispatched to General Eisenhower in New York a telegram which he read. It said:

"The people have made their choice and I congratulate you. That you may be the servant and guardian of peace and make the dale of trouble a door of hope is my earnest prayer. Best Wishes.

Adlai E. Stevenson."

Governor Stevenson did have a grin, however, for the crowd and displayed his ever-present humor to reporters. Asked how about 1956, the next presidential election year, he echoed in a loud voice and with mock surprise "56! Examine that man's head."

As for his immediate plans, he

Continued on Page 16, Column 2

RACE IS CONCEDED

Virginia and Florida Go to the General as Do Illinois and Ohio

SWEEP IS NATION-WIDE

Victor Calls for Unity and Thanks Governor for Pledging Support

By ARTHUR KROCK

Gen. Dwight D. Eisenhower was elected President of the United States yesterday in an electoral vote landslide and with an emphatic popular majority that probably will give his party a small margin of control in the House of Representatives but may leave the Senate as it is—forty-nine Democrats, forty-seven Republicans and one independent.

Senator Richard M. Nixon of California was elected Vice President.

The Democratic Presidential candidate, Gov. Adlai E. Stevenson of Illinois, shortly after midnight conceded his defeat by a record turnout of American voters.

At 4 A. M. today the Republican candidate had carried states with a total of 431 electors, or 165 more than the 266 required for the selection of a President. The Democratic candidate seemed sure of 69, with 31 doubtful in Kentucky, Louisiana and Tennessee.

General Eisenhower's landslide victory, both in electoral and popular votes, was nation-wide in its pattern, extending from New England—where Massachusetts and Rhode Island broke their Democratic voting habits of many years—down the Eastern seaboard to Maryland, Virginia and Florida and westward to almost every state between the coasts, including California.

General Wins Illinois

The Republican candidate took Illinois, Governor Stevenson's home state. In South Carolina, though he lost its electors on a technicality, he won a majority of the voters. And, completing the first successful Republican invasion of the States of the former Confederacy, the General carried Texas and broke the one-party system in the South.

The personal popularity that enabled him to defeat Senator Robert A. Taft of Ohio in the Republican primaries in Texas, and present him with the issue on which he defeated the Senator for the Republican nomination, crushed the regular Democratic organization of Texas that was led by Speaker Sam Rayburn of the House of Representatives and had the blessing of former Vice President John N. Garner.

The tide that bore General Eisenhower to the White House, though it did not give him a comfortable working majority in either the national House or the Senate (the Democrats may still nominally control the machinery of that branch), probably increased the number of Republican governors beyond the present twenty-five.

"My fellow citizens have made their choice and I gladly accept it," said Governor Stevenson at 1:46 A. M., Eastern standard time, and he asked all citizens to unite behind the President-elect. The defeated candidate said he had sent a telegram of congratulation to General Eisenhower.

At 2:05 A. M., from the Grand Ballroom of the Commodore Hotel, General Eisenhower said he recognized the weight of his new responsibilities and that he would not give "short weight" in their execution. He also urged "unity" and announced he had sent a telegram of thanks to the Democratic candidate for his promise of support.

The issues of the unusually vigorous campaign that was waged

Continued on Page 14, Column 3

New York, Wednesday, November 5, 1952.

Eisenhower Wins in a Landslide; Takes New York; Ives Elected; Republicans Gain in Congress

Race Is Conceded

Virginia and Florida Go to the General as Do Illinois and Ohio

Sweep Is Nation-Wide

Victor Calls for Unity and Thanks Governor for Pledging Support

By Arthur Krock

Gen. Dwight D. Eisenhower was elected President of the United States yesterday in an electoral vote landslide and with an emphatic popular majority that probably will give his party a small margin of control in the House of Representatives but may leave the Senate as it is—forty-nine Democrats, forty-seven Republicans and one independent.

Senator Richard M. Nixon of California was elected Vice President.

The Democratic Presidential candidate, Gov. Adlai E. Stevenson of Illinois, shortly after midnight conceded his defeat by a record turnout of American voters.

At 4 A.M. today the Republican candidate had carried states with a total of 431 electors, or 163 more than the 266 required for the selection of a President. The Democratic candidate seemed sure of 69, with 31 doubtful in Kentucky, Louisiana and Tennessee.

General Eisenhower's landslide victory, both in electoral and popular votes, was nation-wide in its pattern, extending from New England—where Massachusetts and Rhode Island broke their Democratic voting habits of many years—down the Eastern seaboard to Maryland, Virginia and Florida and westward to almost every state between the coasts, including California.

General Wins Illinois

The Republican candidate took Illinois, Governor Stevenson's home state. In South Carolina, though he lost its electors on a technicality, he won a majority of the voters. And, completing the first successful Republican invasion of the States of the former Confederacy, the General carried Texas and broke the one-party system in the South.

The personal popularity that enabled him to defeat Senator Robert A. Taft of Ohio in the Republican primaries in Texas, and present him with the issue on which he defeated the Senator for the Republican nomination, crushed the regular Democratic organization of Texas that was led by Speaker Sam Rayburn of the House of Representatives and had the blessing of former Vice President John N. Garner.

The tide that bore General Eisenhower to the White House, though it did not give him a comfortable working majority in either the national House or the Senate (the Democrats may still nominally control the machinery of that branch), probably increased the number of Republican governors beyond the present twenty-five.

"My fellow citizens have made their choice and I gladly accept it," said Governor Stevenson at 1:16 A.M., Eastern standard time, and he asked all citizens to unite behind the President-elect. The defeated candidate said he had sent a telegram of congratulation to General Eisenhower.

At 2:05 A.M., from the Grand Ballroom of the Commodore Hotel, General Eisenhower said he recognized the weight of his new responsibilities and that he would not give "short weight" in their execution. He also urged "unity" and announced he had sent a telegram of thanks to the Democratic candidate for his promise of support.

The issues of the unusually vigorous campaign that was waged by the candidates of the two major parties, with President Truman advocating Governor Stevenson's election, in a speaking tour throughout the country, as an endorsement of the record of his administration and that of the late President Roosevelt, were these:

General Eisenhower asserted that it was "time for a change" from the twenty-year tenure of the Democrats in the White House, with control of Congress for all but two years in that period, the third longest in American history. Governor Stevenson promised to "refresh" his party and the Government and said that would be all the "change" the critical world situation justified.

General Eisenhower forcefully attacked revelations of official corruption in the Truman Administration and charged first negligence and then tolerance of the infiltration of Communist agents in the Government. Governor Stevenson denounced both but defended the Administration as having done its full duty in the circumstances.

General Eisenhower demanded a "new look" at the war in Korea and promised to make an inspection trip to the peninsula if he were elected. He charged that more south Koreans could and should have been trained to man the front lines "where our boys do not belong." Governor Stevenson and the President denounced this as a "cheap trick," and as an injury to the chances for an armistice in the Korean war.

Governor Stevenson and the President assailed General Eisenhower because he declined to denounce Senator Joseph R. McCarthy of Wisconsin and other Republican Senators for "character assassination" and "isolationism." They also accused him of having "surrendered" to Senator Robert A. Taft of Ohio whom he defeated for the Republican nomination, and of abandoning his "principles" in domestic and foreign policy thereby.

Fitzpatrick Concedes State

The great majority of the voters sustained General Eisenhower's position on all these issues. Their desire for a "change" rather than a "refreshment" of the Administration was noted by Paul E. Fitzpatrick, Democratic State Chairman of New York, when at 11 P.M. yesterday, he conceded the state to the Republicans.

This was thirteen minutes after Arthur E. Summerfield, Republican National Chairman, had asserted that General Eisenhower had been elected by a "landslide" that also carried majorities in both branches of Congress.

In states where the issues of corruption and Communist infiltration had been actively debated, the voting majority also sustained the General.

And, by the defeat for re-election in Connecticut of Senator William Benton, who has made a career of attacking Senator McCarthy; the re-election of Mr. McCarthy by a huge margin in Wisconsin; and the re-election of Senator William E. Jenner of Indiana, the voting majority indicated approval of the objectives of what the Democrats and independents have assailed as McCarthyism.

Effect of Korea Issue

There is no way of estimating the effect on yesterday's voters of the angry argument over the Korean war between the two Presidential candidates, with President Truman rising to heights of bitterness hitherto unscaled even by him in his denunciation of General Eisenhower's criticism of the Administration's pre-war policies in the Far East and the General's promise to go to the scene of the war, if elected.

But ever since General Eisenhower made the promise, it had been evident that the Democrats were alarmed about its vote-getting potential for the Republican candidate. Therefore, it is reasonable to conclude that on this issue, which became the central one of the final phase of the campaign, the voting majority preferred the position taken by General Eisenhower.

On the over-all issue of the record of the Roosevelt-Truman Administrations, including the New Deal and Fair Deal programs, that the President insisted was "all Stevenson had to run on," the result of the election will be taken by the Republicans as repudiation of Mr. Truman.

This undoubtedly will be the basis of the proposals to Congress that President-elect Eisenhower will make and that Congress will sustain, if it is controlled by the Republicans.

At midnight that control seemed possible but not certain. The Democrats lost two Senate seats to the Republicans in Connecticut—those of Mr. Benton and the late Brien McMahon—and that of Herbert R. O'Connor in Maryland.

The Republicans held the seats of Senator H. Alexander Smith of New Jersey, John W. Bricker of Ohio, and Irving M. Ives of New York, in addition to those of Messrs. McCarthy and Jenner. But final returns may disclose that the Democrats have taken the seat held by Senator Henry Cabot Lodge Jr. of Massachusetts by electing John F. Kennedy to his place.

There is no way of estimating the effect on yesterday's voters of the angry argument over the Korean war between the two Presidential candidates.

Since the Republicans must make a net gain of two to organize the Senate (that is to elect the chairman of its committees and its officers), and Senator Wayne Morse of Oregon, elected as a Republican, has resigned from the party and may vote on organization with the Democrats, the issue of party control of the Senate was in doubt and may be until Senator Morse decides on his course in that body.

The campaign just ended was unusual in many ways in addition to the fact that no retiring President ever had taken the stump with the intensity and activity Mr. Truman did in defense of his record.

The Republican and Democratic nominees both were reluctant candidates and powerful pressures had to be exerted on both before General Eisenhower would consent to seek the nomination and Governor Stevenson would agree to be drafted by his party convention.

Once nominated, however, each fought as hard as the most ambitious politician to whom a Presidential nomination has come as the consequence of unremitting efforts to acquire it.

General Eisenhower was persuaded to resign as Supreme Commander of the North Atlantic Treaty Organization by assurances that, if he agreed to accept the Republican nomination, he would be chosen by acclamation and elected easily.

Instead, he was obliged to wage a hard battle against Senator Taft that for a time split the Republican party wide open. And though it appeared at last midnight that his electoral and popular majorities would be large, the apparent strength of Mr. Stevenson was such that the General had to put everything into the campaign. Governor Stevenson refused until the Democratic convention had been in session for three days to give the slightest encouragement to those who wanted to draft him.

He said and did a number of things calculated to discourage the effort, including a statement to the Illinois delegation that he was "temperamentally" and otherwise "unfit" to be President.

And, though he was the first Presidential candidate truly drafted in modern American history, the pattern was spoiled by the fact that he got delegate votes on the first two ballots in contest (though against his will and command) with Averell Harriman, Senator Estes Kefauver of Tennessee and Senator Richard B. Russell of Georgia.

Like the other reluctant candidate, however, Governor Stevenson fought as hard as he could to be elected. Beginning with a speech of acceptance that forecast a campaign on the highest level, he was soon trading blows—high ones and low ones—with General Eisenhower.

In the echelon of winners under the General the more conspicuous were:

Senator Harry F. Byrd, Democrat of Virginia, whose state endorsed his refusal to support Mr. Stevenson; Gov. Thomas E. Dewey, Republican of New York, who was among the early Eisenhower drafters and was most active in the successful campaign to carry the state; Senator McCarthy, who was made a national issue.

September 23, 1952

CHECKERS SPEECH (Excerpt)

. . . Pat and I have the satisfaction that every dime that we have got is honestly ours.

I should say this, that Pat doesn't have a mink coat. But she does have a respectable Republican cloth coat, and I always tell her she would look good in anything.

One other thing I should probably tell you, because if I don't they will probably be saying this about me, too. We did get something, a gift, after the election.

A man down in Texas heard Pat on the radio mention that our two youngsters would like to have a dog, and, believe it or not, the day we left before this campaign trip we got a message from Union Station in Baltimore, saying they had a package for us. We went down to get it. You know what it was?

It was a little cocker spaniel dog, in a crate that he had sent all the way from Texas, black and white, spotted, and our little girl Tricia, the six year old, named it Checkers.

And you know, the kids, like all kids, loved the dog, and I just want to say this, right now, that regardless of what they say about it, we are going to keep it.

. . . Now let me say this: I know this is not the last of the smears. In spite of my explanation tonight, other smears will be made. Others have been made in the past. And the purpose of the smears, I know, is this, to silence me, to make me let up.

Well, they just don't know who they are dealing with. I'm going to tell you this: I remember in the dark days of the Hiss trial some of the same columnists, some of the same radio commentators who are attacking me now and misrepresenting my position, were violently opposing me at the time I was after Alger Hiss. But I continued to fight because I knew I was right, and I can say to this great television and radio audience that I have no apologies to the American people for my part in putting Alger Hiss where he is today. And as far as this is concerned, I intend to continue to fight.

. . . Let me say this: I don't believe that I ought to quit, because I am not a quitter.

. . . But the decision, my friends, is not mine. I would do nothing that would harm the possibilities of Dwight Eisenhower to become President of the United States. And for that reason I am submitting to the Republican National Committee tonight through this television broadcast the decision which it is theirs to make.

. . . But let me just say this last word. . . . I am going to campaign up and down America until we drive the crooks and the Communists and those that defend them out of Washington, and remember folks, Eisenhower is a great man. Folks, he is a great man, and a vote for Eisenhower is a vote for what is good for America.

—Richard M. Nixon

America had changed in four years, but the parties ran the same candidates—the only time in the twentieth century that two opponents ran against each other twice in a row.

The fear of communism and nuclear Armageddon had abated somewhat, replaced by a new mood of indulgence. Americans flocked to the suburbs, they drove bigger and shinier cars, and they watched television night after night (over 35 million homes had TVs by 1955). The explosive impact of Elvis Presley in 1956 was an early sign of the incipient power of the baby boom.

But one thing about America had not changed: Ike's invincibility. An early Gallup poll asserted that Eisenhower had a 3-to-2 lead over any Democrat. Under his leadership, the Korean War had ended, McCarthyism had receded, a huge interstate highway system had been authorized, and the economy was roaring.

There was some speculation that Ike's health would keep him on the sidelines after he suffered a heart attack in September 1955. But he put that question to rest in March when he announced his intention to run—mainly because, as his press secretary confided, he dreaded

Left to right:
Dwight David Eisenhower (1890–1969)
Adlai E. Stevenson (1900–65)

"Stevenson for President" cigarettes—a promotion from a vastly more innocent era.

"the god-awful boredom of not being President." In San Francisco, the Republicans happily renominated him, and vice president Richard Nixon survived a "dump Nixon" drive.

Stevenson had to work a little harder for his nomination than he had in 1952, when it had almost been forced on him. Again, his main challenger was Senator Estes Kefauver of Tennessee, who beat him in the Minnesota primary and almost beat him in Florida (mounting evidence that primary contests were growing more important). But Stevenson won impressively in California, and was nominated on the first ballot when the Democrats convened in Chicago. The chief drama of the convention was Stevenson's decision to throw open the selection of his running mate. John F. Kennedy, a young Massachusetts Senator, ran well, but Kefauver won the nomination.

Despite the odds against him, Stevenson ran a dignified campaign. He invoked the slogan of a "New America," and throughout the summer and fall, proposed a series of reforms that would slowly evolve into genuine policy in subsequent administrations—ranging from health care and education reform to defense policy. Eisenhower, confident of reelection, barely exerted himself above what was required; Nixon did most of the campaigning.

As the election approached, Soviet tanks crushed a popular uprising in Hungary, and a crisis over the Suez Canal in Egypt pitted the United States against its allies, England, France, and Israel. Stevenson denounced Eisenhower's foreign policy, but if anything, the mood of crisis solidified Eisenhower's commanding lead. A frustrated Stevenson complained that Americans had turned to Eisenhower for refuge from Eisenhower's foreign policy.

On November 6, Americans loosed the biggest landslide since FDR defeated Eisenhower's fellow Kansan, Alf Landon, in 1936. Eisenhower won 457 electoral votes to Stevenson's 73.

After Adlai Stevenson was photographed with a hole in his shoe, Republicans added it to the list of reasons that an "egghead" should not be elected president.

One of the greatest electioneering slogans of the twentieth century was also one of the shortest.

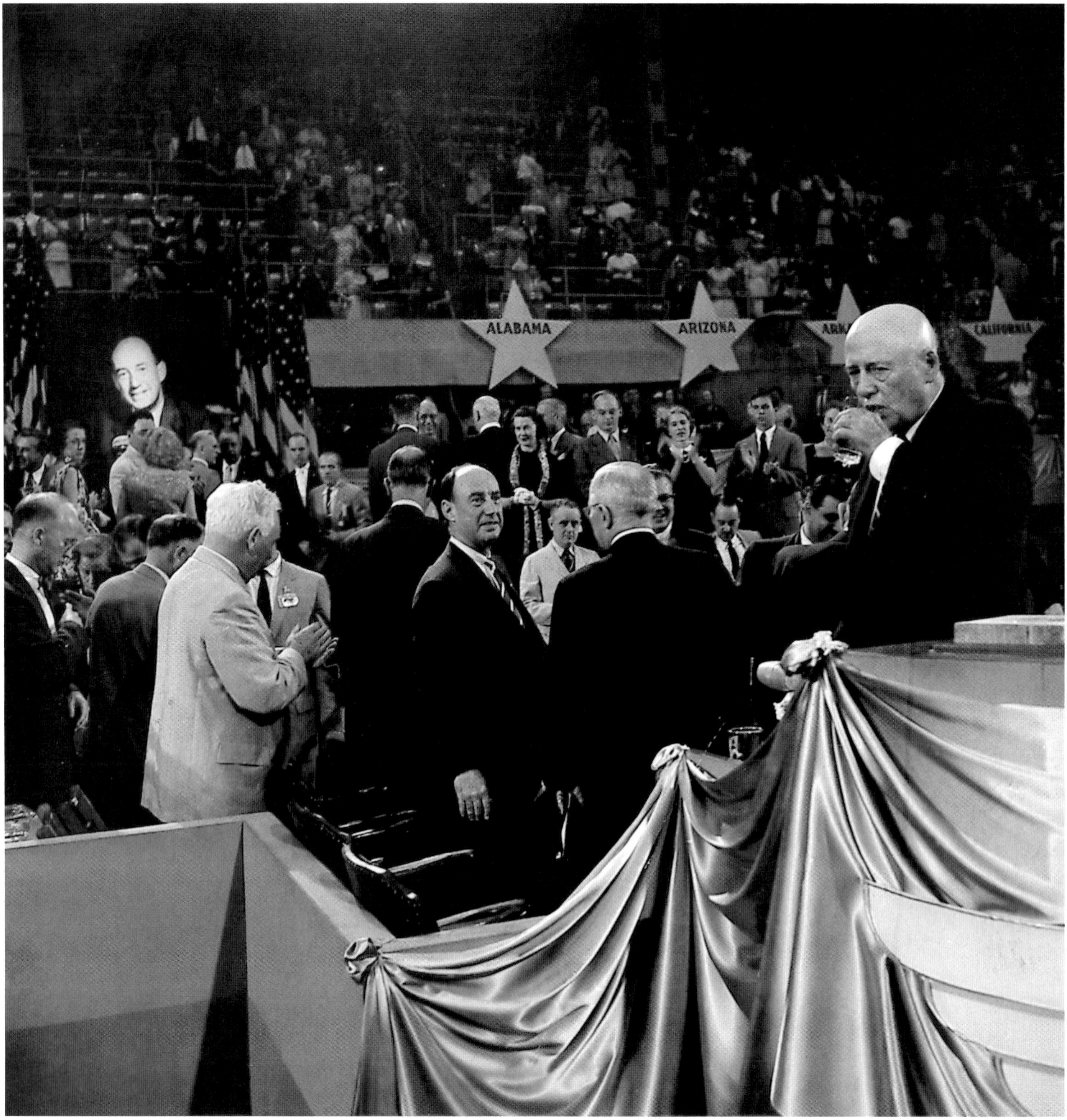

House Speaker Sam T. Rayburn (with water glass on far right) and Adlai Stevenson (center) on the podium at the Democratic Convention in Chicago, August 14, 1956.

In the 1950s, television became a major force in politics. This cameraman sits above the rafters at the Chicago Democratic convention, August 14, 1956.

Adlai Stevenson works on a campaign speech *(above)* in a Florida motel room, May 20, 1956.

Michael and Maureen Dowd of New Jersey ride the ferris wheel with Stevenson during a campaign stop at the Palisades Amusement Park *(right)*, September 9, 1956.

President Eisenhower and the Nixon family pose for photographers *(opposite)* after a breakfast conference in Washington, D.C. September 19, 1956.

WE LOVE
PAT

At a tent rally on his Gettysburg farm, President Eisenhower shares a soda with Leonard Hall, Chairman of the Republican National Committee, September 14, 1956.

Eisenhower socializes with two campaign supporters at his Gettysburg rally, both wearing dresses patterned with "IKE," September 14, 1956.

"All the News That's Fit to Print"

The New York Times.

LATE CITY EDITION
Condensation of U. S. Weather Bureau forecast:
Some cloudiness today; cloudy tonight. Clearing, cooler tomorrow.
Temperature range today: 66—50.
Temperature range yesterday: 65.4—52.2.
Full U. S. Weather Bureau Report, Page 53.

VOL. CVI. No. 36,082. Entered as Second-Class Matter, Post Office, New York, N. Y. NEW YORK, WEDNESDAY, NOVEMBER 7, 1956. Times Square, New York 36, N. Y. Telephone LAckawanna 4-1000 FIVE CENTS

EISENHOWER BY A LANDSLIDE; BATTLE FOR CONGRESS CLOSE; JAVITS VICTOR OVER WAGNER

Suez Warfare Stopped Under British-French Cease-Fire

MAYOR CONCEDES

Javits, Swept In With the Eisenhower Tide, Wins Stiff Contest

Vote for Senator
CITY SUMMARY

	Javits (Rep.)	Wagner (Dem.-Lib.)
Manhattan	270,146	393,462
Bronx	218,895	374,810
Brooklyn	398,088	605,002
Queens	400,832	372,505
Richmond	49,694	32,881
Total	1,337,655	1,778,660
Upstate	2,362,618	1,478,238
Grand total	3,700,273	3,256,898

All E. D.'s of 4,607 in city and 6,522 of 6,525 upstate.

By DOUGLAS DALES

Attorney General Jacob K. Javits was swept to victory yesterday in the Eisenhower Republican landslide in his race against Mayor Wagner for the United States Senate.

Mayor Wagner conceded defeat in a statement at 1:22 A. M. after the trend to Javits' victory became unmistakable.

Mr. Wagner carried three boroughs in the city—Manhattan, Brooklyn and the Bronx—but lost in Queens and Richmond.

The city-wide complete totals gave Mr. Javits 1,337,655 votes to 1,778,660 for Mayor Wagner. The Mayor's total included 233,560 on the Liberal party line. The Liberal line attracted 404,769 votes in the city four years ago, when the party ran its own candidate for the Senate, George S. Counts.

The victor's margin was expected to reach 444,000 with the final results. With all city districts and 6,522 of 6,525 districts upstate reported, Mr. Javits had an edge of 443,375.

Mayor Wagner carried two of the fifty-seven upstate counties, Erie and Albany. Eisenhower carried both.

Everywhere outside the city, Mr. Javits ran substantially behind the President's vote. On the other hand, Mayor Wagner ran well ahead of Adlai E. Stevenson, the Democratic candidate for President.

In view of the size of the

Continued on Page 26, Column 2

PRESIDENT SCORES NEW HIGH IN STATE

Plurality Tops 1,500,000 as He Cuts Rival's City Edge

State Presidential Vote
CITY SUMMARY

	Eisenhower (Rep.)	Stevenson (Dem.-Lib.)
Manhattan	299,929	378,018
Bronx	256,909	343,656
Brooklyn	459,703	558,187
Queens	471,144	313,311
Richmond	64,236	196,653
Total	1,551,921	1,614,825
Upstate	2,766,183	1,127,403
Grand total	4,318,104	2,742,228

All E. D.'s of 4,607 in city and 6,522 of 6,525 upstate.

By LEO EGAN

President Eisenhower swept New York yesterday by a plurality that dwarfed all previous records.

With sixty-one of the state's 11,132 election districts still to report this morning, General Eisenhower's margin exceeded 1,500,000.

The previous record for a Presidential plurality in New York was established in 1920, when the late Warren G. Harding, Republican, defeated James M. Cox, Democrat, by 1,139,927.

All the missing districts are in Republican territory upstate.

Continued on Page 23, Column 1

An International Summary: The Mideast and Hungary

Following are summaries of the leading developments in the Middle East and Europe. The full foreign news report begins on the first page of the second part.

Cease-Fire Is On

Britain and France put a cease-fire into effect and halted their advance in Egypt. Prime Minister Eden told Commons that conditions had been established for an international police force under the United Nations to promote settlement of Middle Eastern issues.

Invaders Hold Canal

The invasion forces claimed control of the Suez Canal Zone. They took Port Said and drove south before the cease-fire became effective.

Egyptians Halt Fight

The Egyptians decided to hold their fire at the deadline in the hope that the United Nations resolution of Nov. 2, providing for withdrawal of all forces behind armistice lines, would be carried out.

Soviet May Send 'Volunteers'

Indications in Moscow were that Soviet "volunteers" who began applying for service with Egyptian forces might go to the Middle East despite the cease-fire. Moscow broadcast a Cairo appeal for aid.

Troop Withdrawal Asked

Asian and Arab states drafted a United Nations resolution calling on Britain, France and Israel to withdraw their troops from Egypt immediately. A special session of the General Assembly called for last night was postponed until this morning.

Hungarian Battle Persists

Stubborn Hungarian revolutionary forces are continuing to fight the Soviet army in Budapest, according to diplomatic reports received in Vienna. Women and children were said to be fighting alongside the men in a house-to-house struggle. The General Assembly scheduled a special session this afternoon to consider Soviet intervention in Hungary.

EISENHOWER SETS RECORD IN JERSEY

Margin of 700,000 Carries All 21 Counties—G. O. P. Wins 2 Hudson Seats

By GEORGE CABLE WRIGHT

President Eisenhower yesterday scored the greatest victory in New Jersey political history.

With most of the state's ballots tallied early this morning, his margin over Adlai E. Stevenson had soared above 700,000, almost double that of 1952. He became the first candidate in modern times to carry all twenty-one counties.

The returns were:

PRESIDENT
4,017 districts out of 4,155.

Eisenhower	1,522,971
Stevenson	821,067

The most startling aspect of his victory was the complete turnabout of Hudson County, for half a century a Democratic stronghold.

This county gave the President a majority of 76,554. In 1952 Mr. Stevenson had carried Hudson by 7,886 votes.

In fact, Republicans swept every county contest. When residents of Hudson awake this morning it is certain that many will find it hard to believe that for the next two years they will be represented in Congress by not one, but two, Republicans. There was no precedent there for that.

A third Democratic incumbent, Representative Harrison A. Williams Jr., went down to defeat in Union County.

Thus, the Democratic representation of six in the House was cut in half. All eight Republican incumbents were re-elected.

President Eisenhower became the first Presidential candidate to carry the solidly Democratic bailiwick of Jersey City since Warren G. Harding did it in 1920. Long the citadel of the late Frank Hague and now of John Kenny, it gave General Eisenhower a majority of 31,527 over Mr. Stevenson. In 1952 the Democratic candidate had carried the city by 8,251.

But the trouncing of the former Illinois Governor was by no means restricted to Hudson. Camden and Mercer Counties, which also went to Mr. Stevenson in 1952, likewise turned their backs to him this year.

Continued on Page 28, Column 5

BUSH RE-ELECTED IN CONNECTICUT

Plurality for Eisenhower of 303,036 Biggest in State in a Presidential Race

By RICHARD H. PARKE
Special to The New York Times.

HARTFORD, Nov 6—President Eisenhower scored an easy victory in Connecticut today. He carried to victory with him Senator Prescott S. Bush, the Republican incumbent.

The President's plurality of 303,036 votes over Adlai E. Stevenson, Democratic candidate, was the greatest margin the State ever has given a Presidential contender. The previous high figure was 136,138 votes, achieved by Prseident Coolidge in 1924.

The President, whose 1952 plurality of 129,363 was considered of landslide proportions, defeated Mr. Stevenson today by 708,995 votes to 405,959, according to complete but unofficial returns.

The Republican sweep was general throughout the state. It carried in Senator Bush by a plurality of 129,544 votes. He defeated his Democratic opponent, Representative Thomas J. Dodd, by 607,330 to 477,876.

The Republicans also retained

Continued on Page 28, Column 5

SENATE IN DOUBT

Democrats Lag in East on War Issue but Gain in the West

By WILLIAM S. WHITE

The Democrats and Republicans fought along a swaying electoral battle line early today for control of the oncoming Eighty-fifth Congress.

Not all the power of President Eisenhower's landslide victory had been enough to put his Republican Congressional colleagues in front.

The Senate race, in which the Republicans were attempting to overturn a present 49-to-47 Democratic margin of control, was an affair of hairbreadth drama.

Small net Republican gains for the House of Representatives were indicated. But whether these would continue or would be enough remained wholly in doubt.

The Republicans needed a net gain of 15 House seats, and the capture of 2 additional and now vacant seats that had been Republican.

The pattern of the Congressional contest was this: The East, more sensitive than other sections to the last-minute issue involved in the Middle Eastern and Central European war crises, on the whole was hitting the Democrats hard. The appeal of "don't change horses in midstream" was strong in this area. In the interior, however, Democratic organizational strength, farm discontent and other factors were turning up great Democratic strength.

Cooper Wins in Kentucky

The position on the Senate in some critical states was this:

KENTUCKY—A gain of one Republican seat in former Senator John Sherman Cooper's defeat of his Democratic challenger, Lawrence Wetherby, for the seat made vacant by the death of Senator Alben W. Barkley. The possibility of another gain for the Republicans in the fact that the assistant Democratic leader of the Senate, Earle C. Clements, was running behind Thruston B. Morton, a former assistant Secretary of State in the Eisenhower Administration.

NEW YORK—A Republican gain in the victory of Jacob K. Javits over Mayor Wagner for the seat being vacated by Senator Herbert H. Lehman, Democrat-Liberal.

OHIO—A Democratic gain in the defeat by Gov. Frank J. Lausche of Senator George H. Bender.

ILLINOIS—Senator Everett M. Dirksen, Republican, ran ahead of his Democratic opponent, Richard Stengel.

PENNSYLVANIA—Joseph S.

Continued on Page 3, Column 1

Coudert Wins in Close Contest; Vote in Queens 7th Rechecked

By CLAYTON KNOWLES

The Republicans emerged from a hard-fought Congressional campaign early today with a possible net gain of one in the state delegation to the House of Representatives.

At 4:20 A. M. a final decision rested on the outcome of the race in the Seventh district of Queens. Here Representative James J. Delaney, Democratic incumbent, claimed victory at 4:15 A. M. by forty votes, but a final tally was unavailable.

An hour and a half earlier, Delaney supporters were conceding the election of Joseph Stockinger, a Republican, but the contest was so close that all 217 districts were being rechecked.

The announced vote for 202 districts was 72,186 for Mr. Stockinger to 72,112 for Mr. Delaney, who ran with Liberal party backing.

The prospect that the Republicans would pick up a House seat in the state, giving them twenty-seven of a total of forty-three, arose when Representative Frederic R. Coudert Jr. staged an eleventh-hour triumph in the Manhattan Seventeenth District.

He prevailed once more over Anthony B. Akers, Democrat-Liberal who had come within 314 votes of defeating him in 1954. This time Mr. Coudert won, 68,862 votes to 66,207.

If Mr. Delaney should go to defeat, the Republicans will have seven of the twenty-two House seats filled in the city.

President Eisenhower's land-

Continued on Page 20, Column 6

PRESIDENT EISENHOWER

VICE PRESIDENT NIXON

G. O. P. MAKES BID TO CAPTURE HOUSE

Picks Up 9 Seats in East, but Drive Eases in West —Midwest to Decide

By JOHN D. MORRIS

Republicans got off to a fast start in their bid to recapture control of the House of Representatives, but appeared to lose steam early today as returns trickled in from the West.

As of 3 A. M., results from yesterday's Congressional races indicated a decided Republican trend, with some major upsets for the Democrats. However, with control of nearly two-thirds of the 435 seats still in doubt, victory for either party was far from certain.

The undecided contests were almost entirely in the Midwest, where the issue of declining farm income was a factor favoring the Democrats, and in the the Far West.

G. O. P. Gains in East

Such returns as were available from those areas indicated possible Democratic gains in Iowa, California and South Dakota.

Eastward, where the only decisive tallies were available, Republicans had picked up nine seats held by Democrats in the Eighty-fourth Congress while holding their own in all other contests where returns were conclusive. One, in New York City, was subpect to a recount. Democrats had failed to capture any Republican seat except one that they took in the Maine election on Sept. 10.

Republican incumbents were easy victors in a number of contests that had promised to be close.

The most outstanding upsets were in New Jersey, where the Hudson county Democratic stronghold of the late Mayor Frank Hague of Jersey City unseated its two Democratic Representatives, T. James Tumulty and Alfred D. Sieminski, in the Thirteenth and Fourteenth Congressional Districts.

Mr. Sieminski lost to Norman H. Roth, Republican. Mr. Tumulty, a 300-pound legislator, was defeated by Vincent J. Dellay, Republican.

A third Democratic incumbent in New Jersey, Harrison A. Williams, lost to Florence P. Dwyer, Republican.

Republicans also picked up one Democratic seat in Connecticut, one in Deleware, one in Pennsylvania, one in Indiana and

Continued on Page 3, Column 2

Stevenson Concedes Defeat and Wishes President Success

Stevenson and Kefauver talks appear on Page 13.

By HARRISON E. SALISBURY
Special to The New York Times.

CHICAGO, Wednesday, Nov. 7—Adlai E. Stevenson conceded the election of President Eisenhower in a statement made public at 12:25 A. M. Central standard time today (1:25 Eastern standard time).

In a telegram to President Eisenhower, the Democratic candidate expressed his understanding of "grave difficulties" that the Administration faced and wished all success to General Eisenhower in the years ahead.

Mr. Stevenson coupled his telegram of congratulations to the President with an appeal to his followers to carry forward in the crusade for what he called a "New America."

He called on America's leaders to recognize that the nation "wants to face up squarely to the facts of today's world."

"We don't want to draw back from them," Mr. Stevenson said. "We can't. We are ready for the test that we know history has set for us."

Mr. Stevenson in his statement took note of the troubled conditions of the world.

"Beyond the seas, in much of the world, in Russia, in China, in Hungary, in all the trembling satellites, partisan controversy is forbidden and dissent suppressed," Mr. Stevenson said.

Mr. Stevenson also took note

Continued on Page 13, Column 5

Electoral Vote by States

	Eisenhower	Stevenson		Eisenhower	Stevenson
Ala.	—	11	Nev.	3	—
Ariz.	4	—	N. H.	4	—
Ark.	—	8	N. J.	16	—
Calif.	32	—	N. M.	4	—
Colo.	6	—	N. Y.	45	—
Conn.	8	—	N. C.	—	14
Del.	3	—	N. D.	4	—
Fla.	10	—	Ohio	25	—
Ga.	—	12	Okla.	8	—
Idaho	4	—	Ore.	6	—
Ill.	27	—	Pa.	32	—
Ind.	13	—	R. Isl.	4	—
Iowa	10	—	S. C.	—	8
Kan.	8	—	S. D.	4	—
Ky.	10	—	Tenn.	11	—
La.	10	—	Texas	24	—
Me.	5	—	Utah	4	—
Md.	9	—	Vt.	3	—
Mass.	16	—	Va.	12	—
Mich.	20	—	Wash.	9	—
Minn.	11	—	W. Va.	8	—
Miss.	—	8	Wisc.	12	—
Mo.	—	13	Wyo.	3	—
Mont.	4	—			
Neb.	6	—	Total	457	74

EISENHOWER VOWS TO TOIL FOR PEACE

Hails Landslide Re-election as Proof Nation Wants 'Modern Republicanism'

Texts of the Eisenhower and Nixon talks on Page 12.

By RUSSELL BAKER
Special to The New York Times.

WASHINGTON, Wednesday, Nov. 7—President Eisenhower hailed his landslide re-election victory today as proof that his "modern Republicanism has now proved itself and America has approved of modern Republicanism."

He pledged in a victory statement early this morning to work with "whatever talents the good God has given me for 168,000,000 Americans here at home and for peace in the world."

Addressing a jubilant crowd of party workers at Republican election headquarters here and the nation, over television, the President declared that so long as the G.O.P. pursued the "ideals, the hopes and aspirations" of the people, it would continue to flourish.

"If it is anything less," he said, "it is only a conspiracy to seize power. And the Republican party is not that."

'Looks to the Future'

Thus, in his moment of triumph, General Eisenhower claimed a sweeping triumph for what his Administration's philosophers had styled the "new Republicanism" and what he himself termed this morning "modern Republicanism."

"Modern Republicanism," he said, "looks to the future and this means it will gain constantly new recruits." So long as it continued to remain "modern," he added, it would "continue to increase in power and influence for decades to come."

So long as it clings to its "modern" ideals, the President declared, it would "point the way to peace among nations and prosperity, advancing standards here at home in which everyone will share."

The President delivered his victory statement at 1:45 A. M., about fifteen minutes after this restive crowd gathered in the mammoth ballroom of the Sheraton-Park Hotel had heard Adlai E. Stevenson concede defeat in Chicago.

General Eisenhower had been waiting upstairs in a third-floor suite for three and a half hours,

Continued on Page 12, Column 1

41 STATES TO G.O.P.

President Sweeps All the North and West, Scores in South

By JAMES RESTON

Dwight David Eisenhower won yesterday the most spectacular Presidential election victory since Franklin D. Roosevelt submerged Alfred M. Landon in 1936.

The smiling 66-year-old hero of the Normandy invasion, who was in a Denver hospital recuperating from a heart attack just a year ago today, thus became the first Republican in this century to win two successive Presidential elections. William McKinley did it in 1896 and 1900.

Adlai E. Stevenson of Illinois, who lost to Mr. Eisenhower four years ago, thirty-nine states to nine, conceded defeat at 1:25 this morning.

At 4:45 A. M. President Eisenhower had won forty-one states to seven for Mr. Stevenson. His electoral lead at that time was 457 to 74 for Stevenson, and his popular vote was 25,071,331 to 18,337,434—up 2 per cent over 1952. Two hundred and sixty-six electoral votes are needed for election.

Victory in All Areas

This was a national victory in every conceivable way. It started in Connecticut. It swept every state in New England. It took New York by a plurality of more than 1,500,000. It carried all the Middle Atlantic states, all the Midwest, all the Rocky Mountain states and everything beyond the Rockies.

More than that, the Republican tide swept along the border states and to the South, carried all the states won by the G.O.P. there in 1952—Virginia, Texas, Tennessee and Florida—and even took Louisiana for the first time since the Hayes-Tilden election of 1876.

For the President and his 43-year old Vice Presidential running mate, Richard M. Nixon of California, who carried much of the Republican campaign, it was a more impressive victory than for the Republican party.

So close were many races for

Continued on Page 2, Column 3

CLARK LEADS DUFF IN PENNSYLVANIA

Democrat's Edge Dropping —President Takes State

By WILLIAM G. WEART
Special to The New York Times.

PHILADELPHIA, Wednesday, Nov. 7—Joseph S. Clark Jr., former Mayor of Philadelphia, was running ahead of Senator James H. Duff early today.

But his margin was ebbing as returns from rural areas and small towns began to offset the lead he piled up in large cities.

President Eisenhower won the state's thirty-two electoral votes by a plurality that was steadily mounting.

Mr. Clark expressed disappointment at the defeat of his party's standard-bearer. He attributed General Eisenhower's victory to his "personal popularity." Mr. Clark's campaign manager, Mayor Richardson Dilworth of Philadelphia, said the President's re-election was due to the "emotion caused by the war situation."

In the event the final tally in the Senatorial race is close, an estimated 50,000 absentee votes cast by servicemen and hospitalized veterans may decide the outcome. Under the law, absentee ballots are mailed to county

Continued on Page 13, Column 6

New York, Wednesday, November 7, 1956.

Eisenhower by a Landslide; Battle for Congress Close; Javits Victor Over Wagner

Suez Warfare Stopped Under British-French Cease-Fire

41 States to G.O.P.

President Sweeps All the North and West, Scores in South

By James Reston

Dwight David Eisenhower won yesterday the most spectacular Presidential election victory since Franklin D. Roosevelt submerged Alfred M. Landon in 1936.

The smiling 66-year-old hero of the Normandy invasion, who was in a Denver hospital recuperating from a heart attack just a year ago today, thus became the first Republican in this century to win two successive Presidential elections. William McKinley did it in 1896 and 1900.

Adlai E. Stevenson of Illinois, who lost to Mr. Eisenhower four years ago, thirty-nine states to nine, conceded defeat at 1:25 this morning.

At 4:45 A.M. President Eisenhower had won forty-one states to seven for Mr. Stevenson. His electoral lead at that time was 457 to 74 for Stevenson, and his popular vote was 25,071,331 to 18,337,434—up 2 per cent over 1952. Two hundred and sixty-six electoral votes are needed for election.

Victory in All Areas

This was a national victory in every conceivable way. It started in Connecticut. It swept every state in New England. It took New York by a plurality of more than 1,500,000. It carried all the Middle Atlantic states, all the Midwest, all the Rocky Mountain states and everything beyond the Rockies.

More than that, the Republican tide swept along the border states and to the South, carried all the states won by the G.O.P. there in 1952—Virginia, Texas, Tennessee and Florida—and even took Louisiana for the first time since the Hayes-Tilden election of 1876.

For the President and his 43-year old Vice Presidential running mate, Richard M. Nixon of California, who carried much of the Republican campaign, it was a more impressive victory than for the Republican party.

So close were many races for both the House and the Senate that control of the national legislature was not expected to be decided until later in the day.

> . . . the first Republican in this century to win two successive Presidential elections.

About the only consolation for the Democrats, other than that it was all over, was that they picked up strength in the Governor races and thus improved their chances of rebuilding for the post-Eisenhower election of 1960.

Starting with the advantage of holding twenty-seven state governorships to twenty-one for the Republicans, the Democrats won the state capitals yesterday in Iowa, Kansas and Massachusetts. Of the twenty-nine governorships at issue, they won twelve to ten with seven in doubt at 3:40 this morning.

The Eisenhower-Nixon sweep not only broke the Roosevelt coalition of the large urban states of the North and the "Solid South," but also carried into almost every group in the nation that was supposed to be strong for Mr. Stevenson and his running mate, Senator Estes Kefauver of Tennessee.

It clearly gained momentum in the last days during the fighting in the Middle East and Eastern Europe. It established the President as the man the nation wanted to lead it through the difficult period of transition in the Allied, Communist and neutral worlds.

The farm "revolt" was there all right in the areas where drought and falling prices had created a hardship situation, but it was not strong enough to sweep the farmers away from their natural Republican moorings.

Mr. Stevenson not only lost in the areas where his foreign policy arguments were supposed to be the strongest, as in New York, but he also lost ground on the civil rights issue in many of the Negro wards in the North.

He lost, too, in the so-called "Polish wards" of the North, no doubt because of the anti-Communist uprisings in Eastern Europe just as he was preparing to concentrate on the argument that the Administration's foreign policy had failed.

The Chicago Story

The story of Chicago illustrates what happened yesterday. Chicago, in Cook County, the home of one of the strongest Democrat Party machines in the New Deal days, actually went for Eisenhower by a projected margin of about 16,000.

The irony of this was that Mr. Stevenson had founded his hope on the assumption that the Democratic Party machine was his main hope. Yet it failed him there, and the same trend was present, if not so marked, through most of the populous cities from the Mississippi to New York, another Democratic "stronghold," which Mr. Stevenson carried by fewer than 100,000 votes.

Outside of a few states of the Old Confederacy, Mr. Stevenson's forces broke against the combination of the President's popularity, the prosperity of the nation, and the ominous international situation, which brought out a record number of voters in a serious frame of mind.

The steel workers of Lorain, Ohio, the Negroes of Ward 32 in Philadelphia and the so-called Polish voters of Ward 21 in Buffalo, all supposed to be strong for the Democrats, shifted the other way.

They didn't "go Republican," but they cut down their margins for the Democrats. And when that happens the coalition that kept the Democrats in power for a generation in the Nineteen Thirties and Forties is badly hurt.

What was particularly impressive was the strength of the President's vote in the Northern and border state cities. Four years ago, he took Bridgeport by 314 votes. Yesterday he carried it by 16,000. He took 55 per cent of the total vote yesterday in New Haven which gave Mr. Stevenson 54 per cent of that city's vote in 1952.

The President now has the opportunity to pursue the three objectives he gave in explanation of his decision to seek re-election: the maintenance of a just and stable peace in the world; the strengthening of what he has called "The New Republicanism"—that is, conservative in fiscal affairs and liberal in human affairs—and finally, the liberalization of the Republican party.

One of the most remarkable aspects of the President's victory is that he apparently was inclined not to seek re-election until after his heart attack a year ago last September. Before then, he repeatedly urged his party not to count on him but to find younger men to carry on the job he had started.

For example, when he was asked after he announced his candidacy last February what his decision was before his heart attack, he said this was something [that] would probably not be disclosed until twenty-five years after his death. However, his associates have said privately that he finally decided to run because, after his convalescence, he felt it was too late to build up a successor who could win and he was determined to do what he could to liberalize his party and complete the program he had started.

The general expectation was that he would make a start toward rebuilding his party in his second term by changing his Cabinet at some key posts. Secretary of State Dulles is now in Walter Reed Hospital in Washington recovering from an operation to remove a cancerous section of his large intestine. He is expected to be given a new post, probably as a foreign affairs adviser to the President.

One of the most remarkable aspects of the President's victory is that he apparently was inclined not to seek re-election until after his heart attack a year ago last September.

There have also been reports that Secretary of Defense Charles E. Wilson has no intention of staying on at the Pentagon through a second Eisenhower term, and Attorney General Herbert Brownell Jr. has told friends he will retire before the President's second-term inauguration on Jan. 20, 1957.

Gov. Christian A. Herter of Massachusetts, who started his federal government career in the State Department, former Gov. Thomas E. Dewey of New York, former U.S. High Commissioner in Germany, John J. McCloy, and General Eisenhower's former Chief of Staff at the North Atlantic Treaty headquarters, Gen. Alfred Gruenther, have all been mentioned as possibilities for any vacancies that may occur in the top four posts in the State and Defense departments.

Meanwhile, Sherman Adams, the Assistant to the President, and Vice President Nixon, who carried the main brunt of the campaigning for the Republicans in the last six weeks, are expected to assume increasingly important roles in the second Eisenhower Administration. The President, who will be seventy at the end of his second term, is forbidden by an amendment to the Constitution from seeking re-election in 1960.

Accordingly, with both General Eisenhower and probably Mr. Stevenson out of the running for the 1960 Presidential election, both parties will be seeking new potential candidates before long. Mr. Nixon and Mr. Adams are expected to be high on the Republican list of G.O.P. possibilities.

The main issues of the campaign were as follows:

Mr. Stevenson asserted that President Eisenhower was too old at 66 to meet the responsibilities of his office for another four years. He characterized him as a "part-time resident" who delegated his Presidential responsibilities to cabinet officials of inferior ability, and, despite two major illnesses in the last year, had chosen as his Vice-Presidential running mate a controversial politician. Mr. Nixon, he declared, would divide the country if he ever succeeded to the Presidency. President Eisenhower dissented on all counts.

The Republicans contended that President Eisenhower alone had the popular following at home and the experience and influence abroad, to guide the nation safely through a period of revolutionary transition in the world. The Democrats charged that, ever since the death of Stalin, the President had failed to understand or deal effectively with the new Soviet leaders, or the rising nationalism of the neutral nations, and had allowed the Atlantic Alliance to split wide open over the present crisis in the Middle East.

On the home front, the Republicans said that they had freed the national economy from unnecessary controls and not only had ended United States participation in foreign wars but also had produced the greatest era of prosperity in the history of the Republic. The Democrats, in reply, said this prosperity, like the Eisenhower "peace," was an illusion. They charged that the Republican appointments policy, tax policy, and farm policy had produced a "farm depression" and hurt "small business."

There were many subsidiary issues, including attempts by Mr. Stevenson late in the campaign to persuade the electorate that the President was remiss 1) in continuing tests of the hydrogen bomb and 2) in rejecting suggestions that the military manpower draft could be continued. However, there was little evidence that these issues had impressed the voters when they went to the polls yesterday.

The voting took place once more under pressure of extraordinary events overseas. Not since the election of 1944, when the Second World War was reaching its decisive phase with the American armies deep in Germany, have the American people gone to the polls so preoccupied with alarming foreign policy developments.

Despite the more hopeful news from Egypt yesterday afternoon, the war scare, combined with good weather over most of the nation, brought out an unexpectedly large crush at the polls.

The President drove to his home in Gettysburg, Pa. early yesterday morning after a meeting with his aides on the foreign situation. He and Mrs. Eisenhower reached the polling place at 11:15 A.M. and were applauded by their neighbors as they left the building. The President then flew back to Washington, though he originally had planned to drive back to the Capital.

Not since the election of 1944 . . . have the American people gone to the polls so preoccupied with alarming foreign policy developments.

Mr. Stevenson cast his ballot at Half Day, Ill., near his Libertyville farm. With him was his son, Borden, a first-time voter. Incidentally, the Census Bureau showed that 7,500,000 Americans reached voting age between the last Presidential election and this.

The Democratic nominee was cheerful and optimistic. He bantered with a small crowd at the polling place and said he had been told that leaders in several cities had reported to him that there was "a very strong Democratic turnout."

The Democratic Vice-Presidential nominee, Senator Estes Kefauver of Tennessee, the "iron man" of the campaign, was the last to stop exhorting the voters. He was in Miami, Fla., shaking hands with everybody within reach. He finally quit campaigning late yesterday morning and flew home to Chattanooga to cast his vote. Vice President Nixon had sent his absentee ballot to his home town of Whittier, Calif. earlier. He was in Washington yesterday.

The Kennedy campaign liberally used the image of the photogenic candidate—particularly in heroic profile.

The new decade began with one of the closest, most hard-fought elections in American history. Voters in both parties shared the sense that Eisenhower's departure had cleared the way for younger leaders. Richard Nixon and John F. Kennedy, both freshmen Congressmen in 1946, aspired to lead this new generation.

No one was better organized than Kennedy, the 43-year old senator from Massachusetts. Since 1958, when he was reelected to the Senate by the biggest majority in the state's history, he had been a frontrunner. Handsome, charismatic, a Pulitzer Prize winner and a well-known war hero (thanks to a well-oiled publicity machine that kept information and photographs flowing to the media), Kennedy was a formidable candidate, notwithstanding his political liabilities.

These included his Roman Catholicism, his relative youth, and the general distrust of his wealthy, powerful father, Joseph P. Kennedy. But JFK proved skillful in neutralizing those weaknesses, and more important, at winning votes. The Democratic primaries had never been so important, and in Wisconsin and West Virginia, Kennedy defeated Senator Hubert Humphrey of Minnesota. The next round was fought at the Los Angeles convention, where he outmaneuvered Lyndon B. Johnson to win nomination on the first ballot. Surprising many, including his brother Robert, he chose Johnson as his running mate, chiefly as a vote-getter in

Left to right:
John F. Kennedy (1917–63)
Richard M. Nixon (1913–94)

Nixon's running mate, Henry Cabot Lodge, was the grandson of the man who had defeated Kennedy's grandfather in the 1916 Senate race.

the South. Kennedy's slogan, the "New Frontier," captured the appeal of youth, the search for new knowledge, and the appeal of the unknown new decade just beginning.

The Republicans met in Chicago, where they nominated Nixon on the first ballot, adding Henry Cabot Lodge as his running mate. Nixon had steadily gained admirers for his loyalty and toughness; in particular, his 1959 "kitchen debate" in Moscow with Nikita Khruschchev impressed Americans. He promised to travel to all 50 states (Hawaii and Alaska had just entered the union), a pledge that he later regretted.

The evenly matched candidates were equally energetic, and the result was a campaign of unmatched excitement and expense. Both followed grueling schedules (Nixon covered 65,000 miles, Kennedy 44,000). Nixon was bruised early on by listless support from Eisenhower. Ike told reporters who asked about Nixon's contributions to major administrative decisions, "If you give me a week, I might think of one."

Kennedy, on the other hand, reacted shrewdly to deflect criticism. He spoke candidly about the separation of church and state before an audience of concerned ministers in Houston. And when Dr. Martin Luther King Jr. was arrested on October 19 in Atlanta, Robert Kennedy intervened to get him released on bail, bringing many African-American votes to the Democratic side just before election day.

Four live television debates were the substantive and theatrical highlights of the campaign. Seventy million Americans tuned in to the first debate, held September 26 in Chicago. Though both candidates were informed and articulate, Kennedy's more relaxed and telegenic appearance convinced Americans that he won the debate, and that translated into votes.

The election went down to the wire. Aided by an unprecedented turnout, Kennedy won by a whisker with 34.2 million votes to Nixon's 34.1 million, and slightly more breathing room in the electoral college, 303 to 219. It was the closest election since 1880. The world's foremost power was poised to enter a daunting new decade with the youngest president it had ever elected.

Every campaign generates an enormous amount of memorabilia—but the intensity of 1960 raised the contest to new levels.

At 43, Kennedy was the youngest man ever to win election to the presidency, and the first born in the twentieth century.

Senator John F. Kennedy and Vice President Richard M. Nixon face off in the second of a series of four live televised debates—the first ever broadcast between Democratic and Republican presidential nominees. The debates ushered in the era of electronic politics, forever changing the way candidates and political parties communicated with voters and ran their campaigns. Kennedy won the debate—and arguably the election—because he looked cooler, more confident, and more handsome on television.

Richard Nixon campaigns in Flint, Michigan, September 23, 1960.

Nixon and Eisenhower hold a rally in New York City, November 2, 1960.

The crowd clamors for a view of JFK in the Bronx, New York, November, 1960.

The Vice President and his running mate, Henry Cabot Lodge (in center), hold a campaign meeting *(left)*, with General Wilton B. Persons, Assistant to President Eisenhower, Washington, D.C., August 1960.

Nixon is welcomed in his hometown of Whittier, California *(bottom)*, as he opens his campaign, August 2, 1960.

John F. Kennedy in a pre-convention huddle at the Biltmore Hotel in Los Angeles *(left)* with Governor Abraham Ribicoff of Connecticut, right; Connecticut state Democratic chairman John Bailey, left; and his brother Robert, July 12, 1960.

The Kennedys motorcade rolls through Manhattan *(below)*; Mayor Robert F. Wagner is pictured in the lower right, October 1960.

JFK campaigns at Commack Sports Arena, Long Island *(opposite)*, November 6, 1960.

"All the News That's Fit to Print"

The New York Times.

LATE CITY EDITION
U. S. Weather Bureau Report (Page 93) forecasts: Cloudy, periods of rain today. Partly cloudy, colder tomorrow. Temp. range: 55—41; yesterday: 53.8—40.4.

VOL. CX..No. 37,546. © 1960 by The New York Times Company, Times Square, New York 36, N. Y. NEW YORK, THURSDAY, NOVEMBER 10, 1960. 10 cents beyond 50-mile zone from New York City except on Long Island. Higher in air delivery cities. FIVE CENTS

KENNEDY'S VICTORY WON BY CLOSE MARGIN; HE PROMISES FIGHT FOR WORLD FREEDOM; EISENHOWER OFFERS 'ORDERLY TRANSITION'

DEMOCRATS HERE SPLIT IN VICTORY; LEHMAN ASSAILED

De Sapio Accepts Challenge for Party Control—Mayor Claims Leadership

Text of De Sapio statement appears on Page 43.

By LEO EGAN

Less than twenty-four hours after the polls closed, the political coalition that gave Senator John F. Kennedy New York's forty-five electoral votes began coming apart at the seams.

Its disintegration was signaled by Carmine G. De Sapio in a statement assailing former Gov. Herbert H. Lehman, key figure in the Democratic reform group, and Alex Rose, Liberal party master of strategy.

The statement accepted Mr. Lehman's election night challenge to a finish fight for control of the party organization in the city and state.

At the same time it appeared to rule out any chance of a Democratic-Liberal party coalition for next year's Mayoral election in New York City and for the Governorship election in the state in 1962 if Mr. De Sapio remains in control of the party machinery.

Kennedy's Delicate Problem

Mr. De Sapio, leader of Tammany and Democratic National Committeeman for New York, consulted Michael H. Prendergast, the Democratic State Chairman, and a number of party leaders in the city and upstate before issuing his statement.

The collapse of the coalition so soon after it achieved its goal gave President-elect Kennedy a delicate political problem before he takes office. At some stage soon he will have to decide whom in New York to consult about appointments for the new Administration.

Thus, in so far as New York is concerned, the election appeared to raise as many questions as it settled. Control of the Democratic party machinery is one of them. Among the others are: What is Mayor Wagner's political future? And what is Governor Rockefeller's?

When told of Mr. De Sapio's statement last night, Mayor Wagner commented that he in-

Continued on Page 43, Column 1

Registration Set-Up Called Faulty Here

By DOUGLAS DALES

Political leaders voiced dissatisfaction yesterday over the way permanent personal registration functioned here Tuesday in its first test in a Presidential election.

Charges were made that thousands of persons had been disfranchised because they were unable to convince election inspectors that they had registered and were eligible to vote.

How many voters may have been so affected was concededly a guess. But a check of the Supreme Courts in the five boroughs indicated that more than 1,300 persons had gone before the justices for orders directing the inspectors to permit them to vote.

"There was a minimum of 10,000 denied the right to vote," Abraham Gellinoff,

Continued on Page 43, Column 5

ASSEMBLY DELAYS U.N. CONGO DEBATE

Postpones It Indefinitely, 48-30, as Soviet Backs Step—U. S. Move Fails

By KATHLEEN TELTSCH
Special to The New York Times.

UNITED NATIONS, N. Y., Nov. 9—The General Assembly voted tonight to postpone the debate on the Congo indefinitely.

The 48-to-30 vote, with eighteen abstentions, was on a surprise move made by Ghana with the help of Guinea and Nigeria and the enthusiastic support of the Soviet bloc.

The United States tried to avoid the adjournment vote by asking for a suspension of the session until delegates could ponder the unexpected request.

Western sources said privately that Ghana's initiative appeared to have been prompted in part by the presence here of President Joseph Kasavubu of the Congo and the likelihood that the Assembly's Credentials Committee would agree to his request for the seating of a Congolese delegation of his supporters.

A Two-Hour Wrangle

Ghana, Guinea, India and five other states have joined in sponsoring a resolution that aims instead at having the Assembly seat a delegation designated by the deposed Congolese Premier, Patrice Lumumba.

The Assembly acted after a two-hour wrangle marked by two table-thumping demonstrations by the Soviet bloc and also by Ghana, both in protest against the efforts of Foreign Minister Pierre Wigny of Belgium to defend his country's position on the Congo issue.

The adjournment request was made by Alex Quaison-Sackey, Ghana's chief delegate. He appealed to the Assembly to hold off any further debate pending the efforts of a fifteen-member Asian-African commission to reconcile the clashing political factions in the Congo and restore some governmental stability.

He said that the commission probably would leave for the Congo in a week and that further acrimonious debate in the Assembly would only hamper the conciliation effort.

However, the adjournment as voted did not stipulate how long the debate should be suspended. United States sources said tonight that they understood this to mean that discussion could

Continued on Page 3, Column 1

WINNER'S PLEDGE

Family Is With Him as He Vows to Press Nation's Cause

Text of Kennedy's statement is printed on Page 36.

By HOMER BIGART
Special to The New York Times.

HYANNIS, Mass., Nov. 9—Senator John F. Kennedy accepted in solemn mood today his election as President.

He pledged all his energy to advancing "the long-range interests of the United States and the cause of freedom around the world."

He made this pledge inside the flag-decked Hyannis Armory at 1:4. P. M., an hour after Vice President Nixon, his Republican opponent, had conceded defeat.

His wife, Jacqueline, stood at his side as the 43-year-old President-elect faced 300 newsmen and massed batteries of TV cameras and gave his victory statement to the nation.

Behind him were arrayed the Kennedy family: his father, former Ambassador Joseph P. Kennedy; his mother, three sisters and three brothers.

No Sign of Jubilation

The Kennedys showed no evidence of jubilation. All wore expressions of solemnity. Mr. Kennedy's margin of victory was too slender to stir much elation. Some of his aides acknowledged disappointment over the startlingly narrow gap in the popular vote.

Mr. Kennedy, after responding to applause with a diffident bow and a smile, first read the telegram from Mr. Nixon conceding defeat and extending congratulations. The Senator had stayed up until 3:50 A. M. awaiting this concession and had gone to bed disappointed when the Vice President withheld it.

Replies to Nixon

Mr. Nixon wired the President-elect that all the nation would give him "united support" in the next four years.

Mr. Kennedy replied to Mr. Nixon:

"I know that the nation can continue to count on your unswerving loyalty in whatever effort you undertake, and that you and I can maintain our long-standing cordial relations in the years ahead."

Mr. Kennedy then read a congratulatory message from President Eisenhower.

In his message the President informed Mr. Kennedy that he would shortly receive suggestions from the President as to the change-over of responsibilities for national leadership.

To this Senator Kennedy had replied:

"I am grateful for your wire and good wishes. I look forward to working with you in the near future. The whole country is hopeful that your long ex-

Continued on Page 36, Column 7

United Press International Telephoto

THE MESSAGES WERE CONGRATULATORY: Senator John F. Kennedy displaying telegrams at Hyannis, Mass. With him are Mrs. Kennedy, his parents and Robert F. Kennedy, left, and R. Sargent Shriver, a brother-in-law.

KHRUSHCHEV NOTE SALUTES KENNEDY

Message of Congratulations Asks for Negotiations on Tensions in World

Text of Khrushchev message will be found on Page 42.

By The Associated Press.

MOSCOW, Nov. 9—Soviet Premier Khrushchev congratulated Senator John F. Kennedy today for his Presidential victory.

He expressed hope that Soviet-United States relations would "again follow the line along which they were developing in Franklin Roosevelt's time."

He urged negotiations aimed at easing the international situation.

[In Bonn, Chancellor Konrad Adenauer said he planned to go to Washington early next year for conferences with Mr. Kennedy.]

Mr. Khrushchev's statements in a congratulatory message to Mr. Kennedy coincided with Moscow's insistence that the policies of President Eisenhower had suffered a rebuff in the election.

The Soviet press contended that the election proved "the American people have blackballed the policy of the 'cold war' and the arms race, that they want changes and expect Washington to pursue a reasonable course in international affairs, a course dictated by life and the balance of forces now prevailing in the world." Mr.

Continued on Page 42, Column 4

Electoral Vote by States

	Rep.	Dem.		Rep.	Dem.		Rep.	Dem.
Alabama	..	5*	Louisiana	..	10	Ohio	25	..
Alaska	..	..	Maine	5	..	Oklahoma	8	..
Arizona	4	..	Maryland	..	9	Oregon	6	..
Arkansas	..	8	Mass.	..	16	Penna.	..	32
California	..	..	Michigan	..	20	Rhode Island	..	4
Colorado	6	..	Minnesota	..	11	So. Carolina	..	8
Conn.	..	8	Mississippi	**	**	So. Dakota	4	..
Delaware	..	3	Missouri	..	13	Tennessee	11	..
Florida	10	..	Montana	4	..	Texas	..	24
Georgia	..	12	Nebraska	6	..	Utah	4	..
Hawaii	..	..	Nevada	..	3	Vermont	3	..
Idaho	4	..	New Hamp.	4	..	Virginia	12	..
Illinois	..	27	New Jersey	..	16	Washington	9	..
Indiana	13	..	New Mexico	..	4	W. Virginia	..	8
Iowa	10	..	New York	..	45	Wisconsin	12	..
Kansas	8	..	No. Carolina	..	14	Wyoming	3	..
Kentucky	10	..	North Dakota	4	..	Total	185	300

*Five electors are pledged to Kennedy and six unpledged.
**Eight electors not pledged to vote for party candidates.

LIBERALS SUFFER SETBACK IN HOUSE

G. O. P. Picks Up 22 Seats to Aid Conservative Bloc

By JOHN D. MORRIS

The House of Representatives will have a more conservative tinge in the Eighty-seventh Congress.

Inroads into the present House Democratic majority of 283 to 154 scored by the Republicans in Tuesday's elections promised to strengthen their conservative coalition with Southern Democrats.

The liberal legislative program to be submitted early next year by the new Democratic President, John F. Kennedy, may consequently face handicaps in the new Congress, which convenes Jan. 3.

In the Senate, Republicans cut the Democratic margin by two seats, to 64 to 36. That chamber remains predominantly liberal in membership, although conservatives dominate key committee posts.

Gubernatorial Shifts

The Democrats achieved a net gain of one governorship and now control thirty-four of the fifty state houses. In twenty-seven gubernatorial contests the Democrats won fifteen and the Republicans twelve, with an exchange of party control in thirteen.

In the House races, nearly complete unofficial returns showed that the Democrats had elected 257 House candidates and the Republicans 175, with five contests still in doubt.

The Republicans captured twenty-nine seats held by Democrats and lost seven of their own, for a net gain of at least twenty-two. For a bare numerical majority of 219 they would have had to achieve a net gain of sixty-five.

Among the eleven states of the Old Confederacy the Republicans maintained their hold on seven seats of the Eighty-

Continued on Page 38, Column 4

NIXON WIRE GIVES HIS 'BEST WISHES'

Sends Kennedy a Message —500 in Capital Hail Him

By BILL BECKER
Special to The New York Times.

LOS ANGELES, Nov. 9—Vice President Nixon conceded today the Presidential election of his Democratic opponent, Senator John F. Kennedy.

About twelve hours after the polls had closed, the Vice President sent the following telegram to Senator Kennedy at Hyannis Port, Mass.:

"I want to repeat through this wire the congratulations and best wishes I extended to you on television last night. I know that you will have the united support of all Americans as you lead the nation in the cause of peace and freedom in the next four years."

Read by Aide

The telegram was read to newsmen by Mr. Nixon's press secretary, Herbert G. Klein, at 9:45 A. M., Pacific standard time (12:45 P. M., Eastern standard time).

The Vice President did not make a personal appearance. Mr. Klein said Mr. Nixon was resting with Mrs. Nixon and their two daughters in their suite at the Ambassador Hotel.

It was obvious that the Vice President had considered his remarks late on election night a virtual concession.

[A crowd of several hundred greeted Mr. Nixon as he arrived Wednesday night at Andrews Air Base, near Washington, after a flight of four and a half hours from Los Angeles.]

Mr. Nixon remained in seclusion most of the morning although Mr. Klein said he was up about 6 A. M. after little more than three hours of sleep. The secretary said Mr. Nixon

Continued on Page 42, Column 5

PRESIDENT SENDS WIRE TO KENNEDY

He Felicitates Senator and Orders Agency Chiefs to Cooperate With Him

By FELIX BELAIR Jr.
Special to The New York Times.

AUGUSTA, Ga., Nov. 9—President Eisenhower congratulated President-elect John F. Kennedy today on his election and then invited him to designate representatives to participate in all Federal policy discussions to assure an "orderly transition" to the new Administration.

The text of the President's telegram was withheld here at the request of Mr. Kennedy. But President Eisenhower is understood to have told the President-elect that he had instructed all heads of Federal departments and agencies to "cooperate fully" with Mr. Kennedy's representatives.

President Eisenhower arrived here for his customary fall holiday in midafternoon after a two-hour flight from Washington.

The President's message of congratulation to Mr. Kennedy was sent from the White House just before he took off for his favorite vacation retreat here at Augusta National Golf Club.

He also sent messages to the defeated Republican candidate, Vice President Nixon, and his running mate, Henry Cabot Lodge, as well as Vice President-elect Lyndon B. Johnson.

In his telegram to Mr. Nixon

Continued on Page 42, Column 7

RESULTS DELAYED

Popular Vote Almost Even—300-185 Is Electoral Tally

By JAMES RESTON

Senator John F. Kennedy of Massachusetts finally won the 1960 Presidential election from Vice President Nixon by the astonishing margin of less than two votes per voting precinct.

Senator Kennedy's electoral vote total stood yesterday at 300, just thirty-one more than the 269 needed for election. The Vice President's total was 185. Fifty-two additional electoral votes, including California's thirty-two, were still in doubt last night.

But the popular vote was a different story. The two candidates ran virtually even. Senator Kennedy's lead last night was little more than 300,000 in a total tabulated vote of about 66,000,000 cast in 165,826 precincts.

That was a plurality for the Senator of less than one-half of 1 per cent of the total vote—the smallest percentage difference between the popular vote of two Presidential candidates since 1880, when James A. Garfield outran Gen. Winfield Scott Hancock by 7,000 votes in a total of almost 9,000,000.

End Divided Government

Nevertheless, yesterday's voting radically altered the political balance of power in America in favor of the Democrats and put them in a commanding position in the Federal and state capitals unknown since the heyday of Franklin D. Roosevelt.

They regained control of the White House for the first time since 1952 and thus ended divided government in Washington. They retained control of the Senate and the House of Representatives, although with slightly reduced margins. And they increased their hold on the state governorships by one, bringing the Democratic margin to 34—16.

The President-elect is the first Roman Catholic ever to win the nation's highest office. The only other member of his church nominated for President was Alfred E. Smith, who was defeated by Herbert Hoover in 1928.

Faces Difficult Questions

Despite his personal triumph, President-elect Kennedy is confronted by a number of hard questions:

¶In the face of such a narrow victory how can he get through the Congress the liberal program he proposed during the campaign?

¶Can so close an election produce any impetus for loosening the conservative coalition of Republicans and Southern Democrats which has blocked most liberal legislation in the House?

¶Will the new President be able successfully to claim a mandate for legislation such as the $1.25 minimum wage, Fed-

Continued on Page 35, Column 1

ATOM BILL BEATEN IN FRENCH SENATE

Debre to Push Compromise on Nuclear Force Plan

By W. GRANGER BLAIR
Special to The New York Times.

PARIS, Thursday, Nov. 10—The Senate early today rejected President de Gaulle's project for an independent French nuclear striking force.

By a vote of 186 to 83, with seventeen abstentions, this conservative Upper House approved a procedural motion to table the national nuclear deterrent bill that had been passed to it by the National Assembly Oct. 27.

Although the Senate's action was a stinging blow to President de Gaulle and a sharp indication of mounting parliamentary opposition, it did not mean that the Government's measure would not eventually become law.

It was announced after the vote that Premier Michel Debré would call for the creation of a mixed committee of Senators and Deputies to work out a compromise measure. Should this conference committee fail to find a compromise, the Government would resubmit its measure to the Assembly for a second reading, and virtually certain approval. The measure would then become law with or without Senate's approval.

The Senate motion to table

Continued on Page 8, Column 1

NEWS INDEX

10 Irish Soldiers Slain in Congo When U.N. Patrol Is Ambushed

By PAUL HOFMANN
Special to The New York Times.

LEOPOLDVILLE, the Congo, Nov. 9—A patrol of eleven Irish soldiers of the United Nations force in the Congo was ambushed in the northern part of Katanga Province yesterday. The bodies of four men were sighted.

[The United Nations Command said that ten soldiers had been slain in the ambush, Reuters reported. The Irish Army announced in Dublin that one private had survived the attack. Reports received by the United Nations in New York said the surviving soldier was "badly wounded," according to United Press International.]

The patrol belonged to the Irish Thirty-third Battalion, which has headquarters in the industrial city of Albertville. The battalion, with a strength of about 550 men, is responsible for maintaining order in a vast area of North Katanga. The region has been the scene of intertribal warfare and clashes between Baluba tribesmen and the gendarmerie controlled by Moise Tshombe, President of Katanga.

United Nations officials here were unable to say who had attacked the Irish patrol. The ambush occurred south of Niemba, a village between Albertville and Kabalo. The zone is described as "Baluba country," but it is not known whether Baluba tribesmen were responsible for the assault.

Announcing the loss, a United Nations spokesman said it brought the toll of dead in the international force in the Congo to about thirty since the world organization's troops arrived

Continued on Page 2, Column 3

Vatican Calls Kennedy Election Proof of American Democracy

By ARNALDO CORTESI
Special to The New York Times.

ROME, Nov. 9—The election of Senator John F. Kennedy, a Roman Catholic, to the Presidency was received with keen satisfaction in the Vatican today.

During the campaign the Vatican remained neutral. Its newspaper, L'Osservatore Romano, abstained from all comment lest it be accused of siding with one candidate against the other.

Today the editor of the newspaper, former Italian Deputy Raimondo Manzini, said:

"Kennedy's victory strengthens the appreciation for the high democratic principles of freedom that guide American public life and assure access to the highest office to every citizen regardless of social class, race, or religion.

"The effective support given by large numbers of Protestant citizens to a Catholic considered suitable for the Presidency has been significant in this respect. Catholics are, of course, satisfied at the solemn confirmation of the principle that the office of President is open to a son of the Catholic Church, which enjoys such large prestige in the United States. Catholics have, however, always admired Nixon's irreproachable attitude of deferential respect for the Catholic hierarchy."

Senator Kennedy's victory was announced under large headlines by the whole morning press in Italy today. In most newspapers it took precedence over the results of the provincial and municipal elections that were held in Italy over the week-end.

Government circles received the news without astonishment

Continued on Page 38, Column 7

New York, Thursday, November 10, 1960.

Kennedy's Victory Won by Close Margin; He Promises Fight for World Freedom; Eisenhower Offers 'Orderly Transition'

Results Delayed

Popular Vote Almost Even— 300–185 is Electoral Tally

By James Reston

Senator John F. Kennedy of Massachusetts finally won the 1960 Presidential election from Vice President Nixon by the astonishing margin of less than two votes per voting precinct.

Senator Kennedy's electoral vote total stood yesterday at 300, just thirty-one more than the 269 needed for election. The Vice President's total was 185. Fifty-two additional electoral votes, including California's thirty-two, were still in doubt last night.

But the popular vote was a different story. The two candidates ran virtually even. Senator Kennedy's lead last night was little more than 300,000 in a total tabulated vote of about 66,000,000 cast in 165,826 precincts.

That was a plurality for the Senator of less than one-half of 1 per cent of the total vote—the smallest percentage difference between the popular vote of two Presidential candidates since 1880, when James A. Garfield outran Gen. Winfield Scott Hancock by 7,000 votes in a total of almost 9,000,000.

End Divided Government

Nevertheless, yesterday's voting radically altered the political balance of power in America in favor of the Democrats and put them in a commanding position in the Federal and state capitals unknown since the heyday of Franklin D. Roosevelt.

They regained control of the White House for the first time since 1952 and thus ended divided government in Washington. They retained control of the Senate and the House of Representatives, although with slightly reduced margins. And they increased their hold on the state governorships by one, bringing the Democratic margin to 34-16.

The President-elect is the first Roman Catholic ever to win the nation's highest office. The only other member of his church nominated for President was Alfred E. Smith, who was defeated by Herbert Hoover in 1928.

Faces Difficult Questions

Despite his personal triumph, President-elect Kennedy is confronted by a number of hard questions:

In the face of such a narrow victory how can he get through the Congress the liberal program he proposed during the campaign?

Can so close an election produce any impetus for loosening the conservative coalition of Republicans and Southern Democrats which has blocked most liberal legislation in the House?

Will the new President be able successfully to claim a mandate for legislation such as the $1.25 minimum wage, Federal school aid and a broader medical assistance to the aged which he advocated from the stump?

In the campaign Senator Kennedy promised a "first hundred days" equal to that great period of reform in the Administration of Franklin D. Roosevelt. But the result made it more than ever likely that he would have to reach an accommodation with the conservative South, which has opposed much of his program within the Democratic party.

Senator Lyndon B. Johnson of Texas, Senator Kennedy's Vice-Presidential running mate, contributed much to Mr. Kennedy's victory and more than justified the controversial last minute tactic of putting the Texan on the ticket over the loud protests of the Northern Democratic liberals.

Johnson's Contribution

Without much question, he was responsible for bringing Texas back to the Democratic fold for the first time since 1918, and for helping to hold North and South Carolina, which most of the experts gave to the Republicans a month ago. Meanwhile, there was nothing to suggest that he had hurt the Democrats, as predicted, in the liberal areas of the urban North.

Not since President Harry S. Truman's surprising victory over Gov. Thomas E. Dewey of New York in the election of 1948—and perhaps not even since Woodrow Wilson's triumph in the photo-finish election of 1916—have there been so many dramatic swings and changes of political fortune as occurred all through the night Tuesday and even into yesterday afternoon.

It is worth recalling also that Mr. Truman's victory, dramatic as it was, came with a plurality of more than 2,000,000 votes—compared with Senator Kennedy's less than 400,000 so far.

Shortly before midnight Tuesday the signs had seemed to point to a substantial Kennedy victory.

Victory Projected Into West

The Senator's national plurality of the popular vote, which had been climbing steadily all evening, was about 2,000,000. The Chicago vote had given him a big lead in Illinois, and the analysts were projecting westward his smashing triumph in the Northeast.

But actually that was the peak of Senator Kennedy's momentum. Just about midnight a slow process of attrition set in that whittled away at his "sure" win until, in the dramatic hours of the early morning, it was clear that this was the closest election in generations.

> Only in New York and Kennedy's home state of Massachusetts did the Democrats win by truly large majorities.

The Kennedy popular vote margin melted to 800,000 by 5 A.M. yesterday, and the trend was still downward. The Senator's Illinois lead dropped from almost 200,000 to around 50,000, and state Democratic leaders began to sound brave when they forecast a final victory margin of "at least" 28,000.

And it became increasingly evident that the magic worked by Senator Kennedy in the East was less effective on the other side of the Mississippi. As returns began coming in from the West, the race drew closer and closer.

The returns were so close in many Western states that it became impossible to get a clear picture. Leads of a few hundred or a few thousand votes changed hands again and again in Nevada, New Mexico, Montana, Washington, Hawaii and Alaska.

By 5 or 6 A.M. yesterday, the Kennedy margin seemed to be facing a real threat in Minnesota as well as Illinois.

Nixon Finally Concedes

It became clear that Senator Kennedy had to win one of the three big undecided states—Illinois, Minnesota or California—to get his needed 269 electoral votes.

At no time did Vice President Nixon have a chance to win 269 electoral votes on his own. Even if all three of the major doubtful states and every one of the smaller western states had fallen to him, he would have been four votes short.

But in such a situation Senator Kennedy would also have been denied a majority. The power to decide the winner would then have rested with fourteen unpledged electors from Alabama and Mississippi who bolted the regular Democratic ticket as a protest against Northern Democratic views.

Throughout yesterday morning the result hung in the balance. Senator Kennedy's margin fell slowly in Illinois and Minnesota, and indeed at one point Mr. Nixon pulled ahead in the former until a last batch of Chicago votes was produced for Mr. Kennedy.

Then at 12:33 o'clock Senator Kennedy clinched Minnesota and the election. Thirteen minutes later Mr. Nixon made his formal concession.

Strength Combined

Senators Kennedy and Johnson won by putting together their combined strength in the great cities of the North and the rural areas of the traditionally Democratic South; but they were remarkably weak elsewhere.

For example, they won eight of the nine so-called large decisive states, but in some of them their margins were tighter than a Pullman window: 6,000–6,500 in Illinois, 22,000 in New Jersey, 60,000 in Texas, 65,000 in Michigan, 131,000 in Pennsylvania.

Only in New York and Kennedy's home state of Massachusetts did the Democrats win by truly large majorities—404,000 in New York and 498,000 in Massachusetts. Each of these margins was larger than Mr. Kennedy's margin of victory in the nation as a whole.

The anomalies in the results were sometimes startling.

Why should Kennedy win by 131,000 in Pennsylvania and lose in neighboring Ohio, with much the same mixture of union and Catholic voters, by 263,000?

Senator Kennedy campaigned on a liberal program but could not have won without the support of conservative Catholics in the North and conservative Protestants in the South.

Contrasts in Jersey

In most areas populated by Catholics, Mr. Kennedy did well, but in some, Hudson County, N.J., for example, his showing was a great disappointment to his managers, while he did remarkably well in the more Republican territory of Essex County, N.J.

While the Senator was heavily supported in the cities of the North, Southern industrial areas such as Charlotte and Winston-Salem, N.C., went Republican. He did well in the Southern "Black Belts," as indeed did Smith in 1928, but he did poorly in the farm belts of the North, where he expected his attacks on Secretary of Agriculture Ezra Taft Benson might even swing some of the Plains States into the Democratic column.

Also, while Mr. Kennedy was regaining some of the Democratic party's lost strength in the South, he managed at the same time to pick up additional strength among Negroes, who have been complaining about the Democratic party's political associations with the South.

Ironically, Senator Kennedy, whose political reputation rested primarily on his arresting and attractive personality, ran about 7 per cent behind the Democratic local candidates on a national basis.

Senator Thruston B. Morton, the genial and relaxed chairman of the Republican National Committee, said yesterday that the main reason why Vice President Nixon had lost the election was that he had failed to hold the Northern Negro vote, which had gone so heavily to President Eisenhower in the two previous Presidential elections.

Chairman Morton's estimate was that the Vice President had got only between 10 to 12 per cent of the Negro vote, while President Eisenhower got about 26 per cent in 1952 and 1956.

Ironically, Senator Kennedy, whose political reputation rested primarily on his arresting and attractive personality, ran about 7 per cent behind the Democratic local candidates on a national basis.

This was not true in the Northeast, where he was near his home base and where his sophisticated manner was quite popular, but it was definitely true in Illinois, Minnesota, Wisconsin, and Indiana, where he ran well behind the Democratic ticket.

Nevertheless, the most striking facts of all lay in the contrasts in the voting returns from the various regions of the country.

In New England, Senator Kennedy split the six states, three to three, but built up a plurality of 592,036 votes.

He swept all six Middle Atlantic States—Delaware, Maryland, New Jersey, New York, Pennsylvania and West Virginia with another huge plurality of 684,549. Then, as the voting moved westward, his power declined.

A Deficit in Midwest

He split the East Central States, winning Illinois by a whisker and Michigan, but lost Ohio and Indiana, and came out of the region with a deficit of 422,904.

He lost six of the eight West central states, Iowa, Kansas, Nebraska, North and South Dakota and Wisconsin and won only two, Minnesota and Missouri. Here again, Vice President Nixon piled up a plurality for the region of 526,235.

In the Mountain states, New Mexico swung to Kennedy last night, but Mr. Nixon took six of the others, and Senator Kennedy won only Nevada. The same trend prevailed here, with the Vice President getting a plurality of at least 160,000.

Even in the Pacific Coast states, Mr. Nixon's plurality was over 22,000, and while Mr. Kennedy had a plurality of 245,000 in the South, where he won everything except Florida, Oklahoma, Kentucky, Tennessee and Virginia, the Republicans piled up a comparatively large southern vote, 5,300,000.

Barry Goldwater, rather unconvincing in this cowboy hat, nevertheless foreshadowed the rise of western conservatism.

Despite a lopsided final result, and the illusion of consensus it created, the 1964 election coincided with growing anxiety among Americans. The shock of John F. Kennedy's assassination a year earlier still reverberated widely across the country. Throughout the summer of 1964, fiery race riots in northern cities and the murders of civil rights workers in Mississippi reminded Americans that a great deal of unfinished business lay ahead.

At the GOP convention in San Francisco, Senator Barry Goldwater of Arizona claimed the nomination, although even many Republicans considered him far right of center. Tensions erupted when Nelson Rockefeller, the moderate Governor of New York, was shouted down by Goldwater supporters during a speech denouncing fanatacism.

Goldwater's acceptance speech, including his famous line, "extremism in the defense of liberty is no vice," confirmed for many observers that he was some distance from the political mainstream.

The Democratic convention in Atlantic City was designed as a coronation, but a split divided the President and Attorney General Robert Kennedy. Kennedy was still incensed after

Left to right:
Lyndon B. Johnson (1908–73)
Barry Goldwater (1909–98)

The Goldwater campaign came up with this clever slogan in scientific shorthand, perhaps hoping to plant subliminal messages of prosperity into the voters' subconscious.

LBJ doused his hope of being named his running mate. Johnson was worried about the possibility of a Kennedy draft, a legitimate worry that deepened when the delegates gave RFK a sixteen-minute ovation at the convention. Johnson was also distressed by the growing rift between Southern Democrats, his old constituency, and African-Americans, to whom he would commit a large part of his social program. In the end, the second slot went to Senator Hubert H. Humphrey of Minnesota.

From the start, Goldwater faced an uphill battle, which he only made steeper by remarking that he wouldn't mind lobbing a nuclear weapon into "the men's room of the Kremlin." He was one of relatively few Senators to vote against the Civil Rights Act signed by LBJ that summer, and he had also voted against the nuclear test ban treaty. Near the end of his campaign, a new Republican star emerged when the former actor Ronald Reagan participated in a televised fundraising campaign for Goldwater. Two years later, he would win election as governor of California.

LBJ's strategy was to work on important legislation, and to make sure people knew that he was behind it. As a young Texan whose life had been deeply shaped by the New Deal, Johnson knew the power of government to make a difference. Most of the programs that defined the War on Poverty and the Great Society were either under way or soon would be. Beginning in September, he campaigned more aggressively, giving folksy speeches around the country.

On November 4, LBJ took 44 states and the District of Columbia, which was voting for the first time. He won 61 percent of the popular vote, the highest percentage in history. Goldwater carried Arizona and five southern states, an early sign that the South was beginning to turn from its historic alliance with the Democratic party. For the moment, LBJ had the landslide he had craved ever since he won a Senate race by 87 votes in 1948. But victory would prove short-lived, both at home and abroad.

An outline of Texas adorns these riding boots, which LBJ brought wherever he went—including Vietnam in 1966.

LBJ's message evoked memories of the New Deal, but also addressed contemporary concerns.

Republican headquarters at the Camelback Inn (owned by a close friend of Goldwater's) in Scottsdale, Arizona, July 31, 1964.

Ben Kaplan, owner of Ye Junk Shoppe, stands proudly in front of his campaign memorabilia display, Times Square, New York, October 13, 1964.

Barry Goldwater jokingly pokes a finger through his no-lens eyeglasses during a photo shoot; he removed the lenses so they would not reflect camera flashes *(left)*, Washington, D.C., August 14, 1964.

Goldwater at a rally in San Francisco for the Republican convention *(below)*, July 10, 1964.

Republican vice-presidential candidate William E. Miller campaigns in Lowell, Indiana, September 7, 1964.

Claudia "Lady Bird" Johnson stumps for her husband in Ohio *(left)*, September 1964.

At East Side Citizens for Johnson in New York City *(below)*, children sort, distribute, and trade campaign buttons, November 1964.

LBJ tosses his cap into the crowd, Indianapolis, October 1964.

USA
USA

A citizen in the voting booth *(above)* in Brooklyn, New York, November 3, 1964.

LBJ squeezes through a throng of supporters in Atlantic City *(left)*, September, 1964.

"All the News That's Fit to Print"

The New York Times.

LATE CITY EDITION
U. S. Weather Bureau Report (Page 78) forecasts: Sunny today; clear tonight. Fair and milder tomorrow. Temp. Range: 63—48; yesterday: 60—48.

VOL. CXIV . . . . No. 39,001. © 1964 by The New York Times Company. Times Square, New York, N. Y. 10036 | NEW YORK, WEDNESDAY, NOVEMBER 4, 1964. | TEN CENTS

JOHNSON SWAMPS GOLDWATER AND KENNEDY BEATS KEATING; DEMOCRATS WIN LEGISLATURE

KENNEDY EDGE 6-5

Keating's Defeat Is Termed a 'Tragedy' by Rockefeller

New York Vote

PRESIDENT

Johnson, Dem. 4,509,514
Goldwater, Rep. 2,089,113
11,330 of 12,439 E.D.'s rptg.

SENATOR

Kennedy, Dem. 3,479,976
Keating, Rep. 2,857,023
11,318 of 12,439 E.D.'s rptg.

By R. W. APPLE Jr.

Robert F. Kennedy was elected to the United States Senate from New York yesterday in his first bid for elective office, overwhelming Republican Senator Kenneth B. Keating.

With more than 80 per cent of the vote counted, Mr. Kennedy held a 6-to-5 lead. Because most of the untallied vote was in heavily Democratic New York City, it appeared that the former Attorney General's plurality might reach 650,000.

Mr. Keating conceded defeat at 11:39 P.M. with the announcement at the Roosevelt Hotel that he had sent a congratulatory telegram to Mr. Kennedy.

Governor Rockefeller, standing beside the white-haired Rochester legislator, said Mr. Keating's defeat was "a tragedy for the state and nation."

Runs Behind Johnson

"Senator Keating, one of the great Senators in the history of New York, has been rolled under by a national landslide," the Governor added. "He waged a magnificent campaign."

Mr. Kennedy ran well behind President Johnson, who seemed to be headed for a record margin of 2.5 million votes or more in the state. The President won all of the state's 62 counties.

It thus appeared that about a million New York voters had split their ticket to cast votes for Mr. Johnson and Mr. Keating — but even this wasn't enough to make the Senate contest close.

A major surprise was the showing of the Liberal party, which had expected to deliver

Continued on Page 27, Column 4

The Election at a Glance

President

	Number of States*	Electoral Votes
Johnson	45	486
Goldwater	6	52

*Includes Dist. of Columbia

President—New York

Johnson	4,509,514
Goldwater	2,089,113

Incomplete

Senator—New York

Kennedy	3,479,976
Keating	2,857,023

Incomplete

The Senate

Newly Elected Senators		Make-up of New Senate	
Democrats	25	Democrats	65
Republicans	5	Republicans	30
In doubt	5	In doubt	5

The House

Democrats elected	261
Republicans elected	127
In doubt	47

UPSET AT ALBANY

Carlino and Mahoney Defeated—Special Session Expected

By LAYHMOND ROBINSON

A surge of Democratic votes swept the Republicans from control of the State Legislature yesterday for the first time in more than a quarter of a century.

The massive victory gave the Democrats a probable working majority of a dozen seats in the Assembly and a half dozen in the Senate.

Not since 1935, in the sweep of Franklin D. Roosevelt's New Deal, had the Democrats had control of both the houses. Not since 1938 had they held control of the Senate.

Toppled from their powerful posts in stunning upsets were Assembly Speaker Joseph F. Carlino of Long Beach, L. I., and Senate Majority Leader Walter J. Mahoney of Buffalo.

Beaten by Outsiders

Both suffered defeat at the hands of virtually unknown Democrats.

Mr. Carlino, the top Republican figure in the lower house for six years and an Assemblyman representing Nassau's Second Assembly District for 20 years, was beaten by Jerome R. McDougal Jr., a car salesman making his first race for public office.

Senator Mahoney, often called the most powerful man in the Legislature, was unseated by John H. Doerr of Buffalo in Erie County's 55th Senate District.

Another high-ranking Republican who lost was Senator MacNeil Mitchell of Manhattan, the most influential New York City member of the two houses.

In some districts in the suburbs and in upstate counties, Democrats captured Assembly and Senate seats for the first time in this century.

Districting Fight Due

At the last session, the G.O.P. had a 10-vote edge over the Democrats in the Assembly, holding 85 seats to 65 for the Democrats. In the Senate they had a 33-25 edge.

Although the Democrats ended this G.O.P. domination, the battle for control could be resumed again in December.

The Governor is expected to call a special session of the Legislature then to adopt a new plan for reapportioning seats in the two houses.

This reapportionment session will be controlled by the present members, with the Republicans in control.

Members elected yesterday do not take their seats until the

Continued on Page 33, Column 3

LYNDON BAINES JOHNSON

The New York Times

HUBERT HORATIO HUMPHREY

TURNOUT IS HEAVY

President Expected to Get 60% of Vote, With 44 States

By TOM WICKER

Lyndon Baines Johnson of Texas compiled one of the greatest landslide victories in American history yesterday to win a four-year term of his own as the 36th President of the United States.

Senator Hubert H. Humphrey of Minnesota, Mr. Johnson's running mate on the Democratic ticket, was carried into office as Vice President.

Mr. Johnson's triumph, giving him the "loud and clear" national mandate he had said he wanted, brought 44 states and the district of Columbia, with 486 electoral votes, into the Democratic column.

Senator Barry Goldwater, the Republican candidate, who sought to offer the people "a choice, not an echo" with a strongly conservative campaign, won only five states in the Deep South and gained a narrow victory in his home state of Arizona. Carrying it gave him a total of 52 electoral votes.

Senator Plans Statement

A heavy voter turnout favored the more numerous Democrats.

In Austin, Tex., Mr. Johnson appeared in the Municipal Auditorium to say that his victory was "a tribute to men and women of all parties."

"It is a mandate for unity, for a Government that serves no special interest," he said.

The election meant, he said, that "our nation should forget our petty differences and stand united before all the world."

Mr. Goldwater did not concede. A spokesman announced that the Senator would make no statement until 10 A.M. today in Phoenix.

Johnson Carries Texas

But the totals were not the only marks of the massive Democratic victory. Traditionally Republican states were bowled over like tenpins—Vermont, Indiana, Kansas, Nebraska, Wyoming, among others.

In New York, both houses of the Legislature were headed for Democratic control for the first time in years. Heralded Republicans like Charles H. Percy, the gubernatorial candidate in Illinois, went down to defeat.

Former Attorney General Robert F. Kennedy, riding Mr. Johnson's long coattails, overwhelmed Senator Kenneth B. Keating in New York.

But ticket splitting was widespread. And in the South, Georgia went Republican; never

Continued on Page 22, Column 1

JOHNSON CRUSHES RIVAL IN JERSEY

Lead Near 900,000, Topping Eisenhower's Record—Williams Re-elected

New Jersey Vote

PRESIDENT

Johnson, Dem. 1,645,844
Goldwater, Rep. 853,708
4,001 of 4,603 E.D.'s rptg.

SENATOR

Williams, Dem. 1,474,523
Shanley, Rep. 891,425
4,001 of 4,603 E.D.'s rptg.

By GEORGE CABLE WRIGHT

President Johnson won New Jersey's 17 electoral votes yesterday in the biggest political victory ever scored in the state.

With 91 per cent of the vote tallied, the President held a record lead of nearly 900,000 votes over his Republican opponent, Senator Barry Goldwater.

Until yesterday, the record plurality for a Presidential candidate in New Jersey was the 756,605-vote margin rolled up by President Eisenhower, a Republican, in 1956.

In sweeping at least 19, and possibly all of the state's 21 counties, Mr. Johnson carried to victory with him incumbent Democratic Senator Harrison A. Williams Jr. Democrats also captured a majority of the state's 15 seats in the House of Representatives for the first time since 1912.

In the present Congress, Republicans hold eight of the seats. On the basis of incomplete returns from yesterday's balloting, Democrats won at least 10 seats.

The Democratic candidate James J. Howard also held a narrow lead over his Republican opponent, Marcus Daly, in an

Continued on Page 32, Column 4

Connecticut Votes 2-1 for President; All Democrats Win

Connecticut Vote

PRESIDENT (Complete)

Johnson, D. 825,416
Goldwater, R. 392,556

SENATOR

Dodd, D. 779,252
Lodge, R. 425,376

By RICHARD H. PARKE

President Johnson led a sweeping Democratic victory in Connecticut yesterday.

His better than 2-to-1 margin over Senator Barry Goldwater eclipsed the previous record plurality in a Presidential race in the state. Mr. Johnson's plurality was 432,860. The earlier record had been set by President Dwight D. Eisenhower in 1956 when he defeated Adlai E. Stevenson by 306,758 votes.

Senator Thomas J. Dodd, the Democratic incumbent, also triumphed easily over his Republican opponent, former Gov. John Davis Lodge. But the 57-year-old Senator ran about 45,000 votes behind the President.

One result of President Johnson's landslide was the defeat of the state's only Republican Congressman, Representative Abner W. Sibal of the Fourth (Fairfield County) District. Mr. Sibal lost the normally Republican district to former Representative Donald J. Irwin, a

Continued on Page 32, Column 1

SOUTH REVERSES VOTING PATTERNS

Goldwater Makes Inroads, but More Electoral Votes Go to the President

By JOHN HERBERS

Special to The New York Times

ATLANTA, Nov. 3—President Johnson carried a majority of Southern states tonight by turning the normal voting patterns inside out.

The rural Deep South, solidly Democratic in the past, voted for Senator Barry Goldwater of Arizona on the Republican ticket. The states on the border of the region, which had gone Republican in recent Presidential elections, returned to the Democrats.

But so strong was the Goldwater tide in the Deep South that seven Republican Congressional candidates rode to victory on the Senator's coattails from districts that had been Democratic since Reconstruction.

The Republicans made their biggest gains in Alabama, where five candidates for Congress defeated Democratic opponents.

President Johnson carried Virginia, North Carolina, Florida, Tennessee, Arkansas and Texas with a total of 81 electorial votes. Senator Goldwater carried Louisiana, Mississippi, Alabama, Georgia and South Carolina with a total of 47 electorial votes.

South Carolina and Mississippi had not voted for Repub-

Continued on Page 24, Column 2

Democrats Are Assured Of Majorities in Congress

House Gain for Democrats

By JOHN D. MORRIS

Democrats strengthened their control of the House of Representatives in yesterday's elections, scoring substantial gains in all regions except the South.

With returns from Congressional races still incomplete early this morning, the trend indicated a Democratic pickup of at least 20 seats and possibly 30 or more.

The Republicans nevertheless scored spectacular breakthroughs in the South, winning five of Alabama's eight seats, one of Mississippi's five and at least one of Georgia's 10.

Those gains were more than offset, however, by the loss of both of their Texas seats and by heavy Democratic gains in other parts of the country.

The House division in the expiring 88th Congress is 257 Democrats and 178 Republicans. This credits five vacancies to the parties last holding the seats. Three were occupied by Democrats and two by Republicans.

With 218 needed for a major-

Continued on Page 21, Column 1

3 G.O.P. Senators Lose

By E. W. KENWORTHY

The Democrats appeared virtually certain today of maintaining a nearly 2-to-1 majority in the United States Senate.

At 3 A.M. the Democrats had won 25 of the 35 contests in yesterday's elections. These, added to their 40 holdovers, assured them of 65 seats when the Eighty-ninth Congress convenes in January.

The Republicans, at the same hour, had won only five seats—in Vermont, Nebraska, Delaware, Arizona and Hawaii—all of which were won by incumbent Senators. These, added to 25 holdovers, assured the Republicans of at least 30 seats.

The party line-up when Congress adjourned last month was 66 Democrats and 34 Republicans.

By 3 A.M. the Democrats had captured three seats from the Republicans.

In New York, Robert F. Kennedy, former Attorney General, a brother of President Kennedy,

Continued on Page 20, Column 1

STATE DEMOCRATS GAIN SIX IN HOUSE

Lindsay and Other Liberal Republicans Keep Seats

By WARREN WEAVER Jr.

Democrats swept through the New York Congressional delegation in yesterday's election, unseating six Republican Representatives and threatening the House seat of a seventh.

In the wake of the Johnson victory, the Democrats increased their strength in the delegation from 20 to 26 while the number of Republicans dropped from 21 to 14, with one district in doubt.

Although they failed to dislodge any of the three New York City Republican Congressmen, Democratic candidates scored victories elsewhere across the state. They took two seats in Nassau County, one in Westchester, one in the Hudson Valley and two in Western New York.

Among the chief Republican survivors was Representative John V. Lindsay of Manhattan, who won by a 65,000-vote margin in his East Side district.

Other Republicans to retain their seats were Representative Seymour Halpern of Queens, who like Mr. Lindsay had opposed Senator Barry Goldwater, and, Representative Ogden R.

Continued on Page 24, Column 3

G.O.P. Grip Broken In Suburban Voting

By JOHN SIBLEY

Traditional Republican bastions in the suburbs crumbled before the Johnson onslaught yesterday, and the President carried with him many local Democratic candidates in nearby New York and New Jersey communities.

Widespread ticket-splitting showed, however, that Republican suburbanites were not forsaking their party so much as they were renouncing its Presidential nominee, Senator Barry Goldwater.

Westchester County, for the first time since 1912, gave a plurality to a Democratic Presidential candidate. Rockland County went Democratic for the first time since Franklin D. Roosevelt carried the county in 1936 and for only the fourth time in 100 years.

Long Island's suburbs, too, went to the President. Mr. Johnson became the first Democratic Presidential candidate in modern

Continued on Page 33, Column 2

ROMNEY IS VICTOR; PERCY'S BID FAILS

Democrats Likely to Achieve Gain in Governorships

By JOSEPH A. LOFTUS

Democrats gave a good account of themselves in 25 contests for Governor yesterday, but it was a Republican who produced the spectacular.

Gov. George Romney, running aloof from Senator Barry Goldwater, set off a Michigan ticket-splitting spree to win re-election and thereby planted himself firmly in the thin front line of 1968 Presidential possibilities.

While Senator Goldwater gathered barely a third of Michigan's votes, the Governor defeated Neil Staebler with more than 55 per cent of the tally.

Strong Goldwater supporters "cut" Governor Romney, but the latter improved on his own 1962 vote totals in the labor-Democratic areas of Detroit and Flint-Saginaw.

The Republicans failed to capture a major prize, the Illinois governorship. The defeated nominee, Charles H. Percy, had figured in Presidential talk for the future.

Gov. Otto J. Kerner won a second term in Illinois despite the failure of Mayor Richard Daley's organization to deliver Chicago majorities as big as those Mr. Kerner won there four years ago.

Nationally the Democrats seemed likely to score a net

Continued on Page 24, Column 4

Summary of International News: Wilson Acts to Nationalize Steel

Following is a summary of foreign news. A full report begins on the first page of the second part.

Labor Offers Program

Britain's new Labor Government offered a program of controversial legislation to Parliament. Headed by a demand for renationalization of the steel industry, the proposals indicate one of the bitterest sessions in parliamentary history.

French Explain Aim

Foreign Minister Maurice Couve de Murville told the French Parliament that the United States and Europe should develop separate, but not necessarily hostile, policies. In Washington, officials predicted that a major crisis for Atlantic unity would arise at a NATO meeting in December.

Bolivian Troops Revolt

A military revolt broke out in Bolivia and appeared to be spreading across the country. A truce designed to open the way for efforts "to resolve the present crisis" facing the Government of President Victor Paz Estenssoro was announced. In neighboring Chile, Eduardo Frei Montalva was inaugurated as the country's 28th President. In Cuba workers will vote Dec. 2 for worker councils.

Soviet Voices Concern

The Soviet Union expressed concern to the United States over the situation along the Cambodian-South Vietnamese border. In Pnompenh, Prince Norodom Sihanouk said his nation was ready to retaliate against any further border incursions by South Vietnamese forces. In Saigon, United States officials raised the casualty toll in Sunday's bombardment of the Bienhoa air base to 76 Americans, of whom four were dead.

WHITE BACKLASH DOESN'T DEVELOP

Vote in Suburbs in North Is Strong for President

By ANTHONY LEWIS

Rich and poor, Protestant and Roman Catholic and Jew, farmer and city-dweller and suburbanite—all showed marked shifts toward President Johnson in yesterday's extraordinary election.

Only in the Deep South did Senator Barry Goldwater score any significant gains for the Republican ticket over four years ago. Riding the crest of the racial issue there, he swung Mississippi, Alabama, Georgia, South Carolina and Louisiana to his party.

The white backlash, on which Mr. Goldwater had counted so strongly, failed to materialize in most parts of the North. Only among voters of Polish and other East European origins were there signs of this resentment toward Negroes, and even this phenomenon was scattered

Continued on Page 26, Column 1

NEWS INDEX

PRESIDENT SEES A UNITY MANDATE

In Victory Talk, He Pays Tribute to Predecessor

The text of Johnson's talk will be found on Page 22.

By CHARLES MOHR

Special to The New York Times

AUSTIN, Tex., Wednesday, Nov. 4—President Johnson said early this morning that his election was a "mandate for unity" and for a "government that provides equal opportunity for all and special privilege for none."

Mr. Johnson, obviously deeply moved by his landslide victory, told a crowd at the Municipal Auditorium here that it was a tribute to "the program begun by our beloved President John F. Kennedy."

Of the returns, Mr. Johnson said, "I doubt there have ever been so many people seeing so many things alike" on an Election Day.

Earlier, Mr. Johnson had said of Senator Barry Goldwater's refusal to concede that it was "purely a matter for the individual involved—whatever reasons he may have, I don't know."

He also said that the election was going "about as we expected."

Mr. Johnson appeared on the Municipal Auditorium stage with his wife and two daughters to a long ovation.

He said that "no words are

Continued on Page 22, Column 6

Salinger Is Losing; Johnson Wins State

By LAWRENCE E. DAVIES

Special to The New York Times

SAN FRANCISCO, Wednesday, Nov. 4—President Johnson captured California's 40 electoral votes in his triumph over Senator Barry Goldwater in yesterday's election.

On the basis of the incomplete count of ballots, however, the President's former press secretary, Senator Pierre Salinger, apparently lost his Senatorial battle to George Murphy, the Republican nominee.

Mr. Salinger late last night refused to concede defeat but said he "would be less than candid if I didn't say the vote doesn't look good." Some of his campaign strategists agreed that the results "looked bad" but declared they would await developments for a few hours before having anything definite to say.

Mr. Salinger, who has been

Continued on Page 34, Column 4

New York, Wednesday, November 4, 1964.

Johnson Swamps Goldwater and Kennedy Beats Keating; Democrats Win Legislature

Turnout Is Heavy

President Expected to Get 60% of Vote, With 44 States

By Tom Wicker

Lyndon Baines Johnson of Texas compiled one of the greatest landslide victories in American history yesterday to win a four-year term of his own as the 36th President of the United States.

Senator Hubert H. Humphrey of Minnesota, Mr. Johnson's running mate on the Democratic ticket, was carried into office as Vice President.

Mr. Johnson's triumph, giving him the "loud and clear" national mandate he had said he wanted, brought 44 states and the District of Columbia, with 486 electoral votes, into the Democratic column.

Senator Barry Goldwater, the Republican candidate, who sought to offer the people "a choice, not an echo" with a strongly conservative campaign, won only five states in the Deep South and gained a narrow victory in his home state of Arizona. Carrying it gave him a total of 52 electoral votes.

Senator Plans Statement

A heavy voter turnout favored the more numerous Democrats.

In Austin, Tex., Mr. Johnson appeared in the Municipal Auditorium to say that his victory was "a tribute to men and women of all parties."

"It is a mandate for unity, for a Government that serves no special interest," he said.

The election meant, he said, that "our nation should forget our petty differences and stand united before all the world."

Mr. Goldwater did not concede. A spokesman announced that the Senator would make no statement until 10 A.M. today in Phoenix.

Johnson Carries Texas

But the totals were not the only marks of the massive Democratic victory. Traditionally Republican states were bowled over like tenpins—Vermont, Indiana, Kansas, Nebraska, Wyoming, among others.

In New York, both houses of the Legislature were headed for Democratic control for the first time in years. Heralded Republicans like Charles H. Percy, the gubernatorial candidate in Illinois, went down to defeat.

Former Attorney General Robert F. Kennedy, riding Mr. Johnson's long coattails, overwhelmed Senator Kenneth B. Keating in New York.

But ticket splitting was widespread. And in the South, Georgia went Republican; never in its history had it done so. Into the Goldwater column, too, went Mississippi, Alabama, Louisiana and South Carolina—all part of the once solidly Democratic South.

But Mr. Johnson carried the rest of the South, including Virginia, Tennessee and Florida—states that went Republican in 1960. He carried his home state of Texas by a large margin and won a majority of the popular vote in the Old Confederacy.

> "It is a mandate for unity, for a Government that serves no special interest."

Nationwide, the President's popular vote margin apparently would reach 60 per cent or more. His popular vote plurality had risen early this morning to more than 13 million.

The President was clearly carrying into office with him a heavily Democratic Congress, with a substantially bigger majority in the House.

The vote poured in, through the high-speed counting system of the Network's Election Service, at such a rate that the leading television broadcasters were calling it a Johnson victory about 9 P.M.

But the only time the Republican candidate ever was in front was early yesterday morning when Dixville Notch, N.H., traditionally the earliest-reporting precinct in the nation, gave him eight votes to none for Mr. Johnson.

After that, in the President's own slogan, it was "L.B.J. all the way."

Election analysis thought that would be the case when the first significant returns came in from rural Kansas, where partial counts of incomplete boxes are allowed. They showed Mr. Johnson running strongly in this traditionally Republican territory.

Their early judgments were strengthened when the President swept early-reporting Kentucky, an important border state that had not gone Democratic in a Presidential election since 1948, and rolled to victory in Indiana, a Republican stronghold since 1936.

Ohio, a state counted upon as a vital part of the Goldwater victory strategy, fell to the President next, with Mr. Johnson compiling a massive lead in populous Cuyahoga County (Cleveland). One Negro precinct there went for the President by 99.9 per cent of its vote.

In sharp contrast, Mr. Johnson at one point in the evening was carrying only 8.9 per cent of the vote in Jackson, Miss., where his civil rights stand was unpopular. Mr. Goldwater compiled an overwhelming victory in that state, winning more than 80 per cent of its vote.

> He won the distinction of being the first candidate from a Southern state to be elected to the White House in more than a hundred years.

But as victory after victory rolled in for the President—all New England, the big Middle Atlantic states of New Jersey and Pennsylvania, Southern states like Texas, Tennessee, and North Carolina, the Western states of Oklahoma, Colorado and Kansas—Mr. Johnson's mounting total became a triumphant march across the nation.

There was nothing spotty or regional about it and long before midnight it was apparent that the President would have the "loud and clear" national mandate.

It was one of the most significant victories in Presidential history. The Goldwater campaign had posed a sharp challenge to almost the entire trend of national policy, domestic and foreign, since the Great Depression and World War II.

What He Proposed

He had proposed a sharp curtailment of Federal Government activities, particularly in the welfare field and in matters affecting the economy. He had called for a foreign policy of "brinkmanship," in which the nation's military might would be used as a threat against the Communist-block nations.

And he had raised doubts whether he would continue to lend Federal influence and authority to the drive for Negro equality in the United States.

Mr. Johnson, in head-on conflict with Mr. Goldwater on almost every campaign issue, thus received decisive endorsement from the nation for the general line of policy pursued by the nation for more than a quarter-century, through Administrations of both parties.

For himself, he won the distinction of being the first candidate from a Southern state to be elected to the White House in more than a hundred years.

And he won a massive vote of approval for the manner in which he had conducted its business since taking over the Presidency when John F. Kennedy was assassinated last Nov. 22.

Rapid Moves Likely

On the impetus of his imposing victory, Mr. Johnson can be expected to move rapidly on a broad front in domestic policy, and to grapple with several serious foreign problems.

He has said that a program of medical care for the aged through the Social Security system will be his first priority in legislative matters. He has also pledged to seek a major education program and to extend his "war on poverty."

In international matters, Mr. Johnson must soon seek positive answers to the problems of establishing some form of international nuclear force that would include West Germany, of reorganizing the North Atlantic Treaty Organization and its forces, and of prosecuting the anti-Communist guerrilla warfare in South Vietnam.

Mr. Johnson voted this morning in Johnson City, Tex., the hill country town where he was born on Aug. 27, 1908, and near which is located his LBJ Ranch. He and Mrs. Johnson voted, like most of the rest of the nation, for Lyndon B. Johnson.

Mr. Johnson's remarkable victory, carrying with it such traditional Republican states as Indiana, Vermont and Kansas, produced unusual examples of ticket-splitting. These testified to the inability of Mr. Goldwater to unify the Republican party behind his conservative program.

In Rhode Island, for instance, Mr. Johnson won a victory, taking almost 80 per cent of the vote. In the same state, voters re-elected Republican Gov. John Chafee, who had fought Mr. Goldwater's nomination, by about 58 per cent of the vote.

In Vermont, Senator Winston Prouty, a moderate Republican, survived the Johnson tide. But the President's sweeping victory in Ohio endangered the senatorial candidacy of Robert Taft Jr., a pre-election favorite, who was running neck and neck with Stephen M. Young, the Democratic incumbent.

Mr. Johnson's coattails were long for some underdog Democrats, notably Gov. Otto Kerner of Illinois, who was re-elected over Mr. Percy, a Republican newcomer who had looked to many in his party like future Presidential timber.

Mr. Johnson's great victory in New York also was a prime factor in the apparent victory of Mr. Kennedy over Senator Keating.

In Iowa, however, one Democrat outran Mr. Johnson, a rare event in yesterday's election. He was Gov. Harold F. Hughes, who took about 63 per cent of the vote to about 60 per cent for the President.

Mr. Johnson's victory was solidly based in the votes of almost all religious and ethnic groups, all income classes, and in every section of the nation. Nor did the so-called "white backlash" against the Civil Rights Act of 1964 materialize to any serious extent.

The backlash was apparent among Polish steelworkers in Baltimore, but Mr. Johnson piled up a heavy vote elsewhere in Maryland to add that state to his total.

In the District of Columbia, with its big Negro population, the President won by about five to one in the first Presidential election ever held in the Federal city.

Paradoxes Noted

In Kentucky, where anti-Catholic voting contributed to John Kennedy's defeat there in 1960, Mr. Johnson ran in some areas as much as 15 per cent ahead of Mr. Kennedy's totals among white Protestant voters.

In New York, he was about five percentage points ahead of Mr. Kennedy's pace among Roman Catholic voters.

New York provided another paradox. Although there was evidence of a slump in Polish-American voting for Mr. Johnson in Maryland, Indiana, Ohio, and Illinois, that ethnic group gave both the President and Robert Kennedy a heavy proportion of its vote in New York.

Even more remarkable was the situation in the South. There, Mr. Johnson carried two states, Virginia and Tennessee, that had gone Republican in 1960, and was leading narrowly in another, Florida.

Mr. Goldwater carried South Carolina, which went Democratic in 1960, and was threatening in Georgia.

But it was an election dotted with such paradoxes. In normally Republican Nebraska, for instance, Mr. Johnson and Democratic Gov. Frank Morrison were elected—but so was Republican Senator Roman Hruska. All three carried the population center of Lincoln by a wide margin.

The explanation for such unusual voter behavior lay in the nature of the Presidential contest.

The nation was voting at the end of one of the most unusual Presidential campaigns in its history. Some called it dull, some called it dirty, some called it unenlightening, but no one disputed that there had been few like it.

It was remarkable, first, in that no Vice President had ever succeeded to office so late in the term of his predecessor as Mr. Johnson did when he took over less than a year ago—Nov. 22, 1963. As a result, almost all of his time in office, following a political "moratorium" in memory of John F. Kennedy, was spent in an intensely political atmosphere.

The campaign was unusual, too, in that Mr. Johnson was the first resident of a Southern state to be nominated by a major party for the Presidency since Zachary Taylor of Louisiana ran on the Whig ticket in 1848 and James K. Polk of Tennessee was nominated by the Democrats in 1844.

President Taylor was both the last Southern resident elected President before today and the last successful Whig candidate.

Mr. Goldwater, the President's Republican opponent, was in many ways an even more unusual candidate. As an apostle of a conservatism that was virtually uncompromised throughout his year-long campaign, he was the most ideological and factional candidate of either major party since William Jennings Bryan ran on a free silver platform in 1896.

As the candidate of a faction that had captured the Republican party, rather than the overwhelming choice of that party's consensus, Mr. Goldwater suffered sharp defections that amounted almost to a party split.

Except for a concilatory speech to a group of Republican leaders at Hershey, Pa., on Aug. 12, Mr. Goldwater made little effort to compromise with the more moderate and liberal sentiment in his party. In Republican National Headquarters and in many of the state parties, a "purge" of non-Goldwater men was carried out soon after his nomination in San Francisco on July 15.

Appeals to Republicans

As a result, many Republicans either withheld public support of the Goldwater-Miller ticket, or defected outright to the Democrats. Mr. Johnson and Mr. Humphrey carefully refrained from attacking the Republican party as such, termed Mr. Goldwater no more than its "temporary spokesman" and openly appealed for dissident Republicans to enter the Democratic coalition this year.

Thus, a Southern Democrat once considered too conservative to win the Democratic nomination, and a small-state conservative long believed to be an isolated figure in Republican politics, made the 1964 race—the 45th Presidential campaign in the nation's history.

Although Mr. Goldwater was the challenger, his outspoken conservatism and controversial views set the tone of the campaign and largely shaped the most hotly debated issues. Most analysts and poll-takers came to believe that the central question of the campaign was not Mr. Johnson and the record of his Administration but Mr. Goldwater and the radical departures he proposed in both domestic and foreign policy.

> Mr. Johnson's victory was solidly based in the votes of almost all religious and ethnic groups, all income classes, and in every section of the nation.

There were few substantive exchanges between the candidates until after the nomination of Mr. Johnson and Mr. Humphrey at Atlantic City on Aug. 26. On Aug. 18, the United States Senate, with the acquiescence of the President, killed a bill that would have suspended the equal-time provision of the law governing broadcasting, and that ended all chance of an actual face-to-face debate between Mr. Goldwater and Mr. Johnson.

Nevertheless, as the campaign developed through the fall months, with both men and their running mates criss-crossing the nation and appearing frequently on television, a dialogue did develop between them on several questions, including the following:

Centralized Government

Mr. Goldwater contended that since 1933, the Federal Government had absorbed more and more power from the states and localities, and that within the Government itself, the executive branch and the Supreme Court had progressively usurped powers that more properly resided in Congress or with the states.

He pledged, however, that he would move slowly in terminating Federal programs and that he would honor both actual and implied commitments between the Government and the people.

Mr. Johnson vigorously defended the Federal Government as the instrument of all the people, pointed frequently to Federal programs in the welfare, conservation, medical and other fields, denied that a strong central government was a threat to the liberties of the people, and accused Mr. Goldwater of running "against the Presidency" instead of for it.

Nuclear Weapons

Mr. Goldwater argued on several fronts. He said the Administration's reliance on missiles instead of manned bombers would eventually bring a sharp reduction in deliverable nuclear capacity. He said the Supreme Commander of the North Atlantic Treaty Organization forces ought to have "more leeway" in the use of tactical nuclear weapons—weapons he said should be considered "conventional."

Later, he modified this to say that commanders in the field already had delegated authority to use nuclear weapons in certain pre-described emergency situations.

Throughout his campaign, Mr. Goldwater implied that the United States ought to have overwhelming nuclear and conventional strength, and should use it in a policy of "brinkmanship" to force Communist governments to stop disturbing the world's peace.

Mr. Johnson and other Democratic spokesmen denied that the shift to missiles endangered American security. They insisted that the nation's strength had never been greater, and that it was measurably increased over that provided in the Administration of President Dwight D. Eisenhower.

The Democrats also insisted that nuclear weapons control should and did remain exclusively in the hands of the President. They termed Mr. Goldwater a "trigger-happy hip-shooter" who could not be relied upon to keep his finger off the "nuclear button."

And they argued that a policy of brinkmanship was not only too risky in the nuclear era but also that the idea of forcing Communist nations to back down from their line of policy was unrealistic and oversimplified.

Civil Rights

Mr. Goldwater, who voted in the Senate against the Civil Rights Act of 1964, on the ground that its public accommodations and equal employment sections were unconstitutional, insisted that such legislation infringed the rights of the people.

He said the solution to the problems of Negro rights could be found only "in the hearts of the people," not in legislation, and he urged that the enforcement of these rights be left to the states.

Mr. Goldwater was believed by many observers to be seeking the so-called "white backlash" vote from white persons alarmed at the pace of the Negro rights drive. His strategists conceded that they hoped to "sweep" the once solidly Democratic Southern states, and both Mr. Goldwater and Mr. Miller campaigned heavily in that region.

Mr. Johnson gave total support to the civil rights bill enacted last summer. He and his supporters derided the idea of leaving civil rights enforcement to the states.

The President campaigned extensively in the South, however, urging Southerners not to let their concern with the race problem bar them from full participation in the economic and social advance of the nation. There also was more than a hint in some Democratic campaign speeches that Southern states that remained adamantly opposed to equality for Negroes might begin to lose lucrative Federal defense contracts and other forms of subsidy.

Morality In Government

Mr. Goldwater charged that there was "moral decay" in the nation and lawlessness in the streets; whether his reference was to hoodlums and juvenile delinquency or to Negro demonstrations was never made clear. He frequently pointed to the Robert G. Baker and Billie Sol Estes cases as examples of lax morality in the Johnson Administration.

When Mr. Johnson's top assistant, Walter W. Jenkins, was arrested on a morals charge last month, and it was subsequently disclosed that he had been arrested on a similar charge in 1959, the Republicans added his case to the others. Mr. Goldwater, however, charged only that the Jenkins case had jeopardized national security.

Mr. Goldwater's thesis was that "moral decay" in the Johnson Administration "trickled down" to the people and was affecting the fiber of the nation itself. Mr. Johnson seldom replied to these charges although he did defend Mr. Jenkins as an able public servant whose personal misconduct had not endangered the national security.

These were the main themes of the campaign—but there were others. Mr. Johnson spoke frequently of his "Great Society" concept, a plan that envisioned massive new Federal programs in education, medical care, conservation of natural resources and urban renewal in the cities.

Mr. Goldwater criticized the Democratic tax cut of 1964 as politically inspired "gimmickry" and offered his own five-year program of tax reduction. He also called Mr. Johnson's "war on poverty" a "cruel hoax" designed only to win the votes of the less fortunate.

Mr. Johnson, however, attributed the nation's rising prosperity to the 1964 tax cut and promised even greater efforts to eliminate poverty, illiteracy and discrimination.

Most Democratic strategists believe, however, that the most telling argument on their side was the widespread belief that Mr. Goldwater would be careless in the use of nuclear weapons, belligerent in his foreign policy, and thus would endanger the peace. This accounted, they believe, for the high percentage of women in both parties who indicated to polltakers that they feared to back Mr. Goldwater.

The two Presidential candidates campaigned in strikingly different manners, although each roamed widely in the nation by jet aircraft and made frequent speeches.

Contrasts Noted

Mr. Johnson was folksy and mingled freely with the crowds; he often climbed on top of his limousine to speak to street-corner throngs through a bull horn. Mr. Goldwater almost never made sidewalk tours, handshaking expeditions and rarely came close to the sizable crowds that turned out to see him. In motorcades, he rode in a closed car, paying little attention to the increasingly sparse turnouts for these events.

On the platform, despite his hard-hitting charges, Mr. Goldwater was deceptively mild, often colloquial, and rarely made any effort to rouse his listeners to excitement. Mr. Johnson, on the other hand, sometimes roared at the top of his voice through an hour or more of almost extemporaneous speaking.

As the campaign advanced, Mr. Johnson's lead seemed at first to widen, then to shrink somewhat, then to return to approximately the level at which polltakers had first estimated it. In the final days of the campaign, for instance, Dr. George Gallup predicted that he would win 61 per cent of the vote, just about the pre-campaign prediction of most poll takers.

Mr. Goldwater insisted to the last, however, that his campaign had started "moving up" before Oct. 15 and was coming to a peak that would bring him victory on Election Day. Neither he nor any of his supporters, however, ever predicted that he could win by more than a few electoral votes.

Senator Eugene McCarthy was relatively unknown until he nearly upset LBJ in the primary—thanks to his antiwar stance and the students who embraced him. Johnson withdrew, leaving the field open.

The 1968 campaign was the most divisive since Lincoln's election precipitated the Civil War. A year of reversals began with LBJ presumed unbeatable. It ended with his presidency in ruins, his designated successor rejected, two national leaders murdered, and Richard Nixon, derided for years as a loser, finally triumphant.

Johnson's *annus horribilis* opened with the Viet Cong's Tet offensive in January, which defied administration predictions of easy victory. The timing was exquisitely bad because Senator Eugene McCarthy of Minnesota had already launched an insurgent campaign against LBJ's war policy. The New Hampshire primary on March 12 stunned the President by giving McCarthy 42% of the vote and 20 of 24 delegates. Four days later, New York Senator Robert F. Kennedy entered the race, to the dismay of McCarthy supporters. Two weeks after that, LBJ shocked the nation by withdrawing. When Dr. Martin Luther King Jr. was gunned down on a motel balcony in Memphis on April 4, riots flared across the country, dividing Americans even further.

As Kennedy and McCarthy fought for the antiwar vote, the Democratic hierarchy tried to jumpstart the campaign of Vice President Hubert H. Humphrey, who mistakenly invoked "the politics of joy" in a tragic year. Just as Kennedy's campaign began to take off, after winning the California primary, he was assassinated in Los Angeles. Incredulous Americans grieved again, severely shaken by the crescendo of violence.

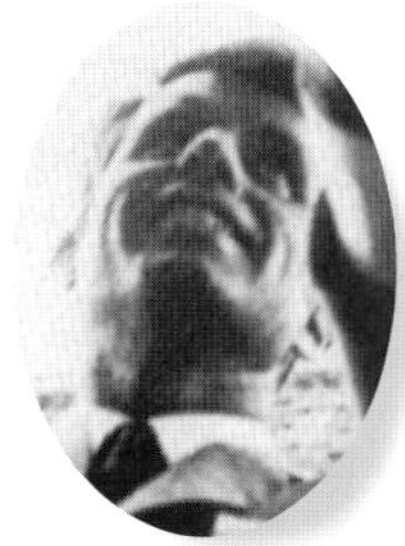

Left to right:
Richard M. Nixon (1913–94)
Hubert H. Humphrey (1911–78)
Eugene McCarthy (b. 1916)
Robert F. Kennedy (1925–68)
George C. Wallace (1919–98)

Nixon's nomination and election capped one of the great comebacks of all time—and stemmed from his remarkable success in presenting humself as a new Nixon.

Robert Kennedy's campaign drew strength and staff from the memory of the martyred president—to LBJ's distress.

The Republican candidates were a disparate group. Michigan governor George Romney was an early frontrunner, but stumbled badly when he claimed to have been "brainwashed" by rosy predictions over winning the Vietnam war. New York governor Nelson Rockefeller did not clearly declare his candidacy until it was too late. California governor Ronald Reagan was too conservative to win over a party still reeling from Barry Goldwater's rout. All were outdistanced by former Vice President Richard M. Nixon, who had rebuilt his career by helping Republicans make impressive congressional gains in 1964 and 1966. He was nominated without serious opposition in Miami Beach, appealing to the "forgotten Americans" who were worried about crime.

The Democratic convention in Chicago was chaotic and bloody. Riots broke out when police attacked thousands of student demonstrators, in the heart of downtown, live on TV. Humphrey won the nomination, but at great cost. With a shattered party, he set about the thankless task of defending the LBJ record while arguing that he would promote change.

Nixon's strategy called for calm reassurance. He refused to debate, and stuck to a relaxed schedule of telegenic events (he would never repeat his 1960 mistake of overcampaigning in remote locations). He led for most of the campaign, but after organized labor dispatched thousands of union members to get out the vote, and Humphey sought more aggressively to settle the war, the race settled into a dead heat. After much posturing in the final week, including Democratic attempts to forge new peace proposals, and Republican attempts to subvert those proposals, Nixon squeaked by with 31.77 million votes to Humphrey's 31.27 million, and 301 electoral votes to 191. Nearly 10 million people voted for the segregationist George Wallace, the ex-Governor of Alabama, who harnessed blue-collar rage on both sides of the Mason-Dixon Line, and won five states in the Deep South.

In his victory speech, Nixon remembered a sign he had seen in an Ohio crowd that read "Bring Us Together." That simple challenge would prove elusive in the years ahead.

Hubert Horatio Humphrey's alliterative name lent itself well to campaign buttons—though the result reminded some of prison bars.

George Wallace ran a strong third party campaign on the American Independent ticket, capturing 46 electoral votes in the Deep South and winning 13.5 percent of the popular vote.

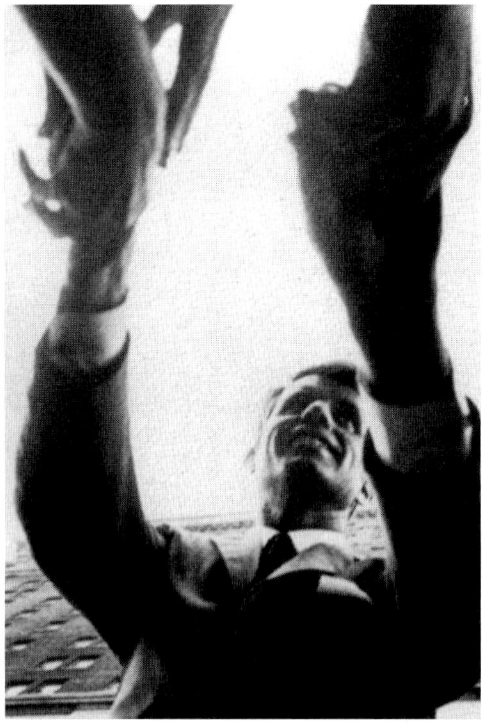

President Johnson reflects after announcing his decision not to seek the election *(far left)*, Washington, D.C., March 31, 1968.

Robert Kennedy campaigns in New York City *(left)*, spring 1968.

Senator Eugene McCarthy in Channel Thirteen's make-up room before an interview, New York City *(right)*, December 4, 1967.

Robert Kennedy reaches into the audience at a rally *(opposite)* in Sacramento, California, March 24, 1968.

Hubert Humphrey speaks in New York City *(left)*, October 21, 1968.

Humphrey addresses the Jewish constituency in Brooklyn *(below)*, October 21, 1968.

Wall Street is thronged with spectators waiting to see Humphrey *(right)*, New York City, October 10, 1968.

A police officer threatens a photographer with a club at the tumultuous Chicago Democratic Convention *(opposite top)*, August 28, 1968.

An overhead shot gives the scope of the chaos outside the convention hall *(opposite bottom)*, Chicago, August 28, 1968.

Democratic strategist Larry O'Brien works behind the scenes at the convention, *(above left)*, Chicago, August 28, 1968.

Humphrey tallies the votes that won him the Democratic nomination *(above right)*, Chicago, August 28, 1968.

George C. Wallace calls his ailing wife, Alabama governor Lurleen Wallace, during his speaking tour in Pennsylvania, *(left)*, April 1968.

Wallace and his running mate, General Curtis E. LeMay, clasp hands on the podium at a Madison Square Garden rally in New York City *(below)*, May 1968.

Women at a Wallace rally in Houston wear matching dresses and wave Confederate flags, October 1968.

Tricia
UNITED
UNITED
UNITED

Richard Nixon is at the center of a Republican rally in Washington *(opposite top)* on November 1, 1968.

Patricia and Julie Nixon christen campaign planes bearing their names at LaGuardia Airport in New York City *(opposite bottom)*, September 1968. Looking on are former Vice President Nixon and Julie's fiancé David Eisenhower, grandson of the former President.

Republican vice-presidential candidate Spiro T. Agnew campaigns in Chicago *(above)*, September 16, 1968.

LBJ and President-elect Nixon are captured in an intimate portrait at the White House *(left)*, November 1968.

"All the News That's Fit to Print"

The New York Times

LATE CITY EDITION

Weather: Rain today and tonight. Cloudy, showers likely tomorrow. Temp. range: today 52-48; Wed. 54-45. Full U.S. report on Page 93.

VOL. CXVIII . . No. 40,465 — © 1968 The New York Times Company. — NEW YORK, THURSDAY, NOVEMBER 7, 1968 — 10 CENTS

NIXON WINS BY A THIN MARGIN, PLEADS FOR REUNITED NATION

SHE KNEW IT ALL ALONG: President-elect Richard M. Nixon holding crewelwork, a facsimile of Presidential seal embroidered by his daughter Julie, who stands beside her fiancé, David Eisenhower. Mrs. Nixon and daughter Patricia completed the family group at the Waldorf-Astoria yesterday.

NIXON'S ELECTION EXPECTED TO SLOW PARIS NEGOTIATION

Allied Diplomats Suggest All Sides May Adopt a Wait-and-See Stance

By HEDRICK SMITH
Special to The New York Times

PARIS, Nov. 6 — Allied diplomats suggested tonight that Richard M. Nixon's election victory would add, at least temporarily, to the delays and complications of getting meaningful Vietnam peace negotiations under way.

The American, the North Vietnamese and the National Liberation Front delegations here had no comment on the election results.

But allied diplomats close to the talks suggested that the Republican victory would probably bring eventual changes in the American negotiating team, encourage delays by the South Vietnamese Government, and induce a wait-and-see attitude by all sides until Mr. Nixon's own approach to the talks became clearer.

The uncertainty about the future relationship between the outgoing Johnson Administration and Mr. Nixon is considered the primary complicating factor.

Eyes on Saigon

"Everybody has to see how Nixon and Johnson are going to handle this period," said one Western diplomat.

The Saigon Government is reported to feel that the Johnson Administration pressed it too rapidly toward expanded talks embracing the Vietcong. It now is expected to use the change-over period in the United States to play for time.

South Vietnamese officials here made no secret that they consider Mr. Nixon more sympathetic than Mr. Johnson to their position.

They have recently dropped hints that they expect no active negotiating on issues of substance until early next year.

Western diplomats now speculate that President Nguyen Van Thieu may delay sending a delegation to the talks here until he has learned Mr. Nixon's views.

But a more common opinion is that Saigon will send a delegation soon and then try to stall until the Republicans take office in January.

The Republican victory,

Continued on Page 13, Column 1

POLICE SEIZE 125 ON C.C.N.Y. CAMPUS

AWOL Soldier Taken From Student Center 'Sanctuary'

About 250 members of the Tactical Patrol Force moved onto the City College campus early today at the request of the administration and arrested more than 100 students and the AWOL soldier they had been guarding in a student center.

Under the direction of Police Commissioner Howard R. Leary, Chief Inspector Sanford Garelik and a number of other high police officials, the arrests were carried out without violence following a warning from the administration to vacate the building.

In all, about 125 persons were arrested, including supporters of the peace movement and Pvt. William Brakefield, who had been in the Finley Student Center, at 133d Street and Convent Avenue, since last

Continued on Page 4, Column 4

Soviet Bids U.S. Confer; Calls for 'Normalization'

By HENRY KAMM
Special to The New York Times

MOSCOW, Nov. 6—The Soviet Union greeted the election of a new President of the United States today with a call for the "normalization" of relations between Moscow and Washington for the sake of world peace.

The demand was put forward in a speech on behalf of the ruling Politburo of the Communist party by First Deputy Premier Kirill T. Mazurov as election returns in the United States showed that Richard M. Nixon had won the Presidency. The occasion was the traditional speech in the Kremlin on the eve of the anniversary of the Bolshevik Revolution.

To underline the importance Moscow attaches to relations with the United States, Mr. Mazurov raised the issue twice. Noting Soviet proposals for mutual limitations on nuclear weapons and delivery systems, the official said:

"It is relevant to recall in this connection that we have expressed readiness to conduct negotiations with the United States on the entire range of these problems. But their positive solution does not depend on the Soviet Union alone."

Review of Soviet Actions

After a review of Soviet actions on the international scene, Mr. Mazurov returned to Soviet-American relations. He said:

"We have always attached great importance to the normalization of relations between the Soviet Union and the United States, which would be important not only to both of our countries but also to world peace."

A public offer to enter into negotiations with the United States for an accommodation on vital issues was regarded as a Soviet reaction to the

Continued on Page 14, Column 1

POSITION ON SINAI DEFINED BY ISRAEL

Note to Jarring Links Issue of Boundaries to Security Needs and Tiran Rights

By DREW MIDDLETON
Special to The New York Times

UNITED NATIONS, N. Y., Nov. 6—Israel has told the United Arab Republic that her attitude toward the boundary problem will be governed by her security needs and the maintenance of full protection of Israeli navigation in the Strait of Tiran.

This is the first time that Israel has defined with any precision her interest in the Sinai Peninsula.

Western diplomats inferred that if Israel's security requirements were fulfilled, including protection of shipping in the Strait of Tiran, the Government would not reject an arrangement that returned a demilitarized Sinai to Egypt. The peninsula has been occupied by Israel since the Israeli-Arab war of June, 1967.

This information was in a memorandum that Foreign Minister Abba Eban gave yesterday to Dr. Gunnar V. Jarring, the United Nations intermediary. Mr. Eban went over the text of the memorandum with Dr. Jarring at meetings yesterday afternoon and last night.

Ambassador Jarring was asked to transmit the memorandum to Mahmoud Riad, the Egyptian Foreign Minister. The clarification of Israel's approach to the boundary problem apparently was intended to rebut Mr.

Continued on Page 2, Column 3

NEWS INDEX

REPUBLICANS GAIN SAFE ALBANY EDGE

Lead in Assembly Put at 77-73 and in Senate at 33-24 Unofficially

By JAMES F. CLARITY

Republican officials said yesterday that they expected to have clear majorities in both houses of the 1969 Legislature.

The Republicans, on the basis of unofficial but reliable vote-counts in the elections for the 150 Assembly and 57 Senate seats, will probably control the Assembly by 77 to 73, and the Senate by 33 to 24.

The official counts of several close Assembly races were not expected to affect lower house control, which the Republicans appeared almost certain to have wrested from the Democrats in Tuesday's election.

Official Count Delayed

The official count of the close races was expected to be completed early next week. The G.O.P. Senate majority was assured, regardless of the final count in a few close races.

But the Republicans' control of the Assembly, which they had lost in 1964, did not appear to give G.O.P. leaders assurance that their programs and legislation or those proposed by Governor Rockefeller would necessarily sail through the Legislature because of the majorities in both houses.

Among the Republicans who captured Democratic seats in the Assembly were several conservatives who, by combining with conservative Democrats, could obstruct, if not defeat, legislation they considered liberally oriented, or objectionable for other reasons.

Three of the newly elected Republican Assembly members

Continued on Page 40, Column 5

The Election at a Glance

President

Needed for Election—270 Electoral Votes

	Number of States*	Electoral Votes
Humphrey	14	191
Nixon	30	287
Wallace	5	45
In Doubt: Alaska, Missouri	2	15

*Includes District of Columbia.

The Senate

Newly Elected Senators		Make-up of New Senate	
Democrats	18	Democrats	58
Republicans	15	Republicans	41
In Doubt	1	In Doubt	1

The House

Democrats Elected	243
Republicans Elected	192

Senate's Liberal Coalition Survives Gains by G.O.P.

By DAVID E. ROSENBAUM

Republicans made a net gain of at least four Senate seats in Tuesday's election, but the balance between liberals and conservatives did not appear to have changed substantially from the present Senate.

One Senate race remained in doubt last night. In Oregon, Wayne Morse, a Democrat, who served four terms, was running a close race with State Representative Robert W. Packwood, a Republican. Observers said it might be days before the outcome was certain.

Depending on the Oregon race, the Democrats will hold 58 or 59 seats in the new Senate to 41 or 42 for the Republicans. In the present Senate there are 63 Democrats and 37 Republicans.

Four conservative Republicans and one conservative Democrat were elected to seats that had been held by liberals or moderates. On the other hand, there was a shift in favor of liberals in at least two states.

Thus it appeared that a majority could still be formed from liberal Northern Democrats and moderate Republicans to pass legislation on such issues as civil rights and aid to education.

The Republicans' net gain of only four seats in the House of Representatives dashed the party's hopes of capturing control of that body.

In the Senate the Republicans picked up seats that had been held by Democrats in Arizona, Florida, Maryland, Ohio, Oklahoma and Pennsylvania. Democrats took Republican-held seats in California and Iowa.

Among the new conservatives was Barry Goldwater, the Republican Presidential nominee in 1964. He defeated Roy L. Elson for the Arizona

Continued on Page 29, Column 2

Election Tables

Tables reporting the vote in national, state and local contests in Tuesday's election are now scheduled for publication in The New York Times tomorrow.

The Times had expected to print them today, but breakdowns in the News Election Service's national and regional computers made a total recheck of the election results necessary. This recheck is expected to be concluded today.

A Loser Concedes and Tries to Smile

By R. W. APPLE Jr.
Special to The New York Times

MINNEAPOLIS, Nov. 6—It was probably Hubert Horatio Humphrey's last hurrah in Presidential politics.

He had tried once before, in 1960, and had been crushed by the superb organization of John F. Kennedy in the West Virginia primary. Now he had lost again, this time to the man whom John Kennedy had defeated, in an agonizingly close finish.

Transcript of the Humphrey statement is on Page 22.

The Vice President—a hearty, sentimental man, given to laughter and to tears—tried to smile as he stood on the stage in the Leamington Hotel's ballroom this morning and listened to his faithful followers shout, "We Want Humphrey!" But what he brought forth was more a grimace than a grin. "Thank you very much," he said in a quavering voice. "It's nice to know."

Mr. Humphrey went through

Continued on Page 22, Column 1

Vice President Humphrey with his wife after conceding

GOAL IS HARMONY

President-Elect Vows His Administration Will Be 'Open'

By ROBERT B. SEMPLE Jr.

President-elect Richard M. Nixon turned yesterday from the business of winning elections to the business of assembling an Administration.

Weary but thankful, he appeared before an elated band of supporters gathered in the ballroom of the Waldorf-Astoria at 11:35 A.M. He expressed his gratitude for their efforts and his admiration for the "gallant and courageous fight" of his opponent.

Transcript of Nixon's remarks will be found on Page 21.

He also extended the hand of friendship to the disappointed partisans of Mr. Humphrey's cause—particularly the young.

Near the end of his eight-minute talk, Mr. Nixon took note of the division in the nation and pledged, in these words, to bend every effort to restore racial peace and social harmony:

"I saw many signs in this campaign. Some of them were not friendly and some were very friendly. But the one that touched me the most was one that I saw in Deshler, Ohio, at the end of a long day of whistle-stopping, a little town. I suppose five times the population was there in the dusk, almost impossible to see — but a teen-ager held up a sign, 'Bring Us Together.'

"And that will be the great objective of this Administration at the outset, to bring the American people together. This will be an open Administration, open to new ideas, open to men and women of both parties, open to the critics as well as those who support us.

"We want to bridge the generation gap. We want to bridge the gap between the races. We want to bring America together. And I am confident that this task is one that we can undertake and one in which we will be successful."

Several hours later the campaign entourage began to disassemble, its members heading home for a brief but long-overdue rest. The candidate himself flew southward for a three-day vacation in Key Biscayne, a peninsula just south of Miami where he rested occasionally during the campaign.

Although he has been urged

Continued on Page 21, Column 1

ELECTOR VOTE 287

Lead in Popular Tally May Be Smaller Than Kennedy's in '60

By MAX FRANKEL

Richard Milhous Nixon emerged the victor yesterday in one of the closest and most tumultuous Presidential campaigns in history and set himself the task of reuniting the nation.

Elected over Hubert H. Humphrey by the barest of margins—only four one-hundredths of a percentage point in the popular vote—and confronted by a Congress in control of the Democrats, the President-elect said it "will be the great objective of this Administration at the outset to bring the American people together."

He pledged, as the 37th President, to form "an open Administration, open to new ideas, open to men and women of both parties, open to critics as well as those who support us" so as to bridge the gap between the generations and the races.

Details Left for Later

But after an exhausting and tense night of awaiting the verdict at the Waldorf-Astoria Hotel here, Mr. Nixon and his closest aides were not yet prepared to suggest how they intended to organize themselves and to approach these objectives. The Republican victor expressed admiration for his opponent's challenge and reiterated his desire to help President Johnson achieve peace in Vietnam between now and Inauguration Day on Jan. 20.

The verdict of an electorate that appeared to number 73 million could not be discerned until mid-morning because Mr. Nixon and Mr. Humphrey finished in a virtual tie in the popular vote, just as Mr. Nixon and John F. Kennedy did in 1960.

With 94 per cent of the nation's election precincts reporting, Mr. Nixon's total stood last evening at 29,726,409 votes to Mr. Humphrey's 29,677,152. The margin of 49,257 was even smaller than Mr. Kennedy's margin of 112,803.

Meaning Hard to Find

When translated into the determining electoral votes of the states, these returns proved even more difficult to read, and the result in two states—Alaska and Missouri—was still not final last night. But the unofficial returns from elsewhere gave Mr. Nixon a minimum of 287 electoral votes, 17 more than the 270 required for election. Mr. Humphrey won 191.

Because of the tightness of the race, the third-party challenger, George C. Wallace, came close to realizing his minimum objective of denying victory to the major-party candidates and then somehow forcing a bargain for his sup-

Continued on Page 20, Column 1

Johnson Vows Aid In Power Transfer

By NEIL SHEEHAN
Special to The New York Times

SAN ANTONIO, Tex., Nov. 6—In a telegram of congratulations this morning, President Johnson informed President-elect Richard M. Nixon that he would do "everything in my power to make your burdens lighter on that day when you assume the responsibilities of the President."

Even as Mr. Johnson's telegram was being transmitted to Mr. Nixon from the President's ranch 65 miles north of here, the machinery had been set in motion for an orderly transition from the old Administration to the new.

Lawson Knott, the administrator of the General Services

Continued on Page 20, Column 3

November 7, 1968

Nixon Wins by a Thin Margin, Pleads for Reunited Nation

Elector Vote 287

Lead in Popular Tally May Be Smaller Than Kennedy's in '60

By Max Frankel

Richard Milhous Nixon emerged the victor yesterday in one of the closest and most tumultuous Presidential campaigns in history and set himself the task of reuniting the nation.

Elected over Hubert H. Humphrey by the barest of margins—only four one-hundredths of a percentage point in the popular vote—and confronted by a Congress in control of the Democrats, the President-elect said it "will be the great objective of this Administration at the outset to bring the American people together."

He pledged, as the 37th President, to form "an open Administration, open to new ideas, open to men and women of both parties, open to critics as well as those who support us" so as to bridge the gap between the generations and the races.

Details Left for Later

But after an exhausting and tense night of awaiting the verdict at the Waldorf-Astoria Hotel here, Mr. Nixon and his closest aides were not yet prepared to suggest how they intended to organize themselves and to approach these objectives. The Republican victor expressed admiration for his opponent's challenge and reiterated his desire to help President Johnson achieve peace in Vietnam between now and Inauguration Day on Jan. 20.

The verdict of an electorate that appeared to number 73 million could not be discerned until mid-morning because Mr. Nixon and Mr. Humphrey finished in a virtual tie in the popular vote, just as Mr. Nixon and John F. Kennedy did in 1960.

With 94 per cent of the nation's election precincts reporting, Mr. Nixon's total stood last evening at 29,726,409 votes to Mr. Humphrey's 29,677,152, smaller than Mr. Kennedy's margin of 112,803.

Meaning Hard to Find

When translated into the determining electoral votes of the states, these returns proved even more difficult to read, and the result in two states—Alaska and Missouri—was still not final last night. But the unofficial returns from elsewhere gave Mr. Nixon a minimum of 287 electoral votes, 17 more than the 270 required for election. Mr. Humphrey won 191.

Because of the tightness of the race, the third-party challenger, George C. Wallace, came close to realizing his minimum objective of denying victory to the major-party candidates and then somehow forcing a bargain for his support on one of them. Although he did not do nearly as well as he had hoped and as others had feared, he received 9,291,807 votes or 13.3 per cent of the total, and the 45 electoral votes of Alabama, Georgia, Louisiana, Mississippi and Arkansas.

Mr. Wallace's support ranged from 1 per cent in Hawaii to 65 per cent in his home state of Alabama, and his presence on the ballot in all 50 states unquestionably influenced the outcome in many of them. But there was no certain way of determining whether Mr. Nixon or Mr. Humphrey was the beneficiary of the third-party split-offs.

Mr. Humphrey's narrow victory in states such as Texas was probably due to Mr. Wallace's strong showing there. Conversely, Mr. Wallace's drain-off in traditional Democratic strongholds, such as New Jersey, probably helped Mr. Nixon.

Strong in the Northeast

The Vice President, staging a remarkable and highly personal comeback drive in the last three weeks of the campaign, after the opinion polls showed him 10 and even 15 percentage points behind, ran extremely well in the northeastern industrial states, including New York, and in Michigan. And he profited from large urban majorities, including Negroes, Jews and Spanish-speaking communities, to take Pennsylvania, Texas and Maryland, and possibly Missouri.

Mr. Humphrey mounted a strong challenge in California, but his only other successes west of the Mississippi were in his home state of Minnesota, Hawaii and possibly Washington, with Alaska still in doubt.

Mr. Nixon's victory, therefore, though marginal in numbers, turned out to be well spread geographically.

He established the Republican party as a formidable and probably permanent political factor in the South and Southern border states, profiting from the Wallace inroads, but nonetheless running extremely well in such states as Kentucky and Virginia. Mr. Humphrey lost everything south of West Virginia and east of Texas to his two rivals, a result that should profoundly shake the Southern Democratic parties.

Hurt in Urban Areas

Yet the broad spread of Mr. Nixon's strength clearly did not extend into the great urban areas where he must perform his works of unity and redevelopment.

After receiving Mr. Humphrey's concession, congratulations and offer of cooperation at noon yesterday, Mr. Nixon replied before television cameras with a statement that implicitly recognized this possible obstacle to his rule. Of all the signs, friendly and hostile, thrust at him on the campaign trail, he said, the one that touched him the most appeared in the hands of a teen-ager one evening in Ohio, reading "Bring Us Together."

He had not campaigned very much in Negro communities and knew of the overwhelming opposition to him by black voters. His running mate for the Vice-Presidency, Gov. Spiro T. Agnew of Maryland, had become, rightly or wrongly, a kind of symbol of white annoyance with the restiveness of the Negro community. Mr. Nixon made no mention of Mr. Agnew as he thanked all those who had contributed to his success and vowed to restore peace between the races.

> The President-elect said it "will be the great objective of this Administration at the outset to bring the American people together."

Yet another challenge before the Nixon Administration will be a Congress firmly managed by the opposition party. Mr. Nixon is the first man since Zachary Taylor in 1844 to be elected President without his party's also winning control of both houses of Congress.

With the net loss to the Republicans of only four seats in the House and four, possibly five in the Senate, the Democrats will organize the legislative agendas of the 91st Congress and command all its committees. By retaining control on Capitol Hill through a change of parties in the White House, they will be in a position to exercise a powerful restraint on Mr. Nixon's budgetary priorities, which in fact means his priorities of government.

President Eisenhower, too, had to deal with a Democratic Congress for six of his eight years in office but his personal and nonpartisan standing among the opposition legislators cannot be compared with Mr. Nixon's reputation on the Hill for tough and highly partisan combativeness. Perhaps because he anticipated some of these problems, the President-elect expressed the hope in his victory statement that he could cooperate with President Johnson as Mr. Johnson dealt closely with President Eisenhower.

The Republicans took only [192] of the 390 contested seats of the 435 in the House, and lost five seats in return, for a final line-up of 243 Democrats and 192 Republicans.

In 34 Senate races, the Democrats gained two seats, in California and Iowa, and lost seats in Maryland, Florida, Arizona, Oklahoma, Pennsylvania and Ohio, with the race of Senator Wayne Morse of Oregon still in doubt.

The political complexion of the new Congress, however, may have shifted another few degrees from the innovative and liberal-minded spirit that prevailed in the first two years of the Johnson Administration. The concern about excessive spending on domestic social programs and about law and order that Mr. Nixon stressed in his campaign has been evident on both sides of the aisles in both Houses for some time.

Yet there was no clear ideological pattern in any of the voting, for President or Congress. Critics of the Vietnam war, for instance, lost some contests and won in others. Energetic Democratic incumbents were able to resist even strong tides to Mr. Nixon in some states while others fell victim to them elsewhere.

Survival for some created new opportunities for leadership of the now leaderless Democratic party. Mr Humphrey indicated that he would not retire from public life, and his efforts to pay off campaign debts may in fact keep him talking for quite a while. But it will be in Congress that a new generation of Democratic leaders now begins to emerge.

Senator Edmund S. Muskie, Mr. Humphrey's running mate, became an exciting new national figure even in defeat, with a broad appeal that extended all the way from some of Senator Eugene J. McCarthy's young admirers to the hard-bitten party regulars of big-city Democratic organizations.

New Leaders Emerge

Senator Edward M. Kennedy, by loyally playing a key role in the revitalization of the Humphrey campaign, further extended his standing as a Democrat to be reckoned with in future years. Senator George S. McGovern's brief bid for his party's nomination after the assassination of Senator Robert F. Kennedy gave him new stature.

Gov. Harold E. Hughes' successful campaign for a Senate seat in Iowa will further add to his reputation as a formidable vote-getter in Republican regions and Alan Cranston of California, though a quiet and professional man, should gain stature from his defeat of the arch-conservative Superintendent of Public Instruction, Max Rafferty.

The Republicans, too, produced some vigorous new Senators such as Charles Mathias of Maryland and Richard S. Schwelker of Pennsylvania, who defeated two incumbents, Senators Daniel Brewster and Joseph S. Clark.

Of more immediate interest, however, was the question of where Mr. Nixon would turn for candidates for position in his Cabinet, his White House policy staff and other key positions. His choice of men and a few crucial appointments, such as a new Chief Justice, may well reveal how far to the right and left he intends to reach in the interests of unity and the "new coalition" of which he sometimes spoke during the campaign.

The old Democratic coalition that Franklin D. Roosevelt put together in the 1930s—united the South with the urban North, racial segregationists with Negroes, big-city machines, labor unions and the offspring of immigrants—was thought this year to be finally breaking apart.

Racial tension and the loss of interest in the economic bounty traditionally associated by the lower middle classes with the Democrats clearly threatened this political alignment, as did the physical shifting of populations out of the cities.

But Mr. Humphrey sang a vigorous last hurrah for the remnants of the New Deal and proved that the old economic arguments—or fears of Republican economic management—were strong enough to hold many Democratic voters from defection. Saddled from the start of the campaign with an unpopular President and an unpopular war in Vietnam, he also managed to wriggle loose from those burdens and held much of his party together at least one more time in opposition to Mr. Nixon.

The results suggest that in many of the big states, this remains a potent appeal. And where the Democrats remain well organized, as in Texas, Missouri or Illinois, or where the unions put their men and money to work, there was shown to be a political mechanism still worthy of the attentions of ambitious leaders.

Above all, the campaign demonstrated that the American political system as a whole could still adjust itself to the most violent strains. The bitter conflict over the war, the unexpected abdication of President Johnson in March, the shooting of the Rev. Dr. Martin Luther King Jr. and of Senator Kennedy in April and June, the riots in the Negro ghettoes and the turbulence, inside and out, at the Democratic National Convention, had spread disgust and disaffection through political ranks.

Yet the excitement of the closing days of the campaign appeared to kindle new emotions and Mr. Nixon pleaded with the young partisans in different branches of the Democratic party to remain within the system and to retain their enthusiasm, even if they felt compelled to continue to oppose him.

The old Democratic coalition that Franklin D. Roosevelt put together in the 1930s . . . was thought this year to be finally breaking apart.

The widespread fear that neither Mr. Nixon nor Mr. Humphrey would win a clean victory and that weeks of bizarre maneuvering would result both in the Electoral College and in the House of Representatives persisted through the long night of return watching and analysis. The close escape at the end may now encourage the forces of reform who wish to alter or abandon the elector system, Mr. Humphrey among them.

But harrowing as the campaign proved to be and narrow as Mr. Nixon's margin unexpectedly came to be, the system held and turned, under the leadership of the retiring President and the defeated Vice President, to the swift and orderly passage of power.

The well-oiled Nixon campaign trampled everything in its path, winning by the widest electoral margin since FDR trounced Landon in 1936.

On the surface, the election of 1972 did not appear to hold great historic significance. A tough incumbent president easily defeated a challenger whose views were out of touch with the majority of the American people. Yet the chicanery of the campaign cast a pall over electoral politics for an entire generation, and in its way, it was as historic as any election of the century.

President Richard M. Nixon remained a formidable candidate in 1972. The Vietnam War had not ended, yet he had "de-Americanized" it by bringing home large numbers of GIs. The groundbreaking trip to China in February was a diplomatic masterstroke, shocking right and left alike with its audacity, and impressing most Americans with its sheer common sense. Domestically, Nixon pursued a centrist course on the environment, the economy and other issues.

His powerful incumbency was strengthened by the ineffectiveness of his challengers. Edward Kennedy—though dreaded by Nixon—had destroyed his chances at Chappaquiddick in 1969, when he drove his Oldsmobile off a wooden bridge after leaving a party, drowning his passenger, a young campaign worker named Mary Jo Kopechne. Senator Edmund Muskie was damaged by weeping in response to a right-wing slur on his wife. Hubert Humphrey had trouble getting traction. George Wallace was shot and paralyzed by a deranged assailant while campaigning in Maryland.

Left to right:
Richard M. Nixon (1913–94)
George McGovern (b. 1922)

McGovern's dovishness failed to connect with rank and file voters, and many traditional Democratic constitutencies deserted him.

Democrats finally turned to a relative unknown, Senator George McGovern of South Dakota, whose last-minute candidacy had added to the confusion at Chicago in 1968. McGovern had appealing credentials as a World War II pilot, but he was far to the left of most Americans and never managed to connect with average Democratic voters. The convention in Miami Beach managed to avoid repeating the debacle at Chicago in 1968, but the party now seemed to many nonpartisan outsiders like a set of malcontents from the margins of American society. New nominating rules championed in Congress had removed the clout of the old bosses, but left the party disorganized. McGovern's acceptance speech was not delivered until 2:48 A.M., thanks to an extended series of satirical nominations for vice president, including TV's Archie Bunker and Mao Zedong. The peacenik platform rivaled Henry Wallace's of 1948, promising withdrawal from Vietnam, amnesty for draft dodgers, support for busing, and a ban on handguns and capital punishment.

From this impolitic beginning, things grew worse. When the press revealed that McGovern's running mate, Senator Thomas Eagleton of Missouri, had suffered from depression and received electric shock treatment, McGovern handled the news badly, first expressing his support for Eagleton, then asking for his withdrawal.

Nixon stayed above it all, following the historic practice of incumbents. Compared to the disorganized Democrats, his campaign was disciplined and well-funded. Americans saw no reason to change course, and Nixon was reelected by one of the widest margins in history. He won 60 percent of the popular vote and every state except Massachusetts and the District of Columbia.

But this overwhelming margin, comparable only to the avalanches of 1936 and 1964, would soon vanish amidst the Watergate revelations and the portrait they painted of a president who either was not in control of his duplicitous underlings, or worse, had told them to break the law and then obstruct justice. By ordering a petty burglary against his hapless opponents, Nixon's henchmen stole his future. When the President was forced to resign rather than face impeachment, one of the great mandates of American history was erased.

Within a year of the election, Vice President Spiro Agnew resigned over a bribery scandal—one of the many problems that would plague the winning team.

As a senator, McGovern had led the effort to open up the selection process and remove the clout of big city bosses—an effort that led directly to his nomination.

Democrats attend the Columbus Day parade in New York City *(above left)*. Senator George McGovern, filling a tobacco pipe, is at center right. Other participants, clockwise, include Bella S. Abzug, Robert F. Wagner, Abraham D. Beame, Sanford D. Garelik, Richard L. Ottinger, Mayor John Lindsay, and at far right, Robert Abrams, October 9, 1972.

President Nixon receives a hug from close friend Sammy Davis Jr. *(left)*, during the Republican Convention in Miami, August 22, 1972.

McGovern campaigns in Brooklyn, New York *(opposite)*, with Senator Edward Muskie (in plaid tie), September 21, 1972.

Campaign workers for Senator George McGovern and President Nixon share a corner *(above)* at 74th Street and Broadway, New York City, October 28, 1972.

Supporters line the streets to welcome McGovern to North Bergen, New Jersey *(opposite top)*, September 20, 1972.

A delegate to the Republican convention expresses her enthusiasm *(opposite bottom)*, Miami, August 23, 1972.

I'M A
RED-HOT
REPUBLICAN

Police guard the Fontainbleu Hotel, site of the Republican Convention in Miami, August 20, 1972.

President and Mrs. Nixon arrive at the Westchester airport, and are greeted by Nelson Rockefeller (waving), October 23, 1972.

"All the News That's Fit to Print"

The New York Times

LATE CITY EDITION

Weather: Cloudy, rain likely today and tonight. Cloudy, cool tomorrow. Temp. range: today 48-60; Tuesday 45-61. Full U.S. report on Page 93.

VOL. CXXII . . No. 41,927 NEW YORK, WEDNESDAY, NOVEMBER 8, 1972 — 15 CENTS

NIXON ELECTED IN LANDSLIDE; M'GOVERN IS BEATEN IN STATE; DEMOCRATS RETAIN CONGRESS

President Loses in City By 81,920-Vote Margin

By FRANK LYNN

President Nixon swept New York State yesterday, but lost to Senator McGovern in New York City by a total of 81,920 votes.

Mr. Nixon's statewide plurality was expected to be about a million votes.

With 11,521 of the 12,948 districts in the state reporting, the tally was:

Nixon 3,712,113
McGovern 2,539,326

With all of the 4,219 districts in the city reporting, the tally was:

Nixon 1,259,244
McGovern 1,341,164

The President's strong showing in the state rivaled the 1956 victory of President Dwight D. Eisenhower, who first brought Mr. Nixon to the national ticket 20 years ago.

The Nixon victory did not appear to carry too far down the Republican line. The Legislature remained Republican, but with no indication of substantially increased Republican majorities.

Three Republican candidates for the Court of Appeals held slight leads but returns were still inconclusive.

The President's capture of the state was only the third time a Republican Presidential candidate had won New York since 1928.

Dozens of sample districts showed last night that the President substantially improved his 1968 showing in virtually all ethnic groups and geographic areas in the state and city.

In many cases, particularly in the cities, Mr. Nixon surpassed Governor Rockefeller's victory margins of two years ago.

In New York City, Senator McGovern carried districts that were predominantly black, Puerto Rican and Jewish. But in the Jewish areas, Mr. Nixon doubled his showing of four years before. In a middle class

Continued on Page 36, Column 2

MANY VOTES SPLIT

G.O.P. Loses Senate Seats in 6 States and Picks Up 4 Others

By R. W. APPLE Jr.

The Democratic party withstood President Nixon's landslide yesterday to retain control of both houses of Congress.

With voters in all parts of the nation splitting their tickets in huge numbers, the Democrats brought off a series of startling upsets in Senate contests to gain at least two seats, similar to their feat in the face of Dwight D. Eisenhower's sweep of 1956.

The Democrats captured previously Republican Senate seats in six states—Delaware, Iowa, Kentucky, Maine, Colorado and South Dakota. Those pickups more than offset Republican gains in the two Southwestern states of Oklahoma and New Mexico and the two Southern states of Virginia and North Carolina.

Two Races Open

Two Senate races remained in doubt this morning—in Alaska and Nebraska. Both seats were held by the Republicans in the last Congress.

The figures for the House were far less complete, but the Republicans were not making the gains they needed to take control. It appeared that they would pick up somewhere in the neighborhood of a dozen seats; they had already gained seven.

At present, the Senate lineup is 54 Democrats, 44 Republicans, one Conservative-Republican and one independent who votes with the Democrats. In the House it is 255 Democrats, 177 Republicans and three vacancies.

Mr. Nixon's coattails proved relatively short this year, as they had in 1968. In state after state, he swept to massive vic-

Continued on Page 34, Column 7

C.B.S. News

Associated Press

President and Mrs. Nixon and Vice President Agnew at the Republican celebration in Washington early today

MARGIN ABOUT 60%

Massachusetts Is Only State to Give Vote to the Dakotan

By MAX FRANKEL

Richard Milhous Nixon won re-election by a huge majority yesterday, perhaps the largest ever given a President.

Mr. Nixon scored a stunning personal triumph in all sections of the country, sweeping New York and most other bastions of Democratic strength.

He was gathering more than 60 per cent of the nation's ballots and more than 500 electoral votes. He lost only Massachusetts and the District of Columbia.

The victory was reminiscent of the landslide triumphs of Franklin D. Roosevelt in 1936 and Lyndon B. Johnson in 1964, although it could fall just short of their record proportions.

Tickets Are Split

Despite this drubbing of George Stanley McGovern, the Democratic challenger, the voters split their tickets in record numbers to leave the Democrats in control of both houses of Congress and a majority of the nation's governorships. Mr. Nixon thus became the first two-term President to face an opposition Congress at both inaugurals.

The turnout of voters appeared to be unusually low, despite jams at many polling places. Projections indicated a total vote of 76 million out of a voting-age population of 139.6 million, or only about 54 per cent. If accurate, that would be the lowest proportion since 51.4 per cent in 1948. The percentage had been over 60 per cent in every election since then.

May Claim Mandate

The President seemed certain, however, to claim a clear mandate for his policies of gradual disengagement from Vietnam, continued strong spending on defense, opposition to busing to integrate the schools and a slowdown in Federal spending for social programs. These are the issues he stressed through the campaign.

The 59-year-old Mr. Nixon, who will be 60 before inauguration on Jan. 20, could also claim a resounding personal vindication against the strong charges of corruption brought against him personally by the opposition.

By coincidence, the greatest triumph of his 26 years in national politics came on the 10th anniversary of his defeat for Governor of California—the time he told newsmen they would not have Nixon to kick around anymore.

McGovern Concedes

Mr. McGovern, 50, conceded defeat before midnight in the East with a telegram of support for the President if he leads the nation to peace abroad and justice at home.

The South Dakotan took credit for helping to push the Administration nearer to peace in Indochina and assured his cheering supporters at the Sioux Falls Coliseum that their defeat would bear fruit for years to come.

The President responded in a brief address from the White

Continued on Page 34, Column 1

Nixon Has a Big Plurality In Jersey and Connecticut

Case an Easy Winner

By RONALD SULLIVAN

President Nixon won the overwhelming victory predicted for him in New Jersey in yesterday's Presidential election, defeating Senator George Mc Govern by a 2-to-1 margin.

At the same time, Senator Clifford P. Case, the liberal Republican, won a fourth term and one of the biggest Senate election victories in New Jersey's history, defeating Paul J. Krebs, the Democratic candidate.

However, incumbent Democratic Representatives survived the G.O.P. onslaught at the top of the ballot in what political leaders described as a remarkable display of ticket-splitting.

The Presidential tally, with 4,142 districts of 5,212 reporting, was:

Nixon 1,440,420
McGovern 862,582

The tally in the race for the Senate, with 3,657 of 5,212 districts reporting, was:

Case 1,112,754
Krebs 627,352

With both Mr. Nixon and Senator Case piling up 2-to-1 margins throughout the state, Republican leaders predicted that the President's margin would rival the 800,000-vote plurality achieved by Dwight D.

Continued on Page 37, Column 3

Hartford Assembly G.O.P.

By LAWRENCE FELLOWS
Special to The New York Times

HARTFORD, Nov. 7—President Nixon carried Connecticut today in a landslide victory.

The President swept the state's eight electoral votes with a plurality of 252,289, approaching the 306,758-vote margin by which the late President Dwight D. Eisenhower carried the state in 1956.

The Republicans also took control of the General Assembly, winning the State Senate by 23 to 13 and the House of Representatives by 93 to 58.

But widespread ticket-splitting enabled three of the four incumbent Democratic Representatives to keep their seats in Washington.

With all of the 169 towns in the state reporting, the Presidential tally was:

Nixon 799,249
McGovern 546,960

Representative John G. Schmitz of California, the

Continued on Page 37, Column 7

Olympic Fund Barred

Voters in Colorado cut off public funds for the 1976 Winter Olympics yesterday. Without the tax money, the International Olympic Committee was all but forced to move the games to another site. Page 31.

M'GOVERN TO BACK MOVES FOR PEACE

But Says He Will Continue to Oppose Policies He Had Deplored in Campaign

By JAMES M. NAUGHTON
Special to The New York Times

SIOUX FALLS, S.D., Nov. 7—Senator George McGovern conceded defeat of his Presidential candidacy here tonight but said that he would "shed no tears" because of the effort his campaign had made to draw the nation close to peace.

The Democratic nominee told 1,200 cheering enthusiasts at 10:40 P.M., Central standard time, that he had sent a telegram to President Nixon pledging support for "peace abroad and justice at home."

Text of McGovern's comments appears on Page 3

He said the President had his "full support" in efforts toward such goals.

But he added in his speech, which was televised, that he would, as the leader of the "loyal opposition," continue to oppose any policies that he had deplored during his long campaign.

"Now, the question is to what standards does the loyal

Continued on Page 3, Column 3

The Election at a Glance

President

Needed for Election—270 Electoral Votes

	*Number of States	Electoral Votes
Nixon	49	521
McGovern	2	17

The Senate

Newly Elected Senators		Make-up of New Senate	
Democrats	16	Democrats	57
Republicans	15	Republicans	41
In Doubt	2	In Doubt	2

The House

Democrats Elected	218
Republicans Elected	154
In Doubt	63

*Includes District of Columbia.

NIXON ISSUES CALL TO 'GREAT TASKS'

At Victory Celebration, He Vows to Make Himself 'Worthy' of Victory

By ROBERT B. SEMPLE Jr.
Special to The New York Times

WASHINGTON, Wednesday, Nov. 8—President Nixon summoned the nation last night "to get on with the great tasks that lie before us" and, in a later statement to a crowd of cheering supporters, pledged to make himself "worthy of this victory."

Mr. Nixon made two statements, both televised.

The first of these was a brief statement from his desk in the Oval Office of the White House in which he pledged himself to secure not only "a peace with honor in Vietnam" but also "a new era of peace" throughout the world; to "prosperity without war and without inflation" at home, and to an America in which all citizens will have "an equal chance."

Text of Nixon's remarks is printed on Page 34

"I would only hope," he said, "that in these next four years we can so conduct ourselves in

Continued on Page 34, Column 3

Victory, 10 Years Later

Spectacular Nixon Vote Considered Vindication in Light of Past Defeats

By JAMES RESTON

News Analysis

It was a spectacular personal victory for Richard Nixon, 10 years to the day, and almost to the hour, after his most humiliating defeat by Pat Brown in the 1962 election for the governorship of California.

Beaten by John Kennedy by the narrowest of margins in the Presidential election of 1960, beaten again for the control of his own state in 1962, finished with American politics by his own angry proclamation exactly a decade ago, here he is now, not only vindicated but triumphant in one of the most decisive victories in the history of American Presidential politics.

In a few days before he will take the oath of office for a second term as President of the United States (Jan. 9), he will be 60 years old. His thirties were a political surprise, even to himself, his forties were an agony of controversy and self-doubt, his fifties were a struggle and at the end a triumph. What now will he do with his sixties? This is the question that even his most intimate associates in Washington cannot answer.

In the world, he has to achieve not only the cease-fire, but the peace he has promised in Vietnam, the "reconciliation and cooperation" with Peking and Moscow that were so central to his victory, the truce in the savage struggle between Israel and the Arab states, and some kind of new economic and political relationship with Japan and the Common Market countries of Europe, who are now challenging the American economic leadership of the modern world.

At home, Mr. Nixon has to deal also now with the minorities who failed to support him in the election: the poor and the blacks who have been left behind in the general prosperity of the nation, the young in the universities who have been over-run but not persuaded or

Continued on Page 34, Column 3

Reid Wins as Democrat; Bella Abzug Easy Victor

By RICHARD L. MADDEN

Representative Ogden R. Reid, a former Republican, was re-elected yesterday as a Democrat in Westchester County, and Representative Bella S. Abzug, a one-term Democrat, won a decisive re-election in Manhattan.

In another key Westchester race, Representative Peter A. Peyser, a freshman Republican, claimed victory over his predecessor in the House, Richard L. Ottinger, a Democrat-Liberal, who was seeking to recapture his former seat.

Mrs. Abzug defeated by about a 2-to-1 margin Mrs. Priscilla M. Ryan, a Liberal and widow of the late Representative William F. Ryan, who had defeated Mrs. Abzug in the Democratic primary in the 20th Congressional District last June.

With about 85 per cent of the vote reported in Westchester, but with large numbers of absentee ballots still to be counted, Mr. Reid led Carl A. Vergari, a Republican-Conservative and the county's District Attorney, by more than 8,000 votes.

Despite the strong vote for President Nixon in the state, incumbent Democratic Representatives generally appeared to be withstanding the Republican tide. One exception was Representative John D. Dow, of Newburgh, a liberal Democrat who had strenously opposed the war in Vietnam.

Mr. Dow, who lost his House seat in the generally conservative Rockland-Orange county area in 1968 and won it back two years ago, was substantially trailing Assemblyman Benjamin A. Gilman, a Middletown Republican.

Representative Otis G. Pike, a six-term Democrat from Suffolk County, won a three-way fight for re-election and another prime target of the Republicans, Representative James M. Hanley of Syracuse, defeated his Republican-Conservative opponent, Leonard C. Koldin.

Representative Lester L. Wolff, a four-term Democrat whose new Nassau County district now takes in part of Queens, led Assemblyman John

Continued on Page 36, Column 6

Mrs. Smith Defeated For Senate in Maine

By BILL KOVACH
Special to The New York Times

PROVIDENCE, R. I., Wednesday, Nov. 8—The 34-year Congressional career of Senator Margaret Chase Smith, the Senate's only woman member, ended last night in a major upset as Democrats showed unexpected strength in New England Senate and Gubernatorial races.

William D. Hathaway, the Democrat who gave up his Second District Congressional office to challenge the 74-year-old Mrs. Smith despite her near-legendary standing in Maine, won the seat in a hard-fought contest.

Mr. Hathaway's stunning victory was part of a Democartic surge that overcame the general New England sweep by President Nixon, and reflected stubborn ticket-splitting by

Continued on Page 21, Column 1

A Rockefeller Loses West Virginia Race

By BEN A. FRANKLIN
Special to The New York Times

CHARLESTON, W. Va., Wednesday, Nov. 8—Secretary of State John D. Rockefeller 4th suffered a sharp defeat yesterday in a bid for the West Virginia governorship. The loss appeared, at least, to have postponed a possible role for him in national Democratic politics in 1976.

Mr. Rockefeller's well-financed candidacy had depended heavily on proposals on the environment in this the second-ranked coal-mining state. These also suffered a setback through his defeat in a race that eclipsed all others here.

Gov. Arch A. Moore Jr., a Republican former Congressman who is the first Governor here who has been constitutionally able to succeed to a second

Continued on Page 23, Column 1

Summary of Other News

Following is a summary of major nonelection news. A full report begins on the first page, second part.

Canarsie School Boycott

Leaders of Canarsie parents who have kept their children out of school for two weeks declared yesterday that "the boycott is over" and called on parents to return their children to school. But the prospect of full classes today remained in doubt since more than 1,000 parents shouted down the same call Monday night.

Bid by Vietcong

Agents of the National Liberation Front have made several recent contacts with Saigon's anti-Government, non-Communist opposition, according to opposition sources.

Britons Protest Price Rises

British Government offices were swamped with complaints of price increases on the first full day of Prime Minister Heath's anti-inflation freeze. But a check of London shops found no wide pattern of violations. Most of the increases involved noncontrolled items.

Soviet Parades Its Arms

The Soviet Union, marking the 55th anniversary of the Bolshevik Revolution, paraded its military might in low-key fashion. The unusually deliberate movements of Leonid I. Brezhnev, the party leader, reinforced speculation that he had been ill.

NEWS INDEX

News Summary and Index, Page 49

Wednesday, November 8, 1972

Nixon Elected in Landslide; M'Govern Is Beaten in State; Democrats Retain Congress

Margin About 60%

Massachusetts Is Only State to Give Vote to the Dakotan

By Max Frankel

Richard Milhous Nixon won re-election by a huge majority yesterday, perhaps the largest ever given a president.

Mr. Nixon scored a stunning personal triumph in all sections of the country, sweeping New York and most other bastions of Democratic strength.

He was gathering more than 60 per cent of the nation's ballots and more than 500 electoral votes. He lost only Massachusetts and the District of Columbia.

The victory was reminiscent of the landslide triumphs of Franklin D. Roosevelt in 1936 and Lyndon B. Johnson in 1964, although it could fall just short of their record proportions.

Tickets Are Split

Despite this drubbing of George Stanley McGovern, the Democratic challenger, the voters split their tickets in record numbers to leave the Democrats in control of both houses of Congress and a majority of the nation's governorships. Mr. Nixon thus became the first two-term President to face an opposition Congress at both inaugurals.

The turnout of voters appeared to be unusually low, despite jams at many polling places. Projections indicated a turnout of 76 million out of a voting-age population of 139.6 million, or only about 54 per cent. If accurate, that would be the lowest proportion since 51.4 per cent in 1948. The percentage had been over 60 per cent in every election since then.

May Claim Mandate

The President seemed certain, however, to claim a clear mandate for his policies of gradual disengagement from Vietnam, continued strong spending on defense, opposition to busing to integrate the schools and a slowdown in Federal spending for social programs. These are the issues he stressed through the campaign.

The 59-year-old Mr. Nixon, who will be 60 before inauguration on Jan. 20, could also claim a resounding personal vindication against the strong charges of corruption brought against him personally by the opposition.

By coincidence, the greatest triumph of his 26 years in national politics came on the 10th anniversary of his defeat for Governor of California—the time he told newsmen they would not have Nixon to kick around anymore.

McGovern Concedes

Mr. McGovern, 50, conceded defeat before midnight in the East with a telegram of support for the President if he leads the nation to peace abroad and justice at home.

The South Dakotan took credit for helping to push the Administration nearer to peace in Indochina and assured his cheering supporters at the Sioux Falls Coliseum that their defeat would bear fruit for years to come.

The President responded in a brief address from the White House, expressing appreciation to his supporters and respect for the supporters of Mr. McGovern, whose name he pronounced for the first time in months. He promised rapid progress toward peace and prosperity.

Mr. Nixon carried into office again his running mate, Vice President Spiro Theodore Agnew, who will now be regarded as a formidable candidate for the Republican Presidential nomination four years hence.

His opponent, Robert Sargent Shriver Jr., has left many with the impression that he, too, will seek to lead his party. Both will celebrate birthdays tomorrow, Mr. Agnew his 54th, Mr. Shriver his 57th.

Unlike four years ago, when he became the 37th President by the slenderest of margins, Mr. Nixon did not suffer even a moment's suspense last night. As predicted by the public opinion polls, he gathered three votes or more for every two for his opponent.

Indeed, in state after state, Mr. Nixon's margin was remarkably close to the combined total won by him and the third-party candidate, George C. Wallace, in 1968. Had Mr. Wallace not been eliminated from contention this year by a crippling bullet, the 1972 contest would have been much closer.

But in the clear field against Mr. McGovern, the President swept almost everything in sight. Projections based on early returns showed him getting between 55 and 60 per cent in the cities, 70 per cent in suburbs and nearly 80 per cent in rural regions.

Mr. Nixon's margins of victory in the states ranged from 52 per cent in Rhode Island and Wisconsin to an estimated 75 per cent in Oklahoma.

Mr. McGovern carried Massachusetts by a margin of 5 to 4. Hubert Humphrey triumphed there by 2 to 1 four years ago.

The South Dakotan carried the District of Columbia and its black majority with a decisive 72 per cent.

The President appeared to have improved his standing with all identifiable groups in the electorate, even blacks and Jews who still gave majorities to the Democrats.

The first-time young voters, upon whom Mr. McGovern had counted throughout his long struggle for the nomination, appeared to have divided their votes 50–50.

The bonds of party loyalty were shattered in every part of the country. The defections of Democrats from New York to California and overwhelmingly in the once solidly Democratic South were so great that the computers projecting early returns for the television networks had no difficulty marking state after state in the Nixon column.

Many Lost Interest

The unanimous verdict of the opinion polls and political analysts had deprived the campaign of much of the customary suspense. Many voters were found to have lost interest in the race, in part because they felt sure of the outcome, often because they felt no enthusiasm for either candidate.

Yet the contest was fiercely fought.

It was by far the most lavishly financed Presidential campaign, with Mr. Nixon's forces spending nearly $50-million and Mr. McGovern's at least $25-million.

The President was the beneficiary of many huge individual contributions, including two of at least $1-million each. Mr. McGovern compensated for the loss of many traditional big Democratic contributors with mail solicitations that evoked an estimated 650,000 individual responses.

And the charges exchanged by the two parties were not lacking in bite.

Mr. Nixon set an idealistic tone at the start, seeking "four more years" to complete what he called the works of peace in the world.

But without mentioning his opponent by name, he accused him of wishing to "stain the honor" of the nation by settling for "surrender" in Vietnam and of proposing a fatal weakening of the country's defenses.

Senator McGovern's lofty appeal was that Americans should "come home" to the ideals of the past, home from foreign adventure and back to a concern for the poor.

But he combined this with bitter attacks upon the President, accusing him of barbaric tactics in Indochina, of corruption and big-business favoritism and of deception of the voters.

The fundamental contrast between the contenders lay in their style of campaigning, clearly reflecting their own agreement with the conventional finding that Mr. Nixon was far in front from the outset.

The President pleaded the press of business at the White House and left most of the stump-running to Vice President Agnew and dozens of other stand-ins.

He held only one news conference during the campaign, ventured into only a few well-prepared urban parades and topped a series of radio speeches with only one long television speech.

Mr. McGovern, by contrast, kept criss-crossing the country, seeking crowds and enthusiasm and money and concentrating his energies on the most populous states with the large blocks of electoral votes.

The bonds of party loyalty were shattered in every part of the country.

He and his running mate, Mr. Shriver, made a daily pitch for free time on television news shows and combined rally appearances with a heavy use of purchased television time.

With the outcome so widely taken for granted, the principal questions on election night turned on the size of Mr. Nixon's majority and the question of how many other Republicans, particularly candidates for the Senate, he could pull along to victory.

The President, in his last bid for national office—and his fifth in 20 years—was also competing against the statistics of history.

A landslide as such is not an unusual phenomenon. The term has been applied to cases in which a Presidential candidate lost no more than 10 states or carried 80 per cent of the electoral votes or at least 53 per cent of the total popular vote. By those standards, there have been 24 landslides in the previous 46 Presidential contests.

George Washington twice and James Monroe in 1820 won the electoral votes of all states. In this century, the record belongs to Franklin D. Roosevelt, who lost only Maine and Vermont in 1936.

The modern records for total electoral votes are Mr. Roosevelt's 98 per cent in 1936 and Lyndon B. Johnson's 90 per cent in 1964.

Johnson the Leader

The data on popular votes date back to 1824. Mr. Johnson's share of 61.1 per cent in 1964 topped Mr. Roosevelt's 60.8 per cent in 1936, Warren G. Harding's 60.3 per cent in 1920 and Herbert Hoover's 58.2 per cent in 1928.

In view of his demonstrated interest in historical firsts, Mr. Nixon was probably also aware of some other possible records that were within his reach.

Since Jefferson, no man who had served as Vice President was ever elected to two full terms in his own right. And no two-term Vice President had ever been elected to two terms as President.

Also, there have been five previous teams that were elected to two terms as President and Vice President, and only one previous Republican team, that of Dwight D. Eisenhower and Mr. Nixon. The others were George Washington and John Adams, James Monroe and Daniel D. Tompkins, Woodrow Wilson and Thomas R. Marshall and Franklin D. Roosevelt and John N. Garner.

Since the creation of the modern major parties in 1854, only two Presidents had begun terms of office with the opposition in control of Congress: Mr. Eisenhower in his second term in 1956 and Mr. Nixon on his first in 1968. No President had ever begun two terms against an opposition Congress.

No two-term Vice President had ever been elected to two terms as President.

Mr. Nixon was ambivalent throughout the 1972 campaign about whether to seek the largest possible mandate for himself or to risk offending some Democratic voters by supporting Republican candidates for Congress.

For the most part, he stressed his own contest, making only token appearances in the closing weeks in states where Republican Senate candidates had complained of the lack of help.

The President yielded to the calculation of his strategists that the Senate might be within reach but that the House was not.

At the same time, he appeared to believe that with a huge popular vote and the ideological support of many Southern and conservative Democrats he would be able to work almost as well with an opposition Congress as with one whose leadership and committees were in the control of Republicans.

Mr. Nixon had drawn much criticism for the partisan vigor with which he tried to capture control of Congress in 1970. In his own cause this year, he remained aloof and serene to the end.

Nixon's Vote on Coast

The President and Mrs. Nixon voted when the polls opened at 7 A.M. yesterday at a schoolhouse near their villa at San Clemente, Calif., and then flew across the country to await the returns at a private dinner in the White House.

Mr. and Mrs. McGovern voted in a church in the Senator's home town of Mitchell, S.D., and then drove to Sioux Falls to await the verdict.

In many states, yesterday's Presidential ballot also carried the names of one or more minor-party candidates.

They were:

American Independent party—John G. Schmitz for President and Thomas J. Anderson for Vice President (33 states).
People's party—Benjamin Spock and Julius Hobson (10 states).
Socialist Workers' party—Linda Jenness and Andrew Pulley.
Communist party—Gus Hall and Jarvis Tyner.
Socialist Labor party—Louis Fisher and Genevieve Gunderson.
Libertarian party—John Hospers and Theodora Nathan.
Prohibition party—Earl Munn and Marshall Inchapher.
Universal party—Gabriel Green.
America First party—Jon V. Mahalchik.

The rise of feminism in the 1970s brought with it a renewed interest in women voters.

Not surprisingly, the best campaigner of 1976 proved to be the one with the least experience in Washington. Voters recently dismayed by the political process wanted a fresh start, and that was the one thing that Gerald Ford could not offer.

Ford began the campaign with a mixed record. His cal m leadership had restored badly shaken confidence in the presidency, but his decision to pardon Nixon was damaging. And despite his long experience in Congress, which would have struck earlier voters as an asset, his campaign fought against the growing sense that the Beltway encircled an alien culture, distinct from ordinary American life.

Jimmy Carter was a highly unlikely candidate. A former one-term governor of Georgia, naval officer, and peanut farmer, he was almost entirely unknown to Americans when he declared his candidacy in 1974. Nevertheless, his early start, his intelligence, and most of all, his candor impressed voters and the news media. A promise never to lie struck home after the Watergate revelations. On top of that, he had a great smile.

Carter not only appealed to moralists, he played the game of politics well. Over the next 22 months, he traveled half a million miles. In particular, he understood the importance of the

Left to right:
James Earl Carter Jr. (b. 1924)
Gerald R. Ford (b. 1913)
Eugene McCarthy (b. 1916)

After his defeat, Gerald Ford wondered whether his decision to drop Nelson Rockefeller in favor of Bob Dole cost him voters.

early primaries and, buoyed by his "Peanut Brigade," he worked hard to win in both New Hampshire and the Iowa caucuses, now crucial to the nominating process. By the time of the New York convention, he had the delegates sewn up, and won on the first ballot. Carter promised a return to honest government, a balanced budget, reduced unemployment, and a variety of centrist reforms.

Despite his incumbency, Ford had a harder time nailing down his nomination. A serious challenge came from Ronald Reagan and the Republican right, relatively quiet since the Goldwater defeat of 1964. Boasting of his outsider credentials, Reagan ran a surprisingly robust campaign, defeated Ford in several major primaries, and only narrowly lost the nomination at Kansas City.

A weakened Ford immediately proposed televised debates—the first since 1960—to raise his standing against Carter, who led in the polls (the vice presidential candidates, Senator Walter Mondale of Minnesota and Senator Bob Dole of Kansas, also debated). The strategy backfired in the second debate when Ford, who had stressed his foreign policy expertise, suggested that the people of Eastern Europe were independent of the Soviet Union. He never really recovered from the gaffe. Carter, too, made a few mistakes, including the decision to talk to *Playboy* magazine. Honest to a fault, Carter confessed to occasional "lust in my heart."

On the eve of the election, Carter's lead dissolved. But the desire for change proved irresistible. Carter won 50.1 percent of the vote to Ford's 48 percent, and 297 electoral votes to Ford's 240. Eugene McCarthy, a retired Democratic senator from Minnesota who was best remembered for galvanizing antiwar sentiment in 1968, ran a weak campaign as an independent. For the first time since Andrew Jackson, the United States had elected a president from the Deep South, and the Democratic coalition was back in business after eight years out of power.

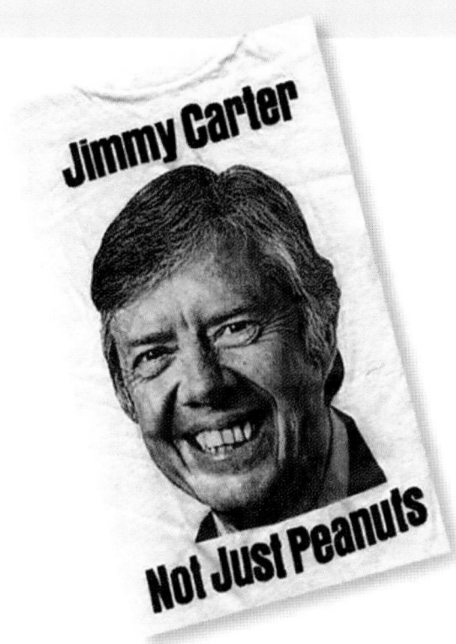

Jimmy Carter's million-watt smile and peanut-farming background enhanced his folksy appeal to voters weary of Washington.

Despite his obscurity, Carter realized earlier than most that Americans wanted revolutionary change in this bicentennial year.

A bumper sticker on this New York City subway entrance *(above)* reads "Nobody in '76," November 3, 1976.

Eugene McCarthy is interviewed on a press cruise *(left)*, Seattle, October 20, 1976.

Jimmy Carter takes questions during a Brooklyn campaign stop *(above)*, September 7, 1976.

Carter causes a traffic jam in front of the 21 Club in New York City *(right)*, July 22, 1976.

President Ford leads a Republican rally at Nassau Coliseum, Long Island, New York, October 31, 1976.

Ford stands out in the crowd while campaigning in Yonkers, New York, October 13, 1976.

McCarthy makes a campaign swing through downtown Hartford for a book-signing *(left)*, August 24, 1976

Nancy and Ronald Reagan listen to President Ford's acceptance speech at the Republican convention, Kansas City, Missouri *(below)*, August 19, 1976.

Gerald Ford—exhausted and hoarse—grimly listens to Betty Ford read his telegram to Jimmy Carter, conceding defeat *(left)*. His daughter Susan looks on. November 2, 1976.

The band plays "Happy Days Are Here Again" as Jimmy Carter greets supporters *(below)* at a victory celebration in Atlanta, November 3, 1976.

"All the News That's Fit to Print"

The New York Times

LATE CITY EDITION

Weather: Partly sunny today; cool tonight. Fair and cooler tomorrow. Temperature range: today 42-58; Tuesday 33-50. Details on page 82.

VOL. CXXVI . . No. 43,383

NEW YORK, WEDNESDAY, NOVEMBER 3, 1976

25 cents beyond 50-mile zone from New York City, except Long Island. Higher in air delivery cities.

20 CENTS

CARTER VICTOR IN TIGHT RACE; FORD LOSES NEW YORK STATE; DEMOCRATS RETAIN CONGRESS

Moynihan Defeats Buckley For New York Senate Seat

By MAURICE CARROLL

Daniel P. Moynihan won election to the United States Senate yesterday and shouted jubilantly to a jostling crowd in his headquarters, "It's time we made some claims on the national Government."

Mr. Moynihan topped a cautious campaign that counted on the normal Democratic sympathies of New York voters by easily defeating James L. Buckley, the Conservative-Republican incumbent.

With 12,407 of 13,844 districts reporting, the vote for Senator was:

Moynihan 2,973,200
Buckley 2,517,292

His long gray hair toppling over his forehead and perspiration gleaming on his roundish face, Mr. Moynihan told several hundred supporters in his jammed storefront office on the Avenue of the Americas: "New York was on the ballot—and New York won."

It took almost 10 minutes for Mr. Moynihan to squeeze through the cheering crowd and step to the platform to claim victory.

Six years ago, the cheers had been for Mr. Buckley, who won an unexpected victory as a third-party candidate. But last night, Mr. Moynihan reconstituted much of the traditional Democratic vote—with the exception of some parts of the black community and some liberals disgruntled over his narrow primary-election victory—and it was his turn to congratulate Mr. Buckley for "gracious" concession.

Then Mr. Moynihan headed for a series of celebrations, but today, his wife, Liz, said, he will go to Harvard to teach his customary class there. He did not interrupt his academic chores during the campaign and will not today, she said.

Mr. Moynihan led by 2-to-1 margins in the traditional Democratic territory in

Continued on Page 19, Column 3

Atlantic City Casinos Approved

By MARTIN WALDRON

New Jersey voters yesterday approved Las Vegas-style casinos for Atlantic City, the first on the East Coast, and residents of the shore resort began celebrating as many bars handed out free drinks.

With 4,991 districts of 5,569 reporting, the vote was:

Yes 1,305,800
No 1,015,126

In the state's Congressional contests, Senator Harrison A. Williams Jr., a Democrat, easily won re-election to a fourth term, while Representative Henry Helstoski, a six-term Democrat from the Ninth District who is under indictment on Federal extortion charges, was defeated. Thirteen other incumbents—10 Democrats and three Republicans—won, as did Joseph A. LeFante, also a Democrat, who succeeded the retiring Dominick V. Daniels in Hudson County.

Two years ago, New Jersey voters defeated by more than 400,000 votes an amendment to the State Constitution that would have allowed casinos anywhere in the state.

Promoters of casinos, including Atlantic City's legislative delegation, scheduled a meeting for 9 A.M. today to begin drafting a law to implement the constitutional amendment voted on yesterday.

The Council of Churches and United States Attorney Jonathan L. Goldstein, who was the most vocal opponent of casinos, had predicted that if Atlantic City got casinos, other areas of the state would demand them also.

Mr. Goldstein also warned that gambling casinos were a magnet for organized crime, and said that loan sharks and prostitutes would flock to Atlantic City if casinos were opened there.

In the midst of the noisy crowd in the headquarters of the Committee to Rebuild Atlantic City, an organization of businessmen and public officials who led the drive for the casinos, Mayor Joseph

Continued on Page 28, Column 1

Weicker Wins a 2d Term Easily

By MICHAEL KNIGHT
Special to The New York Times

HARTFORD, Nov. 2—United States Senator Lowell P. Weicker Jr. scored an impressive re-election victory today over Gloria Schaffer, the state's top Democratic vote-getter and the only woman running for the Senate this year.

With all of the state's 169 towns and cities reporting, the unofficial vote was:

Weicker 787,568
Schaffer 559,109

Despite an intensive effort, Mrs. Schaffer, who is Connecticut's Secretary of State, was unable to generate much excitement during the campaign or close the gap between herself and Senator Weicker, the maverick first-term Republican who earned a nationwide reputation in 1973 as a member of the Senate Watergate committee.

The clear-cut result in the senatorial race was in marked contrast to the voting in the Presidential contest in this state, where President Ford defeated Jimmy Carter by a narrow margin.

Mrs. Schaffer won handily, and sometimes even overwhelmingly, in many of the state's ethnic neighborhoods. She carried the black districts of normally Republican Stamford, for example, the Italian and Polish areas of industrial New Britain and the Italian, Irish and black districts of Hartford.

In the Congressional races, all of the state's four Democratic and two Republican United States Representatives won re-election by wide margins. The Representatives from the three western districts—Stewart B. McKinney and Ronald A. Sarasin, Republicans, and Anthony Toby Moffett, a Democrat—had faced the possiblity of an upset.

The Republicans gained seven seats in

Continued on Page 29, Column 1

United Press International
Jimmy Carter leaves voting booth in Plains, Ga.

Associated Press
Walter F. Mondale waiting to vote in Afton, Minn.

Election At a Glance

PRESIDENT

Needed to Win—270 Electoral Votes

	Number of States*	Electoral Votes
Carter	23	272
Ford	23	160

THE SENATE

33 of 100 Members to Be Elected

Newly Elected Senators	
Democrats	20
Republicans	8
Independent	1
In Doubt	4
Makeup of the New Senate	
Democrats	61
Republicans	37
Independent	1
In Doubt	1

THE HOUSE

All 435 Seats to Be Filled

Democrats Elected	255
Republicans Elected	120
In Doubt	60

*Includes District of Columbia

A guide to election news, page 17.

8 Senators Lose Seats, but Lineup Of Parties Stays About the Same

By DAVID E. ROSENBAUM

At least eight incumbent Senators were defeated yesterday, and a ninth was in a close struggle for re-election.

Nonetheless, the Democrats did no worse than retain their current 61-to-38 majority in the Senate, with one seat held by an independent, and they may have picked up one seat.

In the House, the Democrats' 2-to-1 majority was not substantially changed.

The Democratic Senators who lost were Vance Hartke of Indiana, Joseph M. Montoya of New Mexico, Frank E. Moss of Utah and Gale W. McGee of Wyoming.

The other losers were James L. Buckley, Conservative-Republican of New York, and Bill Brock of Tennessee, J. Glenn Beall Jr. of Maryland and Robert Taft Jr. of Ohio, all Republicans.

Senator John V. Tunney, Democrat of California, was in a close race with S. I. Hayakawa, a Republican, who had been president of San Francisco State College.

Fourth-Term Bids Lost

Senator Moss and Senator McGee, both committee chairmen, were defeated in their attempts at fourth terms in the Senate. Mr. Moss lost to Orrin E. Hatch, a lawyer who has never held public office. Mr. McGee lost to a State Senator, Malcolm Wallop. Mr. Hatch and Mr. Wallop are much more conservative than the incumbents.

But, in Ohio, Mr. Taft was beaten by a liberal, Howard W. Metzenbaum, a former Senator whom Mr. Taft beat in 1970.

Senator Robert T. Stafford, Republican of Vermont, won a narrow victory over Gov. Thomas P. Salmon, his Democratic challenger.

Eight senators, four Republicans and four Democrats, are retiring, but neither party was able to take advantage of the situation to gain in total strength.

Republicans John C. Danforth and John H. Chaffee took Senate seats in Missouri and Rhode Island that are held by retiring Democrats Stuart Symington and John O. Pastore.

Democrats Apparent Winners

But Democrats apparently captured seats in Arizona and Nebraska that are held by Republicans. Dennis DeConcini, a Democratic county prosecutor, was leading in the race for the Arizona seat of Paul J. Fannin, and Mayor Edward Zorinsky was ahead in the race for Roman L. Hruska's race in Nebraska.

In Pennsylvania, Representative H. John Heinz 3d held the seat for the Republicans by narrowly beating Representative William J. Green. Hugh Scott, the Republican leader, is the incumbent.

Senator Philip A. Hart's seat in Michigan was retained for the Democrats by Representative Donald W. Riegle Jr., who defeated Representative Marvin L. Esch, a Republican.

In Montana, Representative John Melcher, a Democrat, easily won the seat now held by Mike Mansfield, the Democratic leader.

The eighth Senate vacancy was that created by the retirement of Hiram L. Fong, Republican of Hawaii. Returns from Hawaii were reported late, but it was widely believed that Representative Spark M. Matsunaga, a Democrat, would win.

In the House, nearly all of the 79 freshmen Democrats, who were the principal targets of the Republicans during the campaign, managed to win re-election.

With half of the House races already

Continued on Page 17, Column 3

GEORGIAN WINS SOUTH

Northern Industrial States Provide Rest of Margin in the Electoral Vote

By R. W. APPLE Jr.

Jimmy Carter won the nation's Bicentennial Presidential election yesterday, narrowly defeating President Ford by sweeping his native South and adding enough Northern industrial states to give him a bare electoral vote majority.

Three of the closely contested battleground states slipped into Mr. Carter's column shortly after midnight—New York, Pennsylvania and Texas. The President-designate lost New Jersey and Michigan, Mr. Ford's home state, while Ohio, Illinois and California were still up for grabs.

New York teetered between the rivals for hours, contrary to all expectations, before delivering a small majority to Mr. Carter—a majority that gave the Democrat a bonanza of 41 electoral votes.

When Mr. Carter finally carried Hawaii by a far narrower margin than customary for Democratic candidates in that Democratic stronghold, it gave the Georgian 272 electoral votes in 23 states, two more than a majority. Mr. Ford had 160 electoral votes in 23 states, and five states were still in doubt.

A Southern Victor

Mr. Carter was the first man from the Deep South to be elected President in a century and a quarter, and Mr. Ford, the nation's first appointive President, was the first incumbent to lose a Presidential election since Herbert Hoover.

Although the President dominated the Plains and Mountain regions, he lost several middle-sized states that he had counted upon. Among them were Louisiana and Mississippi on the Gulf Coast, and Wisconsin, which went to the Democrats for only the second time in a quarter-century as the result of an outpouring of votes from industrial Milwaukee and liberal Madison.

Mr. Carter owed large debts to Mayor Frank L. Rizzo of Philadelphia, who produced the 250,000-vote margin Mr. Carter needed to carry Pennsylvania; to Robert S. Strauss, the Democratic national chairman, who worked tirelessly to put together the Texas operation, and to the South and the Border states as a whole. The Georgian won every Border state and every Southern state except Virginia, which seemed headed for the Ford column.

Division of Popular Vote

The popular vote, which was swelled by a relatively heavy turnout to roughly the same level as four years ago, appeared likely to split 51 percent for Mr. Carter, 48 for Mr. Ford and 1 for others.

With 81 percent of the nation's precincts reporting, the vote was:

Carter ..... 33,684,344—51 percent
Ford ...... 31,665,958—48 percent

In the metropolitan area, Mr. Carter lost both New Jersey and Connecticut, as his backers had feared he would.

All 25,000 voting machines in New York were ordered impounded by State Supreme Court Justice Edward S. Conway. Acting at the request of state Re-

Continued on Page 17, Column 1

Summary of Other Major News

Articles on the first page of the second part of this issue are:

Indian Amendments Pass

The lower house of India's Parliament passed a sweeping set of constitutional amendments that will shift the balance of power in the Government.

No Accord on Rhodesia

Prime Minister Ian D. Smith of Rhodesia and African nationalist leaders failed to agree on a date for independence of the territory.

Burundi Chief Ousted

Burundi's armed forces deposed the President of the small central African country without violence, according to an official broadcast.

Park Tong Sun Disputed

The Gulf Oil Corporation has disputed a statement by Park Tong Sun that he received $1 million a month from his relationships with the oil company.

State U. Social Clubs

National sororities and fraternities will be allowed on the campuses of the State University of New York after a 23-year ban.

Ouster Held Illegal

The Supreme Court in effect affirmed that a company acted illegally in dismissing an employee for refusing on religious ground to work Saturday.

News Summary and Index, Page 45

METZENBAUM BEATS TAFT IN SENATE RACE

Democrat Wins Ohio Contest That Was Clear Test of Philosophies

By WILLIAM K. STEVENS
Special to The New York Times

CLEVELAND, Wednesday, Nov. 3—Robert Taft Jr., bearer of one of the most famous names in national Republican politics, lost his seat in the United States Senate yesterday to former Senator Howard M. Metzenbaum, a Democrat.

The contest between the two was a clear-cut test of orthodox Republican conservatism against classical Democratic liberalism.

With 11,138 of the 13,104 polling places reporting, the tally was:

Metzenbaum 1,637,778
Taft 1,537,830

Mr. Metzenbaum rolled up a sufficient margin of votes in Cuyahoga County (Cleveland) to offset Senator Taft's strength downstate. With 1,700 of 1,727 polling places in the county reporting, the Democrat held a 122,000-vote lead there.

The campaign was a rematch of a 1970 race in which Mr. Taft narrowly defeated Mr. Metzenbaum to win his first Senate term. In losing that election six years ago, Mr. Metzenbaum won 49 percent of the vote.

He also won statewide recognition and sufficient stature within the party to be appointed to the Senate by former Democratic Gov. John J. Gilligan in 1974. Mr. Metzenbaum subsequently ran that year

Continued on Page 24, Column 5

Pro-Statehood Candidate Stages Puerto Rican Upset

By DAVID VIDAL
Special to The New York Times

SAN JUAN, P.R., Wednesday, Nov. 3—In a staggering upset, San Juan Mayor Carlos Romero Barcelo of the pro-statehood New Progressive Party snatched the governorship of Puerto Rico from the incumbent, Rafael Hernández Colón, sending the Popular Democratic Party to only its second defeat since 1940.

The Governor, speaking to weeping campaign workers, conceded defeat and asked the party faithful "to heed this decision, if confirmed by the final official results, as the will of the people of Puerto Rico."

"That is how I accept it," he said, in a brief statement. He also called for unity but added: "The campaign for 1980 begins tomorrow."

The election was all the more surprising because the New Progressives were also on their way to assuming control of both houses of the Puerto Rican legislature as well as retaining the powerful post of mayor of San Juan.

The results reflected less a mandate for statehood than they did voter discontent with the administrative and economic problems under Mr. Hernández Colón's leadership.

In another surprise, the two parties favoring independence were running behind their 1972 pace.

With 66 of 113 precincts reporting, the tally was:

New Progressive Party 312,055
Popular Democratic Party ... 297,632
Puerto Rican Independence Party 33,170
Puerto Rican Socialist Party 4,604

A measure of the trend was seen in Barranquitas, considered a stronghold of the Popular Democrats because it was the birthplace of the father of Luis Muñoz Marin, founder of the Popular Democratic Party and of the Commonwealth. The 78-year-old leader came out of political seclusion to campaign there personally over the weekend. The party was losing there, however, as it was in Mayaguez, called the capital of the Popular Democrats.

In 1972, when 84.14 percent of the electorate voted, the Popular Democratic Party won by 85,631 votes, taking 51.2 percent as against 44.01 percent for the New Progressives. Other parties divided the rest.

Although each major party had pre-election polls indicating it would win this year, other polls had shown a high number of undecided voters.

That there was any doubt at all of a Popular Democratic victory was significant and indicated the changing nature of the electorate, of its perception of the party and of the party itself.

For years, islanders had grown accustomed to more and more prosperity under the "bread, land, and liberty" slogan of

Continued on Page 22, Column 5

Wednesday, November 3, 1976

Carter Victor in Tight Race; Ford Loses New York State; Democrats Retain Congress

Georgian Wins South

Northern Industrial States Provide Rest of Margin In the Electoral Vote

By R. W. Apple Jr.

Jimmy Carter won the nation's Bicentennial Presidential election yesterday, narrowly defeating President Ford by sweeping his native South and adding enough Northern industrial states to give him a bare electoral vote majority.

Three of the closely contested battleground states slipped into Mr. Carter's column shortly after midnight—New York, Pennsylvania and Texas. The President-designate lost New Jersey and Michigan, Mr. Ford's home state, while Ohio, Illinois and California were still up for grabs.

New York teetered between the rivals for hours, contrary to all expectations, before delivering a small majority to Mr. Carter—a majority that gave the Democrat a bonanza of 41 electoral votes.

When Mr. Carter finally carried Hawaii by a far narrower margin than customary for Democratic candidates in that Democratic stronghold, it gave the Georgian 272 electoral votes in 23 states, two more than a majority. Mr. Ford had 160 electoral votes in 23 states, and five states were still in doubt.

A Southern Victor

Mr. Carter was the first man from the Deep South to be elected President in a century and a quarter, and Mr. Ford, the nation's first appointive President, was the first incumbent to lose a Presidential election since Herbert Hoover.

Although the President dominated the Plains and Mountain regions, he lost several middle-sized states that he had counted upon. Among them were Louisiana and Mississippi on the Gulf Coast, and Wisconsin, which went to the Democrats for only the second time in a quarter-century as the result of an outpouring of votes from industrial Milwaukee and liberal Madison.

Mr. Carter owed large debts to Mayer Frank L. Rizzo of Philadelphia, who produced the 250,000-vote margin Mr. Carter needed to carry Pennsylvania; to Robert S. Strauss, the Democratic national chairman, who worked tirelessly to put together the Texas operation and to the South and the Border states as a whole. The Georgian won every Border state and every Southern state except Virginia, which seemed headed for the Ford column.

Division of Popular Vote

The popular vote, which was swelled by a relatively heavy turnout to roughly the same level as four years ago, appeared likely to split 51 percent for Mr. Carter, 48 for Mr. Ford and 1 for others.

With 81 percent of the nation's precincts reporting, the vote was:

Carter 33,684,344—51 percent

Ford 31,665,958—48 percent

In the metropolitan area, Mr. Carter lost both New Jersey and Connecticut, as his backers had feared he would.

All 25,000 voting machines in New York were ordered impounded by State Supreme Court Justice Edward S. Conway. Acting at the request of state Republican officials, with the approval of White House officials, he said the closeness of the vote made the impoundment necessary.

Mr. Carter and Mr. Ford were running a dead heat in Ohio, but the voting pattern in Cuyahoga County (Cleveland) suggested that the Democrat might be able to pull out a very narrow victory. He ran strongly in the Appalachian area.

In Illinois, Mr. Ford's vote in the suburbs and Mr. Carter's vote in the city of Chicago closely matched the figures in the final Chicago Sun-Times straw poll, which showed a virtual tie. But Mayor Richard J. Daley reportedly assured Democratic leaders that the state would tip Democratic.

As advertised, the race was harrowingly close in a large number of states. With the count nearly complete in Iowa, Mr. Carter held a 141-vote lead. As the tabulation wore on in Maine, Mr. Ford led by 31 votes. At one point, Mr. Carter led in Hawaii by 877 votes.

Former Senator Eugene J. McCarthy of Minnesota, running as an independent candidate, appeared to hold the balance of power in at least two hard-fought states, Ohio and Oregon.

From the beginning of the count, most of the states fell as they had been expected to. Kentucky and Indiana, the first two to report substantial returns, appeared to be following the predictions closely, with Mr. Carter approaching 55 percent in Kentucky and Mr. Ford the same figure in Indiana.

Partial returns and interviews with party leaders indicated that the former Georgia Governor was holding his Southern base and leading in the East. But the President was narrowly ahead in the Middle West and the two nominees were virtually deadlocked in the West.

Key Role for Independents

Mr. Carter appeared to be winning enormous margins among both blacks and Latin-Americans; in fact, early figures indicated that Mr. Ford was narrowly ahead among white voters, according to early results of a CBS News survey of voters as they left their polling places.

The CBS News poll, which covered about 10,000 voters and was made available to The New York Times under a special arrangement, indicated that the Presidential balloting was breaking along partisan lines, with nearly 90 percent of the Republicans backing Mr. Ford and more than 80 percent of the Democrats backing Mr. Carter.

Independents held the key, and they were going to the President by a narrow margin. But it was not clear early last night if the trend would continue or be strong enough to give Mr. Ford a victory. Almost a quarter of the independents said they had made up their minds in the last five days of a campaign that perplexed much of the electorate.

Reports from a number of states indicated that labor unions, which had supported the Carter campaign with an unusually sophisticated, computer-designed vote-pulling operation, were playing a major role in the surprisingly large turnout.

The weather was also splendid across the country, and reports of jammed voting places poured in from state after state.

In New York, the turnout was said to be "astonishingly heavy"; in Minnesota, voters appeared at the polls in "fantastically high" numbers; in Rhode Island, there were long lines. Mr. Carter's Illinois manager, Paul Sullivan, declared that "apathy is dead" and said he was "jumping for joy."

Mary Singleton, director of elections in Florida, was saying, before the polls closed, that voting in her state would reach the highest level since 1952, despite months of predictions that as little as half of the voting age population might choose to vote.

President Ford cast his ballot at an elementary school in his old Congressional district in Grand Rapids, Mich., said an emotional farewell to his fellow townspeople and returned to Washington to await the verdict of the voters.

An Emotional Occasion

He wept as he watched the unveiling of an airport mural depicting his life and told the audience, struggling to maintain his composure, that he owed everything to his mother and father. He was obviously completely exhausted.

Mr. Carter was the 11th person to vote in Plains, Ga., the rural hamlet he left 22 months ago to begin a quest for the Presidency that was dismissed as an absurdity by the elders of his party until he won his first primary victories. He spent five minutes marking the long Georgia ballot, then commented that he had voted for "Walter Mondale and his running mate."

"I feel a sense of satisfaction," the slight, 52-year-old peanut farmer said. "I did the best that I could."

Senator Mondale voted in Afton, Minn., and Senator Robert J. Dole, Mr. Ford's running mate, in Russell, Kan.

Mr. Carter, a former naval officer who served a single term as Governor of Georgia, started as a lonely campaigner, short on money, staff and national recognition. But he was relentless in his early effort, meeting voters in two's and three's, and it slowly began to pay off in his campaign against such better-known figures as Senators Birch Bayh and Henry M. Jackson, Representative Morris K. Udall and Gov. George C. Wallace.

He won the Jan. 19 caucuses in Iowa and that gave him a bit of publicity. Then he proved that he could win a primary in New Hampshire, and he dispatched Mr. Wallace in Florida. Finally, victories in two of the big industrial states—Pennsylvania and Ohio—brought the party leaders to his side.

Mr. Ford took office in the shadow of Watergate and won high marks for restoring a measure of candor to the White House. But as the first appointed President, he lacked the strong hold on voters' emotions that most incumbents have, and he had to battle for more than six months to beat back a challenge from former Gov. Ronald Reagan of California, a telegenic conservative who came within a hair's breadth of beating him.

It seemed after the conventions that Mr. Carter would win in a walk—or at least it seemed so from the polls.

But Mr. Carter found the general-election campaign more difficult than the primary campaign, and his lead began to shrink after Labor Day. An interview with *Playboy* magazine in which the Georgian used earthy language and a lackluster performance in the first of three televised debates hurt his cause.

By the time the President emerged from his passive, Rose Garden campaign for 11 days of furious stumping to conclude the campaign, it appeared that he had a chance of pulling off an upset. And when the campaign ended on Monday, the national polls showed the race a toss-up—too close to call.

Tuesday, November 2, 1976

THE NEXT PRESIDENT— A DETERMINED GEORGIAN JAMES EARL CARTER JR.

By James T. Wooten
Special to the New York Times

PLAINS, Ga., Nov. 2—The snow began sometime in the night and by the time he arrived at the Manchester Airport early that morning last February a real New Hampshire blizzard was blowing. He stood impatiently on the slushy tarmac, shivering in the wind, sipping coffee from a styrofoam cup, watching the pilot of his small plane scrape ice from its wings, and listening to an aide sagely suggest that the trip ought to be canceled.

"No way," "he finally snapped. "We're going. People support you only if you ask them to support you and you can't very well ask them if you don't show up"

And so, off he went into the white, white storm, a slightly built Georgia farmer flying into the teeth of a New England winter, looking for one more hand to shake, one more chance to smile and say, "Hi, I'm Jimmy Carter and I'm running for President."

Historians will, no doubt, pronounce his victory today the end result of Richard M. Nixon's White House crimes—something better understood perhaps in terms of a Republican forfeit than a Democratic triumph—and their thesis, no doubt, will be as sound as any other.

Yet, there was in that quick, cold moment on that morning in New Hampshire nine months ago as keen an insight into the remarkable rise of James Earl Carter Jr. as his grueling, two-year campaign for the Presidency would provide.

He believed passionately that if he could talk to enough voters about a "Government as good as the American people," he could win—and from the unlikely beginnings of his pursuit to its heady climax in the voting, he was as stubbornly and as single-mindedly committed to that approach as any man who ever dared dream that dream.

For 99 weeks, through all sorts of storms, including several of his own making, he rummaged about the country, alone at first "and lonely," he remembers, making more than 1,500 speeches in a thousand cities in all 50 states and piling up nearly a half-million miles of travel along the way.

A New Session Ignored

In Philadelphia, in the early days, he called a news conference and nobody came. In New York, later on, the papers missed one of his "major addresses." In Hollywood, Fla., deep into the primary season, a woman watched him lope along the street with his stoop shouldered, plowboy gait and asked after he had passed who he was.

Still, through it all—even into the final hours of election eve, he campaigned fiercely, ignoring the strain and the fatigue, still smiling that smile, still telling the voters about a Government as good as the people.

"He may be a lot of things," his speechwriter, Patrick Anderson, said last month, "but the one thing I know he is is tough. He is probably the toughest guy who ever ran."

. . . No one knows precisely how or exactly when his Presidential pursuit began, not even Mr. Carter himself. "I guess maybe it might have been there all along and I just didn't know it," he said. "Maybe it was a gradual realization, but at any rate, all I know is that it occurred to me one day that running for President might not be such a bad idea."

When he formally announced his "idea" on Dec. 12, 1974, only a month before his one term as Governor was to end, there were very few people who thought it had much merit.

He was, after all, a white Southerner who, despite impressive gestures and stands, would be racially suspect elsewhere in the country. His name was not, after all, a household word. He would run without holding public office and he would begin with very little money and no visible base of support.

But Mr. Carter, Mr. Powell, Mr. Kirbo and Hamilton Jordan, his campaign manager, appraised those factors as assets in a volatile political field, and the candidate hit the road, promising again and again never to lie, never to mislead, never to avoid a controversial issue.

Gains in Presidential Quest

They were hard promises to keep, but as he gathered victory after victory in the winter and the spring—the Iowa caucuses, the primaries in New Hampshire, Florida, North Carolina, Illinois, Wisconsin and finally Ohio—he managed to weather most of the challenges to his credibility.

In doing so, he bared his strategy. Words, skillfully used, could play dual roles for him. Liberals came to conceive of him as one of their own. Conservatives responded to him sympathetically as well. Blacks in Harlem voiced their support. Whites in Mississippi got behind him.

Finally, at the Democratic convention, with the nomination in hand, he brought together on the platform most of the men he had beaten, the ideological symbols of his fractious party, in a feast of unity that included—for good measure—the Rev. Martin Luther King Sr. and Gov. George C. Wallace of Alabama.

The Democratic comeback proved to be short-lived, as Ronald Reagan triumphantly returned from his defeat at the Republican convention in 1976 to capture both nomination and election in 1980. Like Ford before him, Carter underestimated Reagan's strength until it was too late.

Carter's presidency, buoyed by hopes for high-minded politics in the wake of Watergate, had fallen victim to many of the frustrations that had plagued his predecessors. There were notable successes, such as the Camp David negotiations that led to a historic peace agreement between Egypt and Israel. But Americans were frustrated by a stagnant economy and what Carter admitted was a "crisis of confidence." The malaise, to use the prevailing term, was exacerbated by two foreign crises that darkened the Carter presidency late in the term: the revolution in Iran, which prompted the seizure of the American embassy and its personnel for 444 days, and the Soviet invasion of Afghanistan, which led Carter to cancel U.S. participation in the 1980 Moscow Olympics.

Carter also had the same misfortune that plagued Gerald Ford in 1976: a strong challenge within his party. Ted Kennedy, urged to run since 1968, at last decided to do so, and led a vigorous insurgency that deepened the divisions in the Democratic coalition. Carter prevailed at the New York convention, but Kennedy's speech, an elegy to the old brand of

Left to right:
Ronald Wilson Reagan (b. 1911)
James Earl Carter Jr. (b. 1924)
John B. Anderson (b. 1922)

President Carter's winning smile belied the difficulty of the internal and external challenges he faced in 1980.

The independent campaign of an Illinois Republican congressman, John Anderson, excited a small minority of voters but failed to stem the Reagan tide.

liberalism that had defined the Democratic party for much of the century, inescapably recalled the memory of his brothers, and was better received than the President's.

As Carter's fortunes were sagging in the east, Reagan's were rising in the west. In many ways, he was an unlikely candidate. Reagan was 69 years old (the oldest previous President, Andrew Jackson, left office at the same age). To those who remembered Barry Goldwater, it seemed unlikely that a candidate from the Republican right could be viable. To liberals, Reagan's B-movie career in Hollywood offered seeming proof of his shallowness. When Reagan remarked that trees caused pollution, the pundits had a field day.

In fact, Reagan's acting skills were a formidable weapon, and the great mass of voters found him both likable and gentlemanly. The skeptics failed to perceive that Reagan was forming a powerful bond with Americans, eager to forget the political and generational divisions of the '60s and '70s and restore earlier standards of patriotism and faith. He easily won the nomination, and selected one of his rivals, George Bush, as his running mate. Their platform promised the difficult double objective of lower taxes and stronger defense.

The campaign was dominated by news of the continuing Iranian hostage crisis, and growing Democratic despondency. Reagan and Carter held one debate, which failed to stop the Republican steamroller. Reagan also debated John Anderson, a moderate Republican Congressman and independent candidate who drained votes from Carter.

The result was a surprise to no one, but the margin of victory was. Reagan won 489 electoral votes and 51 percent of the popular vote to Carter's 49 votes and 41 percent of the vote; Anderson won 7 percent.

With surprising vigor, the oldest president ever elected launched a new period of Republican primacy. The Democrats still controlled Congress, but the 1980 election signaled an important shift to the right among voters with political ramifications to this day.

Some thought Reagan was unqualified, but in his optimism, his confidence, and his disdain for the problems of the 1970s, he forcefully captured the public mood.

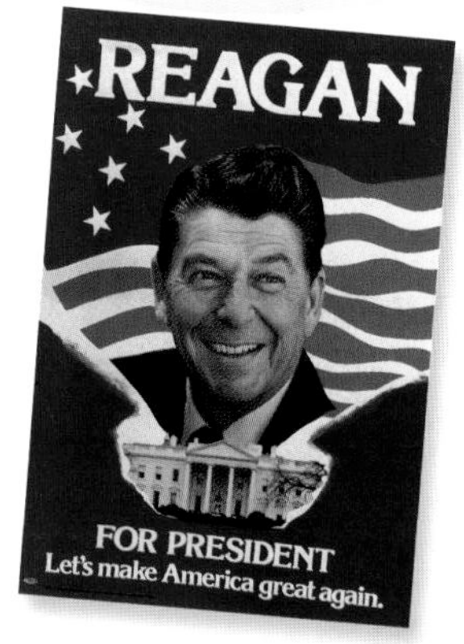

Marion K. Epstein holds a sign *(left)* reminding New York voters of their duty, Manhattan, September 9, 1980.

President Carter makes a campaign stop at the Concord Baptist Church in Brooklyn *(opposite, top)*. Joining him in song are, from left: Representatives Charles Rangel and Shirley Chisolm, and Senator Edward Kennedy, October 20, 1980.

Ronald Reagan leads Republican congressmen in singing "God Bless America" on the Capitol steps *(opposite, bottom)*. In front row were, from left: Senator Bob Dole, vice-presidential candidate George Bush, Senator Howard H. Baker Jr., and Representatives John J. Rhodes and Robert H. Michel, September 15, 1980.

Congressman John Anderson and his daughter Diane (in hat) tour the Gold Star Hat and Cap factory, New York City *(top, left)*, October 9, 1980.

Anderson speaks at a fund-raiser *(bottom, left)* at the Fifth Avenue penthouse of Stewart Mott, a financier of liberal causes, New York City, February 5, 1980.

President Carter attends a Legionnaires' meeting in Boston *(top, right)*, August 21, 1980.

Workers at the Raritan River Steel Company in New Jersey give Jimmy Carter a demonstration *(bottom, right)*, September 9, 1980.

Ronald Reagan stumps in Houston with his old friend Roy Rogers *(above)*, October 29, 1980.

Reagan speaks at Liberty State Park, New Jersey, the Statue of Liberty providing a majestic backdrop *(opposite)*, September 1, 1980.

Jimmy Carter jumps down off the roof of his limo, which he used as a makeshift dais for a speech at an East St. Louis rally *(left)*, November 3, 1980.

John Anderson speaks to a crowd of over 100,000 during a rally for Soviet Jewry at Dag Hammarskjold Plaza in New York City *(below)*, April 27, 1980.

Mr. and Mrs. Ronald Reagan sing "God Bless America" *(opposite)* in San Diego, California, November 3, 1980.

"All the News That's Fit to Print"

The New York Times

LATE CITY EDITION

Weather: Sunshine and clouds today; clear, cold tonight. Sunny tomorrow. Temperature range: today 43-53; yesterday 49-58. Details are on page B6.

VOL.CXXX . No. 44,758

NEW YORK, WEDNESDAY, NOVEMBER 5, 1980
30 cents beyond 50-mile zone from New York City. Higher in air delivery cities.

25 CENTS

REAGAN EASILY BEATS CARTER; REPUBLICANS GAIN IN CONGRESS; D'AMATO AND DODD ARE VICTORS

Rep. Holtzman Defeated; Connecticut Is for Reagan

Javits Is Far Behind

By FRANK LYNN

Alfonse M. D'Amato, a political unknown outside Nassau County six months ago, defeated Representative Elizabeth Holtzman yesterday in a close contest for the United States Senate. The incumbent, Senator Jacob K. Javits, a veteran of 24 years in the Senate, trailed far behind.

The 43-year-old Mr. D'Amato, whose qualifications for the Senate were repeatedly questioned by his opponents, was helped by Ronald Reagan's coattails as the Republican Presidential candidate won the state by at least 130,000 votes. Mr. D'Amato's plurality in a three-way race was about half that.

With 96 percent of 14,058 election districts reporting, the Senate vote was:

D'Amato	2,532,925
Holtzman	2,459,639
Javits	611,163

Murphy and Thompson Lose

Representative John M. Murphy was defeated in his district on Staten Island and in lower Manhattan, and another Democratic Congressman indicted in the Federal Abscam inquiry, Frank Thompson Jr. of New Jersey, also lost.

At 12:55 A.M., an hour after Mr. D'Amato claimed victory at his headquarters in Hempstead, L.I., Miss Holtzman would not concede. "The race remains too close to call, and I remain confident," the Brooklyn Democrat told cheering supporters at her Brooklyn Academy of Music headquarters. She reminded them that she had won her first primary victory in 1972 by 635 votes.

Aides of the Democratic candidate con-

Continued on Page A20, Column 1

Moffett Re-elected

By RICHARD L. MADDEN

Despite a victory by Ronald Reagan at the top of the ticket, Representative Christopher J. Dodd yesterday defeated his Republican opponent, James L. Buckley, to win a Connecticut seat in the United States Senate where his late father served.

With 91 percent of the state's 739 precincts reporting, the vote was:

Dodd	655,509
Buckley	511,316

In the Presidential race, which pre-election polls had indicated would be a toss-up, Mr. Reagan led President Carter, 48 percent to 39 percent, with John B. Anderson, the independent candidate, drawing about 12 percent of the vote.

Mr. Buckley conceded at 9:20 P.M. but told his supporters at a New Haven hotel to "stay involved."

Consistent Leader in Polls

Mr. Dodd, a three-term Democratic Representative from Norwich and the 36-year-old son of the late Senator Thomas J. Dodd, had been a consistent leader in the polls for the Senate seat being vacated after 18 years by Abraham A. Ribicoff, a Democrat who is retiring.

An Associated Press-NBC News poll of voters as they left the Connecticut polls indicated that Mr. Reagan benefited from a strong dissatisfaction with the President's record on defense and the economy. The survey also indicated that Mr. Anderson drew more votes from Mr. Carter than from Mr. Reagan.

In the Congressional races, the Republicans picked up the House seat in the

Continued on Page A20, Column 5

United Press International

Ronald Reagan and his wife, Nancy, waving to supporters last night in Los Angeles after he defeated President Carter

PRESIDENT CONCEDES

Republican Gains Victories in All Areas and Vows to Act on Economy

By HEDRICK SMITH

Ronald Wilson Reagan, riding a tide of economic discontent against Jimmy Carter and promising "to put America back to work again," was elected the nation's 40th President yesterday with a sweep of surprising victories in the East, South and the crucial battlegrounds of the Middle West.

At 69 years of age, the former California Governor became the oldest person ever elected to the White House. He built a stunning electoral landslide by taking away Mr. Carter's Southern base, smashing his expected strength in the East, and taking command of the Middle West, which both sides had designated as the main testing ground. The entire West was his, as expected.

Mr. Carter, who labored hard for a comeback re-election victory similar to that of Harry S. Truman in 1948, instead became the first elected incumbent President since Herbert Hoover in 1932 to go down to defeat at the polls.

Concession by Carter

Despite pre-election polls that had forecast a fairly close election, the rout was so pervasive and so quickly apparent that Mr. Carter made the earliest concession statement of a major Presidential candidate since 1904 when Alton B. Parker bowed to Theodore Roosevelt.

At 9:50 P.M., Mr. Carter appeared with his wife, Rosalynn, before supporters at the ballroom of the Sheraton Washington Hotel and disclosed that an hour earlier he had telephoned Mr. Reagan to concede and to pledge cooperation for the transition to new leadership.

"The people of the United States have made their choice and, of course, I accept that decision," he said. "I can't stand here tonight and say it doesn't hurt."

At a celebration in the Century Plaza Hotel in Los Angeles, Mr. Reagan claimed his victory and said: "There's

Continued on Page A18, Column 1

Republican Majority Is Possible In Senate, the First in 26 Years

By MARTIN TOLCHIN

Bolstered by a conservative tide and a sweep by Ronald Reagan, Republicans cut deeply into the Democrats' Senate majority yesterday and appeared within striking distance of ending 26 years of Democratic control.

"If this trend continues, we may very well control one house of the Congress for the first time in a quarter of a century," Mr. Reagan told cheering supporters in a victory speech early this morning.

The changing party alignment and the lingering effects of tough re-election campaigns were expected to give a more conservative coloration to the incoming 97th Congress. That could affect the outcome of hitherto close votes on military spending, social programs and the controversy surrounding Federal abortion payments.

Party control of the Senate could well rest with Harry F. Byrd Jr. of Virginia, an independent who has previously cast his lot with the Democrats, and with Edward Zorinsky, Democrat of Nebraska, formerly a Republican.

It was a disastrous day for liberal Democrats, women who had won major party nominations and some veteran members of Congress.

In three contests that attracted national attention, Senators Birch Bayh of Indiana, George McGovern of South Dakota and John C. Culver of Iowa went down to defeat, all by conservative Republicans. They and other liberal Democrats had been designated for defeat last spring by national conservative groups and opponents of the Medicaid abortion payments.

Mr. Bayh was ousted by Representative Dan Quayle, Mr. McGovern by Representative James Abdnor, and Mr. Culver by Charles E. Grassley.

In Idaho, Frank Church, a Democrat who is chairman of the Foreign Relations Committee, and who also was designated for defeat by the conservative groups, was trailing Representative Steven D. Symms, another conservative Republican.

Senator Warren G. Magnuson, Democrat of Washington, who turned 75 years

Continued on Page A19, Column 5

The Election At a Glance

Summary of Presidential Vote

Electoral Votes Needed to Win: 270

	States	Votes
Reagan	39	444
Carter	6	45
Undecided	6	49

Summary of Congressional Vote

THE SENATE

	Present 96th Congress	New 97th Congress
Democrats*	59	47
Republicans	41	45
Undecided	...	8
Total	100	100

*includes one independent

THE HOUSE

	Present 96th Congress	New 97th Congress
Democrats	276	210
Republicans	159	163
Undecided		62
Total	435	435

The Collapse Of a Coalition

Carter Failed in Groups That Backed Him in '76

By ADAM CLYMER

The old Democratic coalition deserted President Carter yesterday, with defections reminiscent of the defeat of George McGovern in 1972.

News Analysis

Roman Catholics went against the President, he gained little better than a split among voters from union households, and his margins among Jews, liberals and low-income voters fell well below the percentages that Democrats usually get. That was the message from a New York Times/CBS News Poll of more than 10,000 voters leaving polling booths across the nation yesterday.

And Mr. Carter neither repeated the unusual strength he showed in 1976 among such predominantly Republican groups as white Protestants, nor made the compensating gains he had counted on among blacks or the teachers who had turned out in force to help him win this year's Democratic nomination. In fact, teachers went for Ronald Reagan.

The poll proved the Carter campaign correct in an analysis it made early. All summer long the Carter camp had said that if it could make Mr. Reagan the issue the President could win, but that he risked defeat if he became the issue.

On Election Day, Mr. Carter was the issue. One of the most frequently cited reasons for voting — it came entirely from the Republican's supporters — was: "It's time for a change."

This referendum focused on the economy. In 1976, Mr. Carter attacked President Ford on inflation and unemployment

Continued on Page A18, Column 3

Iran Seeks U.S. Reply on Hostages Via 'Media' but Washington Balks

Teheran Seems in a Hurry

By Reuters

TEHERAN, Iran, Nov. 4 — Iran has called on the United States for a speedy reply "through the mass media" to its conditions for the release of the 52 American hostages.

The request, contained in a message conveyed to the Carter Administration through the Algerian Embassy in Washington, appeared to reflect an urgent desire to end the hostage crisis — and the resulting Western economic boycott — in view of the increasing military pressure by Iraq and growing disarray in the Iranian economy.

[The United States turned the request aside. The State Department commented that Iran's conditions "deserve careful analysis and careful study and they will get it." It said it could not estimate how long this would take. Page A8.]

'Positive Answer' Sought

Prime Minister Mohammed Ali Rajai said in an interview with the Teheran radio today that if the United States "wants to solve the question, it will be obliged to give a positive answer to us."

But Ayatollah Ruhollah Khomeini's son, Hojatolislam Ahmad Khomeini, sought in a separate interview to discourage any idea that a solution was near. He said no clear solution was in sight.

The Prime Minister announced that his Government would take control of the hostages from the militants who seized the American Embassy here a year ago today. A spokesman for his office said a

Continued on Page A9, Column 1

Bill on Assets Is Reported

By ROBERT A. BENNETT

The Carter Administration has prepared a bill that would nationalize American claims against Iran and thereby prevent American individuals or companies from directly suing the Iranian Government for past claims, according to attorneys involved in such litigation.

This, the lawyers said yesterday, is one of several options the Administration is considering to facilitate negotiations regarding the release of the 52 Americans held hostage by Iran. A major demand of the Iranians has been for return to Iran of about $8 billion in Iranian assets that were blocked last year by President Carter.

In line with its policy against discussing publicly details of the Administration's negotiating position, a State Department spokesman declined to comment on the possibility of such legislative attempts.

Skepticism in Washington

But William Rand, a former justice of the New York Supreme Court, said yesterday that Administration officials had discussed the bill with Congressional leaders. Mr. Rand currently is a litigator with Coudert Brothers, a prominent international law firm that is based in New York.

In Washington, however, Congressional aides were skeptical that such a measure, which would establish a Federal claims commission on Iran, would be approved. Many members of Congress,

Continued on Page D12, Column 3

United Press International

President Carter making his concession speech last night at the Sheraton Washington. With him were his wife, Rosalynn; his daughter, Amy, and a grandson, Jason. He called Ronald Reagan's accomplishment "a fine victory."

Summary of Other Major News

Iraqi Affirms Territorial Claims

President Saddam Hussein of Iraq says the war against Iran will continue until all of Iraq's territorial claims are recognized by the Iranians. Page A8.

Delays on Subways to Grow

Subway riders will have to wait longer for trains because equipment shortages have forced cuts in service, the Transit Authority said. Page B1.

Opera Negotiations Hit Snag

Hopes for reopening the Metropolitan Opera were dampened when the chorus's union voted to back demands the Met is resisting. Page C25.

Oh Retires From Baseball

Sadaharu Oh, who surpassed Babe Ruth and Henry Aaron with 868 home runs, retired after 21 years in Japan's professional leagues. Page A27.

Wednesday, November 5, 1980

Reagan Easily Beats Carter; Republicans Gain In Congress; D'Amato and Dodd are Victors

President Concedes

Republican Gains Victories In All Areas and Vows To Act on Economy

By Hedrick Smith

Ronald Wilson Reagan, riding a tide of economic discontent against Jimmy Carter and promising "to put America back to work again," was elected the nation's 40th President yesterday with a sweep of surprising victories in the East, South and the crucial battlegrounds of the Middle West.

At 69 years of age, the former California Governor became the oldest person ever elected to the White House. He built a stunning electoral landslide by taking away Mr. Carter's Southern base, smashing his expected strength in the East, and taking command of the middle West, which both sides had designated as the main testing ground. The entire West was his, as expected.

Mr. Carter, who labored hard for a comeback re-election victory similar to that of Harry S. Truman in 1948, instead became the first elected incumbent President since Herbert Hoover in 1932 to go down to defeat at the polls.

Concession by Carter

Despite pre-election polls that had forecast a fairly close election, the rout was so pervasive and so quickly apparent that Mr. Carter made the earliest concession statement of a major Presidential candidate since 1904 when Alton B. Parker bowed to Theodore Roosevelt.

At 9:50 P.M., Mr. Carter appeared with his wife, Rosalynn, before supporters at the ballroom of the Sheraton Washington Hotel and disclosed that an hour earlier he had telephoned Mr. Reagan to concede and to pledge cooperation for the transition to new leadership.

"The people of the United States have made their choice and, of course, I accept that decision," he said. "I can't stand here tonight and say it doesn't hurt."

At a celebration in the Century Plaza Hotel in Los Angeles, Mr. Reagan claimed his victory and said: "There's never been a more humbling moment in my life. I give you my sacred oath that I will do my utmost to justify your faith."

With 73 percent of the popular vote counted, Mr. Reagan had 31,404,169 votes, or 50 percent, to 26, 295,331, or 42 percent, for Mr. Carter, with John B. Anderson, the independent, drawing 3,862,679, or 6 percent of the national total.

Mr. Reagan also suggested that enough Congressional candidates might ride the coattails of his broad sweep to give Republicans a chance to "have control of one house of Congress for the first time in a quarter of a century."

The Republicans picked up Senate seats in New Hampshire, Indiana, Washington, Iowa, Alabama, Florida and South Dakota and were leading in Idaho. Going into the election, the Senate had 58 Democrats, 41 Republicans and one independent. The Republicans also appeared likely to gain at least 20 seats in the House, nowhere nearly enough to dislodge the Democratic majority.

In the Presidential race, Mr. Carter managed six victories—in Georgia, Rhode Island, West Virginia, Maryland, Minnesota and the District of Columbia—for 45 electoral votes. But everywhere else the news was bad for him. By early this morning, Mr. Reagan had won 39 states with 444 electoral votes, and more were leaning his way.

In the South, the states of Texas, Florida, Mississippi, Louisiana, Virginia, South Carolina, North Carolina, Tennessee and Kentucky fell to the Reagan forces, an almost total rejection of the President by his home region. In the Middle West, the former California Governor took Ohio, Illinois and Michigan, three states on which Mr. Carter had pinned heavy hopes, as well as most others.

But Mr. Reagan's showing was even more startling in the East. He took New York and Pennsylvania, always vital bases for Democrats, as well as New Jersey, Connecticut and several smaller states.

A New York Times/CBS News poll of more than 10,000 voters as they left the polls indicated that the predominant motivation among voters was the conviction that it was time for a change. The biggest issue in their minds was the nation's economy, especially inflation.

"The Iranian thing reminded people of all their frustration," Robert S. Strauss, the Carter campaign chairman said. "They just poured down on him. I don't think there's anything anyone could have done differently."

"It was really a referendum on leadership," countered Richard Wirthlin, the Reagan pollster. "The Presidential debate did not have a tremendous influence on the vote, but it strengthened Reagan's credibility for taking Carter on as sharply as we did in the last five days and drive home the attack on the economy."

The Times/CBS News survey revealed a general collapse of the traditional coalition that has elected Democratic Presidents since the New Deal. It showed Mr. Carter running behind his 1976 performance not only in the South but also among such groups as blue-collar workers, Roman Catholics and Jews.

Pocketbook Issues Stressed

Although the President had tried to make foreign policy, especially nuclear arms control, the principal issue of the election, voters leaving the polls told interviewers that pocketbook issues had been more decisive in their voting. Thirty-five percent of those interviewed said their family financial situation was worse than a year ago, and in that group, Mr. Reagan led the President by 65 to 25 percent.

That kind of voting pattern was particularly damaging to the President in such crucial battlegrounds as Pennsylvania, Ohio, Michigan and Illinois. The dimensions of his defeat carried a number of other Democratic incumbents down with him, including prominent liberal senators like Birch Bayh of Indiana and George McGovern of South Dakota, as well as the House Democratic whip, John Brademas of Indiana.

In addition to the Presidency, 34 Senate seats, 13 governorships, all 435 seats in the House of Representatives and about 7,500 seats in state legislatures were at stake in the election.

G.O.P. Hopes in Senate

Riding Mr. Reagan's coattails, Republican candidates for Congress seemed likely to exceed their advance expectations of picking up 15 to 20 seats and half a dozen in the Senate.

Nationwide, Mr. Reagan's overall margin was greater than Mr. Anderson's vote and his sweep so extensive that he largely put to rest the Carter contentions that the Illinois Congressman was "the spoiler" depriving the President of winning margins in key states.

Mr. Anderson made his concession statement at the Hyatt Regency Hotel in Washington, about an hour after the President spoke, asserting that his campaign had contributed "a new realism" to American politics. His vote total seemed to guarantee him Federal subsidies to help repay his campaign debts. He needed a minimum of 5 percent of the vote to qualify for Federal funds.

All the indications were that Mr. Reagan's solid year of active campaigning had put to rest voter worries about his age.

As expected, he was the solid favorite of men, holding close to a 5-to-3 advantage over Mr. Carter in that group, according to the Times/CBS News Poll. Despite earlier indications that the Californian might be penalized among women by his opposition to the equal rights amendment, he managed to run even with the President in that group. That was the only demographic category in which Mr. Carter ran even with his challenger.

The mood of the two men, as they voted, reflected their advance estimates of the balloting. Mr. Carter had been given a pessimistic overnight report by his pollster, Patrick H. Caddell, who cautioned that this year there had not been the kind of election-eve surge that lifted the former Governor of Georgia to victory in 1976.

Carter Pledge in Plains

Mr. Carter, his voice breaking and tears welling in his eyes, told well-wishers in his hometown of Plains, Ga., "I will not disappoint you." Some in the small crowd were crying.

"I've tried to honor my commitment," he went on, but he had to pause for a moment to regain self-control, "to you."

"God bless you," he said in conclusion.

Mr. Reagan, who has been jaunty and joking over the last several days as aides reported firm momentum since the Presidential debate on Oct. 28, voted at a neighbor's house near his home at Pacific Palisades, outside Los Angeles.

> At 69 years of age, the former California Governor became the oldest person ever elected to the White House.

When reporters asked if he expected to win, Mr. Reagan replied: "You know me. I'm too superstitious to answer anything like that." But his wife, Nancy, nudged him and whispered, "cautiously optimistic," and he echoed, "Yes, I'm cautiously optimistic."

The Carter camp had pinned its final hopes on a big voter turnout and a breakthrough in the Iranian hostage crisis, but Mr. Caddell said the Iranian situation had worked against the President in the last 48 hours.

Assessments of Outcome

His analysis was that after the debate, the President had fallen 5 percentage points behind Mr. Reagan but recovered by last Saturday night. On Sunday, Mr. Caddell said, Mr. Carter was once again down 5 points and 10 points behind by Monday. "It was all related to the hostages and events overseas," he said.

But the Republican pollster, Mr. Wirthlin, differed, saying that the President's credibility had been damaged and Mr. Reagan's strengthened in the debate, laying the basis for the final Republican attacks on Mr. Carter's economic record. His own polling showed a mounting Reagan lead since the day after the debate, he said.

Mr. Wirthlin also attributed the unexpectedly large Republican margins in state after state to extremely effective organizations that got out a heavy vote and to the collapse of the Democratic coalition. "We cracked the unions, blue-collar voters, ethnics, Catholics and the South, just as he had planned," he said.

In the Northeast, Middle Atlantic States and coastal regions of the South, there were showers through much of the day, but most of the country had clear weather, cool in the Northern states and warm and pleasant in the South and Southwest.

Voting officials in major states like New York, Ohio, Pennsylvania, Illinois, Michigan, Texas and Florida reported long lines and fairly heavy balloting early in the day. In Columbus, Ohio, polling officials had to add extra voting machines to handle the crowds.

Most experts had been expecting turnout to fall below the 54 percent of the eligible voters who cast ballots in 1976. Census estimates placed the number of eligible voters at 160,491,000 and the likely turnout at not more than 88 million.

Appeal to Anderson Backers

Low turnout and Mr. Anderson's pull among potential Democratic voters were major worries for Mr. Carter. With a low turnout, Mr. Carter kept warning, "We Democrats can beat ourselves."

"Don't waste your vote," he pleaded to Anderson supporters in a voice raspy from dawn-til-dusk campaigning in the homestretch drive.

For the President, the election year has been an unpredictable roller-coaster. A year ago, before the American Embassy was seized in Teheran, he looked as though he was headed toward almost certain defeat and might not even be renominated. But after the American hostages were taken, patriotic support rallied to him, and he overtook his main Democratic challenger, Senator Edward M. Kennedy of Massachusetts, in the polls and took an unbeatable lead in the primaries.

In mid-summer he was once again far behind, this time trailing Mr. Reagan in the polls by 20 points. But when Senator Kennedy healed the Democratic rift and began vigorously campaigning for the Carter-Mondale ticket, Democratic voters began "coming home" and the polls see-sawed until the debate.

With a low turnout, Mr. Carter kept warning, "We Democrats can beat ourselves."

When surveys showed Mr. Reagan gaining from their confrontation in Cleveland, the President stepped up the frantic pace of his campaigning. But there was too much ground for him to cover. He had to divide time between fighting for the battleground states of the industrial belt from New Jersey to Wisconsin and protecting his crumbling southern base in Texas, Florida, Alabama, Mississippi and South Carolina.

The strain began to show in the final week. "I need you," Mr. Carter kept telling his rallies trying to energize a vigorous push from blacks, Hispanic-Americans and other traditionally Democratic voting groups. His right hand was red and bruised from endless hand-shaking and his face, puffy and lined from the relentless pace he had set.

At the same time, Mr. Reagan concentrated his efforts on the pivotal states, bolstered by increasingly confident projections from his own pollsters.

Mondale, a Humphrey protégé, never quite shook the label that he was an old-school tax-and-spend Democrat, more comfortable in the Capitol than the White House.

The 1984 campaign proved that Reagan was not relinquishing power anytime soon (even though he fell asleep in Cabinet meetings now and then). Despite crises during his first term, including the bombing of the Marine barracks in Beirut, and a willingness to let the deficit soar, the "Teflon President" remained enormously popular.

His prospects for reelection were in no way threatened by the Democratic primaries. At first, eight candidates vied for the nomination, but the field soon dwindled to three: Walter Mondale, Jimmy Carter's vice president and a former Minnesota senator; Gary Hart, senator from Colorado; and Jesse Jackson, the civil rights activist, and the first African-American to attract major interest as a candidate. Mondale was not exactly a dynamic stump speaker (critics called him "Norwegian Wood"), but he impressed voters with his integrity, and bested his rivals after a long primary season. One of its funnier moments included Mondale's invocation of a slogan for Wendy's hamburgers when he said that Hart's proposals made him ask, "Where's the beef?"

A high point of the Democratic campaign was the San Francisco convention. In a stirring speech, Governor Mario Cuomo of New York reminded Democrats of their history of fighting for social justice and punctured some of Reagan's comforting optimism. Another Italo-American

Left to right:
Ronald Wilson Reagan (b. 1911)
Walter F. Mondale (b. 1928)

The nomination of Geraldine Ferraro for vice president was a historic milestone, and remains the most lasting achievement of the Mondale campaign.

from New York, Representative Geraldine Ferraro was nominated by Mondale to be his running mate—the first time a major party had chosen a female candidate for one of the top spots. Though she later encountered difficulties related to her husband's business dealings, Ferraro was a popular choice and enlivened the Democratic ticket.

Reagan repeated the ideas that had brought him to the Presidency, advocating supply-side economics, a strong military, smaller government, and old-fashioned idealism; the Christian Right was also a growing force in Republican politics. Even his gaffes were forgiven. In August he joked into a live microphone that he would begin bombing Russia in five minutes. Mondale attacked the spiraling deficit, and called for new taxes to reduce it: an honest approach, if not exactly a well-liked one.

The candidates debated twice. During the first debate, on October 7, Mondale was sharp and persuasive, while Reagan seemed slow and even disoriented. But two weeks later, Reagan came back sufficiently to reassure voters that the "Great Communicator" was still in good shape. Despite the President's advancing age (he was 73), he remained effortlessly telegenic with the help of a skilled public relations team who produced a film proclaiming "morning in America" and an ad portraying the Soviet Union as a dangerous bear lurking in the woods. Voters responded enthusiastically.

November brought a landslide. Reagan won 59 percent of the vote (54 million) and Mondale won 41 percent (37 million). The electoral discrepancy of 525 to 13 was even more overwhelming. Millions of southerners, Catholics and blue-collar workers crossed party lines to vote Republican, earning the sobriquet "Reagan Democrats."

To an extent, Mondale suffered for his old-school liberalism—the era of the L-word had definitely faded. But it is doubtful anyone would have fared better. Blessed with a bustling economy, a sunny faith in the future, and an imperturbable sense of America's greatness, the Gipper was unbeatable in 1984.

In 1984, the year of "morning in America" and the Los Angeles Olympics, Reagan's popularity was at an apogee.

Jesse Jackson speaks to supporters in New York City *(below)*, April 3, 1984.

The Democratic presidential candidates draw their seating assignments before the start of their televised debate *(right)*, Hanover, New Hampshire, January 6, 1984.

Walter Mondale gestures to the crowd at a rally in Columbus, Ohio *(above)*, October 11, 1984.

Mondale and Ferraro receive deafening applause *(right)* at the Sheraton Centre in New York City, after marching in the Columbus Day Parade. New York politicians—including Governor Mario Cuomo (fourth from left) and Mayor Ed Koch (third from right)—lend their support, October 8, 1984.

The
Sheraton Centre
New York

Nancy Reagan waves to her screen idol at the Republican National Convention in Dallas, August 22, 1984.

George Bush beckons to the crowd at the Dallas convention as balloons fall around him, August 21, 1984.

A billboard in Bladenburg, Maryland *(above)*, urges women to vote,October 1984.

Geraldine Ferraro campaigns in Oregon *(opposite, top)*, October 26, 1984.

Mondale/Ferraro supporters in Amherst, Massachusetts *(opposite, bottom)* cheer for their candidates. October 20, 1984.

MONDALE
FERRARO
MONDALE
FERRARO
FOR
NUCLEAR FREEZE

Ronald Reagan visits a group of construction workers *(left)* during a campaign stop in New York City, October 1, 1984.

Reagan waves to the press while posing in front of a B-1 bomber *(below)*, before addressing employees at the Rockwell International plant, Palmdale, California, October 22, 1984.

The Reagans watch election results *(opposite, top)* at the Century Plaza, Los Angeles, November 6, 1984.

Frank Sinatra joins the President and Mrs. Reagan at an Election Eve rally in front of the California State Capitol, Sacramento, *(opposite, bottom)*, November 5, 1984.

"All the News That's Fit to Print"

The New York Times

Late Edition

Weather: Mostly sunny and cool today, northwesterly winds; mostly clear tonight. Mostly sunny, mild tomorrow. Temperatures: today 50-53, tonight 33-37; yesterday 42-59. Details, page A24.

VOL.CXXXIV.. No. 46,221 | NEW YORK, WEDNESDAY, NOVEMBER 7, 1984 | 50 cents beyond 75 miles from New York City, except on Long Island. | 30 CENTS

REAGAN WINS BY A LANDSLIDE, SWEEPING AT LEAST 48 STATES; G.O.P. GAINS STRENGTH IN HOUSE

Two Parties Still Split Control on Capitol Hill

House Power Battle

By STEVEN V. ROBERTS

Republicans cut into the Democratic majority in the House of Representatives last night, but their drive to shake the control of Democratic leaders seemed to fall short.

If last night's trends hold when the final votes are tallied, the House would continue to pose a major obstacle to President Reagan's legislative agenda, despite his overwhelming re-election victory.

Representative Thomas P. O'Neill Jr., the Speaker of the House, estimated that the Democrats would lose 10 to 12 seats from their majority of 99. In a television interview, he attributed the Democrats' strong showing to widespread desire in the country check Mr. Reagan's more conservative proposals.

G.O.P. Needed 25 Seats

"I believe they wanted the Democrats in there as a safety net," he said. Speaking of President Reagan, Mr. O'Neill said, "He really hasn't had coat tails."

The Republicans needed a gain of about 25 seats to give them a chance to form the sort of coalition with conservative Democrats that enacted many of Mr. Reagan's proposals during the first two years of his Presidency.

In many states, Democratic Representatives survived the Reagan landslide by distancing themselves from the national ticket and stressing their personal records of service to their constituents.

In North Carolina and Texas, the Republicans had a chance to make sweep-

Continued on Page A23, Column 1

Helms Senate Victor

By MARTIN TOLCHIN

Senate Republican candidates grasped President Reagan's coattails yesterday, but early returns indicated that they would be unable to solidify their control of the Senate.

Mr. Reagan, who spent the final week of his campaign appearing in behalf of Senate Republican candidates, seemed unable to translate his dramatic victory into significantly increasing the Republican margin in the Senate. But Democrats were similarly unable to make significant inroads into the Republican margin.

Should this pattern prevail, Mr. Reagan could expect to encounter the same resistance to some of his programs that he experienced in the last two years.

Helms Wins Bid

In the most acrimonious, expensive and closely watched Senate race, Senator Jesse Helms, Republican of North Carolina, leader of the New Right and a foe of abortion and supporter of organized school prayer, defeated Gov. James B. Hunt Jr., a moderate Democrat. The two had exchanged invectives right up to election day.

In Iowa, Senator Roger W. Jepsen, a Republican, was defeated by Representative Tom Harkin, a Democrat, in another campaign in which both candidates engaged in intensive negative campaigning.

Republicans appeared to have won an upset victory in Kentucky, where A. Mitchell McConnell, Jefferson County Judge, was narrowly leading Senator Walter D. Huddleston, a Democrat, although The Associated Press reported

Continued on Page A23, Column 3

The New York Times/Paul Hosefros

President and Mrs. Reagan claiming victory last night in Los Angeles.

MANDATE CLAIMED

Mondale Concedes Loss — Democrats Seek to Avert Realignment

By HOWELL RAINES

Ronald Wilson Reagan won a second term as President yesterday in an election that Republican leaders hailed as a sweeping personal triumph and a mandate for his policies.

Mr. Reagan secured clear landslide victories in both popular and electoral votes as he defeated Walter F. Mondale, the Democratic nominee, in at least 48 of the 50 states.

However, it remained unclear whether the powerful tide of support

Transcripts of speeches, page A21.

for Mr. Reagan ran deeply enough to carry enough Republican Congressional candidates into office to secure the "historic electoral realignment" that the President asked the voters to deliver.

With more than two-thirds of the popular vote counted, Mr. Reagan led Mr. Mondale by about 59 percent to 41 percent.

The President waited until after midnight, Eastern time, to claim the election that continued his tenure as the oldest man to occupy the White House.

Entering the ballroom of the Century Plaza Hotel in Los Angeles to the strains of "Hail to the Chief," Mr. Reagan received a tumultuous welcome from a crowd that chanted, "Four more years."

"I think that's just been arranged," said Mr. Reagan with a grin.

Policy Extension Planned

He said he would use his mandate to extend the economic and military policies of his first term. But, as if answering criticisms made by Mr. Mondale, he said he would also devote his second term to limiting nuclear weapons and to "lifting the weak and nurturing the less fortunate."

"You know, so many people act as if this election means the end of something," Mr. Reagan concluded i an indirect reference to the fact that this was the last election night of his career. "To each one of you I say, it's the beginning of everything," Mr. Reagan said. Then he stirred full-throated cheers by repeating an informal slogan of his campaign, "You ain't seen nothing yet."

Mondale Affirms Principles

Mr. Mondale, looking somber and drained, conceded shortly after 11:20 P.M., Eastern time. After complimenting the President on his victory, Mr. Mondale affirmed his commitment to the principles he had championed in a long, grinding campaign.

"Let us continue to seek an America that is just and fair," Mr. Mondale said. "Tonight especially I think of the

Continued on Page A20, Column 1

Economy the Key Issue

By HEDRICK SMITH

News Analysis

For all the careful orchestration of campaign rallies and political commercials, the televised debates, the partisan clashes over fine points of foreign and military policy, it was the economy that set the basic pattern for President Reagan's stunning re-election sweep yesterday and that fueled Republican gains in Congress.

In a very real sense the election returns followed the well-established script of the Reagan Presidency to make economic policy the central issue of American politics, according to a New York Times/CBS News Poll of 5,051 people as they left the voting booths. For Ronald Reagan vaulted into the White House in 1980 largely on the strength of his biting attacks on the economy under President Carter and his telling question, "Are you better off today than you were four years ago?"

In the midterm Congressional elections two years ago, he suffered a stinging setback with the recession that eroded Republican ranks in the House of Representatives. Now this year, interviews showed, the President won a resounding vote of confidence for his handling of the economy and used it to power a coast-to-coast landslide for a second term in the White House.

His strategists were quick to contend that he had won a mandate for future policies. But the Times/CBS News poll showed that it was the electorate's feelings about the economy more than Mr. Reagan's appeals to traditional values or any specific vision for the future of what he likes to call his "second American revolution" that moved solid majorities in every region of the country into the President's column.

Broad Coalition for Reagan

Indeed, Walter F. Mondale gained more support than Mr. Reagan on his vision of the future, according to the poll. By nearly 2 to 1, however, the voters rejected Mr. Mondale's argument that a tax increase was necessary to reduce the Federal deficit, and Mr. Reagan won a big margin among those who opposed raising taxes.

Most significantly, the Election Day survey found that almost three-fifths of the voters felt the economy was better off today than four years ago, and that

Continued on Page A20, Column 2

PRESIDENT SWEEPS THE TRISTATE AREA

Connecticut Landslide Gives G.O.P. the Legislature

By FRANK LYNN

President Reagan swept New York, New Jersey and Connecticut yesterday. But except for Connecticut, he generally failed to translate his landslide margin into Republican victories in the House of Representatives and local offices.

In Connecticut, the Reagan tide enabled Republicans to gain control of both houses of the General Assembly for the first time in a decade, and to win the post held by Representative William R. Ratchford, a Democrat who was seeking his fourth term.

The President's victory over Walter F. Mondale, his Democratic opponent, in both New Jersey and Connecticut was approaching record proportions of at least 300,000 and 600,000 votes respectively.

He won New York State by at least 500,000 votes, triple his 1980 plurality in the state. He lost traditionally Democratic New York City by 300,000 votes but almost made up the entire deficit on Long Island, with victories of more than 100,000 votes each in Nassau and Suffolk Counties. The President lost only one upstate county, Albany, also a traditional Democratic stronghold.

In a hotly contested House campaign that was the most expensive in the country, Andrew J. Stein, the Democratic Manhattan Borough President,

Continued on Page B4, Column 1

State of Siege Is Imposed in Chile

By LYDIA CHAVEZ

Special to The New York Times

SANTIAGO, Chile, Nov. 6 — President Augusto Pinochet imposed a state of siege in Chile today for the first time in six years.

He acted after months of political unrest and a day after his Cabinet resigned to give him a freer hand to deal with the situation.

"It is precisely to save democracy and liberty that now more than ever it is necessary to be inflexible with respect to the institutional order that rules us," the President said at a ceremony at which he announced a new Cabinet.

Greater Powers for President

Minutes after the ceremony, a nightly curfew from midnight to 5 A.M. was imposed.

The President already had considerable powers to combat terrorism under the previous state of emergency. The press could be censored and political leaders exiled.

The main difference seems to be that under the state of siege the Goverment can hold terrorist suspects without charges for an indefinite period and trials can be delayed indefinately.

The new Cabinet brought only two minor changes. General Pinochet reappointed Interior Minister Sergio Onofre Jarpa, the chief minister, whose decision to step down Monday was followed immediately by the resignation of 15 other ministers.

Mr. Jarpa's resignation had been thought to be in protest against the Government's hard line against the opposition. But his decision to remain in the Cabinet indicated that he agrees with the Government's position.

The Government has taken an in-

Continued on Page A12, Column 1

The New York Times/Jim Wilson and Sara Krulwich

Eleanor Mondale hugging her father as he appeared in St. Paul to make concession speech. Geraldine A. Ferraro was joined by her mother, Antonetta, and a daughter, Laura, in watching results at a Manhattan hotel.

Bradley Wins Handily in Jersey Despite Strong Vote for Reagan

By JOSEPH F. SULLIVAN

Senator Bill Bradley, Democrat of New Jersey, easily won re-election to a second term yesterday.

With more than two-thirds of the votes counted, the 41-year-old Senator led Mary V. Mochary, a 42-year-old lawyer and former Mayor of Montclair, 63 to 37 percent.

Mr. Bradley gained his victory as hundreds of thousands of voters moved between the Democratic and Republican lines on the ballot to give President Reagan an overwhelming margin in the state as well.

Mr. Reagan held a a 64-to-36 percent lead over Walter F. Mondale with more than two-thirds of the votes counted. Mr. Reagan was leading in all 21 counties on his way to capturing the state's 16 electoral votes. The sweep would include Essex, Hudson and Mercer, three counties that he lost in 1980, when he won the state by 400,000 votes over President Jimmy Carter.

Mrs. Mochary telephoned Mr. Bradley at 8:45 P.M., 45 minutes after the polls closed, to congratulate him.

The Republican challenger was outspent by the incumbent, 3 to 1, and had to interrupt her campaign during the final three weeks to accompany her 44-year-old husband, Stephen, to the Stanford University Medical Center in California, where he is awaiting a heart transplant.

Mrs. Mochary said that she planned to leave for California this afternoon.

Mrs. Mochary, who talked to her supporters at the Somerset Hilton Hotel after telephoning Mr. Bradley, said she planned to run for office again, "and I'm not going to lower my sights."

Her comment prompted speculation she was thinking of running against New Jersey's other Democratic Sena-

Continued on Page B4, Column 5

Other News

Trade Talks With Russians

The United States and the Soviet Union plan talks in Moscow in January to explore ways to expand trade between the two nations. Page D1.

Catholics on Capitalism

A commission of conservative Roman Catholic business and professional leaders voiced strong support for American capitalism. Page A16.

Nicaragua Said to Get Soviet Attack Copters

By PHILIP TAUBMAN

Special to The New York Times

WASHINGTON, Wednesday, Nov. 7 — Nicaragua has received a number of Soviet-built attack helicopters in recent days, a senior Administration official said Tuesday night. He said the White House viewed their delivery as a "very serious development."

In addition, Administration officials said they were concerned about a Soviet freighter apparently headed for Nicaragua that intelligence reports indicated was carrying crates that could contain MIG fighter aircraft.

A spokesman for the Nicaragua Embassy denied that helicopters had been delivered or that MIG's were on the way.

A senior Defense Department official said the Administration was considering a variety of responses to the delivery of the helicopters because they could have an important impact on the military balance in Central America.

Although they do not represent as serious an increase in Nicaraguan fire power as would the delivery of advanced fighter planes, he said, they presented a more serious "practical problem."

Specifically, he said, the helicopters, which Soviet forces have used extensively in Afghanistan to combat insur-

Continued on Page A12, Column 1

Wednesday, November 7, 1984

Reagan Wins by a Landslide, Sweeping at Least 48 States; G.O.P. Gains Strength in House

Mandate Claimed

Mondale Concedes Loss —Democrats Seek to Avert Realignment

By Howell Raines

Ronald Wilson Reagan won a second term as President yesterday in an election that Republican leaders hailed as a sweeping personal triumph and a mandate for his policies.

Mr. Reagan secured clear landslide victories in both popular and electoral votes as he defeated Walter F. Mondale, the Democratic nominee, in at least 48 of the 50 states.

However, it remained unclear whether the powerful tide of support for Mr. Reagan ran deeply enough to carry enough Republican candidates into office to secure the historic electoral realignment" that the President asked the voters to deliver.

With more than two-thirds of the popular vote counted, Mr. Reagan led Mr. Mondale by about 50 percent to 41 percent.

The President waited until after midnight, Eastern time, to claim the election that continued his tenure as the oldest man to occupy the White House.

Entering the ballroom of the Century Plaza Hotel in Los Angeles to the strains of "Hail to the Chief," Mr. Reagan received a tumultuous welcome from a crowd that chanted, "Four more years."

"I think that's just been arranged," said Mr. Reagan with a grin.

Policy Extension Planned

He said he would use his mandate to extend the economic and military policies of his first term. But, as if answering criticisms made by Mr. Mondale, he said he would also devote his second term to "lifting the weak and nurturing the less fortunate."

"You know, so many people act as if this election means the end of something," Mr. Reagan concluded in an indirect reference to the fact that this was the last election night of his career. "To each one of you I say, it's the beginning of everything," Mr. Reagan said. Then he stirred full-throated cheers by repeating an informal slogan of his campaign, "You ain't seen nothing yet."

Mondale Affirms Principles

Mr. Mondale, looking somber and drained, conceded shortly after 11:20 P.M., Eastern time. After complimenting the President on his victory, Mr. Mondale affirmed his commitment to the principles he had championed in a long, grinding campaign.

"Let us continue to seek an America that is just and fair," Mr. Mondale said. "Tonight especially I think of the poor, the unemployed, the elderly, the handicapped, the helpless and the sad, and they need us tonight.

"I'm at peace with the knowledge that I gave it everything I've got," the former Vice President concluded.

His running mate, Geraldine A. Ferraro, the first woman to run for the Vice Presidency on a major party ticket, conceded defeat shortly after Mr. Mondale did, saying that her losing candidacy had helped fight discrimination against women.

Addressing a crowd at the New York Hilton Hotel, Mrs. Ferraro praised Mr. Mondale for selecting her, saying he had "opened a door which will never be closed again."

"The days of discrimination are numbered," she said. "American women will never again be second-class citizens."

Mr. Reagan was leading everywhere except in Minnesota, Massachusetts and the District of Columbia, giving him a strong chance of attaining one of the largest electoral vote totals in the nation's history.

The Republicans also retained control of the Senate and made gains in the House of Representatives.

A series of hard-fought contests for House seats emerged as the major focus of the battle joined by the parties in this election. Democratic Congressional leaders predicted that Mr. Reagan's big popular victory would not convert into the large gains that the Republicans needed to assure "ideological control" of the House and to pave the way for a long-term realignment of the power balance between the parties.

More vote for Republicans

Interviews with voters as they left the polls throughout the country indicated that more voters were casting their ballots for Republican Congressional candidates than for Democrats.

The voter interviews by The New York Times/CBS News Poll also showed that Mr. Reagan and his running mate, Vice

President Bush, were leading comfortably in Democratic strongholds in the Northeast and Middle West.

The Republican leads over Mr. Mondale and Mrs. Ferraro were much larger in the Southern and Western states that had hardly been contested by the Democratic ticket.

James A. Baker, 3d, the White House chief of staff, said that Mr. Reagan had apparently secured his second term with a victory of "historic proportion."

Edward J. Rollins, the President's campaign manager, said Mr. Reagan had secured a "landslide victory."

Mr. Baker said Mr. Reagan would use his mandate to push his conservative economic agenda, with additional cuts in Federal spending and "an effort at historic tax simplification."

As Mr. Reagan watched tallies of the vote on television, reporters asked him about the possibility of a summit meeting with the Soviet Union.

"Yes," he said, "it's time for us to get together and talk about a great many things and try to clear the air and suspicions between us so we can get down to the business of reducing, particularly, nuclear weapons."

Asked whether he intended to propose a meeting with the Soviet leader, Konstantin U. Chernenko, Mr. Reagan said, "Let's wait and see if they'll be more specific and definite once the campaign is over."

In electoral votes, Mr. Reagan was threatening the large totals achieved by Franklin D. Roosevelt and Richard M. Nixon.

Mr. Reagan appeared to be comfortably within the large vote margins predicted by polls before the election showing him ahead by 12 to 25 percentage points. The President, who awaited the election returns at the Century Plaza Hotel in Los Angeles, had appealed to voters for a landslide victory that would give the Republicans a chance to overturn half a century of Democratic dominance in Washington.

In electoral votes, Mr. Reagan was threatening the large totals achieved by Franklin D. Roosevelt and Richard M. Nixon. In 1936, President Roosevelt won 523 electoral votes, to 8 for Alf M. Landon, the Governor of Kansas. In 1972 President Nixon scored the next highest total, with 520 electoral votes, to 17 for Senator George McGovern of South Dakota.

With the victory for Mr. Reagan, Democratic and Republican campaign officials turned their attention to the battle for ideological control of Congress. The Republicans were fighting to preserve their majority in the Senate, while cutting into the Democrats' 99-seat advantage in the House of Representatives.

Reagan campaign officials felt that winning back the 26 Republican seats lost in the 1982 election would give conservatives control of the House through a bipartisan majority, and Mr. Reagan and Mr. Bush spent the last week of the Presidential campaign encouraging voters to choose Republican Congressional candidates.

Higher Taxes Rejected

The Times/CBS News Poll showed that Mr. Reagan's handling of the economy was the strongest factor attracting voters to him. Those polled rejected Mr. Mondale's call for higher taxes by a ratio of nearly 2 to 1.

As in 1980, Mr. Reagan drew voters from many customarily Democratic constituencies, although he was overwhelmingly rejected by blacks.

Mr. Reagan also drew support from new groups. Although at the age of 73 he is the oldest man ever to hold the Presidency, he ran well among the young. He won a majority of voters 18 to 24 years old in every region and carried that group in the Middle West by almost 3 to 1.

As he did in 1980, the President also cut strongly into core Democratic groups like Southern whites and Roman Catholics. Despite the A.F.L.–C.I.O.'s yearlong effort on behalf of Mr. Mondale, Mr. Reagan got almost half the voters from union households.

Voting by Sex Not Decisive

The difference in voting patterns between men and women was also evident in this election, but not as a decisive factor. Mr. Reagan carried a solid majority of the men who voted and did not do nearly so well among women.

The Times/CBS News Poll also showed that Mrs. Ferraro did not appear to be a major factor in attracting votes to the Democratic ticket, but neither did she appear to be a handicap.

The strongest issue for Mr. Mondale was nuclear arms control. Blacks were his strongest voter group, with about 90 percent voting for the Democrat. However, in some Deep South states, Mr. Mondale's strength with blacks was offset by the 70 percent level of support for Mr. Reagan among whites.

Mr. Reagan traveled by helicopter yesterday morning from Los Angeles to Solvang, a tourist town near his ranch in the Santa Ynez Mountains north of Santa Barbara. Later, he made the 55-minute helicopter trip back to Los Angeles, where he awaited the returns with friends and family.

Mr. Mondale and his family voted in North Oaks, Minn., on a chilly morning with temperatures in the mid-20's.

Reagan's Popularity Dominated

The Presidential contest was dominated by Mr. Reagan's strong personal popularity. Mr. Mondale and his advisers were continually frustrated by polls that showed many supporters of Mr. Reagan also said they agreed with Mr. Mondale's stronger emphasis on arms control, his opposition to organized school prayer and his support of abortion rights.

At the Democratic National Convention in July, Mr. Mondale took a major gamble by acknowledging that he would raise taxes if elected. The Democrat hoped to get credit for honesty with the voters, and initially the Republicans were rattled, as Mr. Reagan and Mr. Bush issued contradictory statements on tax policy.

But after Labor Day, Mr. Reagan turned Mr. Mondale's words against him, saying his opponent had a two-point economic program. "Raise your taxes and then raise them again."

'Age Issue' Arose Briefly

Mr. Mondale gained in the public opinion polls after the first of two debates between the candidates. At that debate, in Louisville, Ky., on Oct. 7, Mr. Reagan gave a halting performance that raised concerns with many voters about whether he was up to his job.

But the 73-year-old Mr. Reagan appeared to lay the "age issue" to rest in the second debate at Kansas City, Mo., on Oct. 21, joking that he would not try to capitalize on the youth and inexperience of this 56-year-old opponent. Within a week of that debate, Mr. Reagan's lead in the polls began to expand, with particularly discouraging results for the Democrats in California.

The Mondale campaign poured millions of dollars into the most populous state, hoping to use its 47 electoral votes as a starting point to turn the tide against Mr. Reagan nationally. But after closing to within seven percentage points of the incumbent, Mr. Mondale slipped to 14 points behind.

Serenely Confident Effort

Except for his stumbles over the tax issue in July and his weak performance in the first debate, Mr. Reagan ran a campaign of serene confidence. Its most troublesome moments were caused by the Vice President, who became a target of editorial condemnation because of a series of disparaging remarks directed at Mrs. Ferraro by Mr. Bush, his wife and staff.

The Reagan campaign relied on a series of artfully made television commercials and elaborate patriotic rallies, all designed to promote the theme that "America is back" under Mr. Reagan's leadership.

His camp used tens of thousands of red, white and blue balloons, huge loudspeakers and a country-style theme song, "God Bless the U.S.A." to craft campaign events to provide colorful, upbeat images of the President for the nightly television news.

At the Democratic National Convention in July, Mr. Mondale took a major gamble by acknowledging that he would raise taxes if elected.

Mr. Mondale denounced this as a "happy talk campaign" based on the evocation of positive feelings rather than a discussion of issues. But the Reagan team held to its strategy of stressing Mr. Reagan's leadership image over substantive discussion. Despite criticism from journalists, Mr. Reagan did not hold his first news conference of the fall campaign until Sunday.

About a week ago, Mr. Reagan said he was seeking more than re-election. He called for a coast-to-coast victory that would be both a mandate for his "second American Revolution" and a signal for what Mr. Reagan called a "historic electoral realignment."

The 1988 campaign opened with Republicans eager to extend what they were beginning to see as a renewable lease on the White House. Democrats were delighted to campaign against someone other than Reagan, and their hunger for victory was whetted by the president's late-term troubles over the Iran-Contra affair, in which profits from secret arms sales to Iran were diverted to Nicaraguan paramilitary groups.

Each party saw stiff competition for the nomination. Reagan's vice president, George Herbert Walker Bush, was a logical candidate after eight years of loyalty, and a glittering resume (Navy pilot in World War II, Republican Congressman, Director of the CIA). But unlike Reagan, his elite eastern upbringing aroused suspicion among the GOP faithful, and he had to fight against what *Newsweek* called "the wimp factor." Nevertheless, none of his rivals (Bob Dole, Alexander Haig, Jack Kemp, Pat Robertson) mustered enough support, and Bush won the nomination at New Orleans. Bush's choice of Senator Dan Quayle of Indiana as his running mate raised a few eyebrows, for Quayle was young and relatively unknown. But Bush won points for a pledge (that would haunt him) not to raise taxes, and his call for a "kinder, gentler" nation illuminated by "a thousand points of light" waswidely applauded.

The Democrats had an even more crowded field. Many were hoping Governor Mario Cuomo of New York would run, but he refused. Senator Gary Hart of Colorado was the early

Left to right:
George Herbert Walker Bush (b. 1924)
Michael S. Dukakis (b. 1933)

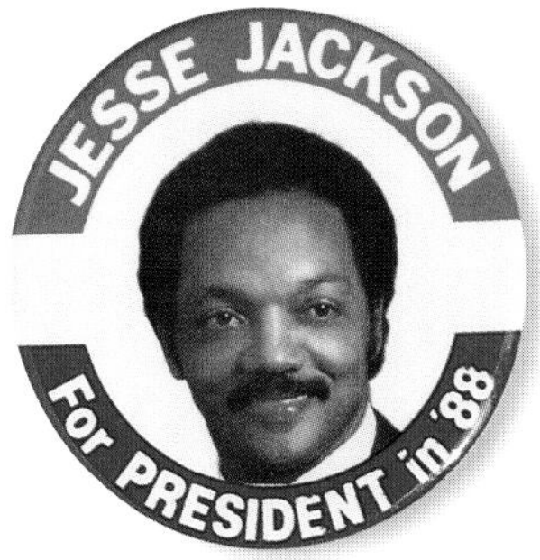

Jesse Jackson's "Rainbow Coalition" broadened the reach of Democrats, and his gospel-tinged oratory electrified the Atlanta convention.

frontrunner, but he flamed out spectacularly after challenging reporters to prove he was an adulterer. They obliged by photographing him on a nautical lark with a girlfriend.

After a grueling primary process, Governor Michael Dukakis of Massachusetts emerged as the top contender, and was duly nominated at Atlanta, where Jesse Jackson gave a stirring speech as the voice of a "Rainbow Coalition." Senator Lloyd Bentsen of Texas was selected as running mate to achieve regional and ideological balance. The platform called for "the restoration of competence" and used Bush's own phrase to attack the "voodoo economics" of the Reagan administration.

Dukakis, the son of Greek immigrants, had presided over the growth of high-tech industries in Massachusetts. Following the Mondale debacle in 1984, he appeared a younger and more modern Democrat. At one point, he outpolled Bush by 17 points, but his technocratic expertise began to grate on voters. He failed to impress a national audience in the second debate when he gave a listless answer to an unexpected question about his imagined response to the hypothetical rape and murder of his wife. And the "Duke" took an undignified and widely televised ride in an army tank wearing an ill-fitting helmet, prompting comparisons with Charlie Brown and worse, undermining his credibility to be Commander in Chief.

Bush pursued his advantage with punishing sarcasm, calling the liberal Dukakis "a card-carrying member of the American Civil Liberties Union," a charge that angered liberals with its echoes of Joseph McCarthy. His campaign also ran a series of controversial television ads focusing on a black man named Willie Horton who committed rape and assault while on a weekend furlough from a Massachusetts jail.

Dukakis traveled everywhere he could, but to no avail. On election day, Bush won 54.6 percent of the popular vote (nearly 48 million) and 426 electoral votes to Dukakis's 46 percent (41 million) and 111 votes. He was the first sitting vice president since Martin Van Buren in 1836 to win election to the presidency in his own right.

This pugilistic pose belies the damaging reputation Michael Dukakis acquired as a technocrat—though he counterpunched well in some of the debates.

A Bush supporter at the GOP convention in New Orleans obscures her view of the "thousand points of light" with buttons.

Candidate supporters brave the cold in Nashua, New Hampshire during the presidential primary, February 16, 1988.

Reverend Jackson leads "New Yorkers for Jesse Jackson" in a march over the Williamsburg Bridge *(above left)*, New York City, April 17, 1988.

Jackson supporters listen to cheers for Dukakis at the Democratic Convention in Atlanta, Georgia *(above right)*, July 20, 1988.

Michael Dukakis meets with Coretta Scott King during a campaign stop in Atlanta, Georgia, July 19, 1988.

Dukakis visits Harlem for gospel music and votes; by his side is Manhattan Borough President and future Mayor of New York City David Dinkins, October 21, 1988.

VICE PRESIDENT OF THE UNITED STATES

Bush pilots a speed boat *(above)* near his summer home in Kennebunkport, Maine, August 1988.

Dan Quayle speaks at the GOP convention in New Orleans as Vice President Bush looks on *(opposite, top)*, August 16, 1988.

Bush and Quayle discuss strategy in Bush's suite prior to a press conference, New Orleans *(opposite, bottom)*, August 17, 1988.

Governor Dukakis hugs his wife Kitty *(left)* after the second of two presidential debates, Los Angeles, October 13, 1988.

The Bush campaign ran this controversial "Willie Horton ad" *(below)* on national television, October 1988.

Horton Received
10 Weekend Passes
From Prison

The Reagans wave good-bye to George Bush as they board Air Force One after the conclusion of the Republican National Convention, New Orleans, August 16, 1988.

"All the News That's Fit to Print"

The New York Times

Late Edition

New York: Today, mostly sunny. High 54-58. Tonight, clear. Low 34-43. Tomorrow, cloudy, windy, showers by late afternoon. High 59-63. Yesterday: High 56, low 43. Details, page D28.

VOL.CXXXVIII . No. 47,684 NEW YORK, WEDNESDAY, NOVEMBER 9, 1988 — 50 cents beyond 75 miles from New York City, except on Long Island. — 35 CENTS

BUSH IS ELECTED BY A 6-5 MARGIN WITH SOLID G.O.P. BASE IN SOUTH; DEMOCRATS HOLD BOTH HOUSES

OTHER HIGHLIGHTS

MISSISSIPPI

Republican to Fill Seat Long Held by Stennis

Lott

As the one-party South fades into history, the Senate seat that John Stennis held for the Democrats over four decades changed hands. Representative Trent Lott, beat Congressman Wayne Dowdy to join another Republican, Thad Cochran, in the Senate.

WISCONSIN

Proxmire's Senate Spot Stays With Democrats

Kohl

Susan Engeleiter, a 36-year-old Republican legislator, was the only woman who seemed to have a chance at the Senate yesterday, but she lost to Herbert Kohl in the race to succeed William Proxmire. Mr. Kohl, a millionaire businessman, persuaded Wisconsinites that he is, as he put it, too rich to be bought off.

BLACK REPUBLICANS

Senate Candidates Lose To Robb and Sarbanes

Republicans nominated two black Senate candidates this year, Alan L. Keyes in Maryland and Maurice A. Dawkins in Virginia. Both lost, as was widely expected, to popular Democrats: Senator Paul S. Sarbanes beat Mr. Keyes while former Gov. Charles S. Robb won in Virginia.

TEXAS

Bentsen's the Winner (For His Spot in Senate)

Bentsen

Michael S. Dukakis had high hopes of carrying Texas when he asked Lloyd Bentsen to be his running mate, but Republicans fought back with the suggestion that the state could do better with George Bush in the White House and Mr. Bentsen on the Senate Finance committee. Texans chose that route, as Mr. Bentsen ran out of luck on the national ticket but retained his Senate seat easily.

THE GENDER GAP

Men and Women Split On White House Choice

The New York Times/CBS News Poll of voters showed that women favored Michael S. Dukakis by a 51 to 49 margin, while men gave the Democrat only 42 percent of their votes.

RHODE ISLAND

House Banking Chief Loses After 14 Terms

Representative Fernand J. St Germain, chairman of the House Banking Committee, lost his re-election bid to a Republican challenger, Ronald K. Machtley. Mr. St Germain was hurt by reports that the House ethics committee has been investigating him.

THE QUAYLE FACTOR

Just How Unpopular Was Senator Quayle?

When pollsters asked voters to choose between Mr. Quayle and Senator Lloyd Bentsen, they picked the Democrat by more than 2 to 1. Over all, the poll made it clear that Mr. Quayle cost Vice President Bush 2 percent of the vote, and perhaps more.

GOVERNORS

Bayh Wins in Indiana; West Virginian Is Out

Bayh

Democrats claimed two new governorships. Arch Moore Jr., who sought a fourth term in West Virginia, lost to Gaston Caperton, a wealthy Democratic insurance executive seeking his first public office. Evan Bayh, 32-year-old son of a former Senator, was elected in Indiana, where the incumbent Republican could not run again.

GUN CONTROL

Maryland Vote Upholds Ban on Some Handguns

The voters had more than candidates on their minds all across the country yesterday. In one ballot issue, exit polls said Maryland voters upheld a measure to ban cheap handguns known as Saturday night specials. Gov. William Donald Schaefer campaigned hard to keep the law despite a $4 million repeal drive by the National Rifle Association.

NEBRASKA

Former Governor Ousts A Republican Senator

Kerrey

A losing incumbent, who had been an underdog from the outset, was Senator David K. Karnes, a Republican. He was appointed to fill a vacancy and served only a year and a half before defeat at the polls by former Gov. Bob Kerrey, a Medal of Honor winner who lost a leg in Vietnam.

National coverage, A24-27.
State by state, A28-30.
The New York region, B4-5.

The New York Times/Paul Hosefros

Vice President Bush striding from the polling place after casting his vote yesterday in Houston.

A Victor Free to Set His Own Course

George Herbert Walker Bush

By GERALD M. BOYD

Special to The New York Times

Man in the News

HOUSTON, Nov. 8 — When George Bush declared last June that he would not raise taxes, skeptical reporters gave him repeated chances to hedge. Could he support higher excise taxes? No, Mr. Bush said. Would he use "revenue enhancers"? No, Mr. Bush insisted.

Finally, when asked if he believed that such a blanket prohibition was wise in the face of uncertain Federal deficit prospects, Mr. Bush slammed the door completely: "I do think it is good public policy; I think it is very reassuring to the working man and woman of this country."

Many friends and associates have long described Mr. Bush as pragmatic, willing to adapt to changing realities. Yet his rigidity on the tax question, maintained throughout the campaign, illustrates a tenacity that is also a critical measure of the man.

Chance to Set Agenda

The same tenacity was seen when he picked himself up off the political floor of Iowa to all but clinch the nomination with a 16-state sweep on "Super Tuesday" just a month later. And when, after a Democratic convention that gave Michael S. Dukakis a big lead in the polls, he fought back to victory.

Now, after 30 years in public service in the shadow of others, that tenacity has given Mr. Bush the chance to set his own political, economic and foreign-policy agendas.

But what is the President-elect's agenda?

In announcing his candidacy last October, Mr. Bush said he would not seek to "make the world over" as President. Instead, his announcement was a personal declaration that "I am the man" to keep the nation safe, to protect its economic well-being and, although he does not say so explicitly, to temper policy excesses of the last eight years.

What He Truly Stands For

Despite hundreds of position papers and thousands of speeches since, what George Bush truly stands for remains an issue.

To some, he campaigned not out of conviction but out of instinct and the competitiveness that leads him to explode with "high-five" celebrations when winning even a horseshoe pitch-

Continued on Page A26, Column 1

MANY SPLIT TICKETS

A Late Drive by Dukakis Fails Despite a Surge in Industrial Areas

By E. J. DIONNE Jr.

George Herbert Walker Bush of Texas was elected the 41st President of the United States yesterday.

The Vice President fashioned a solid, 6-to-5 victory in the popular vote over Gov. Michael S. Dukakis of Massachusetts with a sweep of the once Democratic South. He captured enough major states in other regions to win a commanding majority in the Electoral College.

Of the total of 538 electoral votes, Mr. Bush appeared likely to get from 350 to 415.

Crossover Voting

His solid victory notwithstanding, Mr. Bush did little to help Republican candidates for the Senate. In states like Florida, New Jersey and Ohio, all carried by him and all with Senate races the Republicans had hoped to win, the Republican senatorial nominees went down to defeat.

As a result, the Democrats maintained control of not only the House of Representatives but also the Senate, as voters split their tickets in contest after contest.

The voters stayed away from the polls in unusually large numbers. A preliminary estimate by CBS News indicated that the turnout would be below 51 percent of the population of voting age, which would make it even lower than that of the 1948 Presidential election, the previous post-World War II low.

Concession by Dukakis

In their statements last night, Mr. Bush and Mr. Dukakis were as gracious and positive as their campaigns had been tough and negative.

In Boston Mr. Dukakis, flanked by his family, conceded defeat shortly after 11:15.

"He will be our President," the Governor said of Mr. Bush, "and we'll work with him. This nation faces major challenges ahead, and we must work together."

Barely half an hour later, Mr. Bush claimed victory, declaring before a tumultuous crowd in Houston: "We can now speak the most majestic words a democracy has to offer: 'The people have spoken.' "

The Vice President also again invoked a favored theme of his campaign. "When I said I want a kinder, gentler nation," he asserted, "I meant it and I mean it."

Mr. Dukakis, winning a large majority of the voters who made up their minds late in the campaign, saved himself from an electoral humiliation simi-

Continued on Page A25, Column 1

Lieberman Edges Out Weicker; Lautenberg and Moynihan Win

Joseph I. Lieberman, a Democrat whose campaign advertisements mocked Senator Lowell P. Weicker Jr. as a bear hibernating during important roll call votes, scored a narrow victory over the three-term Connecticut Republican yesterday. But Mr. Weicker, refusing to concede defeat, said he would request a recount today.

With 99 percent of the vote counted, Mr. Lieberman, the Connecticut Attorney General, was 6,500 votes ahead of Mr. Weicker, out of nearly 1.3 million cast. Mr. Weicker, a liberal Republican, soared to national attention in his first term as a member of the Senate Watergate committee.

In New Jersey and New York

In two other races in the metropolitan area, incumbent Democrats — Frank R. Lautenberg of New Jersey and Daniel Patrick Moynihan of New York — kept their Senate seats.

In New Jersey, Mr. Lautenberg defeated his Republican challenger, Pete Dawkins, even though Vice President Bush won the state's 16 electoral votes.

In New York, Mr. Moynihan easily won a third term, rolling up a 2-to-1 margin over his Republican-Conservative challenger, Robert R. McMillan, a Long Island lawyer.

Setback to G.O.P.

Mr. Moynihan claimed victory just 25 minutes after the polls closed, the earliest a major candidate in the state had made such a claim in recent years. The Senator, who won every major county in the state, said he expected the largest Senate plurality in history, more than Senator Alan M. Cranston's 1.6 million votes in California in 1980.

The Lautenberg victory was a setback to Republican efforts to cut the Democratic majority in the Senate. G.O.P. strategists had selected Mr. Lautenberg as one of the country's most vulnerable Democrats.

The New York Times/Stephen Castagneto

Joseph I. Lieberman claiming victory over Lowell P. Weicker Jr. in the Senate race in Connecticut.

Voters in Newark and four suburbs elected New Jersey's first black Representative, Donald M. Payne, a Newark City Councilman. He will succeed a fellow Democrat, Representative Peter W. Rodino Jr., the chairman of the House Judiciary Committee, who is retiring after 40 years in Congress.

Eliot L. Engel, a Democrat, won the 19th District seat in the Bronx and part of Yonkers that Representative Mario Biaggi had held for 20 years. Mr. Biaggi was convicted on corruption charges in two Federal trials.

New Yorkers' approved the largest bond issue in the state's history, a $3 billion transportation proposal. Also, five Charter amendments in New York City passed.

Articles, pages B4 and B5.

The G.O.P. Advantage

Peace, Prosperity and a Disaffected South Were Among the Hurdles Facing Dukakis

By R. W. APPLE Jr.

It has never been easy to oust a party from the White House in times of peace and prosperity. That was the first underlying principle of the 1988 Presidential election.

News Analysis

The second was this: since the mid-1960's the deck has been stacked against the Democrats in Presidential voting. That was when they began to deliver at last on their promises to the nation's blacks, putting right scandalous wrongs but also destroying the old Solid South, one key element of past Democratic majorities, and gravely weakening another — the alliance between blacks and Northern, ethnic, largely Roman Catholic members of trade unions that Franklin Delano Roosevelt had relied upon.

As things turned out, those two handicaps proved to be more than than the Democrats could overcome, despite their feverish endgame.

Gov. Michael S. Dukakis of Massachusetts was widely criticized for his campaign; indeed, the post-mortems started well before the tumult and the shouting had died. In a typical commentary, Sir Gordon Reece, the mastermind of the three election victories of Prime Minister Margaret Thatcher of Britain, said that Mr. Dukakis had made "mistakes of absolutely heroic dimensions."

Failure to Reply

That may well be. And it may well be, as practicing politicians from precinct to Presidential level have been arguing for weeks, that the man from Massachusetts erred most seriously when, mistakenly thinking that he could play bigtime politics by the Marquis of Queensberry rules, he failed to reply early enough to his rival's attacks.

But Vice President Bush began with all sorts of advantages, however obscured they were in those first, eu-

Continued on Page A25, Column 1

INSIDE

Delay on Deficit Plan

A bipartisan budget commission, torn by dissension, has abandoned its Dec. 21 deadline for a deficit reduction plan, its co-chairmen said. Page A32.

Deal Near With Soviets

Six large American companies are on the verge of concluding an agreement on joint ventures that would allow profits to flow to the U.S. Page D1.

Afghan Rebel Offensive

Afghan guerrillas said they were opening a new offensive against Soviet forces along the route from Kabul to the Soviet border. Page A9.

The New York Times, 1983

Kingman Brewster Dies

Kingman Brewster Jr., president of Yale University from 1963 to 1977 and Ambassador to Britain from 1977 to 1981, died in England at 69. Page D29.

News Summary, Page A2

New York, Wednesday, November 9, 1988.

Bush Is Elected by a 6-5 Margin With Solid G.O.P. Base in South; Democrats Hold Both Houses

Many Split Tickets

A Late Drive by Dukakis Fails Despite a Surge in Industrial Areas

By E.J. Dionne Jr.

George Herbert Walker Bush of Texas was elected the 41st President of the United States yesterday.

The Vice President fashioned a solid 6 to 5 victory in the popular vote over Gov. Michael S. Dukakis of Massachusetts with a sweep of the once Democratic South. He captured enough major states in other regions to win a commanding majority in the Electoral College.

Of the total of 538 electoral votes, Mr. Bush appeared likely to get from 350 to 415.

Crossover Voting

His solid victory notwithstanding, Mr. Bush did little to help Republican candidates for the Senate. In states like Florida, New Jersey and Ohio, all carried by him and all with Senate races the Republicans had hoped to win, the Republican senatorial nominees went down to defeat.

As a result, the Democrats maintained control of not only the House of Representatives but also the Senate, as voters split their tickets in contest after contest.

The voters stayed away from the polls in unusually large numbers. A preliminary estimate by CBS News indicated that the turnout would be below 51 percent of the population of voting age, which would make it even lower than that of the 1948 Presidential election, the previous post-World War II low.

Concession by Dukakis

In their statements last night, Mr. Bush and Mr. Dukakis were as gracious and positive as their campaigns had been tough and negative.

In Boston Mr. Dukakis, flanked by his family, conceded defeat shortly after 11:15.

"He will be our President," the Governor said of Mr. Bush, "and we'll work with him. This nation faces major challenges ahead, and we must work together."

Barely half an hour later, Mr. Bush claimed victory, declaring before a tumultuous crowd in Houston: "We can now speak the most majestic words a democracy has to offer: 'The people have spoken.'"

The Vice President also again invoked a favored theme of his campaign. "When I said I want a kinder, gentler nation," he asserted, "I meant it and I mean it."

Mr. Dukakis, winning a large majority of the voters who made up their minds late in the campaign, saved himself from an electoral humiliation similar to those suffered by Walter F. Mondale and George McGovern, the Democratic nominees in 1984 and 1972. He did so by holding Mr. Bush close in key industrial areas and carrying several states, including New York.

Mr. Bush becomes the first incumbent Vice President elected to the Presidency since Martin Van Buren in 1836. His share of the popular vote was 54 percent, CBS News estimated, as against 46 percent for Mr. Dukakis. The Governor's share was the highest for a Democratic Presidential nominee since Jimmy Carter won election in 1976.

The victory by Mr. Bush and his running mate, Senator Dan Quayle of Indiana, confirmed the Republican Party as the dominant forcer in Presidential politics and reflected the country's general satisfaction with the results of eight years of Republican government under Ronald Reagan.

In campaigning to succeed Mr. Reagan, Mr. Bush had promised no major departures, but he had also suggested that he might do some things differently, invoking that vision of a "kinder, gentler nation" and affirming a strong commitment to the environment.

Bush Saw a Referendum

But if these gestures heartened political moderates, the campaign Mr. Bush ran was hailed by conservatives, since the Vice President, once thought of as being at the center of his party, cast the contest with Mr. Dukakis as an ideological referendum. He repeatedly castigated Mr. Dukakis as a "liberal," and highlighted conservative social issues, notably crime.

That same campaign style led some Democrats, including Senator Lloyd Bentsen of Texas, Mr. Dukakis's popular running mate, to predict that a President Bush would have difficulty winning support from a Democratic-controlled

Congress. At the same time, polls showed that the public regarded the campaign as exceptionally negative and blamed Mr. Bush for that more than Mr. Dukakis.

Mr. Bentsen, claiming victory last night in his effort for re-election to the Senate—he appeared twice on the Texas ballot—hailed the campaign he and Mr. Dukakis had run.

> "When I said I want a kinder, gentler nation," he asserted, "I meant it and I mean it."

"He and I waged a campaign that's worthy of the American people," the Senator told cheering supporters in Austin. "We told you the truth, and we stepped up to those issues. We challenged America to do better."

As for Mr. Dukakis himself, his concession statement, although gracious in tone toward Mr. Bush, was also a call on Democrats to continue fighting for their beliefs, "so that every citizen in this country can be a full shareholder in the American dream."

Mr. Dukakis cited city after city he had visited, group after group he had addressed, in pledging to continue that battle himself.

"There is nothing in this world more fulfilling or more satisfying than giving of yourself to others," the Governor declared as he urged young people to pursue lives in public service. "Our hearts are full, we love you all, and we love this country."

Tribute to Reagan

In his victory statement, Mr. Bush paid tribute to President Reagan.

"I thank him for turning this country around and for being my friend," the Vice President said. "He is simply one of the most decent men I've ever met."

Despite the divisiveness of the campaign, Mr. Bush promised to unite the nation. Campaigns are divisive by nature, he said, adding, "An election is a decision, and decisions clear the way for harmony and peace."

The combination of "peace and prosperity" and Mr. Bush's effective, highly disciplined campaign proved potent.

A New York Times/CBS News Poll of more than 10,000 voters after they had cast their ballots yesterday showed that Mr. Reagan's popularity and the generally favorable assessments voters made of the nation's economy were key factors in Mr. Bush's victory.

In addition, the poll showed that Mr. Bush's campaign clearly got through to voters with a number of other central arguments: that Mr. Bush was more experienced than Mr. Dukakis, better equipped to deal with military affairs and the Soviet Union, tougher on crime and more likely to keep taxes down.

But the poll also suggested that there was nothing inevitable in Mr. Bush's victory and that Mr. Dukakis's early, lackluster campaigning had severely damaged his chances for the White House. In the campaign's final weeks, Mr. Dukakis shifted styles, vigorously attacking Mr. Bush and running as a populist who was on the side of average Americans.

The shift came too late, but it nonetheless helped the Democratic nominee. The Times/CBS News Poll showed that voters who decided in the last week of the campaign backed the Governor by a margin of nearly 3 to 2.

Mr. Dukakis, who capped his campaign with a feverish 48-hour swing across the country, did very well among lower-income voters and won back a substantial share of the Democrats who backed President Reagan in 1984. His strength in the closing days of the campaign allowed him to make a race of it in such key states as Illinois, Pennsylvania and California.

Consolation for Democrats

In the wake of another Presidential defeat, Democrats sought consolation in their strength in the Senate and House contests, in which, according to The Times/CBS News Poll, about a quarter of Bush voters backed Democratic House candidates.

The pattern was much the same in contests for the Senate.

In both Ohio and New Jersey, roughly a quarter of Bush voters backed Democratic Senators who won re-election: Howard M. Metzenbaum in Ohio and Frank R. Lautenberg in New Jersey.

Dukakis voters, on the other hand, tended to stick with the Democratic ticket in Ohio and New Jersey, only a tenth of Mr. Dukakis's backers supported the Republican senatorial candidates.

Mr. Bush built his campaign on a powerful foundation. There was, first, Mr. Reagan's popularity, which grew as the campaign went on. The Times/CBS News Poll found that one of the best indicators of voters' choices yesterday was their attitude toward Mr. Reagan. Those who approved of him backed Mr. Bush by more than 4 to 1; those who disapproved of him went about 9 to 1 for Mr. Dukakis. What helped the Vice President in this regard was that many more Americans approved of Mr. Reagan's performance (53 percent) than disapproved (about 40 percent).

There was, as well, the state of the nation's economy. Even in the Midwest, whose economy has gone through a searing transition, roughly four voters said the economy had grown better since 1980 for every three who said it had grown worse. Not surprisingly, Mr. Bush overwhelmed Mr. Dukakis among voters who said the economy had become better.

But the poll also suggested that there was nothing inevitable in Mr. Bush's victory and that Mr. Dukakis's early, lackluster campaigning had severely damaged his chances for the White House.

Behind the Dukakis Gains

Finally, there were the other issues that Mr. Bush's campaign stressed. One voter in five yesterday said that punishment of criminals was among the issues that mattered most to them, a remarkably high proportion for a Presidential election. And these voters went about 2 to 1 for Mr. Bush.

Those figures were a tribute to the power of the Vice President's advertising, which attacked a prison furlough program in Massachusetts as well as the Governor's opposition to the death penalty. Indeed, more voters mentioned crime as an important issue than cited taxes, the issue that Mr. Bush's strategists had once thought would be central to the campaign. Still, those who did mention taxes went substantially for Mr. Bush.

The poll also showed that throughout the country, but especially in the Midwest, where Mr. Dukakis campaigned heavily, the issue of "helping the middle class" was central to his late gains. In the Midwest, it was the most important issue of all, picked by better than one voter in four. And across the nation, the Governor won, by roughly 3 to 1, those voters most concerned about the middle class.

The Governor also focused for weeks on Mr. Bush's choice of Mr. Quayle as his running mate, and, as it turned out, the "Quayle factor" clearly hurt Mr. Bush. While it was not possible to measure the exact impact of voters' comparison between Mr. Quayle and Mr. Bentsen, the poll showed in several ways that it mattered.

For example, 15 percent of voters said it was a key issue, compared with only 10 percent who said the same thing four years ago about the Vice-Presidential nominees. And the poll made it clear that the two Vice-presidential nominations together had cost the Republicans at least one percentage point in the national vote, and could not rule out the possibility that they had cost more. (Notwithstanding all this, the poll also showed that the controversy over Mr. Quayle's joining the National Guard during the Vietnam War had not stopped Vietnam veterans from backing Mr. Bush, 2 to 1.)

Finally, Mr. Dukakis succeeded in another tactic: getting voters to blame Mr. Bush more than himself for the negative cast of the 1988 race. Voters were more likely to say that Mr. Bush had spent most of his time attacking Mr. Dukakis than they were to say that Mr. Dukakis had concentrated his campaign efforts on attacking Mr. Bush.

The Times/CBS News Poll found that one of the best indicators of voters' choices yesterday was their attitude toward Mr. Reagan.

Regional Splits

The Election Day polling portrayed a nation sharply divided along regional lines.

Mr. Bush had expected that his base would be in the South, and it was: voters there supported him by about 3 to 2.

But in the East, the Midwest and the West, the regions of the battleground states, the nominees ran about even in the popular vote, according to the poll.

Then there was the "gender gap." Women gave Mr. Dukakis a narrow majority, but men went for Mr. Bush by nearly 3 to 2.

Mr. Dukakis was helped because black voters, some of whom seemed to hold back on their support during the campaign, finally rallied to him when it counted, on Election Day.

The Times/CBS Poll showed that 87 percent of black voters went for Mr. Dukakis, and 11 percent for Mr. Bush, 3 percent either voted for someone else or did not vote for President.

Black turnout was 10 percent of the electorate, up from 9 percent in 1984.

The poll also lent support to the argument made by some Democrats that a public generally satisfied with the state of the economy was nonetheless worried about the future of that economy. Asked if they were more hopeful or more concerned in this regard, the public split almost exactly in half. The problem for Mr. Dukakis was that even among voters worried about the future, Mr. Bush managed to win about 3 voters in 10.

For Vice President-elect Quayle, who maintained a remarkably low profile in the campaign after polls showed him to be a drag on the Republican ticket, the results were a moment of at least partial vindication.

Going Home

A key to Mr. Dukakis's success in running ahead of Mr. Mondale was his ability to win back Democrats who voted for Mr. Reagan in 1984.

Mr. Dukakis was especially successful in doing this in the Midwest, where roughly 6 Reagan Democrats in 10 supported him. In the East, Reagan Democrats split about evenly. In the South, they gave a narrow advantage to Mr. Bush.

The Vice President, who battled the former television evangelist Pat Robertson in the Republican primaries, won overwhelming backing, about 3 to 1, from voters who said they were fundamentalists.

The election also saw a clear class split among voters, a division that seemed to grow as Mr. Dukakis sharpened his campaign's message. Mr. Dukakis carried voters earning less than $12,500 by nearly 2 to 1. Mr. Bush carried those earning over $100,000 by more than 2 to 1. In the middle, Mr. Bush's vote rose steadily as income rose.

Mr. Bush wanted the contest to be an ideological race, and it was. He carried voters who called themselves conservative by 4 to 1 over Mr. Dukakis, while Mr. Dukakis carried liberals by a similar proportion. Moderates split evenly. The advantage in all this for Mr. Bush was that there were almost twice as many conservatives in the electorate as liberals.

Criticism From Dole

As criticism of Mr. Bush from Democrats died down last night, at least for the time being, there was a little of it within his own party. Bob Dole of Kansas, the Senate minority leader, whom the Vice President vanquished in the primaries, complained about Mr. Bush's failure to help Senate candidates.

"We could have used a little help from the Vice President in some of these states like Florida," Mr. Dole said.

But Lee Atwater, Mr. Bush's campaign manager, vigorously defended him.

"There's not a man in America, in either party, who has been to more fundraising events, more speaking events and participated in more Congressional, Senate, gubernatorial contests than George Bush while he was Vice President," Mr. Atwater said. "The fact of the matter is that the Vice President was in a tough race for President."

Jackson Speaks

Meanwhile, Mr. Dukakis's defeat was likely to set off yet another round of debate within the Democratic Party, which has now lost five of the last six Presidential elections.

A man who is likely to play a major role in that debate, the Rev. Jesse Jackson, urged the party to resist acrimony.

"We must avoid the incestuous finger-pointing and placing of blame that can only divide us," Mr. Jackson said at his election night party in Chicago. "We must hold the President-elect to his promise of a 'kinder, gentler nation.'"

For Vice President-elect Quayle, who maintained a remarkably low profile in the campaign after polls showed him to be a drag on the Republican ticket, the results were a moment of at least partial vindication.

An ebullient Mr. Quayle came downstairs into the ballroom of the Washington Hilton around 12:15 this morning, shortly after Mr. Bush had spoken in Houston.

"We did win one for the Gipper," he told the enthusiastic crowd. "Now we have another task. It is ours, to fall behind George Bush as President."

Wednesday, November 8, 1988

THE 1988 ELECTIONS

Man In the News: George Herbert Walker Bush;
A Victor Free to Set His Own Course

By Gerald M. Boyd
Special to The New York Times

HOUSTON, Nov. 8—When George Bush declared last June that he would not raise taxes, skeptical reporters gave him repeated chances to hedge. Could he support higher excise taxes? No, Mr. Bush said. Would he use "revenue enhancers?" No, Mr. Bush insisted.

Finally, when asked if he believed that such a blanket prohibition was wise in the face of uncertain Federal deficit prospects, Mr. Bush slammed the door completely: "I do think it is good public policy; I think it is very reassuring to the working man and woman of this country."

Many friends and associates have long described Mr. Bush as pragmatic, willing to adapt to changing realities. Yet his rigidity on the tax question, maintained throughout the campaign, illustrates a tenacity that is also a critical measure of the man.

. . . But what is the President-elect's agenda?

In announcing his candidacy last October, Mr. Bush said he would not seek to "make the world over" as President. Instead, his announcement was a personal declaration that "I am the man" to keep the nation safe, to protect its economic well-being and, although he does not say so explicitly, to temper policy excesses of the last eight years.

What He Truly Stands For

Despite hundreds of position papers and thousands of speeches since, what George Bush truly stands for remains an issue.

To some, he campaigned not out of conviction but out of instinct and the competitiveness that leads him to explode with "high-five" celebrations when winning even a horseshoe pitching contest. America is a nation concerned about drugs and crime, so he advocated the death penalty for drug leaders and other get-tough measures; America is patriotic, so he wrapped his candidacy in the flag.

He ran a campaign that was criticized as devoid of substance, deriding his opponent rather than telling Americans what he would do, where he would lead. At times Mr. Bush seemed genuinely troubled by such criticism, but he did not shift tactics, apparently reasoning that what counted most was reaching his final destination.

"It's been too long: we've come too far," he said at one point in the final weeks of the campaign. "I know if I'm elected President I could define that for the country by being kind and gentle and also strong. I think I'd be a good leader."

Entitled to Trust

At one point toward the end of the campaign, Mr. Bush was asked if he did not have a responsibility to tell the American public what programs he would cut to reduce the budget deficit. His answer was an emphatic no, as if his three decades of service entitled him to the public's trust in such important areas of Government.

Today he won that trust. But even as they cast their ballots, voters could not know exactly what their man would do with it. As Vice President, Mr. Bush had donned a cloak of obedience. He ridiculed Ronald Reagan's promises in the 1980 campaign as "voodoo economics," then espoused the same principles in 1988. Once he was the darling of party moderates; now he champions conservatism. . . .

No Clone of Reagan

But no matter how much he has tried to submerge his own political philosophy and accept the President's in the last eight years, Mr. Bush today is not a Reagan clone.

He did not come to Washington, as the former governor of California did, hoping to begin the dismantling of the Federal Government. Mr. Bush has been an insider, who sees a real role for government in making America at peace with itself or, in his words, "kinder and gentler." In particular, he has suggested that he would pursue policies different from Mr. Reagan's in civil rights, the environment and child care.

Mr. Reagan came to Washington with a burning desire to redirect domestic priorities; Mr. Bush's interest has long been in foreign policy, where he is more experienced. One of his first official acts, he has pledged, will be to meet with the Soviet leader, Mikhail S. Gorbachev, to assess superpower relations.

Moderate Advisers

If the measure of a President is the people he surrounds himself with, Mr. Bush also appears to be no ideologue. His closest confidant, James A. Baker 3d, the campaign chairman, has long been a thorn in the side of the Republican right, which has complained that he compromised too often with Congress on issues like raising taxes and was less devoted to the social agenda of the right.

Mr. Bush has raised alarm bells even among some supporters in showing no willingness to concede, even to them, that his selection of Dan Quayle as a running mate might have been a drain on the Republican ticket. But at the same time, he let his advisers push the Indiana Senator deeper into the campaign's shadows.

President Bush relied heavily on his role in Desert Storm to sway the voters—unfortunately for him, many were wrestling with difficult domestic problems.

A year and a half before the 1992 election, there seemed little doubt that George Bush would win a second second term. After the successful American military intervention in Kuwait, Bush's popularity rating ratings soared above 90 percent. By 1992, however, the glow of the Gulf War had faded and the economy had begun to slide into a mild but politically damaging recession. The Democratic nomination, which had seemed almost worthless six months earlier, was now worth fighting over. But it was too late for the party's leaders to enter the race, and Governor Bill Clinton of Arkansas—well organized and well funded—approached the critical early primaries as a clear frontrunner.

In the last weeks before the New Hampshire primary, damaging stories about Clinton's personal life hurt him badly and seemed briefly to destroy his hopes for election. He lost in New Hampshire to former Massachusetts Senator Paul Tsongas, a regional favorite, but he recovered enough in the last week to come in a strong second and to enable his campaign to keep going. In the following weeks, he steadily gained strength so that by early April it was clear that he was to be the party's nominee. President Bush, in the meantime, shook off Pat Buchanan on his right and easily won his own renomination.

Late in the spring, however, everyone's calculations were thrown into chaos by the unexpected popularity of H. Ross Perot, the Texas billionaire who used his own fortune

Left to right:
William Jefferson Clinton (b. 1946)
George Herbert Walker Bush (b. 1924)
H. Ross Perot (b. 1930)

Texas billionaire H. Ross Perot dramatically altered the two-party balance when he launched his suprisingly successful independent bid.

to fund an independent candidacy attacking both parties for their subordination to special interests and their failure to tackle the spiraling federal deficit. By mid-May, he was leading both major party candidates in public opinion polls. Then Perot withdrew from the race on the eve of the Democratic convention, apparently leaving Clinton and Bush to fight it out alone.

Clinton used the Democratic convention effectively to rebuild his public image and to position himself as a determined centrist focusing ("like a laser beam," he often said) on the economic problems of middle-class Americans. A hand-written sign in the soon-to-be-famous "War Room" of the Clinton campaign reminded the staff that "It's the economy, stupid!"

The Republican convention was a less happy experience for President Bush, displaying the party's divisions and giving voice to its most strident cultural conservatives. By the end of August, Clinton led the President by a healthy margin. He maintained that lead by performing well in the presidential debates and by running a disciplined campaign. Aided by his choice of Senator Al Gore of Tennesee as his running mate, he presented himself effectively as a dynamic candidate and made Bush seem an older and more passive figure.

Clinton's eventual victory was not as overwhelming as had seemed likely a few weeks before the election, largely because of the surprising last-minute surge of Perot, who had reentered the race in September and in the end attracted 19 percent of the vote. Even so, Clinton defeated Bush by a substantial margin in the popular vote (43 percent to 37 percent) and a much larger margin in the electoral college (370 to 168).

Bush lost in part because he was an indifferent campaigner saddled with the baggage of his party's internal battles, and in part because the economy had soured late in 1991. But he lost as well because in Bill Clinton he faced one of the most talented, determined, and resilient politicians of his generation.

—ALAN BRINKLEY

Bill Clinton and Al Gore, both Southerners and "New Democrats," ran as an unusually cohesive team, and lifted the number two spot to new prominence.

The Clinton-Gore ticket effectively appealed to young voters through catchy slogans, MTV appearances, and barn-storming bus tours.

Supporters rally for activist Ralph Nader and Senator Tom Harkin of Iowa, Manchester, New Hampshire *(top left)*, February 17, 1992.

A Bush supporter boards a bus outside Bush primary headquarters in Manchester, New Hampshire *(bottom left)*, February 18, 1992.

A man peers into Perot headquarters *(opposite, top)*, Dallas, Texas, June 1992

A Buchanan supporter stands outside a beauty salon in Woodsville, New Hampshire *(opposite, bottom)*, January 24, 1992.

FOR PRESIDENT
FOR PRESIDENT
FOR PRESIDENT

Buchanan
for
President
REDKEN

Dan Quayle tosses a frisbee at the GOP Convention in Houston, Texas, August 20, 1992.

George Bush speaks to a crowd in Des Moines, Iowa, October 27, 1992.

Clinton
TV POOL

Bush admires a doll of his wife, Barbara *(above)*, during a campaign stop in Woodstock, Georgia, August 22, 1992.

Bill and Hillary Clinton share a private moment *(opposite, top)* on the campaign trail, summer 1992.

Al and Tipper Gore celebrate with their children at the Democratic National Convention *(opposite, bottom)*, July 16, 1992.

Clinton visits the Swinging Sixties Senior Center during a campaign stop in Brooklyn, New York, March 30, 1992.

Larry King and Ross Perot pause during a television break on King's live CNN talk show; Perot announced the day before that he was withdrawing from the presidential race, Atlanta, Georgia, July 17, 1992.

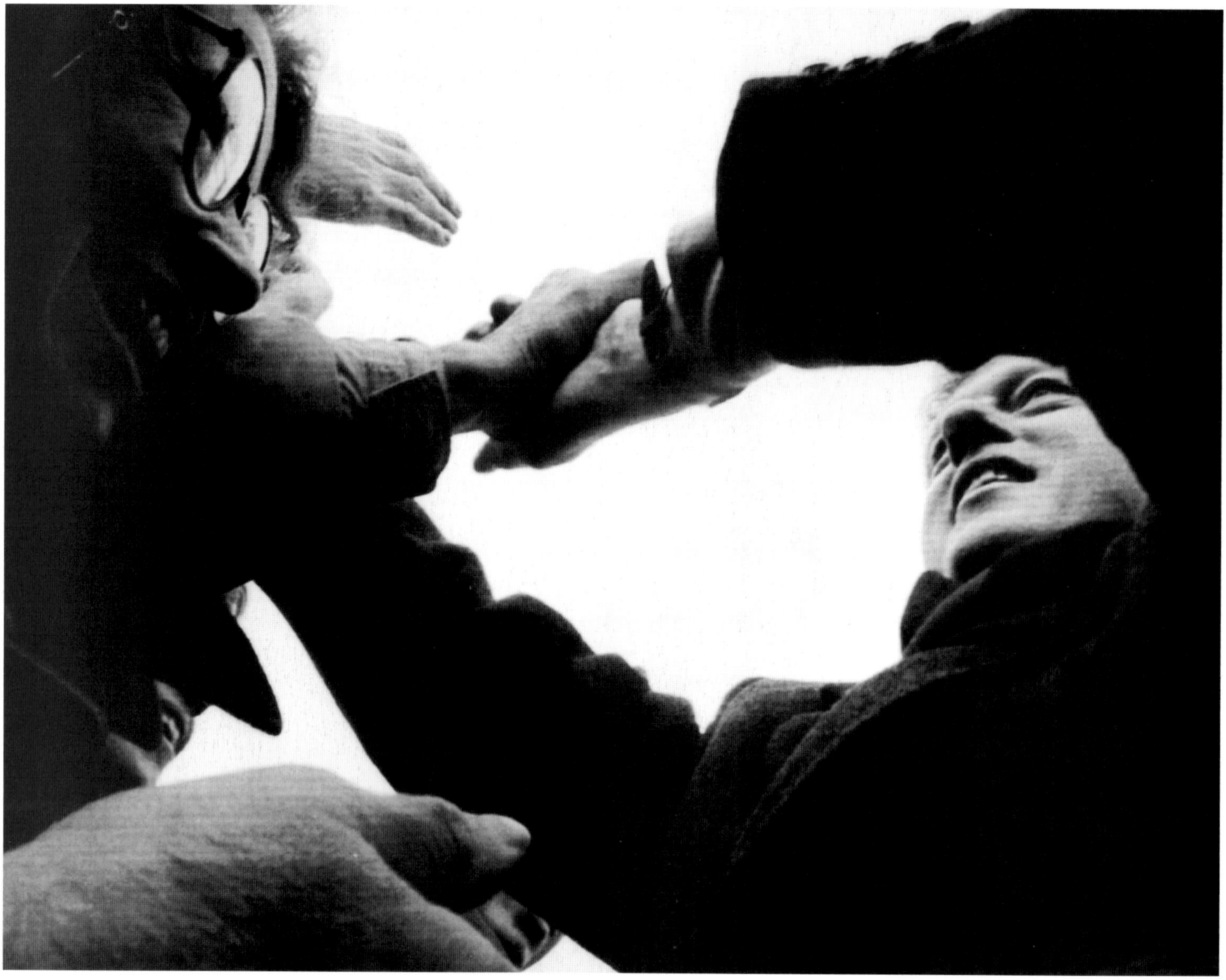

Clinton works the crowd in Cleveland, Ohio, November 2, 1992.

Clinton tries on sunglasses handed to him by a fan, as he leaves his hotel in Kansas City en route to St. Louis, October 10, 1992.

Bush turns back to give a final wave to supporters as he walks towards his helicopter, surrounded by Secret Service agents, Atlantic City, New Jersey, October 22, 1992.

Clinton and Gore celebrate their election victory with an ardent crowd, Little Rock, Arkansas, November 4, 1992.

"All the News That's Fit to Print"

The New York Times

Late Edition
New York: **Today,** brightening after morning fog. High 66. **Tonight,** rain arriving. **Tomorrow,** variable clouds, breezy, cooler. High 60. **Yesterday,** high 55, low 49. Details, page C17.

VOL.CXLII . No. 49,140 Copyright © 1992 The New York Times *NEW YORK, WEDNESDAY, NOVEMBER 4, 1992* *50 CENTS*

CLINTON CAPTURES PRESIDENCY WITH HUGE ELECTORAL MARGIN; WINS A DEMOCRATIC CONGRESS

OTHER HIGHLIGHTS

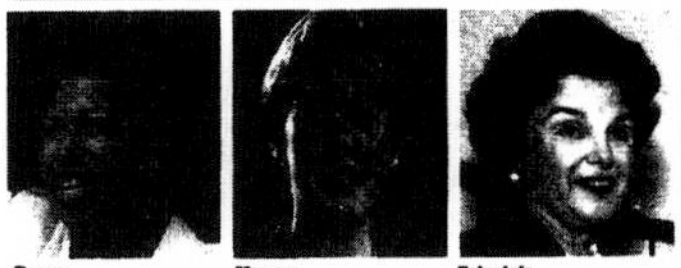
Braun Murray Feinstein

WOMEN IN THE SENATE

'Year of the Woman,' as Predicted

This was to be the "Year of the Woman," and that prediction was borne out in the Senate elections. Carol Moseley Braun, a Chicago Democrat, will be the first black woman in the Senate.

In California, two women were elected to the Senate at once: Dianne Feinstein, the former Mayor of San Francisco, who won a special election to fill the last two years of Gov. Pete Wilson's Senate term; and Representative Barbara Boxer, who won a full six-year term to succeed Alan Cranston. Both are Democrats.

In Washington State, Patty Murray, a Democrat, defeated a five-term Republican Congressman.

But Lynn Yeakel of Pennsylvania, the Democrat who won her primary on a tide of anger over the Clarence Thomas-Anita Hill hearings, fell short in her challenge to Senator Arlen Specter.

SENATE

Newcomers, Upsets And Familiar Faces

Campbell

Ben Nighthorse Campbell, a Democrat, won in Colorado; he will be the Senate's first American Indian.

In Wisconsin, another Democrat, State Senator Russell Feingold, beat Senator Bob Kasten.

Only one Democratic incumbent, Senator Terry Sanford of North Carolina, was defeated; he lost to a one-time close friend, Lauch Faircloth. Two other Southern Democrats who faced tough races, Ernest F. Hollings Jr. of South Carolina and Wyche Fowler of Georgia, survived. So did John Glenn in Ohio, who defeated Lieut. Gov. Michael DeWine in the toughest race of his career.

HOUSE

On Capitol Hill, A Big Freshman Class

In state after state, Democratic lawmakers who clung to Bill Clinton's coattails survived tough Republican challenges. But there will be more than 100 new members in the 103d Congress. They are sure to change the face of Congress, with sharp increases in the numbers of women, blacks and Hispanic lawmakers. Several black women were elected to represent Congressional districts in the South.

THE REGION

Dodd Wins 3d Term; Green and Downey Lose

Senator Christopher J. Dodd, the Connecticut Democrat, turned back a challenge from a businessman, Brook Johnson.

But Thomas J. Downey, a Long Island Democrat whose 18 years in the House made him one of its most influential members, lost to Rick Lazio, a Suffolk County Legislator who had made Mr. Downey's overdrawn checks at the House bank a major issue in his campaign.

New York City's liberal Republican Congressman, Bill Green, lost the seat he has held for seven terms to Carolyn B. Maloney, an upstart Democrat.

BALLOT ISSUES

Return Incumbents? Not Forever, Voters Say

In a display of anti-Washington passions, voters in at least five states — Florida, Michigan, Missouri, Nebraska and Ohio — approved measures to limit the terms of members of the House and Senate. But those measures face an uncertain future in the courts.

THE ELECTIONS: SECTION B

D'Amato Is Victor Over Abrams In New York's Bitter Senate Race

By TODD S. PURDUM

Senator Alfonse M. D'Amato, the battle-scarred Republican incumbent, drew support from just enough Democrats to squeak to a third term over State Attorney General Robert Abrams last night, claiming victory despite an overwhelming landslide for Bill Clinton in New York.

Mr. D'Amato won re-election, after repeated investigations into his conduct in office, in the tightest statewide contest since his own initial victory in a three-way race 12 years ago, according to unofficial returns.

With 97 percent of election districts reporting at 1:30 A.M. today, the vote was:

D'Amato	2,944,182 (51%)
Abrams	2,849,671 (49%)

At 1:20 A.M., Mr. D'Amato appeared in a ballroom of the New York Hilton and Towers, flanked by his mother, Antoinette, and former Mayor Edward I. Koch, and proclaimed proudly: "I'm not a diplomat. I'm your advocate, and I'm going to continue the fight."

The closeness of the race was a painful blow to Mr. Abrams in the face of Mr. Clinton's strength in a state where registered Democrats outnumber Republicans by nearly 3 to 2, and a testament to the fury of a contest in which Mr. D'Amato not only outspent Mr. Abrams by 2 to 1 but also outmaneuvered him at almost every turn in the costliest Senate race in the nation this year. At 2 A.M., Mr. Abrams told supporters in a ballroom of the Sheraton New York that Mr. D'Amato appeared to have won and congratulated him. But he left open the possibility that a final count, including paper and

Continued on Page B12, Column 1

INSIDE

Abortion Curb Is Voided

A Federal appeals court invalidated the Administration's ban on abortion counseling at Government-financed family planning clinics. Page A29.

Report on Women in Combat

A Presidential panel said women should be allowed to serve on most warships but be barred from combat flights and ground fighting. Page A24.

Associated Press
Bill and Hillary Clinton at a Fort Worth rally, hours before the Governor became President-elect.

A Man Who Wants to Be Liked, and Is

William Jefferson Blythe Clinton

By MICHAEL KELLY

It is 2:30 in the morning of Election Day, and Bill Clinton, a middling amateur saxophonist, is playing his true instrument, the crowd.

Man in the News

Thousands of people have come to see him in Fort Worth, and they are wild with emotion, straining so heavily against the heavy steel barricades set up to keep them apart from the candidate that it takes half a dozen large police officers to keep the fences from toppling forward.

The candidate, his boyish face beaming in the moonlight, plunges along the line, grabbing every hand he can, reaching up over the heads to touch in the second and third ranks. The crowd swells and surges as he goes by. In the press, a young woman faints, slumping blank-eyed to the tarmac, but Mr. Clinton is already 10 feet away, still moving and touching, and he doesn't notice.

Garry Mauro, Mr. Clinton's Texas campaign manager and a friend since he and Mr. Clinton entered politics working in the 1972 Presidential campaign of George McGovern in this state, watches in mild wonder. "He's decided he doesn't want to be President," Mr. Mauro says. "He wants to be a rock star."

The communion between William Jefferson Blythe Clinton and the people is the central fact of his life, and of his race for the goal he pursued for three decades, the Presidency.

Thirteen months ago, when Mr. Clinton stood in front of the Old State Capitol in Little Rock and announced his candidacy, he was considered by many an unlikely prospect. He had been elected to five terms as Governor of Arkansas, but running a state with an annual budget smaller than that of the District of Columbia did not seem much of a qualification. Republicans dismissed him, and the Democrats, hoping to regain the White House that had been denied to them for 12 years, pined for someone more glamorous.

After an old friend named Gennifer Flowers and an old letter by the young Bill Clinton raised questions about his integrity, the consensus grew that the candidate was dead, and would be buried in time.

Mr. Clinton, who was always the chief strategist of his campaign, banked on the central faith of his political life: If he could meet enough people, talk to enough people, make the essential connection enough times, he would win. The people

Continued on Page B2, Column 1

Associated Press
President Bush conceding defeat last night in Houston.

Congress at a Glance

As of 2:45 A.M. Eastern time.

Current balance	At stake	Winners	New balance
SENATE			
57 Dem. 43 Rep.	19 Dem. 15 Rep.	19 Dem. 11 Rep. 4 Undecided	
HOUSE			
268 Dem. 166 Rep. 1 Ind.	All 435 seats	222 Dem. 151 Rep. 1 Ind.	

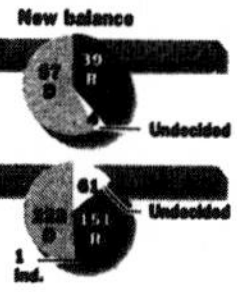

BUSH PLEDGES HELP

Governor Given an Edge of 43% to 38%, With Perot Getting 18%

By ROBIN TONER

Gov. Bill Clinton of Arkansas was elected the 42d President of the United States yesterday, breaking a 12-year Republican hold on the White House.

Mr. Clinton shattered the Republicans' political base with a promise of change to an electorate clearly discontented with President Bush.

Ross Perot, the Texas billionaire who roiled this race throughout, finished third, drawing roughly equally from both major party candidates, according to Voter Research & Surveys, the television polling consortium. His share of the popular vote had the potential to exceed any third-party candidate's in more than half a century.

Faithful Are Won Back

The President-elect, capping an astonishing political comeback for the Democrats over the last 18 months, ran strongly in all regions of the country and among many groups that were key to the Republicans' dominance of the 1980's: Catholics, suburbanites, independents, moderates and the Democrats who crossed party lines in the 1980's to vote for Ronald Reagan and Mr. Bush.

The Governor from Arkansas won such big, closely contested states as Michigan, Missouri, Pennsylvania, New Jersey and Illinois. As polls closed across the nation, networks announced projected winners based on voter surveys. It was Ohio that put him over the top shortly before 11 P.M., followed closely by California. Based on those projections, Mr. Bush prevailed in his adopted state of Texas and other pockets of Republican states around the country.

With 83 percent of the nation's precincts reporting by 3 A.M. today, Mr. Clinton had 43 percent to 38 percent for Mr. Bush and 18 percent for Mr. Perot.

A state-by-state breakdown of those returns gave the President-elect more than 345 electoral votes, a commanding victory in the Electoral College, which requires 270 for election. His victory also provided coattails for Democrats running for Congress in the face of tough Republican challenges: Democrats, who control both chambers, appeared likely to gain in the Senate and suffer manageable losses in the House.

'With High Hopes'

In a victory speech to a joyous crowd in Little Rock, Mr. Clinton declared, "On this day, with high hopes and brave hearts, in massive numbers, the American people have voted to make a new beginning."

He described the election as a "clari-

Continued on Page B6, Column 1

The Economy's Casualty

By R. W. APPLE Jr.

In the end it was the faltering economy, which had bedeviled him all year, that did George Bush in.

News Analysis

From the New Hampshire primary in February, through the party conventions this summer, to the start of the general-election campaign on Labor Day, public opinion held remarkably steady: three-quarters of the American people, according to New York Times/CBS News polls, disapproved of the way the President was handling the economy.

Mr. Bush failed to change their minds with his furious closing onslaught against Bill Clinton's character. More than 7 voters in 10 said in interviews as they left their polling places yesterday that they considered the economy not so good or poor, and a big majority opted for giving the Arkansas Governor a chance to turn it around. Though many had doubts about a man untried on the national stage, they had lost faith in Mr. Bush's ability to do the job, and they found Ross Perot too much of a gamble.

Electoral votes piled up in landslide proportions as Mr. Clinton blitzed through some of the most hotly contested terrain in this election: New Jersey, Pennsylvania, Michigan, Ohio, Illinois and Missouri. He swept New England and the West Coast states of California, Oregon and Washington. With that kind of triumph, leading Democrats said, the pressure on Mr. Clinton to produce big economic improvements soon after taking office will be enormous.

Competing Imperatives

Within days of moving into the White House, for example, he will have to find a balance between competing imperatives: getting a start on reducing the deficit and finding some way to jump-start the nation's stalled economic engine. With Democrats firmly in control of the House and Senate once again, the President-elect will have little excuse for inaction or confusion.

If the partisan coloration of the new Congress will be little different, its diversity will be markedly greater, with four more women and an American Indian, the first ever, in the Senate,

Continued on Page B3, Column 1

New York, Wednesday, November 4, 1992.

Clinton Captures Presidency with Huge Electoral Margin; Wins a Democratic Congress

Bush Pledges Help

Governor Given an Edge of 43% to 38%, With Perot Getting 18%

By Robin Toner

Gov. Bill Clinton of Arkansas was elected the 42d President of the United States yesterday, breaking a 12-year Republican hold on the White House.

Mr. Clinton shattered the Republicans' political base with a promise of change to an electorate clearly discontented with President Bush.

Ross Perot, the Texas billionaire who roiled this race throughout, finished third, drawing roughly equally from both major party candidates, according to Voter Research & Surveys, the television polling consortium. His share of the popular vote had the potential to exceed any third-party candidate's in more than half a century.

Faithful Are Won Back

The President-elect, capping an astonishing political comeback for the Democrats over the last 18 months, ran strongly in all regions of the country and among many groups that were key to the Republicans' dominance of the 1980's: Catholics, suburbanites, independents, moderates and the Democrats who crossed party lines in the 1980's to vote for Ronald Reagan and Mr. Bush.

The Governor from Arkansas won such big, closely contested states as Michigan, Missouri, Pennsylvania, New Jersey and Illinois. As polls closed across the nation, networks announced projected winners based on voter surveys. It was Ohio that put him over the top shortly before 11 P.M., followed closely by California. Based on those projections, Mr. Bush prevailed in his adopted state of Texas and other pockets of Republican states around the country.

With 83 percent of the nation's precincts reporting by 3 A.M. today, Mr. Clinton had 43 percent to 38 percent for Mr. Bush and 18 percent for Mr. Perot.

A state-by-state breakdown of those returns gave the President-elect more than 345 electoral votes, a commanding victory in the Electoral College, which requires 270 for election. His victory also provided coattails for Democrats running for Congress in the face of tough Republican challenges: Democrats, who control both chambers, appeared likely to gain in the Senate and suffer manageable losses in the House.

'With High Hopes'

In a victory speech to a joyous crowd in Little Rock, Mr. Clinton declared, "On this day, with high hopes and brave hearts, in massive numbers, the American people have voted to make a new beginning."

He described the election as a "clarion call" to deal with a host of domestic problems too long ignored and to "bring our nation together." He paid tribute to the voters he had met along the campaign trail, saying they had simply demanded that "we want our future back." The President-elect, who looked euphoric and seemed to savor every cheer, added, "I intend to give it to you."

He also hailed his longtime rival, Mr. Bush, for "his lifetime of public service" and the "grace with which he conceded this election."

"Not very long ago I received a telephone call from President Bush," the President-elect said. "It was a generous and forthcoming telephone call, of real congratulations and an offer to work with me in keeping our democracy running in an effective and important transition."

The crowd hailed the victor repeatedly with cries of "We love you, Bill," especially when he paid tribute to his home state, the object of Republican ridicule throughout the campaign.

Mr. Clinton credited much of his success to his wife, Hillary, who was also a target of Republican attacks. The Clintons and their daughter, Chelsea, were joined by Vice President-elect Al Gore and his family, creating once again the tableau of youth and generational change that they projected throughout the campaign. Mr. Gore and Mr. Clinton embraced in a jubilant bear hug.

Bush Gives Concession

Mr. Bush, looking weary but composed, made his concession speech shortly after 11 P.M. in Houston. "The people have spoken and we respect the majesty of the Democratic system," he said. Mr. Bush congratulated Mr. Clinton, but did not mention Mr. Perot, and promised that his own Administration would "work closely with his team to insure the smooth transition of power."

Vice President Dan Quayle made his concession speech in Indianapolis a few minutes later and like Mr. Bush congratulated Mr. Clinton and hushed the boos. "We must all pull together now. If he runs the country as well as he ran the campaign, we'll be all right."

Congressional leaders said they welcomed the new era beyond divided government. "We welcome the challenge and the responsibility," said Senator George Mitchell of Maine, the majority leader.

There were other signs of change: California elected two women to the Senate, in Representative Barbara Boxer and the former San Francisco Mayor Dianne Feinstein. Illinois also elected a woman, Carol Moseley Braun, to the Senate, as did Washington State, which chose Patty Murray.

Mr. Perot made his concession speech in remarkably good spirits and seemed intent on signaling that he was not leaving the political stage. "This is not the time to get discouraged," he said. "This is the time to redouble our efforts, to make sure we live in alabaster cities undimmed by human tears."

Mr. Clinton's campaign represented the culmination of years of effort by centrist Democrats to redefine their party and reconnect with the middle class. It also represented an extraordinary turnaround for a party that for much of 1991 seemed destined to lose to a President soaring in the approval ratings in the aftermath of the war in the Persian Gulf.

Brown Sees 'Watershed'

"It was a watershed election for America," said Ronald H. Brown, the chairman of the Democratic National Committee. "The case for change was made, and it resonated so much that it broke down traditional political lines. It's a new day." In fact, the voter surveys showed that economic discontent and a hunger for change were two of the engines of the Democratic victory.

Republicans sadly watched Mr. Bush become the third one-term President in 20 years. "He was a good man, he was a good President," said Representative Vin Weber of Minnesota, a co-chairman of the Bush campaign. "But he thought that if he simply did the right thing, people would understand. Whereas, I think Reagan understood the need to communicate your vision."

Lynn Martin, the Secretary of Labor, said of the voters last night, "They understand about world affairs, but they were worried about their own."

But there was also Republican anger. Mary Matalin, deputy manager of the Bush campaign, accused the news media of bias last night in their coverage of the 1992 election. Ahead, many Republicans feared, was a round of soul-searching, finger pointing and a struggle to recast their party for an era beyond the cold war, an era that seems relentlessly focused on domestic needs.

A Grueling Comeback

The voting capped a grueling campaign in which Mr. Clinton came back from seeming disaster in the New Hampshire primary, where questions were raised about how he avoided the draft in the Vietnam War, setting off a round of attacks from his political opponents on his trustworthiness. Mr. Clinton survived with a remarkably disciplined campaign that stayed focused on the economy and what he often called "the forgotten middle class."

Mr. Bush, at the same time, fell from great heights as the economy continued to falter. He spent much of the year trying to convince the voters that the country was in better shape than they thought. Still, the voter surveys showed that seven in 10 voters considered the economy either poor or "not so good," and Mr. Clinton ran strongly among them.

Mr. Clinton, who is 46 years old, becomes the first President born after World War II—a changing of the guard in American politics.

Mr. Clinton also ran strongly among young voters, working women and a variety of other groups that showed the strains in the Republican coalition which had been held together for years by economic growth and a fierce anti-Communism. And his Southern roots, like those of Jimmy Carter in 1976, made him a formidable challenger to the Republicans in the heart of their political base in the South. The big states of Florida and Texas stayed fiercely competitive until the end.

Mr. Clinton, who is 46 years old, becomes the first President born after World War II—a changing of the guard in American politics.

Mr. Clinton's careful strategy to appeal to suburban residents, independent voters and moderates clearly paid off. Nearly half of the suburban voters backed Mr. Clinton, compared with about a third who were supporting Mr. Bush. Mr. Clinton also carried 4 in 10 of the independent voters, with Mr. Bush splitting the rest with Mr. Perot.

Here, and in several other demographic categories, Mr. Clinton broke into groups that for the past decade were clear parts of the Republican Presidential majority—the swing voters drawn to the Republicans by the promise of fiscal responsibility and economic growth. In 1980 and 1988, for example, independents went heavily for Mr. Reagan and Mr. Bush.

The President-elect also won more than half of the voters who consider themselves moderates, suggesting that he had succeeded in his goal of recasting the Democratic Party in a more centrist image. Only 3 in 10 of the moderates backed Mr. Bush, who was widely thought to be hurt by the backlash to the "family values" appeal at the Republican National Convention. Again, that was a far poorer showing than Mr. Bush had in 1988.

Mr. Clinton also succeeded in bringing home many of the Democrats who persistently crossed party lines in Presidential elections in the 1980's: More than half of the Democrats who voted for Mr. Bush in 1988 voted for Mr. Clinton this time around.

Mr. Bush essentially ran even with Mr. Clinton among white voters, but the Democratic nominee, as is the case with most recent Democratic nominees, did far better with black voters.

Mr. Bush ran better than Mr. Clinton among white Protestants, but the Democrat carried about half of the Catholic votes and an even bigger majority among Jewish voters.

'Way Beyond Abortion'

Mr. Bush and Mr. Clinton fared about the same among men, but Mr. Clinton had an edge among women, particularly among working women. Only 3 in 10 of the working women voted for Mr. Bush, according to the poll.

"It goes way beyond abortion," said Ann F. Lewis, a former Democratic strategist and commentator. "George Bush campaigned four years ago on the promise of a kinder, gentler nation, and women are keenly aware that he provided neither."

There was also a distinct generational cast to this election. Mr. Clinton, who carefully courted MTV viewers, carried half of the 18- to 29-year-olds, after a decade in which Republicans worked hard to cement their political gains by building on the loyalty of the young. Baby-boomers, those aged 30 to 44, broke more like all voters, despite Mr. Clinton's status as a card-carrying boomer.

But Americans aged 60 and over showed a clear bias in favor of Mr. Clinton, according to the poll. He also ran well among other demographic groups, including half of the military veterans (despite the furor over his draft status during the Vietnam War), half of the first-time voters, and more than half of union members.

From the beginning of this campaign, in the chilly towns of New Hampshire, the economy was the issue that was front and center, and so it was when voters went to the polls yesterday. Jobs and the economy were cited by nearly 4 in 10 voters as the issue that mattered most in their decision. Health care and the deficit, the latter's prominence probably a reflection of the Perot candidacy, were the second-most important issues, each cited by about a quarter of the voters.

The hostility of the political terrain for Mr. Bush this year was underscored by this fact: fewer than one in 10 voters cited foreign policy as the most important issue to them. Abortion was cited as the determining issue by about one in 10.

Not surprisingly, Mr. Bush carried the anti-abortion vote, after a year when he and his party chose to reaffirm their strong opposition to legalized abortion, as codified in their platform. Mr. Clinton, equally unsurprisingly, carried the votes of those who support abortion's being legal in most or all circumstances.

Mr. Clinton had an edge among women, particularly among working women.

There were also clear regional patterns at work: Mr. Clinton ran strongest in the East and the West, and only slightly less strongly in the Midwest. Mr. Bush's strength was greatest in the South, which was long considered his political "fire wall." But even there, the all-Southern Democratic ticket kept it neck and neck. Mr. Perot's strongest performance was in the West.

The voting ended what had become an epic campaign.

The Clinton forces, who became increasingly convinced that victory was in their grasp over the past week, flew home to Little Rock yesterday morning. There was some weeping, much rejoicing and great weariness on the Clinton plane. James Carville, the strategist who headed the campaign's "war room" in Little Rock, said there was also some weeping Monday night as the group of strategists at the heart of this campaign met for the last time.

"I'm a little overwhelmed," said Mr. Carville, the tightly wound Lousianian who became emblematic of a new, more aggressive Democratic Party. "When you get to the top of the mountain, your first inclination is not to jump for joy, but to look around."

Though Ross Perot organized a new Reform Party for the 1996 campaign, the Texas billionaire only secured 8.4% of the popular vote (down from 18.9% in 1992.)

It would be only a slight exaggeration to say that Bill Clinton was elected to his second term not in November 1996, when the election actually took place, but in November 1995, when congressional Republicans closed down the federal government for several days in an effort to pressure the President into supporting their budget proposals. Few political strategies in recent history have proved so misconceived. One year earlier, Republicans had won control of both houses of Congress for the first time in 42 years, and the Clinton Administration had seemed headed for almost certain defeat in 1996. After the shutdown, public opinion turned quickly and heavily against the GOP, and President Clinton began slowly to improve his standing in the public opinion. By the time the campaign began in earnest the following spring, he seemed virtually assured of reelection.

His prospects were greatly improved by the character of his opponents. The most visible figure in the Republican party was House Speaker Newt Gingrich, the architect of the shutdown and, in its disastrous aftermath, one of the most unpopular political figures in the nation. Not even the Republican presidential nominee—Bob Dole of Kansas, the Senate Majority Leader—could loosen Gingrich's grip on the popular image of his party, particularly since Dole himself aroused little popular enthusiasm. Evidence for that was his humiliating

Left to right:
William Jefferson Clinton (b. 1946)
Bob Dole (b. 1923)
H. Ross Perot (b. 1930)

Despite widespread admiration for his political intelligence and his long career of public service, Dole's campaign never caught fire.

defeat at the hands of the right-wing challenger Pat Buchanan in the New Hampshire primary and his rather plodding march to victory in subsequent contests. Dole tried to rejuvenate his campaign by dramatically resigning from the Senate, but to little avail. Not even the tame Republican convention that summer, in which he chose his erstwhile rival Jack Kemp as his running mate, seemed to improve his prospects.

President Clinton, in the meantime, sailed to renomination without opposition and campaigned almost without reference to his opponents, basking instead in the glow of the impressive prosperity of the previous several years. Ever since the 1994 elections, Clinton had moved determinedly to the political center, preempting many positions that had long been the property of Republicans. He and Vice President Gore focused on a small but popular group of government commitments that they claimed were under threat from the GOP, and that they promised to defend: aiding education, protecting the environment, and sustaining Medicare. Clinton also helped the Democrats raise enormous sums of money and used the funds to pay for television commercials in critical states linking Dole to Gingrich and to all the unpopular programs of the Republican Congress. The Democratic convention in Chicago was a buoyant coronation, and Clinton entered the fall campaign on a wave of good feeling, speaking platitudinously about building "a bridge to the twenty-first century."

The ebullient Democratic campaign flagged slightly toward the end in the face of allegations of improper and illegal fund-raising techniques. That may be one reason why the seemingly forlorn candidacy of Ross Perot, running now as the candidate of the new Reform Party, picked up steam in the final weeks. Clinton's victory was nevertheless substantial: 49 percent of the popular vote to Dole's 41 and Perot's 8, and 379 electoral votes to Dole's 159, making him the first Democratic president since Franklin Roosevelt to win two successive terms in the White House.

—ALAN BRINKLEY

This poster drew on nostalgia for World War II and classic liberalism of FDR—though many Democrats worried about Clinton's drift toward the center.

Bob Dole, with Senator Charles Grassley by his side, is surrounded by reporters as he leaves WHO Radio after an interview, Des Moines, Iowa, February 12, 1996.

President Clinton turns a camera on the press after his arrival at Pease Air Force Base in Portsmouth, New Hampshire, February 17, 1996.

President Clinton works in his office aboard Air Force One, June 12, 1996.

Bob and Elizabeth Dole are showered with confetti after his acceptance speech at the Republican National Convention, San Diego, August 15, 1996.

The Clintons and the Gores wave to the crowd at the Democratic National Convention, Chicago, August 29, 1996.

President Clinton appears on screen from his hotel room after arriving in Chicago for the convention, August 28, 1996.

that

Ross Perot speaks at a Reform Party rally *(above)*, 1996.

Dole is greeted by a crowd of almost 9,000 supporters *(opposite, top)* at Rich Stadium, Buffalo, August 19, 1996.

Dole emphasizes a point at an outdoor rally *(opposite, bottom)* as Jack Kemp listens, 1996.

A sea of enthusiastic faces greet Clinton at a campaign stop in Santa Ana, California, October 17, 1996.

Dole signs autographs for patrons and workers of Wolfie Cohen's Rascal House Restaurant in North Miami Beach, September 28, 1996

Clinton and Dole greet one another before the start of the first presidential debate, Bushnell Theater, Hartford, October 6, 1996.

Perot gestures during a speech, 1996.

A send-off rally in San Diego includes the presentation of Charger football jerseys for Dole and Kemp; Governor Pete Wilson stands behind Elizabeth Dole, August 16, 1996.

President Clinton waves to the crowd, following his remarks at the Bailey Elementary School, Fresno, California, September 12, 1996.

"All the News That's Fit to Print"

The New York Times

Late Edition
New York: **Today,** limited sun, possible sprinkle. High 63. **Tonight,** mostly cloudy, mild. Low 55. **Tomorrow,** cloudy, showers late. High 64. **Yesterday,** high 59, low 45. Details, page B20.

VOL. CXLVI . No. 50,603 — NEW YORK, WEDNESDAY, NOVEMBER 6, 1996 — 60 CENTS

$1 beyond the greater New York metropolitan area.

CLINTON ELECTED TO A 2D TERM WITH SOLID MARGINS ACROSS U.S.; G.O.P. KEEPS HOLD ON CONGRESS

Democrats Fail to Reverse Right's Capitol Hill Gains

By DAVID E. ROSENBAUM

With close races all across the country, Republicans retained control of the Senate and the House in yesterday's elections.

The votes in several states were still in doubt early today, but Republicans were guaranteed of having at least 51 Senate seats in the next Congress. And around 2 A.M., Speaker Newt Gingrich proclaimed that his party had retained control of the House. [Page B3.]

The Republicans won in the Senate by holding most of their own seats and picking up at least two seats in states where popular Democratic Senators are retiring.

In one of the most compelling political contests of the year, Senator John Kerry of Massachusetts was reelected. All other Democratic incumbents who were running also won.

But only one Republican Senator lost, and Republican newcomers won in Nebraska and Alabama, replacing retiring Democrats.

Republicans began Election Day with a 53-to-47 advantage and thus could afford to lose a net of two seats and still have a majority in the 100-member Senate.

Among the Republican Senators who were re-elected were Jesse Helms of North Carolina and Strom Thurmond of South Carolina.

Senator Larry Pressler of South Dakota, a Republican, was the only Senator running for re-election who lost. He was defeated by Representative Tim Johnson, now the state's only Congressman.

Early last night, Senator Robert C. Smith of New Hampshire seemed likely to be defeated by his Democratic challenger, former Representative Dick Swett. But Mr. Smith gained as the night progressed, and shortly after midnight, Mr. Swett conceded defeat.

Among the other Republicans who were re-elected were Mitch McConnell of Kentucky, John W. Warner of Virginia, Thad Cochran of Mississippi, James M. Inhofe of Oklahoma, Fred Thompson of Tennessee and Phil Gramm of Texas.

In Nebraska, Chuck Hagel, a Republican investment banker who has never held elective office, defeated the state's Democratic Governor, Ben Nelson. Mr. Nelson began the year as the odds-on favorite to replace Senator Jim Exon, a Democrat who is retiring after three terms, but Mr. Hagel rallied in the last month.

In Alabama, Jeff Sessions, the Republican State Attorney General, defeated State Senator Roger Bedford.

In an interview on CNN, Senator Trent Lott of Mississippi, the Republican leader, said, "It looks like I will be majority leader."

Other Democrats who held their

Continued on Page B2, Column 1

Monica Almeida/The New York Times

The voters' message was to work together and put aside politics, President Clinton said in claiming victory in Little Rock with Hillary Rodham Clinton, their daughter Chelsea and Vice President Gore.

PEROT A FAR THIRD

President's Success Lay in Ability to Co-opt Republican Issues

By RICHARD L. BERKE

William Jefferson Clinton was reelected President of the United States yesterday, capping a yearlong political resurgence that made him the first Democrat since Franklin Delano Roosevelt to win a second term as President.

Mr. Clinton built a landslide in the Electoral College and won a decisive victory in the popular vote, overwhelming Bob Dole in all regions of the country except the South and the High Plains, where the Republican won several states. The President's sweep carried to California, where Mr. Dole, in an enormous gamble, diverted millions of dollars from other states and stumped doggedly in the final weeks of the campaign.

Ross Perot, the Texas billionaire who ran on the ticket of the Reform Party he had created, finished a distant third, drawing roughly half of the 19 percent he won in 1992.

With 84 percent of the popular vote tallied at 3 A.M. today, Mr. Clinton drew 49 percent; Mr. Dole 41 percent, and Mr. Perot 8 percent. The President surpassed his showing of 43 percent of the popular vote in 1992.

A state-by-state breakdown of those returns gave Mr. Clinton more than the 370 electoral votes he won four years ago, a commanding showing in the Electoral College, which requires 270 votes for victory.

The support for Mr. Clinton did not run deep enough to allow Democrats to declare a reversal of the Republican tide that swept Congress two years ago. The Republicans retained control of the Senate; by early this morning, they appeared headed to keep a majority in the House.

With a Democrat still in the Oval Office and Republicans still dominating at least one chamber of Congress, the nation's political landscape remains competitive and unsettled.

Shortly after midnight, eastern time, Mr. Clinton and Vice President Al Gore and their families emerged before a joyous crowd jamming the streets in front of the Old State House in Little Rock, Ark., where they had their victory celebration four years ago.

"Today the American people have spoken," Mr. Clinton said, recognizing the power of the mixed message that voters seemed to be sending him and Congress.

"America has told every one of us — Democrats, Republicans and independents — loud and clear: It is time to put politics aside, join together

Continued on Page B4, Column 1

TORRICELLI WINS SENATE CONTEST

Defeats Zimmer for Open Seat in Bitter New Jersey Fight

By BRETT PULLEY

Representative Robert G. Torricelli, a Democrat who has served in Congress for seven terms, won election to New Jersey's open United States Senate seat yesterday.

Mr. Torricelli, known for throwing himself into the center of high-profile and volatile issues, defeated Representative Richard A. Zimmer after a race that had become a testament to the ever-increasing expense and negative nature of campaigning. In the end, the race was not as close as the polls had predicted. With 94 percent of precincts reporting at 12:52 A.M. today, Mr. Torricelli had 53 percent of the popular vote, compared with 42 percent for Mr. Zimmer.

In selecting Mr. Torricelli, 45, from Englewood in Bergen County, over Mr. Zimmer, a 52-year-old, three-term Congressman from Delaware Township in Hunterdon County, voters sided with the Democratic candidate's belief that government should play an active role in preserving Medicare, protecting the environment and strengthening education initiatives.

"You have given me the blessing of success, but the burden of being worthy of all that you have given," a somewhat giddy Mr. Torricelli told a crowd of ebullient supporters gathered at a Woodbridge hotel shortly after 10 last night.

He then alluded to the nastiness of the race and his hope that it would not be repeated. "Let this campaign be remembered finally for this," he said, "that it was the beginning of a new civility in the public life of New Jersey."

About half an hour earlier, at 9:30, Mr. Zimmer had conceded defeat and credited Mr. Torricelli with run-

Continued on Page B12, Column 1

The Second Term: Promise and Peril

Many Goals Left for Clinton, and Many Pitfalls

By TODD S. PURDUM

Four years ago Bill Clinton won the Presidency with an outsized agenda and an underwhelming mandate, and the gulf between the two left him struggling in the first half of his term simply to establish his legitimacy. By the midpoint, the President had been reduced to proclaiming his own relevance.

Last night Mr. Clinton won re-election with a larger margin but with a manifesto both smaller and less clear. And if the promise of achievement glistens, potential pitfalls abound, from the ancient feuds of Bosnia to the paper chase of special prosecutors at home.

Campaigning in El Paso last week, Mr. Clinton declared, "This is an election of enormous moment, with great consequences." But for more than a year the President has steadily strived to blur the traditional divisions of American ideology in a politics of pointillism, at once capturing the electorate's vital center and renewing questions about his own.

In this President's effusive view, it is possible to both balance the budget and provide new tax breaks for college education, to force families off welfare and find new jobs for them, to expand the Federal role in everything from encouraging school uniforms to deterring violence on television — all the while declaring that "the era of big government is over."

Surveys of voters leaving the polls yesterday showed that 6 in 10 did not believe he could cut the deficit and pay for his programs at the same time, and that a like number did not believe that their President was either honest or trustworthy. He and his wife, Hillary, face a raft of pending or continuing investigations into their financial and ethical conduct and their party's fund-raising practices. Still, nearly half those surveyed said they were either optimistic or excited about a second term.

"This is not about liberal or conservative," Mr. Clinton told a rally in Little Rock, Ark. last weekend, in one of the most pointed formulations of an argument he made in the last weeks of the campaign, citing Republican and Democratic predecessors alike as his heroes. "We have run by far the most fiscally conservative Government, and we've done more to stand against crime, and we've stuck up for this country in having a strong foreign policy. I think the record will stand on its own.

"This is about whether you're going to be diverted and divided," Mr. Clinton continued, "or whether we're going to find common ground and build that bridge to the 21st century together."

To that end, one of the closest

Continued on Page B5, Column 1

Rail Victim's Widow Captures House Seat

Carolyn McCarthy, whose husband was shot on a Long Island commuter train and who ran on a gun control platform, won a House seat by soundly defeating a freshman Republican. In Connecticut, Representative Gary A. Franks, a black conservative considered a rising G.O.P. star, lost his seat, while voters in New York City rejected a plan to lengthen term limits for elected city officials.

Articles, Pages B14, B15 and B16.

Librado Romero/The New York Times

Bob Dole conceded defeat before supporters in Washington.

Yeltsin Has 7-Hour Heart Surgery And Doctors Say It Was a Success

By LAWRENCE K. ALTMAN

MOSCOW, Wednesday, Nov. 6 — President Boris N. Yeltsin came out of a seven-hour, multiple-bypass heart operation in a hospital here on Tuesday with his doctors declaring the operation a success. They said they were optimistic about the 65-year-old Russian leader's chances of resuming a full workload.

At a news conference in the hospital an hour after the operation, the doctors said the surgery went without a hitch. Mr. Yeltsin's heart was stopped for 68 minutes during one phase of the operation.

Mr. Yeltsin signed a decree this morning reassuming his presidential powers, the Kremlin said. Sergei Yastrzhembsky, his press spokesman, said the President signed the document at 6 A.M. (10 P.M. Tuesday, Eastern time), 23 hours after he had delegated the powers to Prime Minister Viktor S. Chernomyrdin on Tuesday morning, minutes before undergoing anesthesia..

In the operation, surgeons sewed five grafts to restore blood flow to coronary arteries. They had become constricted by the fatty deposits of atherosclerosis that had built up over a period of years and deprived the organ of vital nourishment, leading to two heart attacks.

Even if all goes well for Mr. Yeltsin, it may yet be months before he can run the country again. And when he does return to the Kremlin, many find it hard to imagine that he will be the same forceful leader who has for five years driven Russia away from Communism and toward a market economy. [News analysis, page A12.]

On Tuesday, Mr. Yeltsin was reported in stable condition in an intensive care unit, where he remained connected to an artificial respirator used during the operation. He opened his eyes early Tuesday evening but had not fully awakened from the anesthesia. Patients usually awaken from 6 to 18 hours after such surgery.

Mr. Yastrzhembsky said today

Continued on Page A12, Column 1

An Election Day For 2d Thoughts

More than half the voters yesterday spoke openly about having second thoughts. Those voting for President Clinton said they had confidence enough in the nation's economy to overcome doubts about their candidate's honesty. Bob Dole meanwhile pulled nearly half the wavering voters his way as the campaign ended.

Article, page B1.

Economy Helps Again

Clinton Rode Wave of Discontent in 1992; With Times Better, He Gets to Ride Again

By R. W. APPLE Jr.

News Analysis

Four years ago, a faltering economy persuaded American voters to give Bill Clinton a chance as President. Yesterday, surveys of voters leaving the polls showed, a robust economy persuaded them that he deserved a second term.

Four years ago, only 39 percent of voters said they thought the country was headed in the right direction — a key indicator of the nation's mood. That figure grew this year to 53 percent.

But Mr. Clinton's success in occupying "the vital center," as he called it in his victory statement, in a phrase borrowed from the historian Arthur M. Schlesinger Jr., did not extend to Capitol Hill. He and his party failed in their quest to recapture control of the Senate, and they appeared headed for failure in the struggle for dominance of the House of Representatives. So he and his country face two more years at least of divided Government.

After a campaign filled with fund-raising abuses on a grand scale, Mr. Clinton pledged early action on campaign-finance reform. His Vice President, Al Gore, said he was ready to work with the Republicans, and the President himself said, "It is time to put country ahead of party."

But appeals to eschew partisanship may be lost in the clamor of investigations of alleged scandals in the first Clinton Administration.

The returns showed little diminution in the conservative trend that has coursed through the country since the 1970's. The new Senate will be more conservative than the old. In California, the most publicized initiative of the year, opposing affirmative action, was approved.

Bob Dole did everything he could to refocus the Presidential contest, the last of the 20th century, as Mr.

Continued on Page B4, Column 5

INSIDE

Wall St. Bets on Status Quo

Expectations of a Democratic White House and a Republican Congress drove stocks up yesterday. Page D8.

G.I.'s May Aid Africa Relief

The U.S. is considering sending troops to Central Africa to aid refugees caught in the conflict. Page A8.

On the Internet: www.nytimes.com

Wednesday, November 6, 1996

Clinton Elected to a 2nd Term With Solid Margins Across U.S.; G.O.P. Keeps Hold on Congress

Perot a Far Third

President's Success Lay in Ability to Co-opt Republican Issues

By Richard L. Berke

William Jefferson Clinton was reelected President yesterday, capping a yearlong political resurgence that made him the first Democrat since Franklin Delano Roosevelt to win a second term as President.

Mr. Clinton built a landslide in the Electoral College and won a decisive victory in the popular vote, overwhelming Bob Dole in all regions of the country except the South and the High Plains, where the Republican won several states. The President's sweep carried to California, where Mr. Dole, in an enormous gamble, diverted millions of dollars from other states and stumped doggedly in the final weeks of the campaign.

Ross Perot, the Texas billionaire who ran on the ticket of the Reform Party he had created, finished a distant third, drawing roughly half of the 19 percent he won in 1992.

With 84 percent of the popular vote tallied at 3 A.M. today, Mr. Clinton drew 49 percent; Mr. Dole 41 percent, and Mr. Perot 8 percent. The President surpassed his showing of 43 percent of the popular vote in 1992.

A state-by-state breakdown of those returns gave Mr. Clinton more than the 370 electoral votes he won four years ago, a commanding showing in the Electoral College, which requires 270 votes for victory.

The support for Mr. Clinton did not run deep enough to allow Democrats to declare a reversal of the Republican tide that swept Congress two years ago. The Republicans retained control of the Senate; by early this morning, they appeared headed to keep a majority in the House.

With a Democrat still in the Oval Office and Republicans still dominating at least one chamber of Congress, the nation's political landscape remains competitive and unsettled.

Shortly after midnight, eastern time, Mr. Clinton and Vice President Al Gore and their families emerged before a joyous crowd jamming the streets in front of the Old State House in Little Rock, Ark., where they had their victory celebration four years ago.

"Today the American people have spoken," Mr. Clinton said, recognizing the power of the mixed message that voters seemed to be sending him and Congress.

"America has told every one of us—Democrats, Republicans and independents—loud and clear: It is time to put politics aside, join together and get the job done for America's future."

Paying tribute to Mr. Dole, the President called on the partisan crowd to "join me in applause for his lifetime of service to the United States." Mr. Clinton said he spoke with his rival last night, adding, "I applauded the campaign that he fought so bravely."

Less than an hour earlier, Mr. Dole, accompanied by his wife, Elizabeth, and his daughter, Robin, appeared at a hotel ballroom in Washington that was packed with his cheering supporters.

"Tomorrow will be the first time in my life I don't have anything to do," he said. He added: "It hurts to lose an election. But stay involved and keep fighting the good fight because you are the ones who will make the 21st century the next American century."

At times over the past two years, winning his party's nomination appeared as vital to Mr. Dole as winning the White House. He said last night, "I've never been prouder in my life than to have been the Republican nominee for President of the United States."

The 50-year-old Mr. Clinton offered himself as a vigorous leader for a new century, but the success of his campaign turned largely on his ability to seize a litany of Republican issues as his own: welfare, crime and balancing the budget. Often, the President seemed to be running as much against Newt Gingrich, the unpopular Speaker of the House, as against Mr. Dole. Mr. Clinton's nimble and aggressive political organization, and the fact that he has presided over a relatively hardy economy in peacetime, left Mr. Dole with few openings to make his case.

Perhaps the most striking example of Mr. Clinton's electoral strength was his victory in Florida, where both candidates campaigned strenuously. Mr. Clinton was particularly determined to win Florida because he viewed a victory there as emblematic of the Democrats' breaking the Republican stranglehold on the South.

In addition, the President lost the state very narrowly in 1992, even though he barely campaigned there. The last Democrat to win Florida was Jimmy Carter in 1976.

Besides Florida and California, Mr. Clinton's electoral victories included New Jersey, Connecticut, Ohio, Pennsylvania and Tennessee. Mr. Dole's biggest prize was Texas.

Among women, Democrats, Asian-American and Hispanic voters, Mr. Clinton won more support than he did against George Bush in 1992.

> The 50-year-old Mr. Clinton offered himself as a vigorous leader for a new century, but the success of his campaign turned largely on his ability to seize a litany of Republican issues as his own.

Though his attempt to stage a Trumanesque upset never materialized, Mr. Dole managed to hold his own with some important voter groups.

Independent voters and suburbanites, whom both Mr. Clinton and Mr. Dole courted assiduously, supported those candidates equally, according to a survey of voters leaving the polls conducted by the Associated Press and the television networks.

Voters who waited until the final hours to make up their minds gave their votes to Mr. Dole by 2 to 1. And Republicans stepped forward for their nominee more vigorously than earlier polls had suggested they would.

Mr. Dole, who is 73, said he was offering the nation a chance to return to the values of the World War II generation. But though he won his party's nomination this year, on his third try, he was unable to appeal to a wider audience in the general election, despite a series of self-consciously dramatic gestures.

In one of the most memorable moments, Mr. Dole resigned as Senate majority leader after three decades in Congress. He also put forth an ambitious 15 percent across-the-board tax-cut plan that went against decades of his own strong belief in deficit reduction. He picked Jack Kemp, with whom he has had strained relations, as his surprise choice for a running mate. And in the final weeks, after agonizing in public over whether he was risking his carefully nurtured reputation as a man of rectitude, he began slamming Mr. Clinton as unethical.

Indeed, the survey of voters leaving the polls showed that they were willing to set aside any concerns they had about Mr. Clinton's character in favor of their satisfaction with the humming economy—and their general perception that the country was headed in the right direction.

Democrats hailed the outcome as a triumph for a politician who as recently as four years ago was still Governor of Arkansas.

After a hectic campaign schedule, Mr. Clinton arrived in Little Rock early yesterday morning, only to play hearts with Leon E. Panetta, his chief of staff, and Douglas Sosnik, the White House political director, until the sun rose. He voted just after midday at a renovated train station in his hometown.

Mr. Dole cast his paper ballot just after noon at his hometown of Russell, Kan., before flying to Washington on the last leg of his often sleepless 96-hour campaign marathon.

Even before Mr. Dole formally conceded, his aides and prominent Republicans were engaged in a round of soul-searching as well as searing post-mortems over some major decisions of the campaign, particularly the move to transform the final weeks of the race into essentially a battle for California.

In the wake of the 1994 midterm elections, expectations had been high for the campaign of 1996. Republicans lined up to take on a vulnerable-appearing Mr. Clinton. Many prominent politicians toyed with running as independents, only to back down in the end. And one of the most gripping stretches was in 1995, during Colin L. Powell's will-he-will-he-not process of mulling over a White House bid.

Still, throughout this year, the campaign often seemed more perfunctory than passionate, with the battle over the control of Congress offering the most suspense. The Presidential match-up was largely between two candidates who have long been well known to the American public. And no disruptive world or national events altered the contours of the race.

Mr. Clinton's lead over Mr. Dole in the polls never wavered from October 1995. It was around that time that Democrats succeeded in blaming Republicans for the budget standoff in Congress that led to the Government shutdown.

Nevertheless, Mr. Clinton's reelection was an impressive turnabout for the President. Only two years ago, he was faulted for the Republicans' takeover of the House and Senate, the first time in 40 years that the party gained control of Congress. And only a year ago, he was widely viewed by leading Republicans, and even many Democrats, as eminently beatable.

Mr. Clinton will now be a lame duck, the first Democrat to be subject to the ban on Presidents serving more than two full terms. Increasingly, the attention and speculation will shift to Mr. Gore, who delivered a long introduction of Mr. Clinton in Little Rock this morning and who has left no doubt of his intentions to seek the White House in 2000.

Yesterday's election may also have brought an end to the role of Mr. Perot as a major political player. By piling up more than 5 percent of the vote, Mr. Perot insured that his Reform Party will continue to get Federal financing for a run in 2000. Yet unlike four years ago, when Mr. Perot's message about eliminating the deficit and overhauling the campaign finance system altered the political dialogue, he did not loom large over the 1996 campaign.

This year, according to the survey of voters leaving the polls, voters who backed Mr. Perot in 1992 gave Mr. Dole nearly half their support and split the rest between Mr. Clinton and Mr. Perot.

But in his concession speech, Mr. Perot vowed not to fade away, saying: "We're going to keep the pressure on the major issues. I think they've gotten the word on campaign finance reform, don't you? They've repented and been reborn."

Even after he glides to another term, the specter of scandal still looms over Mr. Clinton. More than half of the voters in the survey said Mr. Clinton was not honest or trustworthy. Seven in 10 of those voters backed Mr. Dole. Six in 10 voters said the President had not told them the truth about the Whitewater case.

Wednesday, November 6, 1996.

DOLE CAMPAIGN ENDS WITH A MISSTEP, CONCEDING BY MISTAKE

By Adam Nagourney

In the final hours of Bob Dole's campaign, the candidate took to appearing with a reproduction of a famous newspaper headline, which gave Mr. Dole hope in the face of discouraging polls. "Dewey Defeats Truman," The Chicago Daily Tribune declared in 1948, the evening before Harry S. Truman won re-election to the Presidency.

Last night, Mr. Dole's campaign weighed into history with its own variation of that famous mistake.

At 9:30 P.M., Mr. Dole's campaign announced, graciously but surprisingly, given that polls in California had not yet closed, that Mr. Dole was conceding the election. A half-hour later, he took it back.

"Due to an error, a statement from the Dole campaign was prematurely released to some news outlets this evening," Nelson Warfield, who is Mr. Dole's press secretary, said in his second statement. "The fact is Bob Dole has conceded nothing."

Mr. Warfield in a telephone conversation last night from the hotel where Mr. Dole was preparing to give his actual statement, was at a loss to explain what had happened.

"A variety of statements were prepared for release," Mr. Warfield said. "Either a gremlin or some other thing caused it to be released." Mr. Dole's campaign had agreed to send out the statement at 11:05 Eastern standard time, five minutes after the polls in California closed.

Instead, the announcement was sent out to major news organizations, and led to some erroneous reports that Mr. Dole had given up. *The Washington Post*, in its first-edition front-page sub-headline, announced, "Dole Aide Concedes Race, Foresees a G.O.P. Congress." Both the Associated Press and Reuters made similar announcements.

On ABC News, Peter Jennings the anchor, announced the concession at 10 P.M., and returned at 10:12 P.M. to announce the retraction. "Poor Mr. Warfield," Mr. Jennings said of the press secretary, who has handled past Dole mishaps with aplomb.

The episode seemed an all-too appropriate ending for Mr. Dole's Presidential campaign, which had been plagued from the start with the kind of incidents that lend themselves metaphors campaigns tend to avoid: from Mr. Dole's fall off a stage in California in September to the flat tire on his airplane this weekend.

. . . The premature concession probably did not pose any serious threat to the 1996 Presidential election. All three networks had already declared Mr. Clinton the winner.

But the practice of declaring the Presidential contest over before it really was over—by networks and by the candidates themselves—has been the subject of much wrangling since President Jimmy Carter conceded the election in 1980 to President Ronald Reagan at 9:50 Eastern standard time, or more than an hour before the polls closed in California.

Consumer advocate Ralph Nader ran a vitriolic campaign against both major parties, and his fringe vote was more than enough to tip the balance to Republican in several states, including Florida.

The 2000 presidential election was one of the most extraordinary in American history—not because of the campaign that preceded it, which was (in the opinion of most Americans) unusually dull and uninspiring—but because of the sensational controversy over its results, which preoccupied the nation for more than five weeks after the actual voting.

The two men who had been the frontrunners for their parties' nominations a year before the election captured those nominations with only slight difficulty. George W. Bush—son of the former president and a second-term governor of Texas—rode his famous name and enormous campaign war chest to overcome a powerful challenge from Senator John McCain of Arizona, a maverick reformer who championed campaign finance reform. Vice President Al Gore, an even more prohibitive favorite in the Democratic race, easily beat back a challenge from former Senator Bill Bradley of New Jersey, who attacked Gore for being too cautious.

Left to right:
George W. Bush (b. 1946)
Albert Gore Jr. (b. 1948)
Ralph Nader (b. 1934)

Despite the background of the Capitol in this button, Al Gore's campaign received a psychological lift when he moved his headquarters from Washington to Nashville.

Voters found Gore and Bush rather bland—unthreatening but also unexciting. Both men ran careful, centrist campaigns, making much of their relatively modest differences over how to use the large budget surpluses forecast for the years ahead. Although polls showed an exceptionally tight race right up to the end, no one anticipated how close the election would be. Gore won the national popular vote by a margin of about 500,000 votes out of about 100 million cast (or .05%). But both candidates remained short of the 270 electoral votes needed for victory because no one could determine who had actually won Florida.

At one point during the long election night, television networks projected that Gore would win Florida—a victory that would have given him the presidency. Hours later, they retracted that projection. Later still, they awarded the state (and the presidency) to Bush, and Gore called to concede. But as Bush's slim lead in Florida began to evaporate in the last stages of vote counting—and as Gore's motorcade was delivering him to a rally in Nashville to make his concession speech—the Vice President called Bush again, this time to retract his concession. After a mandatory recount over the next two days, Bush led Gore in the state by fewer than 300 votes at one point. (Ralph Nader, the presidential candidate of the Green Party, had not done well nationally but drew over 90,000 votes in Florida, which almost certainly denied Gore what would otherwise have been a comfortable victory there.) At that point, the long, controversial, and often bitter post-election battle began—in a state, ironically, whose governor, Jeb Bush, was the Republican candidate's brother.

The technology of voting quickly became central to the dispute. In a number of Florida counties, including some of the most heavily Democratic ones, votes were cast by punch-card ballots, which were then counted by machines. But punch cards are notoriously inaccurate,

George W. Bush is depicted here as representing the Lone Star State and an aspiring family dynasty; the telltale "W" is missing from this button.

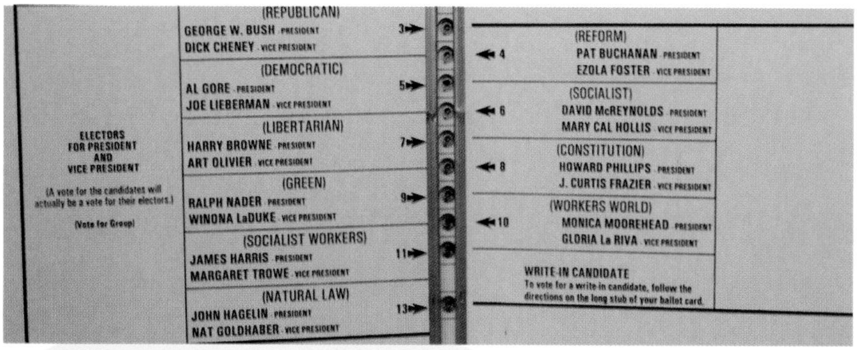

ELECTORS FOR PRESIDENT AND VICE PRESIDENT
(A vote for the candidates will actually be a vote for their electors.)
(Vote for Group)
(REPUBLICAN)
GEORGE W. BUSH PRESIDENT
DICK CHENEY VICE PRESIDENT
3
(DEMOCRATIC)
AL GORE PRESIDENT
JOE LIEBERMAN VICE PRESIDENT
5
(LIBERTARIAN)
HARRY BROWNE PRESIDENT
ART OLIVIER VICE PRESIDENT
7
(GREEN)
RALPH NADER PRESIDENT
WINONA LaDUKE VICE PRESIDENT
9
(SOCIALIST WORKERS)
JAMES HARRIS PRESIDENT
MARGARET TROWE VICE PRESIDENT
11
(NATURAL LAW)
JOHN HAGELIN PRESIDENT
NAT GOLDHABER VICE PRESIDENT
13
4
(REFORM)
PAT BUCHANAN PRESIDENT
EZOLA FOSTER VICE PRESIDENT
6
(SOCIALIST)
DAVID McREYNOLDS PRESIDENT
MARY CAL HOLLIS VICE PRESIDENT
8
(CONSTITUTION)
HOWARD PHILLIPS PRESIDENT
J. CURTIS FRAZIER VICE PRESIDENT
10
(WORKERS WORLD)
MONICA MOOREHEAD PRESIDENT
GLORIA La RIVA VICE PRESIDENT
WRITE-IN CANDIDATE
To vote for a write-in candidate, follow the directions on the long stub of your ballot card.

Some voters in Palm Beach County claimed that they were confused by this redesigned punch-card ballot; the positioning of the holes and the alignment of the candidates led some supporters of Al Gore to vote for Patrick J. Buchanon.

and many voters failed to punch out the appropriate holes adequately, leaving the machines unable to read them. In Palm Beach County, where the ballot was especially poorly designed, thousand of confused voters punched the wrong hole, or punched two holes when they were supposed to punch one. Into this morass, the Gore campaign moved quickly with a demand—sanctioned by Florida law—for hand recounts of punch-card ballots in three critical counties. The Democrats chose not to make an issue of other complaints about the voting in Florida, including charges (which the U.S. Justice Department began to investigate) of intimidation of black voters at the polls.

The Bush campaign, fearing a recount that might wipe out their frail margin of victory, immediately struck back in court (where at first they failed) and through the Republican Secretary of State, Katherine Harris, who had worked actively on the Bush campaign. As the Florida official responsible for certifying elections, she refused to authorize the recounts and declined to extend a deadline for making an official certification. The Gore campaign promptly petitioned the Florida Supreme Court, which voted unanimously to require Harris to permit the hand recounts and to accept the results after the deadline. Such recounts proceeded in two of those counties, but in the third and largest (Dade County, which includes Miami) the local election board—for complicated reasons, which may have included intimidation by Republican demonstrators in the municipal building—abruptly called off the recount, claiming they could not finish in time.

When the new, court-ordered deadline arrived, Harris quickly certified Bush the winner in Florida by a little more than 500 votes. The Gore campaign immediately contested the results in court, asking for the Dade County recount to be reopened. Turned down by a lower court judge,

Joe Lieberman offers support to Al Gore in Nashville, after Gore's statement on the election, asserting that "because of what is at stake, this matter must be resolved expeditiously but deliberately and without any rush to judgment,," November 8, 2000.

George W. Bush pauses during his first speech as president-elect, in which he declared that "the nation must rise against a house divided," Austin, Texas, December 14, 2000.

they prevailed again in the Florida Supreme Court, which ordered hand recounts of all previously uncounted ballots in all Florida counties. Once again, the laborious and controversial process of counting punch cards by hand—which required election boards to agree on a standard for judging "voter intent," since the Supreme Court had declined to set one—resumed.

In the meantime, the Bush campaign appealed desperately to the United States Supreme Court to stop the recounts. To almost universal surprise, the Court issued a stay on Saturday, December 9 (by a vote of 5–4), halting the recounts and calling for arguments before the Court on Monday, December 11. Late on Tuesday, the Court issued one of the most unusual and controversial decisions in its history. Voting 5–4 again, dividing sharply along party and ideological lines, the conservative majority overruled the Florida Supreme Court's order for a recount, insisted that any revised recount order be completed by December 12 (an obviously impossible demand, since the Court issued its ruling late at night on the 12th), and argued that the standards for evaluating punch-card ballots were too arbitrary and unfair to withstand constitutional scrutiny. The four-member minority bitterly protested the majority's reasoning, and the majority itself appeared deeply divided on some crucial issues. Critics of the decision called it one of the most clearly partisan in the Supreme Court's history and predicted that it would be many years before the Justices would be able to repair their damaged credibility. Divided or not, the Court had decided the election. Absent a recount, the original certification of Bush's victory stood—with the actual result of the election in Florida still unknown and, perhaps, unknowable.

The next day, Gore gave a brief and conciliatory concession speech and Bush a subdued acknowledgment of one of the most controversial victories in the history of American presidential elections.

—ALAN BRINKLEY

Election workers recount ballots at the Broward County Emergency Center, Fort Lauderdale, Florida, December 2000.

Senator John McCain of Arizona (center) greets Governor George Bush and Gary Bauer *(above)*, before the first debate of Republican presidential candidates. In the background, from left, are fellow candidates Steve Forbes, Senator Orrin Hatch of Utah, and Alan Keyes, Manchester, New Hampshire, December 2, 1999.

Al Gore joined in the phone canvassing *(right)* at his campaign headquarters in Manchester, New Hampshire, January 31, 2000.

In his office aboard Air Force Two *(top right)*, Vice President Gore receives a briefing on his next campaign event in Atlanta, March 3, 2000.

George Bush meets with the press *(right)* during a campaign stop in New Castle, New Hampshire, June 14, 1999.

Bush greets supporters *(above)* at the State Capitol in Harrisburg, Pennsylvania, August 1, 2000.

Gore addresses the AFL–CIO Pennsylvania state convention in Philadelphia *(opposite, top)*, the day after he secured the Democratic nomination for president, March 15, 2000.

Residents of Pueblo, Colorado greet Gore on his arrival at the airport for a campaign visit *(opposite, bottom)*, February 27, 2000.

PROUD
Working families for GORE

UNION

Texans wave their hats at George W. Bush *(top left)* as he appears on the big screen at the Republican National Convention, Philadelphia, August 1, 2000.

The scene as Al Gore enters the convention hall *(bottom left)* during the final day of the Democratic National Convention, Los Angeles, August 17, 2000.

Nader is feted after receiving the Green Party's presidential nomination at the party's convention in Denver, Colorado, June 24, 2000.

Al Gore introduces Senator Jospeh I. Lieberman of Connecticut as his running mate at a Democratic rally *(left)*, Nashville, Tennessee, August 9, 2000

The Bushes and the Cheneys are showered with confetti at the conclusion of the Republican National Convention *(below)*, Philadelphia, August 1, 2000.

George and Laura Bush step up onstage *(left)* at a rally in Covington, Kentucky, July 28, 2000.

Al Gore gives his wife Tipper a well-publicized, passionate kiss *(below)* at the end of the Democratic National Convention, Los Angeles, August 17, 2000.

THE UNION AND

The two candidates face off on the question of prescription drugs during the first of three presidential debates moderated by PBS anchorman Jim Lehrer, University of Massachusetts, Boston, October 3, 2000.

BUSH

A baby gets an aerial view of Al Gore at a rally in Tampa, Florida *(above)*, November 1, 2000.

George Bush took his message to supporters at the state fair in Pomona, California *(opposite, top)*, September 14, 2000.

After the Bush-Cheney plane touched down in Bangor, Maine, George Bush took to a makeshift stage in an airplane hangar to address supporters *(bottom, left)*, October 2000.

EXIT

90004
WISCONSIN
GORE
Gore
Lieberman
Fire Fighters
GORE

George Bush flashes his W-for-victory sign aboard his campaign plane, days before the election *(opposite, top)*. He is joined by members of his campaign staff, including Karen P. Hughes, communications director, November 6, 2000.

Vice President Gore speaks at a rally at General Mitchell International Airport in Milwaukee *(opposite, bottom)*, part of a frenetic 19-hour trip through four closely contested states, November 5, 2000.

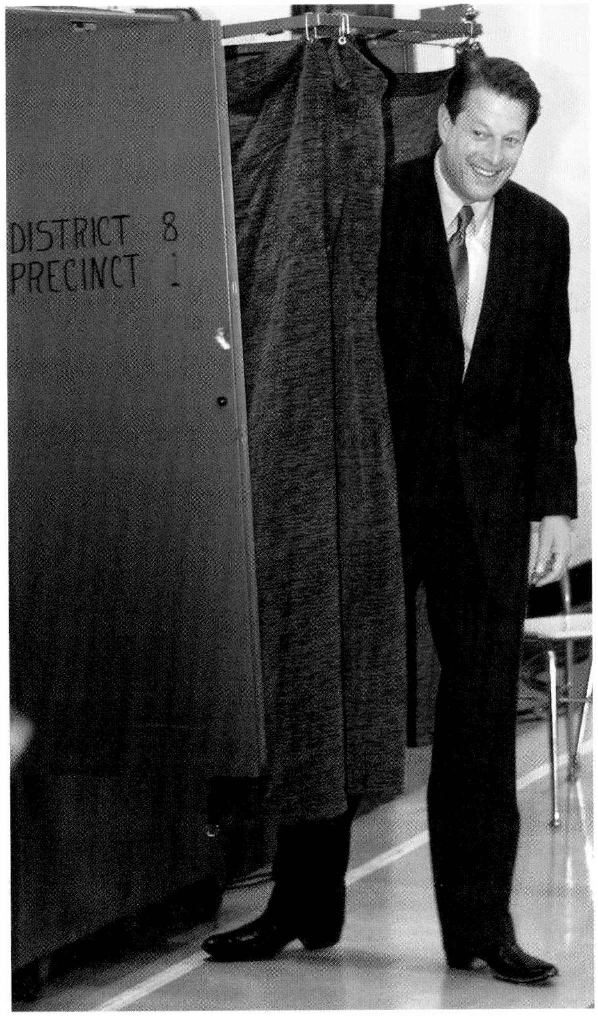

After more than 30 hours of nonstop campaigning, Al Gore votes at Forks River Elementary School in Nashville, *(top right)* November 7, 2000.

George and Jeb Bush follow the returns on Election Night with their father *(bottom right)*, former President George Bush, at the Bush family home in Austin, November 7, 2000.

DEM

Volunteers labor to finish counting ballots at the Broward County Emergency Operation Center *(opposite)* in Plantation, Florida, November 21, 2000.

The canvassing board of Broward County spends the Thanksgiving holiday counting ballots at the circuit courthouse in Fort Lauderdale, Florida *(right)*, Thursday, November 23, 2000.

Afton Gille, a Bush supporter, gets a hand on the bull horn of Charles Clark, a Gore backer *(below)*, at a demonstration in front of the Florida Capitol in Tallahassee, November 26, 2000.

President-elect George W. Bush is joined by his wife, Laura, and Speaker Pete Laney of the Texas House during his victory speech *(above)*, at the Texas House of Representatives, Austin, December 13, 2000.

Vice President Al Gore puts his arm around his running mate, Senator Joseph I. Lieberman, as they and their families leave Mr. Gore's office in the Old Executive Office Building after his concession speech *(opposite, top)*, Washington, D.C., December 13, 2000

Al Gore thanks a crowd of supporters after delivering his concession speech, *(opposite, bottom)*, Washington, D.C., December 13, 2000.

The New York Times

BUSH AND GORE IN EXTREMELY CLOSE RACE; HILLARY CLINTON WINS SEAT, POLLING SHOWS

In Turn in Her Political Life, First Lady Goes to Senate

An Electorate Divided, to the Very End

November 8

The New York Times

BUSH BARELY AHEAD OF GORE IN FLORIDA AS RECOUNT HOLDS KEY TO THE ELECTION

How Gore Stopped Short On His Way to Concede

Recipe for a Stalemate

Florida Democrats Say Ballot's Design Hurt Gore

November 9

The New York Times

GORE CAMPAIGN VOWS COURT FIGHT OVER VOTE WITH FLORIDA'S OUTCOME STILL UP IN THE AIR

2 Game Plans But One Goal

Florida Courts Tread Warily In Ballot Fights

Anger and Chagrin After an Oops on a Ballot

Israelis Track Down and Kill a Fatah Commander

November 10

The New York Times

BUSH AND ADVISERS, CONFIDENT OF A VICTORY IN RECOUNT, URGE GORE NOT TO STAND IN WAY

Democrats Split Over Possibility Of Court Battle

Clinton Seen Issuing Work Rules That Stalled Spending Agreement

Democrats' Eyes on Recounts and Courts

Shopping in Palm of the Hand Is Making Its Holiday Debut

Making Economic Lifeline of a Wartime Trail

November 11

The New York Times

BUSH SUES TO HALT HAND RECOUNT IN FLORIDA

The Limits Of Patience

2 Camps Clash Vote by Vote, Scrap by Scrap

Bush Takes 4-Vote Lead in New Mexico

Chicago Girds for Big Battle Over Its Skyline

Cable-Car Fire Kills 170 Skiers Trapped In Austrian Tunnel

November 12

The New York Times

RECOUNT FIGHT WIDENS AS COURT CASE BEGINS

Strange Bedfellows

In Palm Beach County, Tumult Grew Hourly

To Weary Israelis, a Hijacking Augurs Another Difficult Week

Bodies and Questions in an Austrian Tunnel

November 13

The New York Times

A VOTE DEADLINE IN FLORIDA IS SET FOR TODAY

U.S. Judge Refuses to Block Hand Recount of Ballots

Americans Patiently Awaiting Election Outcome

For Burmese, Repression, AIDS and Denial

Mother Lode of TV Comedy Is Found in Forgotten Closet

Florida Official Has Dual Roles In a Maelstrom

November 14

The New York Times

FLORIDA SAYS NO TO FURTHER RECOUNTS AS BUSH DISMISSES OVERTURE FROM GORE

Seeking the High Ground

Taken Aback, Bush Campaign Sticks to Script

High-Tech Stealth Being Used To Sway Doctor Prescriptions

Uncounted Overseas Votes Carrying a Pro-Bush Profile

November 16

The New York Times

Florida's High Court Rules Recounts Can Go On

Democrats Rue Ballot Foul-Up In a 2nd County

With Tallahassee All Astir, Jeb Bush Keeps a Distance

Holiday Fliers Face The Usual Crowds, Plus Riled Workers

Alas, Vote-Count Machines Are Only Human

November 17

The New York Times

FLORIDA COURT BARS NAMING A WINNER; BUSH LEAD GROWS WITH OVERSEAS TALLY

Sharp Swings In the Battle

G.O.P.'s Help for Absentees In a County Is in Court, Too

Huge Crowd in Hanoi for Clinton, Who Speaks of 'Shared Suffering'

November 18

The New York Times

FLORIDA COURT BACKS HAND RECOUNTS AND ORDERS VOTE DEADLINE OF MONDAY

Bush Camp, Outraged, Vows to Seek Recourse to Ruling

Dimpled Votes Are New Hope For Democrats

Political Fallout After a Legal Finding

Software That Tracks E-Mail Is Raising Privacy Concerns

November 22

The New York Times

BUSH TAKES APPEAL TO U.S. SUPREME COURT; CHENEY IN HOSPITAL WITH MILD HEART ATTACK

In Blow to Gore, Recount Halts In Miami-Dade

Florida Legislators Consider Options to Aid Bush

For Texas and Other States, A Bump Is Sometimes a Vote

Flurry of Activity in Cheney Case Left Bush Struggling to Keep Up

Russia Ending Deal on Arms Negotiated by Gore

November 23

The New York Times

FLORIDA'S HIGH COURT DEALS GORE A SETBACK, DENYING BID TO FORCE A MIAMI-DADE RECOUNT

November 24

The New York Times

U.S. Supreme Court to Hear Florida Recount Case

November 25

The New York Times

With Deadline Near, Florida Recount Grinds On

November 26

The New York Times

BUSH IS DECLARED WINNER IN FLORIDA, BUT GORE VOWS TO CONTEST RESULTS

November 27

The New York Times

U.S. Supreme Court Presses 2 Sides on Vote Case

December 2

The New York Times

GORE LOSES FLORIDA RECOUNT CASE; PUTS LAST HOPE IN STATE HIGH COURT

December 5

The New York Times

Florida High Court Hears Gore's Appeal on Vote

December 8

The New York Times

FLORIDA COURT BACKS RECOUNT; BUSH APPEALING TO U.S. JUSTICES

December 9

The New York Times

SUPREME COURT, SPLIT 5-4, HALTS FLORIDA COUNT IN BLOW TO GORE

December 10

The New York Times

Bush v. Gore Is Now in Hands of Supreme Court

December 11

The New York Times

JUSTICES' QUESTIONS UNDERLINE DIVIDE ON WHETHER HAND RECOUNT CAN BE FAIR

December 12

The New York Times

BUSH PREVAILS

BY SINGLE VOTE, JUSTICES END RECOUNT, BLOCKING GORE AFTER 5-WEEK STRUGGLE

December 13

"All the News That's Fit to Print"

The New York Times

Late Edition
New York: Today, morning rain, then cloudy, high 39. Tonight, becoming partly cloudy, low 32. Tomorrow, partial sunshine, high 40. Yesterday, high 31, low 20. Weather map, Page B13.

VOL. CL . . No. 51,602 | NEW YORK, THURSDAY, DECEMBER 14, 2000 | 75 CENTS

$1 beyond the greater New York metropolitan area.

BUSH PLEDGES TO BE PRESIDENT FOR 'ONE NATION,' NOT ONE PARTY; GORE, CONCEDING, URGES UNITY

AN END TO A QUEST

Vice President Offers to Aid Bush but Admits Disappointment

By RICHARD L. BERKE and KATHARINE Q. SEELYE

WASHINGTON, Dec. 13 — Vice President Al Gore reluctantly surrendered his quest for the presidency tonight, telling the American public that while he was deeply disappointed and sharply disagreed with the Supreme Court verdict that ended his campaign, "partisan rancor must now be put aside."

In a gracious eight-minute televised speech from his ceremonial office next to the White House, Mr. Gore said he had telephoned Gov. George W. Bush to offer his congratulations. He promised to stand behind Mr. Bush, honoring him, for the first time, with the title "president-elect."

"Now the United States Supreme Court has spoken," he said. "Let there be no doubt. While I strongly disagree with the court's decision, I accept it. I accept the finality of the outcome, which will be ratified next Monday in the Electoral College. And tonight, for the sake of our unity as a people and the strength of our democracy, I offer my concession." [Transcript, Page A26.]

The speech was an emotional and political crest for Mr. Gore, 52, who had such qualms about giving up his race for the White House, a lifelong goal, that aides said he was on the telephone with them at least until 1:30 this morning, asking about possible legal avenues that the Supreme Court's decision might have left open. He told his advisers that he wanted to sleep on it before making a final decision.

Many politicians said Mr. Gore's address was as important as the one by Governor Bush that followed. By submerging any bitter feelings and sounding a conciliatory tone, they said, Mr. Gore could help reduce the festering tensions between Republicans and Democrats who cling to the belief that their candidate should rightfully claim the White House.

Mr. Gore declared that he would "honor the new president-elect and do everything possible to help him bring Americans together."

For all his outreach to Mr. Bush, Mr. Gore dropped several not-so-veiled hints that this might not be his last try.

Making clear that he is not about to fade away — or stop fighting — Mr. Gore said, "I do have one regret, that I didn't get the chance to stay and fight for the American people over the next four years, especially for those who feel their voices have not been heard. I heard you and I will

Continued on Page A26

Reuters

"I know America wants reconciliation and unity," said George W. Bush. "I know Americans want progress."

Theme of Reconciliation After Five-Week Wait

By DAVID E. SANGER

AUSTIN, Tex., Dec. 13 — George W. Bush spoke to the nation for the first time as president-elect tonight, declaring that the "nation must rise above a house divided" after one of the closest and most disputed presidential elections in United States history.

Speaking from the podium of the Texas House of Representatives, precisely 24 hours after the United State Supreme Court ended a five-week-long dispute by halting a recount of Florida's disputed votes, and thus preserving Mr. Bush's razor-thin lead, the 54-year-old governor devoted his entire speech to themes of reconciliation.

"I was not elected to serve one party, but to serve one nation," Mr. Bush said.

"Whether you voted for me or not, I will do my best to serve your interests," he said, "and I will work to earn your respect." [Transcript, Page A24.]

A little more than an hour before, Vice President Al Gore called Mr. Bush to say he was withdrawing from the 17-month-long presidential race, and congratulated the Texas governor, who was first elected to office here only six years ago, on being elected the 43rd president of the United States.

Minutes later, in his own speech from his ceremonial office next door to the White House, Mr. Gore said that while he disagreed with the court's ruling "I offer my concession."

Mr. Bush appeared by turns relaxed and slightly nervous, licking his upper lip as he looked around the large chamber, dominated by a huge Christmas tree and filled with his supporters and staff. "I have a lot to be thankful for," he said in a speech that emphasized only common ground between Democrats and Republicans, and made only glancing references to the disputes that punctuated the campaign and its often bitter aftermath. "I am thankful for America, and thankful that we are able to resolve our electoral differences in a peaceful way."

The choice of locale for his speech underscored the theme: The Texas House is under Democratic control.

Mr. Bush used the moment to reiterate some of his campaign themes, talking of making "all our public schools excellent," strengthening Medicare and creating a prescription drug benefit for "all of our seniors." He talked of a "broad, fair and fiscally responsible tax relief" a phrase so vague that it could embrace many varieties of tax cuts — and like Mr. Gore an hour before him, talked of "common ground."

"During the fall campaign, we differed about details of these proposals but there was remarkable consensus about the important issues before us." He spoke of serving "every race and every background," aware that minorities voted overwhelmingly against him in last month's election.

It was not the kind of speech Mr. Bush would have delivered had he won the large victory his aides were predicting on election night. He of-

Continued on Page A24

The 43rd President

George Walker Bush

By ALISON MITCHELL

AUSTIN, Tex., Dec. 13 — Gov. George W. Bush cast his quest for the presidency as a stand against poisonous Washington — its gridlock, its scandals, its bruising partisanship — and in the very last week of his campaign he was barnstorming under bright banners that promised, "Bringing America Together."

Man in the News

But as Mr. Bush was finally able to claim a belated and minuscule victory over Vice President Al Gore, after a debilitating month of bare-knuckled court fighting, it was as if he had somehow crossed through the looking glass.

In the contested aftermath of Election Day, the man who presented himself as a Texas outsider turned to the ultimate Washington insiders to secure his victory. James A. Baker III, Dick Cheney and Andrew H. Card, all from Mr. Bush's father's administration, became the faces of the Bush presidency in waiting, and Theodore B. Olson, the capital's reigning conservative litigator, argued the case at the Supreme Court.

Far from calming the flames of partisanship, Mr. Bush's struggle for victory against Mr. Gore fanned them to an intensity not seen since President Clinton's impeachment. And suddenly Mr. Bush seemed lassoed to the Congressional leaders whom he had once kept so carefully at a distance, as they thundered on his behalf against the "unelected judges" of Florida who were rendering verdicts about the vote.

Now George Walker Bush, 54, comes into office as only the fourth man in history — and the first in more than a century — to assume the presidency without winning the popular vote. Like the only other son of a president to win the office himself, John Quincy Adams in 1824 (who had fewer popular votes than Andrew Jackson), Mr. Bush lost the popular vote in a disputed election to a Tennessean. Indeed, Mr. Bush won office with 271 electoral votes, just one more than the minimum.

Mr. Bush is not facing personal scandal, as President Clinton did. But his situation may be just as searing politically, for Mr. Bush ultimately won through a bruising legal battle over the 25 electoral votes in a state run by his brother, Gov. Jeb Bush of Florida. It was a fight that was finally decided by nine Supreme Court justices, who split bitterly over the issue.

With his speech tonight from the Texas House of Representatives, Mr. Bush began trying to pull the nation together after this grueling ordeal, choosing the House because it is a chamber where the Democrats have a majority. He quoted the words of Thomas Jefferson who won the presidency in 1800 only after 36 ballots in the House of Representatives.

And he said that the rancor and strange circumstances of his election could lead to healing and help him bring the warring Congressional leaders together.

"I am optimistic that we can change the tone in Washington, D.C.," Mr. Bush said. "I believe things happen for a reason, and I hope the long wait of the last five weeks will heighten a desire to move beyond the bitterness and partisanship of the past."

Republicans say Mr. Bush's quick instincts about people and his years of reaching across the aisle in Texas

Continued on Page A25

The 36th Day

The nation's closest presidential race in more than a century is over. Looking back at a five week battle. Looking ahead to the transition. Articles, addresses, and the text of the ruling that ended it all.

THE 43RD PRESIDENT
PAGES A23-36

Another Kind Of Bitter Split

When Jurisprudence Is Pulled Into Politics

By LINDA GREENHOUSE

WASHINGTON, Dec. 13 — The Supreme Court justices who drove off into the night on Tuesday left behind more than a split decision that ended a disputed presidential election.

News Analysis

They also left behind an institution that many students of the court said appeared diminished, if not actually tarnished, by its extraordinary foray into presidential politics.

They point to the contradiction between the majority's action in this case and those justices' usual insistence on deference to the states.

The members of the majority appeared at pains to refute any suggestion that the court had intervened unduly by stopping the Florida recount on Saturday or by ruling Tuesday that it could not resume. It was "our unsought responsibility to resolve the federal and constitutional issues" in the case, the majority said in its unsigned opinion.

And Justice Clarence Thomas, a member of the 5-to-4 majority, told a group of high school students at the court today that "I have yet to hear any discussion, in nine years, of partisan politics" among the justices.

"I plead with you that, whatever you do, don't try to apply the rules of the political world to this institution; they do not apply," Justice Thomas said, adding, "The last political act we engage in is confirmation."

Be that as it may, the events of the last few days were jarring even for people who pride themselves on being realists rather than romantics about how the court works.

One federal judge, a Republican appointee who was a Supreme Court law clerk decades ago, said today that he had long since become accustomed to watching the justices

Continued on Page A32

Now, Lifting the Clouds

By R. W. APPLE Jr.

WASHINGTON, Dec. 13 — The victor and the vanquished turned this evening to the arduous task of mending a body politic riven by the painful presidential election of 2000.

News Analysis

As the two nominees — first Vice President Al Gore and then Gov. George W. Bush of Texas, now the president-elect — appeared on television to appeal to the nation for a measure of unity, they spoke in the context of a Supreme Court decision that had sown the seeds of potential disunity. The court's muddled, if decisive, ruling on Tuesday night gave Mr. Bush his long-sought victory, yet denied him clear, unclouded title to the Oval Office.

Mr. Gore did his best to remedy that by buttressing confidence in the rule of law. Without a trace of rancor, in a speech that seemed both less stiff and more personal than many of his stump speeches, the vice president said, "I accept finality," and pledged to put himself at Mr. Bush's disposal.

"What remains of partisan rancor must now be put aside, and may God bless his stewardship," he said.

The Bush camp could not have hoped for more. And when the president-elect's turn to speak came, he saluted his defeated rival, promising to change the tone of Washington by emphasizing consensus, not confrontation.

"Our nation must rise above a house divided," Mr. Bush declared. "Republicans want the best for our nation, and so do Democrats. We must seize the moment and deliver."

Mr. Bush must live with the knowledge that he won Florida by just 537 votes out of 6 million cast, with a manual recount abandoned, thousands of ballots short of completion, at the order of a court split 5 to 4. Many people noted today that he would take office as the 43rd president by a margin of a single judicial vote, and some people, politicians as well as journalists, vowed to complete the recount on their own.

If such a recount showed Mr. Gore the "winner," it could destabilize the

Continued on Page A28

NEWS SUMMARY A2

Updated news: www.nytimes.com

CNN

"I say to President-elect Bush that what remains of partisan rancor must now be put aside," Vice President Al Gore said last night in his speech.

INSIDE

Judge Upholds Use of Race In University's Admissions

A federal judge upheld the University of Michigan's use of affirmative action in its admissions, ruling that diversity is a critical component of higher education. PAGE A14

Clinton in Ulster Debate

President Clinton found himself in a debate with a group of hard-line lawmakers who oppose a peace accord that he helped forge. PAGE A10

Plant's Genes Are Mapped

Scientists have determined the complete genetic sequence of a plant, a finding that should provide ways to genetically alter crops. PAGE C4

New York, Thursday, December 14, 2000

Bush Pledges to Be President For 'One Nation,' Not One Party; Gore, Conceding, Urges Unity

Theme of Reconciliation After Five-Week Wait

By David E. Sanger

AUSTIN, Tex., Dec 13—George W. Bush spoke to the nation for the first time as president-elect tonight, declaring that the "nation must rise above a house divided" after one of the closest and most disputed presidential elections in United States history.

Speaking from the podium of the Texas House of Representatives, precisely 24 hours after the United States Supreme Court ended a five-week-long dispute by halting a recount of Florida's disputed votes, and thus preserving Mr. Bush's razor-thin lead, the 54-year-old governor devoted his entire speech to themes of reconciliation.

"I was not elected to serve one party, but to serve one nation," Mr. Bush said.

"Whether you voted for me or not, I will do my best to serve your interests," he said, "and I will work to earn your respect."

A little more than an hour before, Vice President Al Gore called Mr. Bush to say he was withdrawing from the 17-month-long presidential race, and congratulated the Texas governor, who was first elected to office here only six years ago, on being elected the 43rd president of the United States.

Minutes later, in his own speech from his ceremonial office next door to the White House, Mr. Gore said that while he disagreed with the court's ruling "I offer my concession."

Mr. Bush appeared by turns relaxed and slightly nervous, licking his upper lip as he looked around the large chamber, dominated by a huge Christmas tree and filled with his supporters and staff. "I have a lot to be thankful for," he said in a speech that emphasized only common ground between Democrats and Republicans, and made only glancing references to the disputes that punctuated the campaign and its often bitter aftermath. "I am thankful for America, and thankful that we are able to resolve our electoral differences in a peaceful way."

The choice of locale for his speech underscored the theme: The Texas House is under Democratic control. Mr. Bush used the moment to reiterate some of his campaign themes, talking of making "all our public schools excellent," strengthening Medicare and creating a prescription drug benefit for "all our seniors." He talked of a "broad, fair and fiscally responsible tax relief"—a phrase so vague that it could embrace many varieties of tax cuts—and like Mr. Gore an hour before him, talked of "common ground."

"During the fall campaign, we differed about details of these proposals but there was remarkable consensus about the important issues before us." He spoke of serving "every race and every background," aware that minorities voted overwhelmingly against him in last month's election.

It was not the kind of speech Mr. Bush would have delivered had he won the large victory his aides were predicting on election night. He offered nothing to the conservative wing of his party, and evoked none of the cultural issues that often divide the two parties.

> "I was not elected to serve one party, but to serve one nation . . . Whether you voted for me or not, I will do my best to serve your interests."

Mr. Bush is expected to travel to Washington next Tuesday, aides said, and meet both President Clinton and Vice President Gore. But his transition is already under way, and with tonight's concession by Mr. Gore, Mr. Bush will now have use of the $5 million transition budget and a large office blocks from the White House. Within days he is expected to start naming his senior staff and top cabinet members, likely starting with Gen. Colin L. Powell, who is expected to be named secretary of state.

Though he briefly invoked the words of Lincoln at the opening of his speech Mr. Bush referred directly to only one of his predecessors, Thomas Jefferson, who took office in a disputed election in 1800.

"I will be guided by President Jefferson's sense of purpose," he said, "to stand for principle, to be reasonable in manner, and above all, to do great good for the cause of freedom and harmony."

"The presidency is more than an honor. It is more than an office," he concluded.

"It is a charge to keep." The last phrase was also the title of a book he published at the beginning of the campaign to introduce himself to the American public.

Jesse Jackson, angry at the Supreme Court's decision, declared that while Mr. Bush would legally serve as president, he had no "moral authority."

Mr. Bush's speech to the nation tonight was no ordinary victory address.

After weeks of legal maneuvering and two rapid-fire decisions by the Supreme Court which effectively ended Mr. Gore's hopes for a recount on Tuesday night, Mr. Bush had much more to accomplish this evening than simply declaring himself the victor on a typical Election Day.

A man who is at his most uncomfortable with formal addresses in formal settings was called on to give one that he knew would set the tone of his first term. It was a night for perfect pitch and appropriate symbolism, "chiefly the olive branch," one aide said.

His words were simple, his rhetoric not as lofty as the speech Mr. Gore gave an hour before. In discussions leading up to the drafting of the speech, aides said he had to be humble, while making it clear that other nations and his political opponents at home should not question his command of the office. It is unclear whether he accomplished that goal; his only reference to America's role in the world was a call for bipartisan foreign policy and "a military equal to every challenge, and superior to every adversity."

He had to appeal to those who, despite a nearly year-and-a-half-long campaign and a five-week recount, still question whether he comes to the job adequately prepared, or risks becoming captive to a talented set of advisors.

This afternoon his aides, led by his communications director, Karen P. Hughes, and his speechwriter, Michael Gerson, were fine-tuning drafts of the speech, knowing they would be judged by how well they closed a breach with Democrats that is far wider today than it was on Election Day.

They were acutely aware that the Republican majority in the House of Representatives is so small as to be virtually useless. That creates a far larger challenge than Mr. Clinton had in 1993, when he enjoyed a substantial Democratic majority—before losing it, for the rest of his presidency, in the 1994 midterm elections. Moreover, the Senate is now divided precisely 50-50, though the vice president-elect, Dick Cheney, will cast the deciding vote if there is a tie.

So it was no surprise that Mr. Bush chose his setting with bipartisan care: The Texas House is controlled by Democrats, and he was introduced tonight by its Democratic speaker, Pete Laney, who praised him effusively as a leader and a partner. Although the Legislature is not in session, many of its members attended.

Mr. Bush is the first president to take office in an election that was for all practical purposes settled by the Supreme Court. And not since 1888 . . . has anyone assumed the presidency after losing the popular vote but winning the electoral vote.

But even such a show of bipartisan comity could not overcome some of the bitterness of today's events. Jesse Jackson, angry at the Supreme Court's decision, declared that while Mr. Bush would legally serve as president, he had no "moral authority." Perhaps that is why Mr. Bush chose to paraphrase Lincoln. "There were also questions about Lincoln's legitimacy," David Donald, the emeritus professor at Harvard and Lincoln's biographer, noted recently.

"Those dissipated, and I hope these questions will dissipate too."

Nonetheless, Mr. Bush is the first president to take office in an election that was for all practical purposes settled by the Supreme Court. And not since 1888, when Benjamin Harrison won the presidential election, has anyone assumed the presidency after losing the popular vote but winning the electoral vote.

Mr. Bush also shares that dubious distinction with two others: Rutherford B. Hayes in 1876 and John Quincy Adams in 1824. Mr. Adams, of course, was also the only other son of a president to win the presidency.

Under very different circumstances, other presidents have faced tasks similar to Mr. Bush's tonight. Another politician who learned his political skills in the chamber where Mr. Bush spoke tonight, Lyndon B. Johnson, faced a similar challenge of unifying the nation after he was thrust into the presidency by the assassination of his predecessor, John F. Kennedy. But the tragic circumstances of his ascendancy created a well of sympathy that Mr. Bush does not enjoy.

Gerald R. Ford had a more analogous job of reuniting the nation after a bitter and partisan division, and hours after President Richard M. Nixon resigned he declared that "our long national nightmare is over."

"Both Johnson and Ford were far more successful in sending out unifying messages than anyone thought at the time they could be," said Michael Beschloss, the presidential historian, who has focused intensively on Johnson's term.

But both men, he noted, were thrown into the Oval Office by fate; Mr. Bush must overcome suspicions among many of his political opponents that he took office by obstructing a reliable recount of the Florida vote. And both Mr. Johnson and Mr. Ford were creatures of Congress and understood how it operated; Mr. Bush, like Mr. Clinton before him, must learn that territory on the job.

Tonight Mr. Bush also had to take firm command of a national agenda, when many suggest that the manner of his election may impose limitations on his powers. He did not refer to that problem, though Mr. Gore, in his speech, addressed the question head-on. He said that while many believed Mr. Bush would be hampered, "I do not believe it need be so." In some ways, Mr. Gore's speech was a more passionate call for the nation to rally around the new president than Mr. Bush's was.

Many of Mr. Bush's advisors say that in the next few months, he must focus on common ground with his Democratic opponents, and win bipartisan passage of some major piece of legislation to show that he is willing to come to the middle. But there is still debate within the Bush camp about what that piece of legislation should be.

He also faces an array of immediate challenges, at home and abroad, that will not wait for Senate confirmations or the selection of roughly 800 senior White House staff.

The economy is clearly slowing, and while Mr. Cheney has several times warned of an impending recession born in the Clinton administration, it will be up to a Bush administration to keep it from happening. Privately some of his advisors worry that Mr. Bush's economic bench is not as deep as his national security bench.

Mr. Bush must overcome suspicions among many of his political opponents that he took office by obstructing a reliable recount of the Florida vote.

His chief economic advisor, Lawrence B. Lindsey, is a respected former member of the Federal Reserve Board, but the search for a treasury secretary has focused on Wall Street.

Whoever gets the job will have to decide with Mr. Bush whether to pursue the kind of deep tax cuts that the Texas governor talked about as a candidate. Many Republicans believe that Mr. Bush's plans will have to be dramatically scaled back given the composition of Congress, though most believe some reductions in estate taxes and the elimination of the marriage penalty could prove low-hanging fruit for Mr. Bush's first few months in office.

Wednesday, December 13, 2000

BY SINGLE VOTE, JUSTICES END RECOUNT, BLOCKING GORE AFTER 5-WEEK STRUGGLE

An Awareness of Hazards

By Linda Greenhouse

WASHINGTON, Dec. 12—The Supreme Court effectively handed the presidential election to George W. Bush tonight, overturning the Florida Supreme Court and ruling by a vote of 5 to 4 that there could be no further counting of Florida's disputed presidential votes.

The ruling came after a long and tense day of waiting at 10 P.M., just two hours before the Dec. 12 "safe harbor" for immunizing a state's electors from challenge in Congress was to come to an end. The unsigned majority said it was the immediacy of this deadline that made it impossible to come up with a way of counting the votes that could both meet "minimal constitutional standards" and be accomplished within the deadline.

The five members of the majority were Chief Justice William H. Rehnquist and Justices Sandra Day O'Connor, Antonin Scalia, Anthony M. Kennedy and Clarence Thomas.

Among the four dissenters, two justices, Stephen G. Breyer and David H. Souter, agreed with the majority that the varying standards in different Florida counties for counting the punch-card ballots presented problems of both due process and equal protection. But unlike the majority, these justices said the answer should be not to shut the recount down, but to extend it until the December 18 date for the meeting of the Electoral College.

Justice Souter said that such a recount would be a "tall order" but that "there is no justification for denying the state the opportunity to try to count all the disputed ballots now."

The six separate opinions, totaling 65 pages, were filled with evidence that the justices were acutely aware of the controversy the court had entered by accepting Governor Bush's appeal of last Friday's Florida Supreme Court ruling and by granting him a stay of the recount on Saturday afternoon, just hours after the vote counting had begun.

"None are more conscious of the vital limits on judicial authority than are the members of this court," the majority opinion said, referring to "our unsought responsibility to resolve the federal and constitutional issues the judicial system has been forced to confront."

The dissenters said nearly all the objections raised by Mr. Bush were insubstantial. The court should not have reviewed either this case or the one it decided last week, they said.

Justice John Paul Stevens said the court's action "can only lend credence to the most cynical appraisal of the work of judges throughout the land."

His dissenting opinion, also signed by Justices Breyer and Ruth Bader Ginsburg, added: "It is confidence in the men and women who administer the judicial system that is the true backbone of the rule of law. Time will one day heal the wound to that confidence that will be inflicted by today's decision. One thing, however, is certain. Although we may never know with complete certainty the identity of the winner of this year's Presidential election, the identity of the loser is perfectly clear. It is the nation's confidence in the judge as an impartial guardian of the rule of law."

What the court's day and a half of deliberations yielded tonight was a messy product that bore the earmarks of a failed attempt at a compromise solution that would have permitted the vote counting to continue.

It appeared that Justices Souter and Breyer, by taking seriously the equal protection concerns that Justices Kennedy and O'Connor had raised at the argument, had tried to persuade them that those concerns could be addressed in a remedy that would permit the disputed votes to be counted.

Justices O'Connor and Kennedy were the only justices whose names did not appear separately on any opinion, indicating that one or both of them wrote the court's unsigned majority opinion, labeled only "per curiam," or "by the court." Its focus was narrow, limited to the ballot counting process itself. The opinion objected not only to the varying standards used by different counties for determining voter intent, but to aspects of the Florida Supreme Court's order determining which ballots should be counted.

"We are presented with a situation where a state court with the power to assure uniformity has ordered a statewide recount with minimal procedural standards," the opinion said. "When a court orders a statewide remedy, there must be at least some assurance that the rudimentary requirements of equal treatment and fundamental fairness are satisfied."

Three members of the majority—the chief justice, and Justices Scalia and Thomas—raised further, more basic objections to the recount and said the Florida Supreme Court had violated state law in ordering it.

The fact that Justices O'Connor and Kennedy evidently did not share these deeper concerns had offered a potential basis for a coalition between them and the dissenters. That effort apparently foundered on the two justices' convictions that the midnight deadline of Dec. 12 had to be met.

The majority said that "substantial additional work" was needed to undertake a constitutional recount, including not only uniform statewide standards for determining a legal vote, but also "practical procedures to implement them" and "orderly judicial review of any disputed matters that might arise." There was no way all this could be done, the majority said.

"Although we may never know with complete certainty the identity of the winner of this year's Presidential election, the identity of the loser is perfectly clear. It is the nation's confidence in the judge as an impartial guardian of the rule of law."

The dissenters said the concern with Dec. 12 was misplaced. Justices Souter and Breyer offered to send the case back to Florida courts "with instructions to establish uniform standards for evaluating the several types of ballots that have prompted differing treatments," as Justice Souter described his proposed remand order. "Unlike the majority," he added, "I see no warrant for this court to assume that Florida could not possibly comply with this requirement before the date set for the meeting of electors, Dec. 18."

Justices Stevens and Ginsburg said they did not share the view that the lack of a uniform vote-counting standard presented an equal protection problem.

In addition to joining Justice Souter's dissenting opinion, Justice Breyer wrote one of his own, signed by the three other dissenters, in which he recounted the history of the deadlocked presidential election of 1876 and of the partisan role that one Supreme Court justice, Joseph P. Bradley, played in awarding the presidency to Rutherford B. Hayes.

"This history may help to explain why I think it not only legally wrong, but also most unfortunate, for the court to have terminated the Florida recount," Justice Breyer said. He said the time problem that Florida faced was "in significant part, a problem of the court's own making." The recount was moving ahead in an "orderly fashion," Justice Breyer said, when "this court improvidently entered a stay." He said: "As a result, we will never know whether the recount could have been completed."

There was no need for the court to have involved itself in the election dispute this time, he said, adding:

"Above all, in this highly publicized matter, the court runs the risk of undermining the public's confidence in the court itself. That confidence is a public treasure. It has been built slowly over many years, some of which were marked by a Civil War and the tragedy of segregation. It is a vitally necessary ingredient of any successful effort to protect basic liberty and, indeed, the rule of law itself."

"We do risk a self-inflicted wound," Justice Breyer said, "a wound that may harm not just the court, but the nation."

Justice Ginsburg also wrote a dissenting opinion, joined by the other dissenters. Her focus was on the implications for federalism of the majority's action. "I might join the chief justice were it my commission to interpret Florida law," she said, adding: "The extraordinary setting of this case has obscured the ordinary principle that dictates its proper resolution: Federal courts defer to state high courts' interpretations of their state's own law. This principle reflects the core of federalism, on which all agree."

"Were the other members of this court as mindful as they generally are of our system of dual sovereignty," Justice Ginsburg concluded, "they would affirm the judgment of the Florida Supreme Court."

Unlike the other dissenters, who said they dissented "respectfully," Justice Ginsburg said only, "I dissent."

Nothing about this case, Bush v. Gore, No. 00-949, was ordinary: not its context, not its acceptance over the weekend, not the enormously accelerated schedule with argument on Monday, and not the way the decision was released to the public tonight.

When the court issues an opinion, the justices ordinarily take the bench and the majority gives a brief oral description of the case and the holding.

Today, after darkness fell and their work was done, the justices left the Supreme Court building individually from the underground garage, with no word to dozens of journalists from around the world who were waiting in the crowded pressroom for word as to when, or whether, a decision might come. By the time the pressroom staff members passed out copies of the decision, the justices were gone.

Index

A

B

C

D

E

F

G

L

M

N

O

P

Q

R

S

T

U

V

W

Y

Photo Credits

page 2 Angel Franco/The New York Times

Introduction

6 James Estrin/The New York Times
7 © Bettman/CORBIS
9 The New York Times Photo Archive
11 © Bettman/CORBIS
13 Times Wide World
15 © CORBIS
16 Times Wide World
18 Barton Silverman/The New York Times
20 The New York Times
21 Associated Press
22 Sara Krulwich/The New York Times
24 Chester Higgins Jr./The New York Times
25 Paul Hosefros/The New York Times

1900

26 *(bottom, both)* Hulton Getty
27 *(top)* Museum of American Political Life, *(bottom)* © CORBIS
28–29 Hulton Getty
30–31 © CORBIS
32 Hulton Getty
33 Library of Congress/Hulton Getty
34–35 Hulton Getty

1904

38 *(top)* Duke University Special Collections Library, *(bottom far left)* Library of Congress/Hulton Getty, *(bottom center left)* © Bettman/CORBIS
39 *(top)* © Bettman/CORBIS, (bottom) © CORBIS
40 © Bettman/CORBIS
41–43 Museum of American Political Life
44 Library of Congress/Hulton Getty
45 Museum of the City of New York/Archive Photos

1908

48 *(bottom far left)* New York Times Photo Archive, *(bottom center left)* Brown Brothers Inc.
49 *(both)* Museum of American Political Life
50–51 New York Times Photo Archive
52 © CORBIS
53 Museum of American Political Life
54 Photo News Bureau
55 Brown Brothers Inc.
56 Library of Congress/Hulton Getty
57 Hulton Getty

1912

60 *(top)* Museum of American Political Life, *(bottom, all)* Hulton Getty
61 (top) Museum of American Political Life, *(bottom, both)* © Bettman/CORBIS
62 American Press Assn.
63–65 Hulton Getty
66 *(top, left)* New York Times Photo Archive, *(bottom right)* Hulton Getty
67 New York Times Photo Archive
68–69 Hulton Getty

1916

72 *(bottom far left)* Hulton Getty, *(bottom center left)* New York Times Photo Archive
73 *(both)* Museum of American Political Life
74 Kellar & White
75 Hulton Getty
76–77 Museum of American Political Life
78–79 New York Times Photo Archive
80–81 Hulton Getty

1920

86 *(top)* Museum of American Political Life, *(bottom far left)* Walter Melicher for Times Wide World, *(bottom center left)* International, *(bottom center)* Times Wide World
87 *(both)* Museum of American Political Life
88 Times Wide
89–90 International
91 Underwood & Underwood
92 Brown Brothers Inc.
93 Times Wide World
94 Minneapolis Tribune
95 Times Wide World
96 Walter Melicher for Times Wide World
97 Harris & Ewing

1924

102 *(bottom far left)* Kadel & Herbert, *(bottom, center left bottom center)* Times Wide World
103 *(all)* Museum of American Political Life
104 Times Wide World
105 *(top)* Kadel & Herbert, *(bottom)* Times Wide World
106 *(both)*Times Wide World
107 Pacific & Atlantic
108 *(both)* Times Wide World
109 Pacific & Atlantic

1928

114 *(bottom far left)* Associated Press,
(bottom center left) Times Wide World
115 *(top)* © Bettman/CORBIS,
(bottom) Museum of American Political Life
116–17 Times Wide World
118 Associated Press
119 Times Wide World
120 Associated Press
121 Arkansas Gazette
122–25 Times Wide World

1932

130 *(bottom far left)* Times Wide World,
(bottom center left) Associated Press,
(bottom center) New York Times Photo Archive
131 *(top left)* Agincourt Press,
(top right, bottom right) Museum of American Political Life
132 Associated Press
133 Times Wide World
134 *(top)* Associated Press, *(bottom)* New York Times Photo Archive
135 *(both)* Times Wide World
136–37 *(top)* New York Times Studios
138 Associated Press
139 Seattle Times

1936

144 *(top)* © Bettman/CORBIS, *(bottom, both)* Times Wide World
145 *(both)* Agincourt Press
146 *(top)* Times Wide World,
(bottom) William Eckenberg/Times Wide World
147–51 Times Wide World

1940

156 *(top)* Duke University Special Collections Library,
(bottom far left) Associated Press,
(bottom center left) Times Wide World
157 *(top, bottom left)* Agincourt Press,
(bottom right) Museum of American Political Life
158–60 Times Wide World
161 Associated Press
162 *(top)* Associated Press, *(bottom)* International
163 Times Wide World
164–65 Associated Press

1944

170 *(bottom far left)* Associated Press,
(bottom center left) The New York Times
171 *(top)* © Lake County Museum/CORBIS,
(bottom) Museum of American Political Life
172 New York Times
173 International
174 New York Times
175–77 Associated Press

1948

182 *(top)* Museum of American Political Life,
(bottom far left) George Tames/The New York Times,
(bottom center left) Associated Press,
(bottom center) Associated Press,
(bottom center right) Edward Hausner/The New York Times
183 *(all)* Museum of American Political Life
184–85 George Tames/The New York Times
186 Ernie Sisto /The New York Times
187–88 Associated Press
189 *(top)* Edward Hausner/The New York Times,
(bottom) Morris Wright for The New York Times
190 Associated Press
191 Arthur Brower/The New York Times
192 Associated Press
193 George Tames/The New York Times

1952

198 *(bottom far left)* Sam Falk/The New York Times,
(bottom center left) George Tames/The New York Times
199 *(top)* Museum of American Political Life,
(bottom, both) © David J. & Janice L. Frent Collection/CORBIS
200–201 Sam Falk/The New York Times
202 George Tames/The New York Times
203 *(top)* Arthur Brower/The New York Times,
(bottom) George Tames/The New York Times
204 The New York Times
205 George Tames/The New York Times

1956

210 *(bottom far left)* George Tames/The New York Times,
(bottom center left) Patrick A. Burns/The New York Times
211 *(top, bottom right)* Duke University Special Collections Library,
(bottom left) © David J. & Janice L. Frent Collection/CORBIS
212–13 George Tames/The New York Times
214 *(top left)* George Tames/The New York Times,
(right) Patrick A. Burns/The New York Times
215–17 George Tames/The New York Times

1960

222 *(top)* Duke University Special Collections Library,
(bottom far left) Patrick A. Burns/The New York Times,
(bottom center left) George Tames/The New York Times
223 *(top)* Agincourt Press,
(bottom left) Duke University Special Collections Library,
(bottom right) © Richard Cummins/CORBIS

224–25 The New York Times
226 George Tames/The New York Times
227 Carl Gossett/The New York Times
228 Mike Liebowitz/The New York Times
229 *(top)* George Tames/The New York Times, *(bottom)* George Tames/The New York Times
230 (top) Associated Press, *(bottom)* Patrick A. Burns/The New York Times
231 Ernie Sisto/The New York Times

1964

236 *(top)* Museum of American Political Life, *(bottom far left)* UPI, *(bottom center left)* Associated Press
237 *(top bottom right)* Duke University Special Collections Library, *(bottom, left)* Agincourt Press
238 George Tames/The New York Times
239 Jack Manning/The New York Times
240 *(top)* Associated Press, *(bottom)* George Tames/The New York Times
241 Associated Press
242 *(top)* George Tames/The New York Times, *(bottom)* Jack Manning/The New York Times
243–44 UPI
245 The New York Times

1968

252 *(top)* Museum of American Political Life, *(bottom far left)* George Tames/The New York Times, *(bottom center left)* William Sauro/The New York Times, *(bottom center)* Neal Boenzi/The New York Times, *(bottom center right)* George Tames/The New York Times, *(bottom far right)* Larry Morris/The New York Times
253 *(top left, bottom left)* Duke University Special Collections Library, *(top right, bottom right)* Museum of American Political Life
254 *(top left)* George Tames/The New York Times, *(top right)* George Tames/The New York Times, *(bottom)* Neal Boenzi/The New York Times
255 George Tames/The New York Times
256 *(top)* William Sauro/The New York Times, *(bottom)* Arthur Greenspon for The New York Times
257 Neal Boenzi/The New York Times
258 *(top)* Barton Silverman/The New York Times, *(bottom)* Barton Silverman/The New York Times
259 *(left)* George Tames/The New York Times, *(right)* George Tames/The New York Times
260 *(top)* George Tames/The New York Times, *(bottom)* Larry Morris/The New York Times
261 Nancy Palmer Agency, *(top)* Michael Evans/The New York Times
262 *(bottom)* Patrick A. Burns/The New York Times
263 *(top)* Associated Press, *(bottom)* George Tames/The New York Times

1972

268 *(top)* Agincourt Press, *(bottom far left)* Librado Romero/The New York Times, *(bottom center left)* Barton Silverman/The New York Times
269 *(all)* Museum of American Political Life
270 Barton Silverman/The New York Times
271 *(top)* Librado Romero/The New York Times, *(bottom)* Associated Press
272 Don Hogan Charles/The New York Times
273 *(top)* Edward Hausner/The New York Times, *(bottom)* George Tames/The New York Times
274 Garry Settle/The New York Times
275 D. Gorton/The New York Times

1976

280 *(top)* Agincourt Press, *(bottom far left)* Neal Boenzi/The New York Times, *(bottom center left)* Teresa Zabala/The New York Times, *(bottom center)* Associated Press
281 *(top, bottom left)* Duke University Special Collections Library, *(bottom right)* © David J. & Janice L. Frent Collection/CORBIS
282 *(top)* Neal Boenzi/The New York Times, *(bottom)* Associated Press
283 *(both)* Neal Boenzi/The New York Times
284 Teresa Zabala/The New York Times
285 Edward Hausner/The New York Times
286 *(top)* Associated Press, (bottom) Teresa Zabala/The New York Times
287 *(top)* Teresa Zabala/The New York Times, (bottom) Associated Press

1980

292 *(bottom far left)* Associated Press, *(bottom center left)* Vic DeLucia/The New York Times, *(bottom center)* Edward Hausner/The New York Times
293 *(top left)* Museum of American Political Life, *(top right)* Duke University Special Collections Library, *(bottom)* © David J. & Janice L. Frent Collection/CORBIS
294 Chester Higgins Jr./The New York Times
295 *(top)* D. Gorton/The New York Times, *(bottom)* George Tames/The New York Times
296 *(top)* Edward Hausner/The New York Times, *(bottom)* Fred Conrad/The New York Times
297 *(top)* Vic DeLucia/The New York Times, *(bottom)* Teresa Zabala/The New York Times
298 Vic DeLucia/The New York Times
299 Teresa Zabala/The New York Times
300 *(top)* D. Gorton/The New York Times, *(bottom)* Marilyn K. Yee/The New York Times
301 Associated Press

1984

306 *(top)* Museum of American Political Life,
(bottom center left) Paul Hosefros/The New York Times,
(bottom center) Vic DeLucia/The New York Times
307 *(top)* Agincourt Press,
(bottom) Duke University Special Collections Library
308 Ruby Washington/The New York Times
309 Paul Hosefros/The New York Times
310 Vic DeLucia/The New York Times
311 Sara Krulwich/The New York Times
312 Paul Hosefros/The New York Times
313 Paul Hosefros/The New York Times
314 D. Gorton/The New York Times
315 *(top)* Sara Krulwich/The New York Times,
(bottom) Sara Krulwich/The New York Times
316 (top) Neal Boenzi/The New York Times,
(bottom) George Tames/The New York Times
317 *(top)* Paul Hosefros/The New York Times,
(bottom) Paul Hosefros/The New York Times

1988

322 *(bottom far left)* Sara Krulwich/The New York Times,
(bottom center left) The New York Times
323 *(top)* Agincourt Press,
(bottom left) Museum of American Political Life,
(bottom right) © Bettman/CORBIS
324 Jim Wilson/The New York Times
325 *(left)* Chester Higgins Jr./The New York Times,
(right) Jose R. Lopez/The New York Times
326–27 Jim Wilson/The New York Times
328 *(top)* Paul Burnett/The New York Times,
(bottom) Paul Hosefros/The New York Times
329 The New York Times
330 *(top)* Jim Wilson/The New York Times,
(bottom) The New York Times
331 Sara Krulwich/The New York Times

1992

338 *(top)* © David J. & Janice L. Frent Collection/CORBIS,
(bottom far left) Monica Almeida/The New York Times,
(bottom center left) Jose R. Lopez/The New York Times,
(bottom center) The New York Times
339 *(top, bottom right)* Agincourt Press,
(bottom left) © Lynn Goldsmith/CORBIS
340 *(both)* Edward Keating/The New York Times
341 *(top)* The New York Times,
(bottom) Paul Hosefros/The New York Times
342–43 Jose R. Lopez/The New York Times
344 *(top)* Monica Almeida/The New York Times,
(bottom) Andrea Mohin/The New York Times
345 Jose R. Lopez/The New York Times
346 Andrea Mohin/The New York Times
347 Joyce Dopkeen/The New York Times
348 Librado Romero/The New York Times
349 Monica Almeida/The New York Times
350 Jose R. Lopez/The New York Times
351 Jim Wilson/The New York Times

1996

356 *(top)* Museum of American Political Life,
356 *(bottom far left)* Jim Wilson/The New York Times,
(bottom center left) Stephen Crowley/The New York Times,
(bottom center) Suzanne DeChillo/The New York Times
357 *(top)* Agincourt Press, *(bottom)* Museum of American Political Life
358 Jim Wilson/The New York Times
359 Keith Meyers/The New York Times
360 Paul Hosefros/The New York Times
361 Stephen Crowley/The New York Times
362–63 Keith Meyers/The New York Times
364 *(top)* Stephen Crowley/The New York Times,
(bottom) Stephen Crowley/The New York Times
365 Suzanne DeChillo/The New York Times
366 Monica Almeida/The New York Times
367 Stephen Crowley/The New York Times
368 Monica Almeida/The New York Times
369 The New York Times
370–71 Jim Wilson/The New York Times

2000

376 *(top)* Museum of American Political Life,
(bottom far left) Stephen Crowley/The New York Times,
(bottom center left) Stephen Crowley/The New York Times,
(bottom center) The New York Times
377 *(all)* Museum of American Political Life
378 *(top)* The New York Times,
(bottom) Ruth Fremson/The New York Times
379 *(top)* Stephen Crowley/The New York Times,
(bottom) Keith Meyers/The New York Times
380 *(top)* Stephen Crowley/The New York Times,
(bottom) Paul Hosefros/The New York Times
381 *(top)* Paul Hosefros/The New York Times,
(bottom) Andrea Mohin/The New York Times
382 Stephen Crowley/The New York Times
383 *(both)* Paul Hosefros/The New York Times
384 *(top)* Chang W. Lee/The New York Times,
(bottom) Monica Almeida/The New York Times
385 The New York Times
386 *(top)* Paul Hosefros/The New York Times,
(bottom) Stephen Crowley/The New York Times
387 *(top)* Stephen Crowley/The New York Times,
(bottom) Keith Meyers/The New York Times
388–89 Stephen Crowley/The New York Times
390 *(both)* Stephen Crowley/The New York Times
391 Andrea Mohin/The New York Times
392 *(top)* Stephen Crowley/The New York Times,
(bottom) Richard Perry/The New York Times
393 *(top)* Richard Perry/The New York Times,
(bottom) Stephen Crowley/The New York Times
394 Vincent Laforet/The New York Times
395 *(top)* Vincent Laforet/The New York Times,
(bottom) Chang W. Lee/The New York Times
396 *(both)* Ruth Fremson/The New York Times
397 Stephen Crowley/The New York Times

Acknowledgments

The New York Times

Combining outstanding photographs with wonderful text, without diminishing either, is always tricky. Both demand respect and attention. In the case of *Campaigns*, the goal turned out to be relatively simple because so many people shared the same vision. We all wanted a book that was beautiful, authoritative, timely, and lively.

Many thanks are owed to many people for their work on this project. At Dorling Kindersley, the publisher, Sean Moore, the editor, Barbara Berger, and the art editor, Mandy Earey, were energetic and creative partners in solving the usual swarm of problems that hovered over the many elements that were integrated to comprise this book. At The Times, in addition to the colleagues who worked intensively on *Campaigns* and are listed on the copyright page, I would like to thank a number of people for their assistance: Thomas K. Carley, Jim Mones, Lee Riffaterre, and Mitch Belitz for administrative support; the large and talented cadre of New York Times photographers who made this book possible in the first place; and for researching and transmitting the images for the 2000 election, Margaret O'Connor, Jose Lopez, William P. O'Donnell, Earl Wilson, Dan Gaba, and Phyllis Collazo.

Finally, extra thanks to Ted Widmer and Alan Brinkley, fine historians whose understanding of presidential campaigns in the twentieth century tells us as much about America as it does about politics.

DK Publishing, Inc.

DK Publishing, Inc., would like to thank the following people and organizations for their invaluable help: Mitchel Levitas of The New York Times for his support in making this book possible and for his invaluable editorial expertise; Russell Hassell for his brilliant design and tireless enthusiasm; Ted Widmer and Alan Brinkley for their insightful text; and Nancy Lee of The New York Times for her astute editorial contributions.

For their unflagging assistance in supplying photographic material and archival information we would like to thank Jeff Roth, Lonnie Schlein, and Paul Hacker at The New York Times. We are also grateful to the following individuals for providing early photographic material and campaign memorabilia: Charles Merullo and Liz Ihre at Hulton Getty; Hanna Edwards at Corbis; David Rubel at Agincourt Press; Zina Davis, Robyn Kelsey, Kevin Lamkins, and Edmund Sullivan, Professor Emeritus and former Director, at the Museum of American Political Life; Janie Morris at Duke University Special Collections Library; and Kathy Lavelle at Archive Photos. Special thanks go to Dave King for his photography of memorabilia at the Museum of American Political Life; Nanette Cardon at IRIS Indexing; and Linda Sullivan at Wordsmart Word Processing. And we are grateful to Pauline Testerman at the Truman Library, Jim Detlefsen at the Hoover Library, Carolyn McMahon at Associated Press, Victor Mongeau at polikicks.com, Jonathan Bennett, and Laurel Girvan.

[redacted]